Survey of
Science Fiction Literature

Survey
of
Science Fiction
Literature

**FIVE HUNDRED 2,000-WORD ESSAY REVIEWS OF
WORLD-FAMOUS SCIENCE FICTION NOVELS
WITH 2,500 BIBLIOGRAPHICAL REFERENCES**

Edited by
FRANK N. MAGILL

Volume Five
Sho - Z
2051 - 2542
Index

SALEM PRESS

Englewood Cliffs

LIBRARY OF CONGRESS CATALOG CARD NUMBER: 79-64639

Complete Set: ISBN 0-89356-194-0
Volume V: ISBN 0-89356-199-1

PRINTED IN THE UNITED STATES OF AMERICA

LIST OF TITLES IN VOLUME FIVE

LIST OF TITLES IN VOLUME FIVE

Survey of
Science Fiction Literature

THE SHORT FICTION OF RUDYARD KIPLING

Author: Rudyard Kipling (1865-1936)
Type of work: Short stories

Stories which prepared the way for many science fiction writers by offering classic examples of the familiar types and setting them in a materialistic universe

Not even a partisan would consider calling Rudyard Kipling "the father of science fiction." Kipling nevertheless deserves some other epithet indicative of his relationship to the genre that emerged during his lifetime and under his influence. "Godfather of science fiction" would perhaps suffice, or "favorite uncle" — something indicating at once lack of direct responsibility together with familial guidance.

Though little of Kipling's enormous production was actually science fiction, at least according to a narrow definition, he did two things which assisted later writers in the genre. First, he wrote classic examples of most of science fiction's "ancestor types" (ghost stories, other-world allegories, fantastic journeys); second, he set these within the materialistic universe which nearly all science fiction ultimately accepts, having little recourse to romantic medievalism or superstition (even when, as sometimes happened, he used medieval settings). He showed what could be done. He is mentioned more frequently than any other writer by such early "hard" science fiction practitioners as Robert A. Heinlein and Poul Anderson. References to Kipling, furthermore, are sympathetic, admiring, and untouched by feelings of competition — another reason for calling him "uncle" rather than "father."

Thus, in H. G. Wells's *The Sleeper Awakes* (1899), one of the first things the sleeper comes across is a book written in phonetic script. After a moment he deciphers the title: "The Man Who Would Be King." "One of the best stories in the world," he observes, passing on to his destiny. The incident is both irrelevant and significant, rather like the relationship of "The Man Who Would Be King" itself to science fiction. That story, first published in 1888, contains no scientific or futuristic elements. It is built entirely upon the confrontation between familiar life and alien habits — those of the Indian princely states, where malefactors may be filled up with red pepper and then somehow "slippered" to death, and those of the utterly unknown realm of "Kafiristan," where "the man" himself goes to make his kingdom. Kipling's combination of strangeness with casual acceptance has been remembered by dozens of later writers, as has his articulation of the intense Faustian ambition that leads Daniel Dravot to a crown, to godhood, and to execution for the crime of being human. Other "Indian" stories by Kipling, such as "The Strange Ride of Morrowbie Jukes" (1885), made a similar impact.

The cardinal fact of "The Man Who Would Be King," however, is that we never find out what really happened, since the tale is told largely by a madman. This technique is characteristic of Kipling, and is the result not of evasiveness, but of an exceptionally strong awareness of the underlying structure of Victorian thought, in which materialism was not yet dethroned, and in which the "Powers that Be" were iron, coal, steam, all remorseless in their tangibility.

Kipling's story "A Matter of Fact" (1892) opens as the crew and passengers of a ship soberly observe by daylight the agonies of a dying sea-serpent. It ends with their return to London, with its suburban villas, clipped hedges, newspapers, and all the trappings of civilization. They decide unanimously to keep their secret, because they understand that belief in established knowledge is as strong as belief in God, and deals as ruthlessly with its heretics. Unsupported observation is not strong enough to offer a challenge; and however much scientists ought to disagree, the truth is that science consists as much of accepted theory as of merely recorded fact. This notion, of course, has been the germ of many a later science fiction story, though few have drawn out the ironies of the situation as well as Kipling.

The same theme of the inability to shake "established" knowledge is developed in "A Madonna of the Trenches" (1924). In this story, the Narrator pretends to suffer from shell shock after a spell in the trenches of World War I. He uses this cover because he knows it is acceptable to the psychological theory of his time; but the real cause of his terror is his having seen the ghost of his Auntie Bella. She neither meant nor did him any harm. But the confirmed existence of the supernatural shakes the foundations of a materialist's world in a way that nothing else can, not death, corpses, or corruption, which are at least expected. Love being stronger than death, however, he cannot understand.

Kipling, in fact, moved in the post-Darwinian world which has created science fiction, and he understood its true fears and hopes better than any other writer. That is why even his smallest fables preserve a resonance in the contemporary world. *The Just-So Stories* (1902), for instance, comically explain "How the Rhinoceros Got His Skin" and "How the Leopard Got His Spots" as they accustom the infant mind to immense stretches of time and to the mechanics of natural selection. The same is true of the "Mowgli" stories from *The Jungle Book* (1894) and *The Second Jungle Book* (1895), which have as their basic concept the "wolf-child," the human, reared by animals, who can then cast an unprejudiced eye on mankind and observe the variations between "civilized" habits and the "Law of the Jungle." In different ways, this idea was seized by Edgar Rice Burroughs, rather to Kipling's amusement, and by H. G. Wells, who imaged the Law-chanting Beast Folk of *The Island of Doctor Moreau* (1896). But in one point Kipling differs from most of his contemporaries, and resembles more his science fiction successors: he did not resent either the Darwinian revolution or the Industrial Revolution. He was a technophile, not a technophobe.

This positive stance toward technological progress is well illustrated by the author's poem "McAndrew's Hymn" (1893), which laughs at the common notion that steam-power kills romance instead of transmuting it. Kipling also proved his point in short stories such as "Wireless" (1902) and "Mrs. Bathurst" (1904), both of which exploit the intensely unreal and counterintuitive impression made on their first appearance on radio and the cinema. The latter seems to bring ghosts to life, while the former calls voices from the abyss.

All the various themes discussed so far are best brought together in Kipling's two unquestioned works of science fiction, "With the Night Mail" (1905) and "As Easy as A.B.C." (1912). In both pieces, one can find the simultaneous conjunction of strangeness and familiarity, the awareness of social structures as shaped by technology, and the growth of romance from human achievement.

"With the Night Mail" makes a particularly determined attempt to develop the first of these three themes. With seeming redundance, Kipling adds to the main story — which pretends to be a journalist's account of an aerial Atlantic crossing in the year 2000 — extracts from the magazine of the future in which the account is supposed to have appeared. He includes letters, official notices, news, reviews, and even nine pages of fantastically detailed advertisements. These contain no narrative and are exactly the kind of thing that readers of contemporary magazines usually skip over. Why include them? They do, of course, provide a glimpse of the future. But the point Kipling is making is that glimpses can be more effective than clear vision, because they are less premeditated.

The imagined advertisements, for instance, are no more truthful than advertisements of any age. One is for synthetic bearings (an example of the failure of which has been given in the main account). Jeweled ones are better and safer, but more expensive, so there is a market for inferior bearings, and a balance is struck, in the future as in the past, between cost and human lives. Other advertisements praise aeroplanes instead of dirigible balloons, and *vice versa*. Detached readers can see that both have their good points, but that manufacturers are incapable of admitting the advantages of their rival's product. In a way, what the "magazine extracts" tell us is not that people do not change, but that they can make successful adjustments. Each novelty causes horror and suspicion; then it is exploited, integrated, and accepted — and finally becomes part of the old stability it once threatened.

The main narrative makes the same point by its juxtaposition of the amazing physical presence of the great metal-clad dirigible (lifted by an as-yet-undiscovered gas and powered by "Fleury's Ray"), and its utterly mundane purpose of carrying mailbags for the General Post Office. The focus of the story is not on technology itself, but on how it is used. The characters are familiar Kipling types, slightly monomaniac in their concern for the details of their profession, and utterly reliable because of their attachment to that profession. They contain within themselves a history and a tradition (sea-chanteys and captains' bridges) of which they are barely aware. Submersibles, radium, and aeroplanes are the top layers of Kipling's imagined future, but, like all good science fiction writers, the author is more interested in such bottom layers as the different economics and career opportunities brought about by an airborne world; the technological shortcuts and bottlenecks of the future society; and the way in which millions of lives can be changed by a single (often disregarded) genius.

One subject, however, which Kipling barely hints at in "With the Night Mail," is politics, which forms the center of its sequel, "As Easy As A.B.C." A.B.C. stands for the Aerial Board of Control, a power mentioned in the earlier story, but dominant in the later one, which is set in the year 2065. The basic assumptions made in the sequel are that aerial transport will erode national frontiers to the point of eliminating them, and that peace and security will send the world back to a kind of pastoralism. What, then, will become of politics, once the State has withered away? There will be none visible, suggests Kipling, since the dominant aim of humanity will be to avoid crowds, maintain privacy, and reject democracy.

In the story, Northern Illinois (there is now no Chicago) cuts off communications in order to force the A.B.C. to take over and restore them, and in the process eliminate the atavistic elements that threaten their privacy. The A.B.C. does indeed take over, rescues the neodemocrats, and takes them off to use on a kind of television show. Chicago's terrible statue of "The Nigger in Flames," dedicated sarcastically to "the Eternal Memory of the Justice of the People," is slagged, and all seems to end well. Kipling, however, leaves several matters hanging. His basic irony is that democracy destroys itself by arousing popular passions (an accurate forecast, in 1912). However, the benevolent despotism of the A.B.C. has weaknesses too. From our twentieth century viewpoint we can see that the men of the future are dangerously indecisive in their kindliness, strangely short of executive talent. Can even a pastoral society run with nobody at the helm? Kipling does not offer an answer.

There is one further story which illustrates Kipling's ability to draw moral dilemmas from particular inventions: "The Eye of Allah" (1926). In this historical tale, a microscope is used to show germs to an audience of thirteenth century clerics and doctors, including Roger Bacon ("the great-grandfather of science fiction"). The Abbot destroys the instrument although he sees its potential for good. By threatening faith and the social order, he believes, it would kill as many people in religious wars as it would save in hospitals. We are forced to agree on that fact. Dare we dispute the Abbot's decision? With this question Kipling once more strikes to the center of science fiction's utility, and to the heart of the ideology of material progress.

T. A. Shippey

Sources for Further Study

Criticism:

Cruse, Amy. "Science and Romance," in her *After the Victorians*. London: Allyn & Unwin, 1938, pp. 163-173. Cruse explores Kipling's use of scientific materials in his fiction.

Sussman, Herbert L. *Victorians and the Machine: The Literary Response to Technology*. Cambridge, Mass.: Harvard University Press, 1968. This work which deals not only with Kipling but also with Wells and Carlyle provides a significant part of the context necessary to an understanding of the rise of Science Fiction.

THE SHORT FICTION OF THEODORE STURGEON

Author: Theodore Sturgeon (1918-   )
Type of work: Short stories

More than 150 pieces of short fiction written since 1939 express Sturgeon's fascination with newness, growth, change, and love in a variety of styles that has consistently given science fiction a greater literary respectability

Sturgeon's Law definitely does not apply to the short fiction of Theodore Sturgeon. More than one-tenth of Sturgeon's 150-plus stories are memorable and worth studying, although, as is the case with so many science fiction writers, careful editing and collecting needs to be done in order to make his rich proliferation of short fiction available to the reader as one corpus. Nevertheless, from the appearance of "Ether Breather" in the September, 1939, *Astounding Science Fiction*, to his most recent stylish fantasy that appeared in October, 1978, in the opening issue of *Omni*, Sturgeon's short fiction in the science fiction genre contains a remarkable unity and consistency; and paradoxically, this thematic unity is related to the author's very proliferation and variety.

Sturgeon's short fiction is also notable for its style. Sturgeon delights in wordplay, shifts of tone, comic sequences, and startling effects. James Kidder, the protagonist in the award-winning 1941 story "Microcosmic God," is an inventor capable of incredible proliferation and variation, who finally turns his inventive skills to the basic problem of how to increase the rate of proliferation itself. Kidder is a mad but gentle scientist; and even though James Blish has called this story atypical of Sturgeon, the relevance of Kidder's problem to the basic theme of proliferation makes the story a logical place to begin. In order to combat the sameness of things, Kidder gains an edge on evolutionary trends by inventing a small intelligent species of his own whose members rush through their life cycles generation after generation at a phenomenal rate. Hence, they produce evolutionary "progress" from which Kidder can benefit. A similar technical inventiveness in literary matters seems to be the property of Theodore Sturgeon.

Nearly thirty years later, Sturgeon invented another "mad scientist" who is somewhat like Kidder in the award-winning story of 1970, "Slow Sculpture." The doctor in "Slow Sculpture" cannot be called doctor since he is a practicing mechanical and electrical engineer and a lawyer by training; Kidder could not be called doctor because he never would waste the time to earn a degree. Both characters demonstrate Sturgeon's feelings about the discrepancy between real craft and style, and mere credentials. But whereas Kidder was shy and chose to isolate himself from the world in order to develop his invention, the inventor of the advanced cancer cure in the later story is portrayed as an angry, frightened man of much greater depth of character. This fear lasts until he can make the meaningful human contact that will give coherence and significance to his inventions. The later story is a love story; it ends with the doctor speaking to the woman he has cured with his skill and who, in turn, is curing him of his sense of isolation. The doctor talks about skill and style, whereas the woman who loves him says that human projects are like growing bonsai trees; they will work out right if you take both time and care and allow things to be what they will be.

Thus with all his craftsmanship and stylish rhetoric, Sturgeon also generates great compassion and feeling in his stories. Another beautiful example is "Thunder and Roses" from the November, 1947, *Astounding Science Fiction*. This narrative, about attempts to preserve some life on earth after a nuclear holocaust, is a finely paced and structured story with hope, love, and terror on all levels — personal, social, and cosmic. The image of brown roses (effected by radiation) with ingrowing thorns that kill the plant is balanced by the meaningful deaths of the human protagonists in order to avert total death.

Obviously, Sturgeon the stylist and literary form-changer is also Sturgeon the lover. Form and content in the overall effects of his work are one, and his continual interest in the nature of change and newness is closely related to his interest in style. In a short essay from 1953 entitled "Why So Much Syzygy," Sturgeon talks about love but also includes telltale references to crafty work and to virtuosity; and, of course, "syzygy" is both a fancy, clever, unusual word (style) and a work for yoking. Sturgeon writes:

> I think what I have been trying to do all these years is to investigate this matter of love. . . . I investigate it by writing about it because, as stated above, I don't know what the hell I think until I tell somebody about it. And I work so assiduously at it because of a conviction that if one could understand it completely, one would have the key to . . . the marvelous orchestration which enables us to keep ahead of our own destructiveness.

The author's emphasis at the end of the statement is similar to the serious concern expressed in "Thunder and Roses." And yet, whether he actually strives for it consistently, Sturgeon works assiduously not at presenting ideas, but at writing images. The result, as in some theories of Renaissance art, is a richly proliferating aping of nature that conveys finally the most valuable idea from nature: its complexity and continually changing newness. Sometimes this newness and proliferation result in something morbid and destructive, such as the curious yet deadly monster in "It" from Sturgeon's first collection, *Not Without Sorcery* (1948). But there is always energy, growth, and newness in these short stories.

In an appreciation that he wrote of Damon Knight for the November issue of *The Magazine of Fantasy and Science Fiction*, 1976, Sturgeon himself praises writers whose style is varied and flexible. Certainly his own short fiction production has seen a variety of styles. But more important is the fusion and interrelationship of the notions of love and survival. In a novel about survival, *The Seedling Stars*, James Blish comments about various species changes in a lively nature: "But why should any of them think of form-changing as something extraordinary, and to be striven for? It's one of the commonplaces of their lives, after all." The commonplace of at least a major portion of Theodore Sturgeon's literary life is that style and loving concern are counterparts of each other. The comic tension of our complex universe allows us to love things as they are, and Sturgeon's complex literary fabrications contribute to the expression of this comic tension.

Donald M. Hassler

Sources for Further Study

Criticism:

The Encyclopedia of Science Fiction and Fantasy. Compiled by Donald H. Tuck. Chicago: Advent Publishers, Inc., 1978, pp. 413-414. Tuck gives a general review of Sturgeon's life and works, including a full bibliography of the author's publications.

Kostolefsky, Joseph. "Science, Yes — Fiction, Maybe," in *Antioch Review*. XIII (June, 1953), pp. 236-240. Although a diatribe against science fiction literature generally, this article gives credit to Sturgeon as one of the best in the field, and one whose works stand up against non-science fiction authors.

Wolheim, Donald. *The Universe Makers: Science Fiction Today*. New York: Harper & Row, 1971, pp. 63-65. Wolheim discusses Sturgeon's fiction generally, with particular emphasis on "The Universe Makers."

THE SHORT FICTION OF THOMAS M. DISCH

Author: Thomas M. Disch (1940-   )
Type of work: Short stories

*The range of Disch's short stories stretches from cruel, sardonic parables to sinu-
ous, mysterious, poetic stories, demonstrating an increasing virtuosity of language and
the discovery of compassion and courage in cruel situations*

Since his stories began appearing during the early 1960's, Thomas M.
Disch has always had an equivocal place in the science fiction field for the
very good reason that he has never really been part of it. He is an American
whose writing sounds English; an ironist in a field where crude heartiness is
still the rule; a humorist in a field where solemnity is more popular than wit.
Disch is self-consciously literary to the point where his work suits the *Paris
Review* better than *Analog*. He has made few concessions to the chauvinist,
technocratic, complacent opinions frequently characteristic of science fiction.
In short, Disch is one of those rarities in the field, someone who sees himself
as a "writer" rather than as a "science fiction writer." His allegiance is to the
art of prose, not to a series of genre assumptions.

It is a surprise to discover, when reading his early short stories, how much
of a genre writer he once was. The 1969 collection, *Fun with Your New Head*,
contains his best stories written up to that time. One of them, "Nada," remains
well known within the field. Almost all the elements in the story are science
fiction clichés. There is the kindly teacher attempting to bring some educational light to slum kids who have been abandoned by every other teacher and
the little girl in the class who is much more intelligent than she is willing to let
on. The teacher becomes fascinated with the girl and discovers, of course, that
she is one of a race of alien beings who live among humans. Only the joking
manner of the story's ending offers any real surprise. Yet "Nada" is a memorable story, because all the details are right. Both the teacher and the girl
really do inhabit the slums. The speech patterns sound authentic; the descriptions of school and streets are well-observed. We sympathize with the teacher
and gain some insight into the dilemma of the girl and her interstellar parents.

However, it is difficult to sympathize with the viewpoint of the author himself. He seems to dismiss the teacher's dilemma with the joke in the punchline
of "Nada." Disch still has a reputation among science fiction readers as being
"cold," of showing how people feel but not seeming to feel anything for the
characters themselves. To the extent that this reputation is justified, it rests
with stories of the vintage of those collected in *Fun with Your New Head*.
Every story has the same distressingly predictable pattern: main character
gains a hint of disaster (or is already in a disastrous situation); disaster arrives;
disaster gets worse and worse. Most of the main characters in this volume's
stories die at the end. It is as if Disch tried to use the superficial qualities of

Kafka's nightmares without noticing Kafka's compassion or complexity of vision.

The pattern is shown at its most predictable (yet most memorable) in "Descending," where a man becomes trapped on an escalator which keeps going down. That is all that happens in the story, but Disch dramatizes the main character's plight so effectively that the reader will watch his step before stepping onto an escalator in the future.

One story in *Fun with Your New Head* gives a hint of the Disch-to-come. "Casablanca" is original in even its elemental science fiction ideas. It is unique as a science fiction story by an American writer for suggesting that the United States could be destroyed in a nuclear war without the rest of the world being destroyed as well. It is certainly the only story which relates the experiences of Americans traveling outside their own country when this happens.

Mr. and Mrs. Richmond are world travelers who happen to be staying in Casablanca. They are walking embodiments of the middle-aged American tourist. What they like most about Casablanca are the cheap restaurants, taxis, and the little parlor which serves better ice cream than any that can be bought in Florida. Their nightmare begins when they cannot find any American newspapers on the stand at their hotel in the morning. They cannot read any foreign languages, so the large black headlines in the French newspapers mean nothing to them. Outrage follows when the hotel manager will no longer accept their travelers' checks. The manager cannot speak English, so the mystery remains unsolved. The Richmonds stay in their room, but they find that they are no longer allowed to use the hotel's facilities, including the corridor toilet. No one, in fact, will cash their travelers' checks, and language problems prevent them for some time from finding out that the country that would honor them no longer exists. The Richmonds discover that exuberant crowds have sacked the U.S. Embassy. A little notice tacked to the door advises American citizens to leave Casablanca as soon as possible. From then on, Disch's characteristic pattern reasserts itself in the story: things simply get worse. Fred's wife disappears and he cannot find her. All his belongings are stolen, and he is thrown into jail. When released, he manages to live on nuts and chocolate. His entire lifestyle has disappeared in a few hours.

The temptation is to regard this as just another of the sardonic nightmares which are featured in *Fun with Your New Head*. But a different note appears at the end of the story. Disch seems to sympathize with Fred, even if he does epitomize everything Disch apparently dislikes about his own countrymen. Fred Richmond might be a victim, like the main characters in the other stories in the volume, but he is a defiant victim. The end of the story gives some hint that he will survive. If he can survive, he is capable of learning and changing. Perhaps he might even understand, eventually, why the people of Casablanca were so gleeful to learn of the destruction of America.

The 1976 collection, *Getting into Death*, presents a much more able writer than the relative beginner of *Fun with Your New Head*. The stories collected in *Getting into Death* truly are "the best short stories of Thomas M. Disch" (which was the subtitle of the British edition of the book). The stories are no longer predictable; they roam clear of stereotypes. Most can be compared favorably with the best "mainstream" fiction. However, these stories still depend on a science fictional frame of mind — a commitment to scientific and cultural ideas as the main framework of human existence. Some fit into the pigeonhole of science fiction, many do not. They all bristle with originality, intelligence, and fierce feeling, plus an element of compassion previously lacking in Disch's stories.

"The Colors" first appeared in *New Worlds* magazine in the late 1960's. In this story, the unnamed main character learns to use the color-machine which his friend Raymond has invented. The color-machine draws up impressions from the well of the user's mind and spills them onto the surface of external reality. The main character is intelligent and discriminating enough to make sense of the well-nigh hallucinogenic experience. Because he is a painter, he soon sees the entire world as the surface of a painting.

In this new, glowing still-life, the most notable object is Helen, the main character's lover: "Her fluorescing flesh could be seen in one sense as a great uncompleted canvas." The surfaces, movements, and gestures which form an entity called "Helen" blend into a kaleidoscopic unity. The main character's unique, obsessive viewpoint removes this love affair entirely away from the territory of conventional romantic fiction. Soon he forgets about Helen's speech patterns, ways of lovemaking, or sometimes whether she is still present as a model for her own image. "The funny thing is," says the narrator to Raymond, "she seems to have so little to do with it herself. I mean, it's not love that connects me and her — it's Helen that connects me and love."

In this way, Disch takes a story about the aberrated views of a color addict and changes it into a splendid eulogy for the idea of love. When Helen leaves the main character, he cannot tell how long she has been gone, and he does not know when she will return. In the middle of his reverie, he is grief-stricken by "the days of her absence" which "had been like the sere March fields before the new grass — with this difference, that love cannot be relied on to recur seasonally: its sere days, when they come, seem to come for ever."

When the main character reaches this point of perception, he has managed to go beyond the colors, to take the images and see the metaphor behind them. Art has saved his mind from chaos, yet elevated it permanently into a new chaos of experience. Helen returns; the "veritable spring" returns. Inevitably, a descent begins. As Helen and her bedazzled lover drift apart, he sees beyond conventional love-sadness and melancholia. In his notion of love, the descent from ecstasy is like a skier speeding down a ski-slope: he enjoys the spectacle of the white landscape and the sensation of speed as much as he enjoyed the serenity of standing on the mountaintop, but now he cannot slow down, and inevitably he must reach the conclusion of the whole experience. The view-point may be very different from the reader's and rather chilling, but the writ-ing is so compelling in its lucidity that it lets us experience this reversed view-point as well as the transformation.

"Transformation" is a word which describes what Disch accomplishes in all the best stories in this volume. "The Asian Shore" (which dates from the early issues of Damon Knight's *Orbit* anthology) is a more complex story than "The Colors," but it shows perhaps a simpler process of transformation.

John Benedict Harris, an American architect, settles in Istanbul for some months. He becomes haunted by a Turkish woman and a small boy. Whenever she sees him, the woman calls out, "Yavuz! Yavuz!" to attract his attention. The small boy seems to lurk in every street and alley. It is as if they have claimed Harris as husband and father. Harris retreats into his room where "He rotted like a jar of preserves left open and forgotten on the top shelf of a cupboard."

At the same time, his own recently published book, *Homo Arbitrans*, haunts him. "It was the thesis of his book that the quiddity of architecture, its chief claim to an aesthetic interest, was its arbitrariness." When Harris tours Istan-bul at the beginning of his stay, he finds beauty in the conventional places, the mosques and monuments. Later, he can find no beauty in anything man-made. He comes to enjoy "the turbaned shafts of marble" which "jutted in every direction but the vertical, . . . or lay, higgledy-piggledy, one atop another." His mind takes on the structure of his own ideas, so much so that he can no longer understand his own book.

He does not leave his room for days on end, but one morning he finds his shoes, soaking wet, lying beside his bed. He takes some photos of an area on the European Bosphorus coast; when they are developed, the photos show an area which Harris soon discovers on the Asian shore. When Harris thinks that he has escaped from his situation, he becomes transformed to fit it. He be-comes an arbitrary, uncomprehending man — an ordinary Turk with a wife and child. He has also broken through many of the barriers which have always separated him from the world in general.

In "The Asian Shore," the process of transformation takes up the whole story. The main character has already begun to change at the beginning of the story, in that he has chosen a sleepy, seedy area of Istanbul in which to stay. In the end, he steps out of our frame of comprehension. In between, Harris experiences a dream-state of mixed ecstasy, metamorphosis, and acute misery. His clear mind watches his own disintegration, defeat, and resurrection. His own ideas destroy him, yet allow him to reach a state which, perhaps, he was always seeking.

Like most of the interesting stories in this volume, "The Asian Shore" brings to life a process of death. Death is the idea at the center of this book, and perhaps at the center of all Disch's fiction. In the *Fun with Your New*

Head stories, he tends simply to kill off characters. In *Getting into Death*, Disch writes joyful, funny, and bracing stories which accept the threat of extinction.

In "Getting into Death," the title story, Cassandra Miller thumbs her nose at death while her relatives grieve over her imminent passing or wait for the reading of the will. In acknowledging sentimental ideas about death and love, Disch wrote "Feathers from the Wings of an Angel," which is a parody of the heartthrob stories which once appeared in American popular magazines.

It is, however, in "Let Us Quickly Hasten to the Gate of Ivory" (which first appeared in Samuel Delany's remarkable *Quark* anthology series) that Disch examines death most clearly, yet most mysteriously. At the beginning of the story, Mickey and Louise, brother and sister, have driven to the cemetery where their mother and father are buried. They park the VW in the parking lot, and stride out across the acres of lawn. They step through and are surrounded by death; Disch punctuates the prose with inscriptions from tombstones carved with comforting clichés such as "Gardens of Memory and Peace," "Until the Day Break," and "Taken to His Eternal Home."

From the beginning, Disch makes it clear what will happen to Mickey and Louise: they will become lost forever in the cemetery. No matter which way they turn, although they walk for miles, they will never find their way back to the parking lot. We expect that Mickey and Louise will meet a horrifying, apocalyptic end.

This is not what happens. In fact, the story does not really end at all. Mickey and Louise do become alarmed when they realize that they have lost their way back to the car, but not because of any possible physical danger, rather because of the impending disapproval of Mickey's wife, Joyce, about their late homecoming. Louise and Mickey find more and more comfort in each other's presence. For the first time, they discuss Louise's divorce and the petrification of Mickey's youthful hopes. This is hardly a tale of incest, but of lost love found. "Tomorrow would find them in the cemetery still," thinks Louise in the story's last paragraph, "In an almost perfect silence they would walk through the cemetery, lost. . . . She fell asleep in her brother's arms, smiling: it was just like old times."

What actually happens in "Let Us Quickly Hasten to the Gate of Ivory"? Do Mickey and Louise die? Have they entered their own heaven, or at least limbo? If so, at what point in the narrative do they "die"? Or do they still have to "die," in the Elizabethan sense?

Certainly they were dead already, trapped in a living death of Joyce's tongue and the impotence of Louise's husband. Now they have discovered a new life. In this story we come close to the meaning of death which suffuses all these stories. Disch fears only one type of death — the death of sensitivity, which we call normal existence. The threat of such an existence is that it destroys love; it preserves the ego by building walls around the personality.

When those walls fall, the result can be physically destructive. It can also transform people and allow them to become their real selves.

It is this glimpse of underlying patterns of existence which makes the stories in *Getting into Death* so much more rewarding to read than those in *Fun with Your New Head*. In *Getting into Death*, the characters are blessed with courage and love, as well as Disch's euphonious prose. The transformation between the two books is fitting evidence that Thomas M. Disch is not only one of science fiction's finest writers, but also the one most likely to keep improving and finally fulfill his true potential.

Bruce Gillespie

THE SHORT FICTION OF WILLIAM TENN

Author: William Tenn (Philip Klass, 1920-   )
Type of work: Short stories and novellas

A collection of short stories and novellas which exploit the comic and ironic potential of the twin themes of time travel and contact with aliens

William Tenn is the major pseudonym used by Philip Klass. Two of the three stories published under his other *nom de plume*, Kenneth Putnam, were absorbed into the Tenn canon when reprinted in book form. Tenn has never been a prolific writer — his output amounts to about fifty science fiction stories (including one novel) and half a dozen fantasies. Most of his work appeared in the period 1946-1959, with a few additional stories in the mid-1960's. Since 1968, when Ballantine Books issued a set of six paperbacks as a showcase of his work, he has written only one short story, for Jack Dann's anthology of Jewish science fiction, *Wandering Stars* (1974). Most of the longer stories which he wrote during the 1950's appeared in *Galaxy*, and his reputation is based primarily on his contribution to the idiosyncratic species of satirical comedy promoted by that magazine. His work in that vein compares with the contemporary work of Frederik Pohl and Robert Sheckley.

Tenn's short fiction appears in six collections: *Of All Possible Worlds* (1955); *The Human Angel* (1956); *Time in Advance* (1958); *The Seven Sexes* (1968); *The Square Root of Man* (1968); and *The Wooden Star* (1968). Of the six stories which remain uncollected, only his contribution to *Wandering Stars*, "On Venus Have We Got a Rabbi," is worthy of note.

There are two main themes which Tenn has exploited liberally for their humorous and ironic potential: time travel and first contact with aliens. These were the two favorite themes of all *Galaxy*'s irreverent humorists, and the work of Tenn and others was made possible by the extent to which pre-1950 science fiction had made their central notions so commonplace. As with all ideative clichés, from the eternal triangle to deals with the devil, these notions had come to embody sets of routine expectations which were infinitely amenable to ironic violations. Tenn was a member of the generation which discovered these story routines ready-made but largely unexploited. Unlike his contemporaries, however, he unfortunately faded out of the picture in the 1960's, once the easy pickings had been well and truly picked, and *Galaxy*'s heyday as the home of incestuous science fiction satire was over.

Several of Tenn's earliest stories feature standard time-travel gimmicks given an extra half-twist. In "Child's Play" (1947), a slip in time allows an unsuccessful lawyer to receive a "Bild-a-Man Set" intended as a Christmas present for a juvenile of the future. He begins experimenting by making simple life forms and quickly builds up to duplicating a neighbor's baby. Flushed with success, he completes his masterpiece — a second self — but gets his comeuppance when an official from the twenty-fourth century comes back to set things right and has no difficulty in deciding which of the duplicates is the inferior specimen to be disassembled.

Another protagonist trying to cash in on the jetsam of a visit from a school-boy of the future is featured in "Errand Boy" (1947), while "Me, Myself and I" (1947), and "Brooklyn Project" (1948) are simple variants on the traditional time-paradox plot in which intrusions into the past bring about changes in the present (of which the population of the present is, of course, quite unaware). The later story, "It Ends with a Flicker" (1956), presents a more sophisticated version of the same plot.

Some of Tenn's time-travel comedies involve scenarios including the curious notion of "temporal embassies" set up to regulate communication between eras and to suppress the problems of potential paradox. In "Flirgleflip" (1950), a scientist who invents time-travel has to embark upon a Machiavellian plot to establish his discovery against the dictates of the temporal controllers who have it scheduled for a later era. Unfortunately, the dupe he sends into the past to make his claim fails to convince the indigenes of his origin, and the integrity of history is successfully protected by the equally Machiavellian ambassadors from the future. In "Sanctuary" (1957), a revolutionary seeks sanctuary from a mob in a temporal embassy, and gains asylum in the future which reveres him as a folk-hero. Unfortunately, he finds the world he has helped to make no more comfortable than his own era, and is soon seeking sanctuary in an embassy from a more distant future.

One of the neatest of these twist-in-time stories is "The Discovery of Morniel Mathaway" (1955), in which an art critic from the future comes to interview the twentieth century's greatest artist. The artist in question is a vain incompetent, who realizes immediately that he has not painted the pictures the critic admires so greatly. Instead of taking the obvious course, however, and stealing the visitor's book of reproductions so he can copy them and thus create the originals, he steals the time machine and goes to reap the rich rewards of adulation, leaving the critic to do the hard work and actually paint the pictures.

The best of all the time-travel fantasies, though, is the longest — "Winthrop Was Stubborn" (1957) — in which five contemporary individuals are sent into the twenty-fifth century in order that five physically similar history students from that era can do some field work. The ill-assorted tourists are treated well by their hosts, but four of them find the age of technological miracles, whose political morality is based on the Utter Sacredness of the Individual and the Individual Eccentric Impulse, quite intolerable. Trouble begins when the fifth member of the group, the aged Winthrop (who hated his miserable twentieth century existence) decides that he likes it far too much to go back. In a world of unlimited *laissez-faire* he cannot be forced to do anything, and his companions face being marooned if they cannot persuade him to let the perfectly balanced exchange take place. Here there is much more than mere plot-trickery as the story becomes a sharp commentary on the ethic of individual freedom and an excellent example of Utopian satire.

Tenn's first humorous contact-with-aliens story was "Consulate" (1948), in which a pair of small-town tradesmen are picked up by a flying saucer, and one of them is then faced with the problem of explaining to his fellow men that the other is now Earth's ambassador to the galaxy. Much more typical of the author's work in this vein, however, are "Betelgeuse Bridge" (1951) and "Will You Walk a Little Faster?" (1951). The first features molluscan confidence tricksters who cheat Earth out of all its radioactive elements by trading in immortality machines which break down as soon as the salesmen are safely away. In the second, aliens who are waiting to take over Earth as soon as mankind has brought to fruition its destiny of racial suicide offer governments free superweapons, making clear their dishonorable intentions but confidently assuming that the offer will be accepted anyhow. This notion of humans as dupes set up to be cheated was to provide Tenn with many plots, and though the tables are sometimes turned on the aliens (as they eventually are in "Betelgeuse Bridge"), the human virtues traditionally fêted in first contact stories are well and truly established.

Some of these stories are pure slapstick, like "Party of the Two Parts" (1954), concerning the difficulties of arresting an amoeba for peddling pornography to a human; the ultracomplicated spy-drama "Lisbon Cubed" (1958); and "The Flat-Eyed Monster" (1955), which is a traditional bug-eyed monster story turned on its head. The stories work better, however, when they are more smoothly subtle, as in the excellent "Bernie the Faust" (1963), a later version of "Betelgeuse Bridge" in which an earthly con artist sells Earth to an alien, realizes what he might have done, and buys it back again, giving the alien a tidy profit. When the alien buys a load of electronic parts with the cash, the con man realizes that he has been double-bluffed, and that the alien was only trying to raise sufficient dishonest money to repair his spaceship. But the last laugh is on the alien, who has bought cheap and shoddy goods foisted upon the dealer by the con man in the normal course of his business, and his spaceship is doomed to break down a second time.

Perhaps the best of all these crazy first-contact stories is *Venus and the Seven Sexes* (1949), which is told from the alien viewpoint. In this novella, the inhabitants of Venus welcome the ambassador from Earth who is supposed to have come to teach them to be civilized. Alas, their visitor is really a hack movie-maker who has been exiled from Hollywood to make a couple of films adapting B-movie romantic clichés to the problems of a species with seven sexes. When he leaves, the aliens look to his films for spiritual guidance, and find themselves on the horns of a sharp philosophical dilemma concerning the right road to civilization.

As with most satirical writers, Tenn is at his best when he is most ruthless, launching all-out attacks on the follies of his fellow-men. In "Null-P" (1951),

·

a postwar America falls prey to the worship of Normality, and a passion for safe mediocrity sweeps the world, bringing a new era of peace, brotherhood, and apathy whose end result is the domestication of man by intelligent and progressive dogs. In "The Masculinist Revolt" (1965), the codpiece comes back in a big way when the males of America revolt against the insidious tide of feminism which has eroded their masculinity. The only ideology that can stand against them is the one which Philip Wylie once attacked as "Momism," and so the banner of mother-love is hoisted against the hosts of *machismo*, with a presidential election to decide the conflict. The most telling of these attacks on favorite American myths, however, is "Eastward Ho!" (1958), in which white men in a postholocaust America find that the Indians have adapted far better to the decline into barbarism. As the Sioux and the Seminoles build great empires, the whites are herded into reservations, the victims of dishonored treaties, until they are forced to send forth the American Navy in the hope that Europe might provide a New World, a land of the free.

Tenn's more serious work tends to sit a little uncomfortably beside his satire — an inevitable consequence of the fact that it makes use of the same conventions that are being satirized elsewhere. "Generation of Noah" (1950) is a routine post-Hiroshima bomb-panic story which seems much less pointed than the acid "Will You Walk a Little Faster?" "The Liberation of Earth" (1953) is a savagely ironic story in which the conquest and reconquest of Earth by warring aliens is supposed to remind us of the evils of colonialism, but the message is blunted when we remember the slapstick treatment of a not-dissimilar theme in "Lisbon Cubed." A more straightforward antiwar story, "The Deserter" (1953), seems rather weak, but "The Sickness" (1955), in which an alien virus provides the means for its victims to transcend their involvement in the bitter hostilities of the Cold War, is relatively effective. The longest of Tenn's stories attempting to use first contact with aliens as a serious theme, "Firewater" (1952), seems to be perpetually embarrassed by the fact that its mildly humorous content is under the restraint of the intention of making a serious point.

Several of Tenn's more serious stories make impassioned claims on behalf of the wonders of parenthood. In "The Dark Star" (1957), the man chosen to be Earth's first space pioneer turns down the moment of glory when he learns that he might be sterilized as a consequence. In "A Man of Family" (1956), the protagonist faces disaster when a drop in his salary negates his legal entitlement to one of his four children. In "The Custodian" (1953), the man evacuating the art treasures of an Earth soon to be consumed by a nova finds new meaning in his task after discovering an infant whom he names Leonardo. Most striking of all, in "Down Among the Dead Men" (1954), the captain of a spaceship wins the support of his crew of recycled corpses when he explains to them that he, like they, is incompletely human because he is sterile and childless. The significance of this particular aspect of Tenn's work is dubious, but

the biographical note in *Of All Possible Worlds* reveals him to have been unmarried in 1955, at the age of thirty-five. The preoccupation is perhaps seen in
its appropriate cultural context in "On Venus Have We Got a Rabbi" and the
nonfantasy story "My Mother Was a Witch" (1966), both of which make
much of the special intergenerational relationships of Jewish families.

Tenn is a writer with a fine sense of irony, a master of a particular brand of
fatalism. Perhaps the story which best exemplifies his world view is "Time in
Advance" (1956), in which criminals who serve their sentences in advance of
committing their crimes get a special discount. Inevitably, the two would-be
murderers who return with licenses to kill find that their opportunity and motive have vanished with the passing years and the weight of experience. Tenn's
universe is one in which a person *can* win, but only in unexpected ways. It is a
universe in which greedy and self-assertive people cannot thrive, and even in
space operas like "The Last Bounce" (1950) and "Confusion Cargo" (1948),
the victories which the central characters achieve are not exactly the ones traditionally prescribed by pulp cliché. This is what gives Tenn's work its special
flavor: an ironic pessimism alleviated by the consciousness that absurdity is
funny and that small triumphs count.

Brian Stableford

Sources for Further Study

Criticism:

Ash, Brian. *Faces of the Future — The Lessons of Science Fiction*. London:
Elek/Pemberton, 1975, pp. 93-94, and pp. 167-168. Ash discusses two
stories of Tenn, "Null-P," and "Liberation of Earth."

The Encyclopedia of Science Fiction and Fantasy. Compiled by Donald H.
Tuck. Chicago: Advent Publishers, Inc., 1978, pp. 254-255. This is a general review of the author's career and life.

THE SHOT INTO INFINITY
(DER SCHUSS INS ALL)

Author: Otto Willi Gail (1896-1956)
First book publication: 1925
English translation: 1929
Type of work: Novel
Time: The 1920's
Locale: Germany, Budapest, Bucharest, and the rocket ship "Geryon" in orbit around the Earth and the Moon

A novel about the first attempt to launch a manned rocket ship into orbit around Earth

Principal characters:
AUGUST KORF, a German inventor of rocket ships
ROMANO VACARESCU, a Rumanian banker
SUCHINOW, a Russian engineer and builder of rockets
NATALJA SUCHINOW, his daughter

The 1920's were the heyday of German rocketry. Konstantin Tsiolkovsky, the Russian pioneer of space travel, had been much earlier, but at that time nobody knew of his work, and he had been neglected even in Russia (although he was later honored by the new Communist government). The work of the American Goddard was not completely unknown, but there was little solid information about him. In Germany, widespread interest in rockets was sparked by the publication of Hermann Oberth's *Die Rakete zu den Planetenräumen* in 1923, of which there were three editions before 1929, the third retitled *Wege zur Raumschiffahrt*. Soon there was a host of other similar books, an especially successful one being *Der Vorstoss in den Weltenraum* (1924) by the flamboyant Max Valier, who was soon to become one of the first martyrs of rocketry. Otto Willi Gail contributed a nonfiction work entitled *Mit Raketenkraft ins Weltenall* (1928), and he also used the theme in several works of fiction.

The most important German novel of space travel was of course written much earlier: Kurd Lasswitz's *Auf zwei Planeten* (1897) translated into English in 1971 as *Two Planets*, a book that contains many shrewd guesses about the actuality of interplanetary travel, including sound mathematical computations. Lasswitz was also one of the first writers to introduce the space station, which was later advanced by the German proponents of space travel. Lasswitz's book was well known in Germany; it sold so well that it was constantly reprinted up until 1933, when the Nazis banned the book for its philosophical-humanitarian content, not for its technological anticipations. Lasswitz was, of course, not only a mathematician but a man with a philosophical inclination, and although he gave much thought to space travel, more than any other author of fiction before him, it was but one element in a much richer and more ambitious novel. Also, in Lasswitz's book the Earthman was not the first to travel in space, but mankind was contacted by a more advanced Martian race.

Subsequent German authors were much more modest in their aims. The novels of the 1920's and 1930's often concentrate on the launching of a rocket ship and the trip beyond the Earth's atmosphere. One of the earliest and best of such novels was Bruno H. Buergel's *Der Stern von Afrika* (1920), subtitled "A Voyage into Space." The same endeavor was also announced in the titles or subtitles of Otfried von Hanstein's *Mond-Rak I, Eine Fahrt ins Weltall* (1929), Walter Vollmer's *Flug in die Sterne. Der Roman eines Weltraumschiffes* (1929) and the later *Start ins Weltall* (1940) by St. Bialkowski. In a number of other novels, space travel was an element essential to the plots: adventures on the Moon or other planets or conflicts in space, for instance in Bialkowski's *Krieg im All* (1935), Thea von Harbou's *Frau im Mond* (1929) (also a successful UFA film), Erich Dolezal's *Der Ruf der Sterne* (1932), C. V. Rock's *Rückkehr aus dem All* (1939), Paul Eugen Sieg's *Südöstlich Venus* (1940), and others. The most successful German science fiction author, Hans Dominik, had written of future worlds where space travel is commonplace in his early short stories published by the boys' annual *Das neue Universum*. However, in his novels, he departed from Earth as a setting in only two cases, *Das Erbe der Uraniden* (1928) and *Triebstoff SR* (1940). In the latter he merely describes the development of a new rocket fuel, a marked step backwards from some of his earlier works.

The Shot into Infinity (1925) is Gail's fictional treatment of mankind's first step into space, followed later by another novel about space travel, the juvenile *Hans Hardts Mondfahrt* (1928, translated as *By Rocket to the Moon*, 1931). By virtue of the fact that Hugo Gernsback had in C. A. Brandt a consultant who was familiar with German science fiction, the novel was translated into English and published in *Wonder Stories Quarterly* (Fall, 1929). It thus became a "noted interplanetary classic," as Don H. Tuck puts it in his *Encyclopedia of Science Fiction and Fantasy*. "Classic" not because of any intrinsic merit the story might have, but classic in the science fiction sense, which might be defined as "any unreadable old story that for some unaccountable reason has caught the fancy of the science fiction fans." As a story, the book is quite hopeless, although it will again be reprinted in a German paperback in 1979.

The hero of the book is the German, August Korf, a latter-day Count Zeppelin destined to increase the fame of German inventors in the world. His motive is to get back at the world for the crushing German defeat in World War I (the peace terms had forced the Germans to turn over their Zeppelins to the victors). Like the heroes of later American space operas by E. E. "Doc" Smith or John W. Campbell, Jr., Korf is a serial inventor (although a more modest one); at first he employs rockets propelled by gun powder (the secret of which is stolen from him — by obnoxious foreigners, of course), and later liquid fuels.

Alas, the first rocket ship ever launched into space is not his; it is a vessel built by the Russian engineer Suchinow, and financed by the Rumanian banker, Romanco Vacarescu. That the first rocket into outer space was launched from Dracula country is an obvious tribute to the rocket pioneer, Hermann Oberth, a Rumanian of German extraction. Unfortunately, Suchinow's attempt, lacking the ingenuity of Germany industry, is simply too feeble. His pilot Skoryna (his daughter Natalja in disguise) remains caught in orbit around the Moon, powerless to get back to Earth.

This situation provides German genius with an opportunity to step in and set a humanistic example. In only four month's time, August Korf whips up a proper rocket ship. Actually the design for Suchinow's rocket ship was taken partially from the plans stolen from Korf. Natalja had previously approached Korf in order to learn his secrets, and adapted the knowledge gleaned in this dishonest way to try out her own ideas (which were unsuccessful). Her additional hard luck was that she happened to fall in love with August Korf, and he with her. From this comes a subplot in which an uncle of the hero searches for the vanished Natalja in Berlin, Budapest, and Bucharest, without being able to solve the secret of her identity. The reader is thus treated to a great surprise when the pilot Skoryna turns out to be Natalja, miraculously still alive after many months in her tiny rocket. Having apparently fallen into some sort of suspended animation, she has been preserved in a frozen state in outer space. Natalja is very weak, however, and after her reconciliation with the hero, who is at first understandably furious and hurt, she dies upon entering the full force of Earth's gravity again. To tie up all the novel's loose ends, her father Suchinow, who had secretly entered Korf's rocket disguised as a reporter, burns up in the atmosphere when he tries to bring his salvaged rocket ship back to Earth.

As fiction, this is all pretty dreadful, with a hackneyed plot and thin, stereotyped characters. Korf, for instance, is described simply as a blonde giant with steel-blue eyes. So all that a reviewer can do is to note the novel's technological details. Even there, Gail is hardly scientifically accurate, speaking, for example, of the limits of Earth's gravity field. He merely incorporates into his novel the thinking of astronautics as it was at the time. His rocket is a three-stage contraption, the first stage burning alcohol, the second a mixture of hydrogen and alcohol, and the third pure liquid hydrogen. The interior of the rocket is, however, pure imagination; it is huge, quite fashionable, furnished like a palace, and manned by a large crew. The equipment is also more fiction than science. Gail's characters move about in the vacuum of space in space suits which are redesigned skaphanders; Natalja is evacuated from her tiny rocket by means of a tunnel that is welded to her ship; the returning rocket ship is deacclerated by atmospheric friction, and lands like an airplane. In the sequel to the book, the spaceships have shrunk and more closely resemble torpedos. In *The Shot into Infinity*, the shot into space is all important for the book; and when it is accomplished, all that remains to be done is to wind down a melodramatic love story.

August Korf returns again in the sequel *Der Stein vom Mond* (1926), translated into English as *The Shot from the Moon* (*Wonder Stories Quarterly*, Spring, 1930). This story boasts a more elaborate plot, but also never rises above the level of the most rudimentary boy's fiction. It mixes rocketry with ancient myth, a mixture that has found it widest appeal not in science fiction but in the fictions passed off as fact by the propagandists of Ancient Astronaut theories such as Erich von Däniken.

The novel begins in Yucatan, where a young girl of European-Indian ancestry, apparently possessed, imagines herself to be one Huitaca, an ancient Mayan empress. The novel is blatantly racist, with a few brief but repellent scenes in which Indians are described as a degenerate and lazy race of blockheads, in contrast to the industrious, intelligent contemporary Europeans. The story describes the glory that was ancient Atlantis and Mu, where people knew how to control gigantic powers, but grew vain in their belief in reason, lost their touch with nature, and started enslaving and exploiting the barbarians around them. When these peoples rose up in revolt, Queen Huitaca called upon the secret powers over the elements. The skies divided, and the Moon, arriving from the outer cosmos, entered its present orbit around Earth, causing great upheavals and floods that tore Atlantis asunder. Huitaca herself fled into space.

These rather wild theories of cosmic catastrophe are based upon the crank theories of Hörbinger's "World Ice Theory" which held that the Moon and the planets consist mostly of ice. Among the sources cited by Gail is not only Fauth-Hörbinger's original *Die Glacial-Kosmogonie*, but other crank works that connect the Atlantis story with the Aryan myth, such as K. G. Zschaetsch's *Atlantis, die Urheimat der Arier* or Rudolf Steiner's *Unsere atlantischen Vorfahren*. These prehistoric happenings, which are told in retrospect, are then confirmed by an expedition to the planet Venus. The old spaceship of Queen Huitaca is discovered there, before it is swallowed forever by the atmosphere of Venus. In this sequel, rocketry has given way to old myths, and space travel is merely used to confirm them. The author never bothers to explain how the spirit of such an ancient person manages to get hold of the mind of a young present-day girl. Here the old mysticism again raises its head, and space travel simply serves to verify this nonsense. The book only presents a childishly diluted and coarsened version of a biblical Eden destroyed by human presumption and by mankind's overweening faith in his own reason.

Whether considered as intellectual constructs or merely entertainment, Gail's novels are not outstanding. Such is the state of many books considered to be "classics" in the genre of science fiction.

Franz Rottensteiner

Sources for Further Study

Criticism:

The Encyclopedia of Science Fiction and Fantasy. Compiled by Donald H. Tuck. Chicago: Advent Publishers, Inc., 1978, p. 178. Tuck cites this novel as one of Gail's best on interplanetary travel.

SINISTER BARRIER

Author: Eric Frank Russell (1905-1977)
First book publication: 1943
Type of work: Novel
Time: 2015
Locale: New York and its environs

The story of events following the discovery that the human race is the property of invisible energy-beings which feed on emotional tensions generated by fear, pain, and hatred

> *Principal characters:*
> BILL GRAHAM, an agent of the U.S. Intelligence Service
> SANGSTER, his superior officer
> HARMONY CURTIS, a doctor
> ART WOHL, a policeman
> PROFESSOR EDWARD BEACH, a scientist

Sinister Barrier appeared in the first issue of *Unknown*, the companion magazine to *Astounding Science Fiction* which flourished briefly in the years before America joined World War II. The story that its submission to John W. Campbell, Jr. inspired the editor to found the new magazine is, however, untrue. Though *Sinister Barrier is* a horror story, it is also a straightforward piece of science fiction. It borrows its plot from the writings of the eccentric and iconoclastic collector of unusual newspaper-items, Charles Fort. Fort published four books documenting his researches between 1919 and 1932, one of which (*Lo!*, originally published in 1931) had been serialized in *Astounding Science Fiction* during 1934; but his influence on science fiction had previously been slight. One of the conclusions he had gleaned from his mock-logical synthesis of the "damned data" which he collected ("damned" in the sense that it was not accepted by orthodox scientists) was that the human race is property, owned by some superior species which has warned would-be extraterrestrial visitors away from Earth. Though there have been other memorable science fiction stories based on Fortean mythology written in more recent times (such as Robert M. Green's "The Dead-Eye Dick Syndrome" and R. A. Lafferty's *Where Have You Been, Sandaliotis?*), *Sinister Barrier* remains the classic example of this curious species. It appeared in book form in England in 1943, and in the United States in 1948.

Sinister Barrier opens with lurid descriptions of the deaths of a number of eminent scientists. All the deaths are diagnosed as suicide or heart failure, but the reader is left in no doubt that the victims have been destroyed by something malevolent and mysterious. One of them, Professor Walter Mayo, plunges to his death from a New York skyscraper to land at the feet of intelligence agent Bill Graham. Graham is instantly suspicious, having known Mayo to be a man of extraordinarily sound mind. He telephones his superior officer, Sangster, and obtains *carte blanche* to begin an investigation.

Graham soon finds out about the other mysterious deaths, and connects them when he discovers that all the dead scientists had been in contact with Professor Bjornsen of Stockholm, and that all had treated themselves before dying with iodine (applied externally), methylene blue, and mescal (applied internally). Graham recruits the help of a policeman named Art Wohl, and learns from a female doctor named Curtis that another eminent scientist involved with Mayo and Bjornsen, Professor Edward Beach, is apparently still alive. Beach works for the National Camera Company at Silver City, Idaho, and is developing a new photographic emulsion sensitive to wavelengths of electromagnetic energy outside the visual spectrum.

Graham sets off for Silver City, but before he gets there the whole city is blown sky-high by a colossal explosion at the National Camera Company plant. From one of the few survivors, he learns that Beach may have survived, and he eventually manages to track down the scientist, who is hiding underground in a remote location. Beach explains to Graham that Bjornsen had discovered a way to extend human powers of sight, allowing him to break through the "sinister barrier" confining visual sensation to its narrow band of electromagnetic frequencies. With his improved vision, Bjornsen, and those who followed his example, were able to see pale-blue luminous globes floating above the surface of the Earth, which would periodically descend to fasten themselves on to the spinal cords of unsuspecting humans, leeching from them some special energy generated by powerful negative emotions. These creatures, dubbed "Vitons," apparently own the human race and milk them of sustenance in the same way that humans own and milk cattle. The Vitons are receptive to human thoughts, but only at close range — they move quickly enough to destroy all trace of Bjornsen's discovery, but are unaware that Beach has survived the Silver City holocaust.

With the resources of the U.S. Intelligence Service at their disposal, Graham and Beach manage to spread their revelation far and wide across America, though thousands of lives are lost in consequence as the Vitons try to silence the media. The immediate reaction of the Vitons to the fact that their existence is known is to provoke an all-out war between the alerted West and the hordes of the "Yellow Empire," whose leaders are under the sway of the telepathic aliens. The Vitons have been responsible for all past wars and virtually all other human miseries and misfortunes, which they deliberately generate in order to produce the negative emotions on which they feed. All people who have disappeared mysteriously have been captured by the Vitons for use in bizarre experiments; such experimental subjects returned to the world of men are schizophrenics.

Despite the war, Graham and his allies battle on to try to develop a weapon which will be effective against the Vitons. Through Dr. Curtis he learns that a particular instrument of medical technology sets up a field which repels the aliens, and this instrument saves his life when the Vitons come to destroy him.

This provides one vital clue to the project, and the other is unwittingly provided by the Vitons themselves when they set up a trap for him by taking over Sangster and his secretary. By this time Beach has already been disposed of. At last, the weapon is ready, and Graham sets out to gun down the Vitons even as the bombs of the Yellow Empire are falling on New York. Civilization is on the brink of collapse, and millions have been slaughtered, but the Vitons are vanquished. Graham is free at last to embrace Harmony Curtis and look forward to the dawn of a new era of peace and prosperity for mankind. All human troubles have been swept away completely.

Sinister Barrier is one of the great paranoid fantasies of science fiction. It is an extremely lurid and crudely written thriller, penned in a ludicrous mock-American style which Russell, a British writer, apparently felt compelled to adopt in order to enhance his chances of selling to the American pulp market. Despite these failings, however, the novel proved to be extremely effective. It is less so today, but this is in some measure due to the fact that its basic premise has become familiar and has lost most of its shock value. Other classic paranoid melodramas, such as Robert Heinlein's *The Puppet Masters* (1951) and Jack Finney's *The Body Snatchers* (1955), have overtaken the theme of *Sinister Barrier* with their own extrapolations of the idea of insidious parasitism.

The notion of invisible horrors lurking beyond the visible spectrum had been used before, but it was Russell who figured out how best to exploit it, by making human beings the unsuspecting victims of such creatures, cruelly used, exploited, and tortured. For centuries, the great majority of men believed that the ills suffered by mankind were the work of malevolent demonic forces, but science fiction had espoused a world view which rigorously excluded such notions until Russell found a way to reimport them. The essential power of the idea was already well-established, and Russell merely built a pipeline for it to flow into the mythos of science fiction, recharged with plausibility. H. P. Lovecraft had been doing the same thing for many years, but had never quite been accepted by the science fiction establishment as conforming to their standards of plausibility.

The notion that men are not really responsible for the sea of troubles that engulfs them has obvious attractions. Russell himself went on to provide an even more bizarre account of the origins of the "madness" which seems in his view to afflict the human race in his second novel, *Dreadful Sanctuary* (1948), in which Earth is seen as the dumping ground for the mental deviants of several other worlds. The rationale of *Sinister Barrier*, meanwhile, was given a new symbolic dressing by Richard S. Shaver in the long series of stories which he wrote for *Amazing Stories* in the late 1940's. In order to put across its point, *Sinister Barrier* employs a kind of "double bluff" in its presentation, with Russell protesting too much in his introduction that *of course* the story is not true, and that just so long as no one believes a word of it, he is safe from

possible reprisals. Ray Palmer, the editor who promoted Shaver, was less subtle in his own double bluff, continually hinting that Shaver's paranoid fantasies
of degenerate descendants of a prehistoric super-race controlling mankind from
caverns beneath America *might* be true. Shaver himself appeared to believe the
stories wholeheartedly. The subsequent fate of the Shaver mystery, which deteriorated into an embarrassing sick joke, shows clearly enough what happens
when such fantasies are dragged into confrontation with reality, but its brief
period of flourishing success testifies to the essential power of the fantasy. The
Fortean elements of *Sinister Barrier* are deployed cleverly enough to serve
their instrumental value without ever pushing the narrative over the edge into
the morass of crank hysteria (something of which Fort — who refused to join
the Fortean society founded to promote his message — would surely have
approved).

Viewed on the basis of its literary merits, *Sinister Barrier* is a very poor
work. As an explication of a particular kind of nightmare, however, it is eminently worthy of attention. It provides an excellent vocabulary of symbols for
the dramatization of the sensation (which we all suffer periodically) that one is
the victim of persecution by forces unknown, unseen, and quite beyond one's
control. When this sensation takes over, it achieves the status of a neurosis, or
even a psychosis, but this does not mean that *Sinister Barrier* is a neurotic
book. The way in which it operates upon the consciousness of the reader is
crude and melodramatic, but this trait is part of the very essence of genuine
nightmares, which must evaporate quickly in the light of reason. If they did
not, they could hardly perform the cathartic function which allows them to be
as stimulating and exciting as *Sinister Barrier* undoubtedly is.

Brian Stableford

Sources for Further Study

Reviews:

Amazing Stories. XXXIX, April, 1965, pp. 126-127.
Analog. XLIV, September, 1949, pp. 151-152.
Authentic Science Fiction. XXII, June, 1952, p. 112.
Fantastic Novels Magazine. IV, May, 1950, p. 117.
Super Science Stories. V, January, 1949, p. 93.

THE SIRENS OF TITAN

Author: Kurt Vonnegut, Jr. (1922-   )
First book publication: 1959
Type of work: Novel
Time: The future
Locale: The United States, Mars, Mercury, Titan

The satirical and comically visionary account of one man's odyssey through the solar system as he searches for the meaning of life and the destiny of man

> *Principal characters:*
> MALACHI CONSTANT, the richest American and a notorious rake
> WINSTON NILES RUMFOORD, a space-time traveler
> BEATRICE RUMFOORD, wife of Winston, wife of Malachi
> CHRONO, son of Malachi and Beatrice
> SALO, an eleven-million-year-old Tralfamadorean messenger

Kurt Vonnegut's deceptively simple and seemingly unsophisticated style reveals a lucid vision of the modern age. His books are restrained in a manner which lures the reader on with unaffected prose and surface humor. It is only when the reader is thoroughly enmeshed in the web of character and incident, and is chuckling to himself about the situation of some fictional being, that his self-satisfied grin begins to fade. Indeed, with the recognition of his own face in the group portrait of humanity, the reader comes to understand Vonnegut's depth and insight. As his characters pursue their own truths and eventually discredit themselves, his readers find themselves inextricably wired into the proceedings. The undertow of his humor pulls the reader down, forcing him to confront cherished dogmas and entrenched values. Kurt Vonnegut has been the gadfly of modern existential man, and has only recently emerged from the literary "underground" into the mainstream of contemporary letters.

The Sirens of Titan represents an early stage of Vonnegut's writing; written in 1959, it is an occasionally heavy-handed attempt at "social significance" satire. Here, in his second novel, the writing is more clearly science fiction than either his earlier or later work. The genre lends itself to the breadth of Vonnegut's vision and is a compatible form for his treatment of such broad subjects as war, religion, human contingency, and other existential problems. His use of science fiction enables him to draw upon many of the progressive beliefs man has developed through science itself, allows him to take the reader through space and time, and encourages him to create deranged worlds which are actually the logical extension of contemporary American values.

With a style free of esoteric mystification, Vonnegut telegraphs his punches. While there is much to be discovered between the lines, his major targets are clearly delineated. In *The Sirens of Titan*, Vonnegut wastes no time in presenting his themes. His comic, nightmarish vision is an honest portrayal of man-in-the-world which attempts to affirm hope for mankind in general. If there is a major thrust to this book it is the relentless convergence upon the question of life's ultimate meaning or the purpose of life itself. The story is constructed in a manner which forces the reader to encounter both internal and external realities of an absurd, chaotic universe. It is a look backwards to an unenlightened time, one described by the narrator as "the nightmare ages." This was a time of outward searching. Mankind wanted to know who was in charge, what life was all about. Since the actual search of the heavens yielded nothing, all that remained was inner reality, a new frontier which would eventually yield "goodness and wisdom."

Nevertheless, the action of the novel begins in a time of spiritual impoverishment. Not only does the author set out his themes early in the story but he also outlines the course of events. Winston Niles Rumfoord, a man whose private spaceship chanced a collision with an "uncharted chrono-synclastic infundibulum," and his dog, Kazak, are about to materialize within his palatial mansion somewhere in Newport, Rhode Island. Because of their intrusion into this time-funnel, the man and his dog exist as a type of "wave phenomenon — apparently pulsing in a distorted spiral with its origin in the sun and its terminal in Betelegeuse." Traversing the universe in this Einsteinian time-space warp, they exist simultaneously in all times and places with which the wave-phenomenon makes contact. This simultaneity of existence enables the man to experience the future, the present, and the past all at once. Because he can predict the future, his periodic materializations are significant.

If Winston Niles Rumfoord could effectuate change in the course of cosmic events he would be much more than a fortune teller. Unfortunately, he, like everyone else, is subject to the whims and fancies of the meaningless universe. As the story begins, Vonnegut's existential hero, Malachi Constant, is present for one of the materializations. In this meeting Constant learns that his ultimate destiny will take him to a satellite of Saturn called Titan; but first he will marry Beatrice Rumfoord on Mars, go to Mercury, and come back to Earth again. The remainder of the book is a gradual unfolding of this design. The plot of *The Sirens of Titan* follows Malachi Constant through a series of interrelated events that tempt the reader to interpret Vonnegut's universe as predetermined.

Yet, as the narrative develops, it is clear that the author's underlying concern is really with man's incapacity to master his own destiny in spite of insight into the overall design. Many paradoxical elements in Vonnegut's plot development create the basis for comic irony or black humor. Through the exposition of characters and events he takes issue with the comfortable belief that there is a benevolent force in the universe rewarding the good and punishing the bad. For some, organized religion provides a preordained purpose to existence; these people are a recurring target of Kurt Vonnegut's trenchant wit.

Malachi Constant, soon to be involved in a rather difficult trek throughout the universe, is the "richest American — and a notorious rakehell." An unimpressive character born into greath wealth, he inherited a fortune from a physically and morally unattractive man whose only explanation for his great success was that he had had an enormous quantity of "dumb luck." Noel Constant, through an investment technique that consisted of breaking down sentences of the Gideon Bible into capital letters, dividing the letters into pairs, putting periods between the letters, and then investing in corporations that had those initials, had become a millionaire. In the end, without ever understanding why his method worked, he died and passed on his money and investment technique to his son. Malachi, singularly unconcerned with understanding the nature of his good fortune, completely accepts both his good luck and his riches without question.

Cosmic irony, as seen in the success story of Noel Constant, is continually on hand in Vonnegut's books. Vonnegut's characters often find themselves questioning what is real, what is imaginary, and whether or not the difference really matters. Although they are equally trapped in a world which provides little in the way of purposeful order, a conflict arises between those characters who embody passive acceptance of reality, and those who demand meaning in a world that has none to offer. Neither Malachi nor his father understand the nature of their luck. They passively accept it, recognizing that some people are lucky and some people are not. The belief that God or Harvard Business School is responsible for great wealth or luck is rejected outright. The issue of an absurd universe cannot be evaded by reaching out for higher appeal or hope that transcends humanity. Vonnegut irrepressively satirizes those who believe that there is a definitive relationship between being good and doing good, between good works and rewards, and between bad works and punishment. The universe is indifferent; that is simply the way it is. There is little reason behind it, and what reason there is is far from holy.

When Malachi's luck leaves as mysteriously as it had arrived, his fortune is lost. Not understanding his bad luck any more than his good luck, he opts to go to Mars with two recruiters for the Martian army. Simultaneously, Beatrice Rumfoord, knowing her husband's prediction that she would marry Malachi on Mars, is insulating herself against every contingency. Nevertheless, she is abducted.

The second segment of *The Sirens of Titan* is a continued assault on rationality. Although the setting has changed to Mars, Vonnegut's vision remains focused on the existential constructs of an absurd universe. The lack of cosmic understanding is as predominant on Mars as on Earth. Recruits from Earth have been systematically relieved of their memories, fitted with antenna implants which control actions and induce great pain for disobedience, and are being trained for an impending invasion of Earth. Just who is in command and why the invasion is to take place is not known. What is clear to the reader is that the invasion is doomed to failure — it will be, in essence, a mass suicide.

Vonnegut's creation of an anti-Utopia on Mars is a vehicle of situational satire. His abhorrence of war is made clear in all of his work, and the military is one of his consistent targets. Here, in *The Sirens of Titan*, the meaningless invasion of Earth and its concommitant death and destruction parallel the Dresden experience, a theme to be found directly or indirectly in each of his books. The lack of freedom, the blind obedience, and the arbitrary control of thought and action are somewhat exaggerated, yet not entirely unlike our traditional military values. Furthermore, the brainwashing and implantation of pain-inflicting devices are metaphorically similar to our own uninitiated recruit's experience.

Up to this point, most of Vonnegut's characters either acquiesce in the human condition or deceive themselves through belief in some cosmic absolute. The thesis that people cannot bear freedom to any large degree is not a profound literary pronouncement. Likewise, the heroic resistance of one individual to societal oppression is old hat. Through the use of the Martian anti-Utopia and the creation of Unk, Vonnegut seems to be parodying the Orwellian mode.

Malachi Constant's identity on Mars is Unk. Unk is a resistor who, in spite of continual punishment and brainwashing, attempts to maintain his individuality through the forbidden process of remembering. Learning that his wife, Beatrice, and son, Chrono, are on Mars, Unk attempts to desert the invasion force, find his wife and son, and fly off somewhere to find some meaning to it all. Unfortunately, his attempt is thwarted and he ends up on a spaceship that is programed to take both Unk and his "buddy," Boaz, to Mercury.

Winston Niles Rumfoord, the true force behind the suicidal invasion by the Martian army, is successful in the first phase of his plan to reorganize the values of people on Earth. Capitalizing on the Martian army's total defeat on Earth, Rumfoord creates a new religion built on collective guilt, which is named "The Church of God the Utterly Indifferent." Since the religion is based on "luckless" equality, all persons are required to handicap themselves so as to avoid any advantage over others. Against this background, the major tenet of the religion is that man does not need, nor will he get, help from God.

Vonnegut's characters go through various forms of torment as they are unwittingly used by superior forces. Unk is brought back to Earth through a series of Rumfoord's contrivances only to find himself the long-awaited "Space Wanderer." As a pawn to Rumfood's purposes, Unk is now the Messiah figure of the new religion which paradoxically is unified around the defilement of that most pernicious of persons — Malachi Constant. In a religion that denies luck as a force in human life and has a world view based on everyone being a victim of a series of accidents, Malachi Constant represents the unfair advantage obtained by so many prior to the Martian War.

The idea that there can be a "religion" based on the belief that there is chaos in the universe and that everyone is equally victimized by a series of accidents is an example of Vonnegut's use of bitter irony. It is in the last segment of the novel that the author lands the *coup de grâce*. After being united with his family and learning his true identity, Malachi Constant sets out for Titan with Beatrice and Chrono. Here they meet Salo, a robot messenger from Tralfamadore, whose mission had been to deliver a message from his planet to the end of the universe. Unfortunately, Salo's spaceship malfunctioned and he became grounded on Titan. For 200,000 years, Salo waited patiently for his replacement part to be delivered to Titan. Since Salo had the ability to watch events on Earth, messages from his home planet were transmitted to him by way of tremendous structures which civilizations had built on Earth. Stonehenge, for example, was actually a message in Tralfamadorian meaning "replacement part being rushed with all possible speed." The replacement part, Chrono's good luck piece, after fifty thousand years of human history, had arrived.

The resolution of *The Sirens of Titan* answers the question set out at the beginning of the book. The meaning of human history, the ultimate destiny of mankind, resides in the pragmatic design of the distant planet Tralfamadore to deliver a replacement part to one of their spaceships. Even for Salo, whose whole purpose for existing was to deliver the message across the galaxy, and who was instrumental in helping Rumfoord bring about the Martian War, there is a grimly humorous discovery. After waiting so long for the replacement part, Salo, who had faithfully followed his orders not to open the message, tears the container open in a fit of rage. The message contains a single dot which, when translated into English, means "Greetings." Upon discovering this, he takes himself apart, throwing his parts in all directions.

Vonnegut, by the end of the story, presents the reader with a teleological universe that remains fitfully chaotic and uncontrollable. Even with insight into the future, man is powerless to control his own external destiny. The events that take place appear to be subordinated in a hierarchical fashion to pragmatic circumstances which, although not predetermined, remained fixed in time. Yet the events do not fit into any overall structure of cosmic purpose. Malachi Constant is the pawn of Winston Niles Rumfoord; Winston Niles Rumfoord is the pawn of Salo and the Tralfamadorians; the Tralfamadorians seem to be pawns themselves. None of Vonnegut's characters seem to have more than a limited ability to see and an even smaller ability to understand why things are the way they are. But Vonnegut's final judgment is not one of despair. Malachi Constant's utterance to Salo after Beatrice's death that "a purpose to life, no matter who is controlling it, is to love whoever is around to be loved," indicates the author's ultimate faith in mankind's ability to create meaning. The only possible solution is the discovery of an internal center of meaning. The truth must be found within each individual.

The Sirens of Titan cleverly succeeds in the ironic juxtaposition of the comic spirit and Existentialism. The ultimate cosmic joke, that all Earthly events from Stonehenge to the Great Wall of China to the Martian War were the result of direct intervention by the inhabitants of a distant planet trying to transport a spare part to one of their spacecraft on Titan, is the darkest of humor. Vonnegut's universe is born of paradox. There is an intermingling of mystery, chaos, and predetermination. His use of comic irony helps the reader tolerate the painful apprehension of an absurd universe.

There is no question that Vonnegut, in *The Sirens of Titan*, tends to moralize. In his overwhelming concern for humanity he is sometimes guilty of oversimplifying many complex issues. It might even be said that he includes too much in the story — various side issues and discussions might just as well have been skirted or left alone. Satire and irony are themselves wonderful vehicles of social commentary, but in using them, the author runs the risk of being potentially obscure, misunderstood, or boring. Vonnegut may or may not be guilty of any combination of the three, but the uncertainty in judgment perhaps speaks for itself. Yet, an analysis of *The Sirens of Titan* must be concluded with praise. In spite of criticisms made, the overall effect of the novel is to assert a positive belief in humanity. *The Sirens of Titan* is the product of a skilled artisan who is able to point out the problems of man and society without negating man as an individual.

Clifford P. Bendau

Sources for Further Study

Criticism:

Ketterer, David. *New Worlds for Old; the Apocalyptic Imagination, Science Fiction, and American Literature*. Bloomington: Indiana University Press, 1974, pp. 296-333. Ketterer discusses *The Sirens of Titan* in comparison with other novels of the same genre.

Lawler, Donald J. *"The Sirens of Titan*: Vonnegut's Metaphysical Shaggy Dog Story," in *Vonnegut in America; an Introduction to the Life and Work of Kurt Vonnegut*. Edited by Jerome Klinkowitz and Donald L. Lawler. New York: Delacorte, 1977, pp. 61-86. This is an excellent analysis of *The Sirens of Titan*, and probably in more depth than any work yet written.

Schatt, Stanley. *Kurt Vonnegut, Jr*. Boston: Twayne, 1976, pp. 30-42. This major work of criticism on Vonnegut gives some discussion of *The Sirens of Titan* as a part of his major novels.

Reviews:

Analog. LXV, May, 1960, p. 175.

Galaxy. XX, December, 1961, p. 144.

Magazine of Fantasy and Science Fiction. XVIII, March, 1960, pp. 91-92.

SF Commentary. I, January, 1969, pp. 19-23.

SIRIUS
A Fantasy of Love and Discord

Author: Olaf Stapledon (1886-1950)
First book publication: 1944
Type of work: Novel
Time: Mainly the 1930's and early years of World War II
Locale: England and Wales

The tragic — and at times warmly, poignantly comic — story of a superdog, his brain artificially mutated to reach human levels of intelligence, whose powers involve him in perpetual conflict with both civilization and his animality, until he achieves, through love and suffering, an identity of "spirit" that is neither man's nor dog's but his own

Principal characters:
THOMAS TRELONE, a Cambridge physiologist
SIRIUS, a German Shepherd bred by Thomas
PLAXY, the daughter of Thomas, who grows up with Sirius
ROBERT, the narrator, a novelist in love with Plaxy
ELIZABETH TRELONE, wife of Thomas, mother of Plaxy
GEOFFREY ADAMS, a parson in the slums of London
LLEWELYN PUGH, a Welsh sheep farmer
THWAITES, a sadistic English sheep farmer

Sirius was the latest of Stapledon's four major works of science fiction, following *Star Maker* (1937), *Odd John* (1935), and *Last and First Men* (1930). Here again Stapledon transposes human nature and society to an extreme perspective that challenges empirical norms of "reality." But this time, departing from the cosmic and superhuman perspectives of his earlier fiction, he finds his angle of vision in a more familiar world: the realm of animal, and specifically canine, nature. The eponymous hero is a dog whose artificially mutated brain matures to reach all but the very highest levels of human intelligence; and the novel is the biography of this "super-super-dog," as he moves continually between the conflicting worlds of his experience: between the wild Welsh moorlands and urban civilization, between the feral nature of his animal self and the humanly conditioned milieu of his searching mind.

His life-quest pursues the endless question of his self-doubt: is it possible for so divided a being (and the division, of course, is ultimately man's as well) to overcome the conflict that threatens to destroy him, to achieve survival and hope for the future through a more transcendent sense of identity and purpose, a viable harmony of natural instinct and undeceived intelligence? To ask that question is to be reminded that Stapledon was a philosopher and a social reformer with a Utopian conscience, a thinker who used fiction as an experimental workshop to test the value of ideas and their consequences. Yet what sets this novel apart in the rather austere Stapledon canon is its emotional warmth. For *Sirius* is also a love story, the history of the lifelong, indomitable love of Sirius and Plaxy, his human twin in education. Perhaps it is this aspect of the

tale which sustains, at the deepest level, the interest of readers and has transformed what might otherwise have been a grotesque speculative fable into a
minor classic of the genre.

The story is told by Robert, a young novelist and R.A.F. airman who is in
love with Plaxy. He has gone in search of her after she mysteriously leaves
him because of some secret anxiety. It is her loyalty to Sirius that has led to
this estrangement, and the novel opens when Robert locates Plaxy at a Welsh
sheep farm and first encounters her dog-companion. Stapledon is careful to
present Sirius from the start as not only a marvelous canine, but also as a
person (Robert's first awareness of him is as a strange voice speaking to Plaxy).
It is Robert's need to understand and accept this paradox of a supersheepdog
who is not only his mental but also his spiritual equal — and a rival for his
beloved's affections — that moves the novelist to recover and reconstruct in
narrative form the inseparably bound histories of Plaxy and Sirius.

Sirius is the creation of Plaxy's father, the physiologist Thomas Trelone.
He has succeeded, through careful interbreeding and hormone injections in
both mother and pup (together with some cranial surgery), in producing a dog
with a massively complex brain, in a braincase large enough to contain it (it
rises domelike as high as the dog's ears) and a body strong and supple enough
to support this weighty head and respond to its varied neural demands. Sirius
is predominantly a German Shepherd, a breed that enjoyed great popularity in
the period between the two world wars; and some facts about its place in
canine history may throw some light on Stapledon's way of conceiving his
protagonist.

Developed in its present form shortly before the turn of the century, the
German breed became established as a superior sheepdog in England just before World War I. The simultaneous rise of anti-German feeling led to British
adoption of the neutral, but genealogically inaccurate, name Alsatian (the
name also used in the novel). In the 1920's numerous popular myths grew up
around the breed: it was reputed to be the bravest, most intelligent, most faithful and trainable of dogs. There were rumors of a superdog being bred from
this stock in Switzerland. Descent from the wolf was widely believed to be the
genetic strain responsible for its strength and versatile skills (as late as 1930
the official name for the dog in England was Alsatian Wolf Dog, though actually there is nothing distinctively lupine in its traits or physical makeup).
Stapledon makes good use of the legend of wolf-ancestry in giving symbolic
resonance to the conflict in his hero: not only is Sirius said to be "wolf-like"
in appearance but an atavistic "wolf-mood" is the great peril of violence in his
nature that his intelligence must learn to overcome.

But why this creation in the first place? And why a dog rather than another
mammal — an ape, for instance, an anthropoid by nature and gifted with
greater manipulative abilities? In a cynical moment Sirius suspects that he was
created for trivial motives, "for fun"; but Trelone's declared intention is to

produce a truly "social animal," one expressing its intelligence through social functions and relationships. (A further ambition, revealed late in the novel, is to lay the groundwork for artificially stimulated brain-growth in man.) Since the objective is "sociality," Thomas insists that dogs, by virtue of their temperament and freedom of access to human society, are the best candidates for his experiment.

This reasoning, of course, overlooks — or helps the reader to overlook — the notoriously poor equipment of dogs for semiotic learning and communication. They are also without much capacity for disciplined observation of the external world, being not only without color vision but unable to make precise discriminations of visual form (line, figure, proportion, and the like). Aware of these deficiencies, Stapledon wisely refrains from any ridiculous descriptions of a bespectacled puppy poring over the print of a text; we are simply told later that the grown Sirius loves to retire to his books, has made his way through H. G. Wells's *The Outline of History*, often examines musical scores, and holds strong critical opinions about the poetry of T. S. Eliot. We are willing to suspend disbelief in these prodigious accomplishments for a very simple reason: our imaginations answer to the silent power of literary convention. For that convention decrees that apes and monkeys are (as in Kipling) antic and senseless mimics of human speech, while dogs and their wild relatives, foxes and wolves, are among the most literate and eloquent of animal talkers.

Nevertheless, the liabilities inherent in the premise of an intellectual dog would be fatal if Stapledon did not consistently turn them to fictional advantage. For it is the constant disparity between the human thought-language of the dog and his less than human adequacy in dealing with the correlatives of his thought in the physical world, and especially in dealing with that reality as it is mediated by his man-derived hopes and expectations, that defines Stapledon's projection of his theme: the body-mind conflict. Because Stapledon always keeps us in concrete touch with this paradox, Sirius succeeds as a character, however disbelievable he might be as a "creature." He seems never more human than in his doggish weaknesses and his resolute determination — at times foolish, at others heroic (or both) — to master them. Our sympathy is firmly established in the chapters about his early upbringing, when he shares his first discoveries of reality with the child Plaxy.

Trelone, unlike his prototype in fiction, the scientist-hero of *Frankenstein*, is acutely aware of his responsibilities in providing for his creature's psychological adaptation to human society. He therefore slows the physiological processes of the dog's maturation in order to bring up the pup in close union with Plaxy; he is to be raised as her equal in love and respect. The clumsy attempts of the puppy to imitate Plaxy when she first stands and walks; the jealousy of the two children for the affections of the mother (Elizabeth); the "doggedness" of the puppy in learning to write with the help of a pencil-holding mitten; the elaborate ruse by which Sirius, overcoming a childlike fear of strange animals, wins his first dogfight, hoping thereby to be admired both as clever hero and fierce beast — all of these episodes owe their comedy to the fact that the "dogged" protagonist does not yet know his true nature as we are being made to know it. He himself will soon discover it inescapably.

Sirius, therefore, does not merely grow up, he grows as a character; and this growth consists in the emergence of his unique animal personality from an illusory humanity. In this respect *Sirius* is true science fiction while so many animal stories — even good ones, Jack London's *The Call of the Wild*, for example — are not. In all such fiction the dog-hero's mind is little more than a simplified version of what human responses would be in like circumstances. The context of consciousness may be altered, but not the modes of perception. Stapledon thus makes use of the literary convention only to win an initial tolerance for his steadily increasing departures from it. In *Sirius* we share a dog's gradual discovery that he does *not* perceive as human beings perceive: he learns that he has compensating powers of sensation and understanding that human minds cannot equal. Plaxy's may be the only pair of hands he will ever have, but his powers of smell reveal aspects of reality — and even of human reality (people smell "sour" to him when they are pretending or prevaricating) — to which human minds are insensitive, precisely because of their self-delusive powers of manipulation and control.

On this point and also in presenting his hero's passion for music (Sirius invents an art of his own based on frequencies above those heard by man), Stapledon is mixing scientific truth with primitive superstition; he is taking advantage of the belief that dogs are "psychic," that they not only hear and smell things beyond man's perception but can also sense spiritual reality (ghosts and demons especially) that is hidden from man. But Stapledon, of course, gives to this notion of canine intuition a direction of meaning unanticipated in popular tradition. One source of the growing faith of Sirius in the inward reality he comes to call spirit, a reality of power beyond material causation, lies in the disparity we have traced between his pride in conceptual thought and his canine frustrations in managing physical things. His doggishness also provides a positive source for this conviction through his perception of certain inspirational values (love, for example) as inhering in shapes of sound, in harmonies of fragrance, in organic life itself, in all animality and even perhaps in all matter. And the human species, too, might discover this truth (or its equivalent) if it were not so far gone in exclusive love for itself as to believe that man alone, of all forms of life on earth, is worthy of spirit.

Even those who love him most, Trelone and Plaxy, prove unequal to the challenge of the unprecedented reality that Sirius longs to reveal to them. Trelone finally shows the same limitations of mind that proved fatal to his predecessor, Victor Frankenstein. He does compassionately acknowledge the conflict in Sirius, but he is willing to define that opposition as simply one between canine nature and supercanine mind, not as an existential dialectic of spirit and body that also defines his own being. When Sirius, yielding to his sense of alienation, suffers his first seizure of wolflike wildness (he kills a ram and pony on the moors), Trelone quickly bustles his creature off to Cambridge, confident that a scientific career — as both subject and researcher — will cure these "subjective" ills.

Sirius is appalled however, by the "self-deception" and complacent lack of understanding that he finds infecting university life. In reaction against science, he turns his energies to religion for spiritual enlightenment. A sojourn in the slums of London, assisting a dedicated but anachronistic parson (Geoffrey), only makes him more intensely aware of the pervasive stench of human poverty, duplicity, and injustice. And Sirius himself is to feel the injustice of "the tyrant species" when he returns to his moorland world after war breaks out in 1939. He is then persecuted and assaulted by a sadistic sheep farmer. Sirius kills his attacker, but his retaliation, begun in self-defense, ends in unnecessary murder. He is unable to deny, as he confesses to Plaxy, that he delighted in the power and bloodlust of the kill.

After Trelone dies in an air raid and Elizabeth dies a short time later, Plaxy comes to recognize that she alone stands between Sirius and his wolf-madness. To save him she knows what she, like it or not, must do. It is impossible for a reader to approach the marriage of Plaxy and Sirius, delicately treated though it is, without feeling some degree of instinctive revulsion. But the point to grasp is that the characters, too, feel much the same aversion to the physical grotesqueness of their union. Before this time they have each led healthy sexual lives with their own kind. The one pathological element to enter their love may be said to come from outside their cottage, from the mean and nasty minds, diseased with superstition, of their Welsh neighbors. Under these circumstances, *not* to have given themselves to each other would have been to doubt or deny their love, to betray its innocence. We note that when the "bride" looks at herself in the mirror it is not bestialization that she dreads so much as the fear that she is becoming, in her hardened defiance of her neighbors, as ugly with hate as they seem in her eyes. This scene, indeed, holds a clue to the emotional necessity of the act for both lovers as individuals.

We may remember that in the great fairy tale that stands as the archetype for Stapledon's story, Beauty has to commit her love to the Beast *before* she knows that he is an enchanted Prince. The psychoanalytical interpretation of Beauty's action, as of all such episodes in "animal bridegroom" tales, is that the ugliness of the Beast really stands for the Oedipal fear and repression of sexuality, a repression that has to be in some way exposed, confronted, and made to contribute emotionally to mature sexual love if the latter is to be free of childhood inhibitions. It is therefore entirely logical that Plaxy, when Robert arrives on the scene, should be willing and able to reciprocate his love without guilt and, after the tragic death of Sirius, to become Robert's wife.

Regrettably, Stapledon is not quite novelist enough to develop this situation as drama, to render it effectively in terms of character. Robert remains faceless as a personality, and Plaxy comes alive only in relation to Sirius. Yet this is her primary function: she is his *anima* in the Jungian sense, and her release from fear is also his liberation from hatred of man into a brief wholeness of being, the one fulfillment possible for him in a civilization (and this is the relevance of the wartime setting) that will recognize as real no power of "spirit" but the spirit of its own protean lust for dominion. The real wolves in this world are the men who at last hunt Sirius down and kill him on the moors. But he does not die in despair; he has mastered, by accepting, his own conflict of body and mind, and he knows that his artificially created "spirit," precisely because of its potential for creative uniqueness, has the reality of all true being and will always have counterparts in the cosmic scheme of things. And "the bright gem of community" that was "Sirius-Plaxy" holds the promise of a renewal of hope for society; it is an augury of that greater human marriage of science and religion, of man and cosmic powers, that Stapledon, throughout his varied career, had never ceased to prophesy. At the end, as Plaxy stands over a dog's dead body, singing a strange dissonant requiem (Sirius's own creation) while the colors of the moorland dawn explode around her, we may remember that those colors, like all others, Sirius himself had never seen but had taken on faith, knowing in other ways the spirit of their beauty.

John Kinnaird

Sources for Further Study

Reviews:
Kliatt Paperback Book Guide. VII, April, 1973, p. 28.
Luna Monthly. XLVII, Summer, 1973, pp. 31-32.

THE SKYLARK SERIES

Author: Edward E. Smith (1890-1965)
First book publications: The Skylark of Space (1946); *Skylark Three* (1947); *Skylark of Valeron* (1949); *Skylark DuQuesne* (1966)
Type of work: Novels
Time: The twentieth century
Locale: The Earth, various worlds of other stars, other galaxies

The story of a group of friends who, with the aid of spaceships of ever-increasing size and power, roam the cosmos and save nations, worlds, and galaxies from threats of conquest

> *Principal characters:*
> RICHARD BALLINGER SEATON, PH.D., a young scientific genius
> DOROTHY VANEMAN, his fiancée, later his wife
> MARTIN REYNOLDS CRANE, a multimillionaire explorer-archaeologist-sportsman
> MARGARET SPENCER, his eventual wife
> MARC C. DUQUESNE, PH.D., a brilliant but blackhearted scientist
> BROOKINGS, President of World Steel
> DUNARK, Crown Prince of Kondal

The Skylark of Space was written by Edward E. Smith some ten years before it was published in *Amazing Stories*, the early chapters including some contribution by Lee Hawkins Garby, who helped him out with the romantic interest. It failed to find a market until Hugo Gernsback created a magazine specializing in "scientifiction" — a home that might have been made specially for this novel. It was serialized in Gernsback's magazine in 1928, and proved to be a great hit with the readers — it was the most popular story Gernsback's *Amazing Stories* ran, and became an important influence on the direction taken by the science fiction pulps.

A sequel, *Skylark Three*, was serialized in *Amazing Stories* in 1930, and the third part of the trilogy, *Skylark of Valeron*, appeared in *Astounding Stories* in 1934-1935. *The Skylark of Space* was first published in book form in 1946, *Skylark Three* in 1947, and *Skylark of Valeron* in 1949. After *Skylark of Valeron*, Smith began work on the Lensman series, and it was not until the 1960's, after a string of failed novels, that he decided to return to the *milieu* of his first triumph by writing *Skylark DuQuesne*. This fourth novel was serialized in *If* in 1965 and reprinted in book form the following year, by which time Smith was dead. His work has enjoyed a spectacular posthumous boom, with paperback editions of his major series being frequently reprinted in the United States and Great Britain, and with two series of pastiches being developed by other writers around characters from minor novelettes.

It is difficult today to appreciate the effect *The Skylark of Space* had on its original audience. We are now familiar with space opera on a grand scale, and that familiarity very rapidly bred contempt when it was realized that a preoccupation with scale for its own sake provided only a tenuous illusion of inventiveness and ideative extravagance. Galactic empires are now conventional stage sets for exotic futuristic romance, and no longer inspire awe. We have grown used to the idea that the universe is so vast that our entire galaxy is merely an insignificant speck within it, and we are so far past the stage of being excited by it that we can casually cultivate a disregard for its implications.

In 1928 it was different. It was only in 1912 and the years following that Slipher discovered the galactic red-shifts, and Leavitt, Hertzsprung, and Shapley calibrated the yardstick that made measuring interstellar distances relatively simple (via their work on Cepheid variables). The general theory of relativity had been published as recently as 1917, and Millikan had popularized the idea of "cosmic rays" in 1925. Edward E. Smith understood none of these things (despite his Ph.D.) — and, indeed, he seems even to have been unaware of the difference between velocity and acceleration — but such news nevertheless had some impact on his imagination, causing an excitement which he found it possible, albeit in a rather crude manner, to communicate to other readers equally naïve. To Smith and to his readers, the knowledge of the immensity of the universe was new and inspiring, and there was a new and special delight in the thought of exploring that immensity.

In the first paragraph of *The Skylark of Space*, a copper bath containing an unknown metal whose properties Richard Seaton is attempting to discover takes off and flies at enormous speed into the unknown. When he awakens his friend Martin Crane to the possibilities opened up by this event, the two make haste to obtain legal control over the metal and to set up business on their own, building a spaceship. Their scheme is bedeviled by the exploits of one of Seaton's ex-colleagues, Marc DuQuesne, and his allies in the crooked cartel known as World Steel, who are determined to seize the discovery for themselves. Brookings, the president of World Steel, wants to take over the world; DuQuesne wants to take over the universe.

Seaton and DuQuesne each build a starship. DuQuesne uses his to kidnap Seaton's fiancée, Dorothy Vaneman, but ends up in deep trouble, marooned in the gravitational grip of a dead star hundreds of light-years from Earth. Seaton rescues them, but has to search for new supplies before he can return to Earth. He becomes embroiled in a war between Kondal and Mardonale, the two nations of the planet Osnome, and wins it for Kondal, being then acclaimed as the Overlord of Osnome. These encounters set the pattern for the whole series: Seaton and DuQuesne are locked in a long battle, which Seaton always wins by having the bigger and more powerful ship, and in the intermissions between rounds of their personal conflict, Seaton takes time out to fight more extravagant battles involving whole worlds and entire races.

In *Skylark Three*, Seaton saves his Kondalian friends again, this time from invaders from Urvan. After threatening to blow up Urvan and annihilate the

Urvanians if they refuse to capitulate to his demands, he forces a peaceful resolution, and is hailed as Overlord of Urvan. This petty squabble fades into insignificance, however, when he has to face the threat of the Fenachrone, who have just set out to conquer the universe. After absorbing the scientific knowledge of several friendly races, including the extremely advanced humans of Norlamin, Seaton is ready to confront the new threat, and duly does so. The Fenachrone are too nasty to join his burgeoning galactic club, so he annihilates them to the last alien (though a few escapees are invented in order to play a minor role in *Skylark DuQuesne*).

In *Skylark of Valeron*, DuQuesne, after duping the Norlaminians into giving him a ship as good as *Skylark Three*, takes over Earth. Seaton cannot stop him because he has had to escape an attack by disembodied intelligences by entering the fourth dimension, where he is temporarily inconvenienced by a race of sea horselike aliens. When Seaton (now back in *Skylark Two*, having abandoned *Skylark Three* to the attack of the pure intelligences) returns to normal space he is a long way from home, and is further delayed by having to intervene to save the human inhabitants of Valeron from the depredations of some chlorine-breathing amoebas. Eventually, though, he builds himself a new and even bigger *Skylark* (this time the size of a small world), saves Earth, and packs DuQuesne and the disembodied intelligences off on a trip to the edge of the universe in a prison of force. There, for thirty years, the matter rests.

The spirit of these early books is one of sheer exuberance. The forces at Seaton's disposal grow mightier as he conquers new "orders" of radiation and absorbs into his own brain the knowledge of other races. By the end of *Skylark of Valeron*, he seems all-powerful, able to materialize more or less anything he wishes by the power of thought. This is wish-fulfillment fantasy taken to the ultimate, and the other aspects of the series also reflect the childish mode of thought where wishes are everything: the lavish violence, the incessant narcissism, and the sharp and easy distinction between *us* and *them* all reflect his juvenile phase. Smith delights in blowing up stars and annihilating whole races, and has no difficulty in selecting his targets: "Humanity *über alles* — *homo sapiens* against all the vermin of the universe!" cries Seaton enthusiastically as he embraces Valeron's cause. This is hardly adult thinking — indeed, it is hardly thinking at all. The "science" in the stories is, of course, all pretense, a jargon of apology for the development of an absolute power fantasy. Smith is not merely careless of authentic science, but actually contemptuous of it; when Seaton pauses to wonder why there are human beings on so many worlds, Crane puts on his anthropologist's hat and explains that "the ultimate genes must permeate universal space itself."

Skylark DuQuesne is not cast in quite the same mold as its predecessors. The style is more flippant, the plot is sprawling and confused. Curiously, the book is infected by a strong mock-feminist ethic and is brimful of liberated ladies — even Dorothy, who exists in the original trilogy mainly to be kid-

naped and constantly to reassure Seaton that he is utterly wonderful, takes to
going into battle, packing a pair of long-barrelled .38's beneath her bouffant
skirt. The elements of the plot, however, are unaltered. There are more races
of menacing aliens to be annihilated in the batlike Llurdi, and there are more
chlorine-breathing amoebas; there are millions of enemy worlds to be
destroyed, though they cause no more than the usual trouble:

> They died in uncounted trillions. The greeny-yellow soup that served them for air boiled
> away. Their halogenous flesh was charred, baked and desiccated in the split-second of the
> passing of the wave front from each exploding double star, moments before their planets
> themselves began to seethe and boil. Many died unaware. Most died fighting. Some died
> in terrible, frantic efforts to escape. . . .
>   But they all died.

The only major change made in this scenario is that it is DuQuesne who
replaces Seaton as the savior of humanity's universe — Seaton (who was
always a bit squeamish) finally wilts under the pressure. DuQuesne's reward is
to be given his own little galactic empire to rule according to his own principles, which seem to comprise little more than rigid autocracy and a strict program of eugenic selection. He accepts his rule gracefully, explaining that he no
longer wants Earth, which is hopelessly decadent, or the home galaxy, which
is now filled with "damned sissies."

The fact that Smith was prepared in the end to favor DuQuesne over Seaton
came as no more than a mild surprise in view of the political ethics implied by
his earlier novels, but it would be too harsh to criticize him unduly on these
grounds. Even at the age of seventy-five, Smith retained an outlook in his
fiction that was too naïve to permit questions of moral philosophy to have any
real meaning. His stories, like the games played by small children, are actually
totally isolated from the concerns of the real world. They have exactly the
same virtues as such games, and should be considered in the same light. Their
brutality is the innocent brutality of fantasy — a safety-valve for the expression and release of impulses which have to be repressed in real life. They are
not (mercifully) any kind of a prescription for real life.

The *Skylark* books are aesthetically and intellectually vacuous, and can no
longer offer the same kind of revelatory consciousness-expansion that they
once did. This should not, however, prevent us from recognizing the historical
importance of *The Skylark of Space* within genre science fiction, the power of
its influence on subsequent work done under the label, or the fact that it really
did have something valuable to offer its teenage audience in 1928. The contemporary Smith revival is harder to understand, but it seems probable that the
audience is still composed mainly of preadolescent teenagers with a considerable appetite for extravagant power fantasy, and that the total lack of intellectual and moral sophistication exhibited by the novels provides them with an
advantage in the literary marketplace that more recent works do not have. It

must be remembered that, although there is a constant supply of new naïve readers, naïve writers are no longer as common as they were in 1928.

Brian Stableford

Sources for Further Study

Criticism:

Ellik, Ron and Bill Evans. *The Universe of E. E. Smith.* Chicago: Advent Publishers, Inc., 1968. This book offers a complete discussion and analysis of all of the Skylark and Lensman novels of E. E. Smith.

Reviews:

Amazing Stories. XXIII, December, 1949, pp. 149-152 and XXXIII, May, 1964, pp. 126-127.

Analog. XLIV, September, 1949, p. 152 and October, 1949, pp. 141-142.

Fantasy Book. I, 1947, p. 41.

Galaxy. II, June, 1951, pp. 54-55.

Science Fiction Quarterly. I, August, 1951, p. 86.

Startling Stories. XIX, March, 1949, p. 161-162.

Super Science Stories. V, September, 1949, p. 101.

Thrilling Wonder Stories. XXXIV, August, 1949, pp. 158-159.

Worlds of If. IX, December, 1958, pp. 110-111.

SLAN

Author: A.E. van Vogt (1912-   )
First book publication: 1940
Type of work: Novel
Time: Approximately the thirty-fifth century
Locale: Unidentified location, probably North America, and Mars

The adventures of a mutant boy searching for others of his kind in a future world where the mutants are feared and killed by humans

Principal characters:
JOMMY CROSS, a young slan boy
KIER GRAY, dictator of the Earth
KATHLEEN LAYTON, Kier Gray's slan daughter
GRANNY, an old junk woman
JOHN PETTY, chief of the secret police
JOANNA HILLORY, a tendrilless slan in charge of capturing Jommy

Mutants have always been popular subjects in science fiction, but until van Vogt's *Slan* they had never been given book-length treatment. Before, mutants were depicted as isolated freaks or monsters to be hunted down and killed by a fearful human community. Van Vogt retains the mutant's isolation and humanity's fear of them as his theme; but whereas previous mutants in fiction had been the only ones of their kind, the author's slans number in the millions. Slans are human in appearance, except for two tendrils growing from the backs of their heads, and they represent the next evolutionary step beyond man. They are the Cro-Magnons and humans are the Neanderthals. Telepathic and superior in intellectual capacity and strength to man, slans are feared and hunted by humans.

In the melodramatic first chapter, a nine-year-old slan boy, Jommy Cross, is charged by his soon-to-be-murdered mother, "You live for one thing only: to make it possible for slans to live normal lives." The sentiments are noble, but as Jommy grows older, the tales of slan experiments and other atrocities performed on human beings make him question the worth of saving his martyred race. But his questions always lead him back to a belief that true slans are merely a misunderstood race.

His doubts, however, are compounded by his discovery of the existence of slans who are tendrilless and lack the power to communicate telepathically. Their twin missions are to rule the earth and to exterminate all true slans. The confusion this causes within him spurs Jommy to intensify his search for true slans.

Because of the intense anti-slan propaganda of the government, the tendrilless slans, like the humans, believe that all slans are the creations of Dr. Samuel Lann ("slan" is derived from his first initial and last name), a scientist who had used a machine designed to mutate offspring on his wife, who afterwards bore the first slans. Lann realized the births of his children were only a part of the billions of abnormal births occurring worldwide as a result of an evolutionary explosion, and had nothing to do with his machine. Nevertheless, believing them to be "machine made," humans turned on the slans and forced them into hiding. Because their tendrils could not be disguised for long, the slans were compelled to alter their genetic structure to remove them, "insuring that [the tendrils would] . . . not turn up for many generations." Thus the slans were protected from humans by becoming tendrilless. Yet only Kier Gray and a few others knew that tendrilless and true slans were of the same race, so Jommy must still solve the mystery.

In his symbolism, van Vogt is as obvious as he is confusing. He is obvious because with the introduction of Kier Gray, "absolute dictator of the entire planet" and persecutor of slans, van Vogt provides his story with a Hitler to complement the Jews that the persecuted slans represent; he is confusing, because in the final chapter Kier Gray is revealed to be a slan. He is the persecutor of his own people, and his claim that he is helping them from within the system is inadequate and illogical in the face of the fact that he has more than a thousand slans killed each year. Jommy Cross, however, is constant throughout as a Christlike figure. He is greeted by everyone from his mother to Kier Gray as the savior of his people. He, like Christ, has his "moments of doubt," but despite the evidence against them, he never loses his faith in his people.

Jommy's search for the true slans, while trying to remain undetected in human society, takes him through fifteen years of adventures. And when all is said and done, adventure *is* the main attraction of the book. Nine-year-old Jommy narrowly escapes death at the hands of an angry mob, being rescued by Granny, an old junk woman who then forces him to steal for her after threatening to turn him over to the government. Fifteen-year-old Jommy finds his father's secret invention, an atomic handgun, and uses it to escape from the tendrilless slan organization. Both the humans and the tendrilless slans have offered rewards for his death. Each chapter ends with a mystery unsolved or a life at stake. And throughout the story there hangs the threat of a three-sided war between the true slans, the tendrilless slans, and the humans.

Action and excitement are present on every page because van Vogt never allows the pace to slacken. All the heroes survive, but the plot comes through badly. In setting a fast pace, van Vogt often places his characters in situations where escape is impossible without the convenient introduction of a new, super powerful weapon, or the sudden alteration of a character's personality to the point where he or she is almost unrecognizable. Van Vogt seems to prefer the latter method since some of the characters experience inadequately explained personality changes. Joanna Hillory, the first tendrilless slan to capture Jommy, inexplicably changes from a blind hatred of "snakes" (the tendrilless slans's name for true slans) to an intense devotion to Jommy and his mission to save the true slans — all on the basis of a brief encounter where she and Jommy hold each other at gun point. Also, Jommy changes Granny from a dangerous old woman into a docile and helpful comrade using hypnotism and his telepathic powers. These transformations are too convenient to fit into the story and give the surrounding events a feeling of being forced and artificial. Van Vogt sacrifices good plotting and consistent characterization at the altar of action.

The author does find time to comment on the nature of man when faced with the unknown. The characteristic reaction of both humans and tendrilless slans toward anything new or different is to destroy it. Near the end of the novel Kier Gray points out that after the first slans were born and "nature's part of the work ended, it remained for intelligence to carry on. And that's where the difficulty came." Man is the cause of his own troubles and must accept the responsibility.

Although the novel's main viewpoint is Jommy Cross's, Kathleen Layton is the focus of a subplot, and much of the book is devoted to her. Kathleen is a slan girl being openly reared in Kier Gray's palace as, according to Gray, an experiment. He "wanted to see if human beings who grew up with a slan might not come to realize that kinship was possible." But neither she nor the other council members know this; they believe that she is being allowed to live only for the purposes of scientific study. She is menaced throughout by John Petty, chief of the secret police, a one-dimensional character whose obsession is to kill Kathleen. The strength of his "queer fanaticism" is unjustified by van Vogt, and therefore seems contrived simply to add excitement to the story.

The sections dealing with Kathleen usually center around meetings between the council and Kier Gray where her fate, and that of all slans, is in question. These meetings show Kathleen's confusion concerning whether Kier Gray is keeping her alive for personal or political reasons. She eventually flees the palace and meets Jommy. Van Vogt has been inevitably building up to this climactic moment: two true slans, after spending all of their lives isolated from their kind, meet. In his typical way of dealing with emotions, van Vogt becomes melodramatic: the couple find each other and fall in love, only to be separated by Kathleen's death at John Petty's hands. The entire episode takes place in an unrealistically short time, with the only emotions resulting from van Vogt's use of a stereotypical male/female relationship (they have just met and Kathleen is already cooking for him). Unfortunately, the "surprise" ending where Kathleen is brought back to life and revealed to be Kier Gray's daughter cheapens the emotional effect of her death, giving the novel a trite ". . . they lived happily ever after" quality.

In a 1947 essay about writing science fiction, van Vogt emphasized the importance of "ideas." In *Slan*, however, his "ideas" are usually nothing more than sensationalized inventions or superhuman powers, and he is interested in them only insofar as they further the action of the story. As a result they are inadequately conceived and explained. Because such "ideas" in the novel as anti-gravity devices and interplanetary travel had already been used in so many other science fiction stories as to have become conventions of the genre, van Vogt feels that it is unnecessary to explain them. But he does elaborate slightly on two of his main "ideas," atomic power and the slans's remarkable capacities. Jommy's father invented a handgun powered by atomic energy, based on a theory which "rejected the notion of critical mass." Jommy uses this theory to harden steel incredibly and to build a new space drive. Yet only two brief paragraphs of analogies and double-talk elucidate this revolutionary theory. Likewise, the slans's telepathic abilities, stamina, and intellect are briefly dismissed as being the result of physical differences (such as tendrils, two hearts, and the like) after one generation of evolution. In other words, van Vogt inspires more awe than understanding of science. The reader is told to accept these "ideas" simply because van Vogt says it is so.

This attitude explains the personality changes as well. Since it is the author's world, he can make it any way he wants to. Apparently he wants it to be like 1940 America, because the inclusion of futuristic paraphernalia is the only thing that distinguishes the setting from the 1940's. People still drive cars, cities still exist, there are still isolated farming communities, weapons are the same, and incredibly, humans have yet to reach the moon (although van Vogt concedes that the slans, because of their superior intelligence, have colonized both the moon and Mars).

That van Vogt would try to pass this story off as life 1,500 years in the future can partially be explained as lack of imagination and a degree of naïveté on his part. But the story could also reflect the audience for which he was writing. When *Slan* first appeared serially in *Astounding Science Fiction*, the largest pulp science fiction magazine of the 1940's, the author probably felt he must gear his story to the magazine's large juvenile readership. Nevertheless, the initial impact of *Slan* was impressive, although the novel's value as a science fiction "classic" has lessened as the ideas used in it become outdated, or clichéd. For example, van Vogt's mention of atomic weapons five years before Hiroshima may have seemed prophetic at the time, but prophecies are not so interesting forty years later. The Kier Gray/Hitler analogy also would have had greater immediacy to an audience in 1940. But if van Vogt's fiction has not worn well with the passage of time, his historical importance as one of the primary writers during the "Golden Age" of science fiction is undeniable.

Kent Craig

Sources for Further Study

Criticism:

Ash, Brian. *Faces of the Future — The Lessons of Science Fiction*. London: Elek/Pemberton, 1975, pp. 117-118. Ash comments and gives criticism of the works of van Vogt.

The Encylopedia of Science Fiction and Fantasy. Compiled by Donald H. Tuck. Chicago: Advent Publishers, Inc., 1978, pp. 430-432. This article gives a review of van Vogt's life and career, with a full bibliography of his works.

Wilson, Colin. "The Vision of Science," in *The Strength to Dream: Literature and the Imagination*. London: Gollancz, 1962, pp. 94-117. Wilson reviews science fiction literature in relation to "the mainstream" of literature, giving some discussion of van Vogt's contributions.

Reviews:

Amazing Stories. XXVI, April, 1952, pp. 152-153.

Analog. XLIX, May, 1952, pp. 158-159 and XLIX, July, 1952, pp. 159-160.

Chicago Sun Book Week. December 29, 1946, p. 7.

Galaxy. IV, April, 1952, p. 120.

Magazine of Fantasy and Science Fiction. XXI, October, 1961, p. 82.

New York Herald Tribune Weekly Book Review. February 9, 1947, p. 18.

San Francisco Chronicle. December 8, 1946, p. 15.

Startling Stories. XXV, March, 1952, p. 139.

SLAUGHTERHOUSE-FIVE

Author: Kurt Vonnegut, Jr. (1922-   )
First book publication: 1969
Type of work: Novel
Time: Before, during, and after World War II, and the future
Locale: The United States, Germany, Tralfamadore

The Dresden fire-bombing from the point of view of Billy Pilgrim, the Tralfamadorians, and Vonnegut as narrator

> *Principal characters:*
> "VONNEGUT," the narrator
> BILLY PILGRIM, a man who becomes unstuck in time
> VALENCIA MERBLE, the girl he marries
> MONTANA WILDHACK, his mate on Tralfamadore
> PAUL LAZZARO, the man who kills Billy
> ROLAND WEARY and
> EDGAR DERBY, would-be heroes
> BERNARD V. O'HARE, Vonnegut's World War II buddy
> MARY O'HARE, his wife
> THE TRALFAMADORIANS, green creatures from outer space

Slaughterhouse-Five, on first reading, may seem an uneasy blend of the realistic and the science fiction novel. As Vonnegut explains in the opening chapter, he at first planned an epic novel about the fire-bombing of Dresden by the Americans in World War II. Realizing that war is confused, anticlimactic, and antiheroic, Vonnegut expresses this confusion in the experience of his protagonist, Billy Pilgrim, who comes "unstuck in time" and in disconnected episodes travels to his past, his present, and his future, not necessarily in that order. Only when he is captured by the Tralfamadorians, strange green creatures from outer space that are shaped like plumber's helpers, does he achieve any kind of unity and coherence of perception. For the Tralfamadorians, every moment is like any other moment, for they can see all experience at once. "So it goes" is the response to death and destruction, and the phrase recurs again and again. Even the fire-bombing of Dresden becomes bearable when seen as one of a series of random events, when the Oz-like Dresden that was destroyed still exists in another moment of time.

The "present" of the novel and the focal point of the action is World War II, an event, for Billy, now in the past. Written in 1969, *Slaughterhouse-Five* is a commentary on all wars, but especially on the Vietnam War. There is no heroic action. Eighteen-year-old Billy, along with Roland Weary, also just eighteen, is captured by the Germans. Weary constantly jeers at Billy for his lack of heroism and constantly romanticizes his own role in the war. He dies on a prison train from gangrene of the foot, but not before he convinces Paul Lazzaro that Billy is responsible for his death and elicits Lazzaro's promise of revenge. From prison camp they are sent to Dresden, where they are lodged in underground slaughterhouses, Billy in the Slaughterhouse-Five of the title.

Slaughterhouse-Five / VONNEGUT

There they survive the fire-bombing to emerge into a science fiction-like "moonscape" haunted by death, including the incongruous shooting of "poor old Edgar Derby" for "looting" a Dresden teacup that has somehow survived the bombing.

The war action develops on a reasonably straight chronological level, with flashes of Billy's past and future juxtaposed to related events in the war. Billy becomes an ophthalmologist (reinforcing the main themes of vision and perception) and marries the fat and hideous Valencia Merble, daughter of the richest ophthalmologist in Ilium, New York. They have two children, Barbara and Robert. Billy's life is relatively uneventful until after his daughter's wedding, when he is kidnaped by the Tralfamadorians and taken to live in a geodetic dome on exhibition on a simulated Earth environment. Billy is provided with a mate, Montana Wildhack, a luscious model for, among other things, pornographic pictures; the two have a child. But Billy also continues his life on Earth, coming back to preach the Tralfamadorian philosophy. He dies when he is shot by Paul Lazzaro as he addresses a huge crowd in Chicago in 1976. The juxtaposition of past and future events with the action of the war creates an ironic perspective on both.

Perhaps the most important and complex character in the novel is "Vonnegut," for in *Slaughterhouse-Five* he has not one, but two *personae*. There is the narrator of the framework "with his memories and his Pall Malls," and the Vonnegut who interacts with the characters in the novel, who was also in World War II: "That was me. That was I." Vonnegut observed in the preface to *Happy Birthday, Wanda June* (1970) that he is a character in all of his novels; in addition he has at least one alter ego per novel. These characters move from book to book, and so do places (like Ilium, the name deliberately ironic) which reinforce his Tralfamadorian vision of life, which in *The Sirens of Titan* (1959) he calls the *chrono-synclastic infundibulum*. That is, according to the Tralfamadorians, who also appear in *The Sirens of Titan*, a point in the universe where all contradictory opinions, be they ever so disparate, meet and harmonize. It is this point of view that the Tralfamadorians teach Billy Pilgrim.

Yet despite this personal identification, Vonnegut treats characters — and they treat one another — with a great deal of detachment. People are "machines"; they are referred to in abstract terms. Robert, Billy's son, is usually referred to as "the Green Beret," reflecting also the dehumanizing effect of war. A Russian soldier, also a prisoner, who encounters Billy views him as "a curious scarecrow" and attempts to talk to "it." Two of the very few people capable of real love or hate are Mary O'Hare, Bernard V. O'Hare's wife, and Paul Lazzaro. Neither is willing to accept death as "so it goes." Both try to change "the past, the present, and the future" which Billy cannot change, Mary by refusing to accept the heroic view of warfare, and Lazzaro by his insistence on personal hatred. Paradoxically, through his hatred he arrives at an antiwar stance: it is ridiculous to kill someone *unless* you hate his guts. "Vonnegut" accepts Mary's view that wars are made glamorous by "dirty old men" and fought by "babies" and alters his original concept of his novel. Billy accepts Lazzaro as simply an agent of the inevitable.

"Vonnegut" himself observes, despite his assertion that all the characters are based on real people, that there are "almost no characters" in *Slaughterhouse-Five*, and very little drama, because the people in it are "so sick" and so much the "listless playthings of enormous forces." War, he continues, discourages people "from being characters." But the major reason there are "almost no characters" is that *Slaughterhouse-Five* is a novel of ideas. Characters function as explanation and often have symbolic names, such as Roland Weary, whose name is a combination of a once heroic name and an accurate description of his real state. In *Slaughterhouse-Five*, what is to be explained is that life and death are inexplicable.

It is no accident that the alter ego closest to Vonnegut's own identity is Kilgore Trout, the "cracked Messiah" with a genuine incapacity for hatred, whose novels Billy has read and whom he seeks out. Trout is an obscure, mad, misunderstood science fiction writer. Yet his madness is that of the sacred idiot. Interspersed through *Slaughterhouse-Five*, as well as through Vonnegut's other novels, are the plots of Trout's novels, "prophetic books" within prophetic books. *Slaughterhouse-Five* even includes a novel by Trout with a plot similar to its own, a glimpse of the situation from Trout's bizarre point of view. In like manner, earthly reality and history appear in *Slaughterhouse-Five* in part from the use of real and imaginary books and documents — *The Execution of Private Slovik*, a history of Dresden, Bertram Copeland Rumfoord's history of World War II — not for the illusion of realism, but as another kind of "prophetic book" commenting on the action. *Slaughterhouse-Five* is thus about the inexplicability of all wars, from Biblical to Vietnamese. One of Trout's novels, *The Gutless Wonder*, tells of a robot who pilots a bomber, remarkable in 1932 for predicting "the widespread use of burning jellied gasoline on human beings." Trout's novels add another of Vonnegut's perspectives to *Slaughterhouse-Five*.

Yet another perspective appears in the difference between characters appearing in *Slaughterhouse-Five* and their appearance in other novels: Bernard V. O'Hare, Rumfoord, Eliot Rosewater, and Howard W. Campbell. O'Hare and Campbell appear in *Mother Night*, a black comedy about tracking down Nazi war criminals, in which O'Hare is the villain, or as much of a villain as Vonnegut ever creates; and Campbell, we learn, was an undercover agent for the Allies — the American Nazi pose was his cover. Rumfoord appears in *The Sirens of Titan* as a benevolent if eccentric millionaire and so does Eliot Rosewater in *God Bless You, Mr. Rosewater*. Their presence implies other views and perspectives on the events described in *Slaughterhouse-Five*.

This is the Tralfamadorian perception, to which Billy Pilgrim is converted.

Tralfamadorians have an Emersonian perception of reality, a Blakean fourfold vision. Their metaphor for Earthling vision is apt: a man who is able to perceive the world only through the hole at the end of a six-foot piece of pipe. Earthling time is opposed to Tralfamadorian time, and Billy Pilgrim becomes unstuck in Earthling time. Though he has complete perspective of his life from start to finish, he has no control over what moment he will experience next. Billy first appears in the novel as a possibly mad middle-aged man, writing letters to the editor about his Tralfamadorian experience, letters which state the theme and structure of the novel. Billy thinks of himself as "prescribing corrective lenses for Earthling souls," "Earthling" in this context implying the Tralfamadorian view of man.

While praising Trout's ideas and the Tralfamadorian perspective, Vonnegut at the same time criticizes the idea of science fiction as prophetic book or salvation; thus, when Billy Pilgrim and Eliot Rosewater turn to science fiction to find some meaning in life, Vonnegut parodies their attempt. Kilgore Trout is eager to see evidence that the things he writes about actually exist. Billy dies in 1976, and Lazzaro is then an "old man"; actually, both would be in their fifties. Parodying future prophecy novels, Vonnegut notes that by 1976, "He [Billy] has to cross three international boundaries in order to reach Chicago" from New York. When Billy makes a speech to the Tralfamadorians, pointing out how terrible Earthlings are and what a threat they are to the universe, the Tralfamadorians are not impressed. "Science fiction had led him to expect" that aliens would be terrified of Earthling "ferocity" and "spectacular weaponry." But the message of science fiction is all wrong. The Tralfamadorians know that one of their own test pilots will press a button and the whole universe will disappear. Nor will the Tralfamadorians attempt to prevent it. It has always happened, and it always will. There is, of course, the paradox that it is the characters who could only exist in science fiction who point out the flaws in science fiction; and Vonnegut's own attitude is equally paradoxical. He dislikes being put in the category of science fiction, yet he is sharply critical of writers who refuse to be aware of the twentieth century technological ethos.

When Billy finally accepts the Tralfamadorian vision, he tries to get others to accept it and is at first thought insane. He becomes a prophet, himself a "cracked messiah." Only in the future is he taken seriously. Billy is in some ways a Christ-figure, but Christianity is not enough of a solution for modern man's dilemmas: *The Brothers Karamazov* contains "everything there was to know about life," yet "that isn't *enough* any more." As "Vonnegut" observes, the epigraph of "the little Lord Jesus,/ No crying he makes" applies only to Billy's singular lack of tears at the unhappy moments of his life. Characters in the novel are searching for some meaning in life, though they have no common solution. Billy's mother, like many Americans, is "trying to construct a life that made sense from things she found in gift shops." Kilgore

Trout writes *The Gospel from Outer Space*, a reinterpretation not so much of the Gospels as of people's attitudes towards them. Billy's "Tralfamadorian adventure with death" is strongly reminiscent of the resurrection as described in St. Luke's Gospel, in which Christ demonstrates his reality by eating. The difference between Tralfamadorian and Christian interpretations is that the idea of resurrection and heaven is comforting, whereas the idea of endless repetition is not — at least, as Billy discovers, not as an idea coming to the average person out of the blue. Nor is the concept pleasant to "Vonnegut," who observes toward the end of the book that he does not relish the idea of spending eternity perpetually visiting various moments; though if it is true, he is "grateful that so many of those moments are nice."

Billy does not always attain or keep his Tralfamadorian vision. He is the alter ego who is furthest from the "real" Vonnegut, appearing in the novel primarily as a young man or as an innocent. Yet his awareness is occasionally Vonnegut's. He does not have entire foreknowledge or self-understanding, and his foreknowledge can inhibit another's actions. When Valencia offers to lose weight and wants to become attractive to him, he tells her he likes her the way she is, not because he really believes so, but because he has the foreknowledge that the relationship will be "bearable." He accepts with like passivity life with Montana Wildhack in the geodesic dome.

Vonnegut's outlook might be described as Calvinism in reverse gear. A similar sort of determinism appears in his other work. In *Slaughterhouse-Five*, Vonnegut says, "I was the victim of a series of accidents, as are we all," and the Tralfamadorians assert, "Only on Earth is there any talk of free will." But what is determined is not cosmos but chaos. As the Tralfamadorians put it, man should not ask "why" — "There is no *why*."

If there is no *why*, then what moves the artist to create, to say as Vonnegut does repeatedly through the novel, "Listen!"? At the beginning of *Slaughterhouse-Five*, Vonnegut compares himself to Lot's wife, who did look back, "because it was so human," and refers to the novel as a "failure," inevitable since it was "written by a pillar of salt." The flaw in the concept of the chrono-synclastic infundibulum and the "so it goes" philosophy is that one cannot go back in time, except in art, nor even in art if books are written by a "pillar of salt." Dresden will always be like Dayton, now, and not like Oz. Kilgore Trout's final desperate cry to Vonnegut (in *Breakfast of Champions*, 1973) is *"Make me young."* "Mustard gas and roses" is throughout *Slaughterhouse-Five* the smell of death, but it is also the breath of the artist.

Vonnegut creates cosmic and darkly comic chaos, luring the reader into the awesome emptiness of space, peopled with the bizarre creatures "science fiction had led him to expect" there, to demonstrate that there is no comfortable escape — whether past, present, or future — from reality, and that only from a point of vision completely outside Earth can man attempt to live with or account for such horrors as the Dresden fire-bombing. Yet the novel ends on a tentatively hopeful note, at the moment in time with Billy in a horse-drawn wagon after the bombing, lying relaxed in the sun and listening to a bird call. Even though both Billy and the reader are aware that soon someone will discover the pathetic condition of the horses and that when Billy sees them he will weep for the only time in the whole war, this moment of peace will still remain, the bird will still question *"poo-tee-weet?"* happily. By journeying into the cosmos for a perspective on incomprehensible Earthling warfare, Vonnegut has created one of the best of the twentieth century's war novels.

Katharine M. Morsberger

Sources for Further Study

Criticism:

Festa, Conrad. "Vonnegut's Satire," in *Vonnegut in America; an Introduction to the Life and Work of Kurt Vonnegut*. Edited by Jerome Klinkowitz and Donald L. Lawler. New York: Delacorte, 1977, pp. 133-149. Festa analyzes Vonnegut's satire.

Harris, Charles B. "Time, Uncertainty, and Kurt Vonnegut, Jr.: A Reading of *Slaughterhouse-Five*," in *Centennial Review*. XX (1976), pp. 228-243. Harris gives a good analysis of the entire novel.

Schatt, Stanley. *Kurt Vonnegut, Jr.* Boston: Twayne, 1976, pp. 81-96. This major work on Vonnegut places *Slaughterhouse-Five* in perspective with his other works.

Tilton, John W. *Cosmic Satire in the Contemporary Novel*. Lewisburg, Pa.: Bucknell University Press, 1977, pp. 69-105. This work, although dealing with a number of other authors, discusses *Slaughterhouse-Five* at great length, citing it as a major American novel.

Reviews:

American Scholar. XXXVIII, Autumn, 1969, p. 718.

Commonweal. XC, June 6, 1969, p. 347.

Luna Monthly. XXVI-XXVII, July-August, 1971, p. 41.

New Republic. CLX, April 26, 1969, p. 33.

New Worlds. CXCV, November, 1969, p. 30.

Saturday Review. LII, March 29, 1969, p. 25.

Time. XCIII, April 11, 1969, p. 106.

Venture. III, November, 1969, p. 105.

SOLARIS

Author: Stanislaw Lem (1921-   )
First book publication: 1961
English translation: 1971
Type of work: Novel
Time: An unspecified future
Locale: A space station hovering over the planet Solaris

A detailed and ingenious description of the human efforts to come to grips with the problems posed by the mysterious ocean covering the surface of Solaris, attempts which end in bitterness and frustration

> *Principal characters:*
> KRIS KELVIN, a psychologist
> RHEYA (HAREY in the original), his dead wife, materialized by the Solaris ocean
> DR. SNOW (SNAUT in the original), a cyberneticist
> DR. SARTORIUS, a research physicist

Whatever else Lem's fiction might be, whether in the realistic or in the humorous, absurd mode, there is one thing central to it: particular models of thought relating specific incidents to a larger design — a style that leads from particulars to universals. This fact is perhaps nowhere clearer than in *Solaris*, which is, in terms of the number of translations it has had, and the critical comment it has evoked, Lem's most important novel. Andrei Tarkovsky, the Soviet director, has rendered it into a widely discussed film that shifts the focus from Lem's burning curiosity about pure knowledge to the human problems of the characters confronted with the Solaris phenomena and to some rather general sentiments about the responsibility of science and scientists. While Tarkovsky's film has received wide critical acclaim, Lem himself does not approve of it, since it totally neglects the cognitive aspects of his novel, and concentrates on things that are at best of secondary importance to him. He has, in fact, never seen the film in its entirety.

The central thematic and philosophical interest of the novel concerns the attempt to solve the riddle of the planet Solaris. The planet revolves around a blue and red double-sun somewhere in the galaxy, and its surface is, aside from some bare islands, entirely covered by a colloidal ocean. This ocean gives rise to a wealth of different formations, which almost never repeat themselves. They are classified and described by the Solarists, the scientists engaged in the exploration of this biological phenomenan. Scientific interest was first aroused when Solaris' orbit was found to be stable, although this contradicted the fact that it revolved around a double sun. The stabilizing factor could only be the ocean, which somehow influenced gravitational fields and stabilized the path of the planet, a feat well beyond the scope of terrestrial science. This astronomical discovery led to a flourish of scientific literature about the planet, but not to any generally acceptable results. Investigation suggested that the ocean was a biological, not simply a physical phenomenon, and even that it was possibly a sentient being. As a result of this rather vague conclusion, the scientists became frustrated, and at the time of the novel, Solaris studies have declined.

The research station on the planet is manned by three people. When the novel's hero, the psychologist Kris Kelvin, arrives on the planet, he finds Gibarian dead of suicide, Dr. Snow half-crazed with fear, and Sartorius in seclusion. Snow greets Kelvin suspiciously, and Kelvin has a hard time convincing him that he is not a phantom. The scientists have begun to observe the materialization of their deepest psychological secrets, things suppressed and forgotten, because they are invariably shameful. Gibarian was plagued by a giant Negro woman; that which haunts the other two is not revealed to the reader, although Snow suggests some fetishistic objects, aberrations of the mind that have become flesh and blood. For Kris Kelvin it is Rheya (Harey in the original), a young woman who killed herself after a quarrel between them, who is materialized by the ocean.

She first appears in the station, not knowing what happened to her, and, they resume their relationship where it left off. To the hero, the return of a person he knows to be dead is horrifying. She has aspects of a succubus, a demon of hell, sent to torment him, which is all the more cruel since she herself is perfectly innocent and does not know her true nature. Quick-witted Kelvin packs her off into a rocket and blasts her into space, only to find her soon returned, still loving him, and with no recollection of his attempt to dispose of her. The duplicate Rheya is a creature formed of neutrinos instead of atoms (though down to the molecules not different from another woman), and she is inextricably bound to the psyche from whose deepest memories she has been created; she cannot stand being separated from her beloved for even a few moments, and when separated she is capable of tearing her way with superhuman strength through steel doors. When injured, her torn tissue has an extraordinary regenerative power, renewing itself in a very short time. Even a suicide attempt with liquid oxygen proves ineffective. Apart from that, she is psychologically quite human, hurt where a normal woman would be hurt, loving as the real Rheya would have loved. If she is a tool created by the ocean for some sinister purpose, she herself does not know what that purpose is. This innocence is what makes her situation so tragically poignant. Whatever the ocean may have intended her to be, she is a woman deeply in love, and the longer she is near Kelvin, the more human she becomes.

Contrary to his first horrified impulses, panicked into murder by her appearance, Kelvin comes to love the replica of his dead wife, though she is incorporated in another material substratum. For Lem, love appears to be something spiritual, more a matter of the mind than of the flesh, with fulfillment rarely possible. Years later, he was to reverse the Rheya situation in the dazzling novella "The Mask," told from the point of view of the woman, a killer-robot programed to pursue and kill the man she has come to love. Sexual fulfillment again being impossible, she is united with her beloved only in death. She finds him covered by an innocent sheet of white snow, not knowing whether she would have killed him if she had found him alive. These are highly romantic affairs with death close by, based on spiritual affinity rather than on physical attraction. This aspect of *Solaris* is presented as a tender, though feverish, high strung love story that shades over into the visionary. It is a science-fiction version of the romantic theme of love beyond death, with the dead female returning not as a vampire, and indeed quite without necrophilic overtones, but by the scientific marvel as a "Phi-creature" or phantom of the ocean.

She is, however, not an exact copy of the dead woman, for she knows things, reconstructed from Kelvin's memory, that the real Rheya could not possibly know. The core of her being remains a mystery, for beyond the normal human tissues and cells that mask the true purpose of the Phi-beings, the electronic microscope reveals only the emptiness of space. When Rheya learns that she is not a normal human being, she is shattered. She reacts to the situation with noble self-sacrifice, knowing that her love for Kelvin has no future. When the physicist Sartorius finally discovers an anti-field for the destruction of the neutrino fields, and the new demons can be exorcized by physics, Rheya asks Snow for her own destruction. Tragic as the story is, and as painful as it is to Kelvin, it is nevertheless one that can be communicated to others without shame. What Snow and Sartorius have to hide must be more horrifying, and Lem wisely refrains from giving more than hints and suggestions. What the ocean reveals to human beings is, in Snow's words, their deepest shame, their folly and their ugliness; it acts as a psychic mirror for the "knights of the Holy Contact" who set out to discover other worlds, and yet encounter only themselves.

In *Solaris*, Lem has successfully combined his central epistemological position with the individual story of a love transcending the limits of life. Of course, the tender and tragic love story remains secondary to the philosophical problem, and the characters are basically building blocks in Lem's epistemological construction. There is also no social environment in the book; the only thing the reader learns about the society that sends scientists to Solaris is that there is a UN convention against the use of X-rays (which is broken by the Solarists). Lem establishes a "pure" experimental situation, undiluted by any social interference, that is concerned with human essentials, not with social accidents. This ideal situation allows him to study his abstract characters and their problems in depth, as representatives of the cognitive situation of mankind.

Interesting as the planet Solaris is in all its particulars, it is only an illustration of rather abstract problems, a concretization of highly unusual and distinct particulars that, as always with Lem, goes beyond the specific case and points towards the general predicament of mankind: the limits of human knowledge, and what takes its place when no final knowledge is possible. "Genius and mediocrity alike are dumbfounded" by the teeming diversity of the oceanic formation of Solaris, some short-lived and explosive, others regular and relatively stable; some superficial formations, others giant structures reaching miles into the atmosphere. At their simplest, they reproduce things that are brought into contact with their surface; at their most complex, they perform complicated functions, bizarre metamorphoses and movements. Sometimes they are thought of as gigantic limbs or organs of the colloid ocean, but all such comparisons are futile. Most interesting of these forms are the symmetriads with their property of illustrating, sometimes contradicting, various laws of physics, and which seem to represent spatial analogons to transcendental equations.

These descriptions and classifications fill thousands of volumes in the vast Solaris library. They became especially numerous after the enthusiasm of the theory-formulating fathers of Solaristics became frustrated, because of their auspicious lack of success at arriving at any explanation, and their failure to achieve contact with the ocean. Then the routine workers came and began observing and filing away masses of repetitious information. However, all the data remain frustratingly phenomenal, while the meaning remains as hidden away from human understanding as ever. The phenomena are described with lucid clarity, but the essence is deeply mysterious. This abyss between observation and interpretation provides the central tension not only of this novel, but of Lem's whole work. This is no variation of the "there are things not meant for man to know"; man is meant to know everything that he can, but there are things that he cannot know, because of the structure of his mind and body and the structure of the universe.

The apparent futility of the Solaris studies does not result in facile despair. The effort is not wasted; experiments must be made, even if they yield no immediate results, but only raise man's failure to understand to a higher level of nonunderstanding, a frequent occurrence in the pursuit of scientific truth. Man must go on hoping and acting on incomplete data. In this respect, Lem is somewhat of an existentialist; in spite of a positive attitude toward science, he is well aware of the absurdity of existence. Although there are reviewers who prefer the banal conviction that he is antiscience, this is very unlikely in view of the intimate knowledge of scientific theories he displays in his fiction and nonfiction.

Thus, Lem is not so much concerned with results as with processes and ways of thinking. This approach gives his writing its energy and dynamism, despite a general lack of plot action. All the descriptions of the Solaris ocean are merely phenomenal and aesthetic, not even scratching the surface of the phenomenon. Explanations are metaphors and similes rather than literal descriptions of processes. This is the deep paradox of Solaristics: man can only resort to the terminology and conceptual apparatus available to him, totally inappropriate though it is for grasping the essence of the situation. In seeking the truly alien, man must always rely on himself and what is familiar to him, because there is nothing else. His cognitive situation is comparable to that of a creature inescapably caught in a net; he may expand that net somewhere, deform it, but try as he might, he will not get out. The mountains of data collected on the Solaris ocean over nearly a hundred years prove unable to answer the innocent question of a schoolgirl: "And what is it for?" There is no lack of theories, but all are equally unproven if unrefuted.

It has come to be generally accepted that the ocean is sentient but the nature of that sentience remains a mystery. From the early optimistic theories about imminent contact, Solaristics has branched into various subfields, with a scientific orthodoxy, heroes, authorities, heretics, and the features of a cult rather than a science. All these theories share, however, one thing: they can neither be refuted nor validated, and any explanation merely replaces "one enigma with another, perhaps even more baffling." This reflects the normal progress of science, made poignant here by the extremity of the situation, by the very size and grandeur of the problem that inevitably leads from the physical into the metaphysical.

In dramatizing the problem, Lem polemizes both the physical and metaphysical against the intellectual pretensions of man, who merely wants to extend his rule over the cosmos and refute the banal solutions offered elsewhere in science fiction. As a rule, other science fiction worlds are purely phenomenological, alien only in appearance, but essentially anthropomorphic: xeno-biological oddities, exotic as they may be in their forms, are psychologically as close as the people in the supermarket next door. For Lem, the true alien has alien principles, laws and purposes not accessible to human reason; this requires a program that is contradictory and unrealizable. So, with a mighty effort, he tries to describe what cannot be understood by man, and which therefore always turns into a mirror, onto which man projects his own thoughts, hopes, and fears. No matter how far the voyage, we meet only ourselves, projecting our own meaning into the alien world. Where science must be silent, its surrogates step in. Not willing to accept the irrevocable loss of Rheya, Kelvin constructs for himself the metaphysical comfort that Solaris is an imperfect god, and he waits for another miracle, the return of Rheya. The essence of that which cannot be grasped intellectually, can nevertheless be accepted emotionally through a quasi-religious belief and appreciated aesthetically. Kelvin's final contact with the ocean is an aesthetic acceptance. Faced with the absurdity of existence, man must nevertheless continue the struggle and at least preserve his dignity. Kelvin's anguish is similar to that of Berton, the helicopter pilot, who was the first person to confront the psychic emanations of the ocean when he saw the face of a giant child. Berton makes all his statements dependent upon whether the commission investigating his case will take him seriously, "because the contents of my hallucinations belong to me, and I don't have to give an account of them, whereas I am obliged to give an account of what I saw on Solaris." There are not many characters in science fiction who speak like this and not many authors who achieve such a convincing fusion of intellect and emotion as Stanislaw Lem does in *Solaris*.

Franz Rottensteiner

Sources for Further Study

Reviews:

Amazing Stories. XLV, January, 1972, pp. 111-112.

Analog. LXXXVII, June, 1971, pp. 169-170.

Galaxy. XXXI, May-June, 1971, pp. 95-102.

Kirkus Reviews. XXXVIII, August 1, 1970, p. 829.

Library Journal. XCV, November 1, 1970, p. 3806.

Luna Monthly. XVII, October, 1970, p. 30.

Magazine of Fantasy and Science Fiction. XL, May, 1971, pp. 42-43.

Publisher's Weekly. CXCVIII, August 17, 1970, p. 50.

SF Commentary. XXIV, November, 1971, pp. 25-34.

Science Fiction Review. XLII, January, 1971, p. 41.

SOLNTSE ZAKHODIT V DONOMAGE
(The Sun Sets in Donomaga)

Author: Ilya Varshavsky (1909-1974)
First book publication: 1966
Type of work: Short stories

Twenty humorous or melancholic tales arranged in three sections mainly reflecting the human problems of a Utopian future, dystopias, parodies, and jokes

Ilya Varshavsky, former sailor on a trader, an engineer and inventor, the coauthor of a book about life and his adventures, and a contributor of notes to a popular science magazine in his youth, had not written for years when he published his first science fiction story in 1962. It was the result of a bet: Varshavsky wanted to show his son that writing science fiction was quite easy. And maybe it really was easy for him; at the age of fifty-two he discovered his special talent for the science fiction short story, a talent that readers almost instantly acknowleged. He became one of the best known Russian science fiction writers, and probably the leading writer of short stories.

His first story collection *The Molecular Cafe* (*Molekulyarnoye kafé*) appeared in 1964, followed by *The Man Who Saw the Antiworld* (*Chelovek, kotory videl antimir*) a year later. *The Sun Sets in Donomaga*, the third collection, completed the initial phase of his work.

Varshavsky arranged the stories in these early collections into thematic sections; in the third book these sections are entitled "Eternal Problems," "Donomaga," and "SF in Its Own Gravy." "Eternal Problems" is the most heterogenous section. It contains texts of several different styles: humorous stories, melancholic "optimistic tragedies," and even a story using a plot which can be classified as "worker's heroism." The characteristic uniting them all is the world in which they are set, a future world that for at least two decades was the background of most Soviet science fiction. It is a world with space flight, highly developed science and technology, and either worldwide Communism or a stable and peaceful coexistence of the two systems devoid of the burning political and social conflicts of the present. Varshavsky welcomes this world, but he does it implicitly; the stories are not strictly Utopian. Instead of simply praising the social achievements of Communism, his more serious tales focus on individual psychological and personal problems.

One short tale, "On the Atoll" sympathetically tells of an astronaut and his family who are infected by an extraterrestrial disease. Therefore, they must live in isolation on a tropical island, hoping that scientists will find a vaccine against the disease. Alas, this story ignores the real conflicts arising between people in such a situation, showing only a somewhat melancholic, but optimistic idyll.

An old astronaut, the hero of "Take Your Decision, Pilot!," who belongs to the flying staff in name only, waits in vain for his chance to fly a spaceship again. Younger pilots, to whom he is a living legend, have taken over his work. In an episode in which he is ordered to fly as second pilot, he suffers from the physical stress he can no longer tolerate; but accidentally he hero-ically saves the ship and fulfills his own fantasy. Though he knows he will never be allowed to fly again, he cannot leave the reserve staff, for that would mean accepting the loss of that which gave his life meaning. The story is a variation of the well-known account of a man who, having dedicated himself totally to his work, encounters a great loss when he can no longer perform the duties of his job. Varshavsky presents the heroic adventure characteristic of such a tale, but he also exposes it for what it really is: a compensatory fantasy.

"Lazy-bones" is a heroic adventure in reality. A young man, by way of some electronically amplified telepathy, mentally directs the work of a robot in a mine. He dislikes the work and never lives up to his potential. When the robot becomes defective, the man must find it in the mine, which is located on a planet inhabited by dangerous animals. Although he brings this adventure to a glorious end, the hero decides to quit his job, for he prefers physical work. Thus, in this story Varshavsky argues against the Utopian idea once common to much science fiction written in socialist countries: that all human work could, and should, be reduced to thinking and pressing buttons.

The other three stories in this section are humorous, if less interesting. In "Cadet Ploshkin," the title character plays a joke on a harsh, grumbling old space captain by passing himself off as a girl; the story is well-told, but as trivial as a camouflaged sailor's tale. "The Uneating" and "Sashka" are more original. The Uneating are alien beings, potentially intelligent, but as they have neither enemies nor the need to eat, they do nothing but stagnate. When fleas are imported to their planet by a Terran expedition's dog, they must look for defenses against the parasites and thus they develop a civilization. In "Sashka," a teenage girl genius invents a computer which works by bacteria instead of electronics. The story relates how Sashka convinces the leading builder of a spaceship to use her invention, and what results from that decision.

The section "SF in Its Own Gravy" is of interest mainly to science fiction fans; the artistic achievement of most of these stories is small, and the ideas are quite flat. "The Conference" presents a robot civilization where scientists declare that intelligent organic life is impossible. "The Game" explains the Universe and human history as the result of a very simple game between God and the devil. "The Shot" exploits the time travel paradox (the traveler kills his own ancestor). In "Mr. Haram in Hell" our world is substituted by an "antiworld" where every relation is inversed, and the author uses it only to tell some shallow jokes. "The Biotrangulation of Lyokochka Rasplyuyev" tells of a hero transported "wirelessly" by supernormal powers (or maybe by some new invention) from another town home to his wife, without any important consequences. Somewhat more interesting is "The Event in Chine Road," in which the inhabitants of a small town go mad for some time, losing their middle-class manners and morals and doing whatever they want. However, the best text in this section is not a story, but an imaginary "Lesson on Parapsychology," which parodies the arguments of parapsychologists.

Varshavsky's two former collections consist mainly of humorous or melancholic tales on conventional science fiction themes and more or less grotesque parodies. It has not been the straight, perhaps too conventional, parodies that have won him the attention of readers and critics, but the type of tale represented in the third book only by "Take Your Decision, Pilot!," "Lazybones," "On the Atoll," and to a lesser degree "Cadet Ploshkin" and "The Uneating." They are stories written around a fantastic idea, sometimes Varshavsky's own invention, but more often a conventional one from science fiction or science. Varshavsky takes such ideas out of the context of science fiction or abstract popular science and places them in an environment more closely related to real life, with ordinary people as characters. For example, in Varshavsky's first collection one can find a number of "cybernetic" stories of a world where all life is penetrated by automatization and computerization. These tales of electronic *enfants terribles*, sad robots, and people isolated from what we would call real life were stimulated by the enthusiastic belief that applied cybernetics would entirely change life for the better in a very short time. This conviction occurred not only in science fiction literature, but also in the public's mind because of the Soviet public's sudden confrontation with cybernetics in the 1960's when it could no longer be rejected as a "capitalist pseudo-science." In his stories, Varshavsky gave the new cybernetic wonderland perspective by showing the flaws, excesses, and implications of some of the ideas of its enthusiasts and turning attention away from technology back to human relations and feelings.

These stories were not dystopian; some, however, came close to dystopia. So when Varshavsky first published *The Sun Sets in Donomaga*, a cycle of dystopian tales, or "warnings" as they are called in the Soviet Union, he could include in the "Donomaga" section of the book one of his early robot stories, "Phantoms." In the entire cycle, he continues to doubt the paradise of cybernetics and other modern sciences and technologies. But he does so the hard way, setting the conflicts in the imaginary country Donomaga which is the opposite to the world of the other stories. In the real world, unexpected problems may occur or things must be reevaluated and looked at realistically, but social development is progressive; in Donomaga things are so wrong that this country is doomed.

The first two stories present Donomaga as the usual "Brave New World" created by misused science. In "No Alarming Symptoms" a mathematician is not only practically immortal (his organs are perpetually regenerated), but his brain is cleaned artificially of "useless" memories. In "Phantoms" the hero, cared for by robots and automats who have replaced human contacts, loves a girl who is merely an image on the television screen created by some computer. The heroes of both stories have lost their humanity, one by his will, the other because he lacks all human contact. In a sense, they both have become robots themselves.

The next four texts are of less literary value; the ideas are unoriginal and undeveloped. "Preliminary Investigations" is the story of a man who, under the influence of drugs, has to create crazy ideas that will be transformed by a computer into science fiction stories. The parody is acceptable but completely out of place among the dystopias. "The Judge" presents an electronic judge; "The Violet" describes a reservation where the last living plants are displayed; "The Sun Sets in Donomaga" chronicles the fate of the last man living in Donomaga, fed, controlled, and tortured by a computer.

Only the final story of the Donomaga section, "The Heir," is a fitting conclusion to the volume. Donomaga first isolated itself from the rest of the world and then destroyed itself testing a new weapon. Only an old man has survived by chance. His sole companion is an intelligent computer with whom he continually argues about the causes of the catastrophe without ever understanding them. He also tells the computer about his lonely walks through the empty city that continues its own automatic life. Even more than the man himself, the computer fears that the old man might die, leaving it alone. This alternative version of the last man/computer theme is convincing for creating instead of the usual crude terrors, a gentle tone that announces the total silence to come.

In spite of the very uneven artistic quality of the stories collected in *The Sun Sets in Donomaga*, it has been a success. The stories point out unexpected aspects of problems and themes widely discussed in the Soviet Union at the time of publication, presenting at the peak of the Russian science fiction boom ideas previously familiar only in a few foreign works available there. Above all, the stories tell of ordinary people instead of abstract space heroes, technology, or pure "ideas."

Varshavsky constantly expressed a kind of commentary on science fiction itself; indeed, his work could not have arisen outside the context of the genre. The incident which stimulated his first story is symbolic for all his work. The close connection with the current ideas of science fiction, however, did not stop Varshavsky from showing, in his best stories, real situations, hopes, and dangers in an emotionally convincing and sometimes unexpected way. In this, his third book, all the general characteristics and themes of Varshavsky's prose were gathered for the first time. They were to be synthesized on a higher level in his following works.

H. Walter

SOZDAN DLA BUZI
(Created for Storms)

Author: Henrich Altov (1926-   )
First book publication: 1970
Type of work: Short stories

A collection of short stories by the foremost Soviet writer of idea science fiction in the 1960's

All present definitions of science fiction are incomplete because it does not exist as a single subject. Or maybe we have yet to grasp this subject as something unified. Science fiction is so diverse that those who attempt to classify or systemize it, no matter how difficult the task, will achieve much more than those who try to synthesize it. It is hard to comprehend even the structural range of science fiction. We know, for example, *situation science fiction* (fantastic elements consist of the description of an alien planet, for example); *character science fiction* (an alien creature familiar to human beings, or a human being among absolutely alien intelligent creatures); *plot science fiction* (traveling in time is an obvious example). There also exist such types as futuristic, paradoxical, metaphysical, and psychological science fiction. Among these types *idea science fiction* is worthy of notice. It by no means implies a return to the times of the violent and inaccurate pulp era when a hypothetical scientific idea was a guarantee of success, as was the case with the authors published in *Amazing Stories* (where "an idea" provided everything necessary for literature).

Nevertheless, the contemporary science fiction of ideas has something in common with that of John W. Campbell, Jr.'s, time: despite the literary art of a writer the idea of his book dominates and determines the dynamics of the plot and the evolution of the book's characters. In Soviet science fiction a most prominent representative of such *idea science fiction* is Henrich Altov.

It would be no exaggeration to call his scientific fiction a "magic box" of original scientific and technological ideas and hypotheses. Not that each of his stories satisfies the tastes of academic critics, but none is trivial. Among Altov's stories there are no standard or worn out topics. And that is rather important today, when the wonderful literature founded by Mary Shelley, Edgar Allan Poe, Jules Verne and H. G. Wells is being corroded by stereotypes.

To provide a better understanding and an emotional perception of Altov's stories, some biographical details are helpful. He is a professional inventor, holding dozens of patents, and the creator of a practically new branch of science — the theory of invention. His monographs containing "the algorithm of invention" are used as textbooks by hundreds of experts in various fields of knowledge. He is the founding father and permanent head of the public laboratory of scientific invention where scientific fiction is an obligatory subject.

Altov is the author of a unique "Register of Topics, Plots and Situations in Science Fiction" comprising several thousand sections and subsections alone. In addition, Altov is one of undisputed leaders of Soviet science fiction of the 1960's. He is an unorthodox person, a tireless fighter against intellectual stagnation, inertness, and stereotypes in the field of technical invention. He is also an ardent and uncompromised partisan of science fiction literature as "a media for message," and those who read his stories inevitably become sympathetic to the author's ideas.

It would be a simplification to describe Altov and his stories as being devoted only to the problems of invention and the people involved in them. The writer presents characters able to view problems from a rather strange angle, who are considered fanatics at first, but in the end appear as far-sighted and prudent persons. To approach ordinary things from an unusual point of view is Altov's credo as a writer. Through his impeccable logic and sincere inspiration he easily involved his readers; very often it is difficult to conclude whether the vision presented is a reality or Altov's fantasy. On the whole Altov remains a science fiction writer and not a theoretician, despite the fact that he has published a number of interesting though debatable articles about the fate of forecasts and anticipations of Verne, Wells, and Alexander Belyaev.

Altov has been most successful with novelettes. In his short stories one often notices an oversaturation of ideas. Short stories are too narrow for his thoughts. He has achieved perfection in describing psychological problems, is a master of dialogue, and keeps the plot of his stories under control, but he fails to control his ideas. Although the stories are not boring, they may prove exhausting to the reader, as if he had spent a day working in the library. His stories are not for amusement. They fully correspond to the classical addition formula: "good (science fiction) = good science + good fiction." Some of his stories are considered classics in Soviet science fiction and have been included in several anthologies.

The collection of stories *Sozdan dla buzi* is compiled in such a way that it makes a complete appraisal of the creative work of Altov possible. The book comprises two earlier collections: *Legends About Star Captains* (1961) and *Scorching Mind* (1968). Combined under one cover, the stories represent an ideal anthology which might have been entitled "The Complete Altov."

The first group of stories can be classified as contemporary science fiction: the action takes place in the present and major characters are taken from everyday life. All of the characters are real people, sometimes presented with a psychological trustworthiness, in other cases as superficial individuals. But all of them are authentic people, not mere book personalities expressing the author's thoughts. We see our own world combined with extremely fantastic situations, and the subtitle "science fiction stories" is accepted without any doubt.

The reader is astounded by the waterfall of ideas, thoroughly worked out and easily presented, which are related to fundamental science and to "ordinary" engineering designs: some are absolutely trustworthy, and others are completely insane. This brainstorm approach can even give the reader ideas unknown as yet to the author. Of course there are too many ideas, and it is hardly possible to absorb the book in one reading. But in a previous work, Altov used an epigraph from Francis Bacon to warn his readers: "Read not to contradict and confute, not to believe and take for granted, not to find talk and discourse, but to weigh and consider." Although it may sound too categorical, it contains Altov's entire philosophy.

At first glance, each of these stories seems based on a particular problem of invention, but as that is solved Altov gives the reader a glimpse of "a distant prospect." Behind the barrier of definite technological ideas one can see daring and limitless dreams about distant stars, future human biological evolution, or instant "self-assembling" machines.

In the story "Created for Storms," the major character represents a new science. When this story was being written, this new science was only on the verge of recognition. Its label is "science about science," or how to teach scientists to think. As an engineer-inventor and not a theoretician, Altov sets only engineering problems for himself. The story has three such problems: to construct a ship having a speed of 600 mph; to create an apparatus allowing man to fly with individual wings; and one intriguing "problem" which is not fully disclosed by the author.

The three problems cannot yet be solved by modern science. Altov develops the action according to all the rules of brainstorming: the experiment is carried out with the help of cranky inventors, who are a mockery of the scientific community. The inventors are convinced that they are to deal only with special effects, using life-size models for a science fiction movie to be filmed. They are expected to create basically new and fantastic machinery for the film. The experimental institute provides money and creates an unexpectedly favorable atmosphere for the inventors. no criticism on the part of experts, no mockery, no cold indifference. In short, they have complete freedom.

The inventors do what is expected of them. They construct an unusual "ship" capable of a fantastic speed on water (indeed, it is a marvelous idea to create an artificial tsunami wave and then to harness it). Then people take off into air using the artificial wings with the aid of electricity. An optimistic end leads us to believe that the third problem also will be solved by human intelligence free of numerous barriers.

If one considers the idea of switching people to electric power, it becomes clear that this is not simple engineering science fiction. Altov has presented one of the morally and psychologically acceptable versions of cyborgization. Such casual mention of the solution of the second problem is worth dozens of stereotypical novels on the same topic.

The story entitled "Crazy Company" presents a group of "cranks," who try to breed pterodactyl, by absolutely scientific methods. At present, bionics is a very popular science, but Altov's characters dare to "copy" prehistoric animals for subsequent studies. They do not create models, but real live animals, which have been extinct for millions of years.

One of the most interesting is the story entitled "Little Donkey and Axiom." In it Altov deals in his usual manner with rather unusual problems of "uselessness of distant space flights" (because of an inevitable outdating of information obtained in such flights) and of constructing machines of the future capable of changing themselves in order to adapt to the necessities of the rapid progress of human society.

It is difficult to single out a key story in Altov's work, but "Scorching Mind" might serve the purpose. What is an intellect? Is it possible to "transplant" intellect? What are the means of intensifying the human brain's activity? These are some of the problems raised in the story. One of them, concerning an optimum concentration and mastering of knowledge, receives an original solution in the story. "The human brain is an amazing device. The task is to provide enough fuel for it."

Superintellectual characters are not exceptional in science fiction. Nevertheless, in "Scorching Mind" an earthly solution becomes striking in its simplicity and unexpectedness. There is no need to search for super abilities or to breed genetically a "homo superior" race; it is enough to give an ordinary human brain a possibility for normal activities. One of the story's characters declares: "The level of genius is the normal level for the human brain. It is not yet so, but it should be." Altov is the first to raise the problem of "intelligence as a necessity," which is in keeping with this remark from a story by the Strugatsky brothers: "To think is not a pleasure, it is a duty." Although it is a modest story in terms of idea and plot, "Scorching Mind" raises the problem of *the necessity* to be a genius.

Saturated with the ideas of Altov, the reader comes to the story "Clinic Sapsan" ready to accept the absolutely scientific idea of a practically limitless extension of human life. The reader will be positive that this is not fiction or a groundless fantasy, but it will take place according to the author. Ignore the technicalities; it is worthwhile to put the book aside and reflect upon the problem oneself.

This book contains interesting examples of Altov's "hard-core" science fiction. Soviet science fiction of the 1960's would have been impossible without such stories as "Heroic Symphony," "Proving Ground," "Star River," and "The Port of Stone Storms." They possess everything that attracts both the veteran science fiction fans and the newcomers to this type of literature: Distant space flights, acquaintance with extraterrestial intelligent beings, an experiment to overcome the light barrier, courageous and traditionally austere "space vets," romanticism, and star winds of far voyages.

No matter how traditional his plots and situation are, Altov never misses a chance to introduce something new and unexpected. Independent of Poul Anderson ("Call Me Joe") and Arthur C. Clarke ("Meeting with Medusa"), he meditates about the prospects of distant biocontrol from the Earth of the automatic research devices on Jupiter ("General Designer"). He introduces a brilliant hypothesis that spherical star clusters are galactic cities united by an unknown intellect ("The Port of Stone Storms"). In a laconic manner he illustrates the idea of "Dyson's sphere" and discovers a moral aspect overlooked by other authors ("Nine Minutes").

In Altov's literary heritage a special place is occupied by lyrical mythology. In Soviet science fiction literature he was the first to try creating "myths of the future" (stylized as ancient original myths), legends about spaceflight pioneers. These stories do not resemble mythological reconstructions of our universe (in the style of Cordwainer Smith or Roger Zelazny); they are more reminiscent of folklore-type legends presented in an ingenious and interesting manner, such as the story of the daring astronauts Icarus and Daedalus who fly through the Sun.

Two science fiction essays, "Can Machine Think?" and "Discovery Machine," are appropriately included in the collection, and their titles speak for themselves. Alas, this anthology is the most recent science fiction work of Altov. If we disregard fragments of his yet unfinished novel, *Third Millennium* (the published chapters show that it is supposed to be a large futuristic panorama in the manner of *2001*), the Soviet science fiction reader has had no further encounters with Altov. At present he is entirely occupied with his scientific activities. He has explained the reason for his departure from literature through one of his literary characters: "A bright idea voids everything else for me, like bright sun makes the star disappear. Probably, that is why I've failed to become a writer."

Vl. Gakov

SPACE LORDS

Author: Cordwainer Smith (Paul M. Linebarger, 1913-1966)
First book publication: 1965
Type of work: Thematically related short stories
Time: The remote future
Locale: Earth and various other planets, in and out of the solar system

Reprints of five stories originally published in magazines in the early 1960's, an important segment of Smith's "future history" of the Instrumentality of Man

In the 1970's Cordwainer Smith became recognized as one of the most original writers of science fiction, as well as a man whose life was hardly less interesting than his stories. "Cordwainer Smith" was only one of several pseudonyms used by Paul Linebarger. Although Linebarger was born in the United States, much of early life was spent in China, where his father was an American adviser to Sun Yat-sen, nationalist leader and first president of China. As a result, Linebarger, who was Sun Yat-sen's godson, spent his formative years in a culture that must have seemed as exotic to Americans of the time as his stories were to a later generation. He traveled extensively both in the Orient and in Europe, learning six languages and finding time to take a doctoral degree in political science. His writing began as a sideline to his several vocations as university professor, government executive, and officer in U.S. Army Intelligence.

According to J. J. Pierce, a recent editor of his stories, Smith's writing of science fiction began in his teens with a short story now lost. But readers of the genre first noticed his work with the publication of the story "Scanners Live in Vain" in 1950. In the 1950's and early 1960's stories followed which made it clear that in Cordwainer Smith a major talent had appeared. One important component of that talent was Smith's ability to establish an atmosphere unique to science fiction, that of the alien society, and to create that atmosphere in a unique way. Some background in the methods of the science fiction genre is necessary to understand Smith's particular technique.

As a method, the role of extrapolation in science fiction has been widely discussed; through its use, writers create a setting in the future by assuming that some present trend will continue or intensify, while they hold other factors in society constant. For example, in one series of stories, Larry Niven assumes that human institutions, desires, and abilities will remain as they are now with the single exception of perfected procedures for transplanting bodily organs; thereafter the effects of this single variable are explored.

But ultimately such explorations of the future are limited. When we look at the span of human history in the past, we realize that at some point not only will abilities and institutions change, but human desires themselves will be different, creating a society as odd to us as ours would be to an Egyptian peasant from the days of the Pharaohs. Of course, these changes will occur not only in the large components of society, but in trivial ones as well. Whatever diversions may exist ten millennia from now, we may well doubt that people will light up tobacco cigarettes in their spare moments, as a character does in Isaac Asimov's Foundation series. Therefore, the writer who sets a story in the far future has a massive task before him, one in which extrapolation will not be of much help. The canvas of the far future society will be much broader than that of, say, George Orwell's *Nineteen Eighty-Four*, yet every detail must be something strange and wondrous.

Several methods are useful for depicting a setting that is radically rather than slightly different, and exotic in many ways, not only in one. The first uses familiar words and terms but in odd juxtapositions, as in Robert Heinlein's celebrated sentence, ''The door dilated.'' The noun ''door'' and the verb ''dilate'' are familiar words, but when we read them as subject and predicate we know that the story in which they are contained presumes a society different from ours in a fundamental way. The reader receives much the same feeling in a Robert Silverberg story in which the bartender has one for himself, not by drinking the alcohol but by transmitting it directly into the bloodstream. Here again, all the parts of the action are familiar, but they are combined in an unexpected unity.

Another method of establishing an exotic setting is that favored by Cordwainer Smith. It starts with terms that are strange in themselves. Some of these terms are recognizable deformations of words changed by time: thus the place-name Meeya Meefla hints at its origin as Miami, Florida. Other terms become clear as the story unfolds: we learn that ''underpeople,'' a word found in many of the tales, is the name for human-shaped intelligent beings derived from the lower animals. C'mell, for example, is a character whose name shows her feline ancestry by its initial letter — for ''cat.'' And still a third group of terms is never explained, contributing strongly to the air of mystery, to the sense of a deep and hidden background that marks the work of Cordwainer Smith. Alpha Ralpha Boulevard, for instance, is a name that tantalizes, since its first part is familiar, and the reader has the feeling that the whole would make sense if perhaps just one piece of its history were known. Or again, a strange machine is known as the Abba-dingo. The definite article makes the name sound like a title, like something unique, yet the source of its name and even its original purpose are hidden from us. As these examples suggest, Smith is especially masterful at evocative and haunting names — C'mell, Lord Jestocost, Charlie-is-my-darling, Mother Hitton — they seem to come from another world, which is just the effect the author is aiming for.

This sense of a mysterious background is crucial to the success of Smith's fiction, since many of his stories (including all those in *Space Lords*) take place in the remote future, perhaps ten or fifteen thousand years hence.

Smith's stories, like those of the early Heinlein or Ursula K. Le Guin, form a connected future history operating through a single vision. Mankind has spread throughout the stars in that scheme, but unlike many centuries-spanning epics, Smith's interstellar society is not static. Over the series of his tales, changes continue to occur in technology, human relations, and politics. In only the field of technology, for instance, starships propelled by the pressure of light on huge sails give way to planoforming — travel through something like that science fiction standby, hyperspace. The planoforming concept is especially rich in details: the go-captains whose subconscious minds navigate the ships, the pin-lighters whose telepathic perceptions guard the ships, the cat-partners who serve the pin-lighters. Yet even all this gives way to something like teleportation.

Nostalgia is a common human response to technological change; people feel sentimental, for example, about the obsolescence of gleaming transcontinental passenger trains and regret seeing the profession of railroad engineer lose its luster and prestige. Yet it is a measure of the skill of Cordwainer Smith that he can make us feel nostalgic about the passing of a profession that is entirely fictional and located in a future far beyond the extent of our lives, as he does for the scanners, spaceship pilots in "Scanners Live in Vain."

Political institutions change as well as technology. In "Alpha Ralpha Boulevard" we see a lasting (and boring) Utopia yield to a world in which the human need for challenge has been rediscovered. In several stories, the under-people, little more than slaves, press for and eventually achieve freedom and respect. Methods of judicial proceedings change, ways of punishment change.

This variety of changes allows most of Cordwainer Smith's stories to be placed roughly in chronological order in his outline of future history. The order of the five stories in *Space Lords* coincides neither with their order of composition nor their arrangement in the book. Following Pierce's chronology, the order of the stories should be "The Dead Lady of Clown Town" first, "Drunkboat" second, and then three stories whose order relative to one another is difficult to determine: "Mother Hitton's Littul Kittons," "The Ballad of Lost C'Mell," and "A Planet Named Shayol." In this order they span most of the changes noted above.

Despite all this change, Cordwainer Smith can hardly be called a writer of hard science fiction; his emphasis is not on technological advance. Nor is he a sociological writer; institutional changes are not his prime concern. Rather, through all his stories, through all the exotic and even bizarre settings, we understand his characters and sympathize with them because he is concerned with the human heart — even when that heart lies within the body of a beast.

It is no disparagement to say that in the main Smith has only one theme: love. That theme, in its varied forms, is so rich a subject that thousands of years of storytellers have not exhausted it, but it is rare to science fiction. When one thinks of writers in the field who have dealt with the subject, Theodore Sturgeon and Ursula Le Guin come to mind, but past them, the list is not very long. No writer in the genre exercises greater skill in characterization or motivates those characters in mature human relationships better than does Cordwainer Smith.

The three central stories in *Space Lords* clearly show Smith's favorite theme. "The Dead Lady of Clown Town" places a simple love theme within a larger plot about the resistance of the underpeople to their oppressed status. At the center stands D'joan, a girl of dog ancestry, whose resemblance to Joan of Arc goes deeper than her name. But unlike the maid of Orleans, D'joan leads an army of underpeople whose only weaponry is love for mankind. We see her struggle through the human eyes of Elaine and the Hunter, whose comparatively mild punishment for their part in the uprising points up the savagery of D'joan's martyrdom at the stake. The story displays love between man and woman, love between intelligent species, and, in the mechanical person of the Lady Panc Ashash, even the love of machines for humans, all against a background of civil insurrection.

The caring of being for being in these stories suggests that Smith proposes a definition of humanity based on the expression of kindness and affection: beings who can do that, whatever their nature, share in humanity.

"Drunkboat" shows the power of the bonds of love; they fuel the teleportation of a traveler through space to the side of his beloved, whose life he believes to be in danger. Here love triumphs not only over distance, but over technology as well, since the story hints that a controlled form of teleportation will replace the planoforming ships.

"The Ballad of Lost C'mell" deals again with the underpeople. It concerns only a single incident in their long struggle to be treated as intelligent beings, and in that sense can be thought of as a companion piece to "The Dead Lady of Clown Town." C'mell's love is returned; the seventh Lord Jestocost, a member of the shadowy but powerful Instrumentality, allows himself to be used to penetrate the Instrumentality's secrets because of his affection for C'mell, and he later on becomes a champion of the rights of the underpeople. Their largely unstated love is made the more poignant by being illegal, by being repressed by both of them, and by being to the last unconsummated.

Perhaps Smith's most interesting concept, one that appears in story after story, is the Instrumentality of Man. While not a government, the Instrumentality exercises a supreme power, even over planetary governments. It is something like an aristocracy, and is perhaps hereditary. Its members are telepathic, intelligent, but not supermen. Their most outstanding characteristic is their collective dedication to a set of ideals that remains shadowy, and there is something about them more like a religious order than a country gentry. In the end, the suggestion of a religious dimension to the Instrumentality may be the most revealing, for an instrument is designed for a purpose, designed to be used for something. And there is an ambiguity about their name: are they an instrument through which mankind works, or is mankind the instrument, the tool through which a divine providence achieves its purposes? Smith, a sincerely religious man, may have answered yes to the second question. His theme of an all-pervading and all-conquering love fits comfortably within the Christian conception of divine benevolence. His raising of beasts and even machines to a share in the communion of people of good will suggests the coming of a new creation. Had Smith lived longer, we might have seen in his work an imaginative picture of the end, in St. Paul's words, towards which all creation strives. As it is, he has given us unforgettable stories of incidents that occur along the way.

Walter E. Meyers

Sources for Further Study

Reviews:

Analog. LXXVI, January, 1966, pp. 146-147.

Magazine of Fantasy and Science Fiction. XXIX, October, 1965, p. 92.

National Review. XVII, September 21, 1965, p. 835-836.

THE SPACE MERCHANTS

Authors: Frederik Pohl (1919-   ) and Cyril M. Kornbluth (1923-1958)
First book publication: 1953
Type of work: Novel
Time: The near future
Locale: The United States, mostly New York City, with scenes in Antarctica and on
the Moon

*A satirical melodrama set in a world controlled by large corporations which are
opposed by a subversive World Conservation Association*

> *Principal characters:*
> MITCHELL COURTENAY, a young advertising executive
> DR. KATHY NEVIN, his estranged wife
> FOWLER SCHOCKEN, his boss, head of the world's largest advertising
>   agency
> B. J. TAUNTON, Schocken's most powerful competitor
> JACK O'SHEA, pilot of the first round-trip voyage to Venus
> HESTER, Courtenay's secretary
> HEDY, a sadistic torturer
> GUS HERRERRA, a synthetic yeast worker and a subversive

The Space Merchants has always been justly famous as the principal example of the social criticism found in science fiction of the Cold War period. Frederik Pohl and Cyril Kornbluth were veterans of both the radical youth movements of the 1930's and the science fiction fan community when they wrote this novel, the first product of a collaboration which continued until Kornbluth's death in 1958. Pohl also had experience in the advertising business; Kornbluth was a reporter and pulp writer. These useful backgrounds contribute to this novel's agreeable combination of social insight and readability.

Mitchell Courtenay is a relatively well-to-do man. He can afford his own two-room apartment even though he lives alone. He can even afford to wash his face with fresh water. He is able to do these things only because he is a senior executive and member of the Board of Directors of Fowler Schocken Associates, the largest advertising agency in the world. And although Courtenay does not know it yet, the agency has just taken control of the Venus Project. Before the working day begins, Fowler Schocken will appoint him to head it.

Schocken Associates' control of the Venus Project will be even more lucrative than the company's account with the United States Government. In this future world, business' growing domination of politics has reached a logical conclusion. Whole continents are organized as industrial trusts, and even in the United States social services such as police protection and mail delivery are performed by private corporations as profit-making ventures. The term "cutthroat competition" has also come to mean the literal cutting of throats. Industrial feuds are an accepted business practice, although the rules governing them are honored more in the breach than in the observance. Congress represents industrial interests, rather than geographic, popular constituencies. Ideal-istic after his own fashion, Courtenay believes in Sales and their continued growth as the highest of ideals. In a world short of space, food, and natural resources, the profits which Schocken Associates will earn by exploiting Venus and its colonists seem a reasonable return for the agency's efforts to ease humanity's lot on Earth by providing a source of raw materials and an outlet for surplus population.

However, the Venus Project is fragile; it is expensive and will require diverting tax money and technology from consumer goods. The potential dan-ger from the public is compounded by the threat from Schocken's political enemies, led by B. J. Taunton, head of his own ad agency; Taunton is trying to steal control of the project, which Schocken has stolen from him. Finally, there are the "Consies": members of the World Conservation Association, fanatics who oppose nearly everything good and useful, including the Venus rocket, as additional assaults on an already polluted ecosphere which has been stripped of natural resources.

This is the skeleton on which the novel is built. But its almost simple plot elements — vast power and melodramatic adventures to steal or protect that power — are distinctly secondary to the descriptive detail and texture with which Pohl and Kornbluth depict a world where the crassest of commercial values has attained complete ideological hegemony. From the first chapter, taut writing, incidental observations, and critical minutiae provide a vivid pic-ture of this highly stratified society from the viewpoint of one of its most privileged members. Who else would know that a junior executive wearing an oaken ring was living beyond his means?

Courtenay is a bright young man who energetically begins fulfilling Schocken's faith in his ability to manage the huge Venus Project. As the price for this efficiency, he is lured to an Antarctic resort in search of a disastrously lax associate, knocked out, and kidnaped. When he wakes up, he has been reported dead, his identity has been obscured, and he is on a labor freighter bound for the synthetic yeast factories of Costa Rica. Having lost his privi-leged status, Courtenay now discovers what the life of a consumer is like.

There is far more working than consuming in Costa Rica, but Courtenay uses his meager spare time and sharply honed ability to manipulate people to establish contact with the subversive Consie organization. Since he is a whiz at writing propaganda, the organization arranges for him to travel to their New York headquarters, where he then reestablishes contact with Schocken Asso-ciates. Schocken himself refuses to believe Courtenay's story, but that obstacle is overcome when Schocken is murdered by Taunton.

In one of the novel's few inconsistencies, the agency head has willed con-trol of Schocken Associates to Courtenay through several intermediaries and dummy corporations. Now aware that his wife, Kathy Nevin, is a member of the Consie Central Committee, and converted to the conservationist cause himself, Courtenay uses his new power to complete the Venus Project and then to turn it over to the Consies. He is discovered at the last minute and barely escapes. Courtenay and his wife, whose marriage had nearly ended, find a new love and purpose as members of the expedition to a new planet.

If melodrama serves the interest of satire here, satire also serves the interest of melodrama. Courtenay is a powerful businessman, close enough to the top of the world's most powerful corporation to inherit the founder's wealth and political power. He can be sophisticated and charming, but he is also efficient, even ruthless. At the same time, he is disturbingly innocent. With a naïveté reminiscent of *The Perils of Pauline*, Courtenay always acts as if the system were straight, the deck unstacked. Each step of the adventure reveals new facets of the social structure built on this monopolistic economic and political base, and each new facet becomes a snag over which Courtenay trips into the next phase of his adventures. Innocent to the last, he is eventually denounced as a Consie and almost literally carried off to join his wife. The blastoff into the sunset provides an appropriately romantic conclusion. (It is also worth mentioning that Pohl and Kornbluth have reversed at least one melodramatic convention. Their archetypal innocent is male, and he is saved by his exasperated but thoroughly competent, beautiful wife.)

While a work of political satire written in an overtly commercial medium (and during an era of great political repression) can hardly be expected to include a complete political program, the Consies are not shown to be motivated by any consistent philosophy. Although they are not the fanatics Courtenay at first believed them to be, the Consies are a limited resistance movement resembling nothing so much as a rightwing caricature of the Communist Party — even when seen through relatively friendly eyes. They are organized into underground cells and a pyramidal hierarchy. They are serious, intellectual, and dull. Courtenay himself rises through their ranks by adapting his advertising skills to political propaganda and overtly replacing reason with appeals to ambition and to the senses. (The dangers of *this* manipulative technique were only beginning to be discussed at the time the novel was written.) Differing on so many real political and economic issues, both the established system and its enemies share the view that their only hope lies in establishing a frontier where only one side or the other can be permitted to develop.

The innocence of this philosophy, even in rebellion, and Courtenay's basic loyalty to the original, idealized image of the *status quo* revealed by it, is hardly limited to either this novel or to science fiction. The regeneration of a once honest system of social relations on an unspoiled frontier is as old a component of American thought as the Puritan settlement of Massachusetts. But two competing systems of social relations can produce contention and bloodshed — as the 600,000 dead in the American Civil War testify. Telling the story through Courtenay's eyes (in which the blastoff for Venus on the novel's last page is simply the confirmation of his alienation from the world of

Schocken Associates), Pohl and Kornbluth evade such sticky political questions, turning instead to science fiction's traditional reliance on technological solutions to social problems. The social forms the Consie settlers on Venus will adopt are presented only in the general terms of conservation and less social stratification. Here too, Pohl and Kornbluth are hardly alone: the years since World War II have been hard on utopian speculation, and the belief in *The Space Merchants* in escape is a mark of relative optimism.

Such a critical perspective should not be permitted to detract from the novel's accomplishments, particularly when viewed against the backdrop of political repression characterizing the early 1950's in the United States. The book's strength lies in the depiction of a world very much like our own, exaggerated enough to be satirical, but close enough to reality to seem uncomfortably plausible even after the passage of twenty-five years. Moreover, Pohl and Kornbluth effectively use much of the freedom generated by science fiction's first steps beyond the genre magazine ghetto.

Not only do the authors join the hard sciences of physics, chemistry, and mathematics with the "softer" science of psychology, but they also depict the everyday man and woman sympathetically. Workers and consumers are presented with a sensitivity often absent in the genre; and the choice of an elitist narrator provides reasonable justification for much of the inevitable stereotyping of minor characters. Portrayed as victims of merciless exploitation, ordinary people are nonetheless capable of some resistance and a certain independent dignity despite the fashion in which the authors give the Consie leadership to dissident members of the ruling elite. Here too, Pohl and Kornbluth are simply reflecting a problem in political theory and practice which has bedeviled democratic thinkers for a long time, and none of *them* has managed a solution either.

Finally, the novel is truly innovative in its focus on the necessary interaction between the process of industrial production, to which social and political critics had long devoted attention, and the then relatively unexamined cultural artifacts and institutions like advertising and mass communications, which teach people how to make sense of the world. In the real world such institutions shape human perception with a powerful hand, but they are subordinate parts of larger industrial conglomerates rather than Pohl and Kornbluth's central organizers. Nevertheless, actual production and the promotion of products in the culture at large are necessarily linked.

As it gets older, *The Space Merchants* may suffer the fate of too much satire. Written to warn of the consequences "if this goes on," the book may soon be read in a world where "this" *has* gone on, and all its dire consequences are no longer satire but reality.

Albert I. Berger

Sources for Further Study

Criticism:

Livingston, Dennis. "Science Fiction Models of Future World Order Systems," in *International Organization*. XXV (Spring, 1971), pp. 254-270. Livingston analyzes *The Space Merchants* and seven other works and discusses societal models presented within each of them.

Reviews:

Analog. LII, November, 1953, pp. 148-149.

Chicago Sunday Tribune. June 21, 1953, p. 6.

Galaxy. VI, August, 1953, pp. 114-115.

Magazine of Fantasy and Science Fiction. V, July, 1953, pp. 84-85.

New York Herald Tribune Book Review. July 5, 1953, p. 8.

New York Times. September 6, 1953, p. 13.

San Francisco Chronicle. July 19, 1953, p. 19.

Speculation. XXXI, Autumn, 1972, pp. 30-31.

Times Literary Supplement. February 2, 1973, p. 129.

THE SQUARES OF THE CITY

Author: John Brunner (1934-   )
First book publication: 1965
Type of work: Novel
Time: The 1960's
Locale: The modern city of Vados in the country Aguazul

A novel describing the tensions created by the development of a modern city within the borders of a backward South American country whose plot is based on an actual chess match between the international grand masters William Steinitz and Mikhail Ivanovich Tchigorin

> Principal characters:
> JUAN SEBASTIAN VADOS, President of Aguazul and mayor of the city of Vados
> BOYD HAKLUYT, a traffic analyst
> MARIA POSADOR, the widow of a political opponent of Vados
> DONALD ANGERS, head of the highway department
> ALEJANDRO MAYOR, Minister of Information
> ESTEBAN DIAZ, Minister of the Interior and chief opponent of Vados
> "FATS" BROWN, a lawyer and opponent of President Vados

The Squares of the City is a difficult novel to analyze since it contains a multitude of themes which, at least in the beginning, seem only loosely connected with one another; indeed, one wonders at first if it can be called a science fiction work at all. As the novel opens, Boyd Hakluyt, a traffic analyst, is called upon by the city council of the Ciudad de Vados to redesign an already model traffic pattern in order to eliminate several unsightly areas of the city created by the influx of peasants. President Juan Sebastian Vados built the city where nothing had previously stood, but in so doing, he altered the course of the river upon which the peasants in the area relied for their farming, thus forcing them from their homes, and they turn to Ciudad de Vados. Given this situation, *The Squares of the City* seems at first to be an investigation of contemporary South American politics.

This first impression is further underscored by the lack of technological trappings usually expected of a science fiction novel. Besides the remarkable achievement of the city itself, there is little in the novel that centers on new scientific advances. Brunner seems to have done this deliberately to make the point that what takes place in the city is possible with our present technological and social tools. However, by downplaying any futuristic aspects of his fictional world, Brunner has created a novel that is indistinguishable from numerous mainstream novels dealing with the same theme.

What Hakluyt learns about the political situation surrounding his employment sounds like a fictional description of the present world. In order to build his city, President Vados hired a large number of foreign experts, attracting them by granting them citizenship and special privileges. As a result, there are two classes of people in Ciudad de Vados: foreign-born citizens (assisted by a few natives) who control the government and economy, and poor natives (aided by a few foreign sympathizers) who threaten the established order. These two groups are organized into opposing political parties, the Citizens' Party and the National Party. Hakluyt unwillingly becomes involved with both groups, and much of what follows is based on the fortunes of members of each party. Again, there is nothing in such a plot that would seem to justify labeling *The Squares of the City* science fiction.

Even the characters Hakluyt encounters underscore the political nature of the novel. They are spokesmen for the various factions within the city and for the larger social view that Brunner presents. Donald Angers, for example, one of the foreign-born citizens, is occasionally very articulate in defense of the Citizens' Party:

> But I think you might try to understand people like me, the foreign-born citizens. We — we hitched our wagon to the star of Ciudad de Vados, as the saying goes. We put our hearts and souls into this city. We gave up all the other things our lives might have held for us — chances of possibly greater wealth, greater success, elsewhere — because we saw in Ciudad de Vados something we could shape to our own desires.

The foreign-born citizens were offered a dream by Vados and they accepted the challenge. Now that the dream has the chance to become reality, they see the influx of peasants and their demands as an ominous threat which may destroy the dream and make their sacrifices meaningless.

On the other hand, "Fats" Brown is frequently more effective than Angers in voicing the view of the National Party:

> He gestured with his now empty bottle; he had been sucking enormous gulps between sentences. The movement took in the big-eyed children and the back-bowed women and the shabby men playing chess, the barrows and the baskets and the fruit and corn and clay pots and trinkets. "Riles me! I'm a citizen, same as Angers I got my stake here, same as him. But it's these poor bastards' own damn country, and they don't get much of a share.

For Brown, the poverty and filth that the peasants of Aguazul are forced to live in is inexcusable when millions of dollars are being spent to "clean up" the city. The people of Aguazul should have prior claim on the resources of the nation rather than the citizens of Ciudad de Vados.

Each person that Hakluyt meets tries to convert him to one of these two positions. Hakluyt, however, does not want to take sides in what he sees as a local political fight; he wants to isolate himself from the feud and simply carry out the terms of his employment, yet neither side will let him remain neutral. In fact, given the nature of his job, neutrality is impossible. As characters around him become victims of political tricks, he realizes that his employers are themselves caught up in the fight. President Vados hopes to buy time for his city. The country is too poor to solve the problems posed by the peasants, and, therefore, all he wants from Hakluyt is a method of removing the festering blights from Ciudad de Vados. He is willing, in other words, to accept a short-term, inadequate solution to save the city.

Esteban Diaz, however, wants to start immediately on long-term solutions. He is not against the city, but he insists that the peasants be allowed to share in the achievement that Ciudad de Vados represents. Himself of peasant stock, Diaz uses his position as Minister of the Interior to oppose Vados' own short-term plans; and he has enough popular support so that Vados cannot eliminate him. Actually, Vados and Diaz respect each other's ideals, and both are ruled by a desire to avoid civil war; thus, a finely established balance of power exists between them.

As a traffic analyst, Hakluyt is responsible to Diaz, but as an employee of Ciudad de Vados, he is responsible to Vados. Each man tries to direct Hakluyt's actions. Hakluyt finally becomes an unwilling agent of Vados when he accepts the President's order to draw up a plan that has no professional basis. Freedom of action for Hakluyt and the people of Ciudad de Vados has thus slowly evolved into a major theme.

Approximately a third of the way through the novel, it is revealed by Maria Posador that Alejandro Mayor is using subliminal perception to color the thoughts of the people in favor of the policies of Vados. As the political battles become more heated, it appears to Hakluyt that many of the members of the parties are themselves being used by the leaders. He starts to draw analogies between the characters around him and the pieces in a chess game, even to the point of noticing that the members of the Citizens' Party tend to have light skin colors while those of the National Party are darker. Finally, when Hakluyt is drugged and then set up to be killed by Maria Posador (a plot that fails), he suspects the manipulation of Vados and confronts the president. He learns that Diaz and Vados have been playing a chess game, with the city as its board and real people as its pieces, in order to avoid civil war. Hakluyt is, of course, horrified, and after several pious parting remarks, he arranges to leave Ciudad de Vados just in time to see the chess game and the city fall apart.

The idea of an author manipulating his characters' actions to correspond to a chess game is both unusual and interesting, and has the potential to be developed into a rather fascinating science fiction story. However, Brunner introduces the chess game framework too late in the story for the device to be effective. As a result, a series of questions are never answered. Why did Vados and Diaz use people for their game? When forced to kill several players, each expresses what seems to be serious guilt; yet they continue to play the game in the same fashion. How was the manipulation accomplished — was something more than subliminal perception involved? Vados tells Hakluyt that if sufficient information is known, any individual can be manipulated. But what kind of information is needed, and how is it used?

Even more important is the question of what is to happen to both Ciudad de Vados and Aguazul. Hakluyt starts to flee the city but returns to tell Maria

Posador about the chess game. But how will such knowledge be of use? The chess game is already disrupted, and neither Vados nor Diaz will be in a position to take it up again. Brunner raises important political and social issues in the course of the novel, but abandons them before any solution is even suggested. It is as if the author uses the science fiction ending to avoid these issues. For most of the novel the reader has seen a world plagued by the basic problems which characterize most countries that now exist; Brunner presents these important issues in all their complexity. Having done so, however, the ending appears to beg the questions which the novel itself raised.

The unsatisfactory ending may be the result of Brunner's attempt to combine a plot based on a chess game with a social and political theme. The two elements simply did not mix well. On the one hand, there is the exploration of serious issues which daily confront the world, while on the other, there is the need to be faithful to a predetermined plot structure not of the author's making and the desire to let the reader into the secret at the end of the novel. One or the other of these elements could have been developed into a successful novel, but the two together seem irreconcilable. There are no answers to the social and political conflicts at the end of the novel, and the chess game, tagged on to the end as it is, seems to have no basis in the hundreds of pages that come before that ending. It appears as an interesting game played by the author that has no bearing on the novel itself.

Stephen H. Goldman

Sources for Further Study

Reviews:

Analog. LXXX, September, 1967, pp. 167-168.

Galaxy. XXIV, June, 1966, pp. 147-152.

Magazine of Fantasy and Science Fiction. XXX, April, 1966, pp. 34-35.

New Worlds. CLXIII, June, 1966, p. 146.

THE STAINLESS STEEL RAT NOVELS

Author: Harry Harrison (1925-   )
First book publications: The Stainless Steel Rat (1961); *The Stainless Steel Rat's Revenge* (1970); *The Stainless Steel Rat Saves the World* (1972)
Type of work: Novels

Three broad but incisive satires of adventure novels in general, and space opera in particular

In his career of more than twenty years, Harry Harrison has written much science fiction of value: his *Make Room! Make Room!* (1966) was a notable member of the 1960's rush of overpopulation stories; his Deathworld novels showed inventiveness and surprising moral comment; his *Tunnel Through the Deeps* (1972; in England as *A Transatlantic Tunnel, Hurrah!*) and *Bill, the Galactic Hero* (1965) displayed something too rare in science fiction — a sense of humor. But in his stories of the Stainless Steel Rat, Harrison has written tales for two audiences: those who read purely for escape and mindless adventure (and some critics have so read them); and those who enjoy satires of subtlety and sophistication, with a broad range of clichés as their target.

The adventures of James Bolivar diGriz, the Stainless Steel Rat, are a blend of science fiction and the derring-do of an Ian Fleming novel; diGriz is much like James Bond without 007's promiscuity (DiGriz has a jealous wife expert in armed and unarmed combat). The resemblances between the two characters reveal the accuracy of Harrison's burlesque: both Jameses share a love of clandestine action in hostile societies; both love gadgety weapons; both have difficulties maintaining their carefully worked-out cover identities; and both are backed by powerful organizations that come to their rescue as dependably as the U. S. Cavalry.

DiGriz lives in a peaceful future society in which, thanks to genetic and psychological manipulation, most people obey the rules down to the Keep-off-the-Grass signs. But there are always exceptions. As diGriz explains early in the first novel, buildings always have had and always will have rats in the walls; as society's laws become tighter — as the buildings change from wood to concrete — the rats become tougher and cleverer. DiGriz is a criminal: in a stainless steel world, he is a stainless steel rat.

At least he begins that way. The proper hero must be on the side of law and order, so by Chapter 3 diGriz has been captured and converted by the Special Corps, a transplanetary agency for law enforcement. In the human part of the galaxy, only this elite organization is crafty enough to foil the super-criminals of the time. (Given the age's strict system of surveillance and the populace's general docility, the few crooks left must be super to survive.) The Special Corps fulfills its duty by recruiting the law-breakers it captures: "set a thief," becomes the first of many clichés punctured in the trio of novels.

The hero must be law-abiding (in general), or at least on the side of good, but he must have a touch of *picaro* about him, just a touch of the *Übermensch* undisturbed by the fussy regulations of the bureaucracy. Hence, Harrison captures the reader's sympathy for diGriz from the beginning by making him careful not to kill: the Stainless Steel Rat offends only against property. Harrison adds the luster of such myths as Jesse James and Bonnie and Clyde, while satirizing them by making bank robbery diGriz's favorite illegal activity. Several times Harrison wryly gives his hero a naïve economic justification for his thefts (which continue after his enlistment in the Special Corps): banks are insured, insurance rates do not go up much, the police get exercise, and the public gets entertainment. The loot is his fee for these useful public services.

Like the best heroes of a 1930's space opera, diGriz has inexhaustible energy and ingenuity. Not that he is simply invulnerable: he can be wounded or outsmarted, and often is. But the cliffs from which he hangs are as outrageously *ad hoc* as his escapes, and herein lies much of the humor of the parody.

DiGriz habitually carries a whole medicine chest of chemical aids with him. Since, in the pulpiest of the pulp traditions, we are never told at the beginning of an adventure what the hero has in his little black bag, he can and does pull from it just what he needs at the moment. If he is tired, it is a stimulant pill that refreshes him; if he is drunk, it is a tablet that will leave him sober and only a little hung over. If he must enter a villain's lair where they will attach a device that causes excruciating pain, he takes a shot beforehand that selectively deadens the nerves that carry the pain stimuli while leaving his motor nerves free to function. At one point the reader may think, "Aha! Now they've got him!" DiGriz is stripped naked and his feet are manacled to a table. But no, the Stainless Steel Rat bites down on his artificial tooth (which has never been mentioned before), and a jolt of chemical is released that provides him with the Herculean strength he needs to burst his bonds and fight off his captors.

DiGriz' offensive armament is equally impressive and inexhaustible, and just as hilariously contrived. He always has dozens of tiny bombs of exactly the right kind at his disposal. When he enters a Cliaand military base in *The Stainless Steel Rat's Revenge*, he has smoke bombs to hide his actions, explosive bombs to knock a hole in the wall, and sleep-gas bombs to render the guards senseless. The bank robbery at the beginning of that novel is accomplished with a gas that temporarily blinds everyone (the Rat himself has nose filters that protect him from its effects while leaving his appearance unchanged). To make his escape from the bank, he sets off a "screamer," a device that emits a variety of sound waves so intense that people flee from the vicinity (the Rat has ear plugs). Thus his reputation for farsighted planning and thorough preparation remains unsullied, as does his aversion to violence: although bullets whiz and bombs explode, no innocent bystander ever suffers an allergic reaction to a gas or gets pierced by a shot from a blinded policeman.

In one 1930's melodrama, the crew of a spaceship exploring Jupiter loses power while descending through the atmosphere of the giant planet. They fall until they reach a point of equilibrium, from which they can neither descend nor ascend. With no possibility of aid reaching them, it appears they face slow starvation. But what is courage if not grace under pressure? On the spot, they invent a machine to convert matter into energy, and escape their peril. The Stainless Steel Rat is their worthy descendant. His brain and hands are equally quick, and although he has never seen them before, he can drive a car and fly a helicopter of our own time well enough to escape from pursuers. He can invent a machine to foil a plot before which the rest of the galaxy remains helpless, not after years of study, but after only a couple of days in hiding.

Naturally, a man of his mettle needs opponents capable of measuring his strength; and if the actions of these opponents do not always make sense, that is one of the conventions of the genre and part of the fun of the parody. In *The Stainless Steel Rat*, diGriz is on the trail of a woman, Angelina, who is a psychotic criminal mastermind. To disguise himself, the hero has his legs shortened and bent to change his height and walk. Plastic surgery remodels his limbs and features — from the bone out. The coloring of his skin, hair, and eyes is changed; his voice is "deepened and roughened." Under this new identity, he tracks down Angelina and appears to gain her confidence. Later, of course, we find out that Angelina has known who he is all along. How she knew is not important, but of paramount importance is a stern rule of pulp adventure fiction: you must not make things easy for the hero.

Rather, you show the hero's cleverness and courage by his careful planning; you show the villain's prowess and wickedness by easily overturning the hero's plans; and you have everything come out right in the end by a last-minute rescue. Faithful to these precepts, diGriz commands the service of the omnipresent and omnipotent Special Corps. They arrive in the nick of time to free him from the deadly Angelina in *The Stainless Steel Rat*, and they do more: they rehabilitate Angelina and recruit her, thereby freeing a character of her obvious ability to marry diGriz, bear his twin sons, and rescue him herself in the following two novels.

The latter of these, *The Stainless Steel Rat Saves the World*, contains the definitive *deus ex machina*, one spectacularly and characteristically science fictional. Harrison is too good a writer not to warn the reader: when one becomes aware that the novel involves time-travel, one is advised to beware of lurking grandfather-paradoxes. The novel finds diGriz chasing the evil and mysterious He, a warped genius who has somehow achieved immortality. (We never do find out who He is, where He came from, or how He acquired his powers: He is as self-sufficiently nasty as Ming the Merciless, and his passion, of course, is to rule the world.)

The abominable He has begun reshaping time, in a way reminiscent of Fritz Leiber's *Change War*, for the purpose of eliminating the Special Corps, who defeated He the first time around. To accompany an insane megalomania, He has a special hatred for diGriz, and has created a time loop in which He hopes to catch the Rat. Everything goes according to plan, and diGriz and a few associates are trapped on the Earth of twenty thousand years from now only minutes before it will be blown to bits. Only a time-helix, a recently invented time-travel device, can save him now, and he has neither the machine nor the means to make one. The reader can perceive what will happen next by imagining the hoariest cliché possible: a time-helix pops out of the air. DiGriz uses it to return to his own time of A.D. 34,500, where he boxes up a time-helix and sends it back in time so that it will appear to rescue him just when he needs it.

Perhaps the most entertaining thing about the series is the perfectly straight-faced manner in which Harrison romps through the burlesque. No science fiction technique is too hallowed and no detail too unimportant to serve as the subject and vehicle of his satire. For example, when diGriz is tracking He in 1975, the Rat has an instrument that will detect the kind of equipment He is using, and supply a vector giving the direction. DiGriz is in Hartford when the instrument first registers, and he quickly shifts his position to obtain a different vector. The intersection of the two lines thus established will mark the location of He by well-known methods of triangulation. The only problem is, the process places the location of He's equipment in New York City, yet diGriz took his sightings from the opposite ends of his hotel-room window: diGriz has "triangulated," all right — his triangle has two sides one hundred miles long and a base of about three feet.

DiGriz's improbable triangulation is typical of the wildly nonsensical humor the stories offer. It is surely healthy to laugh at oneself, as satirists have always known. And the therapy that satire affords makes us more aware of the hidden expectations with which we approach a literary work. The tales of the Stainless Steel Rat expose both what we see and what we ignore in adventure stories: not just science fiction adventure, but any kind. And even those readers who prefer their swash abundantly buckled can be grateful to Harrison for making it possible to read adventure stories with a saner, cooler perspective. The Rat is certainly worth his weight in Stainless Steel.

Walter E. Meyers

Sources for Further Study

Criticism:

Aldiss, Brian W. *Billion Year Spree: The True History of Science Fiction*. Garden City, N.Y.: Doubleday, 1973, pp. 308-310. The exploits of slippery Jim DiGriz feature humor and imagination, according to Aldiss.

STAND ON ZANZIBAR

Author: John Brunner (1934-   )
First book publication: 1968
Type of work: Novel
Time: Approximately 2010
Locale: The United States, Yatakang (major Eastern power), Beninia (undeveloped African nation)

A multidimensional view of mankind's future as population continues to explode, and the military-industrial-communications complex continues to exploit the populace

> Principal characters:
> NORMAN HOUSE, a black ("Afram") junior executive with General Technics Corporation
> DONALD HOGAN, a research generalist later transformed into a fighting machine
> CHARLES ("CHAD") MULLIGAN, a sociologist, author, troubleshooter
> ZADKIEL OBOMI, the sage tribal chieftain of Beninia
> SUGAIGUNTUNG, a molecular biologist in Yatakang
> GEORGETTE TALLON BUCKFAST, the cyborg head of General Technics Corporation
> SHALMANESER, a miniaturized heuristic computer

John Brunner's *Stand on Zanzibar* is a massive book which creates with density of naturalistic detail the illusion of an entire near-future world, closely extrapolated from contemporary science, technology, and social trends.

Borrowing liberally from John Dos Passos' technique in *Manhattan Transfer* and *U. S. A.*, adapted to the mass media theories of Marshall McLuhan and Harold Innis, Brunner surrounds his main lines of narrative with descriptive, expository, and media-oriented chapters which blur the traditional relationship between foreground and background. Thus the protagonist of the novel becomes in a sense the whole world, continually modulating, though its changes proceed in a generally dystopian direction, much as was theorized by Herbert Marcuse in *One-Dimensional Man.* Amid the sensory overkill which gives the reader a dose of "future shock," the image is conjured up of a world out of control, careening along the pathways of common usage and least resistance, toward a catastrophic conclusion it keeps staving off.

Extrapolated less than fifty years forward, the novel's world is a plausible extension of our present, differentiated from our time largely by means of advances in technology and deteriorations of the social fabric. Overpopulation, the main cause of the problems, results in shortages in affordable living space, such that even young executives must share the costs of an apartment. Legal limitations on breeding, especially for those with genetic defects, are supported by concomitant changes in social mores, especially in the United States. Sex has become almost totally recreational. Black marketeers thrive on childless couples. "Right Catholics" with more than two children per couple can find themselves the victims of vigilante action.

Racial and international tensions are continually at flash point, as urban insurrections, guerrilla insurgencies, and the cold war among the major powers continue. Superfluous men may be drafted, or trip out on drugs. Returnees from military training sometimes turn their training to good use, sabotaging the system. "Muckers" who go crazy, killing and maiming anyone in their way, are a common and expected sight in both East and West, a result in part of intolerable crowding and frustrations. The woman's lot has not improved, though women now have the option of becoming "shiggies," hiring out their services as bedmates to men in exchange for a place to live.

Technological development has been spotty. Space research is dormant, and transportation in general has been shoved aside in favor of communications developments which reduce the need for travel. Besides videophone and computer access, the average consumer has available a device which produces the illusion of his own presence at news events and travelogues, as well as entertainment programs. Called "Mr. and Mrs. Everywhere," it also allows one to choose one's appearance and freeze the age of one's image.

Raw materials and energy resources have not yet been stripped completely, but they continually threaten to fail, and the search for them continues everywhere, including the floor of the Atlantic Ocean. With the quantity of live births deemphasized, there is an almost frenetic interest in the quality of people's "prodgies" (progeny and prodigies). Research into genetic manipulation is pursued frantically, and a breakthrough is achieved in Yatakang by Dr. Sugaiguntung.

In case the reader cannot interpret this news for himself, Brunner has written numerous references to news articles from our time into the book which comment on the action explicitly, as do excerpts from the books of Chad Mulligan, Brunner's "house radical." Like Austin Train in *The Sheep Look Up*, he goes Robert Ardrey and C. Wright Mills one better with his wit, wide-ranging observations, and hectoring style long before we meet him as an active character. Thus, a broad perspective of events is kept before us, which turns the book's dystopian warnings in the direction of more "neutral" or matter-of-fact, in some ways even more frightening, extrapolation.

The central lines of the narrative, presented in chapters called "continuity," concern three men. Norman House, a token black, is trying to prove himself in an executive rat race he knows he will lose. He is given the impossible job of rescuing the Mid-Atlantic Mining Project and channeling it through the too-peaceful nation of Beninia. Donald Hogan, his apartmentmate, has sold his soul to the government by accepting pay for his interdisciplinary research, which obligates him to let them activate him as a spy or saboteur whenever they need him. He undergoes "eptification," which transforms him into a fighting machine to "rescue" Dr. Sugaiguntung and "liberate" his secret. Chad Mulligan, the renegade sociologist, is recycled from the fog of alcoholism into which he had retreated from the world, in order to identify the cause of

Beninia's mysterious, perpetual peacefulness. This in turn requires him to solve the problem of the stalled, self-programming GT computer, Shalmaneser.

Patterned on familiar commercial fiction, all three stories rise above their models to some extent by balancing the melodrama inherent in them with a fresh approach to everyday activities. Brunner gives the standard formulas a twist, intertwines them, and eventually melds them into the novel's conclusion. Norman may rise to the top like a Harold Robbins hero, but his success is not truly sweet. Only a "miracle" saves him, as Mulligan uses *his* imagination to persuade Shalmaneser to use *its* imagination, to "pretend" that Beninia really is as peaceful as people say. Though Norman becomes a hero for the moment, the world is still coming apart at the seams, and Shalmaneser's awakening self-consciousness may cause more problems than it solves.

Donald, once he has been "eptified," or turned into a fighting machine, finds that he enjoys the Superman side of his Clark Kent image. Unlike the James Bond type character, however, he has a conscience, and a consciousness of the world beyond his escapades. Sent to "rescue" Sugaiguntung and "liberate" his secret, Donald loses his kidnap victim's life, partly because he is imperfectly programed, and he blames himself for his failure. Unable to shrug it off like a Len Deighton or John Le Carre hero, he becomes schizophrenic, fencing off his old self from the new "machine," Donald Hogan Mark II.

Chad's triumphs, the most explicitly science-fictional in nature, are especially ironic given his long-standing view of man as a botch and a botcher of things. Fascinated by the Shalmaneser problem for its own sake, he proceeds from its solution to the disappointing, but perfectly appropriate discovery that the peacefulness of Beninia's citizens has a physiological cause. Their sweat-glands give off a tranquilizing scent, which can be synthesized as a pacifier and sold at a profit. Thus, it may be possible for man to stave off global suicide for another generation. But man is no closer to learning how to behave in a civilized manner, and Chad heads back to the bottle.

Around these stories, sometimes touching them, illustrating them, parallelling or crossing them, Brunner has woven additional strands of exposition. Chapters labeled "context" explore social theory, with Mulligan frequently acting as a mouthpiece for the author. "The Happening World" consists of chapters, presented as if in a television script, which chart noteworthy day-to-day events across the world, along with contemporary advertisements which may be equally representative of reality. "Tracking with Closeups" comprises short biographical sketches of people who are sometimes involved in the action of "Continuity," but more often of representative characters from a vast and mainly anonymous population.

All three types of background interact with the continuity, if not directly, at least by means of counterpoint and juxtaposition. Brunner's use of mass media terminology and concepts lends a sense of immediacy to the events, just as

Orson Welles's radio version of *The War of the Worlds* did in 1938. But for all of this borrowing from television and cinema, the general effect is distinctly literary, a modernist variation of the epic simile and catalog of Homer. Indeed, in his heaping up of detail, none of which would have to be pointed out in a visual presentation, Brunner is heir to the literary tradition of naturalism. Also naturalistic is his deterministic interpretation of social science, which resembles that theorized by Zola in "The Experimental Novel." Having set up his world and his characters, Brunner can pretend that they simply act out what they were programed to do, that he has nothing to do with their actions.

However, Brunner's mass media-influenced technique provides more than commentary and illustration, which proves confusing to some readers. Some give up on examining the seven-page table of contents. Some mistakenly read one series of chapters, rather than mixing them, as the straightforward read-through does. Others experience a sense of "future shock," with both fact and fiction about an imaginary world seeming to come at them from every direction, assailing all their senses. Brunner's intention, however, is to equalize the balance between foreground and background and thereby achieve a unity of effect centered on the socio-politico-economic roots of the world's malaise. The highlighting of technique itself is the real advance of this novel over its predecessors.

Hogan, House, and Mulligan are not so much heroes as representative men, explored more at length than the snapshots of "Tracking with Closeups" permit, but essentially the same sort of people, differentiated more by situation and focus than by innate superiority. None of these individuals really makes the policies he carries out, those which govern social life in 2010, as in 1968. They do what they must — to survive, to make a buck, to salvage self-esteem; and the sum total of their actions leads to everyone's being a little worse off than before. Whatever their running around may have accomplished, world population continues to grow, so that if everyone were able to stand on the island of Zanzibar at the beginning, those on the perimeter would be knee-deep by the end.

By reversing the traditional balance between foreground and background, Brunner makes a bumbling protagonist of his world, a world which is heading toward a pathetic, if not a tragic, fall. It is a world governed by mechanistic, not humanistic considerations. Progress is identified in terms of efficiency and economy, so that individuals rise and fall by following the line of least resistance, rather than by consciously seeking to do evil. If Shalmaneser is the logical symbol of this process, it is reduced to the absurd in the person of ninety-one-year-old Georgette Tallon Buckfast, most of whose original body parts have been replaced by transplants and prosthetics. But even she only represents a process, like the all-but-immortal corporation she directs.

The real menace may well be Western capitalism, symptomatically extreme in America, as Brunner makes more explicit in *The Jagged Orbit* (1969), *The*

Sheep Look Up (1972), and elsewhere both in and out of fiction. *Stand on Zanzibar* is no less censorious, but it is less didactic, less directive in its social message, which is both a weakness and a strength. Although the reader may not fully understand it, his complicity in helping to put together the fragments of this both familiar and unfamiliar world may have a more lasting effect on the conscious level, reorienting the reader's observation of his own contemporary society, as well as the nature of the science fiction novel.

As social prophecy, the book has already failed to some extent. While we seem so much closer to some of its "predictions," the author did not foresee — or include — other "accidents" of history such as the political tightening up of oil supplies and the rise of Eastern, feminist, and ecological consciousness. However, the book is not destroyed by the success or failure of specific projections. The tenor and direction of the 1960's, and the society it reflects, have not been checked in this decade.

The emphasis, however, is not so much on the social message itself as on the way the world is represented. Brunner's technique is admirably suited to depicting what looks like a whole world, which is supposed to loom larger than its individual components. By infusing a future world with mass-media, Brunner succeeds in evoking the malady diagnosed by Alvin Toffler's *Future Shock* (1970), better in fact than he did in a later novel, *The Shockwave Rider* (1975). The technique is not all-purpose; in his own hands and those of others, approximations of it have been less successful. In *Stand on Zanzibar*, however, he has given us a textbook example of how a futurological imagination can employ modernist literary devices to produce a science fiction masterpiece.

David N. Samuelson

Sources for Further Study

Criticism:

McNelly, Willis E. "The Science Fiction Novel in 1968," in *Nebula Award Stories IV*. Edited by Paul Anderson. New York: Doubleday, 1969, pp. xiii-xxv. McNelly evaluates *Stand on Zanzibar* and compares it to other works of science fiction.

Spinrad, Norman. "*Stand on Zanzibar: The Novel as Felon in Science Fiction: The Other Side of Realism*. Edited by Thomas D. Clareson. Bowling Green, Ohio: Bowling Green University Popular Press, 1971, pp. 181-185. Spinrad asserts that this novel is a film in book form. He gives an in-depth analysis, providing a clearer understanding of the work.

Reviews:

Amazing Stories. XLIII, Deptember, 1969, pp. 123-126.
Books and Bookmen. XIV, June, 1969, p. 57.
Kirkus Reviews. XXXV, July 15, 1968, p. 773.
Magazine of Fantasy and Science Fiction. XXXVI, February, 1969, p. 22.
New York Times Book Review. LXXIII, October 27, 1968, p. 68.
Publisher's Weekly. CXCIV, July 29, 1968, p. 56.
Times Literary Supplement. June 12, 1969, p. 643.

STAR
(STAR OU PSI DE CASSIOPÉE)

Author: Charlemagne Ischir Defontenay (1819-1856)
First book publication: 1854
English translation: 1975
Type of work: Novel
Time: Unidentified
Locale: The distant planet Star

A kind of historical, literary, geographical, and ethnological chronicle of the planet Star, in the constellation Cassiopeia

> *Principal characters:*
> THE NARRATOR
> STAR, a planet
> TASSUL,
> LESSUR,
> RUDAR, and
> ELIER, the satellites of Star

Published in 1854, *Star* is the book of a visionary, a man who would have revolutionized the newly emerging genre of science fiction if his work had received a quarter of the attention it deserved. Hardly a prolific writer — this was his only novel — C. I. Defontenay went almost completely unnoticed until 1949 when Raymond Queneau, in *Pen Strokes, Numbers and Letters*, ranked *Star* among the masterpieces.

Star is not a novel in the strict sense of the word, but rather a series of texts in various forms, such as poetry, drama, and chronicle. After an introduction in three short parts which tells of the discovery of an aerolite in the heart of the Himalayas, there is some account of the Starian books, and then the trip to the world of Star begins.

Book I tells of the beauties of the planet and its specific location in space. The animals, plants, and finally the wondrous humanity of this world are presented. There is also a map of the planetary system of Star, in which no fewer than four different-colored suns revolve.

In Book II the ancient history of the peoples on Star, along with the birth of civilization among three peoples, the Salvelces, the Tréliors, and the Ponarbates, is examined. Then comes the discovery of the Nemsèdes, or Longevouses, whose life span extends over several millennia. The Nemsèdes plan to make use of their knowledge and wisdom for all the Starian peoples. But this happy time soon ends because the "Slow Plague" makes its appearance and decimates life on the planet, bringing the Starian race to the brink of extinction. The process is accentuated by Farnozas, a doomsayer, who has sworn to make his race disappear from the face of the world in order to escape the plague. But happily another Starian by the name of Ramzuel invents an antigravitational spaceship and manages to escape from Star at the last possible moment, accompanied by his family and the last three living Longevouses. In the meantime, as Ramzuel's vessel heads toward Tassul, Star's closest satellite, the Repleus (subhuman yet above the beasts), who are the most resistant to the "Slow Plague," set themselves up as masters of the depopulated world.

Book III describes the life of the Starian emigrants on Tassul. But soon the number of Ramzuel's descendants becomes so great that part of them have to emigrate to Lessur, the second satellite. Then Rudar, the most inhospitable of the worlds orbiting Star, is explored — and finally Elier, a strange transparent globe made entirely of crystal. But homesickness weighs more and more heavily on the hearts of the emigrants, who decide to return and reconquer their own world.

At the beginning of Book IV they reassert themselves as masters of the Repleus, who have lapsed into barbarity. Thanks to the spaceships, the "abares," this reconquest is quickly achieved. Little by little a federation of states with very close ties takes shape. An interplanetary civilization is being born on Star at this time under the shrewd leadership of the three ever-present Longevouses. They founded the "cult of mankind" in order to avoid the dangers posed by religion, and also to free it to develop a love of the arts, the only activity worthy of its greatness.

Book V contains an account of one inhabitant of Tassul who visits Tasbar, the intellectual capital of Star, for the first time. This is followed by a short play concerning the mores of the Repleus and Cétracites (half-breeds resulting from the coupling of Starians with Repleus) and, finally, a six-canto historical poem recounting the loves of Elia, one of the most famous Starian actresses.

The work ends with a three-poem epilogue in which the author expresses his hopes for the future of the human race and relates what moved him to write the book.

It is easy to see that C. I. Defontenay has undertaken a difficult task, one that is as immense as it is risky to carry out. He has attempted to construct a world and its history within the limits of a modest-sized novel when compared with other works in the same vein (*Last and First Men*, by Olaf Stapledon, for example). The wager has been won against all odds, since *Star* remains as fascinating after 125 years as the day it was published — an accomplishment that appears all the more impressive when the subsequent development of science fiction is taken into account.

With the exception of the Narrator himself, the principal characters in *Star* are Star itself, together with its four satellites. This casts Defontenay in the role of the forerunner of writers such as Edgar Rice Burroughs, J. H. Rosny Aine, and Jack Vance, whose powerful imaginations have often made their created universes so fascinating that little by little they relegate the leading characters in the story to minor roles.

Star is an amazing planet, illuminated by four suns whose different colors perform a kaleidoscopic ballet in the skies. The flora and fauna on Star mix gigantism with delicacy, the whole pervaded by an unprecedented strangeness. Two good examples are the "tarrios," huge trees whose roots reach to the bottoms of the seas and whose crowns are lost in the clouds. There is also the "psargino," a weird animal that flees from predators by inflating itself like a living balloon. The creation of the Starian world in a few dozen pages is so perfect that it almost eclipses the description of the Starian peoples, whose perfection seems lackluster when compared with the wonders of the planet itself.

It is different on Tassul. Here, as a matter of fact, nature is dull and monotonous. But the picture is enhanced by the Tassulians, hermaphrodites who have developed a kind of socialist society. It should be noted here how delicately Defontenay speaks to his readers about these strange beings.

On Lessur, the center of attention shifts from the world and its inhabitants to focus on the scented breezes that constantly caress the satellite and its fauna. The result is extraordinary; on this small world, it often happens that the inhabitants really do make love to the whole orb of Lessur!

But Defontenay's biggest surprises are to be found on Star's last two satellites, Rudar and Elier.

Rudar is indeed Hell. Surrounded by a dark, opaque atmosphere that hides the beauties of the universe from its inhabitants, the satellite has a dreary landscape. But the most frightening thing about Rudar is that death in physical form is part of its fauna. It is a grotesque creature, the worst enemy of humans and animals. In his description of these "deaths" Defontenay treats us to the most psychedelic pages in his novel during the course of which these terrifying beings, whose only food is the souls of humans and the vital forces of animals, take shape before our very eyes.

At the other end of the beauty spectrum lies Elier, a world of transparent crystal that gloriously reflects the light from the four suns in the Star system. On this small globe everything is transparent; a play of light constantly emanates to include all of humanity and all of the flora and fauna. Even the dust coming from space seems to be an offense to this fragile beauty. Observing the splendors of Elier, one gets the impression that Defontenay tried to create an image of beauty so perfect that it would become as alien to the human race as the "deaths" prowling Rudar.

The Narrator's role, albeit unobtrusive, is nonetheless important; throughout the work he maintains a restraint that is most admirable.

Defontenay's technical skills, too, are considerable. He knows how to break a rhythm whenever it threatens to become monotonous, by inserting short plays, prose poems, and even a war chant into the main flow of the story. This device not only keeps the reader's attention; it also allows him to see the different strata of Starian society through the eyes of the Starians themselves. The short play entitled "The Celsinore" is an interesting attempt to understand the mentality of the nonhuman (or at least not entirely human), Repleus and Cétracites.

The presence of the Cétracites, completely integrated into the Star social system as voluntary slaves (and as a rule happy with their lot), suggests that we look for Defontenay's pattern for the spirit and art of Starian culture in ancient Athens. But if so, it is an Athens stripped of the scourge of war that serves as the basis for the author's conception. One might think that Defontenay would be satisfied to continue down the path trod by so many Utopians before (and after) him. But that would be a mistake. *Star* is not strictly speaking a Utopia, even though it is obvious that the author has set his ideas down in the form of a model of a more equitable and more humane society. The story belongs to another well defined genre, the space opera. Is Defontenay the creator of space opera? Why not? Many elements of the form appear here for the first time in the history of science fiction: antigravitational spaceships, an interplanetary federation, and above all, the typical attitude, or *approach*. Furthermore, in its ideology *Star* is a *modern* space opera, a space opera stripped of ray guns, pirate spaceships, and blown-up planets, but exhibiting hideous extraterrestrials even before they were invented!

Star is a plea for tolerance among the races that make up the universe. Defontenay's humanistic concerns make this novel one of the most modern written in the "prehistory" of science fiction. It has been published in English as recently as 1975 and without the reassuring "old classic" label.

Richard D. Nolane

STAR MAKER

Author: Olaf Stapledon (1886-1950)
First book publication: 1937
Type of work: Novel
Time: From 1937 to the death of the last galaxy
Locale: England and the cosmos

Using his "hypertelescopic imagination," the Narrator transcends the limitations of time and space and searches for the ultimate source of creation (the Star Maker) and for answers which relate man to this creator and the rest of the universe

> *Principal characters:*
> THE NARRATOR, an Englishman living in the suburbs of London
> BVALLTU, his traveling companion

Except as a prose narrative drawing from the author's imagination more than from sources in history, *Star Maker* scarcely meets the requirements of a novel. In his Preface to the work, Stapledon remarked that *Star Maker* "is no novel at all." Plot is nonexistent; there are no characters. The Narrator, seemingly a rather prosaic married Englishman, becomes a mere disembodied point of view ultimately identified as "I, the cosmic mind." The setting is the entire cosmos and the time frame is approximately five hundred billion years, from the creation of the cosmos to the complete physical quiescence of the universe.

Stapledon described his book as "an imaginative sketch." And while there is some reference to various scientific principles and theories — the Big Bang theory of creation, relativity, the Dopler effect, and so on — it is primarily a work of fantasy rather than science fiction. Perhaps *Star Maker* is most appropriately described as Stapledon's attempt to construct a myth based on known or plausible attributes of man and his universe, a myth consistent with scientific understanding. In the Preface to his earlier novel, *Last and First Men* (1931), Stapledon described a "true myth" as a vision which, given a specific culture, attempts to give voice to the loftiest ideals of that culture.

This is Stapledon's purpose in *Star Maker*. The myth takes the form of a quest, a search not so much for knowledge about the cosmos and man's relationship to it, as for the proper attitude which should come as a result of this knowledge. The Narrator begins in isolation, ignorance, and bitterness. With an act of will and "hawk-flight of the imagination," he becomes both part of a community of questors, and eventually an aspect of the cosmic mind as he makes the spiritual voyage to confront the Star Maker (the "absolute spirit" in all things) in order to have the meaning of the universe revealed. He "awakes" back on earth, enlightened with knowledge which will help him and the rest of mankind to endure the dangers of the present and furnish guidelines for the future.

In something resembling a mystic trance, the Narrator moves away from earth. Traveling at speeds much faster than light, this "disembodied, wandering view point" visits innumerable worlds and establishes telepathic contact with various beings. This mental intercourse allows him to live through the experiences of his hosts and to grasp the reality of the alien worlds. Moving initially to worlds essentially similar to his own, he and his traveling companion, Bvalltu, are able to travel through time as well as space and visit many strange worlds, staying sometimes for days, sometimes for centuries — observing the cycles of progress and regression, lucidity and ignorance, love and hate, civilization and barbarism.

One of the more interesting worlds they visit is a sea-world inhabited by a symbiotic race of fishlike creatures, "ichthyoids," and spiderlike crustaceans, "arachnoids." After eons of competition and war, these creatures "moulded" one another to create a "well-integrated union." The Narrator compares this society to the human race and argues that it was mentally more flexible and had a greater capacity for community. The complete union of the dual race came about when it developed telepathy and genetic research, two essential activities which the Narrator suggests are necessary for man to overcome his limitations, to achieve true community, and to "wake" to the meaning of the cosmos. The themes of telepathy and genetic research recur in Stapledon's other works also.

In his travels, the Narrator comes upon worlds populated by sentient beings whose collective personality is the consequence of a group rather than a single individual. In this world, the basis of intelligence is sometimes a flock of sparrowlike creatures whose individual bodies are linked as a single individual with human intelligence. The Narrator visits other worlds composed of plant-men, organisms simultaneously animal and vegetable. In many of the worlds he visits, he finds situations and problems similar to those which threaten the Earth. These worlds are able to solve their problems only by overcoming both a pernicious individualism and a traditional "tribal spirit" (nationalism). In the fortunate cases, these societies "awake" — a central image in all of Stapledon's works — to a "new lucidity of consciousness and a new integrity of will" in order to create a world community, communistic in essence and permitting the expression of the general will of the inhabitants. The Narrator observes that this awakened stage is perhaps the happiest of all the ages throughout the existence of a world. In turn, these societies develop into galactic Utopias whose inhabitants work to "awaken" themselves more fully, contact and "awaken" other galaxies, and increase the self-awareness of each individual "world spirit." All this is accomplished through telepathy, which unites the whole galaxy.

At one point, the Narrator and his companions merge to form a "single mobile view-point" and travel back in time to the birth of the stars. In the beginning, it is discovered that stars somehow are alive after some worlds attempt to move their neighbor stars out of their customary orbits, only to have the stars nova. The Narrator says, "Stars are best regarded as living organisms." Each star is conscious of other stars as conscious beings. The stars' purposes are basically twofold : to participate in discovering the nature of the cosmos, and to "execute perfectly their part in the communal dance." This latter activity recalls the medieval and renaissance notion of the music of the spheres. In his *Religio Medici* (1643), Sir Thomas Browne (1605-1682) writes,

> For there is a music wherever there is a harmony, order or proportion; and thus far we may maintain the music of the spheres; for those well ordered motions, and regular paces, though they give no sound unto the ear, yet to the understanding they strike a note most full of harmony.

The stars dance to this music. Ultimately, they connect telepathically with the minded worlds and establish the galactic mind. Finally, the Narrator discovers that even the nebulae are "conscious," and that they relate to one another by gravitational action and light pulsation. Indeed, the entire universe is one interconnected organism, all part of the Star Maker's creation. In the initial explosion creating the millions of galaxies, each galaxy was hurled apart, but each remembers and feels itself a part of the single spirit of the whole.

In coming to this understanding, the Narrator seeks to confront the source of all creation, the Star Maker, and, for an instant, manages to get a glimpse of the star of stars:

> I saw, though nowhere in cosmical space, the blazing source of the hypercosmical light, as though it were an overwhelmingly brilliant point, a star . . . this effulgent star was the centre of a four-dimensional sphere whose curved surface was the three-dimensional cosmos.

The Narrator is crushed by his love and longing for a union with this infinite spirit. He worships the Star Maker, but is not loved in return, as the Star Maker neither loves nor needs love. The Narrator realizes the "rightness" of this experience. It is appropriate for the creature to love the creator, but it would be narcissistic for the creator to love its creature, for that would be merely to love part of itself. The Narrator finally realizes that "the virtue of the creature was to love and to worship, but the virtue of the creator was to create, and to be the infinite, the unrealizable and incomprehensible goal of worshipping creatures."

Continuing with the metaphor of the Star Maker as artist, the Narrator tries to relate "the myth of creation," and here he is at an even greater loss for words. His description must be symbolic and take the form of myth and parable; yet he relates the activities of the Star Maker moving from juvenile and immature creation to mature creation. His first cosmos is a "toy" of mere rhythm; others follow, some nonspatial, some without time, some with simultaneous temporal dimensions which might or might not overlap, and some with life. In his mature creations (of which our cosmos is one), he made creatures which were free and recalcitrant to his own purposes. This marked a climax of sorts in his creative activity — "And he saw that it was good." However, the Star Maker moves on to create cosmos after cosmos, some almost totally inaccessible to the mind of the Narrator. Finally, he has a chance to see the ultimate cosmos — a cosmos standing in relation to our cosmos as we stand in relation to a single atom. Even here, however, its creatures suffer grief and agony; but as he protests, the Narrator understands that this is as it should be, and he is filled with mixed emotions — horror and anger, yet acceptance, and even praise. He learns that the Star Maker's temper is not one of sympathy but of contemplation. His creatures live not to be loved or hated — although this is included — but to be appraised by their maker. This is as it should be; this vision of the eternal spirit compels adoration.

The climactic encounter over, the Narrator wakes up back on his hill in the suburbs of London. The anxieties and uncertainties remain. The world's madness is closing in upon him, and he understands that the magic circle of community built up in his relation with his wife is the only certain foundation upon which to build. In lines reminiscent of Matthew Arnold's poem "Dover Beach," the Narrator sadly describes the world's delirium as it seems to be rushing headlong into a new, more horrible catastrophe than World War I. How does one confront such times? The Narrator has learned that he must be guided by two principles: first, to strive for a human community and second, to awake to the "hypercosmical reality" revealed in the Star Maker, to struggle to win some additional increment of lucidity before "the inevitable darkness."

The movement of the novel is in the Narrator's attempts to overcome his sense of spiritual crisis, to come to a state of wakefulness. This crisis has essentially two dimensions: the need to overcome those obstacles which keep man from realizing some kind of true community with his fellow man, and the necessity of putting oneself in harmony, in the correct spiritual attitude toward the universe. It is a movement from protest and rebellion to acceptance and serenity. The mechanism for the resolution of the crisis is the imaginative voyage itself, which lets the Narrator see all of experience from a godlike perspective. Thus, in his visit to the Other Earth and his experience with the Other Men, whose culture is based on taste and gustatory experience, the Narrator is able to witness the horrible effects of racism — each race insisted that its unique "flavor" was the only valid sign of spiritual worth — of industrialism, of ethnic prejudice, and other farcical events which suggested life on earth. The idiotic behavior of the aliens constantly gives the Narrator an opportunity to compare events on this world to events on Earth. The invention of radio-brain-stimulation on Other Earth provides an opportunity for the Narrator to explore the dangers of mass communication and mass culture as it is used for propaganda and brainwashing and for creating the Other Fascism.

Time and again, the Narrator sees race after race struggle to achieve the "bliss of true community" only to fall short because of the folly of either individualism or the mob-spirit. The cyclic pattern becomes universal; a race emerges from barbarism, progresses to a point of lucidity, and then, through some folly or general loosening of will and integrity, civilization takes a downward spiral into almost subhuman savagery, only to begin the cycle again. The Narrator questions the meaning of all that he sees.

Finally, the inability to grasp the significance of man's life, the awareness of man's insignificance compared to the stars, the realization of the ultimate impermanence of Utopia, and the eventual death of all that is valuable, coupled with the vision of his creator coolly contemplating the suffering and ultimate death of his creations, stirs the Narrator into spiritual rebellion. The other movement of the novel is the movement to overcome this protest. In addition to teaching his readers the nature of and need for true community, the Narrator learns how to justify the Star Maker's ways to man. Ultimately it involves questions of evil, suffering, and death, which are resolved when seen from a cosmic perspective.

Stapledon's message was essentially the same in all of his works. Seen from a cosmic perspective, man indeed may be of a very low order of existence, and this point of view makes all the difference. We do not condemn others for not allowing insects to live out their full life because we are not convinced of the intrinsic worth of an insect's life; we are able to accept the death of some animals because we do not credit them with cosmic importance. However, we are convinced of our own importance. But from the cosmic perspective, the assumption that man is the ultimate order of creation seems absurd and based on failure of imagination. As Stapledon explained in his *Philosophy and Living* (1939), it is ridiculous for man to demand that the universe be moral, that God be good. We must learn to deal with the seemingly logical conflict between our two fundamental religious experiences, between moral protest which attempts to alter the universe and the cold clear ecstasy of acceptance, the tragic view of life.

In each instance, the Narrator's moral protest to what he regards as wholly alien to the cosmic spirit is seen to be a manifestation of pride, selfishness, or simply ignorance. He learns to accept the perfection of the spirit. He learns that the Star Maker may seem hostile to the less-awakened, but to those who have attained lucidity, the entire tragic drama is not only necessary but also a source of joy. There is no question that the basic attitudinal frame of *Star Maker* is one of acceptance. The individual accepts, even welcomes the final defeat. On several occasions, the Narrator witnesses the effects of passive resistance and death. Rather than defend themselves or retaliate, in the process wounding their communal spirit, whole worlds choose annihilation. Yet they die praising the universe, the Star Maker, the Star Destroyer. Just before his death, Stapledon published *A Man Divided* (1950) in which he argued that nothing is merely lost in pain and suffering, that the agonies as well as the joys "are gathered up in the whole single music of existence." We must view the human condition from the point of view of the Star Maker.

Yet with its mind-boggling imaginative *tour de force*, this is a rather curious message for a science fiction novel. Published on the eve of World War II and foreshadowing some of the Nazi horrors, the novel abjures the fervor of moral protest in favor of a passive acceptance and a celebration of a detached acceptance and contemplation. Using the Narrator's own metaphor, life is turned into art. The Star Maker is an artist; his worlds are artistic creations. Because they have a structure, a beginning, middle, and end, these universes can be contemplated as aesthetic objects. However, they can be seen as such only from a standpoint outside history, from the standpoint of eternity. From inside the work, from the point of view of history, the final curtain has not fallen. There are still choices to be made and potentialities to be realized. This is the arena of action, not contemplation. Man creates his future; history is nothing but man acting. Can man afford the luxury of viewing life as if it were a complete work of art, as if it were finished?

The tragic view of life assumes the existence of limits, finalities, and absolutes. Science fiction, while recognizing limits, is essentially the fiction of the possible. There are few limits and fewer certainties; there is almost always that not-yet-existing future where almost anything can happen. With all of its incredibly fertile possibilities, *Star Maker* is essentially a conservative work. Like Oedipus, in Sophocles' tragic drama, the Narrator learns that man and, indeed, the entire cosmos are rather limited phenomena. He learns that freedom and even joy come in man's recognition of his "awakening" to necessity; and, in that awakening to lucidity, he will rejoice.

Charles Elkins

Sources for Further Study

Criticism:

Moskowitz, Sam. *Explorers of the Infinite: Shapers of Science Fiction*. Cleveland: World, 1963. This general sketch examines the themes of Stapledon within the traditions of science fiction.

Review:

Kliatt Paperbook Book Guide. VII, April, 1973, p. 28.

STAR MAN'S SON 2250 A.D.

Author: Andre Norton (1912-   )
First book publication: 1952
Type of work: Novel
Time: Two hundred years in the future
Locale: The United States after an atomic holocaust

After America has been ravaged by an atomic holocaust, the remaining bands of men and women, reduced to savagery, attempt to rediscover their world and survive the radioactivity that remains

Principal characters:
> FORS, a young mutant member of the Puma Clan
> LURA, a member of a race of large, telepathic mutated cats
> ARSKANE, a scout for a Negroid race, once pilots, who have been driven out of their settlement by volcanic activity
> BEAST THINGS, hideous creatures mutated from rats and led by a newly mutated genius

Although *Star Man's Son 2250 A.D.* is Andre Norton's first science fiction novel, it was neither her first published work nor her first excursion into space and time. Originally having planned a career in the field of juvenile adventure and having legally changed her name from Mary Alice to Andre in 1934 to accommodate this male-dominated market, she had written *The Prince Commands* (1934), *Ralestone Luck* (1938), *Follow the Drum* (1942), and *Sword is Drawn* (1944) — all juvenile historical novels — before *Star Man's Son 2250 A.D.* Then in 1947, she published her first science fiction work, the short story "People of the Crater"; it appeared in the first issue of a short-lived magazine, *Fantasy Book*. The story was later included as "Garan of Tav" in one of her most successful collections, *Garan the Eternal* (1972). When *Star Man's Son 2250 A.D.* appeared in 1952, it marked Norton's first recognized (and very auspicious) entry into the field; Donald A. Wollheim, in *The Universe Makers: Science Fiction Today* (1971), indicates that by 1970 the novel had sold more than one million copies in the Ace paperback edition.

The novel is not formidable in its complexity and can justifiably be labeled a juvenile work with all-ages appeal. It focuses on the fortunes of Fors, a mutant, and his alienation from a community of explorers known as the Star Men. Born of a Star Man and a plainswoman amid the fragmented future of postholocaust Earth, his unusual senses and silver-white hair mark him as an outcast in an age when any deviation from the norm is cause for fear. Striking out on his own with his companion, the mutated cat Lura, Fors is the prototype of many Norton protagonists to come.

Norton's heroes and heroines are frequently outcasts, disenfranchised and alone with only a few close companions. Often they are hounded by the established order: Fors is pursued because he defied the tribe and stole his father's pouch and maps from the Star Hall, just as Murdoc Jern and Eet are harried in *The Zero Stone* (1968) and its sequel, *Unchartered Stars* (1969). In other works, the principal characters are isolated by holocaust or conflict, as in *Storm Over Warlock* (1960) and *Ordeal in Otherwhere* (1964). Most often, they are set apart by special powers: Fors has acute hearing and night sight; in *Forerunner Foray* (1973), Ziatha's psychic abilities are the source of her persecution and alienation.

Yet, whatever the reasons for their separation, Norton's characters are uniformly isolated and driven. Fors ventures out into the radiation-scarred blue lands to prove his value as an explorer, and it is not unexpected that he, as well as other characters in the Norton canon, are beseiged by fear. While Fors's fear of the unknown and of the dread mutated rats, Beast Things, is effectively presented, it is the tragic hero of *The Beast Master* (1959), Holsteen Storm, his native Terra destroyed and his personal and racial origins lost, who is Norton's most accurate presentation of the agonizing terror that almost paralyzes many of her characters. The characters' reactions may seem almost excessive until one realizes that it is not fear of physical harm that shakes them, but fear of the deprivation of self.

C. G. Jung, in *Archetypes and the Collective Unconscious,* identifies this fear and its numerous variations as the greatest of human fears. Fors dreads the loss of identity within his clan, which is why he must return for their judgment at the end of *Star Man's Son 2250 A.D.* even though he has been offered safer alternatives by Arskane and others. He fears the loss of his own place within his own destiny. His restlessness and his need to explore and to seek knowledge is linked to the Star Men. Thus, when he is originally passed over by his tribe in their rites of passage, he must strike out on his own to preserve himself from the nonexistence the tribe has dictated for him, but he must also return and complete the circle for an affirmation of his growth and wisdom.

In his journey into the shattered shell of Cleveland and the blue lands, Fors also illustrates other central features of Andre Norton's fiction: lack of prejudice and stress on internal value. The cat, Lura, and the Negro, Arskane, are both alien in appearance and nature, yet they are Fors's strongest allies and deepest friends. Norton's characters come in all different sizes and shapes, but their most important qualities are internal. In *Breed to Come* (1972), Fertig, the protagonist, is a mutated cat; in *The Beast Master* (1959) and its sequel, *Lord of Thunder* (1962), the main character's best friends are telepathic animals and his allies are a race of aliens with horns. The longlived Zacathans, a reptile race, are the wise and honored historians of the galaxy in *Storm Over Warlock* (1960), *Ordeal in Otherwhere* (1964), and *Forerunner Foray* (1973). In *Catseye* (1961), intelligent cats, foxes, and a kinkajou are the salvation of the human Troy, and in *Star Guard* (1974), a race of serpents are the comrades of a group of human mercenaries in a battle against other humans. It is this truly humanistic attitude that has also made Norton, along with C. L. Moore, one of the pioneers in the use of realistic female protagonists in science fiction.

Alone, frightened, alienated, threatened, searching — Norton's characters are always admirable; their ethical systems may shake with fear and weaken, as Fors's and Arskane's do in the middle of the plot, but ultimately, they are vindicated and are more attractive for their frailty. Despite their varied shapes and talents, these characters achieve a genuine nobility. Thus, Fors creates his own rites of passage and his own myths, for which he is awarded a high symbol of recognition and identification — a multipointed star as opposed to the traditional five-pointed one — by the Star Men at the end of *Star Man's Son 2250 A.D.* Indeed, like so many of Norton's characters, he heals himself and those around him and gains a dignity and freedom that comes only from the exaltation of self. Most of all, Fors and all of Norton's protagonists discover a sanctity of ideas and ethics, and they come to recognize their own special places within the patterns and rhythms of elemental law. They carry that recognition into a hopeful future that they have been instrumental in establishing.

Roger C. Schlobin

Sources for Further Study

Reviews:

Analog. LI, April, 1953, pp. 157-158.

Galaxy. VII, April, 1954, pp. 119-120.

Kirkus Reviews. XX, August 1, 1952, p. 455.

New York Times. August 31, 1952, p. 12.

Saturday Review. XXXV, November 15, 1952, p. 60.

STAR ROVER

Author: Jack London (1876-1916)
First book publication: 1915
Type of work: Novel
Time: 1913
Locale: The United States

A strong-willed convict learns how to separate his spirit from his body and thus experiences his previous lives

Principal characters:
DARRELL STANDING, a strong-willed convict
ED MORRELL AND JAKE OPPENHEIMER, other convicts
WARDEN ATHERTON, a prison warden

Called a dreamer as well as a social reformer, Jack London was aware of the profound tragedy of life, yet fascinated by the evolutionary history of man. Coinciding with this dual vision was a kind of caveman philosophy that has caused many critics to view London as a shallow and often vulgar adolescent. Such a view, however, is itself limited. Like Frank Norris and the other naturalist writers, London saw a close relationship between humanity and the jungle, between civilized man and brute man; and, utilizing his great skill as a storyteller, he examined that relationship in a plethora of stories and novels, all of which are marked by individualistic struggle and primitive violence. Sled dogs of the far North, prize fighters, gold miners, ruthless sea captains — these are his protagonists. As such they reflect his preoccupation with the cult of "red blood," that elemental instinct in man and animal to cling to life.

One such protagonist is Darrell Standing of *Star Rover*, a stalwart convict who, as the novel opens, is in California's Folsom Prison awaiting the hangman's noose. Narrating his own story, Standing begins by stating that throughout his life he has had an awareness of other times and places — indeed, that all people have hazy recollections of such other times and places. "Not in utter nakedness, not in entire forgetfulness," wrote Wordsworth, and Standing points to that passage as a basis for his theory that children of three, four, and five years of age are in a state of becoming — in a flux of spirit. Through their childish voices scream the voices of their shadowy progenitors from all the way back to pre-Adamic time, blending the snarls of beasts with the cries of humans. And it is the beast — the red wrath — in Standing that has undone him.

A former university professor of agronomics, Standing, in what he refers to as a purely private matter, murdered one of his colleagues. For that crime he was sentenced to life imprisonment at San Quentin — a sentence later changed to the death penalty when he more or less accidentally strikes a guard. Because of his intelligence and his indomitable spirit, he has been marked as an incorrigible and has spent much time (a total of five years) in solitary confinement. His situation is complicated when, through the deviousness of another prisoner, he is erroneously implicated in an escape attempt. Warden Atherton, who by all standards is the villain of the piece, believing that Standing hid some dynamite during the escape attempt, tries vainly to get him to tell where it is. Since there really was no dynamite, Standing cannot comply. As the contest between Atherton and Standing intensifies, the latter is put permanently in solitary and spends longer and longer periods trussed up almost beyond endurance in a kind of satanic straight jacket.

Instead of weakening, as Atherton hopes, Standing seems to grow stronger and learns how to flex his muscles when he is being laced into the jacket so that when he relaxes later, he gains some space for his tortured body. Helping to sustain him are two other convicts in permanent solitary — Ed Morrell and Jake Oppenheimer. The three of them communicate with one another through a tapping code that they have ingeniously worked out — even to the point that Standing can teach Oppenheimer how to play imaginary games of chess.

It is Ed Morrell who, when Standing is on the verge of death from the jacketing that he has undergone, tells him of the "little death," a method of escaping the physical torments of the jacket through astral projection. The method is to will, slowly and painstakingly, each part of the body dead, until at last the spirit is released from its physical confines. Following Morrell's instructions, Standing succeeds beyond his wildest expectations and finds himself treading interstellar space, touching all the stars that he passes. He has proved to himself that the realm of the spirit is more real than that of the body — that the soul exists eternally. As a child, Standing had on occasion displayed knowledge of objects and events that mystified those around him. Now, all of that strange knowledge is explained. Darrell Standing is more than Darrell Standing; he is — or was — many individuals in many ages.

Now that he has found a means of escape, Standing continually taunts Warden Atherton and the guards to put him into the jacket as tightly as they can and for as long as they want. Each time they do, he journeys back through time and relives former incarnations.

His first incarnation finds him in the Paris of centuries ago as Count Guillaume de Sainte-Maure. Going against the wishes of certain powers in Rome, he plans to marry an Italian duchess. Forced to duel with four Italian swordsmen, he quickly and skillfully disposes of three of them, but the fourth by a fluke runs him through. Before he hits the ground, however, he is back in his solitary cell being awakened by the Warden and a guard.

His second incarnation places him on the early American frontier, moving West with his parents in a wagon train. At the instigation of Mormons, Indians attack the wagon train, and a long seige takes place. The Mormons, tricking the people of the wagon train into thinking that they are being rescued from the Indians, massacre them all, and another of Darrell Standing's lives comes to an end.

Another time Standing finds himself as Adam Strang, an Englishman living some time between 1550 and 1650 and sailing the seas near Korea and Japan. His ship is wrecked, but he and several companions succeed in reaching the Korean shore. Because of his fearlessness and strong will, Strang gains a position of power and marries a woman, the Lady Om, from the Emperor's court. Two priests, Yunsan and Chong Mong-ju, are contending for control of the Emperor at this time. Yunsan wins out, and he and Strang become friends. Chong Mong-ju bides his time, however, and eventually gains power, forcing Strang and the Lady Om into forty years of living as beggars. Through a quirk of fate, Strang succeeds in killing Chong Mong-ju as he himself is killed.

Jerusalem is Standing's next stop as a star rover. Born Ragnar Lodbrog, a North Dane, he is captured by the Romans and made a slave. Although the details are not given, he gains his freedom and becomes commander of a Roman legion under Pontius Pilate. He falls in love with Miriam, a woman who becomes a follower of the prophet Jesus. Pilate himself is depicted as an intelligent and understanding governor who is unsuccessfully attempting to keep politics and religion separate. He does everything that he can to keep the mob from crucifying Jesus, but in the end he gives in to their demands and orders the crucifixion. This incarnation ends with Lodbrog, rejected by Miriam, going off with his soldiers to Syria.

The last journey Standing describes is one to a desert island where, as Daniel Foss, he is once more shipwrecked. Living a Robinson Crusoe existence, Foss learns to accept his lot and becomes content enough. He builds an enormous pyramid from which to watch for passing ships. At the end of his eighth year, a ship does come to the island, and he is rescued.

Such star roving has enabled Darrell Standing to survive the horrible torture of the jacket and to defeat Warden Atherton's efforts to crush his indomitable spirit. As he nears the end of his story, he reflects on Pascal's view of humanity as being one man and not a conglomeration of individuals. What Pascal believed, Darrell Standing has lived — and he approaches his execution with the equanimity of a man who knows that his spirit will now go in another direction — that of future star roving.

Darrell Standing is an idealized self-portrait of London — a version of Nietzsche's blond beast. In all of the ancestral incarnations that he undergoes, he is ever the willful, self-sufficient individual who faces life with a Zarathustrian belly laugh. Yet in his final comments, he sees the story of man as the story of the love of woman. He has, he says, in his many lives crossed the seas for her and climbed mountains for her, killed for her and died for her. The several pages devoted to this idealization of woman appear almost as an afterthought. They certainly do not derive from what has gone before, nor do they contribute significantly to the overall theme of racial memory as the wellspring of human will.

Other aspects of *Star Rover* that militate against unity are its episodic structure and its scathing attacks against prison conditions in California. Still, London's style — compact, vivid, and forceful — serves in a redeeming role and makes the novel worth reading. The novel is not vintage London, perhaps, but London nonetheless.

London in this novel presents two of the popular themes of science fiction: psychic phenomena, now being investigated as the "soft" science of parapsychology; and the ever-popular time slip in the context of reincarnation, long familiar to philosophers but here introduced — though not maintained — as star travel.

Wilton Eckley

Sources for Further Study

Reviews:

Atheneum. II, July 31, 1915, p. 77.

Boston Transcript. October, 1915, p. 22.

Dial. LX, January 6, 1916, p. 30.

Independent. LXXXIV, November 15, 1915, p. 270.

Nation. CI, November 4, 1915, p. 548.

New York Times. October 17, 1915, p. 389.

Spectator. CXV, August, 1928, p. 280.

STARLIGHT: THE GREAT SHORT FICTION OF ALFRED BESTER

Author: Alfred Bester (1913-   )
First book publication: 1977
Type of work: Short stories

Sixteen stories with introductions by the author, drawn from the whole of his career in short science fiction from 1941 to 1975; with two essays, one of them auto-biographical

Alfred Bester has never been a prolific writer, and his important short stories can be found in only a few volumes. Eleven stories were collected in *Starburst* (1958) and seven in *The Dark Side of the Earth* (1964). These two collections were reassembled, with six stories dropped, and five stories and two essays added, in the more recent books *The Light Fantastic* (1976) and *Star Light, Star Bright* (1976); these two volumes were in turn reissued as a single omnibus volume, *Starlight: the Great Short Fiction of Alfred Bester* (1977). It is the best introduction to Bester's short fiction, more especially as each story and essay is accompanied by a witty and informative preface, often detailing its genesis.

Bester had his first short story, "The Broken Axiom," accepted in 1939. It was published in a pulp magazine, *Thrilling Wonder Stories*, while he was still a law student. He published another thirteen stories by 1942, and then followed his friend, Mort Weisinger, the editor of *Thrilling Wonder Stories*, into the comic book business, where he worked on *Superman*, *Batman*, and *Captain Marvel*; later he wrote for radio, working on such series as *Charlie Chan* and *The Shadow*. He did not return to science fiction until 1950. Between 1950 and 1959 Bester wrote two novels and fifteen or so stories that gained for him a near-legendary status among science fiction *cognoscenti*.

Bester's early stories now read like the merest apprentice work, and only two have been collected. "Hell Is Forever" (1942) is a colorful, brash fantasy, heavily laden with pop psychology; it is of novella length, 35,000 words, and tells of six decadents, rather conventionally *fin-de-siècle* in their interests, who bargain with a devil to get their hearts' desires; in each case their inner corruption turns the fulfillment around so that it becomes an eternal punishment. Verbal fireworks of a rather sophomoric variety abound.

"Adam and No Eve" (1941) is a much tauter work, in which an obsessed scientist, despite warnings, insists on testing his new rocket ship that utilizes an experimental catalytic fuel; the ship takes off successfully, but the catalysis process spreads rapidly across the face of the Earth, and by the time he returns, the world has been destroyed by fire. The charred and dying protagonist crawls into the now sterile sea, but the organic compounds that make up his body will, it is implied, be sufficient to begin a new cycle of life. This is an entertaining twist on the old science fiction variants of the Adam and Eve legend. Life does not need a man and a woman to be set in motion; it only needs amino acids. Though neither of these stories is of the highest quality, both interestingly prefigure the themes that were to dominate Bester's later and more productive period, 1950-1959.

Although Bester is among the most generous and imaginative inventors of future *milieux*, sketched in economically with surprising and telling details, his stories nearly always focus on the psychology of their protagonists, who are generally doomed and obsessive figures, working out various fantasies in their own lives, very often with ironic results. Verbal pyrotechnics are often accompanied by a lurid atmosphere of violence.

Perhaps it is the balance Bester maintains, like a clever juggler, between inner and outer worlds that has led to his becoming something of a hero figure not only to readers of conservative, hardcore science fiction, who appreciate the frenzied creativity with which Bester creates futuristic technologies and lifestyles, but also to the more downbeat fans of the so-called New Wave, which stresses inner rather than outer space, and the soft sciences like psychology, biology, and sociology over the hard sciences such as engineering and physics.

The typical Bester hero, the "Besterman," is driven and obsessed. He is science fiction's closest equivalent to the dark, sardonic, vengeful protagonists of Jacobean drama. The heroes of his first two novels are stamped of this metal, and examples proliferate in the stories too. "The Pi Man" (1959) features a hero with an extrasensory perception; he senses the patterns of things. Faced with an asymmetry in anything, from the ways chairs are placed around a table to the day's stock exchange figures, he is driven to compensate; this involves behavior ranging from massive share manipulation, through ending sentences in foreign languages, right down to "abominable acts." The story involves a girl, but its center is the nonstop, compulsive rush with which the hero goes through life adjusting its phenomena. The story itself, like most of Bester's, is told in staccato, restless, onward-thrusting sentences, which mirror this disturbed state.

"Fondly Fahrenheit" (1954) is perhaps Bester's most remarkable story. Vandaleur, a soft-centered aristo, owns an android, a synthetic man of great sophistication; it is worth a fortune and cannot be jettisoned, but it is a murderer. Vandaleur flees with it from planet to planet, but always the android kills, horribly, when the temperature soars. This exotic murder story is greatly enrichened by the relationship between owner and android. The homicidal mania is catching, but who is projecting it onto whom? The narrative voice changes person unnervingly; sometimes the android is "he," sometimes "I," sometimes "we"; the two are effectively one. In this modern variant of *Frankenstein*, the question is bluntly put: Who is the monster, the artificial man or its human mentor? Again, the jittering, syncopated prose rhythmically suggests the hysteria and lunacy that are the subject of the story.

The most recent story (*Starlight* contains only two stories from the 1960's and two from the 1970's) is "The Four-Hour Fugue" (1974). The man with the world's most sensitive nose, the top chemist in the all-important future perfume industry (Earth stinks), mysteriously disappears at regular intervals. During these periods, murders take place. It happens that the chemist (who remembers nothing of these occasions) has been morbidly attracted by the pheromones (body chemicals) given off by people who have a death wish. This theme of genius and madness going hand in hand is an old one. Bester's genius lies not in the creation of new themes, but in his adroit rendering of old themes in new terms. The science fiction content is not merely random; it allows him to isolate the themes and embed them in an imagery more bizarrely *à propos* than any that is readily available in the traditional realistic story. He creates imaginary worlds, sometimes wastelands (as in "Adam and No Eve"), sometimes full of color, which are the external correlatives of the states of mind that are his central concern.

"Time Is the Traitor" (1953) again focuses on a genius. This time the protagonist, Strapp, is a man who, acting as a highly paid industrial adviser, can subconsciously weigh the factors involved in decision making with extraordinary accuracy. A calm, unspectacular man on the surface, he is emotionally ruined within; between jobs he commits many acts of violence and sexual assault; the violence always against men called Kruger, the assaults always against buxom, black-haired women. A friend discovers that Strapp is searching through the galaxy for a replica of the women he once loved, who was killed in an accident brought about by the original Kruger. The friend discovers where the body is buried, has cells cloned from it, and creates an exact duplicate of the dead girl, even with the same memories. Strapp meets her, assaults her, and again turns away indifferently in savage disappointment. His mind has created a false past, and ironically, even the real thing now seems *ersatz* to him.

This obsessive need to rediscover and relive the past often appears in Bester's work. Hence, perhaps, his interest in time travel stories, of which the wittiest is "The Men Who Murdered Mohammed" (1958), where a psysicist who discovers his wife in the arms of another man, instead of killing her on the spot, invents a time machine and kills her ancestors. Returning to the present, he finds the embrace continuing; enraged, the returns to the past, and carries out more and more elaborate massacres of famous historical figures, each time only to find his wife still being kissed when he returns. The moral of this macabre tale, which is told with a mordant sense of humor, is that each man's universe of time is subjective.

Indeed, Bester's tales tend to have morals, and these are mostly ironic, or even cynical. Perhaps part of their appeal to readers of science fiction (many of whom were drawn to the genre as adolescents because of its wish-fulfillment elements) is that in Bester's moral fables it is precisely the conventional

power fantasies of lonely adolescents that are first created and then demolished. Chief among them are: to relive the past, but with the maturity and
knowledge you have now; to be loved by many compliant women; to be God;
and to be the last man alive. All four appear in the long, amusing story
"5,271,009," in which a diabolical Wandering-Jew figure attempts to bring
maturity to a brilliant but emotionally flawed artist by allowing him literally to
live out his fantasies. As in the early tale "Hell is Forever," each fantasy fails
to satisfy when made real. In "Hobson's Choice" (1952), neurotic time travelers search through the ages for the perfect world and never find it. One home-
sick Japanese constantly wishes to return to Hiroshima in 1945; it may be hell,
but it's home (The point is made memorably, but the means are a little cheap.
Bester's stories are occasionally flawed by his tendency to reach for effects
that, though strong, are overly facile.) "They Don't Make Life Like They
Used To" (1963) has the last man and the last woman in the world meeting in
New York. All other humans are dead and the survivors adjust to their loneliness by re-creating their past around them and conducting a remarkably se-
date, old-worldly courtship. But the inheritors of Earth are giant warlike insects, and when they arrive in New York the fantasy crumbles, and the couple
fling themselves into a fierce, mutual rape.

God figures recur, sardonically, in "Something Up There Likes Me" (1973)
and "Oddy and Id" (1950) — in the former case as a computer in a satellite, in
the latter as another "Besterman" with a strange talent (this time the ability to
project good luck). Both are likable and benign on the surface; in both cases
the results are disastrous.

"Disappearing Act" (1953) is another tale of people whose fantasies are
given flesh. Shell-shocked soldiers in a hospital learn how to travel into imaginary, subjective pasts, to the bewilderment of the army brass, who cannot
understand the disappearances. But this time the moral is reversed, and it is the
fantacists who triumph. The world, entirely given over to the war machine, has
lost all its poets, and only a poet can find out how the soldiers are performing
the trick.

Again, the moral is simplistic. It is not possible to isolate Bester's strengths
as a storyteller purely by pointing to his themes, or even to the skill with
which he works out the ironic reversals. Half the fun of any good Bester story
is in the incidentals along the way, which are created with great vivacity. In
"5,271,009," for example, the basic story, which is primarily a piece of pop
psychoanalysis, is of no special interest. The story lives through the characterization of the cynical therapist who imposes the *rite de passage* that cures
the artist. His classical tags, his caricatured, sprightly gauntness, his daffy
multilingual urbanity are what is memorable, along with the amazingly accurate and quite unexpected seventeenth century pastiche (an argument about free
will *versus* predestination) that takes place in one of the artist's fantasies.

Bester, who contributes entertaining commentaries to all these stories in

Starlight, is well aware of this facet of his art. He calls it the "rare show quality." It is the wild metaphors, the vigorous, onward-rushing, staccato prose, the voice, in short, of the born *raconteur*, that we remember best; and very noticeably, this is also the voice of the native New Yorker, the sardonic, Jewish comedian. At their best, the stories blaze with a coruscating display, though at times it is almost too flashy. Sometimes we feel that the glitter is that of cut glass, not diamonds. It is when Bester shows passion as well as wit that the stories really resonate, and this, usually, is when he focuses on the "Besterman," the ruined, obsessive malcontent, resourceful and self-destructive, as in the novels *The Demolished Man* and *The Stars My Destination*, and in "Fondly Fahrenheit," "The Pi Man," and "Time is the Traitor."

The stories are of course minor works, but in their ebullience and wit they remain among the liveliest products of the kind of lurid pulp science fiction that lived so long and so well in those magazines with the equally lurid covers. In these stories Bester does not transcend his pulp origins, but by adding his literacy and his great fluency to the pulp ingredients, he gives it a spice excelled by a few or none of his colleagues, before or since.

Peter Nicholls

Sources for Further Study

Reviews:

Starburst:

Amazing Stories. XXXII, October, 1958, p. 145.

Analog. LXII, February, 1959, pp. 141-142.

Fantastic Universe Science Fiction. X, September, 1958, pp. 118-119.

Magazine of Fantasy and Science Fiction. XV, August, 1958, pp. 106-107.

The Dark Side of Earth:

Amazing Stories. XXXVIII, December, 1964, pp. 123-124.

Analog. LXXVII, August, 1966, p. 166.

Magazine of Fantasy and Science Fiction. XXVII, December, 1964, p. 72.

THE STARS MY DESTINATION

Author: Alfred Bester (1913-   )
First book publication: 1956
Type of work: Novel
Time: The twenty-fifth century
Locale: The Earth, the Sargasso Asteroid, Mars, and outer space

The heroic adventures of Gully Foyle, whose evolution from apathetic drifter to world-conqueror epitomizes the genesis of a new, more than human race

> *Principal characters:*
> GULLY FOYLE, the strongest man in the world
> OLIVIA PRESTEIGN, the woman he loves
> PRESTEIGN OF PRESTEIGN, her father and Foyle's most powerful enemy
> ROBIN WEDNESBURY, Foyle's first teacher
> JISBELLA MCQUEEN, Foyle's second teacher
> JOSEPH, leader of the Scientific People

Superman, one of science fiction's favorite subjects, clearly fascinates Alfred Bester. Most of his short stories and all of his novels define various ways in which humanity might develop beyond itself. Of all Bester's many looks at superman, however, the most extensive, original, and provocative is undoubtedly his second novel, *The Stars My Destination*. The novel's protagonist, Gully Foyle, is an extraordinarily concentrated embodiment of both the negative and the positive aspects of superheroism.

The Stars My Destination presents two images of superman, the exterior and the interior. Externally, superheroism appears to be a terrifying combination of psychological fixation and physical strength. On this level, Gully Foyle is an action-adventure hero with the self-imposed mission to avenge himself on the crew of the *Vorga*, a rocket ship which abandoned him to die in space. Foyle's obsession with vengeance is so strong that he becomes a bionic superkiller and develops his latent abilities to teleport himself across unheard-of distances and activate the world's most powerful explosive, PyrE. By the end of the novel Foyle has not only succeeded in revenging himself on the *Vorga*'s crew; a definite superman, he has also defeated the villainous commercial, political, and military establishment, and drastically altered the interplanetary balance of power.

The action-adventure Foyle is an awe-inspiring but profoundly repulsive monster who frightens and disgusts everyone except the psychotic murderess, Olivia Presteign, and the weirdly mystic Scientific People; even Foyle loathes and fears the "tiger" superhero of this book, who is more than human solely by virtue of being much stronger and much meaner than ordinary people. But Bester saves this exterior level of his novel from being merely a depressing demonstration of might makes right by borrowing extensively from Alexandre Dumas' grandly romantic historical novel, *The Count of Monte-Cristo*. Bester has acknowledged that when he was writing *The Stars My Destination* he was thinking about the adventures of Edmond Dantès, the simple Corsican sailor who fought his way back from betrayal and abandonment to become the elegant, influential Count of Monte-Cristo. Dumas provided Bester with a great many exotic settings and intriguing plot twists, giving *The Stars My Destination* a dramatic flair which superman stories often lack.

The central portion of Bester's novel is especially close to Dumas' story. Here Foyle, like Dantès, is imprisoned in a supposedly escape-proof rockbound fortress where, again like Dantès, he encounters a fellow prisoner who teaches him how to escape and survive in the outside world. Once out of prison, Foyle finds a vast secret treasure which he uses to finance his revenge on his enemies, exactly as Dantès did. He further imitates Dantès by establishing a protective cover identity as a frivolous, mysterious, glamorous, aloof, and wealthy social butterfly, while he pursues his grim quest; "Geoffrey Fourmyle" is strikingly like "the Count of Monte-Cristo."

Because of the vividness, power, and variety with which Bester invests the action-adventure elements of his novel, many readers never realize that *The Stars My Destination* is anything more than the external story of Foyle the supermonster. It is particularly important not to stop with this one view of the book, however, because Bester's basic thesis is that the exterior, superficial image of superman is a very dangerous and destructive distortion of humanity's true potential. The interior, symbolic level of *The Stars My Destination* tells of how Foyle himself learns to reject the *macho* image of heroism. In fact, on the symbolic level, Foyle becomes a superman precisely because he grows completely beyond this way of thinking.

Bester unfolds the symbolic dimension of Foyle's career simultaneously with the action-adventure dimension, and thus compels us to solve the same problem that confronts his characters. We, too, must make sense out of the apparently contradictory character of Gully Foyle. While he heightens the drama of the action-adventure story by borrowing from *The Count of Monte-Cristo*, Bester illuminates the symbolic level of his novel by alluding to William Blake's poem, "The Tyger." Indeed, Foyle is so insistently and continuously identified with Blake's image of the Tiger that the English title of this book, *Tiger! Tiger!*, seems thoroughly appropriate. We meet Foyle "in the forests of the night," the outer space where he awaits rescue and the inner blackness of his initially undeveloped consciousness. We watch as he flares into rage and, "burning bright" with the fury of one brutally spurned, sets out to find and destroy the *Vorga*'s crew. Almost immediately he encounters the Scientific People, who instantly recognize his essential character and bestow on him the "fearful symmetry" of a tattooed tiger-mask, so that his face will perpetually signal the terrible energies of the superhero. But the significance of Blake's Tiger is that he radiates not just rage, but the untameable energy of the life-force itself; it is this primal vitality, rather than mere destructiveness, which the Scientific People mark in Foyle and which makes him a superheroic "nomad" who vaults beyond stereotypally masculine values.

Bester represents Foyle's movement toward "the stars" of his full potential by gradually changing the symbolic meaning of the fire and flame images which always accompany him. At first Foyle seems to burn only with anger; but increasingly, he and we understand that he is more deeply and truly aflame with compassion, self-sacrifice, and a great yearning to escape his obsession with revenge. This is the meaning of the Burning Man, whose growing presence in the novel symbolizes Foyle's growing capacity to love. The Burning Man is the interior image of superman, the liberating, regenerative savior who delivers humanity from its own brutality. On this symbolic level, everyman is potentially superman, for we are all "nomads" who must perpetually journey from old selfhood to new, allowing the old identity to sacrifice itself in order that the new one may be born. The Burning Man looms before each of us, calling us to "jaunt" into new life as Foyle did. Moreover, *The Stars My Destination* suggests that this psychological leap is a social as well as a personal necessity; it is the only way our *macho*-idolizing culture can avoid incinerating itself.

Bester uses a third kind of fire image to emphasize the social consequences of our ideas about superheoism. Like the Tiger and the Burning Man, PyrE symbolizes the great potential of Foyle's developing consciousness. But it also represents the infinitely greater potential of the whole world outside of Foyle, for it is "the equivalent of the primordial protomatter which exploded into the Universe." The external, action-adventure superman and the society he terrorizes can merely savage each other in their lust to control PyrE's unimaginable power, and with it the universe. They cannot really tap the cosmic energy because only the Burning Man, with his self-sacrificing commitment to caring, growth, and intuitive vision, comprehends what Dylan Thomas called "the force that through the green fuse drives the flower." At the end of the novel Foyle distributes bits of PyrE to common people everywhere, encouraging us to believe that they, too, will learn to reform and regenerate their worlds by first reforming themselves.

Bester proposes that as society's greatest hope lies in the liberated individual consciousness, so its greatest problem is the pressure to conform. *The Stars My Destination* includes many memorable caricatures of the conformist mentality: perhaps the most devastating are the men who become "Mr. Prestos," reshaping their own minds and bodies to the plastic uniformity approved by Clan Presteign. Just before Presteign first encounters Foyle, he swears in the 497th Mr. Presto:

> After six months of surgery and psycho-conditioning, he was identical with the other 496 Mr. Prestos and to the idealized portrait of Mr. Presto which hung behind Presteign's dais . . . a kindly, honest man resembling Abraham Lincoln, a man who instantly inspired affection and trust. Around the world purchasers entered an identical Presteign store and

were greeted by an identical manager, Mr. Presto. He was rivaled, but not surpassed, by the Kodak clan's Mr. Kwik and Montgomery Ward's Uncle Monty.

No one is free in Terran society, which oppresses every woman and denies even Presteign of Presteign the right to worship according to his personal beliefs. Such a world makes "normal" humans indistinguishable from the robots who serve them. And it produces a great multitude of psychological cripples who think of themselves as freaks because they are not exactly like everyone else. In Robin Wednesbury, Jisbella McQueen, Saul Dagenham, and the Presteign clan, *The Stars My Destination* presents haunting case studies of the wounded and warped psyches which a "Mr. Presto" society inevitably causes, and of the serious injuries these damaged souls inflict on their environment.

If Gully Foyle were nothing more than an action-adventure hero, he would magnify society's problems, not solve them. On this level, Foyle is Nietzsche's kind of superman, asserting his personal will, wits, and muscle at the expense of everyone else. As Burning Man, however, he relates to society in a much more complex and constructive way; he grows into heroism by identifying with society's victims so profoundly that his liberation becomes at least in part their own. He and Robin Wednesbury teach each other the social power of a completely alert and communicative intuition. He, Jisbella McQueen, and Saul Dagenham learn together how to inform and control the wisdom of the head with the warmer, healing wisdom of the heart. The Presteigns are less reformable, but they at least learn with Foyle that the *macho* sense of superheroism leads only to personal and social destruction, not to "the stars" they desire.

Because Foyle's evolution is fundamentally cooperative, an experience shared and nurtured by many people in his world, he escapes the egotism which fragments and destroys his great literary predecessor, Ben Reich of *The Demolished Man*. Indeed, Foyle's career makes full sense only when it is viewed as continuing and completing the story which Bester began in *The Demolished Man*. From this perspective, Bester's first two novels (which were published only two years apart) form a single epic exploration of the death of false superman and rebirth of true superheroism. *The Stars My Destination* opens where *The Demolished Man* closes; centered on an embryonic mentality, the hero is alone and virtually inarticulate in the blackness of his undeveloped psyche. Reich is reduced to this state because he compulsively distorts and rejects intuition and compassion in himself and others; by contrast, Foyle, who learns to integrate these traits with every aspect of his life, impels himself into a completely new, richly promising dimension of selfhood.

In describing Foyle's climactic "jaunt" into superheroism, Bester writes in a dazzlingly original and effective style which is itself a giant step beyond the level of most science fiction writing. Bester is consistently one of the best stylists among science fiction authors; but in *The Stars My Destination* he outdoes even himself. This is particularly true of the novel's concluding scenes — everything from Foyle's trip to Mars to his final return to the Sargasso Asteroid and the Scientific People. In these last several scenes the novel rises to a level of sustained technical brilliance matching the brilliance of its imaginative vision. Here Bester makes us believe that Foyle's inner and outer worlds are truly exploding, because he describes it in language which explodes into new patterns and reproduces the synesthesia, or fusion of senses, which Foyle experiences. The effect of these last brilliant scenes is to introduce Foyle, and us, to the aesthetics of superheroism — a wonderful new sense of color, sound, movement, and above all, control. *The Stars My Destination* thus concludes with a fully realized superman, intellectually, emotionally, morally, and aesthetically complete and integrated to a degree of which ordinary humans can only dream.

The excellence of Bester's writing throughout this novel, especially in its concluding scenes, makes it clear that Foyle is not the only superhero here; Bester himself shoots to the stars in this work. In the depth and range of its study of the human condition; in the originality of its evolutionary optimism; in the complexity of its references to literary, mythic, and psychological patterns; and in the perfect matching of style to substance, *The Stars My Destination* is a masterpiece. As such, it continues to impress readers and writers alike. One of the most imitated novels in science fiction, it nonetheless retains its freshness, power, and suggestiveness even through several readings. Bester has written nothing else which equals this work.

Jane Hipolito

Sources for Further Study

Criticism:

Scholes, Robert and Eric S. Rabkin. *Science Fiction*. New York: Oxford University Press, 1977, pp. 67-68. The plot of *The Stars My Destination* is compared to that of *The Count of Monte Cristo*. Bester is commended for his style of narrating which is described as "exciting."

Reviews:

Fantastic Universe Science Fiction. August, 1957, p. 113.

Infinity Science Fiction. II, October, 1957, pp. 105-107.

Luna Monthly. XXIII, April, 1971, p. 24.

Magazine of Fantasy and Science Fiction. XIII, August, 1957, p. 107.

STARSHIP TROOPERS

Author: Robert A. Heinlein (1907-   )
First book publication: 1959
Type of work: Novel
Time: The twenty-seventh century
Locale: The Philippine Islands, Western United States, and various locations in the galaxy

The story of the making of a soldier in the Mobile Infantry, illustrating the highest form of citizenship in a Utopian society based on liberation principles

Principal characters:
JUAN (JOHNNY) RICO, the narrator, once a spoiled eighteen-year-old, who becomes a career officer
HENRY DUBOIS, a retired colonel, Rico's high school instructor in "History and Moral Philosophy"
SERGEANT ZIM, Rico's topkick in boot camp

The last of thirteen "juveniles" Heinlein wrote for Scribner's, *Starship Troopers* was turned down by them because of its controversial treatment of the nature of war. However, the novel has numerous parallels with its predecessors, and sums up many of the author's concerns in adult novels as well. A fitting transition to the even more controversial works of the last part of Heinlein's career, it is technically the slickest of these books for young adults, which aids in making attractive its dogmatic philosophical message.

Five thousand years have passed since Sargon of Akkad (2340-2305 B.C.), placing the action of this book some seven hundred years from now, in an Earthwide Utopian society reminiscent of *Beyond This Horizon* and the "First Human Civilization" of the "Future History" stories. Affluence is widespread, perhaps universal, but technological advances in warfare and space travel exist alongside twentieth century educational methods and business practices. Government is worldwide, as is the use of Standard English, and racial, ethnic, religious, and sexual prejudices are practically things of the past. Johnny Rico is all but oblivious to them, and we find out near the end of the book, because his "native" language is Tagalog, that he is from the Philippine Islands.

The big difference between people is sociopolitical: citizenship is limited to those who have undertaken voluntary Government Service, which may mean risking their lives in experiments or exploration in such places as Antarctica or bases on other planets. Most commonly, however, it means military service, in which those who have no clear calling or special training windup as soldiers in the Mobile Infantry. The survivors are held worthy of voting for and serving in government office, a privilege weighed lightly ("sour grapes?") by the average person, if Johnny Rico's report is reliable. The military, in particular, is held in peacetime disrepute by civilians, whose special scorn is reserved for the infantry.

This scorn is unmerited, however, from the standpoint of Rico, whose character was built by his MI training. His story illustrates the truth of Mr. Dubois' lectures in Johnny's high school class in History and Moral Philosophy. One exception to the rule of voluntarism, this class was compulsory, but no one had to pass it, and no one seemed to think much of it either. Flashbacks to Mr. Dubois, however, and his hectoring style of instruction, punctuate crucial stages of Johnny's growing up in the narration. Interpolations in the action, they are in a sense what the book is really about: the responsibility of the citizen to risk his life for his fellows, to accept his duty toward the race.

The nature of this Utopian society is not shown in detail, and the reader has to take on faith that "it works," a justification almost every society can make for itself before it collapses. What we are shown, however, is the making of a soldier, though the MI may have more in common with the U. S. Marines of today than with the Army. As Alexei Panshin has pointed out, this novel is as slickly structured as a training film with the sincere "voice over" of a young man who has experienced what is being shown. In his own words, Johnny Rico tells us of his adolescent uncertainty, basic training, major battles, and acceptance of the call to be a career soldier, with appropriate nudges by his superiors and the memories of Dubois' lectures. The presentation is episodic, weaving back and forth in time, effectively documenting not only the processes of training and fighting, but also the growth of the narrator's commitment.

The narrative begins in the middle of things, as "Raszak's Roughnecks" raid a planet of "skinnies," humanoid co-belligerents with man's implacable enemies, the biologically communist "Bugs." Along with exciting action, the reader is given a feel for the new technology of warfare, along with the traditional camaraderie, anxiety, and group dynamics of a well-knit military unit, and the possibly surprising offhand reference to the fact that the pilot of the spaceship is a woman. The next eight chapters recount Rico's past, from his halfhearted enlistment (no one is drafted, and it is absurdly easy to resign at almost any time) through boot camp to graduation and the first taste of combat. We see him through survival training (dropped naked and unarmed in a mountain wilderness), corporal punishment (he both witnesses and experiences flogging), the use of powered suits which make a man a genuine "fighting machine," and the hanging of an AWOL murderer ("the MI takes care of its own in more than one way"). Along the way, Rico not only learns how to fight; he also learns (or relearns) the nature and value of war, the need for absolute discipline, and unflinching philosophy of punishment, the equation of survival with morality, and the inadequacies of twentieth century society.

After returning us to the raid which opens the book, Rico recognizes that his real family now is the MI; the death of his mother, when the Bugs level Buenos Aires, makes him realize that, but fatherly discipline and advice have been proffered him all along the line. Becoming a career soldier — as everyone else seemed to know he would before he did — Rico goes to Officers Candidates School to learn the other side of the command relationship. He becomes a probationary Lieutenant just in time to participate in a key attack on a Bugs outpost planet, which proves to be a turning point in the war. Then he moves on to take over his old outfit, but not before he has met again Sergeant Zim, his old topkick in boot camp, who serves under him in the attack, and Sergeant Rico, his own father, who serves under him in what are now *"Rico's Roughnecks."* Like the son, the father also had to prove his manhood, whatever his bad opinion of government service in the beginning of the story.

The arm of coincidence is long, not only in terms of the identity of Rico's sergeants, but also in terms of the timing with which various incidents occur as he fluctuates on his way toward becoming a man. In a retrospective narration, much of this seems inevitable, however, especially if we consider Rico's apparent purpose in telling the story. He is showing us not the glamor of war — which is still a dirty business, then as now — but rather its inevitability; he stresses the need for people to develop not only the capability to survive, but also the responsibility to protect others by personal sacrifice, if necessary.

The coincidences are part of the novel's sentimental texture, carefully contrived for emotional effect. Other events rendered in this way include moving military rituals, a syrupy letter from Rico's mother offering him comfort which produces the opposite effect, a letter from Mr. ("Colonel") Dubois congratulating him on getting "over the hump" (which the letter itself helps him do), and the controlled communal anger at the AWOL soldier (who, still technically "on duty," killed "a baby girl," and for good measure was named "Dillinger"). In addition to moving the reader, these elements go further, in fact, toward explaining the growth of Rico's character than what we know of his private life, or even the lessons hammered home by his instructors.

Johnny Rico's private life is off limits, for the most part; he seldom mentions it. His parents and best friends are little more than shadows, where they occur, his interaction with them being the least effective aspect of the book. His "real" family has indeed become the military, but even in the MI we only see his public face. As a recruiter for selfless idealism, he never lets us catch him or his fellows with their pants down, figuratively or literally. Though he claims to find women "marvelous," and the best reason worth fighting a war for, sex for him seems almost perfectly sublimated in warfare.

The philosophy of the state, however, as outlined by Dubois, and supported by Rico's training, is given in some detail. He learns that violence is quite effective at settling things, and that war, moreover, is "controlled violence to enforce orders." He comes to accept that nobility is the willingness to sacrifice oneself, that value is relative to what something costs and what it can be used for, and that punishment is essential in training the "moral sense." He buys the line, finally, that morality is an elaboration of the survival instinct, which conclusion, we are told, can be buttressed by "scientific evidence," even worked out mathematically as a balancing of rights and duties.

In the process of drilling these attitudes into Rico, Heinlein levels some heavy criticism at twentieth century organization of society. The communist system is attacked retrospectively, in the form of the Chinese Hegemony (which lost to an Anglo-Russian alliance), and in the present, its logical extreme is the enemy mankind must fight, the "Bugs" with their "hive mind." American society also comes in for some lumps, but the existing system is said to be based on its twentieth century ideals, backed up with the courage of their convictions. People are held responsible for their actions, in other words, which calls for a system of rewards on the one hand, and obligations and punishments on the other, with no exceptions. Flogging is not limited to the military, executions are not shied away from (both being public acts), and criminal activity is simply not tolerated, whether from adults or "juveniles."

People are not necessarily better at heart in this society, but their antisocial behavior is strictly limited, without regard to race, creed, sex, or national origin. That such a system, imposed after a final world war, actually could erase class and race conflicts, much less engender inequalities, is a dubious proposition. Indeed, despite the lip service given women's rights, war still "makes a man out of you" and women are more or less possessions to be protected. The system might well, of course, maintain such an equilibrium, once it was established, especially since those in charge are the ones who have proved themselves willing to fight. But the proof of the system is not really that "it works," perpetuating the *status quo*, so much as that it functions well to protect itself against outside attack. True to the nature of utopias in general, though much to the despair of many modern utopists, "war is the health of the state."

War demonstrates the Social Darwinist tenet of the "survival of the fittest," and man's toughness is extolled as the only thing which keeps him alive and gives him the "right" to expand out into the galaxy. Without a challenge, such as the Bugs, man would tend toward flabbiness, as is illustrated by the affluent Earth society's having neglected to train its civilians nearly as well as its infantry. The schools come in for their usual abuse in Heinlein's fiction; nothing is ever as good as education on the spot, gained largely through experience. Deficient in schooling, Johnny is still bright enough to master (in quick time) history, tactics, ordinance, engineering concepts, and, not without struggle, mathematics, once he sees the need for them. The extreme example of this challenge and response theory, however, is the rest planet, Sanctuary, an Edenic replica of Earth, but with radioactivity seemingly too low to challenge man's gene pool. It is specifically referred to as a potential Utopia, but simultaneously as a world in danger of stagnation and decay.

Nowhere, perhaps, is the challenge of Heinlein's Social Darwinism met more forthrightly than in war itself, or rather, the institution of the Mobile Infantry. Although men do get killed, casualties are relatively light because of the men's training and equipment, and the survivors clearly have something going for them. There are relatively few officers or support personnel since everybody fights; moreover, every unit takes risks to salvage its injured and imprisoned, and the training process aims at an ideal balance of obedience and initiative. At least in part, their security stems from their powered suits, which illustrate Heinlein's undiminished talent at invention and the description of process. Like any other technology, they may be doomed to eventual obsolescence, but at this frozen moment of history, they are all but invincible. More important, the suits function symbolically as exact extensions of the human body, which is thus directly involved in battlefield action, not distanced from the enemy by electronic devices. Although the MI depend on spaceships for travel and pickup, each man is personally responsible for his own suit, so that survival, even for a long period on his own, clearly depends on an individual's responsibility to himself.

Like the state, the Heinleinian individual is at his peak in a state of warfare, whether against enemy soldiers or the wilds of a "frontier" planet. Racial expansionism in either case is paralleled by the expansiveness of the individual, in this as in other Heinlein works. Among the earlier juvenile novels, *Space Cadet* (1948) was the prototype for this book's emphasis on how military discipline builds character, while *Farmer in the Sky* (1950) and *Tunnel in the Sky* (1965) both gave lessons in basic survival against natural enemies. *The Puppet Masters* (1951), an adult novel, posited a similar was against a "hive" mind, and *Beyond This Horizon* also stressed the advantages of a "volunteer" society and militia.

Most of Heinlein's novels are "success" stories, in which success hinges on mastery of oneself within the liberty allowed by the society, which must in turn maintain itself within the limits of a hostile universe. The big change in this book is a matter of presentation. Although characters lectured each other before, they did not speak quite so insistently with the voice of auctorial authority. And rarely did Heinlein show as much control over the form of this narrative; virtually everything in this book contributes to the overall effect of an emotional appeal to self-reliance. If the Heinleinian matrix were actually imposed on society, it might well lead to Fascism, but within the Utopian framework of his fiction, its libertarian ideals are vibrantly appealing.

David N. Samuelson

Sources for Further Study

Criticism:

Showalter, Dennis E. "Heinlein's *Starship Troopers*: An Exercise in Rehabilitation," in *Extrapolation*. XVI (1975), pp. 113-124. Heinlein's theme is
that rights must be based on responsibilities in a society.

Tucker, Frank H. "Major Political and Social Elements in Heinlein's Fiction,"
in *Robert A. Heinlein*. Edited by Joseph D. Olander and Martin H. Greenberg. New York: Taplinger, 1978, pp. 172-193. The social and political
themes dominate this work.

Reviews:

Analog. LXV, March, 1960, pp. 155-159.

Galaxy. XIX, October, 1960, pp. 145-146.

Kirkus Reviews. XXVII, October 15, 1959, p. 792.

New Worlds. CXVII, August, 1960, pp. 2-3.

New York Times Book Review. January 31, 1960, p. 32.

San Francisco Chronicle. November 8, 1959, p. 25.

SF Commentary. IV, July, 1969, p. 48.

Springfield Republican. November 15, 1969, p. 4D.

THE STOCHASTIC MAN

Author: Robert Silverberg (1936-   )
First book publication: 1975
Type of work: Novel
Time: Approximately 2000
Locale: New York City

Lew Nichols is drawn deeply into the lives of Paul Quinn, the future President, and Carvajal, a seer of future events, with crushing effects on Nichols' life

> Principal characters:
> LEW NICHOLS, a probabilist and stochastic technician
> SUNDARA NICHOLS, his wife
> PAUL QUINN, a politician
> MARTIN CARVAJAL, founder of the Center for Stochastic Processes
> and a seer

Creators of science fiction have freely used the physical and life sciences as a rich media of growth for their imaginations. If the work is not filled with projected technological engineering wonders of some future time, it will certainly deal with present physical or biological theories and their potential effects. Seldom does an author step into the realm of mathematics, and when that topic is broached, it is to discuss some application of a mathematical tool. It is, therefore, a rare and exciting treat to find a novel that has mathematical theory as its foundation. In the novel, *The Stochastic Man*, Robert Silverberg makes excellent use of the conflicting mathematical models used to describe the world as we perceive it.

There are presently two mathematical models of our physical surroundings. They are the deterministic model and the probabilistic or stochastic model. Determinism is the older of the two viewpoints and states that all events can be described by mathematical laws (for instance Newton's laws of motion). Armed with the correct set of equations and with the absolute knowledge of the state of a system at this moment, we could, according to this view, correctly predict the system's state for all future time. That is to say, using a correct set of mathematical statements or equations and starting with a handful of small marbles all resting quietly in one's hand, the motion of each marble could be described precisely from the time they are all dropped until they come to rest on the floor. Determinism is not far removed from the concept of predestination.

As one might guess, deterministic solutions of such problems are difficult and, at times, quite impossible. This difficulty leads to the probabilistic view of physical events. In this theory, the motion of the marbles or of, say, a molecule in a liter of water, is without deterministic laws. The motion is assumed to be as random as it appears. In this model, any change of direction of any one marble is as arbitrary as flipping a coin. It would appear that by adopting this view, one has given up describing the events mathematically.

However, there is predictable behavior here, not on any one change of direction or flip of the coin, but after many changes, we find certain predictable occurrences. The coin, for instance, will turn up heads about the same number of times as tails. It is the long-term observable trend which we call "stochastic" behavior. One may think of stochastic behavior as knowledge of future events through incomplete knowledge of the present. It is the ability to predict outcomes in random occurrences.

If determinism parallels predestination, one could look for a corresponding parallel to the stochastic view. A temptation is to choose an existential type of situational ethic, of complete freedom of action without governing laws. This would be more in line, however, with a type of randomness without stochastic behavior which is unlike any model used to describe observed events mathematically. A totally random universe would be the universe found by the dead Rosencrans and Guildenstern and would produce coins which were balanced, but would continue to yield heads on every flip.

In *The Stochastic Man*, Robert Silverberg is able to discuss each of these philosophies within the body of a well-told story. He personifies the viewpoints of determinism, stochastic behavior, and total randomness with main characters and discusses the effect of the philosophies based on the extremes of determinism and total randomness.

Lew Nichols, the stochastic man, lives in the New York of 1995. He is a probabilist, "a stochastic technician," and a projection consultant. For a large enough fee, he will tell clients whether "particle chips will continue to be a growth industry" or "whether it's a good idea to open a tattooing parlor in Topeka." He is right more often than wrong.

Nichols makes his projections based on the data gathered by a "platoon of hired gallups" (pollsters) only after having analyzed that data using probability theory. However, even with these sophisticated efforts, there seems to remain a measure of witchcraft in his leap from analysis to projection. Nichols possesses some unexplainable ability to make this step.

This talent or gift is making Nichols a wealthy man. He and his extraordinarily lovely wife, Sundara, live in New York City, which has become to the 1990's what Beirut was in the 1970's. Warring, armed boroughs have replaced the administrative units. Racial and idealogical groups turn against each other, transforming the city into a battleground. The two-group relationship between Lew and Sundara (two-, three-, or more-group contracts have replaced the traditional marriage concept) is loving, open, and sharing. They share each other in evenings with other groups, as happily as they share the powdered bone (a doped calcium) they smoke.

In the summer of 1995, Nichols meets Paul Quinn. Quinn (call me Paul) is a politician with enough ego and talent to elicit a Nichols' projection of a successful presidential bid for Quinn. With his compelling, hypnotic personality, Quinn wins people as easily as elections. Shortly after meeting Quinn,

Nichols agrees to allow his lucrative business to survive on its own while he works with Quinn's campaign team.

In 1997, with the help of Nichols' projections, Quinn moves easily from Albany to New York City as mayor of that troubled city. Plans are immediately drawn for the presidential elections of the year 2000. Nichols remains part of the Quinn team and ignores his more lucrative consulting firm for the ego-gratification he obtains through Quinn's political climb.

Late in March of 1999, Nichols is introduced to Martin Carvajal, "a faded-looking little man, fifty-five or sixty years old, a slight insignificant person with a narrow oval head sparsely thatched with short gray hair." Carvajal has contributed large sums of money to Quinn's campaigns. He became wealthy through speculation in the stock market. Some, however, feel his consistency is so great that the term speculation can no longer apply. At the end of their first meeting, Carvajal leaves a list of three suggested actions which Quinn should follow in the next few months. According to Carvajal, these actions will enhance Quinn's political future. As the months pass, Nichols realizes these suggestions were, in fact, accurate predictions.

This, of course, intrigues Nichols, who seeks Carvajal in his "small grimy flat in a squat dilapidated ninety-year-old apartment house just off Flatbush Avenue in deepest Godforsaken Brooklyn," an area of the city which had become beyond reclamation. Carvajal confides that he can, at his choosing, see future events. He sees the future as others remember the past.

At approximately the same time, Lew and Sundara meet Caraline Yarber, a Transit creed "proctor." Transit is a new religion of nonattachment, a system of thought which denies determinism and combines elements of Buddhism, Fascism, Zen, Tantra, Platonism, Gestalt therapy, and "Poundian economics." It denies the experience of a lifetime but points toward a continuation of this experience until finally finding release "from the wheel of karma" and reaching the "annihilation that is Nirvana." The main emphasis of this movement is transition to "unpredictable, even eccentric behavior."

Nichols' life now rapidly degenerates into total chaos. He is enticed by his own stochastic nature to follow Carvajal. He wishes to learn to see, as Carvajal, the future. Sundara is drawn by her heritage to follow the Transit creed. She is pulled into wild, mindless acts. Lew and Sundara divorce, and Lew gives himself completely to Carvajal. Carvajal promises to help Lew to see the future in exchange for Lew's complete obedience. Nichols is to follow Carvajal's commands no matter how unreasonable they may appear. These commands are based, after all, on what Carvajal has seen. The events are predetermined. The commands become more and more ludicrous and unpredictable.

Nichols is fired from Quinn's team, denounces Carvajal, and goes off alone to recover. During this rest period, he experiences a vision for the first time. He returns to Carvajal in time to fulfill Carvajal's own prophecies of his own death. Carvajal's millions are left to found the Center for Stochastic Processes; Nichols is designated as director. The goal of the Center is to build a brotherhood of "seers," "extending and refining the capabilities of . . . vision."

The novel starts with a fine statement of the distinction between the philosophy of determinism and randomness as applied to physical phenomenon. The Narrator recalls being seventeen and seeing the world as a "gigantic dice game, without purpose or pattern, into which we foolish mortals interpose the comforting notion of causality for the sake of supporting our precarious, fragile sanity." He is convinced that it is only important to live for the moment. But he later recognizes this attitude as adolescent, a defense against fear, and begins to accept the principle of cause and effect. However, he recognizes that one must transcend that principle and see "that many important phenomena refuse to be packed into neat causal packages but can be interpreted only by stochastic methods."

In contrast, Carvajal is the personification of determinism. He can see the future, and that future is totally determined, undeniable. No change in the predestined events will occur no matter how one may try to avoid them. If Carvajal sees Lew divorcing Sundara, then Lew will divorce Sundara. If Carvajal sees the rather conservative Lew shaving his head, then it will be shaved even though protested. "A paradox, then. From Carvajal's point of view his every action was guided by rigid deterministic criteria; but from the point of view of those around him, his behavior was as irresponsibly random as that of any lunatic."

Sundara, through her dedication to the Transit creed, becomes total randomness. Her every effort is to avoid prediction. She behaves without reason and explanation, "Her behavior was as wild, as unpredictable, as motiveless as Carvajal's"; but they were crazy randomness from opposite directions, Carvajal's behavior governed by blind obedience to an inexplicable revelation, Sundara's by the desire to break free of all pattern and structure.

Quinn appears as the stochastic middle. His actions cannot be determined day by day because he reacts as a politician must to the demands of the voters. So day by day his actions seem random. However, there is no doubt about Quinn's final destination. Everyone knows he will be president, some say he will be the nation's first elected dictator.

Silverberg agrees that determinism, with its unyielding knowledge of what must be, produces actions which are indistinguishable from actions of total randomness without stochastic laws. Both extremes are ultimately destructive. Silverberg takes a strong stand against philosophies based on either determinism or cynical randomness. His observation that both extremes lead to precisely the same destructive end is clever and delightful. The characters are thoughtfully developed with the exact purpose of separating the three possible models of our experience. Robert Silverberg has well established his ability with the more often encountered tools of science fiction. With *The Stochastic*

Man, he has exhibited the breadth of his knowledge and creativity by allowing mathematics, "The Queen of the Sciences," to move toward a position of royalty in science fiction.

Ray C. Shiflett

Sources for Further Study

Reviews:

Best Sellers. XXXV, December, 1975, p. 271.

Kirkus Reviews. XLIII, July 15, 1975, p. 805.

Library Journal. C, October 1, 1975, p. 1848.

New Statesman. XCI, June 18, 1976, p. 821.

Publisher's Weekly. CCVIII, August 4, 1975, p. 52.

Times Literary Supplement. July 30, 1976, p. 950.

THE STRANGE CASE OF DR. JEKYLL AND MR. HYDE

Author: Robert Louis Stevenson (1850-1894)
First book publication: 1886
Type of work: Novella
Time: The 1880's
Locale: London

Dr. Jekyll's transformation into the evil Mr. Hyde becomes a metaphor for man's divided nature

Principal characters:
    HENRY JEKYLL, a prominent London doctor
    UTTERSON, his friend and lawyer
    DR. LANYON, a skeptical colleague of Dr. Jekyll
    ENFIELD, a friend of Utterson, who first brings Hyde to his attention
    MR. HYDE, Henry Jekyll's alter ego

The Strange Case of Dr. Jekyll and Mr. Hyde, perhaps Robert Louis Stevenson's best-known story, is not one that the author himself particularly liked. It has been dramatized repeatedly: Richard Mansfield appeared in a stage version in 1887, the year after the novella's publication; there have been three films, starring John Barrymore (1920), Fredric March (1932), and Spencer Tracy (1941) in the title roles. There have also been two television productions: the version with Jack Palance (1968) was the most faithful of the adaptations, though it also incorporated a number of changes; and a musical version starred Kirk Douglas (1973). Unfortunately, it is the dramatizations which most people know and which have popularized the myth. In the original, for example, there are no women in Jekyll's life — or in Hyde's.

Stevenson was constantly aware, as were most Victorian writers, of the "war among the members," as Stevenson calls man's constant struggle between good and evil, made more difficult by society's refusal to acknowledge the existence of evil impulses in a "good" person, and of society's insistence on labeling anything to do with sexual impulses as evil. "The beast in Hyde," Stevenson wrote to John Paul Bocock on January 1, 1888, " . . . is the essence of cruelty and malice and selfishness and cowardice, and these are the diabolic in man — not this poor wish to love a woman, that they make such a cry about." So Stevenson, perhaps for this reason and certainly for dramatic effectiveness, keeps Hyde's evil unspecified.

The concept of the double, or the *Doppelgänger*, was a prevalent one in the nineteenth century. Victor Frankenstein and his creation are a subtle treatment of this theme, as are Cathy and Heathcliff in Emily Brontë's *Wuthering Heights* (1848). The expression of human duality, however, modulated from the Romantic concept of another person as the reflection of one's own nature, one's Platonic soul-mate, to more ambiguous treatments of the theme. In such works as James Hogg's *The Private Memoirs and Confessions of a Justified*

Sinner (1824), Melville's "Bartleby the Scrivener," Poe's "William Wilson," Conrad's *The Secret Sharer* (1912), and James's "The Jolly Corner," the duality becomes more somber and elusive, the other self becomes not soul-mate but a shadowy reflection of one's own unseen evil nature, of alternate or unknown lives. In *The Strange Case of Dr. Jekyll and Mr. Hyde*, and in Oscar Wilde's *The Picture of Dorian Gray* (1891), the consciousness of evil becomes unbearable, and the duality is not vague, surreal, supernatural, or subliminal, but an expression of the nature of evil itself. This evil nature then splits off as a separate entity: in the one, Mr. Hyde, and in the other, Dorian's portrait. Of course, in numerous Victorian novels there are characters representing polarities of human nature, from Thackeray's sardonically ambiguous portraits of Amelia and Becky to the vapid blond heroine and dark villainess of a thousand forgettable novels, but in Stevenson and Wilde, the two characters are one.

Wilde's novel is fantasy; the process by which Dorian's evil deeds are reflected in the portrait is never explained and no explanation is necessary. Stevenson's tale is quite different. Here, man is using his reason and his scientific expertise to isolate his evil nature, in the form of a drug, which, when mixed in solution and drunk, will change the human form from the good person to the evil one. And, as in many another work of science fiction, the process gets beyond control. What distinguishes Stevenson's work, and what has been most lost in the dramatizations, is his oblique method of telling the tale; his ironies and multiple interpretations are made possible by a succession of narrators and points of view, some of the narrative being in the first person and some in the third. Novella rather than short story, it is a very carefully constructed work.

So familiar has the basic plot become, that it is difficult to imagine its impact on a reader coming to it with no previous impressions. This is to be regretted, for Stevenson builds up mystery and almost unbearable suspense. Much of the narrative is told from the perspective of Utterson, a no-nonsense lawyer, austere with himself but tolerant of others' foibles. Inclined to "Cain's heresy," he is usually indifferent to the sins of others. First told about Hyde by a friend, he is disturbed to find Hyde's connection with his friend and client Henry Jekyll, all the more so because Hyde is named in Jekyll's will, a peculiar and "fanciful" document which offends the lawyer's sense of order and rationality. All is left to Hyde in the event of Jekyll's death or disappearance. Utterson is haunted by Enfield's description of Hyde, and has a vivid nightmare about him, in which he sees him as a human juggernaut moving through the city at night bent on some harm to Jekyll. Even Utterson has his fanciful and uncontrolled side, and Hyde is established as a hauntingly evil personality.

Briskly intent on clearing up the mystery, Utterson systematically searches for Hyde. He is concerned that Hyde may be blackmailing Jekyll, doubly so when, after the murder of Sir John Carew, he goes with the police to Hyde's lodgings and finds evidence of his connection with Jekyll. Confronting Jekyll, he demands the truth. Jekyll assures Utterson that he has done with Hyde, and

offers a letter from Hyde as evidence. Utterson, finding further that the letter
is possibly Jekyll's forgery, fears that Jekyll may indeed be more involved
than he is willing to admit. As Jekyll's behavior becomes more bizarre, Utterson's detachment begins to go, and after one last attempt at a rational explanation — that Jekyll must be suffering from an illness that has destroyed his
mind — he breaks down the door of Jekyll's laboratory, to find only the dead
body of Hyde. Suspense builds again as Utterson goes home to read the two
sealed documents which will solve the mystery, one from a close mutual
friend, Dr. Lanyon, and one from Jekyll himself. There he learns how and why
Dr. Henry Jekyll became Mr. Hyde.

Stevenson's use of multiple levels of narration provides suspense and irony;
his use of settings conveys the emotional content of the narrative, a counterpoint to Utterson's matter-of-fact character and the detachment of the third-
person narrator. The entrance to Jekyll's laboratory, seen from a side street, is
in a "certain sinister block of building." "About three o'clock of a bleak winter morning," Hyde, hurrying through "a part of town where there was literally nothing to be seen but lamps" brutally tramples a small child. When Utterson
first sees Hyde, the night is clear, cold, and clean; the city is unnaturally quiet,
with an air of expectation, and the sounds of Hyde's footsteps suddenly stand
out distinctly from the background. Soho, where Hyde lives, resembles the
scene of Utterson's nightmare, a district hidden by shifting and impenetrable
brown fog, broken only by a momentary and unpredictable light and by the
street lamps, necessary even by day. The fog is so dense that, as it envelops a
man, it cuts "him off from his blackguardly surroundings," a foreshadowing
of the transformation from Hyde to Jekyll. Hyde's rooms are furnished with a
luxury that is normal for Jekyll's residence but jarringly decadent in Hyde's
quarters, the retreat of a gentleman with a secret to conceal. Jekyll's chemistry
laboratory is the old anatomical theater, described in terms reminiscent of the
cadavers that once lay there, ill-kept, and lighted "dimly through the foggy
cupola."

Utterson retreats from the night and fog to his fireside and a glowing bottle
of wine, to clear his spirit of the fogs of London. But the wine itself is a
reminder that Jekyll, too, knows good wine and is a foreshadowing of Jekyll's
fatal draught, which, at first the "reddish hue" of wine, turns to a "watery
green." Hyde downs the potion in a proud combination of toast and challenge
to Lanyon. As Hyde, he toasts the dead Sir Danvers Carew, but as he turns
into Jekyll, he bursts into tears. And Poole, Jekyll's butler, offered a glass of
wine when he comes to fetch Utterson on the final night, leaves his glass
untouched.

He and Utterson go out into a windy, cold night, lit by a moon awry "as
though the wind had tilted her." As they break down the laboratory door, the
wind scatters the clouds that have concealed the moon. There is a moment's
suggestion of normality in the tough, well-made door, and the description of a

cozy room, with a fire and a table laid for tea, a room quiet and commonplace — except for the "glazed presses full of chemicals." Idyllic calm and an illusion of peace precede many of the appearances of Hyde, and this idyllic illusion is recapitulated in Jekyll's own description of his final transformation. On a "fine, clear January day" in Regent's Park, the air filled with the song of birds and the scent of spring, Jekyll, sitting peacefully and comfortably on a park bench, uncontrollably metamorphoses into Hyde.

Significantly, it is Jekyll's own complacent reflections, not the drug, that have caused the change. This time, he has been indulging his appetites in his own person, as he did before he discovered the drug. He is contemplating his excesses, "the animal within me licking the chops of memory," and thinking that after all, he does more good than other men, too. At the very moment he yields to this prideful throught, he is transformed back to Hyde.

From the beginning, Hyde is seen as demonic, a Satanic figure, and to the end Jekyll preserves the illusion of innocence common to those in the thrall of evil, the self-deception that only Hyde is guilty. In contrast, Utterson is a man who is "humbled to the dust by the many ill things he had done," a man who recognizes that "in the law of God, there is no statute of limitations." Hypocrisy, in *The Strange Case of Dr. Jekyll and Mr. Hyde*, repeatedly smooths over evil. Jekyll himself is hypocrite, doing what he calls good, but with a secret propensity to evil. Though Jekyll keeps saying that he is done with Hyde forever, he is tempted again and again. His terror after the murder of Sir Danvers Carew is a fear for his reputation, since he still holds Hyde solely responsible. Though he renews his charities and turns to religion, though he sees himself as "the chief of sinners" as well as "the chief of sufferers," he ultimately does not take full responsibility for the character of Hyde, and because he refuses to be responsible for his evil, he is doomed by it. Hyde, dead, does not turn back into Henry Jekyll; Hyde is a "self-destroyer" as Utterson says, but so, of course, is Jekyll. Even in his extremity, as he desperately seeks Lanyon's aid to turn back to Jekyll, his pride asserts itself. As he prepares the draught, he boasts of "a prodigy to stagger the unbelief of Satan," retaining his hubris about the experiment.

Jekyll's own narrative develops the themes of the spiritual nature opposed to material nature and of responsibility for the creation of Hyde. Before the experiment, Jekyll was "already committed to a profound duplicity of life." Claiming not to be a hypocrite — "both sides of me were in dead earnest" — he nevertheless is motivated by this very hypocrisy to experiment with a method of pursuing his excesses while keeping the façade of the good Henry Jekyll. He senses that there are two sides to man and speculates that man's personality may be even further fragmented. It is the dual nature of man, the sinful side of which is emphasized in the strict Calvinism with which Stevenson grew up, that colors the moral atmosphere of *The Strange Case of Dr. Jekyll and Mr. Hyde*.

In his first change into Hyde, Jekyll paradoxically experiences "an un-known but innocent freedom of the soul" even though he is "sold a slave to my original evil." At first, Hyde is not only a young man but physically weak; evil leaves its stamp in the form of a physical ugliness and repellence. As Hyde takes over more of Jekyll's personality, he becomes physically stronger. Yet, Jekyll embraces Hyde's development as natural. When he finds that he can no longer control this self, he repudiates it.

It is man's nature, and not science, which determines his use or misuse of scientific method. Jekyll realizes that if he had begun with higher aims, he might have split off and strengthened his good side. As it was, with the evil side split off and left to develop itself, the development can only be in the direction of evil. In sending Hyde out to perform his misdeeds, Jekyll assumes that he is "beyond the reach of fate." He soon finds that, with a common memory, Jekyll shares Hyde's evil, but Hyde does not share Jekyll's good. Though Jekyll at last chooses to go with his better nature, he does not have the strength. His motives are still mixed; he is trapped, and his final and irretriev-able fall occurs in the person of Henry Jekyll. He grows increasingly more detached from and repelled by his alter ego as the fate he had thought himself free of closes in inexorably. Hyde becomes "the creature" and "it"; "He, I say — I cannot say I," writes Jekyll in the last pages of his confession. De-spairing, Jekyll realizes to his horror that Hyde is caged within himself, a graphic and moving symbol of original sin. But to the last, Jekyll will not accept responsibility for his sinful side. When he ceases to be Henry Jekyll, all that follows "concerns another than myself."

Stevenson's tale is as powerful an exemplum as Chaucer's "Pardoner's Tale," but the various dramatizations and popularizations have by and large diminished its moral force. Stevenson's dead Hyde does not metamorphose into the "good" Dr. Jekyll, and there are no mourners to give him a final benediction. Stevenson's original is a study in damnation as compelling as any of the Calvinist sermons against which he rebelled.

Katharine M. Morsberger

Sources for Further Study

Criticism:

Aring, Charles D. "The Case Becomes Less Strange," in American *Scholar*. XXX (Winter, 1960-1961), pp. 67-78. Aring attempts to shed new light on various aspects of Stevenson's story.

Borowitz, Albert. *Innocence and Arsenic: Studies in Crime and Literature*. New York: Harper & Row, 1977, pp. 26-32. This critic examines the structure and theme of *The Strange Case of Dr. Jekyll and Mr. Hyde* as an example of a skillfully constructed mystery story.

Eigner, Edwin M. *Robert Louis Stevenson and Romantic Tradition*. Princeton, N.J.: Princeton University Press, 1966, pp. 143-164. Eigner compares Stevenson's writing to that of earlier romantic authors and notes the differences in techniques.

Keppler, C. F. *The Literature of the Second Self*. Tucson: University of Arizona Press, 1977, pp. 8-9. Keppler presents a brief psychological look at Dr. Jekyll.

Miyoshi, Masso. "Dr. Jekyll and the Emergence of Mr. Hyde," in *College English*. XXVII (1966), pp. 470-474, 479-480. The subtle literary techniques involved in the Jekyll-Hyde transformation are examined by Miyoshi.

Saposnik, Irving S. "The Anatomy of Dr. Jekyll and Mr. Hyde," in *Studies in English Literature, 1500-1900*. XI (1971), pp. 715-731. Saposnik presents a detailed character study of Jekyll and Hyde and the techniques involved in delineating them.

STRANGE RELATIONS

Author: Philip José Farmer (1918-   )
First book publication: 1960
Type of work: Thematically related short stories

   A grotesque, fantastic, and richly comic sequence of five short stories based on "family relationships"

   The five tales in this collection vary in length from a nine-thousand-word short story, "Daughter," to a rather expansive novella, "Father," which is three times that length. They were written originally for the science fiction magazines, though "Son" appeared first in *Argosy* as "Queen of the Deep." "Mother" and "My Sister's Brother" have also been included in major anthologies, and Farmer regards "My Sister's Brother" as his best and favorite work after the Hugo Award winner, "Riders of the Purple Wage."
   All the stories bear the names of family relationships and look to themes of incest and sexual taboo, as indicated by the title of the collection. But even beyond these clues, all of the tales have an obvious Freudian, psychoanalytical cast to them. Each of the human protagonists has deep personal problems and psychosexual maladjustments. Each is a definite psychological type, very realistically conceived and boldly presented for sexual frankness in the 1950's. With the exception of "Son," the tales move from a more or less explicitly psychosexual encounter with an alien life form, including weird sex acts, to rather systematic speculations on ecological themes. Highly influenced by Stanley Weinbaum's classic of 1934, "A Martian Odyssey," Farmer has always had a flair for portraying fascinating make-believe environments and populating them with strange animal and plant forms.
   Though it was first published in 1953, very little in the story of "Mother" seems dated, except perhaps for the obvious and deliberate portrayal of the central characters, human and alien alike, in terms of stereotypes of the 1950's. The human mother, Paula, is a domineering female scientist, cold, competent, and calculating. Her son, Eddie, is the classic overprotected child, recently divorced from his wife because his mother-fixation broke up the marriage. Eddie is dependent and infantile; his deepest wish-fulfillment is to be (s)mothered.
   Embarking on a scientific expedition simply to escape their problems, Paula and Eddie crash-land on the planet Baudelaire only to find themselves among a race of intelligent vegetables who exist only in the female sex and are completely sedentary in their adult phase. Males consist of any "mobile" life forms, and are captured when they wander into the vicinity by the powerful and manifold tentacles of the females. This accident happens to Eddie and Paula, each being captured by a different Mother.
   The deftness with which Farmer characterizes Mother Polyphema's maternal psychology and sexuality is masterful. Eddie lives inside the

stomach/womb of his Mother, is fed like her own sluglike babies on her own stew, becomes her mate (the sex act suggests rape and violence — to "impregnate" her Eddie has only to tear apart the tissues in the womb-spot in the wall), and he sucks at will on the "nipples" on the wall for drugs and chemicals.

Because Polyphema is so elementally maternal, Eddie comes to identify her as his real mother. Progressively, he adapts himself to his uterine environment (since he cannot escape anyway), and he transfers his allegiance from his human mother, who is captured and killed by the giant plant because she represents the threat of competition for Eddie's loyalty. Polyphema comes to regard Eddie as the perfect lover. He becomes progressively more childlike and by the end of the story has been altered by his dependent existence into a baby physically as well as psychologically. Yet, because of Eddie's mother-fixation, this retrogression to the womb is the perfect happy ending. He has everything he wants for his body and psyche, so does Mother, and the fable ends on a deeply ironic awareness that it has all been a sly satire of the love story.

According to a legend circulated popularly among his fans, the sequel to "Mother" was eagerly awaited, only for Farmer to play a trick on his readers as he has done so often in his career. Though an honest sequel, "Daughter" is also mainly a literary joke. The tale is a not-very-disguised retelling of "The Three Little Pigs," embellished with a number of puns in pig Latin to reinforce the humorous message; the alien carnivore who kills and devours Mothers, for example, is called the "olfway." Father Eddie communicates with his Daughters via a language called "Orsemay," and the last line of the story is "The Wolf and the Three Little Pigs" rendered in pig Latin.

As in the previous story, the descriptions of the Mothers' biology, as well as the olfway's, are fascinating and show off Farmer's skill in portraying the interaction of life forms that have never existed and never will, but whose elemental relations (eating, procreating) strike some subconscious, archetypal resonance in his readers. Whereas two sisters perish because they are thoughtless, vegetative "bubble-heads" (again the satire on 1950's types), Daughter is a highly adaptable organism who adds to her Mother powers the scientific principles of biology and chemistry which she had learned from her human father. She alters her body structure to better protect her brain from the enemy, and is able to destroy the olfway in an acid of her own devising. Daughter has also learned to think imaginatively from Father's "no-so" stories, that is, from make-believe tales, one of which is specified as "The Three Little Pigs." Thus, the tale circles back, paradoxically and self-consciously, on its own fictional origins, and comments on the necessity for the creative interaction of science and imagination in a manner at once serious and flippant.

"Father" is an outstanding psychoreligious fable based on a common science fiction theme, "encounter with an alien god." On another planet in the same universe as that depicted in the preceding two stories lives an alien being with the godlike powers to turn his world into a perfect paradise for all living creatures. Father arrived from another location ten thousand years ago and has not changed his new world since; nothing has been born, because nothing dies without being reborn, for Father controls resurrection as a superscientific biological process still beyond mankind's control. Although nothing is born or really dies, it is an interesting Freudian touch that all the animal forms are now female. Father is the only male until he causes some Earthmen to crash-land there; he need a replacement caretaker for this world so he can travel to another. Father is, in fact, an evil deity because he feeds off his all-powerful capacity to play god, to make reality perfect and undying for inferior species. And like some cosmic vampire, he needs new worlds on which to feed.

With the convincing portrayal of Bishop André, Father's intended replacement, a special psychological dimension is added to the story. In many works, Farmer has analyzed the psychosexual problems caused by an overzealous religious upbringing (the hero of *The Lovers*, Sarvant in *Flesh*). Bishop André was beaten by his overly strict father and forced to be the perfect young Catholic. Now the influential churchman has impossible standards of moral perfection, purity, and self-control. There are many similarities between the Bishop's and Father's obsessions with perfection and control.

However, not every Christian is a neurotic-become-suicide like the Bishop. "Father" has a third major character, Father John Carmody, a sort of Friar Tuck figure who is the likable, and very human hero of several other tales. One is always aware that Carmody lucks out because he is superlatively human, not because he is a priest. There is always a danger the Bishop will abandon his fellow humans to take on the powers and responsibility of the alien Father because of his traumatic psychic and family history. André needs to be perfect, to be god in fact, to satisfy the childhood demands of his real father to be perfect and never commit a sin. With John, there is never any such danger; it is only a matter of time and energy before the wily priest will figure out the truly deceitful nature of the alien superbeing. In some ways, Farmer has merely worked out a Freudian formula which proposes that our first gods are our parents. Indeed, the alien god's powers are so great on his world that he is as far above his subjects, the stranded humans included, as a parent is above a small child. The conflict with such an authoritative figure leaves André seemingly no way out except suicide. He wants to make sure that he will not be manipulated psychologically to do the god's bidding. Yet even here, John Carmody generously defends his friend's motives and views him as a heroic martyr.

"Son" is in many ways the converse of "Mother." It is set during an imaginary flare-up of the Cold War. A Russian submarine torpedoes an American ocean liner in the Pacific and captures one survivor named Jones. Like Eddie in the earlier tale, this male hero is mother-dependent and has failed in his marriage. However, Jones's brief encounter turns out differently. Though equipped with sophisticated artificial intelligence and able to project a domineering Mother-personality to keep her victim under control, the submarine is involved with the human only in a psychological drama, strictly at the level of a personality conflict. Unlike the other four tales, "Son" explores no biological or sexual dimensions. Ultimately the hero breaks away from the submarine's influence, sabotages her machinery, and is "reborn" after his sojourn in her belly (verbal images of the inner space of the sub as both womb and tomb abound); Jones emerges a mature adult able to cope with the problems of life and marital love. Unlike Eddie's submergence and regression into the elemental and instinctual, Jones's fable is a male maturation myth, and the hero emerges both literally (the hero finds himself on the ocean's surface after he defeats her) and figuratively (he is no longer a mother's boy).

The last tale, "My Sister's Brother," is one of Farmer's best, especially in its unique and remarkable description of an alien sex act which is at once oral and phallic. This story takes place on Mars and shares with its Weinbaumian predecessor *(A Martian Odyssey)* an ecological approach to the description of Mars. Starting with an explanation of the famous Martian canals, Farmer portrays strange giant plant forms, a complex subterranean hive-society peopled by insectlike decapods whose multiforms (larvae, pupae, several kinds of worker adults, fertile male and female forms) are responsible for all the food, atmosphere, and water systems on the planet. The life-support system of the whole planet, in fact, is envisioned by Farmer as one complex but interrelated series of plants, decapods, and hives. The male decapod is one of the fascinating creatures in the system; he is so violent and anarchic that he is used strictly for sexual purposes and must be kept securely caged.

However, the most remarkable being of all is the heroine Martia, who is an explorer-scientist from another star system and is therefore as much a stranger to Mars as Lane, her human counterpart. She belongs to a race of humanoid aliens who are all females. They make love by exchanging their wormlike larvae, which ensures genetic exchange. Being both fetus and phallus, the larva performs what amounts to oral intercourse during sexual intercourse (since these aliens have only one orifice — the mouth — which must serve many purposes). Isolated with a human male, Lane, in the strange, hostile world of Mars, Martia offers to share with Lane the sexual act of her species. Ridden with fanatic Christian neuroses, he finds it repulsive and responds by killing the larva. Yet Martia forgives Lane, and the story is gentler and less satirical in tone than "Mother." If "My Sister's Brother" is an exposé of the violent *machismo* that underlies the purportedly "rational" values of our culture, it is no less a moving story of a love that might have been, based on a well-realized but totally different biological and psychosexual principle than our own.

For almost thirty years Farmer has justly been regarded as a pioneer writer who has helped science fiction achieve a new level of realism and maturity in dealing with human sexuality. Even today, some twenty-five years after the first appearance of the earliest of these stories, their combination of psychological realism, speculative sexuality, and sly social satire make them still seem provocative and contemporary.

S. C. Fredericks

Sources for Further Study

Reviews:

Amazing Stories. XXXIV, September, 1960, pp. 135-136.

Analog. LXVI, January, 1961, pp. 163-165.

Books and Bookmen. XII, December, 1966, p. 60.

Worlds of If. X, September, 1960, p. 88.

STRANGER IN A STRANGE LAND

Author: Robert A. Heinlein (1907-   )
First book publication: 1961
Type of work: Novel
Time: The early twenty-first century
Locale: Earth (area once known as the United States), Mars, and "Heaven"

A satirical view of human behavior observed by and involving the first human being born on Mars, who returns to Earth to claim his birthright; he founds a church which combines both of his upbringings and which results in his martyrdom

Principal characters:
>VALENTINE MICHAEL SMITH, the Man from Mars, "archangel Michael"
>JUBAL HARSHAW, a doctor, lawyer, and hack writer who unofficially adopts Michael
>GILLIAM BOARDMAN, a nurse, then Michael's lover and chief apostle
>BEN CAXTON, a newsman who helps rescue Michael from hospital isolation

Stranger in a Strange Land is a curious book which marked the shift in Robert Heinlein's fiction away from the extrapolative, mimetic mode he had helped to develop, toward the querulous philosophizing and garrulous cuteness of his later novels. Though critics might carp, the move proved commercially successful. As social upheavals in the 1960's led to revaluations of life and literature, social organization, and science fiction, *Stranger in a Strange Land* itself became an underground classic, the first "best seller" to emerge from the science fiction genre.

Perhaps more complicated than complex, the novel depends at least partly for its effect on readers' fastening on to one of its contradictory strands to the neglect of others. While commentary within the book seems to make it "about" any number of things, the central concerns are the conduct of life and the establishment of general authority. Thus the framework of the narrative is the age-old myth of the dying god, on which are strung at least three familiar subsidiary storylines.

The strand which introduces the book is the cops-and-robbers adventure story, with science fiction gimmicks of the 1930's and 1940's (aerocabs, videophones, programed kitchens) constructing a "nostalgic" future. Smith, orphaned child of *three* parents from an ill-fated expedition to Mars, where he was reared by the Martians, is returned to Earth and held in protective custody by the world government. Risking their jobs and lives, Ben Caxton and Gilliam (called Jill) Boardman spirit him away to the mountain hideaway of Jubal Harshaw, who engineers Smith's freedom and begins the task of educating him in human customs.

The second strand is the *Bildungsroman*, the novel of education or development, which takes Mike from social childhood to maturity as he learns about people, laws, customs, money, love, manipulations, religion, and, finally, laughter. Strand three, developed simultaneously, is a satire of human customs, with special relevance to the mid-twentieth century as seen in futuristic guise from the alternating vantage points of Mike and Jubal, each of whom has some claim to be the novel's title character.

The dominant thread, however, is the myth of the dying and resurrected god, surrounded by attendant apparatus. Beginning "Once upon a time" in traditional fairy-tale fashion, the book presents a reworking of the mythical hero: orphaned in infancy and reared by strangers, he is brought back to his rightful kingdom, where he makes peace with his "father," wins the hand of more than one fairy princess, begins to reorganize society, hands down codes of behavior, and prepares for his martyrdom. His adopted father, Jubal, is his toughest convert, but once he has been won over by Michael's self-sacrificing and the efficacy of his teachings, he turns to spreading the gospel by writing a book of roughly the same scope as this one.

Smith's teachings of the Martian language and the magical-mystical powers of the mind it unlocks are sold to the public in the guise of religion, since churches are relatively free from regulation and public censure. In its carnival-like presentations, Mike's church takes its teachings from Jubal's writings and from Mike's life on his own after leaving the safety of Jubal's roof, but it is clearly a delicious parody of mass-marketed Christianity, the Church of the New Revelation (Fosterite). Although Fosterites are burlesqued in Heinlein's presentation, Jubal recognizes their legitimacy as a church which brings about the happiness it promises. Mike's Church of All Worlds promises — and delivers — even more, and is always treated with respect in the narrative.

Although its teachings are supposedly rooted in Martian language concepts, they are very close to literal readings of various human scriptural injunctions. "Waiting is," "I am only an egg" and "grokking to fullness" have the qualities of Eastern wisdom to them, for they are alleged to belong to a long-lived, egg-laying, ghost-dominated, alien race. However, taking literally such Christian commandments as "love one another" and "this is my body; take and eat" leads to consequences which would not have pleased the Church Fathers, much less their cultural descendants. Love and sex are shared in common by members of the church's inner circle; rather than "waste food," moreover, the friends of someone who has departed (such as Mike at the end of the novel) practice ritual cannibalism.

Central to the religion is the verb "to grok," which gained wide currency in the 1960's. Literally it means "to know, completely, holistically," which has traditional mystical associations that Heinlein made use of earlier in his career. Knowing completely, however, seems to mean to know the divine presence in someone else, and in yourself, so that he finally translates the term as "Thou Art God," another catch-phrase made popular by the novel. Assuming such divinity, moreover, gives one the ability to sense good or evil, as ultimates, in a thing or another person and even the right or the obligation to rid the world of that in which one "groks wrongness."

This is the most controversial of Smith's teachings, especially in terms of its effects on the real world of the novel's audience. Granted that in the story Mike is superhuman, perhaps even an angel granted that in the text death is not an ending, but rather a shift or translation to another plane of existence. However, the perfection of his followers, in both the novel and its audience, may be in doubt. They are left with the possibility of actions followed by bloody consequences without the assurance of a comic Heaven offstage. There have been, in fact, followers of the book's purported teachings for whom free love, "water sharing," and even ritual killing have seemed justified. Also, there were fascinated readers in the younger generation for whom this wish-fulfillment fantasy was at least a vicarious answer to a society which demanded their sacrifice in an Asian land war, which opposed their protests against that war, and which tolerated assassinations of political leaders who might have stopped it.

A scriptural acceptance of the novel, however, disregards the strands of parody and satire, the ironic distance between Mike and Jubal and the narrator, and the libertarian patriotism of the author. Since so much is mocked in the novel, and the tone toward Mike's church is almost reverent, it is relatively easy to forget the difficulty such a church would face in the real world — without a fabulously rich "angel" as its founder and patron saint. Even though Jubal becomes a reluctant convert after Mike's martyrdom and apparent spiritual resurrection, Jubal's strictures against organized religion, his sense that this religion is fit only for angels, and his dissatisfaction with the humorlessness of church members all operate to undercut the literal acceptance of Mike's teachings, even within the text.

Outside the text, it should be obvious that there are no Martians, nor is there a bureaucratic Heaven where Fosterite "Archangels" (Church leaders) and Mike himself go after they "discorporate." Furthermore, since the book was written well before the assassination of John F. Kennedy and subsequent massive involvement in Vietnam, its political relevance to the 1960's can be at most that of a parable. And though the author might oppose the draft on libertarian principle, he also opposed pacifism, refusal to fight for one's country, and the kind of organized resistance to "legitimate" authority to which the reading of this book became linked.

Despite Heinlein's attempts to disassociate himself from what the book appeared to stand for, *Stranger in a Strange Land* is a very personal novel. Its structural concern, like those of Heinlein's "juvenile" novels with adolescent heroes, is with education for the proper conduct of life. Like its predecessors, it has two versions of the Heinleinian "competent man," an older and putatively wiser one in Jubal, a younger and supremely gifted one in Mike. But whereas the relationship between the two types was once straightforward, here it is fraught with difficulties. Jubal begins as Mike's mentor, the traditional adviser of hero myths and Heinlein juveniles. But the teacher becomes the pupil at the end; having done his part to create Mike, he is taken over by his creation despite his own skeptical rationality.

The significance of this structural reversal lies in the character of Jubal and his relationship to the author. Whereas in earlier books the focus was on the hero of the action, here the focus is dual. As the archetypal hero, Mike is the story, so to speak. However, Jubal is who it happens to, the major viewpoint character, who reacts to and rationalizes the actions of the Man from Mars. Although there is also an omniscient narrator, Jubal is implicitly the teller of the tale even before he begins to dictate his version at the end.

Jubal parallels Heinlein in a number of ways. He is a writer who revels in his commercial success. He is supremely competent — we are told. He is opinionated about everything, often iconoclastically. For the most part he is an unregenerate individualist. He was also born about the same year as his creator. Other parallels are more conjectural. Jubal is an intellectual who has learned to manipulate, rather than change his society. And he is a victim of *anomie*, rootless, lacking social norms and values, accepting only empirical evidence, and wanting something to believe in.

Michael gives him something to believe in, and Jubal accepts it in the end, but only after a long struggle. Mike's religion requires total commitment, up to and including death, which goes against the grain of Jubal's commitment — and Heinlein's — to the individual ego. For Jubal, as a writer, is a natural solipsist, recognizing his own free will, but not that of his characters or, in practice, that of his employees. Heinlein similarly has trouble breathing life into characters who do not fit his mold of the "competent man," and has shown his fascination with the theme of solipsism in other stories as well as this one.

Reading Heinlein into Jubal gives us a sense of the author's struggle for control of this novel. Knowing his own creative participation, like Jubal's in the forming of Mike, he is led by it to a directive contrary to his own survival as controlling consciousness. A drive to reassert control can then be posited in the mocking openings of chapters told from the long view of the omniscient narrator, the Martians, or the figures in Heaven, which essentially disestablish any ground level of reality, and set the reader free to choose his own.

Such a process might explain, if not excuse, some of the aesthetic failures in the book, such as its vacillating tone, its arbitrary changes of viewpoint, and its indeterminate position on the message that it carries. It suggests, too, why subsidiary characters, even ones as important as Ben and Jill, may not be believable human beings: they are not real to begin with in Heinlein's imagination, so they can simply serve several plot functions for the sake of narrative economy.

But the strength of the story and of the metastory — that subtext of who is to be master, author or material — certainly surmounts many of these problems for the reader who is caught up in the same problem as Heinlein was, of why life is worth living. If one does not accept the essentially authoritarian answer represented by Valentine Michael Smith, there is still plenty of entertainment in the chase, in the satire, and in the longing for omnipotence and omniscience which the book at least partly satisfies on a vicarious level.

David N. Samuelson

Sources for Further Study

Criticism:

Cansler, Ronald L. "*Stranger in a Strange Land*: Science Fiction as Literature of Creative Imagination, Social Criticism, and Entertainment," in *Journal of Popular Culture*. V (Spring, 1972), pp. 944-954. Cansler discusses *Stranger in a Strange Land* as an example of changing cultures.

Christopher, Joe R. "Lazarus, Come Forth from that Tomb," in *Riverside Quarterly*. XXIII (August, 1975), pp. 190-197. Christopher concentrates on the structure of Heinlein's work.

McNelly, Willis E. "Linguistic Relativity in Old High Martian," in *CEA Critic*. XXX (March, 1968), pp. 4-6. McNelly explores the pervasive religious theme of *Stranger in a Strange Land*.

Plank, Robert. "Omnipotent Cannibals in *Stranger in a Strange Land*," in *Robert A. Heinlein*. Edited by Joseph D. Olander and Martin H. Greenberg. New York: Taplinger, 1978, pp. 83-106. Plank calls *Stranger in a Strange Land* "innovative," but not Heinlein's best work in this analysis of the novel.

Slusser. George E. *Robert A. Heinlein: Stranger in His Own Land*. San Bernardino, Calif.: Borgo, 1976, pp. 17-33. Slusser discusses Heinlein's use of personal power in *Stranger in a Strange Land*.

Reviews:

Amazing Stories. XXXV, December, 1961, pp. 130-131.

Analog. LXVIII, January, 1962, pp. 159-162.

Booklist. LVII, July 15, 1961, p. 695.

Galaxy. XX, June, 1962, pp. 193-194.

Kirkus Reviews. XXIX, June 1, 1961, p. 473.

Magazine of Fantasy and Science Fiction. XXI, November, 1961, pp. 77-79.

New Worlds. CLV, October, 1965, p. 124.

New York Times Book Review. August 4, 1961, p. 19.

THE SWORD OF RHIANNON

Author: Leigh Brackett (1915-1978)
First book publication: 1953
Type of work: Novel
Time: The near future, and one million years in the past
Locale: Mars

Bearing the mythic sword of Rhiannon, Matt Carse is cast one million years into the Martian past to work out both his own fate and that of Rhiannon, the ancient "Cursed One"

Principal characters:
> MATT CARSE, a well-respected archaeolgist turned renegade and grave robber
> BOGHAZ HOI, an ancient Martian thief of Valkis, companion and ally of Carse
> LADY YWAIN, an ancient Martian princess of Sark, first the adversary and then the beloved of Carse
> RHIANNON, an extremely ancient Martian, known as the "Cursed One" because he gave knowledge and power to lesser Martians

The Sword of Rhiannon is very nearly a paradigm of much of Leigh Brackett's romance-adventure science fiction. Were it not for the mythic elements embodied in the story and the resonance of the major characters and incidents, one might be tempted to categorize the work as "space opera." But the elements of familiar myths are interwoven in original ways and, given the brevity of the novel, the sometimes stereotypal main characters ring true. So, although the work requires a fairly strong "suspension of disbelief" and certainly has enough swashbuckling action, it transcends the limits of "space opera."

There are five attributes which, together, make *The Sword of Rhiannon* a significant work of literature in addition to a well told story. One is the fine construction of the narrative; Brackett's prose is subtly rich in connotation, so that the brevity of the book results in neither a thin plot with sketchy characters nor a series of telegraphic sentences the meaning of which must remain simple and superficial. The narration is utterly to the point, with no disgressions to complicate the plot; what is told is told fully if briefly.

The simplicity of plot and verbal economy result in evocative glimpses of various alien life forms and also in a peculiar variation on the kind of character Brackett seems to prefer in her adventure-narratives. In *The Sword of Rhiannon*, readers discover a number of races which evolved independently on Mars: the native human Martians found in many of Brackett's stories about the Low Canals; the half-human, half-serpentine Dhuvians who become extinct by the end of the tale; the half-human, half-seallike Swimmers who must be the prototypes of the "children of the sea" in the *Ginger Star* trilogy; and the half-human, half-avian Sky Folk who also appear, somewhat changed, in that more recent longer work. Within the world created by *The Sword of Rhiannon*, these halfling races are interesting because they postulate, on Brackett's Mars, a theory of independent evolutions to sapient life and because they reveal the richness of Brackett's imagination.

Most of Brackett's readers are familiar with Eric John Stark, the son of Earthborn human parents orphaned very young and then reared by the non-human natives of Mercury's twilight belt, finally to become a renegade mercenary with his feral upbringing almost always in conflict with the patina of civilization that is his heritage as a man. Brackett wrote about Stark before she created Matt Carse, but it is apparent that Carse is a variation on Stark, differing from him primarily because of the demands of *The Sword of Rhiannon*. Carse is, if compared to Stark, a bit too civilized (though "the primal ape" in him comes to the surface more than once); but because *The Sword of Rhiannon* tells of an archaeologist's dream as well as an adventurer's, the narrative requires a protagonist with a formal education and some success in the discipline of archaeology, for only an archaeologist could recognize the authenticity of the sword of Rhiannon, its inestimable value, and his own subconscious wish to go, literally, back into the past he has studied and imagined.

In addition to a strong, intelligent, resourceful hero, a tight narrative construction, and a number of evocative characterizations, *The Sword of Rhiannon* has a fourth literary attribute, its setting, which makes the book a notable one. Implicit in most of Brackett's fictions about Mars is a long and mysterious past (with great cities and kingdoms the ruins of which make grave-robbing a pursuit of the avaricious and not only the activity of ghouls). The Mars of the not-too-distant future — where the beginning and end of *The Sword of Rhiannon* are set — is an incredibly ancient and still-dying world, where the vertical succession of seaport ruins attests to the inexorable evaporation of a great body of water. All that is left is a vast arid depression, some few canals the only remnants of a great sea, and decadent Martian towns — Jekkara, Valkis, Barrakesh — still clinging to life and old ways next to the black waters of the Low Canals. Brackett's *The Secret of Sinharat* reveals the ability of some of the very ancient Martians to perpetuate their individual lives by transferring their life-essences to younger "hosts" when their most recent bodies grow too old and frail. What *The Sword of Rhiannon* adds to this familiar Mars is a vicarious experience of its past; when Matt Carse first scrambles out of the tomb of Rhiannon he knows, because of his archaeological background and the evidence of his senses, that he has somehow traveled back to a warm, moist, green, fertile Mars that could not have existed fewer than a million years before his birth.

The first ten pages of the novel establish the setting as Brackett's familiar Mars: late at night in the dark streets of Jekkara, Matt Carse hears someone following him and allows his pursuer, an unsuccessful grave-robber of Barrakesh, to fall into his ambush in a deserted part of the Low Canal town. When Carse forces Penkawr to take him to the treasure that the little native Martian claims to have discovered, the two make their way into the higher, older part of Jekkara — the long-abandoned seaport — and the setting itself foretells Carse's journey into the past. Seeing the treasure that Penkawr has hidden in the ruins, Carse immediately realizes that the sword is the sword of Rhiannon and that Penkawr has discovered the tomb which many believe to be mere legend; Carse demands a two-thirds share of the profits and Penkawr, angry at the Earthman's arrogance but well aware of Carse's ability to sell artifacts at higher prices than a Low Canal thief, grudgingly agrees to the terms of the partnership.

The influence of setting on plot becomes more apparent when the two arrive at Rhiannon's tomb. Inside, surrounded by artifacts as well-preserved as they are ancient, Carse seems to fall into a trance of archaeological awe. Penkawr takes advantage of the other's inattention, and pushes Carse into a black sphere of nothingness in the actual burial chamber. Helplessly, feeling confusion, disorientation, and some strange probings that seek to force their way into his conscious mind, Carse sinks into what must be a bubble in time; when he emerges from it, still holding the sword that lured him, Carse digs his way out of the tomb and looks out upon the setting of his real adventures, out upon a strangely transformed Mars.

It is the Mars of an archaelogist's dream: greenery surrounds him, the breeze is moist and warm, and the port of Jekkara gleams on the edge of a great sea. Matt Carse has traveled a million years into the past.

Throughout the remainder of the story, this ancient Mars determines most of the strictly arranged incidents of the plot at the same time that it explains away most of the mystery that seems to shroud the Mars of Brackett's more usual temporal settings. What happens is simple enough: Carse makes his way to Jekkara, becomes entangled with Boghaz Hoi of Valkis, and becomes with Boghaz a galley slave on a ship of the Lady Ywain, princess of Sark. Expectedly enough for a Brackett hero, Carse then kills the Dhuvian who was Ywain's chief protection, leads a successful mutiny, and, keeping Ywain as prisoner, heads the vessel west to the home of the Sea Kings of Khondor. There he meets Emer, sister of the ruler of the Khonds, a young woman who spends much time with Swimmers and Sky Folk and who (perhaps because of this association) telepathically detects a trace of Rhiannon in the recesses of Carse's mind. The plan Carse proposed — to go to the tomb of Rhiannon and bring its treasures to Khondor — fails and, because a group-entry into Carse's mind reveals that he does indeed harbor the spirit of Rhiannon the Evil One, Carse is condemned to die and plans are laid for a mass attack by the Sea Kings upon Sark. But trusty Boghaz the master-thief brings Carse the sword of Rhiannon and they escape, taking Ywain with them, just before the news of Carse's "possession" and its threat becomes universal knowledge among the Khonds.

While imprisoned and awaiting his death, Carse permits Rhiannon to communicate with him. He learns that the ancient spirit had been waiting more than a million years to undo his sin, that he cannot except with Carse's consent wholly possess the Earthman's person, and that Rhiannon is the one guise under which Carse may hope to obtain his freedom. So Ywain, Boghaz, Carse, and the non-Khond oarsmen of the Sark vessel leave Khondor; closely pursued by the fleet of the Sea Kings, they barely make it to Sark; once there, with Carse pretending to be Rhiannon reincarnated, they take Ywain's father and go to Caer Dhu so that Rhiannon may reclaim the miraculous technology he gave the Dhuvians. At precisely the crucial instant, Rhiannon does take charge of Carse's being (the Dhuvians knew what Carse did not: that the halflings of Caer Dhu had turned against their benefactor and used his weapons against him), and destroys Caer Dhu and all its inhabitants. In a moment of panic, Ywain's father runs into the field of Rhiannon's weapon, dies, and leaves Ywain the ruler of Sark. But neither she nor her people want her to rule, so, after letting Boghaz use his part in the destruction of the Dhuvians to set himself up as king of Valkis, Carse-Rhiannon and Ywain return to Rhiannon's tomb. They witness the return of the Quiru and the liberation of Rhiannon; they step into the bubble of time, guided by a grateful Rhiannon, and step out into the Mars of Carse's lifetime. Carse has Rhiannon's sword and the woman whose courage never failed her, and Ywain has the man she desires and a world, though now dying, that is still her own.

The story as related here is clearly melodramatic, and so would the book be, if its plot were its dominant feature. But *The Sword of Rhiannon* is more than melodrama: even the plot is structured carefully around Rhiannon and his sword, and two other attributes — its use of mythic elements and its evident influence on subsequent science fiction — raise the novel well above the level of "space opera."

After a superficial reading, one cannot help recognizing the Prometheus myth: rebellious Rhiannon gives to the Dhuvians knowledge and power against the wishes of his fellow Quiru, and for his act is imprisoned alive in a time-defying tomb. Then there is the *Prometheus Unbound* analogy, since Rhiannon does in the end obtain both the forgiveness of the other Quiru and the freedom to join them as an equal. The Dhuvians are quite literally the children of the snake, and not much imagination is needed to connect them with the serpent of Eden. Once this connection is made, Rhiannon's godlike qualities make him into a type of Lucifer, though his return to temporal Mars in order to set things aright once more is reminiscent of the harrowing of Hell. If one seeks meaning from these mythic elements by supposing there to be a one-to-one relation between each myth and *The Sword of Rhiannon*, one will find only confusion. What is notable about the novel is Brackett's use of various myths for artistic reasons — and results — of her own.

At one level, Rhiannon is Prometheus, but he is "bound" by his fellow Quiru and his own mistake in judgment (a tragic character), and "unbound" by his sincere repentance and the will of an Earthman (a comic character in the sense that a comic plot is resolved by reintegration with one's society). That the comic and tragic *mythoi* coexist in *The Sword of Rhiannon* is evidence that Brackett refuses, thematically, to accept and then depict a fictional world wherein good and evil are as simplistically separable as black and white. This thematic ambivalence is also apparent in Brackett's depiction of the Dhuvian halflings; they are children of the serpent, true, but they are the ones who are tempted and succumb — they are hardly, even in their dealings with Sark, Tempters in their own right. If Mars under Dhuvian rule is analogous to some sort of Hell, then the dual-natured Carse-Rhiannon who restores the world to the peoples of good will is analogous to the divine-and-yet-human Christ who released all those souls from the Hell to which only their Original Sin of being human condemned them. As for Lucifer, Rhiannon is his antitype, because his *"Non serviam"* is directed to the luminous Quiru: he disobeys precisely in order to do service to the lesser beings of Mars. And once the technological nature of his service is recognized, a more modern myth appears: "technology without good will and wisdom is a tool of destruction."

Recognizing these mythic elements in *The Sword of Rhiannon*, yet refusing to be detailedly exegetical about them, one can still appreciate Brackett's use of myth. For one thing, she makes each element of myth — not each myth itself and in its entirety — serve its purpose in her narrative. For another, she captures the subconscious attention of her readers by providing characters and incidents very closely related to the psychological truths, the veracity of which are (in Western cultures) universally accepted. Thus, *The Sword of Rhiannon* is at its surface a fast-paced entertaining narrative of adventure and is at its deeper thematic levels a narrative that compels readers' attention because it addresses itself to matters important to the subconscious parts of their minds. In such a thin volume, Brackett's words seem to do a great deal.

A final noteworthy attribute of *The Sword of Rhiannon* is its influence, both on Brackett's subsequent works and on the works of others. Thematically, the destruction of Caer Dhu and the consequent waning of Sark suggest the truth that, though good may conquer evil, some of the good must be lost even in victory (this is the same truth that pervades *The Lord of the Rings*: though Sauron is defeated, Middle Earth must pass away). In the context of Brackett's other Martian fiction, the destruction of Caer Dhu explains the decadence of "modern" Mars. Having the technology of Rhiannon for ages and controlling the empire of Sark, the Dhuvians kept the rest of Mars from developing its own technology; once the Dhuvians were annihilated, the other peoples of Mars had to fall back on their static ways, and these ways were insufficient to cope with the inexorable changes — like the evaporation of the sea — that, for want of intelligent intervention, ground Martian civilization down to the level of the Low Canals. So, *The Sword of Rhiannon* is the distant background in Brackett's other Martian tales.

The cohabitation of one body by two minds (when Carse is literally at the command of Rhiannon within him) and the prevalence of telepathy and other psychic powers (always by the agency of some jewel) would not seem so notable if Marion Zimmer Bradley's *Darkover* novels did not rely so heavily on what is suggested in *The Sword of Rhiannon*. Bradley's Darkovan telepaths each have a matrix jewel or starstone to focus and amplify their psychic powers, and it is a common Darkovan practice to embed a matrix jewel in the hilt of a sword. With just these two facts in mind, it is difficult not to remember the several mentions of a smoky jewel, almost with a life of its own, in the hilt of Rhiannon's sword. It is equally difficult to perceive the incident in which Emer, using her black pearl like a Darkovan telepath, first discerns the presence of Rhiannon within Carse as inconsequential. And when she and six of the wise ones (three Swimmers, three Sky Folk), using a large cloudy jewel — it is even called "the stone of thought" — to bring their minds together, to force the great Rhiannon to admit his presence in the mind of Carse, it becomes clear that the scene is virtually the prototype of Bradley's matrix circles.

By virtue of its finely constructed plot, its appropriate characterization, its rich setting, its use of mythic elements, and its effect on subsequent science fiction, *The Sword of Rhiannon* must be considered an important book.

Rosemarie Arbur

SYMZONIA

Author: "Captain Adam Seaborn" (possibly a pseudonym of John Cleves Symmes, 1780-1829)
First book publication: 1820
Type of work: Novel
Time: 1817-1818
Locale: Mainly the Antarctic seas and an inhabited region on the Earth's inner surface

The story of a sea voyage in a new kind of paddle steamer, which takes its crew to a continent within the Earth through an opening at the South Pole

> *Principal characters:*
> CAPT. ADAM SEABORN, the narrator and master of the ship *Explorer*
> MR. BONETO,
> MR. ALBICORE, and
> MR. SLIM, mates aboard the *Explorer*
> THE BEST MAN of Symzonia

In 1818, Captain John Cleves Symmes sent a circular to various institutions of learning in Europe and America announcing that the Earth is hollow and that access to the interior can be gained by either of two openings situated at the North and South Poles. In 1823 he petitioned the U.S. Congress to finance an expedition into the interior of the Earth. He made a number of converts to his theory, including James McBride, who collaborated in the production of *Symmes's Theory of Concentric Spheres* (1826), and Jeremiah N. Reynolds, whose work in promoting polar exploration (a cause which he continued to espouse after losing faith in Symmes) was known to Edgar Allan Poe.

It is not certain that Symmes was the author of *Symzonia*, though it makes explicit use of his ideas (frequently cited as "Symmes's sublime theory"); but the literary historian J. O. Bailey has argued strongly that it should be so attributed, and also that Symmes's theory was an important influence on Poe. The idea of the hollow Earth remained popular in America for many years and formed the basis of numerous imaginative novels, though it is probably an exaggeration of Symmes's importance to credit all hollow-world stories specifically to his inspiration. When the poles were actually reached and no openings were found, the idea lost its fashionability, but even today one sometimes hears doubts expressed about the veracity of "official" reports of polar exploration. The flying saucer enthusiast Brinsley le Poer Trench (now Lord Clancarty) was at one time convinced that UFO's emanated from the interior of the Earth.

Symmes's theory, as the title of the book he wrote with McBride testifies, states that the Earth is not uniformly solid but comprises a series of concentric spherical shells located one within another, both inner and outer surfaces of each one being habitable. His main argument in support of this case was an appeal to divine economy; such an arrangement would make room for the accommodation of the maximum possible number of intelligent beings. (Similar arguments had been used by Swedenborg and others to justify the assertion that all the physical bodies in the universe must be inhabited.) The appeal of the theory is entirely aesthetic. Though Symmes was willing to produce some abstruse and rather bizarre arguments in optical science to explain how the sun's light could be transmitted into the inner world, he made no attempt to overcome the principal scientific objections to his theories — chiefly the fact that there would be no gravitational attraction to anchor his intelligent beings to the inner surfaces of his shells.

The novel is Captain Seaborn's account of the voyage of his vessel *Explorer*, an improved species of paddle steamer, ostensibly commissioned to hunt seals in the Antarctic but actually intended by its master to find and cross the threshold of the inner world. The story begins in the style of a conventional traveler's tale, with sober descriptions of the Falkland Isles and the habits of Gentoo penguins. As the *Explorer* approaches the Antarctic ice field (which, in Symmes's theory, is a mere ring of ice surrounding a region which is virtually tropical in the summer months), Seaborn's third mate, Mr. Slim, foments rebellion and mutiny. However, the threat is averted because the other mates, Boneto and Albicore, are made of sterner stuff, and because some of the crewmen (who bear names such as Jack Whiffle and Will Mackerel) are unswervingly loyal.

The *Explorer* discovers a new Antarctic continent which the heroic captain claims for America and names Seaborn's Land. As he then sails southward, his magnetic compass becomes temporarily disturbed until the ship is heading due north again. Mr. Slim becomes less troublesome, believing that they have crossed the pole in safety, but in fact the ship is now on the inner surface of the Earth's outermost shell. The first land the explorers touch is the uninhabited Token Island, but eventually they come to the continent which Seaborn, mindful of his inspiration, names Symzonia.

The inhabitants of the inner continent seem to know little of optical science and marvel at Seaborn's telescope; they are apparently more advanced in other sciences, however, for they possess dirigible airships. They are at first apprehensive of Seaborn (who comes ashore alone) but are reassured when they see him fall to his knees and implore God for assistance. They are wondrously intelligent, and some of them learn English within a week in order to converse with Seaborn and show him the Symzonian way of life.

The Symzonians live in Utopian harmony, ordering their affairs in a rational and highly moral manner. Their chief executive is the Best Man, who works in collaboration with a council of "worthies," that refers back once every four years to a great assembly of all the worthies in the land. This grand assembly turns out to comprise almost the entire population (or, at least, all the male population — women are hardly mentioned save as objects of beauty) because those who are found unworthy tend to be exiled from the nation. There are three orders of worthies: the Good, who are certified for moral probity; the

Wise, who are rewarded for contributions to science and philosophy; and the Useful, who are skilled craftsmen. All must be nominated for this honor by their neighbors, but must not seek election overtly or covertly. Men found to be vain, hypocritical, tyrannical, or deceitful are judged unworthy and banished.

Seaborn's own worthiness is suspect, especially as his skin is not as purely white as that of the Symzonians, who wonder on this account whether he might not be descended from darker skinned deviants expelled from Symzonia in the distant past. Seaborn privately wonders whether the whole population of the outer world may have such an origin, but he attempts to give his hosts a glowing picture of his own society, conceding that there *are* External nations comprised entirely of depraved men (Britain is his cardinal example), but that his own America is much more like Symzonia. He does observe that though the Symzonians are perfectly virtuous and quite nonaggressive, they possess powerful engines of destruction with which they can defend themselves. The Symzonians account for these as the relics of an ancient war against another Internal continent, Belzubia, but are not sure whether this war ever really happened, or whether it is a myth.

Seaborn's conversations with the Symzonians, especially with the genial Best Man, make continual ironic comparisons between the External and Internal worlds. The author allows himself ample opportunity for pouring scorn on all the traits in human nature of which he disapproves (he is something of a puritan, attacking tyranny, dishonesty, and depravity and launching occasional tirades against the demon drink). All this becomes wryly satirical in tone because of the narrator's inner struggle to conceal his own un-Symzonian impulses and to hide the facts about his native society. When he is shown how the Symzonians reduce priceless pearls to a kind of decorative lacquer he knows that he will not be allowed to remove any if it is known that he wants them because of their crude commercial value, but he cannot resist pocketing a few, regardless. In the end, the Symzonians translate some of the great works of External literature which Seaborn bestows upon them, realize that his world is by their standards hopelessly corrupt, and promptly expel him from their midst.

It is not easy to take all this seriously. There is a certain honest Utopianism about the portrait of Symzonian society, but the author's attitude is occasionally tongue in cheek. J. O. Bailey, introducing a facsimile reprint of the novel in 1965, complains that the Library of Congress catalog had described the original edition as "a burlesque on Symmes's Theory of Concentric Spheres," and refers to the book as "dull and earnest," but it is not easy to decide whether either remark is pertinent. If one were to assume that the author were *not* Symmes, then the novel can perfectly well be read as a Gulliverian skit on travelers' tales. The comic element in the story becomes much more obvious as the book progresses, until in the final chapters (after Mr. Slim has destroyed all evidence of Symzonia, and the *Explorer* has been wrecked) Seaborn is reduced to penury after placing his affairs in the treacherous hands of one Mr. Slippery, a crooked lawyer. The book thus becomes Seaborn's desperate attempt to earn a little money in order to clear his debts and ends with a hopeful declaration of his willingness to lead another expedition into the interior of the Earth, either to Symzonia or in search of Belzubia. Even if the author *is* Symmes, the book may be evidence that, unlike many proponents of pseudoscientific fantasy, he had enough of a sense of humour to reflect somewhat wryly upon himself and his ideas. The continual reference to the "sublime theory" may be sarcastic, or may be a double bluff — hyperbole masking sincerity — but it is difficult to read it as a straightforward expression of admiration.

Because of this difficulty in interpreting the intentions of the author, it is not easy to place *Symzonia* in the tradition of American science fiction. Is it to be taken seriously as the first major American Utopian novel and perhaps as an important precursor of the work of Poe? Is it, conversely, to be regarded as a late example of Gulliveriana? One thing that is certain is that it is much more lively and interesting than some later literary works whose function is to provide propaganda for the hollow-Earth theory (Emerson's *The Smoky God*, for example). *Symzonia* lacks the bizarre intensity of the authentic crank, such as is displayed by that other hollow-Earth classic, John Uri Lloyd's *Etidorhpa*, but is hardly a pure adventure story in the vein of Edgar Rice Burroughs' *Pellucidar*. Perhaps, rather than try to arbitrate between alternative readings of the text in search of the correct one, readers and critics would be better advised to celebrate the fact that its ambiguity offers them two books for the price of one.

Brian Stableford

THE SYNDIC

Author: Cyril M. Kornbluth (1923-1958)
First book publication: 1953
Type of work: Novel
Time: The future, probably the twenty-second century
Locale: The United States and Ireland

A liberal society run by organized crime is threatened with extinction by the gradual return to power of the traditional, bureaucratic government it replaced

Principal characters:
CHARLES ORSINO, a young bagman for the Syndic
LEE FALCARO, a psychiatrist, niece of the Syndic's chief
F. W. TAYLOR, Charles's mentor, an important member of the Syndic
COMMANDER GRINNEL, the ruthless commander of the Government forces
MARTHA, a witchgirl who helps Charles escape from savages in the wilds of Ireland
KEN OLIVER, a citizen in Mob territory who helps Charles and Lee return to New York

The Government, having become too restrictive and bureaucratic, has been expelled from the United States by the combined forces of the Mob and the Syndic, the two factions of organized crime. The Mob, with its headquarters in Chicago, dominates the Western United States, while the Syndic, based in New York, controls the East. The Syndic itself is not a traditional government. Rather, it represents a carefree way of life, a liberal attitude toward morality, a Utopian social system. Insisting upon the right of individual freedom of choice, the Syndic deems indulgence in sex, drinking, and gambling socially acceptable, thereby removing the guilt and frustration attached to secretive indulgence in forbidden pleasures. In turn, this philosophy has rid Eastern society of rapists, alcoholics, and compulsive gamblers. Furthermore, the Syndic prides itself on having abolished petty regulations and laws and on preserving order by maintaining high public morale. Syndic leaders argue that they have not destroyed legality and morality but that they have replaced the Government's system with a less rigid, less puritanical, more realistic social order.

Autonomy and peaceful relations have been preserved for about a century when the Government begins an attempt to reinstate itself, striking out initially by sabotaging Syndic operations and murdering two Syndic members. A third murder attempt proves unsuccessful. The potential victim, Charles Orsino, is a rather insignificant junior member of the Syndic who operates as bagman for the 101st New York Police Precinct. When a Syndic investigation of the violent attacks reveals a network of Government spies within its ranks, the organization's leaders are unable to ignore the danger any longer and hold a family council meeting to discuss appropriate action. Charles, overeager to prove his worth, volunteers to become an internal spy on Government activities. His offer is accepted.

Charles immediately begins a period of concentrated personality conditioning directed by Lee Falcaro, an attractive young psychiatrist whose uncle, Edward Falcaro, is the Syndic chief. The torturous programing is designed to equip Orsino with a new personality. He is molded into Max Wyman, a man rejected by the woman he loves for a Syndic leader and, consequently, driven to alcoholism by his self-consuming hatred of the Syndic. The makeover is so thorough that Charles, as Wyman, is able to withstand intense scrutiny, lie detector examinations, and deinhibiting drugs to convince Government authorities of his defection to their side. He is ultimately recruited as an assassin for the Government by Commander Grinnel, a brutal, calculating, ambitious officer of the Navy. In keeping with Lee's plan, only when Grinnel administers the Government oath of citizenship to him does Charles remember his true identity and consciously begin his mission.

Grinnel and Charles, now knowingly posing as Wyman, travel to Ireland, a base for Government activities. There Charles soon discovers that the social order in Government regions differs radically from that to which he is accustomed. He is shocked and repulsed by slavery, poverty, misery, and violence. Passing an alley where he sees a man assaulting a woman, Charles instinctively rushes to the woman's aid and overpowers her assailant. As it happens, the woman rescued is Lee Falcaro who subjected herself to the same conditioning she practiced on Charles. She has entered Government territory as Lee Bennett, an avowed enemy of the Syndic. Having never been deprogramed, she still believes herself to be an enemy and betrays Charles when he identifies himself as a Syndic spy. Quickly apprehended by the authorities, Charles manages a rather clumsy escape in a stolen jeep and drives deep into the overgrown Irish countryside where he is promptly seized by a band of savages on the orders of the young witch who rules them. Most of Europe has become unpopulated wilderness dotted by scattered primitive ouposts like the one to which Charles is taken. Cultural achievement and scientific technology are virtually unknown; superstitious beliefs and pagan customs prevail. This crude society, like the Government's system, functions according to dictatorial rule with obedience exacted from the people by threats of harsh punishment.

Charles is held captive by the natives for several weeks before he escapes with Martha, the witch queen's younger sister, who, like her sibling, possesses incredible mental powers, among them clairvoyance. With Martha's aid, Charles locates, deprograms, and rescues Lee. To ensure that Lee and Charles flee from the Government forces unnoticed, Martha sacrifices herself and is mercilessly gunned down by Grinnel.

Having no other recourse, Lee and Charles steal a boat and set out for home. When they are stopped by one of the Mob's ore boats commanded by James Regan, a prominent Mobster, they realize that the Mob and the Government have become allies. In a desperate escape effort, Charles kills Regan. Then he and Lee plunge into the chilling waters of Lake Michigan and swim to shore. They are discovered and cared for by Ken Oliver, an artist, disillusioned by the social scheme of the Mob network in which he is trapped. Oliver has witnessed the Mob's gradual adoption of the Government habit of placing increasing limitations on its people — travel passes, permits, passwords, taxes, ordinances. While the Syndic gives people freedom of choice in an effort to boost their morale, a Mobster is expected to evince public spiritedness whether he feels it or not by having a few drinks each evening at a local tavern and by placing regular wagers on the horse races. In befriending Charles and Lee, Oliver seeks to break out of this pattern of mindless conformity.

Charles and Lee regain their strength at Ken's apartment while he forges travel passes for them. Their departure is hastened by the Mob's announcement that it has summoned a new police investigator (actually the Government officer, Commander Grinnel) and authorized his use of any method necessary to apprehend James Regan's killers. Protected by disguises and the forged travel passes, the two Syndic spies manage to slip aboard an Eastern bound train, but not before Charles kills Grinnel in retaliation for Martha's murder.

Charles and Lee return to New York advocating full-scale war, convinced that both the Government and the Mob must be destroyed to protect Syndic ideals. F. W. Taylor, a Syndic leader and Charles's guardian, listens to their recommendations but denies that such action is either feasible or desirable. He confesses that their assessment of a growing threat has merely confirmed his suspicion that the Golden Age of the Syndic way of life has passed and that the glory of Syndic ideals is fading. Even so, according to Taylor, nothing, including war, can prevent its happening and, in his opinion, no one should try to prevent it. He perceives the decline as simply part of a cycle. He solemnly warns against too much inhibiting control and too many binding rules, even if and when such control and such rules are initially conscientiously instituted in the interests of the people. He asserts that no one has the right to decide what is best for others and reminds them of the devastating consequences when anyone has tried to do so in the past. Taylor further points out that any attempt by the Syndic to make such decisions would fit it into the mold of those very organizations it opposes, the Government and the Mob. Whereas Charles and Lee, young and idealistic, consider the demise of the Syndic lifestyle unthinkable, Taylor, recalling historical trends, views it as a predictable outcome for any social order. Nevertheless, Charles and Lee leave the interview unconvinced. Taylor predicts that they will alert other Easterners to the dangers they perceive and passionately struggle against them despite the inherent futility of their resistance.

As in much science fiction, the strength of *The Syndic* does not reside in Kornbluth's handling of traditional elements of fiction such as the plot, which is overloaded with melodramatic action, or the character development, which is shallow. For, after all, the characters and what happens to them are of little consequence. What matters most is the fate of mankind as a whole. The impact of the novel, therefore, lies in Kornbluth's view of man's destiny.

Kornbluth's concerns are social and cultural. Though there are references to technological advances, the scientific focus in the novel is on the social and behavioral sciences rather than the physical sciences. In each of the four social structures Charles Orsino encounters — Syndic, Mob, Government, and primitive — the common man is somehow manipulated. Superstition is the controlling force in the primitive culture; the Mob and the Government make effective use of social conditioning, propaganda, and violence; and the Syndic maintains order by granting favors to sustain high morale. In short, the citizens of all four societies are merely marionettes. The message suggested by the reader's glimpse of each puppet community is verbalized at the end of the novel when Kornbluth speaks through Taylor about the futility and absurdity of man's efforts to shape the future. In *The Syndic*, Cyril Kornbluth has utilized the classic method of social science fiction: employing a breathtaking adventure story of the future as a vehicle to convey penetrating social commentary for the present.

Suzanne Edwards

Sources for Further Study

Reviews:

Amazing Stories. XL, August, 1965, pp. 157-158.

Analog. LIII, April, 1954, p. 148.

Authentic Science Fiction. XLI, January, 1954, p. 150.

Fantastic Universe Science Fiction. I, March, 1954, pp. 158-159.

Galaxy. VII, March, 1954, p. 117.

Imagination Science Fiction. V, March, 1954, p. 146.

Kirkus Reviews. XXI, August 1, 1953, p. 506.

Magazine of Fantasy and Science Fiction. VI, January, 1954, p. 95.

New York Herald Tribune Book Review. October 25, 1953, p. 23.

New York Times Book Review. November 15, 1953, p. 37.

New World. CXLVI, January, 1965, pp. 120-122.

San Francisco Chronicle. January 17, 1954, p. 25.

THE SYNTHETIC MAN

Author: Theodore Sturgeon (1918-   )
First book publication: 1950 (as *The Dreaming Jewels*)
Type of work: Novel
Time: Probably the early twentieth century
Locale: The United States

An examination of what makes a human being identifiably human

> Principal characters:
> HORTON BLUETT (KIDDO)
> ARMAND BLUETT, his foster father
> KAY HALLOWELL, his childhood friend
> HAVANA,
> BUNNY, and
> ZENA, carnival dwarfs
> PIERRE MONETRE (MANEATER), a former physician and present owner of a carnival

There is in science fiction criticism the often-repeated opinion that the genre is at its best as short literature. Such a belief frequently points to the fact that short stories are invariably more successful than novels, which often seem to be simply padded versions of short stories. Indeed, the shorter forms of fiction do appear to be the more desirable because they are geared toward the development of single ideas and single actions. Thus, for a genre such as science fiction, which is basically idea-oriented, the use of the short story would seem to be a perfect match between form and content. Those critics who hold that the novel is rarely suited to science fiction point out that the novel demands far more detail in development of idea and action than might be proper for the writer's purpose. More often than not, the central issue in a science fiction story is the presentation of a change or the threat of change. If the author follows the dictates of development required by writing a novel, he or she is forced to diminish the focus on the change and thus on the basic characteristic that produces a science fiction story in the first place.

The issue of short story *versus* novel as a medium for science fiction can clearly be seen in *The Synthetic Man*, which was Theodore Sturgeon's first attempt at a novel-length work. While some of the novel's problems might be viewed as the result of inexperience, many of its weaknesses illustrate how difficult it is to translate the characteristics of science fiction to the novel.

The Synthetic Man is based on an interesting premise: there exists throughout the Earth an alien life form that looks to human beings like jewels. These jewels are capable of creating perfect duplicates of any object (including the human form), living or not, that they so desire. This premise is well-suited for Sturgeon's major theme: what is true humanity? The author hints that some of the characters are aliens, and, since the reader is in doubt as to the identity of the synthetic men, he is forced to observe the characters' behavior and try to deduce from their actions their basic "humanity" or lack of it.

The problem that Sturgeon sets up is further complicated by the fact that the alien jewels are also capable of in some way becoming part of and transforming actual human beings. Such a thing has already happened to the protagonist, Horton Bluett. As an orphaned boy, he was given a handmade Punch jack-in-the-box which contains two perfectly matched alien jewels for eyes. It is obvious from the introduction of this toy named Junky that a special bond exists between it and Horton. When Armand Bluett tries to destroy it and, later, when a thief tries to steal its eyes, Horton reacts both physically and mentally. He feels that any threat to Junky is a threat to himself.

To further underscore the feeling of Horton's difference, Sturgeon opens the novel with a successfully eye-catching opening sentence: "They caught the kid doing something disgusting out under the bleachers at the high school stadium, and he was sent home from the grammar school across the street." Such an opening immediately arouses curiosity and focuses attention on Horton.

The other characters are rather typical and flat. There is Armand Bluett, a sadistic hypocrite who adopts Horton because the adoption has potential value as a public relations device, a gesture to illustrate his interest in the less fortunate. Early in the novel, Bluett shows just how inhumane human beings can be; as such a symbol, he fills his role well. But later, when Sturgeon brings Bluett back to play the role of a melodramatic lecher, the characterization lapses into boring stereotyping.

This same overuse of a character can be seen in Pierre Monetre. Monetre is introduced as a young doctor who was used as a scapegoat by hospital officials for a patient's death. Used to having everything his own way, Monetre becomes bitterly cynical and outdoes Bluett in sadism. Although at one point Horton believes that Monetre is one of the entirely synthetic creations of the jewels, he turns out to be, like Bluett, a natural human. Once again the reader is taught that there are many people who do not deserve to be called human.

Finally, since Sturgeon wishes to explore the good as well as the bad qualities of humanity, he presents the reader with a number of characters who display ideal traits. There are the two dwarfs, Havana and Bunny, who seem to exist in the novel so that the cliché, "although they are small they have hearts as big as all outdoors," can be suggested. And there is Solum, a creature synthesized by the jewels and tortured by Monetre, who proves that being human is not necessarily limited to those who look human. And there is Zena, the dwarf who is also a synthesized being. Sturgeon gives to Zena the most humane characteristics of any character in the novel. She is capable of deep love and has an abiding desire to aid the very race she has been copied from. More important, Zena is capable of self-sacrifice in order to help not only Horton but all of humanity as well.

If the list of these characters reads like that of a melodrama, it is because that is exactly what *The Synthetic Man* becomes. The novel is flooded with such people, and the plot starts to emphasize the struggles of stage heroes and heroines against stage villains. Such characters might work well in a short story, but in a novel, which demands far more complicated characterizations, the melodramatic tone soon outweighs any serious attempt on Sturgeon's part to develop his original theme.

Thus, by the end of the novel the original question of Horton's relationship both to the jewels and to humanity is lost. Instead, it is replaced with a plea to the jewels to restore Zena to life. When they do, as a result of a soaring speech from Horton on Zena's basic goodness, the reader is told that what makes one human is how well he acts in his relationships with other people, a moral the reader was ready for after the second chapter. Even more unhappily, the jewels themselves are left in the background. What they are, why they do what they do, and what they think of mankind are questions that are ultimately avoided. Given the fact that the use of carnival "freaks" could have accomplished much the same thing that the synthetic creations of the jewels accomplish, one must wonder why Sturgeon bothered with them in the first place.

The Synthetic Man would probably make a fine short story, since the shorter form would have forced Sturgeon to trim away all the unnecessary elements which are included merely to draw out the story; more importantly, a short story would hopefully have focused more clearly on Horton and the jewels.

Stephen H. Goldman

Sources for Further Study

Reviews:

Amazing Stories. XXXV, November, 1961, pp. 144, 146.

Fantastic Stories. XIV, May, 1965, p. 124.

Magazine of Fantasy and Science Fiction. XXI, October, 1961, p. 80.

New Worlds. CXII, November, 1961, p. 128

SYZYGY

Author: Michael G. Coney
First book publication: 1973
Type of work: Novel
Time: Unspecified, but apparently two or three centuries in the future
Locale: The village of Riverside on the colony world Arcadia

An account of events following the conjunction of the six moons of Arcadia, which happens once every fifty-two years, with disastrous consequences

> *Principal characters:*
> MARK SWINDON, a scientist
> JANE WARREN, the sister of his late fiancée
> ARTHUR JENKINS, a psychiatrist
> TOM MINTY, a delinquent youth

The word "syzygy" comes from the Greek, and means connecting together, as by a yoke. In astronomy it is used to describe the alignment of the Earth, the sun, and the moon (or, by extension, any other group of heavenly bodies). The term also enjoyed a transient period of application in biology, referring to a mode of sexual congress in microorganisms which eventually turned out to have been illusory, grounded in observational errors made as a result of the poor preparation of microscope slides. (In this second meaning it crops up occasionally in science fiction stories by Theodore Sturgeon.) It is possible that Michael Coney's title — which he does not bother to define in the text — carries both meanings, in that the key event around which the plot is organized is the strange breeding cycle of planktonic organisms instigated by the alignment of the six moons of a colony world.

Syzygy is developed as a mystery story whose pattern is reminiscent of Isaac Asimov's classic "Nightfall." The six moons of Arcadia come into conjunction once every fifty-two years, and they are about to do so for only the second time since human colonists first came to Arcadia a hundred and thirty years before. The first such conjunction was attended by a kind of madness which seized all coastal settlements on the world, resulting in rioting, murder, and destruction of homes and property. No convincing explanation was ever found for this outbreak of violence, and most of those involved in the unexplained events surrounding the first alignment are reluctant to talk about it. As the second conjunction approaches, the colonists grow anxious since there are now many more, well-populated, coastal settlements on Arcadia.

The first-person narrator, Mark Swindon, belongs to a research project established close to the village of Riverside. His own work involves a long-term experiment to determine the feasibility of "farming" the fish upon which the village's economic fortunes depend; in addition, several of his colleagues, in particular psychiatrist Arthur Jenkins, are there to observe what happens during the conjunction and, if possible, to determine its cause.

The subplot of *Syzygy* involves Swindon's onetime engagement to a girl from Riverside named Sheila Warren, who, under rather suspicious circumstances, fell from a cliffside path to her death on the rocks surrounding an inlet called Anchor Pool. Swindon is presently involved in an uneasy relationship with Sheila's younger sister Jane, but he spends much of his time brooding about Sheila's death, wondering how and why it happened, and suffering from vague feelings of guilt. This subplot integrates well with the main plot and helps keep the pace of the narrative going well enough to conceal one or two weaknesses in its construction.

As the moment of alignment approaches, the level of plankton in the river estuary increases enormously, as does the number of sharklike predators called blackfish. The alignment also triggers a breeding-phase in the planktonic organisms which causes their integration into huge globular entities. In order to protect themselves from fish that might eat them, the plankton attract and control the blackfish, although *how* they do this is not made entirely clear, and the author's description of the situation is deliberately blurred in order to conceal the inadequacy of its logic. In addition, the plankton develop the ability to function as telepathic "relay stations" which transmit images and emotions from one human mind to another. Thoughts and feelings which are ordinarily concealed or repressed in people's minds become public property, which naturally generates anger and ultimately leads to outbursts of violence, although the people involved do not understand what is happening to them. The planktonic breeding-units possess minds which are to some degree sentient, and just as Swindon and Jenkins realize what is happening and try to alert the villagers to the danger they are in, the plankton "minds" develop the capacity to combat human attempts to destroy them. Thus, when several villagers try to destroy one of the globes in Anchor Pool, they are killed.

At this point the government of the colony is alerted, and decides to poison the coastal waters. This arouses the ire of the fishermen, whose livelihood is under threat, and seems likely to add to the violence which is quickly coming to a boil. Swindon fears that any attempt to attack the minds must necessarily fail, and will only serve to make things worse. As panic grows in the village the frustration of the fishermen finds a focus when rabble-rousers seize upon a rumor that Swindon may have murdered Sheila in order to seduce Jane. They come hunting for him, but he is warned to flee by the delinquent Tom Minty, who had earlier played a part in spreading the rumor. The hunt serves to distract the villagers from fighting among themselves, but it leaves Swindon in a very awkward situation.

Eventually, Jenkins and Minty find a partial solution to the situation. Local land animals are unaffected by the planktonic relay system because they all include in their diet a particular plant which contains an inhibitory drug — a kind of tranquilizer — and people who can be persuaded to take the drug also become immune. The remainder, however, are ultimately "taken over" by the plankton minds and are seized with a fervent desire to walk into the sea, where the predatory blackfish await them as their "reward" for protecting the breeding-units. The climax of the book involves the attempt to distract the attention of these would-be victims long enough for the alignment of the moons to pass and the minds to break up.

Coney's story suffers from the faults which almost invariably afflict suspense stories which depend on events within alien life systems. The author is aware of these problems and tries to deal with them, but the evolutionary rationale which he presents in order to account for the existence of the planktonic minds is inadequate. In the first place, he is dealing with an enormously oversimplified ecological situation which includes only one marine predatory species, one prey species, and apparently one plankton species (though whether this is based on a misunderstanding of the nature of earthly plankton is not clear). Any scheme of relationships dealing with such an artificial situation is almost certain to be incompetent, and Coney's understanding of the theory of natural selection seems to be rather limited as well. He cannot explain why the particular behavior pattern required by his plot should be necessary in order to provide the plankton with the necessary selective advantage.

However, one must remember that virtually all biological speculation in modern science fiction is based in crude analogical thinking. Very few science fiction writers have any substantial knowledge of evolutionary genetics, and it is perhaps curious that there should be so many science articles in science fiction magazines dealing with theoretical physics (which actually makes only a minute ideative contribution to science fiction itself) while none at all deal with the science whose hypotheses ought rationally to be involved in the modeling of every alien world. As things are, the *ad hoc* construction of alien life systems to serve other thematic requirements has become as conventional in postwar science fiction as the use of faster-than-light space travel and time travel into the past (both of which notions similarly lead the analytical mind into logical contradictions). What is really significant about *Syzygy* is not that it goes beyond scientific theory but that it does so in order to make a point which is central to a whole series of modern science fiction novels which deal in what might be described as "ecological mysticism."

Though ecological mysticism is not confined to stories about the colonization of other worlds, this particular kind of plot framework is ideally suited to it. The colonization theme represents science fiction's "frontier mythology," and has changed in its emphases quite markedly during the last fifty years of the genre. In the 1940's, stories of colonization were marked by an enthusiastic pioneering spirit which looked ahead to a glorious future of galactic civilization. In the 1950's there was a dramatic trend towards an affectation of "realism" as pioneers had to struggle desperately against harsh and hostile environments (usually the deserts of Mars) in order to establish the first footholds for the long climb to glory. In the 1950's the colonists always won, but the problems they faced were usually straightforward ones, which could be solved by hard work, community spirit, and an attitude of friendly tolerance toward alien neighbors.

In the 1960's this mock-realism gave way to a new species of romanticism, which still assumed that colonization would be difficult, but which conceived of the problems of adaptation in different terms. The notion of adapting to a new and alien way of life was very often charged with a quasireligious mythology of "rebirth." The implication of the new tradition was (and is) that man is ill-adapted to his environment in both the biological sense and, metaphorically, in the spiritual sense. The emergence of this new trend at a time when we are, in the real world, simultaneously preoccupied by ecological problems and problems of personal alienation is not surprising. Archetypal examples of the new tradition which use the colony scenario are Mark Clifton's *Eight Keys to Eden* and John Brunner's *Bedlam Planet*, but the mode of thought extends to the mystification of ecological relationships seen in such novels as Robert A. Heinlein's *Stranger in a Strange Land*, Frank Herbert's *Dune*, Ursula K. Le Guin's *The Word for World Is Forest*, and Piers Anthony's *Omnivore*.

Syzygy embodies the theme neatly. It faces its human characters with the problem of adaptation to new circumstances by an imaginative device which releases the maladaptive elements in human nature, whose repression is the price we pay for harmonious social relations. In this context the character of the protagonist is well-designed; his own network of frayed and twisted social relations is ideal for such exposure. Conventionally, Coney rejects out of hand the notion that we might combat such troubles and end them. The only solution he can see is a fundamental change in human nature itself, and though his suggestion that this might be affected by a drug serendipitously discovered in the immediate environment seems disappointingly banal, it can hardly be said to be unrealistic in an age when valium has replaced religion as the opiate of the masses. Other writers have "discovered" answers to the problem which are much more audacious and imaginatively inspiring (such as the literal metamorphoses which figure in Ray Bradbury's "The Million Year Picnic," and Robert Silverberg's *Downward to the Earth*), but the very ambition of such solutions restricts them to being brilliant dramatizations of the implications of our *malaise* rather than constructive exercises in eupsychian exploration. The fact that Coney's *deus ex machina* is less than inspiring is a reflection of the limitations of the contemporary speculative imagination rather than evidence of his own limitations as a writer.

Syzygy is a reasonably well-paced novel whose climax is suitably melodramatic, if not very convincing. The writing is occasionally clumsy; *Syzygy* was the author's first published novel, and manifests a lack of skill that he has since overcome. This is a novel whose significance lies in its typicality rather than its originality, but it is by no means an uninteresting work.

Brian Stableford

Sources for Further Study

Reviews:

Books and Bookmen. XIX, July, 1974, p. 110.

Renaissance. V, Fall, 1973, p. 14.

Times Literary Supplement. March 15, 1974, p. 269.

T ZERO

Author: Italo Calvino
First book publication: 1967
English translation: 1969
Type of work: Thematically related short stories
Time: Primordial beginnings of Earth forward into the indeterminate future
Locale: Various

Witty and intellectually brilliant fictions which feature reversals, transpositions, and exaggerations of various scientific accounts of reality presented through mind-stretching, almost allegorical characters whose remembrances cast surprising light on the present and future

Principal characters:
> QFWFQ, a consciousness which has existed both unformed and formed since the most ancient times and whose memory contains and narrates these stories
> SIBYL, a female companion/soothsayer
> U(H), the wisest of Qfwfq's ancient male companions
> ORG-ONIR-ORNIT-OR, queen of the birds, onetime wife of Qfwfq
> VUG, female companion of Qfwfq in the crystal world
> ZYLPHIA, female companion of Qfwfq with whom he makes love in a Volkswagen
> SIGNOR CECERE, the reckless male driver of Volkswagen, a speed demon
> PRISCILLA LANGWOOD, an idealized lover of Qfwfq living in Paris
> ABBÉ FARIA, a prisoner in the Château d'If
> EDMOND DANTÈS, another prisoner, narrator of the final story, possibly another incarnation of Qfwfq, another authorial *persona*; also the hero of *The Count of Monte-Cristo*
> ALEXANDRE DUMAS, the author of *The Count of Monte-Cristo*

Each of the eleven tales of *t zero* could stand individually as a story or fable, but the collective impact of this extraordinary collection is greater than the sum of its parts. The organization of the book into three sections, the development of its distinctive narrative style, and the expanding temporal perspectives and thematic motifs from beginning to end make the book a unique science fiction work. Calvino has been particularly fortunate in having a fine translator, William Weaver, whose English version of Calvino's *Cosmicomics* won the National Book Award for translation. Weaver is clearly attuned to the special Calvino blend of scientific fact, technical terminology, and philosophical fantasy, and he provides a lively English rendering of difficult and demanding material. The style varies from vivid description to nearly formulaic scientific description: ". . . that various t_1's of Q_1 L_1, $E(a)_1$, $E(\frac{1}{a})_1$ which have the power to determine the fundamental qualities of to." The readable, fascinating style incorporating this unusual range distinctively extends the normal understanding of the science fiction genre while creating fiction of great originality and philosophical scope.

The contents of the book are symmetrically divided into three parts; the first and last sections contain four tales each, while the intervening second section contains three stories, each of them about division. Part One, "More of Qfwfq," generally describes ancient origins, primordial elements, and early stages of consciousness. Part Two, "Priscilla," moves evolutionarily up the scale to cellular and sexual reproduction. Part Three, "t zero," progresses into a mental reality of acute self-consciousness in a present or future of indeterminate possibility. The development of the book is therefore, on one scale, from the inanimate and elemental origins of the universe, through the beginnings of life (mitosis, meiosis) and consciousness, toward an overwhelming awareness of rationality portrayed in scientific formulae and imaginary realities in the final stories. These perspectives and temporal dimensions complexly interpenetrate and overlap, however, so that even within the various parts and individual tales, multiple evolutionary phases and intellectual-emotional-scientific developments are presented.

In Part One ("More of Qfwfq"), "The Soft Moon" offers an account of prehistoric origins of the world which reverses history, throwing present technology into an ancient time and suggesting that the most primitive surface of the Earth was actually "plastic and cement and metal and glass and enamel and imitation leather." Unfortunately, at one time the moon went soft, covering the entire surface of Earth with a hot, syrupy stuff so that when "the storm of meteorites was over, the earth around us was unrecognizable, covered by a deep layer of mud, a paste of green proliferations and slippery organisms." Sibyl had predicted that such a change could never occur, but her apparently sound predictions were contradicted by actual events. Sibyl, who represents the best of the ancient "scientific" learning and the timeless impulse toward prediction or prophecy, is shown at the end of the story to be foolish and degraded in her certainty, "fat, disheveled, lazy, greedily eating cream puffs," while Qfwfq (the narrator) recognizes that all our modern cities and all our inventions of technologies and materials can be simply understood: "After hundreds of thousands of centuries we are trying to give the Earth its former natural appearance." The soft moon's gloppy covering which buried the original surface of Earth has hidden forever the perfect glass, steel, and plastic of the ideal golden days. Thus Calvino begins the book with a type of Fall from a golden age through the accident of the soft moon. He presents time as circular and the mission of life as an almost Platonic imitation of ideal forms which can never be fully recovered. It is a Fall outside traditional religious and mythic contexts which reverses and redefines the original "natural" aspects of Earth and places human endeavor within an eternal cycle of effort to imitate or return to perfection.

"The Origin of Birds" moves forward on the evolutionary scale in both traditional terms and in Calvino's curiously inverted scheme. The male character U(h) presents a different type of wisdom or knowledge from that of Sibyl;

and Or, queen of the birds, with whom Qfwfq falls in love, is the first of a series of romantic feminine spirits which attract man through desire for the beautiful and unattainable. Sexual and emotional yearning becomes a counterpart to the rational and technological impulse, and symbolically the first two stories are opposite, with the soft moon falling to cover the earth's surface and the original birds lifting desire beyond that buried surface.

"Crystals" describes another evolutionary phase in which Qfwfq moves with his female companion Vug. It presents the male-female pair burdened with mutual awareness of loss. The story begins in New Jersey where Qfwfq is a commuter watching the skyscrapers clustered crystalline along the Hudson. Then it flashes back to a molten world where he and Vug expected the full Earth to become a perfect crystal world. It concludes in a fallen and imperfect present in which one can still perceive the crystals, but only in corrupt and impure form: ice for a glass of whiskey, the luminous television tube, the condensing of tiny silver crystals on photographic plates, the thin sound of a transistor radio.

The first section concludes with "Blood, Sea," a story in which Calvino caps the series of inversions of perfection by suggesting that all that was outside has become internalized: what once swam in the molten seas of unformed Earth now swims inside our bodies in the stream of our blood. At the same time he introduces another parallel metaphor, the flow of automobiles, moving along artery highways like the flowing of water or of blood through the veins of a moving world. The automobile — especially as part of a long, endless line of moving cars — develops in the rest of the book as a symbol of modern life isolated in the technological age, driven through the world in a situation where deviation is awkward or impossible, and where one is forced to make cramped love on the carseat. In fact, the first section finishes with an unconsummated sexual climax suddenly converted to a familiar image of death on the highway. The Volkswagen in which Qfwfq (whose very name begins and ends with the same letter) and Zylphia are passengers is ripped apart; they are as vulnerable as unprotected single cells in the sea. As their vehicle is laid open and destroyed, ". . . the sea of common blood which flows over the crumpled metal isn't the blood-sea of our origin but only an infinitesimal detail of the outside, of the insignificant and arid outside, a number in the statistics of accidents over the weekend."

Despite the death scene at the end of the first section, the unifying narrative consciousness of the book through the voice of Qfwfq continues. The second section ("Priscilla") is preceded by an array of richly suggestive quotations from scientific and philosophical works which explore the continuity of death and birth, and in a more personal, Freudian sense, love and death. As Qfwfq's voice resumes, it is with an ellipsis: ". . . And when I say 'dying of love,'" as though his voice had continued speaking during his death but beyond our hearing in the intervening pages.

"Mitosis," the first story in this part, is Qfwfq's account of himself in a prelapsarian condition, rendered here as the completeness of the single-cell state. Under these conditions, love begins in completeness, not in the more familiar longing, yearning, or desiring something of someone absent or outside oneself. The climax of love under this aspect occurs as a wrenching of one's own fullness, so that "at the climax of the love story my memory dissolves, frays, goes to pieces, and there's no way for me to remember then what happens afterward." Qfwfq adds that in this case, "not remembering the story becomes the very story itself." Yet in the final sentence of the story, the "afterward" materializes out of a timeless past or unspecified future, the unknown "other," like an Eve taken from Adam's rib, "Priscilla Langwood."

"Meiosis" describes the multicellular phase, a new condition of awareness involving an outside presence in which one finds "void, separation and waiting." The narrator intends to describe a relationship between himself and Priscilla, but while the love of "Mitosis" was difficult to express in its fullness, this love is even more difficult because of its complex and contradictory nature. The narrative becomes philosophically entangled, the language abstract and paradoxical. In the process of finding himself incomplete and drawn to Priscilla, Qfwfq is, in the center of the book, nullified. The "t zero" of the title becomes an emotional, moral, and philosophical index, linked to time increasingly as the book progresses. In "Meiosis" it is clearly seen in the genetic processes of evolution:

> A present doesn't exist, we proceed blindly toward the outside and afterward, carrying out an established program with materials we fabricate ourselves, always the same. We don't tend toward any future, there's nothing awaiting us, we're shut within the system of a memory which foresees no task but remembering itself.

The nature of divided love as conveyed in this story is deterministic and limited, more limited than the previous evolutionary phase, before selection had limited the possibilities:

> This is how we live, not free, surrounded by freedom, driven, acted on by this constant wave which is the combination of the possible cases and which passes through those points of space and of time in which the rose of the pasts is joined to the rose of the futures.

Having read this story and become accustomed to a philosophic and romantic-lyrical style, it is particularly surprising at the very end to discover that all these intellectual thoughts and romantic sexual yearnings for Priscilla have been the thoughts and emotions of something less than human. Qfwfq tells us suddenly that he is a camel.

"Death" is the last story in the "Priscilla" section. Calvino concludes here, as in part one, not speaking of generative power, or the life-force aspects of existence, but instead zeroes in on the inevitable movement toward nullification which gives life its definition. He begins by stating that living forever was the great risk, but was avoided:

> . . . the spell is broken, the eternals are dead, nobody seems prepared any longer to renounce sex, even the little share of sex that falls to his lot, in order to have again a life that repeats itself interminably. The victors — for the present — are we, the discontinuous.

In the final lines of "Death," Calvino moves from history (memory) to prophecy, and his shift from textured mental metaphor is dramatically symbolized by a change of subject from the organic to the mechanical:

> The circuit of vital information that runs from the nucleic acids to writing is prolonged in the punched tapes of the automata, children of other automata: generations of machines, perhaps better than we, will go on living and speaking lives and words that were also ours; and translated into electronic instructions, the word "I" and the word "Priscilla" will meet again.

The last group of stories repeats and recapitulates the sequence of motions established in each of the first two parts. Its title ("t zero") designates a situation seen at the mathematical level of abstraction, a level of description appropriate to machines or automata. Paradoxically, the L, X, and A in Calvino's scientific formulation actually refer to a primitive situation — a lion hunter with a bow and arrow — but the hunter holds technological implements in his hands and points forward in time with the tools of death.

Calvino insists, first of all, upon the unpredictable and indeterminate nature of this particular situation, but makes clear that all events take place within a space-time continuum which inevitably repeats itself. The final four stories are in fact symmetrical repetitions of the first four: "t zero" corresponds to the intersection of earth and surface in "The Soft Moon"; "The Chase" is a variant of the pursuit described in "The Origin of Birds"; "The Night Driver" reconstructs the sense of romantic possibility present in "Crystals"; and "The Count of Monte-Cristo" restates in literary terms the organic rendering of "outside-become-inside" which was introduced in "Blood, Sea."

The major difference in the final group of stories rests in their indeterminate endings; the first stories, recounted as histories, had definite conclusions. The first tales progressively highlighted differences between past and present, with change and loss over time; these last stories, while apparently presenting the possibility of change, most dramatically through death or escape from imprisonment, conclude with an inconclusive emphasis on static confinement. In the final words of "The Chase," for instance, not even murder makes any difference in the real situation: "Absolutely nothing has changed: the line moves in little, irregular shifts of position, I am still prisoner of the general system of moving cars, where neither pursuers nor pursued can be distinguished." The statement applies equally well to the lion and the hunter, or to potential lovers

X, Y, and Z in "The Night Driver." To these figures even the finality of highway death statistics is denied them as they continue

> speeding back and forth along these white lines, with no points of departure or of arrival to threaten with their sensations and meanings the single-mindedness of our race, freed finally from the awkward thickness of our persons and voices and moods, reduced to luminous signals . . . indistinguishable from all the other signals that pass along this road. . . .

The final story, "The Count of Monte-Cristo," is at once the most concrete and the most complicated in the volume. It restates the problems of time, individual identity, and the changelessness of existence in which one may become trapped as history narrows possibility and time becomes repetition. Calvino completes what he refers to as "the circuit of information that runs from nucleic acid to writing" with a fiction about fiction, a box within a box. The author Alexandre Dumas becomes a character in a story by Calvino about a prisoner who is actually a character in Dumas' novel, in Calvino's book trying to escape from the Château d'If (which is itself a real chateau fictionalized first by Dumas). This prisoner, Edmond Dantès, is trying to escape from both literal and literary imprisonment, and his method lies in imagining all the possible fictions which could have composed his prison. This final story rewrites the fiction of Dumas in a reversed fashion, much as "The Soft Moon" rewrote scientific reality, offering imaginary escape by reimagining reality. The characters in the last story are the most vivid and tangible in the book. Partly this is the result of the detailed reality they accrue from Dumas' novel, but they are also surrounded by sounds, textures, and physical details of the prison which Calvino describes more completely than most other physical environments in the book.

Calvino is perhaps most optimistic in this concluding tale, for he realizes in his own language, building upon a story already told and character already invented, a point where real escape and genuine freedom may be possible: "the place of the multiplicity of possible things." His last story, like the entire collection, celebrates the amazing complexity of each single situation in time, t zero, so much like every other t, in language or in science, and yet in context unique, miraculously different and unpredictable at the moment we discover it: "and this, then, is a sign that here an opportunity of escape exists: we have only to identify the point where the imagined fortress does not coincide with the real one and then find it." In the labyrinthine sentences and philosophical mazes of his prose, Calvino constructs a surreal set of nullifying space-time moments which constantly escape and therefore define our comprehension.

Richard Mathews

TARZAN OF THE APES

Author: Edgar Rice Burroughs (1875-1950)
First book publication: 1914
Type of work: Novel
Time: 1887-c.1908
Locale: West Africa

Orphaned on the coast of West Africa where his parents were marooned, John Clayton is reared by great apes, grows up to be the greatest hunter and fighter in the jungle, and later discovers that he is actually Lord Greystoke

Principal characters:
TARZAN OF THE APES
JOHN CLAYTON, his father, killed by apes
ALICE CLAYTON, his mother
KALA, the ape who becomes his foster mother
KERCHAK, a vicious ape whom Tarzan kills
JANE PORTER, a young lady from Baltimore with whom Tarzan falls in love
PROFESSOR ARCHIMEDES Q. PORTER, her father
MR. PHILANDER, his assistant
LIEUTENANT D'ARNOT, a French naval officer

Tarzan of the Apes is one of the world's most popular fictional characters. Not only have the Tarzan books sold tens of millions of copies, but Tarzan also has been popularized through motion pictures, radio programs, television, newspaper comics, comic books and big little books, toys, and an extraordinary amount of merchandising, from bubble gum cards to men's bikini underwear to soft drinks. Edgar Rice Burroughs' community in California was even renamed Tarzana after the author's hero. And there is no end in sight, with a 1978 illustrated Tarzan calendar as only the latest example. And Tarzan is just as popular overseas. Even in Africa, where one might expect a backlash against the jungle fantasies, Tarzan books and movies (many of the latter being unauthorized films made in India) are popular; Nigeria has a Tarzan Transport Company and numerous lorries named Tarzan.

Unfortunately, the Tarzan imitations, spin-offs, and satires have made Burroughs' hero into a frequent figure of buffoonery in the popular mind. Though the latest films and a television series have tried to counteract the prevailing image, most of the motion pictures have been a travesty of the books, transforming Tarzan into an inarticulate Neanderthal with a vocabulary as limited as that which Burroughs ascribes to the apes. This Tarzan lives in a tree house, converses in grunts and monosyllables, has an adopted son named Boy (Jane overruled his initial desire to name the child Elephant) whom he found in a plane wreck, and travels with a comic chimp named Cheeta. Consequently, Tarzan has almost become a joke, a cartoon which is a parody of the original.

In fact Burroughs' Tarzan is extremely intelligent and is fluent in English, French, German, Swahili, Latin, and Bantu as well as "apeish." When engaging in jungle adventures, he sometimes reverts to the primitive and "sloughs off" the veneer of civilization, but otherwise he is Lord Greystoke, a polished gentleman who dresses immaculately and lives on a thriving plantation in East Africa. His son (lineal, not adopted) is named Jack and is known as Korak the Killer. There is no Cheeta, though Tarzan is sometimes accompanied by a monkey named Nkima.

Besides debasement by mass culture, the Tarzan books have had to survive the prejudice of librarians. The first books received quite respectable reviews, but because Burroughs later came to be considered a "pulp" writer, many libraries refused to acquire his books, though they had no such reservations about Zane Grey and others whose works are far less subtle and complex than Burroughs'. Thus, while Tarzan movies were celebrated as fine family fare, the far superior books were condemned as "subliterary" and ignored by scholars. Nevertheless, the stories have been kept alive for two-thirds of a century by enthusiastic readers, who contribute their own scholarship in a number of "fanzines" such as *ERB-dom*, *The Burroughs Bulletin*, and *Dum-Dum*. Public attention was focused again on the books in 1961 when a librarian in Downey, California, banned the Tarzan novels on the grounds that Tarzan and Jane were not married and therefore the books might tempt readers to live in sin. Readers protested that Tarzan and Jane were married at the end of *The Return of Tarzan* (in the movies, P. Dempsey Tabler as Tarzan married Karla Schramm as Jane in 1921), and the controversy incited people to go back to Burroughs' original narratives. As a result, his works were resurrected in several paperback editions, and a Burroughs revival was launched. Coinciding with an academic acceptance of popular culture, Burroughs was at last made respectable.

Tarzan of the Apes was followed by *A Princess of Mars* (1917) and *The Outlaw of Torn* (1927). Written between December 1, 1911, and May 14, 1912, it was published complete in the October, 1912, issue of *All-Story* magazine. Every major publisher rejected it in book form until *The New York Evening World* ran it as a newspaper serial, after which A. C. McClurg issued it in hardcover in 1914. Despite the reservations of scholars, it is the most significant American novel of either 1912 or 1914, both in its lasting influence and in its own right. It is very much a product of its time, for its primitivism reflects the literary naturalism of the late nineteenth and early twentieth centuries, particularly in the work of Frank Norris and Jack London, while its romantic adventure in an exotic locale shows the influence of H. Rider Haggard, Rudyard Kipling, W. H. Hudson, R. B. Cunningham Grahame, and Joseph Conrad, as well as Theodore Roosevelt's African safaris and cult of the strenuous life.

At the same time, in Tarzan, Burroughs created a timeless myth, a modernization of the noble savage, a man who escapes the pressures and degeneracy of civilization to discover the self-reliant freedom of his primitive progenitors in the jungle, which is a fallen garden of Eden. He is akin to Thoreau at Walden, unencumbered with possessions, free from wage slavery and social conformity, drawing his vigor from unspoiled nature. He is Huckleberry Finn on his raft, fleeing from the constraints of "sivilization." Burroughs' fantastic Africa is a perpetual frontier uncorrupted by cities, suburbia, and bureaucracy, in which Tarzan is at once explorer, conquistador, untamed mountain man, and Indian. Naked, armed only with a knife and rope, he is an invincible hunter and killer. A superb athlete, magnificently muscled, he is the ultimate macho male. He is both king of the beasts and ruler of the warrior Waziri. In the treasure city of Opar, he has limitless wealth. At the same time, he is a Victorian gentleman, heir both to the Clayton fortune and to its sense of honor. Thus he is simultaneously Lord Greystoke and Lord of the Jungle, literally noble and savage.

The novel opens like one of Joseph Conrad's tales of hearsay: "I had this story from one who had no business to tell it to me, or to any other." Proceeding like a realistic if exotic narrative, the story unfolds of how John Clayton and his wife, Lady Alice, en route to a colonial post and an assignment to stop a rival European power from exploiting and tyrannizing the natives, are marooned on the west coast of Africa by mutinous sailors. There they build a cabin and survive for more than a year. Their son is born in 1888, on the same evening that his mother is frightened into insanity by a giant ape. A year later, she dies; and on the same day, her husband is killed by a great ape named Kerchak. Kala, a female ape whose infant just died, carries off the Clayton boy and leaves her dead offspring in the cradle. Nursed by Kala and raised as an ape, the boy is at first handicapped by his slow growth, but he ultimately develops into a superman. Using his brain to compensate for his lesser physique, he becomes the greatest fighter in the jungle, eventually kills Kerchak (as well as innumerable other apes and lions) and becomes leader of the tribe.

If one pauses to reflect, *Tarzan* is full of improbabilities. Despite numerous legends about feral children, the chances of a human infant's surviving as the adopted child of a female ape are nil. Conceivably he might be suckled on ape milk, but once weaned, he would soon die from malnutrition. Assuming he could adapt to a diet of fruit, it would be a long time before he would be able to tear into raw meat. In fact, Tarzan eats not only freshly killed animals but dines on carrion, buried for days or weeks. From such a diet, combined with running nude and barefoot and swimming in African streams and lakes, he would inevitably suffer from amoebic dysentery, parasites, snail fever, and every variety of tropical disease, including malaria. From his battles with great apes and other animals, he would be a mass of scar tissue and no doubt be crippled by unset broken bones. From a childhood entirely deprived of human contact, conversation, and culture, he would be psychologically retarded, mentally stunted, and emotionally crippled. Yet Tarzan boasts a magnificent physique, superb health, godlike features, acute intelligence, a profound sense of honor, and great emotional sensitivity.

The interior of Tarzan's Africa is a geographical fantasy. Modern cities do not exist; his is entirely an Africa of savage tribes in a primitive, lost world, dotted, however, with the ruins of monumental cities of oriental splendor — sub-Saharan equivalents of Ankor Wat, Baalbek, or Persepolis — and inhabited by the descendants of lost Atlanteans, Roman legionnaires, and Crusaders.

These are the fantastic elements that allow the Tarzan books to be considered, in a sense, science fiction. Some of the sequels are out-and-out science fiction, such as the volumes in which Tarzan encounters the ant men and is shrunk to their size and in which he journeys to Pal-ul-don, a land of prehistoric monsters, and to Pellucidar, a primitive world within the hollow earth (reminiscent of John Cleves Symmes, Edgar Allan Poe, and Jules Verne).

Nevertheless, Burroughs incorporates enough verisimilitude into a fast-paced narrative teeming with rapid, cliff-hanging episodes that the reader suspends disbelief. Though Burroughs never went to Africa, he read extensively about it, and his descriptions of flora, fauna, and village life are graphic, evocative, and even poetic. *Tarzan of the Apes*, though less spectacular than some of its sequels, is the most compelling, largely because it concentrates on Tarzan's education and shows the world from his limited but developing perspective. Entirely self-taught, Tarzan is a *tabula rasa* who uses his reason to deduce techniques of survival. Forced into the water by a lioness, he learns to swim. Amusing himself with plaiting grasses, he learns to make a rope and in time discovers the uses of a noose in hunting. At about the age of ten, he finds his parents' cabin, learns to manipulate the door and lock, and becomes fascinated by the books inside. There, sitting by his parents' skeletons, he pores over a picture alphabet and gradually makes the connection between the pictures and the letters or "bugs" that accompany them.

From this "look-see" beginning, Tarzan eventually teaches himself to read and then to write until after some years he has become fluent in written English. Burroughs makes Tarzan a sort of cryptographer who deduces from the combinations of letters the meaning of words and the structure of language. This is, of course, impossible. Even if he could learn the words that accompany the pictures, he would be unable to teach himself grammar and verb conjugations and to understand abstractions or words for which he has no point of reference, yet he deciphers with little difficulty a letter of Jane's containing such statements as, "It seems that an old bookworm who has a book and curio shop in Baltimore discovered between the leaves of a very old Spanish manuscript a letter written in 1550 detailing the adventures of a crew of mutineers of a Spanish galleon bound from Spain to South America. . . ." He can also write his name, which means "white skin" in the language of the apes (their ability to talk strains credulity, though fortunately Burroughs rarely has them converse in direct dialogue), though there is no way he could make the connection between ape sounds and the letters of written English.

From the cabin he also takes his father's knife and discovers by accident that he can use it to kill, thus compensating for his lesser physique. He also discovers wrestling holds. When a community of black Africans settle nearby, Tarzan spies upon them and learns their culture and the use of bow and spear. When one of them shoots Kala, Tarzan kills him in revenge and then begins a program of terrorizing the superstitious savages. These sequences, together with the minstrel show comedy of Jane's black maid, could justify charges of racism; but in Burroughs' defense, one can observe that such treatment was customary in 1912, and that Burroughs was far less racist than Senator Beveridge of Indiana or President Theodore Roosevelt; and in later books, the Africans, especially the Waziri, are presented as magnificent warriors, courageous and honorable. They are still primitive but are otherwise admirable. Burroughs repeatedly denounces the tyrannic exploitation of Africans by the Belgians and other colonial powers.

At first, Tarzan is ashamed of his body and appearance, thinking himself an inferior ape, but from books he learns that he is a man and thus comes to feel superior to his tribe. To keep from looking like a hairy ape, he shaves with his knife. The symbol of mankind is clothes (though later, as Lord Greystoke, Tarzan feels confined by them and regains a sense of freedom by stripping to a loin cloth and returning to the jungle), so he steals a breechcloth from an African. From his perspective, human practices often seem senseless, such as cooking meat; even as Lord Greystoke, he prefers it raw. He cannot comprehend a burial. Who cares about a pile of old bones? Tarzan's alien view often gives Burroughs a satiric perspective on supposedly civilized values.

Tarzan grows into manhood utterly self-reliant, fearless, loving the "joy" of fighting. (Burroughs' books abound in violence and champion the warrior code, even while they condemn warfare and satirize man's inhumanity to man.) At this point, another party of whites is marooned at the same spot as his parents. They consist of the Porters from Baltimore and (by wild coincidence) Tarzan's cousin William Clayton, the present Lord Greystoke. Tarzan saves them collectively and individually from assorted perils, and falls in love with Jane Porter, who responds to his chaste ardor when he rescues her from "a fate a thousand times worse than death" at the hands of an ape who intends her for his harem. He also saves a treasure that Professor Porter came to Africa to discover. When a French rescue ship arrives, Tarzan saves Lieutenant d'Arnot from cannibals (his own unknown heredity prevents him from succumbing to cannibalism, and one motif of the book is the strength of heredity over environment), but while he nurses d'Arnot back to health, the Porter party returns to America. D'Arnot teaches Tarzan French and takes him to Paris, where he quickly becomes a polished gentleman. Meanwhile, Jane is about to be forced into marriage to a bounder who has her father in debt. Driving a French car, Tarzan arrives in time to save Jane both from marriage and a forest fire. But in a moment of weakness, she rejects both the primitive

Tarzan and the immaculate Frenchman that he has become and promises to marry William Clayton. At this point, a telegram arrives indicating that fingerprints (the infant Tarzan's on the diary his father wrote in French) prove Tarzan is Lord Greystoke; but *noblesse oblige* causes him to pretend he is still the son of Kala. Here the novel ends.

In *The Return of Tarzan*, Monsieur Jean C. Tarzan returns to France, disillusioned with mankind. (Despite his glorification of the heroic and honorable, Burroughs frequently expresses a low view of human nature and denounces mankind as more cruel and savage than wild beasts.) As Tarzan soliloquizes in the sequel,

> Mon Dieu! but they are all alike. Cheating, murdering, lying, fighting, and all for things that the beasts of the jungle would not deign to possess — money to purchase the effeminate pleasures of weaklings. And yet withal bound by silly customs that make them slaves to their unhappy lot while firm in the belief that they be the lords of creation enjoying the only real pleasure in existence.

In France, he becomes as foolish as the rest, chain-smoking, drinking too much absinthe, pursuing the Russian wife of a French count, and enjoying the pleasures of Paris before World War I. After fighting a duel with the count, he returns to Africa, has adventures among the Arabs, and sails to Capetown. When evil Russians push him overboard, he swims ashore, and in a series of adventures becomes the leader of the Waziri, who take him to the treasure city of Opar, a stranded colony of the sunken Atlantis. Jane meanwhile postpones her marriage to Clayton and goes on a year-long cruise around Africa. Her ship is wrecked, and she and Clayton face more perils in the jungle until Tarzan rescues them. Clayton conveniently dies, and Tarzan and Jane are married. The narrative seems complete.

But Burroughs wrote innumerable sequels, for a total of twenty-four Tarzan novels, plus appearances by Tarzan in *The Eternal Savage* and a juvenile, *The Tarzan Twins*. At first, the plot device is to have Jane abducted and Tarzan rescue her, but eventually Burroughs tires of Jane and simply omits her. He has Tarzan discover new lost civilizations and fight Germans in World War I and Japanese in World War II. The chronology is askew; *The Son of Tarzan* was written in 1915, when Tarzan himself would be only twenty-seven years old, yet Jack is fully grown and marries at the end of the novel. Though Tarzan becomes a grandfather, he never ages; in one of the books, he is made immortal. Despite the melodramatic plots, Tarzan is a complex hero, torn between the two worlds of civilization and savagery and not fully at home in either. He is not without a touch of the classical tragic hero, and at times reminds one of a lonely, rootless, wanderer, an Odysseus without an Ithaca.

Robert E. Morsberger

Sources for Further Study

Criticism:

Fenton, Robert W. *The Big Swingers*. Englewood Cliffs, N.J.: Prentice-Hall, 1967. Fenton attempts with mixed results to show the relationship between Burroughs' life and the Tarzan books.

Henighan, Tom. "Tarzan and Rima, The Myth and The Message," in *Riverside Quarterly*. III (March, 1969), pp. 256-265. *Tarzan of the Apes*, says Henighan, "successfully crystalized the longings of urban man for the primitive, the natural, and the animal self."

Lupoff, Richard A. *Edgar Rice Burroughs, Master of Adventure*. New York: Canaveral, 1965. This book, while devoting too much space to plot outlines, is valuable in that it shows the continuing influence of Burroughs.

Slate, Tom. "Edgar Rice Burroughs and the Heroic Epic," in *Riverside Quarterly*. III (March, 1968), pp. 118-123. Slate draws a parallel in literary method and subject matter between *Tarzan* and traditional epics like the *Iliad*.

Reviews:

Nation. XCIX, October 1, 1914, p. 409.

New York Times. July 5, 1914, p. 299.

Springfield Republican. July 9, 1914, p. 5.

TAU ZERO

Author: Poul Anderson (1926-   )
First book publication: 1970
Type of work: Novel
Time: From the twenty-third century to countless billions of years in the future
Locale: Deep space

An awesome epic of endurance in which fifty space colonists traveling in a slower-than-light spacecraft survive the collapse of the present universe and find a new home in the new cycle of creation

Principal characters:
> CHARLES REYMONT, constable of the expedition
> INGRID LINDGREN, first officer
> CHI-YUEN AI-LING, a planetologist
> BORIS FEDOROFF, chief engineer
> ELOF NILSSON, an astronomer
> LARS TELANDER, captain
> NORBERT WILLIAMS, a chemist
> JANE SADLER, a biotechnician
> EMMA GLASSGOLD, a molecular biologist
> JOHANN FREIWALD, a machinist
> MARGARITA JIMENES, a colonist

1971 Hugo Award nominee *Tau Zero* embodies Poul Anderson's most ambitious concept — human beings outliving eternity, surviving the universe which bred them. As usual, Anderson runs scientific and personal crises in parallel. On the one hand, he applies strict Einsteinian physics in what James Blish has called "the ultimate 'hard science fiction' novel." On the other hand, he tests his characters with an unprecedented challenge of will. (Their hardships are torments of mind and spirit only; there is no physical privation or mayhem in the book.) The author brings the two levels of his story together to praise humanity's stubborn courage battling entropy. He sees man's purpose in his capacity for wonder and for struggle against all odds throughout all ages of the cosmos.

The idea of new beginnings has long fascinated Anderson (see, for example, "Flight to Forever," 1950; "Wildcat," 1958; "Epilogue," 1961; and *After Doomsday*, 1962). In *Tau Zero* he describes a beginning of uniquely absolute newness. A spacecraft carrying twenty-five couples, representing a racial and ethnic cross-section of humanity, is launched at the star Beta Virginis, thirty light-years distant. The *Leonora Christine*, their spacecraft, travels close enough to the speed of light to take advantage of the time-dilation effect. But because of an accident en route, the ship never reaches its destination. The ship's only salvation is to keep traveling faster and faster beyond its own galaxy and time until the voyage continues past the dissolution of this universe and the formation of the next. The novel takes its title from the factor tau in the equations for relativistic spaceflight — tau approaches zero as the ship's velocity approaches the speed of light.

Inspired by Olaf Stapledon's *First and Last Men* (1930), Anderson conveys the feeling of this stupendous voyage by an imaginative and effective stylistic device: the time scale of *Tau Zero* is a logarithmic progression. Shipboard time is logarithmically related to elapsed cosmic time. (Recall that log N increases very slowly as N approaches infinity: log $10=1$ but log $10,000,000,000=10$.) The opening chapter takes place in a few hours on the clock of the universe, the next in a few days, and so on at an ever-increasing pace until the eons fleet by in heartbeats.

This breath-stopping sweep of events is rendered in vigorous, poetic language. No one else infuses astrophysics with such passion as Anderson. His images are Bonestell spacescapes painted in sensuous words. His are the beauty and terror of the infinite spaces where icy winds of passage rush past the pitiless stars.

To prevail against this immensity is the measure of mankind's true stature. Much is made of the contrast between the tiny ship ("She was not, after all, anything big or important in the universe.") and the trackless sea of space through which she sails on waves afoam with supernovae. Although man is fallible and his works finite, there is nevertheless an inherent dignity in his existence. He is a free and responsible being, able to meet the endless challenges of nature.

The voyage of the *Leonora Christine* is a metaphor for the lifespan of individuals, groups, and the universe itself. Adventure befalls her as it did Dante "midway in this journey of our life." Singular as her destiny is, Anderson equates it with the common lot of creatures. Everyone and everything that exists must die and be reborn. The spirit in which one's fate is met is all that really matters.

Tau Zero is structured as a true *Magnus Annus* with a gigayear calendar longer than the ancients ever dreamed. Major events in the ship's last bizarre year are keyed to the seasonal festivals of vanished Earth such as Christmas, Midsummer, and Halloween. The last holiday is an especially appropriate moment for smashing and recasting the universe because it marks a cardinal interface in Celtic mythology. This was the feast of Samain, the night when the doors between the worlds of the living and the dead stand open. What better point to cross the cosmic threshold by reversing the polarity of every natural constant.

The turning of the mystical cycle is also linked to a more intimate process. While the universe decays, an unborn child develops. The climax of *Tau Zero* parallels *eschaton* and childbirth in exciting and economical fashion. Welcoming a new life is a "pledge of confidence" in the future, a perennial motif in Anderson stories. But the infant girl, whose "first cry responded to the noise of inward-falling worlds," is never named in the book. The potential mythical significance of this last child born in the old universe is left to the reader's imagination.

The death and rebirth scenario likewise applies to civilizations. The placid twenty-third century Earth which launches the expedition is a clean, orderly, and just world dominated by international peacekeeper Sweden. Nonetheless, Earth is slowly stagnating. Extrasolar colonization is supposed to provide the spark for renewed creativity, but even this remedy must eventually fail as history has repeatedly demonstrated. Anderson's hero Charles Reymont knows that institutions are as mortal as men: "I'm only certain that nothing is forever. No matter how carefully you design a system, it will go bad and die."

Yet renewal is always possible, as the *Leonora Christine*'s voyage so splendidly proves. The ship's crew is the human race in miniature, a parliament of mankind that represents the full range of ethnic and personality types. Each member carries the weight of public as well as private history on his shoulders. Although the balanced composition of the group seems too schematic, it is nevertheless plausible. Genetics, politics, and shrewd public relations would dictate just such an arrangement.

Conditions foster the expression of national stereotypes. Thus Anderson shows us a patient Chinese, a sentimental Russian, a fiery Hispanic, a proper Englishman, a serene Indian, a feisty Irishman, and so on. Some of these portrayals — boorish American Norbert Williams and arrogant Swede Elof Nilsson — are less than flattering to the parent nationalities. Only stateless "interplanetary citizen" Reymont stands outside the pattern. He is a Western-flavored universal man, the only one who consistently sees beyond cultural barriers to the common humanity they all share.

Many of the characters' names contain allusions or wordplays — Anderson is fond of studding his work with references to history, myth, or the arts. Note Charles Reymont (Charlemagne and "king's mountain"), Lindgren (green linden branch), Freiwald ("free forest"), and Margarita (the Faust legend). The author even allows himself a wry jest by calling a Jew Yeshu ben-Zvi after two rejected Messiahs. The ship herself bears the most significant name of all. Leonora Christine Ulfeld was a seventeenth century Danish princess who survived twenty-two years of solitary imprisonment with sanity intact and wrote celebrated memoirs upon release. Like the *Leonora Christine*'s people, she endured and triumphed.

The turning of the mystical cycle is also linked to a more intimate process. While the universe decays, an unborn child develops. The climax of *Tau Zero* parallels *eschaton* and childbirth in exciting and economical fashion. Welcoming a new life is a "pledge of confidence" in the future, a perennial motif in Anderson stories. But the infant girl, whose "first cry responded to the noise of inward-falling worlds," is never named in the book. The potential mythical significance of this last child born in the old universe is left to the reader's imagination.

Anderson is even more interested in his characters' principles than in their genes or ethnic backgrounds. *Tau Zero* is a running debate among conflicting philosophical and religious viewpoints. Believers such as Glassgold the devout Jew, Telender the staunch Protestant, and Jimenes the stubborn Catholic fence with agnostic Williams, humanist Lindgren, and Marxist Fedoroff. Pessimism and optimism, hedonism and nihilism take the platform in turn. (At one point Anderson slyly puts some of his own political convictions into Williams' drunken mouth — not a move calculated to win them approval.) It is the task of Reymont, " 'pragmatism personified,' " to synthesize the positive elements from each system into a battle plan for survival. Ironically, the man constantly criticized as narrow and unfeeling proves himself the bravest dreamer of them all.

Reymont's tireless efforts to make people survive in spite of themselves arouse much resentment. He compels them to complete "as hard a task as human beings ever undertook." Knowing that their plight is too desperate to be solved by sentimental impulses and vague good will, he relies on authority symbols and becomes the *de facto* king of the expedition. He and Lindgren, his beloved, provide role models of courage in public even as they comfort one another in private. She tempers his rigor; but although her tact and sensitivity are important to success, his determination and leadership are absolutely indispensable. Reymont himself takes the ship's helm at the moment of rebirth, a responsibility and an honor he deserves more than anyone else on board. But once the crisis is past, he gladly surrenders his crown.

To Reymont, the voyage is "our way of fighting back at the universe." There is no trace of fashionable resignation in his defiant soul: "I think we have a duty — to the race that begot us, to the children we might yet bring forth ourselves — a duty to keep trying, right to the finish." Instinct wins the field where reason falters. The crew earns a glorious future for themselves and their offspring.

The magnificence of this communal victory outshines individual failures. Although the colonists are supposed to be Earth's best stock, they are riddled with flaws. *Tau Zero* is built out of the tensions between the grandeur of the cosmos and the fraility of man, between the sublime experience of the group and the pettiness of its members' quarrels. Anderson restates his view that real heroism is rarely glamorous (see also "No Truce with Kings," 1963). "Stubbornly ordinary" behavior persists under the most extraordinary circumstances. This should be a source of pride, not shame. Despite embarrassed reactions from some, there is no scandal in "having regular bowel movements . . . while creation happens."

Years of close confinement under the threat of death bring sexual impulses to the fore: most conflicts on board are bedroom skirmishes. (Anderson reused this plot in *The Avatar*, 1978, with deplorable results.) Fortunately, *Tau Zero* is not the great intergalactic pornography novel it might have been in other hands. Friendship, affection, and even romantic love manage to develop despite the permissive atmosphere. Reymont's feelings for Lindgren and Ai-Ling are generously and happily resolved. By the story's close the crew has put aside jealousy for the sake of the larger enterprise. "With all the work ahead of us," says Reymont, "Personalities have no importance whatsoever."

The ramifications of the *Leonora Christine*'s triumph are just as fascinating as the odyssey itself. Past historic cultures share a universal lost paradise myth and thus are based on a sense of failure. What kind of civilization would the descendants of men who had outlived their culture create? Will they become a benign Elder Race as Reymont envisions? What epics will they write about their ancestors? Will they divinize them? (They are conveniently assorted for a pantheon.) And most intriguingly of all, will future ships repeat the *Leonora Christine*'s feat, propagating our species forever and ever, human world without end?

Tau Zero is a science fiction heir of the Northern heroic tradition. Without denying the possibilities of suffering, failure, and death, Anderson says that men can nevertheless go on living with hope, love, and even ribald laughter. For those whose hearts are bold enough, the heat death of the universe can be a prelude to resurrection.

Sandra Miesel

THE TEMPLE OF THE PAST
(LE TEMPLE DU PASSÉ)

Author: Stefan Wul (Pierre Pairault, 1922-   )
First book publication: 1957
English translation: 1973
Type of work: Novel
Time: An undetermined past
Locale: A distant planet

The crew of a damaged spaceship, swallowed by a gigantic sea monster soon after being wrecked on an uncharted planet, attempt to escape from their bizarre captivity

Principal characters:
MASSIR, the captain of a wrecked spaceship
JOLT, a probationary physician
RAOL, a crewman
THE MONSTER

Stefan Wul is noted for his meteoric career in the French science fiction field. In the three years he was active, he published eleven novels in a series aimed at a popular readership, plus six stories in magazines. At that point, he left the field; and it was only after a silence of twenty years that he returned to it with his huge twelfth novel, *Noo*, published in 1977.

The Temple of the Past is, perhaps, the epitome of the "multidirectional novel," a somewhat underrated form pioneered by Wul. Multidirectional fiction can be described as those stories which include a large number of the stereotypes often found in the genre in its rawest state. These stereotypes may be used for humorous purposes since they generate situations out of the leftover scraps of the plot; but they are part of the serious action, and thus it takes a great mastery to maintain such an uncertain balance between the comic and the serious. An excellent example of this technique can be found in Fredric Brown's grotesque novel *What Mad Universe*, even though the author in that book resolutely opted for a humorous treatment of the subject.

Wul, on the contrary, chooses to remain serious in *The Temple of the Past* as he leads the reader into an intentionally unrestrained adventure that falls just short of a joke on every page. Massir, Jolt, and Raol are the only survivors in a damaged rocketship which finally falls on a planet covered by a chlorine atmosphere. As the ship lies on the bed of a liquid chlorine ocean, she is suddenly swallowed by a gigantic monster. The castaways quickly realize that they are prisoners inside the monster's stomach. Because of the particular conformation of the creature's digestive track and because the beast lives permanently in liquid chlorine, they are completely trapped.

Only one solution is left to the astronauts: to make the monster leave its natural habitat for solid land. In order to compel it to do so, Massir devises a way to alter genetically its bodily structure and transform it into an amphibian. After much action the operation succeeds. The castaways kill the monster at the proper time and wait for it to decompose so that they can try to make their rocket spaceworthy again. During the long repair period, they discover that the monster had laid eggs before it died; they now hatch into a species analogous to lizards and wholly different from the parent. This new species is intelligent and revers Jolt and Massir as gods (Raol having died in the beast's belly). Jolt unfortunately also dies in an accident, leaving Massir alone with the realization that he will never be able to leave. He thereupon locks himself in a translucent block made of indestructible matter and goes dormant to await possible rescue millennia later. Centuries later, a Terran expedition lands on the planet where the red lizards rule and discovers the "Temple of the Past." There, in its center, lies the body of Massir, a human being six meters tall, born ten thousand years ago in fabulous Atlantis.

As this synopsis indicates, Wul was not afraid to present extreme situations of a kind which would have been disastrous to any author of lesser talent. The central figure of the novel, Massir, is also the primer move behind the story. He first appears as the classic embodiment of the fearless, space-wise old-timer, a type characteristic of low-grade space opera. He then progressively singles himself out by his dynamic spirit and his opportuneness; it is he who first has the idea of transforming the monster. However, he gradually loses his whole human dimension to become, not only an indifferent character, but a mere device for continuing the story, a key to ignite the plot.

Jolt, perhaps the most humane of the three, judging by his behavior, is the working-hand directed by Massir's brain. A physician (although on probation, which gives scant credibility to his untried knowledge), Jolt puts into practice Massir's stupendous ideas. He is as necessary as his companion to the evolution of the novel, since he is the only one able to transform the monster; but he lacks the conviction in reasoning and the imposing presence that distinguishes Massir. As for Raol, that unfortunate is the novel's only complete stereotype. He is barely competent enough to relieve the other two from time-consuming tasks when the verisimiltude of his scenario commands it. The author wisely does away with him as soon as his role in the plot is fulfilled.

Finally, there is the monster. When the conclusion of the novel reveals Massir to be six meters high, the monster suddenly achieves immoderate proportions. Although its only reactions are those caused by the astronauts in the depth of its stomach, it manages to originate, in spite of itself, a new species of intelligent lizards destined to rule the planet. The only achievement in this incredible adventure belongs to the monster, despite the fact that it is indisputably the most stupid and the least conscious character. This is the obvious product of the author's underlying humor.

The divisions of the novel are typical of action literature. The first part relates in a lively and effective style the shipwreck and the subsequent discovery of the monster; the second part depicts the monster's mutation; the third shows the attempts of Massir and Jolt to put the rocket back in operation while the red lizards look on; the fourth and shortest section is the conclusion. Ever since the novel's initial appearance, this ending has provoked controversy: does it add a gratuitous twist to a novel which is already essentially complete? Wul himself confesses that he is not sure how the idea of making Atlanteans out of the astronauts occurred to him (although in its time it was certainly more original than it seems today). In any event, this confession gives credence to the proposition that this particular kind of ending had already become the author's distinctive finishing touch; several of his novels conclude in a similar way, expecially *L'Orphelin de Perdide* (*The Orphan on Perdide*), the ending of which offers one of the most memorable time-paradoxes in French science fiction.

During an interview Wul stated that the central idea of *The Temple of the Past* occurred to him while he was reading a newspaper article about how two German soldiers had remained confined for over ten years in a Wehrmacht warehouse in the underground part of Warsaw. One went blind and the other mad. Wul simply transposed their story into a damaged rocketship, combined it with the Jonah myth, and gave his captive heroes an ingenious but time-consuming method of escape. The idea of having the monster undergo a speedy mutation is doubtless the most original part of the novel and a valuable contribution to science fiction. It also appears that *The Temple of the Past* is the only Wul novel that develops an idea never previously used in the genre, even though it also utilizes a number of stereotyped characters and situations. This central idea is, moreover, part of a theme common to the author's work: man's struggle against an utterly hostile environment. Generally, the human being facing the problem survives in a manner that is somewhat crazy, yet thoroughly logical. In his stories, Wul continually demonstrates the superiority of human intelligence over aggressive nature. In the character of Massir, this novel develops this proposition to its fullest extent. Mutations are frequently present in Wul's works, and the one which occurs in *The Temple of the Past* is twofold: first the sea-monster is transformed into an amphibious being, and then Massir himself is stripped of his humanity to become a God and creator of an intelligent species. He is a highly representative example of that group of capable professionals and self-made men that the author admired so much.

In *The Temple of the Past*, the plot is inextricably bound to the environment. There are actually four subenvironments which fit inside one another like Chinese boxes. The first is the lost rocketship, inside which the three survivors face their first problem. Once they solve that, Massir and his companions realize they must struggle against another environment which has swallowed the former: the monster. The third deadly environment is the liquid chlorine ocean which contains the monster. At last, escaped from the monster, the two remaining Atlanteans have to face yet a fourth environment, which contains the other three: the planet itself. Each passage from one environment to the next is like a test imposed upon Massir on his road to deification.

Much of Wul's uninterrupted popularity with his readers springs from the writing itself. Wul is first of all a painter, and the scenery in *The Temple of the Past* is of the highest importance. He is a painter who uses his colors sparingly, however; much of the detail must be filled in by readers themselves. The author's chief talent lies in his ability to create a whole universe out of a few words or sentences, a universe to which everyone can relate. However, he is also a painter clever enough to understand that, in the picture of an utterly alien world, the small details can often spoil the whole. It is therefore often more effective to provide subtle shapes and then let the reader fill in details. The four subenvironments that form *The Temple of the Past* give the author four opportunities to demonstrate his artistry in depicting the ruin inside the spaceship or the feelings of the monster as it lazes in liquid chlorine. The account of the astronauts' adventures inside the monster is wonderfully vivid and surrealistic. Wul is inspired by his passion for creating unforgettably bizarre settings. His books remain in one's memory primarily because of their strong and visual quality.

The Temple of the Past represents a rather unique situation in French science fiction of the late 1950's. At that time every national novelist was under the spell of the major Anglo-Saxon authors, whose translated works were overflowing the market. Even amid such competition, Wul immediately drew special attention to his work by flouting certain rules of the genre and by deliberately utilizing science fiction devices considered obsolete. Twenty years later, the spell of his work still remains. During those twenty years, French science fiction has greatly changed. Its Anglo-Saxon framework has fallen apart and it has grown increasingly intellectual and introverted. Thus, Wul appears as a writer of influence, a storyteller whose attractive pictures still pleasantly divert from the nightmares grown in hothouses that many contemporary writers offer.

Richard D. Nolane

Sources for Further Study

Reviews:

Galaxy. XXXIV, November, 1973, pp. 83-84.

Library Journal. CXVIII, November 15, 1973, p. 3476.

New York Times Book Review. September 23, 1973, p. 39.

TERMUSH, ATLANTERHAVSKYSTEN
(Termush)

Author: Sven Holm (1940-   )
First book publication: 1967
Type of work: Novel
Time: Shortly after World War III
Locale: The Atlantic coast, either in France or America

After an atomic war, a few rich survivors retreat to Termush, a protected hotel-clinic on the Atlantic coast

> *Principal characters:*
> THE DIARIST, a former professor
> MARIA, his mistress
> THE SPOKESMAN, who speaks for the more aggressive guests at Termush
> THE DOCTOR, the hotel physician

Termush describes a universe of barrenness and destruction, a place where people live at a barely subsistent emotional level. With a steady hand and a clear head Sven Holm presents a society in dissolution. The story of doom is told simply and laconically in language that is brisk, clean, and even. The very objectivity creates an atmosphere of immense eeriness and foreboding.

The book is written in the form of a diary consisting of thirty-one short entries that give us in clinical detail the story of the people at Termush, from the moment they leave the shelters six days after the last explosion of the holocaust to the moment they leave their refuge at Termush to seek a new one at sea. The diarist describes the ruin of human existence, but does so in a language free from tension, reproach, and misery; it is cool and sterile in its artistic control. One feels the scientist behind the diarist in his concise use of language. Despite this detachment, one feels the fear and weakness of the people described, together with their intense desire to survive. The narrator's own sense of the precariousness of the future transmits itself to the reader from episode to episode in this aloof, precise report from a no-man's-land in a work evoked by a doomsday vision.

This academic, objective style makes no attempt to probe the inner beings of the Termush survivors; there is little insight into, or personal envolvement with, their problems on the individual level. Perhaps the narrator's previous career as a university professor and his obsession with logical deduction have alienated him from the subjective side of human experience. Nor does he tell much about the personalities of his subjects. They tend to become mere representatives of ideas rather than human beings — although this may actually be appropriate for these dehumanized creatures.

The people at Termush cling to hope — without any real reason to do so. They have no foreseeable future, but reject the inevitability of their fate. They cling to life only because they fear death; they are concerned only with prolonging their useless existence. Refusing to consider their own mortality, the patients fill their time with a continual round of trivial occupations, and in doing so, they have become totally self-absorbed. The rest of the world — all of those outside of their sanctuary — are of no interest to them. Termush and what it stands for belongs to *them* and not to those who are in most need of the spa and its resources. The residents believe that since they possess the money and the power, they have the right to live in their "paradise" protected by angels with flaming swords (the staff) and to bar all "sinners" from admittance.

The diarist does not adhere to a straightforward story line, but rather focuses on half a dozen concerns, moving back and forth between them, juxtaposing them, and gradually working out the chronology as he goes along. These matters include: the static, almost paralytic world that emerges after the holocaust; the structure of power at Termush; the patients' fervent attachment to life; his own intense love affair with a childless widow named Maria; to a lesser degree, the world outside Termush and the sea; and, bringing it all together, the gradual disintegration of all these things as reality inexorably closes in on the group.

Much of the development of the novel lies in the slowly developing consciousness of the diary writer himself. On first returning to his room after the catastrophe, he is struck by strange feelings of insecurity, created, not by the disaster itself, but by the fact that nothing seems to have changed. He is especially fascinated by the changelessness of the sea. These initial reactions give the reader an insight into how his former life, so similar to those of the other guests, prepared him for this one. They delineate the social life and attitudes of the group and they fix the image of Termush in the reader's mind. The insecurity of the guests is underscored by their inability to understand the implications of their "subscription to life," and their narrow obsession with simple physical survival. Suddenly forced to live and imagine a new existence, they are unable to relate to it or to what is really happening in the world — some because they *cannot*, others because they *will not*. The reality slowly forces itself on the narrator, however; he likens the new world to a time of fables; nothing definite remains, neither scientific truth — such as the stability of the atom — nor psychological validity. His detachment from the world has become total. As he writes: "The world has spun full circle and the survivors must exist without it."

These thoughts lead him to question "normality" — his own, and even the concept itself. Who are the normal? Those who just continue to live as usual or those who collapse under these new pressures? He begins slowly to break under the psychic difficulties that this new situation has laid upon him. He begins having nightmares; he gives up fighting the restrictions the staff places on the guests; and more and more he desparately clings to Maria in their strange, passionate love affair. The narrator's emotional deterioration is paralleled by the other guests at Termush: One runs away because of claustrophic fears (the shelters); another commits suicide; two rape a girl; and the entire group conspire to persecute a solitary sick man.

At the beginning of the book, the reader's attention is directed to a playground where children play in a world of dreams, a place where the fantasies are both naïve and tender, relieved of all practical logic and everyday affairs. But something incredible and dangerous is hinted at in this absence of problems, in the speed and precision with which the children handle all situations in the here and now. The feeling grows that something lies behind it all; some unseen danger can be felt in this very lack of disharmony. How is it possible to deny reality so completely? As the story progresses it becomes obvious that this playground scene is intended as a metaphor of the situation at Termush and that the vague threat inherent in it is, indeed, very real. The guests live in a playworld of games and meaningless rituals; they enjoy immediate pleasures and mete out intense, trivial punishments. And their games, too, must eventually end.

The well organized life at Termush gradually breaks up. At first the staff had been friendly, hospitable, and flexible. Gradually they become more rigid and authoritarian. They begin to publish and enforce regulations; they begin to punish infractions, even trivial ones, with increasing severity. From a pleasant, luxurious resort hotel and clinic, Termush is gradually transformed into a virtual prison. And much of the increasing authoritarianism is the result of actions by the patients themselves.

The event that precipitates the breakdown of the power structure at Termush occurs when another guest, not one of the exiles, learns the story of the refugees. This shocking development splits the group into three factions: the Management, "rulers" of the hospital, complete with army, who become increasingly guardlike and "protecting"; the Hawks, the strongest of the patient "parties," a large group of egocentric, aggressive, and organized patients; and the Pidgeons, the weak opposition party, humanistic, but quiet and reserved, generally disorganized and indecisive. The first meeting between the three groups results in a victory for the Management and the Hawks, when the spokesman for the latter says: "An inspired lie should be preferred to a malignant truth."

These words become the basis for the censorship that is imposed on the entire group. Given the opening, the Management, in its zeal for protection, imposes its will totally, utilizing manipulation and censorship to force acceptance of its "vital lie." And it is all done in the name of "democracy." As one humanistic doctor (probably Holm's spokesman), says: "Democracy is based on the vote and therefore [he] did not put his faith in democracy."

Thus, Termush suddenly no longer represents an institution that protects its guests, but a minisociety governed by bureaucrats who control everything in the holy *name* of protection. Through the incidents surrounding the punishment of a sick man who gained access to Termush on false premises, Holm shows that the hotel is a microcosm of society; "Termush had become a living town, with streets and alleyways and a stake set up in the market place. The residents formed a united people; no one was going to intervene and destroy its moral code."

This intruder is not the only one to be punished by the cold intolerence of the society. Every tampering with its vital lie is suppressed. A normal life is impossible, but most of the guests refuse to accept the fact of the unreality imposed by force on all who do not want to share it. Ironically, in doing so they destroy whatever possibilities may still exist to live meaningfully in the new reality. In the words of Jørgen Elbed and H. Neiiendam: "It is impossible to live a real life, when you have choked up the source of the mind and with that the sources of cognition."

Because the guests at Termush have lost their past and refuse even to look at their present, their negative personal qualities are exaggerated and forced out into the open where they clash with those of their fellow patients. The result is a continual tension and conflict that gradually destroys the system that it was designed to protect. The Management and the Hawks lose their grip on power, and the vital lie begins more and more to crumble. The people are moved to ask themselves why they stay at Termush. They are forced to acknowledge to themselves, and to one another, that they have no future. Some cling to the Management's fanciful promise that a yacht will arrive to take them to an immaculate shore, but most just deteriorate, mentally and emotionally.

In the end the outside world that they had tried so long to ignore forces itself upon them and drives them from their retreat. By that time they have no will to exist; they rather meekly seek a new refuge in the sea — the only thing in the world that has stayed the same. But whether this exhausted and dispirited band can survive is highly problematical. The last lines of the diary are hardly hopeful: "Outside the sea is still; there is no darkness and no light."

The final image of the group drifting aimlessly out to sea is a powerful one. In the end it probably does not matter whether they survive; they have been essentially dead from the start. Sven Holm's point is that there is more to survival than mere continuation of physical existence. Protected by their wealth and social status prior to the holocaust, they had never had a meaningful relationship with society as a whole. Their reaction to the bomb was simply to emphasize their privileged state and ignore their fellow men. *Termush* chronicles the ultimate implications of such a choice. It is impossible for any group or individual to become isolated from the fate of society. If attempted, the psychological, moral, and ultimately practical price for such a course of action is enormously high and sooner or later it must be paid.

Erik H. Swiatek

Sources for Further Study

Reviews:

Observer. June 1, 1969, p. 28.

Spectator. CCXXII, May 23, 1969, p. 687.

Times Literary Supplement. June 12, 1969, p. 643.

THAT HIDEOUS STRENGTH

Author: C. S. Lewis (1898-1963)
First book publication: 1946
Type of work: Novel
Time: The mid-twentieth century
Locale: England

The conclusion of C. S. Lewis' Perelandra Trilogy, *in which the lords of the un-fallen planets intervene on Earth, Merlin reawakens, and Arthur's successor unites their forces to prevent the establishing of a dictatorship in Great Britain*

Principal characters:
    ELWIN RANSOM, a former university professor of philology
    MARK STUDDOCK, a fellow in sociology at Bracton College
    JANE STUDDOCK, his wife
    MERLINUS AMBROSIUS, the magician of Camelot
    JOHN WITHER, Deputy Director of the National Institute of Co-ordinated Experiments

C. S. Lewis was in every respect an unusual man: among the many sides of his personality were those of world-respected scholar of medieval and Renaissance literature and avid reader of science fiction. He had little patience with those who saw the two interests as contradictory; he enjoyed science fiction without condescension, applying the same standards to Martian or medieval romances alike.

That Hideous Strength forms the third part of Lewis' "space trilogy," following *Out of the Silent Planet* and *Perelandra*. But the term "space" is misleading: the setting of *That Hideous Strength* is entirely in England, and as Lewis himself pointed out, it can be understood without having read the earlier two works. It demonstrates, better than the first two parts of the trilogy, Lewis' mastery of what might be called synthetic mythology: putting together bits of earlier traditions to form a new, satisfying, and complete whole. Better than any other of his works, *That Hideous Strength* shows that the past, in the hands of an artist who knows and respects it as Lewis did, is alive and powerful.

A prominent skein from the past in Lewis' weave is the picture of the eldils. It is wrong to consider them angels in the sense of the rosy cherubs of quattrocento art. Only if we use "angel" as a generic term meaning any noncorporeal intelligent being, will it serve to categorize Lewis' creations. The author's source for the eldils was medieval angelology, which, following the fourth century writer, Pseudo-Dionysius, reckoned nine orders of angels, each with specific functions. Among the concerns of the angels were the planets, each of which was associated with a spiritual being in a relationship analogous to that of the body to its soul. Far from being only a part of theology, these angels held an important place in the theory of physics. Thinkers before the announcement of Newton's Laws of Motion observed that things kept moving only as long as force was applied; the continuous motion of the planets therefore required a continuous application of force, and the angelic powers were postulated as the source of the motive energy. This idea brought a satisfying symmetry to the picture of the universe: just as humans had individual guardian angels, and as nations had principalities watching their affairs, so also did the planets have their tutelary spirits, or "powers." Lewis borrows some details of this scheme for his trilogy, utilizing the planetary powers as his eldils, beings of great might and energy. But he made some changes, too.

Whereas Dante had suggested that the power ruling Earth was Fortuna — chance — Lewis amended the system to include elements of the Eden story by identifying the ruling power of Earth as Satan. Since that spirit's rebellion, Earth had been cut off from communication with the rest of the beings of the solar system; hence, it is "the Silent Planet." Finally, the use of the powers provided Lewis with a connection to the most popular mythology of our time (although he had no notion that it would become so) — *The Lord of the Rings* by his friend and colleague, J. R. R. Tolkien. The powers, or eldils, of Lewis' Thulcandra, Malacandra (Mars), and Perelandra (Venus) are the same sort of being as Tolkien's Valar.

Like the eldils, who appear in all three parts, the figure of Elwin Ransom serves to unite the parts of the trilogy. Ransom, a philologist like Tolkien, undergoes an astonishing transformation through the three books, as if Lemuel Gulliver were to turn into Lord Wellington. We first see Ransom as a vacationing professor, a little tweedy, between thirty-five and forty years old. During his stay on Mars in *Out of the Silent Planet*, he is fearful, bumbling, and more than a little comic. He is also principally an observer. The second volume, *Perelandra*, turns Ransom from an onlooker to a participant, as he struggles with the possessed body of Weston, his kidnaper in the first work, and succeeds in keeping the Earth's rebellion from spreading to Venus. During that volume Ransom grows considerably in inner strength and dignity, and at its conclusion he receives a wound. Upon returning home, he realizes that his wound, like that of Frodo in *The Lord of the Rings*, will not be healed on Earth.

Already it can be seen that Lewis' imagination worked well at selecting pieces from a variety of sources, borrowing the resonances of those sources, and adapting them to his own purposes. Ransom's wound adds still another mythology to *That Hideous Strength*: that of Camelot. In the final book, Ransom acquires another name, Mr. Fisher-King, bringing us again into the atmosphere of medieval romance. Although Lewis could have had a variety of sources for this detail, the one which most closely resembles *That Hideous Strength* is *Parzival*, a thirteenth century poem by Wolfram von Eschenbach, and the source as well of such diverse later renderings as Wagner's *Parsifal* and parts of T. S. Eliot's *The Waste Land*.

The Fisher King in Wolfram's *Parzival*, Anfortas, is wounded like Ransom, and the fertility of his land suffers as a result. Wolfram makes Anfortas gather around himself both an order of celibate knights (Ransom is unmarried) who carry out dangerous missions, and a group of chaste women who serve the Holy Grail. Like the Fisher King, Ransom is surrounded by an aura of magic: radically changed by his experiences, he now appears as a robust youth of twenty or so; he speaks to animals and communes regularly with the eldils; and throughout the novel he directs the activities of the band he has assembled.

But Ransom is no longer the central figure: his wound has made him immobile, and, more important, his near-apotheosis takes him somewhat out of the human sphere. Because he has become less understandable to ordinary mortals, Lewis has wisely moved him to the periphery of the action. At the center of the story is a more ordinary couple, Mark and Jane Studdock. The structure of *That Hideous Strength* depends on a careful arrangement of opposites in this conflict of good and evil, and that pairing process extends even to the Studdocks. Feeling the emptiness of her marriage and a rising fear of its failure, Jane is drawn with reluctance to the circle surrounding Ransom at St. Anne's-on-the-Hill, while her husband Mark edges toward complicity in the work of the National Institute for Coordinated Experiments (N.I.C.E.) at Belbury. They are each attracted and repelled by what they find in their new surroundings, and we see the progress of the plot to its climax chiefly through scenes in which they figure.

The conflict in the plot is provoked by the villains, the officers of N.I.C.E., who have been as misunderstood by some readers as has the angelic machinery. For instance, J. B. S. Haldane, the eminent biologist, saw N.I.C.E. as a caricature of and attack on science itself. He pointed out that the only real scientist in the novel is repelled by the Machiavellian plans of N.I.C.E., refuses to have anything to do with the organization, and is murdered by its Security Police. Haldane, as innocent of literary insight as he was of political judgment, missed the whole point. Preeminent among the leaders of N.I.C.E. are not physical scientists, whose link with reality is maintained by contact with their subjects, but behaviorists: psychologists, sociologists, and politicians. And even these disciplines are represented by corrupted examples. Lewis' point is not that science *per se* is a threat to humanity, but that any threat to human freedom and dignity will, in these times, present itself as scientific, just as in an earlier age it might have presented itself as religious.

Thus the leaders of N.I.C.E., bureaucrats rather than scientists, seek power, not knowledge. And one source is as good as another. If science will not give them all the power they want, they are willing to turn to magic. The Institute has located in Belbury, near a small college, on the strength of information that Merlin lies sleeping nearby, and is soon to awaken. If they could manage to win the half-demonic Celt to their side, their plans would proceed even faster. But they are frustrated when Merlin revives before they expect and joins Ransom's group at St. Anne's.

Merlin is one of the Lewis' most successful characters. He is soundly and convincingly from another time, barbaric in some ways, yet at the same time direct and more honest. He is both humorous and awe-inspiring, and at the same time manages to cement into place the two myths mentioned earlier. As a living, breathing figure from Camelot, he brings with him all the suggestions of splendor and tragedy from the Arthurian cycle. But he points us in another direction as well: we find out that the language Ransom uses with him is the speech of Atlantis, the True West, the Numenor of *The Lord of the Rings*. While Ransom and Merlin speak, the shades of Arthur and Gandalf hover nearby.

The villains are likewise well drawn. The Devil worship carried on in secret by the leaders of N.I.C.E. represents their total rejection of human values. If their plans succeed, they will form the Inner Party of an Orwellian dictatorship, beginning with England, but eventually clutching the whole Earth, and even the other planets. The comparison with *Nineteen Eighty-Four* is not adventitious; in *That Hideous Strength* we see Oceania in the making. Had Haldane looked clearly, he would have noticed Lewis' plain identification of the real villain: an attitude in philosophy that Lewis traces through Hegel and Hume and the Logical Positivists, an attitude that trickles down to popular thought as the notion that all human behavior is relative, and no actions are good or bad in themselves. Lewis argues that when such principles are embraced, only the ruthless will prevail. What begins in N.I.C.E. as a series of experiments on animals is but a prelude to similar ones on prisoners (in the name of rehabilitation), in which the methods for control of the general population will be worked out.

The brilliant characterization on the side of evil, matching that of Merlin, is Lewis' portrait of John Wither, Deputy Director of the Institute. Wither is the consummate opportunist. Throughout the many scenes in which he appears and the many speeches which he utters, he never commits himself to a statement. With the practice of years he has so guarded himself from engagement with his fellows that he has trimmed away his own being little by little, until his own bodily existence is not much more than a relative thing. As a portrait of evil he reminds one of Screwtape, the senior devil in Lewis' *The Screwtape Letters*, and the picture is all the more frightening when we realize that Wither has done this to himself with his eyes open all the way.

Fortunately, Wither and his henchmen do not succeed. They fail for two reasons. First, Weston's invasions of Mars and Venus in the first two novels have broken the quarantine, and the powers of the unfallen planets can act on Earth in self-defense. The second reason, equally as important, is that despite the philosophy of N.I.C.E., there is a reality beyond situation ethics: nature herself turns against them.

Throughout the novel, the villains, especially Wither, have prostituted language and its outlets: one of the aims of N.I.C.E. is the control of newspapers and radio, and one of Mark's first assignments is the manipulation of public opinion through a campaign of lies. Similarly, inhumane experiments on beasts have formed a major part of their work. At a climactic banquet scene, the directors and supporters of N.I.C.E. are subjected to a second confusion of tongues. As they discover that Babel has come again, the experimental animals escape from their cages and ravage the guests. The narrator points out that their aims have succeeded in an unexpected way: they wanted language divorced from meaning, and now they have it. As they were no respecters of the persons of the beasts, so the beasts return their treatment. The scene closes as it began, with reminiscences of the Old Testament: the village, the site of the new Tower of Babel, now suffers the fate of Sodom and Gomorrah.

In gathering together strands from a variety of sources, the story Lewis weaves benefits from the colorful richness of medieval philosophy, the tales of King Arthur, the Old Testament, and *The Lord of the Rings*. *That Hideous Strength* caps a trilogy that begins on the loom of science fiction, showing, if any further proof were needed, that the genre provides an adequate framework for a tapestry of any subject, especially if the weaver has the skill of C. S. Lewis.

Walter E. Meyers

Sources for Further Study

Criticism:

Hilton-Young, Wayland. "The Contented Christian," in *Cambridge Journal*. X (July, 1952), pp. 603-612. Hilton-Young analyzes the mythmaking employed in *That Hideous Strength* and compares Lewis to other modern religious novelists.

Moorman, Charles. "Space Ship and Grail: The Myths of C. S. Lewis," in *College English*. XVIII (May, 1957), pp. 401-405. Moorman looks at Lewis' use of Arthurian mythology in *That Hideous Strength* and compares its treatment to the cosmic myth of the first two novels in the trilogy.

Norwood, W. D. "C. S. Lewis, Owen Barfield and the Modern Myth," in *Midwest Quarterly*. VIII (Spring, 1967), pp. 279-291. Norwood finds that the romantic fantasies of the earlier Lewis novels shift to a historical realism in *That Hideous Strength*.

Spacks, Patricia Meyer. "The Myth-Makers Dilemma: Three novels by C. S. Lewis," in *Discourse*. XI (October, 1959), pp. 234-243. Spacks criticizes the science fiction framework in *That Hideous Strength* for trivializing the Christian meaning for the non-Christian reader.

THEY'D RATHER BE RIGHT

Authors: Mark Clifton (1906-1963) and Frank Riley
First book publication: 1954
Type of work: Novel
Time: The near future
Locale: San Francisco and its environs

The story of an artificial intelligence with miraculous psychotherapeutic abilities

> Principal characters:
> JOE CARTER, a telepath
> PROFESSOR BILLINGS, an aged scientist
> PROFESSOR HOSKINS, a younger scientist
> MABEL, an ex-prostitute
> HOWARD KENNEDY, a plutocrat
> BOSSY, an intelligent machine

Most of the novels which have won the Hugo Award went on to achieve considerable financial if not always critical success. The most striking exception is *They'd Rather Be Right*, which won the award for novels published in 1954. It is, indeed, the poorest of the award-winning novels, and won in a poor year (though the other candidates included Poul Anderson's *Brain Wave* and Frederik Pohl and Cyril M. Kornbluth's *Gladiator-at-Law*, both of which have proved far more durable). Its eclipse is, however, at least partly due to an accident of fate. The original *Astounding Science Fiction* serial was actually a continuation of a story published some months earlier in the same magazine called "Hide! Hide! Witch!" and the book version should really have carried both stories. Unfortunately, the earlier story had been written by Mark Clifton in collaboration with Alex Apostolides rather than with Frank Riley, and its incorporation would presumably have caused complications in the matter of rights. Thus, the book version (somewhat revised from the serial version) published in 1957 and reprinted as a paperback a year later under the title *The Forever Machine* is rather unsatisfactory, omitting much important introductory material.

"Hide! Hide! Witch!" tells the story of how Professor Billings, Dean of Psychosomatic Research at Hoxworth University, is commissioned to build a servomechanism capable of anticipating future eventualities and preparing strategies to cope with them. Billings is restricted in this work by the close supervision of security agents, and his society is one which has for many years been subject to rigid "opinion control," where "freedom of speech" is protected by the rigorous suppression of all "subversive opinions," not only in politics but in science too. (The story is very much a product of the period of Joseph McCarthy — it makes much of the metaphor of witch-hunting — and of the security blanket which descended upon scientific research in the wake of the hydrogen bomb leak.) Billings knows that his masters have no idea how much they are asking in giving him this commission, nor do they suspect the enormous potential of a machine such as they require. Nevertheless, the commission represents a warrant for genuine research, and holds the potential for a considerable step in technological progress. In order to make headway he recruits a cyberneticist, Professor Hoskins, and one of his students, who happens to be the world's only telepath. (The student, Joe Carter, is the subject of an earlier story by Clifton and Apostolides, "Crazy Joey.")

Together the three manage to build a machine which can do what is required of it — and much more. They name the artificial intelligence "Bossy" because of its imagined resemblance to a cow. As soon as the measure of their achievement is known, however, there is an outburst of hostility against the notion of a machine that can outthink a man, and there is soon a mob outside the gates of the university, howling for blood. Carter, Billings, and Hoskins are forced to go into hiding, carrying with them the various parts of their machine.

They'd Rather Be Right itself continues the story with Joe Carter managing to get the professors into hiding on "Skid Row," where they are accommodated by an ailing ex-prostitute named Mabel. With the help of another petty criminal, Doc Carney, who believes them to be counterfeiters, they gather new supplies of equipment. They reassemble Bossy and restore her to working order. Joe intends to use Bossy to administer "psychosomatic therapy" to a volunteer in the hope that clearing away the psychological problems of an ordinary human being might turn that human being into a telepath like himself. (In this respect, too, the novel was very much a product of its time — the *psi* boom was at its height in the pages of *Astounding Science Fiction*, and editor John W. Campbell, Jr., was still receptive to the idea of miraculous new therapeutic techniques such as the one invented by his protégé L. Ron Hubbard.)

Billings and Bossy begin working on Mabel, promising her the possibility of a cure for her arthritis. At first, progress is slow, but once Bossy has absorbed everything Billings knows and is able to carry on alone (after perfecting the psychotherapeutic techniques), things move faster. Mabel is, indeed, cured of her physical ailments — including her age. She becomes a beautiful girl apparently no more than twenty-one years old. Her newfound sanity, alas, is a little too dramatic, and leaves her naïvely incapable of understanding human mores. She wanders out into the street naked, and is picked up by the police. The police psychiatrist tires to have her committed as a lunatic, but she is rescued in a courtroom battle by a lawyer hired by the powerful industrialist Howard Kennedy. Joe Carter, convinced that Mabel's latent psionic abilities are now ready for full expression, goes to see Kennedy. He finds the millionaire surprisingly cooperative, because, immune from public opinion by virtue of his wealth, he has long harbored utopian plans for the reinstitution of scientific progress as a means to creating a better society. Kennedy gives the fugitive professors a laboratory in which to work, protection from harassment, and the services of his public relations staff to manipulate opinion on Bossy's behalf.

Using Mabel as an advertisement for Bossy's potential as a benefactor of mankind, Joe and his colleagues prepare for a public demonstration of her power. This time, Billings is the guinea pig, but the plan goes awry when Bossy, after a long struggle, rejects him as incurable. Here the didactic element of the theme is hammered home: psychotherapy can only work if the subjects sincerely want to achieve sanity, and this must involve a willingness to abandon even their most treasured convictions if these should prove to be unrealistic. Even Billings, champion of the oppressed against the hostility of the witch-hunters, finds this price too high, for he cannot give up some of the articles of his scientific faith. The moral of the story becomes plain: anyone who holds firm allegiance to any set of principles, whether moral, political, or scientific, is unsuitable material for Bossy's immortalizing process, while the only people who qualify are the downtrodden and bewildered, who have lived their lives in a state of ethical and theoretical doubt and cynicism. Clifton and Riley, as the title of the novel suggests, have little confidence in the ability of their fellow men to accept the challenge of a superior intelligence, believing that ordinary people will invariably cling to the "knowledge" to which they have already committed themselves.

The reason that Billings is not sufficiently openminded to be a candidate for immortality is that his scientific philosophy is a "single-value" system; in other words, he has a view of reality in which statements are either true or false. According to Bossy, all truth is relative and the principle of the excluded middle is an error. This particular line of attack was already a familiar one to readers of *Astounding Science Fiction* in the 1950's, when Campbell was convinced that orthodox physicists were far too narrow-minded in refusing to take an interest in the various brands of pseudoscience that he found fascinating. A. E. van Vogt had already popularized the supposed supremacy of "non-Aristotelian logic," and though Clifton, Apostolides, and Riley never mention Korzbyski in either "Hide! Hide! Witch" or *They'd Rather Be Right*, there seems to be something of the spirit of *Science and Sanity* moving through the plot.

After the failure with Billings, Joe Carter has to wait for Doc Carney to decide that *he* wants to be immortal, but he runs into more trouble when the Army claims Bossy as a vital factor in national defense. The question now being debated throughout the world is who should control Bossy and who is entitled to be made immortal. Joe knows that as soon as the public realizes that there are only a few people who *can* be made immortal — and who they are — the old hostility will break out again, redoubled in force. The altruistic inventors agree to evade the problem by making sure that *everyone* gets Bossy, and Kennedy's factories begin secretly retooling for mass-production, using instructions and blueprints kindly provided by Bossy herself. The story ends with Joe Carter speaking on television to the people of the world, telling them that Bossy is theirs to do with exactly as they wish, that she is not a threat but a challenge, and that she is the ultimate tool adequate to each and every purpose, if only people will decide what that purpose is to be.

It is not too difficult to understand why *They'd Rather Be Right* won a Hugo in 1955. All the Hugos for that year were taken by writers from *Astounding Science Fiction*, and *They'd Rather Be Right* is the archetypal *Astounding Science Fiction* novel of the period, combining all the magazine's idiosyncratic concerns in a single story. Most of those concerns were to fade away as the intellectual and political climate changed and such writers as Rhine and Korzybski went out of fashion. Today, the novel seems to be espousing some rather dubious causes and tilting eccentrically at windmills. It is a work which speaks eloquently of its time and its place of origin, but it is no longer convincing.

The injury done to the novel by its preoccupation with fashionable crusades is perhaps made clear by the fact that it loses one of the narrative threads with which it started, and completely fails to explore any of the abundant additional possibilities opened up by the notion of an artificial superintelligence. The narrative thread that is lost is Joe Carter's quest to overcome his loneliness, which is the focal point of "Crazy Joey" and the key to his motivation throughout the main narrative. He does, indeed, find companions when Mabel acquires *psi* powers and when Doc Carney belatedly joins the gang. By the time this happens, however, it is dismissed in a few cursory paragraphs. Joe and Mabel fall in love, of course, but this observation is simply thrown into the narrative in an offhand manner — the attention of the authors is elsewhere. Indeed, for a novel which sets out to be the scourge of narrow-mindedness, the narrative seems to stick very close to a single track, never paying much heed to corollaries and new horizons.

On the credit side, however, the story is one of the first to deal with the theme of artificial intelligence in any but the most superficial manner, and its championship of mental flexibility against dogmatism has not altogether lost its timeliness. Perhaps the most important aspect of the book is the challenge which it presents to the reader, for implicit in the assumptions made by the authors is the notion that its likely audience have more in common with Professor Billings than with Mabel or Joe Carter. The real didactic element in the novel is not so much the observation contained in the title but the question implied by that observation: would *you* rather be right?

Brian Stableford

Sources for Further Study

Reviews:

Analog. LXI, June, 1958, pp. 142-143.

Fantastic Universe Science Fiction. IX, June, 1958, p. 118.

Galaxy. XVI, July, 1958, p. 107.

Magazine of Fantasy and Science Fiction. XIV, April, 1958, p. 94.

THIS IMMORTAL

Author: Roger Zelazny (1937-   )
First book publication: 1966
Type of work: Novel
Time: The indefinite future
Locale: The Earth after a nuclear war

An evocative rendering of how an aware, highly intelligent, and godlike human being makes his home in an often malignant universe

> *Principal characters:*
> CONRAD NOMIKOS, the immortal
> CASSANDRA, his young wife
> CORT MYSHTIGO, a Vegan emissary visiting Earth
> PHIL GRABER, an ex-revolutionary poet
> HASAN, the Assassin
> DON DOS SANTOS and
> DIANE, revolutionary leaders

Roger Zelazny's first novel, *This Immortal*, won the Hugo Award for Science Fiction in 1966; it was originally published in a shorter version as ". . . And Call Me Conrad" in *The Magazine of Fantasy and Science Fiction* in 1965. It exhibits many of the faces of this protean writer, who is poet, preacher, prophet, myth-user, and game-player.

This Immortal, like most of Zelazny's work, is a stylistic mosaic, ranging from terse, economical dialogue often depending on the unsaid and the space of silence, to the poetic use of interlocking images, and a rare quality of passion. The novel opens, for example, in the tough, compact prose of detective fiction similar to that of the early Amber novels, with a conversation between Conrad and his wife Cassandra. It makes us acutely aware of the distance between Conrad's sense of himself and the image others, even his wife, have of him. At once, the combination of external dialogue and internal monologue reveal to us that he is clever, impulsive, devious, and cautious. Conrad is obviously far more than he pretends to be, and what is left unsaid is sometimes as important as what is said. Yet at the novel's close he presents a paean to his friend Phil which is not only a deeply felt tribute and praise, but also a haunting commentary on the cycles of life and death, gain and loss. Conrad's memories of ancient Greece and the music he pipes to the satyrs in a hidden glade similarly reflect in precious rhetoric the song of a dying Earth.

The novel's structure is multileveled as well. It is science fiction: a dramatization of the effects of a nuclear holocaust and the dystopia which results, incorporating techniques such as treatments which retard or reverse aging (the Sprung-Samser treatments), artificial products and procedures extrapolated from contemporary procedures (simicokes and simicoloring), and a variety of futuristic vehicles and weapons. It is also a mystery story — why is the Vegan emissary really on Earth, and who is trying to kill him? — as well as a mythic fantasy, the tale of a mutant immortal demigod battling mythic beasts and superhuman foes.

The setting of the novel is an Earth devastated both physically and psychologically. It is a postcatastrophic world — Earth after the Apocalypse. A cataclysmic atomic war has wasted the entire planet, leaving only a few habitable places, mutating existing life forms, re-creating many mythical figures out of men and beasts, and destroying most of human culture. Yet even more serious is the shock to man's consciousness. Alien contact has forced man to realize both that he is not the *only* conscious animal in the universe, and that he is, in fact, an inferior one. So most of Earth's survivors have chosen servitude to the higher Vegan civilization over a primitive struggle to rebuild their own culture. The novel questions whether man can survive these shocks emotionally, psychically, and spiritually as well as physically.

The plot of *This Immortal* centers on Conrad Nomikos, who is both keeper of the past (he is the Commissioner of Arts, Monuments, and Archives) and protector of the future (as Konstantin Karaghiosis, one of his many names, Conrad has been the rebel leader of the Returnist Radpol, those who have fought to keep the Vegans from turning Earth into a museum-resort and have convinced the Earth *émigrés* to return and rebuild the planet). Conrad is a mutant who is immortal, invincible, and wise (the demigod); a demon who destroys as well as creates; and a Herculean monster-slayer of many forms and names (the significance of the original title).

The novel begins nearly a century after the "Three Days" atomic holocaust has devastated Earth and driven most surviving Earth people to colonies on other planets. An absentee government on Taler has turned the remaining habitable areas of Earth into a combination museum and resort. In a classic older man/younger woman scene, Conrad, who is more than two hundred years old (though he appears to be in his twenties), is explaining to his twenty-year-old wife Cassandra that he must leave her for a while. He has been chosen by the "Earth director" to take the Vegan Cort Myshtigo on a tour which will recapitulate the course of human history, in Egypt, Greece, Rome, Western and Eastern Europe, Mexico, and the United States. Myshtigo, the blue Vegan emissary, has credentials in philosophy, philanthropy, and enlightened journalism. And although it is unclear exactly what Myshtigo is doing on Earth, all agree that the future of the planet depends upon his visit.

Other travelers include Don Dos Santos and Diane, new leaders of the Returnist movement who are convinced that the Vegan is a surveyor bringing Armageddon with a checkbook and are determined to kill him; Phil Graber, Conrad's oldest friend; poet and Returnist Tom Paine, whose *Call of Earth* and *Articles of Return* were the redeclarations of independence and constitution for the Radpol during their initial success at keeping the Earth autonomous; and Hasan, the Assassin who has never failed, master of weapons and the last mercenary of Earth, the chosen one of the dark god Angelsou, the voodoo god of death. Hasan fought with Conrad against the Vegans' first attempt to make the Earth their playground and now fights against him to kill Myshtigo.

We see many of Conrad's powers on the tour's first stop in Egypt: as the group travels through Old and New Cairo to Luxor, Karnak, and the Valley of Queens, he oversees the dismantling of the great pyramid of Cheops to convince Myshtigo that Earth will be destroyed rather than be turned into a Vegan resort (Conrad says that they are viewtaping the destruction to run it backward as "The Building of the Great Pyramid," but we learn later that the blocks have been numbered so that the pyramid may be reassembled). He also fights the boadile, destroys Hasan's robot golem, which possesses strength and speed five times that of a human being, goes into a murderous rage when he learns that Cassandra has been killed in an earthquake, and discovers that his pseudo-telepathic wish-fulfillment is really telepathy.

It is on the next stop, however, in Greece (as the group travels to Athens and from Lamia to Volos), that we fully realize the convergence of life and myth which has occurred in these last days of Earth. It is Phil, who once stood in the Theater of Dionysus in Athens and charismatically read a hymn to Pan, who believes in "The Big Cycles"; who recognizes that the age of heroes, demigods, and strange beasts has come again; who sees this new age in Laurentian terms as a descent into the same darkness out of which humanity rose; and who focuses our attention on the mythic quality of the events.

What we see is the emergence of mythic beasts and plants: satyrs, centaurs, vampire flowers, winged horses, sea serpents, and spiderbats. Here is Zelazny the myth-user. Outer forms objectify inner metaphysics: as a science fiction writer, Zelazny is more concerned with inner than with outer space, and religion and myth become history. As he has used myths in other works (for example, Egyptian mythology in *Creatures of Light and Darkness*, Buddhism in *Lord of Light*, and the Faust myth in "For a Breath I Tarry"), here he uses both ancient and modern Greek myth, drama, and folklore to provide fictional content and substance.

Conrad is described as a ruined spirit of place who is living a folksong both as a demon and as a demigod who denies Carlyle's dictum about heroes and ideals. He is hero and antihero at once, expedient and practical as well as intuitive and idealistic; he is a many-named, arbitrary lawkeeper. He is in fact a Pan-avatar (and thus a representative of Dionysus as well), paradoxically both destroyer and protector of the world. His left profile is that of a demon, his right that of a demigod, and his physical description (hairline peaked at the brow, fungus growth on his face, one leg shorter than the other, a limp) and attributes (he calls the satyrs to him, and standing with his back against an enormous and ancient tree which is surely the Tree of the World, he plays for them the last song he had ever made, the song of the dying Earth) are those of Pan. But whether Conrad is Pan or simply a mutant child, whether, like Nathaniel Hawthorne and Henry James, Zelazny provides a "rational" alternative for those who would reject the mythic, Myshtigo is certain: "You destroy only what you mean to rebuild. Probably you are Great Pan, who only pretended to die."

While in Greece, Conrad must do Herculean battle against cannibalistic tribesmen and their chief, Procrustes; survive the burning rock; and conquer the Black Beast of Thessaly (paralleling Hercules' fourth labor of slaying the wild boar of Arcadia). He is also reunited with his century-old son Jason, the archetypal shepherd and seer, dreamer of dreams, teller of stories, and singer of songs, and his lost hunting dog, the hell-hound Bortan. Yet, although these physical dangers are trials enough, the greatest difficulty is a question of ethics: should the Vegan be kept alive? Paradoxically, keeping Myshtigo alive is both morally right and politically essential; finally Conrad learns that Myshtigo is indeed surveying Earth, but only so that it may be given its autonomy and thus have its cultural integrity preserved. The irony is extended by the fact that, although Conrad keeps him alive, Myshtigo is dying anyway from a rare disease; yet, before he dies, he appoints Conrad the administrator of Earth.

The ending is by far the weakest part of the novel. First Bortan appears after having been lost for a century to rescue Conrad from one of the Hot Places, the Valley of Sleep (his second trial), and to help him battle the Black Beast of Thessaly. They are both rescued by the sudden reappearance of Cassandra, who has been saved by her premonitions and miraculously arrives at the exact moment when the Beast appears about to destroy Conrad; it is a transparent use of *deus ex machina*. This is followed by an awkward telling rather than showing of what happens later to the other characters, an obvious and uncomfortable attempt to tie up the novel's "loose ends" in a brief sequel.

Yet Zelazny the prophet has given us a vision of a postcatastrophic dystopia, and incorporated both an alien viewpoint and that of Emerson's man as a god in ruins. If man, the ritual dreamer, is to be himself, he must pierce the Melville-type pasteboard masks of the universe; he must choose freedom rather than peace. Though only the Earth endures, man becomes himself as he aids in its preservation.

Clark Mayo

Sources for Further Study

Reviews:

Galaxy. XXV, December, 1966, pp. 131-133.

Magazine of Fantasy and Science Fiction. XXXI, December, 1966, pp. 34-35.

Manchester Guardian. January 4, 1968, p. 11.

New Worlds. CLXIX, December, 1966, p. 153.

Observer. December 17, 1967, p. 21.

Punch. CCLIV, February 14, 1968, p. 248.

SF Commentary. XX, April, 1971, pp. 28-29.

THREE HEARTS AND THREE LIONS

Author: Poul Anderson (1926-   )
First book publication: 1961
Type of work: Novel
Time: 1938-1943 in this universe, the Middle Ages in another
Locale: California and Denmark, and the Holy Empire and Faerie

Holger Carlsen, an American-trained, Danish-born engineer, finds himself transported to a parallel medieval and magical universe where he plays a pivotal role in the ultimate battle between Law and Chaos

Principal characters:
> HOLGER CARLSEN, an engineer-turned-knight whose deeds of bravery save two worlds
> HUGI, his comic but valiant dwarf guide and companion
> ALIANORA, Carlsen's virgin swan-may love interest
> SIR CARAHUE, a Saracen knight who is seeking the man who bears the device of three hearts and three lions

Poul Anderson's *Three Hearts and Three Lions* is one of those novels that blurs the distinction between fantasy and science fiction. While primarily a swashbuckling tale of sword and sorcery, there are just enough ties to the science and engineering of the here-and-now to warrant a science fiction classification. Without worrying about the straitjacketed pigeonholing of such classification, however, *Three Hearts and Three Lions* emerges as a delightful new variation on a very old theme and stands as an outstanding example of romantic speculation.

The basic plot is familiar enough. A knight-errant, with his comic sidekick and his fair lady, travels about doing assorted good deeds and ultimately saves the world from the bad guys. Anderson has, first of all, changed the ground rules to allow for magic in his universe. Thus, sorcery is added to swordplay, and the range of opposition to the hero significantly increased. This touch allows the hero's sidekick to be a dwarf named Hugi, who communes with the animals, and his lady a swan-may — a young girl who changes into a fierce swan at will — named Alianora. The opposition includes a witch, sorcerers, a giant, a troll, a dragon, a werewolf, Morgan le Fay, a water-sprite, and the Wild Hunt. The rather episodic nature of the plot first leads the hero to find out what he must do, then to the conclusion of his task, while facing an ever changing set of adversaries. The hero, Holger Carlsen, and his quest provide the unity the novel requires.

But Anderson takes his complications a step further by providing a realistic frame for the sword-and-sorcery plot. An unnamed Narrator, presumably Anderson himself, presents Carlsen's story to the reader as it was presented to him. The Narrator first met Holger in 1938, when they worked together in California. Holger was a Danish-born, American-educated engineer, and when World War II broke out he returned to Denmark to join the resistance movement. During a particularly important operation involving the smuggling of an unnamed but vital individual out of Germany, Holger was wounded by a stray bullet and knocked out. When he came to he was in another world: a world of swords and sorcery, witches and werewolves, giants and trolls. He was stark naked and completely isolated, except for a huge horse bearing clothing, armor, and weapons, all of which fit him surprisingly well.

Following this miraculous transport to another world — a standard feature of parallel or multiple-universe plots — Carlsen begins to learn the ground rules of his new location. First he encounters a witch, Mother Gerd, who conjures up a spirit to find out how he can return home. The spirit's message is ominous: apparently Holger's only way to return lies within Faerie.

It seems that this world is divided into two opposing factions: Chaos, the side of magic and evil; and Law, the side of right and good. The forces of Chaos are mustering their strength in Faerie, the part of the world that they control, for one final, massive assault on Law. Carlsen naturally sides with Law, and the prospect of a journey to the heart of the enemy camp is hardly inspiring. But he resolves to do so, since it is his only hope of returning home.

Mother Gerd provides him with a guide, the dwarf Hugi, and Hugi introduces him to Alianora, a beautiful girl with the magical ability to turn into a swan at will. They accompany him on his trip to Faerie. As soon as they cross the border, their first adventure begins. A strange knight demands to see Holger's coat of arms (until that time hidden from view) and, upon seeing three hearts and three lions blazoned on Holger's shield, attacks him fiercely. Defeating the strange knight with fighting skills that he did not know he possessed, Holger and his companions are amazed to discover that the opponent's suit of armor is empty — Holger was fighting against magic.

Next comes a meeting with Duke Alfric, one of the leaders of Faerie, and a stay at his magic castle. Holger tells the Duke of his problem, and Alfric ostensibly tries to help him. But actually Duke Alfric cunningly plots to remove the mysterious bearer of three hearts and three lions from the coming war by trapping him in Elf Hill, a sort of time-warp that makes a hundred years pass like a single night. Alerted by Alianora, Holger fights his way to freedom, but he must face the fact that he will receive no help from the forces of Chaos. He must find another way to return to this world.

The bulk of the remainder of the novel is devoted to a series of episodes involving Holger solving some problem or defeating some enemy. First, he defeats a fire-breathing dragon by throwing a helmet full of water down its throat, causing a minor boiler explosion. Next, he rejects the amorous advances of the beautiful Morgan le Fay, who for some strange reason seems to know him. A giant named Balamorg is defeated and turned to stone in a riddling contest reminiscent of two episodes in J. R. R. Tolkien's well-known novel *The Hobbit*. A nobleman's werewolf daughter is discovered and disposed of. A lake spirit who briefly captures Holger is defeated by the burning of a magnesium knife under water. Morgan le Fay is again rejected, after offering in good faith to resolve the knight's problems, and finally Holger and Hugi kill an apparently invincible troll while outrunning the dreaded Wild Hunt itself.

Along the way Holger consults with a good magician and finds that his destiny is somehow bound up with the magic sword of Cortana, similar to Arthur's sword Excalibur, and a Saracen knight who has been seeking the unknown bearer of three hearts and three lions. The mysterious Sir Carahue, the Saracen, will not say if he is friend or foe of the unknown knight, only that he seeks him desperately and that he will know him when he sees him. Out of a natural caution Holger has the magician disguise his features and invites Carahue to accompany him on his quest for the great sword.

Ultimately, the quest succeeds and Holger is revealed as Ogier le Danske, the Defender, an epic figure who is the only man capable of defeating Chaos in the last battle. Sir Carahue has been his loyal ally in some remote past, and together they ride to the war. Alianora, who loves and is loved by Holger, is left to mourn for the faithful Hugi, slain in the final encounter with the troll, and await Holger's return.

Victorious though he is, however, Holger does not reap the rewards of victory. At the very moment of his success, when he has decided that he would prefer to stay in that world rather than return to this one, he is mysteriously back in World War II, in the same battle he had left. Ogier the Defender, having defeated the forces of Chaos in that world, is needed to defeat the forces of Chaos, otherwise known as the Nazis, in this world.

Anderson bases his plot on the premise that our myths, legends, and stories might be based on real happenings in some parallel universe. Drawing on Arthurian legend, Scandinavian tales and folklore, and the great medieval *chansons*, Anderson adds a modern twist by giving logical scientific explanations for many of the seemingly magical occurrences. He thus explains the dragon's fiery breath, the curse of a giant's gold, the genetics of the werewolf, and several other inexplicable phenomena.

The only real flaw of the novel is its episodic structure. Several of the episodes in the lengthy middle section seem to exist for their own sake; there is no movement of plot or characterization, and no apparent thematic need for them. This can probably be explained by the similar structure of many of Anderson's epic sources, and, more importantly, by the publisher's requirements for the novel version. As was the case with much science fiction of the 1950's, the shorter version of *Three Hearts and Three Lions* that was published in the *Magazine of Fantasy and Science Fiction* in 1953 led to many requests for more adventures of Holger Carlsen. This so-called "give-us-more syndrome" of the hard-core science fiction fans led to expanded novel-length publications of many popular shorter works. This expansion often led to novels significantly weaker in structure and style than the seed story. The episodic nature of the plot of the novel version of *Three Hearts and Three Lions* can probably be traced to this cause.

Two elements of the novel stand out as particularly well handled. First, Anderson clearly delineates characters by their manner of speaking. Hugi and Alianora, for example, are especially distinctive, speaking a lower and upper class Scottish respectively. Carahue speaks throughout with a formalized Arthurian diction. Somewhat less care has apparently been taken with Holger himself, however, since he begins with a comic Danish accent ("These mat'ematicians vork their brains so hard, no vonder they snap into metaphysics ven off duty. Eqval and opposite reaction.") and ends up sounding more like a standard middle-class American of the 1950's ("You're nuts, I tell you!" Holger protested. "Any fool —").

Second, Anderson handles the descriptive details of medieval weaponry and fighting extremely well. From the fit of the clothing to the use of sword, shield, knife, and lance, the author provides details that ring true. This can be partly explained by the fact that Anderson was one of the founders of the Society for Creative Anachronism, a group of medieval enthusiasts who attempt to re-create the ambiance of the Middle Ages through role playing. As an SCA knight, Anderson would probably have gained experience with simulated weapons such as those Holger uses. In any case, he has been able to lend just the right touch of verisimilitude to his narrative.

Throughout *Three Hearts and Three Lions* Holger Carlsen maintains the reader's interest. His sense of humor, analytical ability, courage, and above all plain common sense are endearing and admirable. At the same time his human failings are clear, and some of his problems are of his own making. We follow the blossoming of his love for Alianora with a smile, and we question with him the motives of Sir Carahue. In short, Anderson has created a fully-rounded sympathetic character with whom the reader can identify. The plot, the characters, and the language combine to make a delightful piece of romantic entertainment.

David Stevens

Sources for Further Study

Criticism:

Erisman, Robert O. "Trolls and Witches of a Coexistent Cosmos," in *New York Times Book Review*. August 17, 1961, p. 27. Erisman finds this novel an imaginative journey to an alternative universe with a Middle World atmosphere.

Reviews:

Amazing Stories. XXXVI, February, 1962, p. 138.

Analog. LXVIII, October, 1961, pp. 163-165.

Booklist. LVII, July 15, 1961, p. 694.

Galaxy. XX, February, 1962, pp. 190-191.

Kirkus Reviews. XXIX, April 15, 1961, p. 386.

Luna Monthly. XVIII, November, 1960, p. 16.

New York Herald Tribune Book Review. September 17, 1961, p. 14.

THE THREE STIGMATA OF PALMER ELDRITCH

Author: Philip K. Dick (1928-1982)
First book publication: 1965
Type of work: Novel
Time: 2016
Locale: New York, Mars, Luna, Sigma 14-B

An account of the events following Palmer Eldritch's return to the solar system from Proxima Centauri, and his marketing of a new hallucinogenic drug

> *Principal characters:*
> LEO BULERO, chairman of the board of P. P. Layouts
> BARNEY MAYERSON, a Pre-Fash consultant
> RONDINELLA FUGATE, his assistant
> PALMER ELDRITCH, a wealthy industrialist
> FELIX BLAU, a detective

Philip Dick published *The Three Stigmata of Palmer Eldritch* at the height of his most prolific period, three years after *The Man in the High Castle* and three years before *Do Androids Dream of Electric Sheep?* It is a key book in the Dick canon because it combines some of the major preoccupations seen separately elsewhere in his work. It associates the shifting realities and private universes already featured in such works as *Eye in the Sky*, *The Man in the High Castle*, and *Martian Timeslip* with the theological speculations later to become predominant in such works as *Our Friends from Frolix-8* and *A Maze of Death*, achieving the association by way of the altered consciousness induced by a hallucinogenic drug. In common with so many Dick stories it portrays the absorption of the victims of induced alienation into a shared fantasy world where they must function without the supportive certainties that sustain ordinary people in their everyday lives and must react as they can, whether in anguish or with fatalistic acceptance.

The principal setting of the novel is an Earth slowly being consumed by the heat of the sun, its surface temperature rising slowly but inexorably. The only pleasant environment left is in Antarctica, but in the great cities life goes on while houses and workplaces, now mostly underground, can still be kept cool. Colonies have been planted on various planets and satellites in the solar system, and colonists are conscripted by the United Nations in the hope of preserving the race in the long term. Life in the colonies is even worse than life on Earth — most of the environments are inordinately hostile, and even Mars, where it is possible for the colonists occasionally to go out on to the surface, offers a severely depleted landscape and extremely restricted resources.

Colonists find life tolerable only because they have a convenient means of escape in the form of their "Perky Pat" layouts, which capture the social environment of the idle rich of twentieth century Earth. The colonists can actually enter into this social environment temporarily by the use of a drug named Can-D, which allows them hallucinatory identification with Pat herself, or her boyfriend Walt. Only the Perky Pat layouts make life worth living for the colonists, and groups compete with one another to supply the layouts with the minaturized apparatus of the leisurely life. P. P. Layouts, which markets the miniaturized artifacts, is an immensely wealthy corporation, all the more so because (illegally) it also manufactures and distributes Can-D.

P. P. Layouts is run by Leo Bulero, who is trying to become a superman by undergoing E therapy at the Eichenwald clinic of Dr. Denkmal. This process stimulates the evolutionary potential of individuals so that they develop larger frontal lobes and superior intellectual ability. Its principal side-effect is that hair on the head is lost and replaced by a horny rind. E therapy is extremely expensive, but Bulero shows no trace of any advanced mental faculties at any point in the story.

In order that the official sector of P. P. Layouts can maximize its profitability, Perky Pat's miniature world is subject to continual changes in fashion. Clothes and domestic appliances continually go out of style, encouraged by disc jockeys operating from artificial satellites circling the colony worlds, and by the natural competitiveness of the layout owners. P. P. Layouts does not entirely control fashionability, bit it can almost invariably anticipate changes in fashion thanks to its team of precognitive "Pre-Fash consultants," who assess the marketability of products submitted for possible miniaturization. Bulero's New York consultant is Barney Mayerson.

The story begins with Mayerson waking up with a hangover. He has to ask his automatic suitcase-psychiatrist, Dr. Smile, to identify the girl he has been sleeping with (it is his new assistant, Rondinella Fugate). The true extent of his personal problems quickly becomes clear. He has been drafted as a colonist, and has only a limited period of time to fail his medical on grounds of excessive vulnerability to stress — hence the suitcase-psychiatrist. Roni Fugate is after his job, and is soon presented by an opportunity to advance her case. Mayerson turns down a set of ceramic pots submitted as candidates for miniaturization on the grounds that he cannot foresee them becoming fashionable. Roni Fugate can, and contradicts him. The true reason for his turning them down is that they are the work of his ex-wife, and that they have been brought in for appraisal by her new husband. Mayerson feels extremely guilty about having thrown out his ex-wife because her pregnancy threatened his standard of living.

News reaches Earth at this time that a spaceship has crashed on Pluto. Its sole occupant is Palmer Eldritch, an industrialist who left the system ten years previously in order to bring off a mysterious deal with the inhabitants of Proxima Centauri. Both Barney Mayerson and Roni Fugate foresee that in approximately forty percent of possible futures Palmer Eldritch will be murdered, and that his murderer will be Leo Bulero.

Bulero's motive for this possible murder soon becomes apparent. Eldritch has brought back from Proxima a lichen similar to that from which Can-D is extracted. He intends to take over the business which P. P. Layouts has monopolized for so long by marketing his own drug, Chew-Z, first as a replacement for Can-D to be used with Perky Pat Layouts, but with the subsequent possibility of rendering the layouts redundant because Chew-Z is inherently more powerful than Can-D. Eldritch appears to have the support of the United Nations in his plan, because they have already seized a cargo of Can-D and seem to have no intention of declaring Chew-Z to be illegal.

Bulero tries to fix a meeting with Eldritch, and eventually manages to gain an interview on Luna. He is, however, rendered unconscious by Eldritch's guards and given an injection of Chew-Z. He finds himself in an apparently illusory environment where Eldritch confronts him in the shape of a little girl. Dr. Smile is also present, and Bulero appeals to the suitcase-psychiatrist for help. Smile promises to alert Barney Mayerson to Bulero's predicament, and apparently does so, illusion or no. (From this point on, reality and illusion become gradually more entangled for all the characters.) Mayerson contacts Felix Blau of the Tri-Planet Police Agency, and Blau concludes that Bulero has been removed to an artificial Earth satellite called Sigma 14-B, but Mayerson decides not to attempt a rescue.

Bulero builds himself an "escape-ladder" from the illusory environment, and confronts Barney in New York, but this too is part of the illusion and soon dissolves. He then kills the little girl and marches off across the surface of Sigma 14-B, eventually discovering two apparently alien beings who claim to be ultra-advanced products of Denkmal's E therapy, set to guard a monument commemorating the long-ago slaying of Palmer Eldritch by one Leo Bulero, hero of the solar system. Bulero wants to believe that he has somehow seen the future, but when a dog appears and urinates on the monument he knows that Eldritch is mocking him. The illusion cuts off, and he is delivered back to the very moment of time when it commenced. He is released by Eldritch and returns to Earth, again to confront and remonstrate with Barney Mayerson.

The new addition to his burden of guilt proves to be the last straw for Mayerson, who stops trying to evade the draft and volunteers for immediate transportation. This move, however, renews his usefulness to Bulero, who commissions him to become a pawn in an attempt to discredit Chew-Z. He is to take the drug in front of witnesses and subsequently to infect himself with an epileptic disease which he is to claim as a side-effect.

Once on Mars he begins to follow through with his plan, buying Chew-Z from a simulacrum of Palmer Eldritch (clearly recognizable by virtue of an artificial arm, a rebuilt jaw, and artificial eyes). When he takes the drug he finds himself back on Earth, trying to patch things up with his forsaken wife. The illusion ends all too soon, and Eldritch appears again to point out that he can try again and again as often as he takes Chew-Z. Forgetting the second part of Bulero's plan, Mayerson grabs more Chew-Z and precipitates himself back into illusion (if, indeed, he has been free of it).

This time he finds himself apparently in the future, in Bulero's office, long after the death of Palmer Eldritch and the banning of Chew-Z. Before long, however, the Leo Bulero and Roni Fugate he meets there begin to undergo a transformation, becoming simulacra of Palmer Eldritch. He himself becomes such a simulacrum, and speaks to Palmer Eldritch in his own person. He finds himself in Eldritch's form aboard a spaceship which he already knows is scheduled to be attacked and destroyed by Leo Bulero, and believes that he is to die in Eldritch's place. But again the illusion seems to end, and he wakes on Mars.

Mayerson's fellow colonists have enjoyed their first experience of Chew-Z, but have been made slightly uneasy by a "creepy presence" which seemed always to be with them in their dream. Mayerson has no doubt about the nature of that presence: it is Palmer Eldritch (or what came back from Proxima wearing his substance). It is also God, and it is evil.

Mayerson goes out on to the surface to survey his new domain. There he is threatened by a predator, which in the end declines to eat him because he is "unclean." Mayerson can only take this to mean that he has undergone a kind of transubstantiation, and is now tainted by the *persona* of Palmer Eldritch. He sees Eldritch, who confesses that he is really an alien inhabiting Eldritch's body, and that Chew-Z has been introduced to humankind as the means of his procreation. Mayerson's flesh — and, indeed, the flesh of other men — has become the body of the being identified with Eldritch, by a process likened to the miracle of transubstantiation by which wafer and wine become the body and blood of Christ in the Catholic Mass. Mayerson is now capable — along with many others (including even Blau, who has not taken the drug) — of exhibiting the three stigmata which are the symbol of his infusion: the arm, the jaw, and the eyes.

As with all Dick's novels, *The Three Stigmata of Palmer Eldritch* has flaws in its makeup. Characters are introduced only to be unceremoniously abandoned (for instance, Richard Hnatt, who brings the pots to Mayerson in the opening sequence). Ideas are invoked which never really function within the story (for instance E therapy). Dick always seems to gather his materials uncertainly, never sure of what he will need to use, nor how he might use it. The plot of the novel has incongruities: why, for instance, does an Eldritch agent buy the pot designs from Hnatt if Chew-Z will make the layouts redundant?

Such incongruities can, however, be made to function in creating the essential sense of dislocation, as when the call for help sent by Bulero by way of the illusory Dr. Smile seems actually to have reached Earth. Bulero, of course, never "really" returns to reality after that point, but the message also seems to be real for Mayerson — who has yet to take the drug — and Blau, who never does take it. This paradox may not have been planned by the author, but it proves vital to the working of the novel, creating the circle by which illusion feeds back into reality and reality can eventually drain slowly away into illusion. The purely temporal concerns of the characters — Will Leo Bulero kill Palmer Eldritch? Will Barney Mayerson put his past behind him and make a new life on Mars? — are shortcircuited by their transcendence of the parameters of the situation, a transcendence which is also a literal alienation.

The conventions of science fiction readily invite the fusion of the notion of altered states of consciousness with that of alternate realities. The former notion has always been associated with mystical experience, with personal transcendence and with the central questions of theology. The fusion of the two ideas provides a route by which metaphysical issues, including theological questions (which were, of course, rigorously excluded from virtually all prewar science fiction) can not only be reintroduced into science fiction but can become central concerns. Dick is not the only writer who has taken this opportunity, but he has certainly been one of the most effective, largely because he has been neither evasive nor halfhearted in his efforts.

The Three Stigmata of Palmer Eldritch no longer seems such a startling work as it once did, but it is a more powerful work than the more delicate *Our Friends from Forlix-8* or the more explicit *A Maze of Death*, and it remains the most dramatic explication of its theme.

Brian Stableford

Sources for Further Study

Criticism:

Gillespie, Bruce. *Philip K. Dick: Electric Shepherd*. Melbourne, Australia, Nostrilla, 1975. This is one of Dick's most popular works.

Reviews:

Analog. LXXV, August, 1965, pp. 132-133.

Books and Bookmen. XI, September, 1966, p. 40.

Galaxy. XXIII, August, 1965, pp. 187-192.

National Review. XVII, March 9, 1965, p. 200.

New Worlds. CLX, March, 1966, p. 157.

Observer. April 3, 1966, p. 27.

Punch. CCL, March 9, 1966, p. 363.

Times Literary Supplement. March 24, 1966, p. 363.

334

Author: Thomas M. Disch (1940-   )
First book publication: 1972
Type of work: Novel
Time: 2021-2026
Locale: New York City

A sequence of thematically related short fictions focused around an apartment house at 334 East 11th Street, New York City, which describes a bleak but believable near future

> *Principal characters:*
> MRS. NORA HANSON, tenant of apartment 1812, 334 East 11th Street
> SHRIMP AND LOTTIE, her daughters
> BOZ, her son
> MILLY HOLT, Boz's wife
> AMPARO MARTINEZ, Lottie's daughter
> AB HOLT, Milly's father
> ALEXA MILLER, the Welfare Department executive responsible for 334 East 11th Street
> BIRDIE LUDD, Milly's onetime boyfriend
> BILLY HARPER, a school friend of Amparo
> JANUARY, Shrimp's lover

334 is the account of a future which lies at the " event horizon" of the time of its writing — in other words, the time which an individual newly entered into adulthood could reasonably expect to experience in old age. The future which lies within this horizon is the one in which some of us, at least, have a direct personal interest, and the question of what life will be like in that future has personal significance. There is a sense, therefore, in which all novels set fifty or sixty years in the future are didactic, because they are hypothetical explorations of the world which we are making for ourselves to live in.

334 is an especially pertinent novel in that the claims which it makes are based on relatively unambitious assumptions regarding new discoveries and epoch-making events. It assumes that things will go on much as they are, changing consistently but without any major break in history. Various trends are extrapolated, but the philosophy is very much a matter of *plus ça change, plus c'est la même chose*. Disch also eschews the melodramatic affective aggression by which so many science fiction writers dealing with the prospects of the near future exaggerate particular potential crises, such as overpopulation, pollution, and exhaustion of resources. *334* is one of the most seemingly realistic of all futuristic novels, and by virtue of its realism the claims which it makes become disturbing in the extreme. It is a strikingly plausible novel in that it gives us an impression of what the future might really feel like to live in, and is for that reason more frightening than any melodrama.

The story is built loosely around the tenants of unit 1812 of an apartment block at 334 East 11th Street, which is administered by the Welfare Department of a governmental organization called "Modicum." The apartment occupies the center of the stage only in the final part of the book, but the characters whose stories are told in the five preliminary sequences are each connected in some way with one or another of the people who have lived there. The final section, which accounts for about forty percent of the book, is the matrix which frames the other stories and unites them into a coherent thematic whole.

The central character of the book, though she is only briefly the protagonist, is Mrs. Nora Hanson, born in 1967, a widow and the mother of three children (a fourth, her first son, born in 1984, has died before the story opens, clubbed to death by police during a riot in 2001). The surviving children are Shrimp (Shirley), born 1986; Lottie (Loretta), born 1989; and Boz, born 2003. Shrimp and Boz both leave the apartment during the period of time covered by the story, but its population is temporarily maintained by Lottie's children, Amparo and Mickey. When they, too, leave, Mrs. Hanson is faced with eviction and this precipitates the crisis of the book.

The opening sequence, "The Death of Socrates," first appeared in a substantially different magazine version some years before the remainder of the material. It tells the story of Birdie Ludd, a tenant of 334 who is for a brief time in love with Milly Holt (who eventually marries Boz). The story is about Birdie's desperate attempt to win sufficient social credit to be approved for procreation. Points can be gained by performance in various tests of intelligence and creativity, or by special achievements of various kinds, and points are deducted for physical debility and family histories of hereditary disease. Birdie has lost his initially adequate score because his father has contracted diabetes, and after retaking the various tests he finds that he has been downgraded several more points. He obtains a grant to produce a piece of writing which might regain the lost points, in the meantime forming a curious relationship with a prostitute who scrapes a meager living by catering to sadists. Her one attraction as a companion is that she, too, has an inadequate credit score. His written piece does win him several points, but leaves him one frustrating point short of adequacy. In a fit of anguished rage he vents his frustration on the girl, and goes despairingly to enlist in the army, this being the only way left to him to win the point that will assure his status.

The prostitute, Frances, plays a minor but vital role in "Bodies," whose main character is Milly Holt's father Ab. Ab works in the morgue at Bellevue Hospital, and makes money on the side by selling bodies to an agent who supplies the needs of necrophiles. His livelihood is threatened when he sells the body of a girl who is subsequently discovered to have been insured by cryonic preservation. He is warned in time by his accomplice, Juan Martinez (Lottie's husband), and has to sweat out a few desperate hours waiting for an adequate replacement. Frances dies just in time for him to switch the identity bracelet and present her to the driver from Macy's as the insured body. The disease which has killed both girls is a multisymptomatic cancer called lupus, which is claimed to represent "the auto-intoxication of the human race in an environment ever more hostile to human life." It is a kind of side-effect of modern civilization and its so-called benefits.

"Everyday Life in the Later Roman Empire" is set in a broader historical context, and takes the reader outside the world of the downtrodden and their lives of quiet desperation. Its main character is Alexa Miller, the civil servant responsible for 334 East 11th Street. Alexa has her own 334 — the year 334, to which she "escapes" by means of the drug Morbehanine, which creates a hallucinatory environment that becomes stable and immutable once constructed. She justifies this escape as a project in "Historical Analysis," but seems to be too successful in analyzing the predicament of both her worlds by analogy with one another. She and her story display a parallel between the world of the 2020's and that of the declining Roman Empire, about to be overwhelmed by the barbarians. Explicit reference is made to Oswald Spengler's *Decline of the West*, which identifies both these historical periods as similar points in the cycle of cultures. (*334* is, in fact, saturated with a deepseated Spenglerian pessimism.)

This view from outside is followed by two pieces which contrast somewhat with the cold brutality of the first two stories. Here *angst* gives way, to some extent, to *weltschmerz* as, without any amelioration of the pessimism, a note of sentimental sympathy begins to creep in. "Emancipation" focuses on the predicament of Boz and Milly. Boz is rendered impotent by Milly's commitment to her job as a peripatetic school "hygiene demonstrator" (an instructress in sexual technique). After a brief encounter with a "Republican" (a homosexual), which offers no solution to the problem, Boz and Milly seek psychiatric advice and are persuaded of Boz's desperate need to become a mother. Milly conceives, the foetus is transplanted at the earliest possible moment, and eventually Peanut makes her debut in the world — an ending which, if not entirely happy, represents a kind of fulfillment.

"Angouleme," the briefest sequence in the book, features schoolboy Billy Harper and his decision to commit a routine "existential murder" after the fashion of Raskolnikov. At first he has the support of several friends from the Alexander Lowen school (including Amparo Martinez and Tancred Miller), but soon he finds himself forced to act alone. In confrontation with his chosen victim, though, he realizes the essential futility of his scheme, and abandons it.

The final section of the book, which provides the setting for the whole, deals directly with Mrs. Hanson and her daughters, and their various hopeless attempts to import some meaning into their lives. The brief elements of the section are categorized under various headings and arranged according to internal logic rather than chronology. The section has both a contents page and a schematic diagram showing the pathways by which Mrs. Hanson, Shrimp, and Lottie can be followed through the maze of their relationships, mapping the exemplary passages on an axis which extends from "monologue" through "reality" and "fantasy" to "another point-of-view." We witness Shrimp's awkward relationship with January, a black female revolutionary, and Lottie's involvement with various religious cults following the death of her husband (who committed suicide when his part in the illicit body-trade was about to be revealed). Lottie, seeking messages from Juan and prophecies of things to come, is several times warned of a fire, but cannot tell whether this is to be actual or symbolic. As things turn out, it is both. In 2026 Mrs. Hanson is the last remaining tenant in apartment 1812, and is given notice to quit since the building is now underoccupied. She tries to fight, and with all rational decisions taken from her, she finally sets fire to her furniture, piled in the corridor outside her door. Lottie returns at this point and perceives her destiny, trying to immolate herself on the pyre. Both end up in Bellevue, Lottie defiantly scoffing at her own feeling that the end of the world is nigh, Mrs. Hanson quietly and methodically listing her reasons for applying for permission to die.

334 is an extremely impressive book. What is perhaps most remarkable about it is its sheer density of experience. Its social environments are fleshed out so well as to be almost tangible; the innovations which are introduced into them are so subtle and so intricately interwoven with familiar elements as to be unobtrusive. Few works of science fiction are quite so elaborate and cohesive, or so engrossing to the reader.

334 tells us, with detailed argument and conclusive finality, that the last vestiges of utopian hope for our own future are now dead. At the beginning of "Bodies," Ab Holt argues with a hospital porter named Chapel about work, and argues that people never really *make* anything — they merely move things about. He demolishes Chapel's resistance with vague references to energy-economics and the kinetic theory of heat, and Chapel concedes, noting silently that "It was science all right. Science battered everyone into submission if it was given its way." *334* does not pretend to be a prophetic work in respect of this claim, for what it alleges is not that this is going to happen but that it already has, and that all that remains is for the process to proceed to its inexorably logical conclusion.

Chapel is perhaps the least perturbed person in the whole novel, utterly passive in his attitude to life and the world. His one preoccupation is following television soap operas, whose characters include people named Billy Harper and Mrs. Hanson. The implication is that Chapel's mode of escapism is to make the problems of the real world appear lessened by transposition into the fabric of fiction. In a curious fashion, Chapel's situation parallels that of the reader of *334*, reading about characters named Billy Harper and Mrs. Hanson, and perhaps exorcising his or her own anxieties about the future which looms on the event horizon by transposing them into fiction. Whether its effect is cathartic or not, *334* certainly warrants description as a tragedy rather than a horror story, for nowhere in its pages is there the least hint that things might, if we act now, turn out otherwise.

Brian Stableford

THROUGH THE LOOKING-GLASS

Author: Lewis Carroll (Charles L. Dodgson,1832-1898)
First book publication: 1871
Type of work: Story for children
Time: Probably 1862
Locale: A room, a garden, and a chessboard reflected in a mirror

A story constructed around an imaginary chess problem, set in a world beyond a mirror

> *Principal characters:*
> ALICE
> THE WHITE KNIGHT
> THE RED QUEEN
> THE WHITE QUEEN
> TWEEDLEDUM AND TWEEDLEDEE
> HUMPTY DUMPTY

Through the Looking-Glass is not science fiction by any stretch of the imagination. It is, in fact, because it so comprehensively avoids any such imaginative elasticity that it warrants discussion in a book whose subject matter *is* science fiction. (This may, of course, seem paradoxical, but no pertinent discussion of *Through the Looking-Glass* can hope to avoid the occasional paradox.)

The story of Alice's second dream-adventure is a nonsensical one which has never been surpassed for sheer brilliance, for there is no other work which defies sense quite so artfully. It is the sense which it opposes, and to which it is so magnificently antipathetic, that provides a strange link between the substance of the story and the historical and philosophical roots of science fiction. For the "sense" which is mirror-reversed in *Through the Looking-Glass* is very much the sense of nineteenth century rationalism: the regime of logic and mathematics which brought order to the positivistic world view of Victorian science. The irrationality of the story is a mischievous spirit which could not have existed in any other age, a response to the *tyranny* of reason which imposed itself upon nineteenth century natural philosophy more oppressively than in any other age (including our own). For that reason, we can, if we wish, view it as a curiously heroic irrationality, marvelously quixotic in its tilting at the giant Mill of systematic logic.

The first reason, therefore, why *Through the Looking-Glass* invites discussion in connection with science fiction, is that they are both responses (albeit very different ones) to the evolving edifice of natural philosophy. There is, however, a further factor which must also be taken into account: a curious and magnificent irony. For it transpired that the mills of antitheistic rationalism, when they came to grind exceeding small, discovered that the fundamental reality of the universe embodies modes of action which are reminiscent of the twisted logic of Carroll's looking-glass philosophers. The analogy was drawn in an enthusiastic manner by Eddington, and several popularizers of modern physics and its world view have found it convenient to refer back to it. (Bertrand Russell and George Gamow are notable examples.) The bewildered Alice has become the twentieth century's Everyman, confronting accounts of reality which unrepentantly deny the convictions of common sense. Just as Don Quixote himself has been redeemed by the twentieth century discovery that windmills, first representatives of large-scale technology, really did represent a race of giants who threatened to subjugate the human race, so the irreverent spirit which infects *Through the Looking-Glass* has triumphed over the dogmatic self-confidence of such nineteenth century intellectuals as Marcellin Berthelot, who declared in 1887 that there was no more mystery about the universe.

The story is a light-hearted fantasy ostensibly designed to amuse the children who meant so much to the Reverend Dodgson. Its mood throughout is one of playfulness, though there are traces of a sober undercurrent. By the time it was published, Alice Liddell herself was nineteen years old and a very different person from the seven-year-old Alice he had adored. *Through the Looking-Glass* is a reflective novel in more respects than one, edged with a nostalgia whose sadder aspect is made explicit by the verses which act as prologue and epilogue to the story, the first expressing the opinion that all the children will forget their friend in growing older, and the second saying of that younger Alice: "Still she haunts me phantomwise,/ Alice moving under skies/ Never seen by waking eyes." The tale contains Carroll's caricature of himself as the White Knight, who helps Alice and who speaks to her in a kindly and affectionate manner which contrasts sharply with the attitudes of other characters in the two books where she takes the star role. *Alice's Adventures in Wonderland* was also nostalgic, recalling for publication in 1865 a fantasy improvised during a boat trip in 1862 which took its place as one of the author's most highly-treasured memories, but there is not within its pages the same sense of something not merely past but also lost. Both works are dream stories but the second is much more self-consciously so and seems preoccupied with the flimsiness and insubstantiality of dreams in those moments where it calls attention to itself. Though it is not obtrusive there is a single moment when the casual wordplay takes on a covert sharpness, when Alice points out to Humpty Dumpty that "one can't help getting older." He — following the practice common in the Looking-Glass world of taking all grammatical conventions over-literally — replies that "*One* can't, perhaps . . . but *two* can. With proper assistance, you might have left off at seven."

Most of the ingredients of *Through the Looking-Glass* are carried over from *Alice's Adventures in Wonderland*: the deck of playing cards is replaced by the chess pieces, and there are more familiar creatures equipped with personalities, principally the flowers in the garden and the passengers in the train. (There was also to have been a wasp in a wig, but this passage was cut at the suggestion of the illustrator John Tenniel and has only recently been rediscovered and published.) The principal innovation in the framework of the story is the intrusion of nursery rhyme characters such as Tweedledum and Tweedledee and Humpty Dumpty. It is these characters who introduce a fresh note into the story and provide it with its most memorable moments, though the Red and White Queens have the best lines. It is Tweedledee who tells Alice that she is a figment of the Red King's dream, and Humpty Dumpty who discourses on the problem of meaning and the logic of naming things.

Though manifest in the story as amusing absurdities and conversational tricks, these sections refer to real philosophical problems. Alice meets Tweedledum and Tweedledee in "the wood where things have no names," and some of the remarks made by Humpty Dumpty reflect philosophical disputes about the significance of names and the status of general terms — arguments which seem sufficiently bizarre to the nonphilosophical mind to lend themselves easily to the creation of an atmosphere of surreality. The question raised by Tweedledee's claim about the Red King's dream reflects metaphysical arguments of the type raised by Bishop Berkeley, who maintained that only ideas have real existence and that for the world to maintain its integrity, consistency, and solidarity, there must necessarily be a God to maintain all entities and events (including those unobserved by humans) simultaneously in mind. Carroll, of course, gives the argument an extra twist (as does the ancient anecdote about the disciple of Chuang-Tzu who dreamed he was a butterfly) because the Red King, if he is not the dreamer in whose imaginary world Alice is a character, must be presumed to be a character in the solipsistic *milieu* of *her* dreams.

From today's standpoint, very little seems to be made in *Through the Looking-Glass* of the inversion inherent in Alice's being in a mirror world. In the earlier Alice story, a different kind of inversion was employed — the inversion of relative sizes which had long been a standard ploy in humorous and satirical fiction, serving the ends of writers such as Cyrano de Bergerac, Jonathan Swift, and Voltaire. The left/right inversion was, however, an innovation with no particular consequences as far as Carroll could see except the reversing of the clock-face and the lettering of the poem "Jabberwocky." There are, however, other inversions of a metaphorical kind in the story — notably the White Queen's reference to "living backwards" and its difficulties, a notion which has formed the basis of several science fiction and fantasy stories, including ones by F. Scott Fitzgerald, J. G. Ballard and a novel by Philip K. Dick. Science, of course was later to reveal that mirror-inversion was by no means as trivial a matter as Carroll supposed. The discovery of the importance of optical isomerism in organic chemistry puts Alice's suspicion of looking-glass milk into an entirely new perspective, and recent claims that it is not merely life but the universe itself that is asymmetric have been based on Yang and Lee's discovery of "the fall of parity" in certain subatomic transactions.

This is, of course, only one aspect of the story which finds a strange echo in modern physics. Another is the way that the Red Queen's allusion to having to run twice as fast to get anywhere, because you have to run quite hard just to stay in the same place, relates to the imaginative implications of Einstein's theory of relativity. Along with the White Queen's "jam tomorrow and jam yesterday — but never jam today" this has also become a significant catch-phrase in our habitual description of our contemporary existential situation. In this respect the book contains a sentence which may surely stand as the definitive commentary on itself, where the Red Queen, objecting to Alice's description of a piece of paradoxical hyperbole as "nonsense," replies: "You may call it 'nonsense' if you like . . . but I've heard nonsense, compared with which that would be as sensible as a dictionary!"

There is no irony more pleasing than the fact that succeeding generations have found in the linguistic trickery by which Carroll's characters convert sense into nonsense a vocabulary quite pertinent to the description of the real world — not only the "electric wonderland" of post-Maxwellian physics but also the world of everyday life. (This may be the one thing that the world of post-Maxwellian physics and the world of everyday life have in common, except, of course, that the latter is an epiphenomenon of the former.) There is, it seems, unreason in all things, if only one can find the phrases which capture it. Other writers besides Carroll have perceived this, but no one else took quite the attitude to the discovery that he did. (Another, perhaps rather unkind, attempt to describe the relation in which *Through the Looking-Glass* stands to science fiction might be to argue that science fiction writers characteristically take notions fit only to amuse small children and pretend that they are of some philosophical significance, while *Through the Looking-Glass* does the opposite. No one would seriously assert such a thing, however, because it is far too patronizing in its implied contempt for small children.)

Ideas from *Through the Looking-Glass* crop up so frequently in twentieth century writing that it is not surprising to find many echoes of it in modern science fiction. Science fiction writers have written stories which echo, in a rather more determined manner, games of chess — Poul Anderson's "The Immortal Game" and John Brunner's *Squares of the City* are notable examples — and there are several stories inspired by the language of "Jabberwocky," including Henry Kuttner and C. L. Moore's "Mimsy were the Borgoves" and James Blish and Robert A. W. Lowndes's "Chaos Co-ordinated." These do not, in themselves, provide evidence of kinship between Carrollian fantasy and science fiction, but in the latter examples at least there is an anarchic spirit which suggests the nature of the actual kinship, which lies in the fact that each species of fantasy, in its own way, seeks a kind of freedom from the shackles of blinkered rationalism.

Brian Stableford

Sources for Further Study

Criticism:

Auerbach, Nina. "Alice and Wonderland: A Curious Child," in *Victorian Studies*. XVII (1973), pp. 31-47. Auerbach's study of *Through the Looking Glass*, although emphasizing characterization, makes an effort to place the story in context with its times.

Ettleson, A. Carr. *Carroll's* Through the Looking-Glass *Decoded*. New York: Philosophical Library, 1966. Ettleson's explication of *Through the Looking Glass* is particularly significant in its interpretation of the novel's symbols.

Henkle, Roger B. "The Mad Hatter's World," in *Virginia Quarterly Review*. XLIX (1973), pp. 107-111. The fantasy atmosphere of Wonderland is the focal point of Henkle's study.

Matthews, Charles. "Satire in the Alice Books," in *Criticism*. XII (1971), pp.105-109. The fantasy world of Alice provides insights into the real one. Matthews shows how the author uses the novel for his satirical views.

TIME AND AGAIN

Author: Jack Finney (1911-   )
First book publication: 1970
Type of work: Novel
Time: 1970 and 1882
Locale: New York City

A time travel adventure that captures the texture and style of urban America in the 1880's through the reminiscences of the narrator

Principal characters:
SIMON MORLEY, a commercial artist
KATIE MANCUSO, his girl friend in the twentieth century
JULIA CHARBONNEAU, a beautiful young girl of the past
JAKE PICKERING, a municipal clerk, the chief villain
RUBE PRIEN, a recruiter for a top secret government project
DR. DANZINGER, a project designer

This cleverly contrived adventure story bubbles with enthusiasm for a bygone era, New York City in the 1880's. The time traveler Simon Morley, a commercial artist in the New York of 1970, journeys into the past ostensibly to solve a mystery for his girl friend, but, as events unfold, he becomes embroiled in more than sleuthing. The story's major strength lies in the historical authenticity and realism of the numerous detailed descriptions of people and places in Manhattan during the winter of 1882. Occasional plot weaknesses are distracting but effectively eclipsed by Finney's entertainingly informational writing. As a study in historical perspective, the novel can be well compared to MacKinlay Kantor's *If the South Had Won the Civil War* (1961), Ward Moore's *Bring the Jubilee* (1953), Edward Bellamy's *Looking Backward*, all of which comment on life in the late nineteenth century.

Illustrated with photographs and reproductions of old prints, the story offers considerable suspense from the outset, when Simon Morley is approached by a government agent, Rube Prien and invited to participate in a top secret government project. Bored with his job and intrigued by the tidbits of information supplied by Prien, Morley accepts the challenge. He soon learns that he has been recruited to bring about a fuller comprehension of history by visiting the past and observing, but not changing, events.

Morley passes his preliminary tests, selects the time period he wants to visit, and then undergoes a training period intended to make him thoroughly familiar with the past. He crosses the time barrier from his residence in the Dakota Hotel facing Central Park West, a nineteenth century apartment building so hedged in by other buildings that he sees basically the same panorama viewed by 1882 occupants. Dressed in period costume, he reads copies of 1882 newspapers and magazines and lives in the style of the times until the process begins to work. After much playacting, an initial attempt succeeds under hypnosis and Morley makes his first short trip into the past, which he finds very pleasant. No sense of danger inhibits Morley's attempts since the tone of the novel is one of enjoyment and nostalgic wonderment. Images surrounding the transition are pleasing rather than disturbing. Each trip is progressively longer and of greater meaning and reality to Morley until he feels himself to be not only an observer of the times but also an involved participant who can mentally and emotionally remain in the past.

Morley's girl friend, Katie Mancuso, an antique dealer, supports the project and helps him in his preparations. Before his initial trip, they review facts of everyday life and look at old 3-D stereoscopic views of New York that make the 1880's more real and meaningful. Unbidden, Katie accompanies him on his first long trip, acting as his companion as well as his major link to the twentieth century. As a love interest, however, she eventually fades from the picture, for Morley becomes enamoured of Julia Charbonneau, the niece of his landlady in 1882 Manhattan.

Once settled in 1882, Morley discovers why a forebear of the Carmodys, Katie's foster parents, committed suicide after losing a multimillion dollar fortune in the 1890's. His investigations unearth a blackmail plot and entangle him with villains and corrupt politicians. The consequences almost cost Morley and Julia their lives as they escape from a disastrous fire and from New York policemen instructed to shoot them on sight.

Morley's antagonist, Jake Pickering, a low-paid municipal clerk, is a colorful character, a "John Bull of a man," who is first encountered in the New York City Post Office by Katie and Morley on Jan. 23, 1882. They observe him mailing a letter whose contents had puzzled the descendants of Andrew Carmody, a wealthy New York financier. A note written on the blue envelope at a later date, revealing that sending the letter had caused the destruction by fire of the entire world, was meaningless because fire had destroyed the key word in the sentence. While trailing Pickering, Morley learns that the missing word is "building" and that the four-story World Building was set ablaze with great loss of life as a result of Pickering's attempt to blackmail Carmody. (Carmody had embezzled city funds as a building contractor, and Pickering wanted a share of the profits.)

From his hiding place next to Pickering's office in the World Building, Morley could have interfered in the confrontation between the two rogues and prevented the holocaust, but he refrained because his role at that point was still one of observer only. Consequently, he is an eyewitness reporter who supplies a series of detailed, dramatic impressions in first person narrative. He is not, however, an absolute spectator, an ideal in time travel concept, because he has brought Julia with him to witness the revelation of Jake's true character and must engineer their escape during the subsequent blaze. Morley also functions here as an artist who sees things both as they are and as they might have been if he had interfered in history. The author's use of Morley in this sense throughout the narrative gives a double focus to episodes that make each a moving, dynamic portrait of controlling forces.

Though the narrative concentrates on the 1880's, much action centers on the twentieth century project planners and their motives in furthering Morley's investigations into the Pickering-Carmody conflict. The chief among them, Dr. Danzinger, Colonel Esterhazy, Dr. Rossoff, and Rube Prien, evaluate Morley's findings and check to see if anything in the present was changed by his influence on past events. They believe in the "twig-in-the-stream" theory; that is, the past as a flowing continuum like a mighty river cannot be significantly changed by a twig thrown into it or by a man sent back through time. To their shock, the theory is challenged when another time traveler, Ted Brietel, inadvertently causes the eradication of a close friend by something said or done on a sojourn into the past. Dr. Danzinger, the project architect, wants all future trips canceled but is opposed by other board members who reason that Brietel's experience may be a fluke.

Morley then makes two more trips. The last is forced upon him by military opportunists who discover that Carmody, as a minor adviser to President Cleveland, influenced the President not to annex Cuba. They want Morley to alter the past by exposing Carmody's true identity and past deeds (he is actually Pickering who, after the financier's death in the World Building fire, masquerades as Carmody) so that he can never be Cleveland's adviser. Cuba can then become an American possession and Castro's coup obliterated from time. Ethically opposed to the plan, Morley returns to prevent a fateful meeting that would have eventually resulted in that time travel project.

His secret decision, however, cuts him off from the present because it finally establishes his dissatisfaction with the twentieth century. He returns to his true love, Julia, and to a more attractive life in the 1880's where people are not troubled by an environment that has yet to be mutilated by atomic war and global pollution. Morley can appreciate that era because, unlike Bellamy's hero who escapes from it, he is not a Utopian but an ordinary man capable of enjoying the simple delights of a less hectic and complicated era.

Finney's handling of character ranks among his most important contributions. His three-dimensional descriptions are far more impressive than his pictorial backdrop. He uses a full range of sensory impressions to capture nuances of speech and individuality among a wide variety of nineteenth century personalities. Voice inflections, speech mannerisms, and hand and body gestures show the reader, rather than tell him, how lifelike the characters are. The reader learns how to spit tobacco juice into cuspidors and otherwise to dress and behave appropriately while observing accurate human prototypes.

Few of these characters of Finney's are poor or unfortunate though his hero does mention beggars, slum tenants, and destitute children that he sees on his many walks through the city. Their plight is faithfully presented and the reader feels a certain pity; but social commentary is minimal. The prevailing viewpoint that the 1880's is a better era than the 1970's, despite shortcomings, dictates a shift in the narrative to a more pleasing scene whenever social ill threatens unduly to upset both Morley and the reader. For example, while wandering through a Manhattan tenement district, Morley quickly retraces his steps when his curiosity turns to disturbing empathy. This reaction contrasts sharply with that of the hero in Bellamy's *Looking Backward*, who unceasingly decries the social injustices of the late nineteenth century.

The act of walking ties together many disparate scenes, some of which, like Morley's and Julia's stride along the Ladies' Mile on Fifth Avenue, are only incidental to the plot. Digressions are understandable when one considers that the author is capturing the essence of an era through a character fascinated by the most commonplace details of daily living because he is an anachronism. Nevertheless, there is occasionally too much emphasis on minutiae, especially in the description of the World Building fire. Too many detailed newspaper accounts of singular incidents, particularly those involving New York City firemen, pad the text. While these descriptions are interesting to read, they betray an uneven sense of proportion.

The descriptive language used also contrasts sharply with that of Bellamy. Realistic, conversational, and embellished with figures of speech, it reflects a glamor alien to Bellamy's labored prose. Finney's sensual delight in Bellamy's horror makes *Time and Again* an ironic commentary on *Looking Backward* and a more satisfying introduction to the late nineteenth century.

Anne Carolyn Raymer

Sources for Further Study

Reviews:

Analog. LXXXVI, February, 1971, pp. 166-167.

Best Sellers. XXX, July 15, 1970, p. 151.

Book World. June 28, 1970, p. 6.

Library Journal. XCV, October 1, 1970, p. 3304.

Luna Monthly. XXVI–XXVII, July–August, 1977, p. 32.

New York Times Book Review. August 2, 1970, p. 24.

Publisher's Weekly. CXCVII, March 9, 1970, p. 81.

Time. XCVI, July 20, 1970, p. 76.

THE TIME MACHINE

Author: H. G. Wells (1866-1946)
First book publication: 1895
Type of work: Novel
Time: From 1895 to 30,000,000 but primarily the year 802,701
Locale: Richmond, a suburb of London

A scientist invents a machine that transports him to the year 802,701, where he witnesses the conflict between the cannibalistic Morlocks and the gentle Eloi, and then to a more distant future where he encounters a giant crab, and finally to the year 30,000,000 where he witnesses the death of the sun

> *Principal characters:*
> THE NARRATOR
> THE TIME TRAVELLER
> THE ELOI, a fragile, childlike race that lives on the surface of the Earth
> WEENA, a female Eloi who befriends the Time Traveller
> THE MORLOCKS, a semihuman race that lives in subterranean caverns and feeds off the Eloi

The Time Machine is H. G. Wells's first — and many of its readers would add his greatest — "scientific romance." Certainly it is his most ambitious, at least in its temporal scope. Certainly, also, it exemplifies the principles underlying his science fiction more clearly and expounds them more fully than does any other work he afterwards attempted in that genre.

The book opens on a comfortable drawing-room in suburban London. The house belongs to the Time Traveller, elsewise identified only as an "Eminent Scientist." His dinner guests regard him as a fellow too much given to paradox. They are therefore not disappointed to hear him holding forth in favor of an idea wholly novel to them: that space has a fourth dimension, which is time. As outrageous as they take this notion to be, they find its sequel even more so. They absolutely reject the possibility of traveling in time. After all, one of them argues, man cannot move about freely in time as he can in space. The Time Traveller, of course, has an answer to this and all other objections. Man, he points out, was not at liberty to defy the laws of gravity until he invented the air balloon. Why, then, might he not construct some vehicle that would enable him to travel at will through time? Going to his laboratory for a moment, the Time Traveller returns with a miniature of just such a vehicle, and setting it in motion, causes it to disappear into the past or the future. His guests, however, have no difficulty dismissing this demonstration as they did his philosophical arguments; they look upon it as a conjuror's trick. And after viewing the full-scale machine that the Time Traveller is in the process of building in his laboratory, they leave his house as unconvinced as they were when they arrived.

A week later, another group of representative Victorian types, including some of those who had attended the previous gathering, convene at the Time

Traveller's Richmond home. The scientist himself is late in joining them; and when he does appear, quite dishevelled, he startles everyone by announcing that he has just come back from the future, where — since four o'clock that afternoon — he has spent eight days. He proceeds to give his spellbound, if incredulous, listeners a report of what he has witnessed and been through.

Aboard his time machine he had ventured into the future slowly at first; but soon abandoning caution, he had accelerated his pace until "the palpitations of night and day merged into one cóntinuous greyness." Finally, out of sheer impulsiveness, he had brought his machine to an abrupt stop: in 802,701. By that time, present-day Richmond had become "a tangled waste of beautiful bushes and flowers, a long-neglected and yet weedless garden." Idyllic though this description may sound the words ominously evoke Darwin's "tangled bank" as the image of a teeming evolutionary struggle for existence. The Time Traveller, however, is as yet unaware that such a struggle is still going on — indeed, that the Darwinian imperative for survival has recently reasserted itself among the descendants of man in all its primeval force. Seeing before him a "garden" whose inhabitants, the Eloi, are a fragile-looking, fruit-eating, and apparently androgynous species, he immediately assumes that he has come upon a new "Golden Age." To be sure, there is something decidedly satirical about this notion of his. For the Eloi are far from being Hesiodic giants on the Earth. They are "child-like" (in a somewhat sentimental sense) not only in demeanor but also in physical stature and intelligence. Even so, it seems to the Time Traveller that they have achieved a communistic ideal of mutual love and cooperation.

The reception that the Eloi accord the Time Traveller is an example of a number of details which recalls William Morris' *News from Nowhere* (1891). Nor is Wells's deliberate parody wholly unaffectionate. The Eloi, basking in the idleness of their "comfort and ease," are not, after all, a totally unappealing travesty of Morris' ideal of a society free from technologized industrial labor with its noise and pollution and its social injustices. This appeal, however, serves only to make Wells's implied critique all the more poignant. The utopia of "ease and delight" for the Eloi, while it incarnates (albeit parodistically) Morris' dream of returning to a preindustrial age, is a fool's paradise. It is quite literally undermined by a world throbbing with the pulse of machinery, the continuing operation of which may still supply the Eloi with some of life's necessities.

The denizens of that underground world are the Morlocks, "lemur-like" beings whose prolonged stay in tunnels beneath the earth has sensitized them to sunlight and left them white and pallid. These Morlocks, as the Time Traveller eventually discovers to his horror, emerge at night to prey upon the hapless Eloi. That realization causes him to modify his hypothesis about 802,701. He had hitherto supposed that the Eloi were the sole descendants of man, whose "too-perfect security . . . had led . . . to a slow movement of degeneration, to a general dwindling in size, strength, and intelligence." Now he surmises that over a span of hundreds of thousands of years, homo sapiens had split into two completely different species as a result of the segregation of the "Capitalist" from the "Labourer." Confined to the brutalizing environment of subterranean factories, the workers had evolved into the hairy and apelike Morlocks. Their descendants had been the economic victims of an aristocracy which, living "in ease and delight upon the labours of [the] fellow-man, had taken [Darwinian] Necessity as [its] watchword and excuse." Exploitation, that is, had been justified on Spencerian grounds according to certain Social Darwinist notions about "the survival of the fittest." But in the course of evolutionary time, the same kind of necessity had reversed this arrangement. Compelled by hunger, the Morlocks were finally ascending as the predators in a strict biological sense.

The world, previously appearing to be an Edenic paradise regained, now reveals itself to the Time Traveller as a Darwinistic hell. As this truth gradually comes home to him, his feelings undergo an alteration. His shift in attitude, moreover, signals an ambivalence on Wells's part that is typical of his science fiction. The Eloi slowly cease to be the object of his — and Wells's — satiric scorn, which begins to focus on the Morlocks. Recognizing at last that the Eloi have replaced the "Labourer" as victim, the Time Traveller sides with them against their oppressors. He develops a particular sympathy for an Eloi named Weena (the Wellsian diminuitive of "Rowena" — as in *Ivanhoe*), and undertakes to defend her with mace and fire against the Morlocks' nocturnal onslaught. But he fails in his efforts to protect her. As the morning dawns with no Weena to be found, he proceeds, grief-stricken, to the statue of the White Sphinx, which, with its wings menacingly uplifted, presides over 802,701. There he wrests his time machine from the Morlocks and sets his course for a yet more distant future, which might unriddle what has ultimately become of Man.

He halts, briefly, eons later. The Darwinian struggle of predator and prey is still very much in evidence. The Eloi and the Morlocks, however, are not. Instead, the Time Traveller observes "a thing like a huge white butterfly" and a giant "crab-like creature." Feeling one of the latter's antennae brushing his cheek and deciding not to risk the danger, he hurriedly takes off again, this time for the year 30,000,000. Here he barely has a chance to notice what life forms exist before the sun goes into a prolonged eclipse. This and other phenomena that he witnesses confirm the calculations of "the younger Darwin" along with those of Kelvin. The solar system, in accordance with the second law of thermodynamics, is in the throes of its heat-death; but as the sun cools, it is simultaneously drawing its planets back into it, as G. H. Darwin had predicted it would in his theory of tidal evolution. Life on land, meanwhile, has almost played itself out. Apart from the "liverworts and lichens" which seem to predominate, the Time Traveller sees only one lone animal, a round-bodied and tentacled monstrosity poised ambiguously on the verge of the ocean.

He thus returns to the present with a vision which is, as a whole, apocalyptic. Furthermore, its details conform to a devolutionary pattern. It broadly recapitulates, in reverse, the stages of the evolutionary ascent to homo sapiens. To be sure, it does not do so with exactitude: the animal species that the Time Traveller encounters in the future do not precisely correspond to those of the past. Wells does nothing, that is, to encourage an idea which he regards as delusory: that cosmic processes are exactly repetitive, or cyclical. He does, however, present a vision of life degenerating by degrees — from forms still recognizably human and beings similar to anthropoid apes, through gigantic reptilians and insects, down to primitive plants — and finally retreating into the oceans from which it arose.

The Time Traveller offers his listeners the alternative of taking his story "as a lie — or a prophecy." By and large, they refuse to believe any part of it. The Medical Man, conceding that the flowers the Time Traveller has brought with him from 802,701 resemble no species known to botanists, wants to analyze them. The Editor is more skeptical yet: he brands the entire tale "a gaudy lie."

These responses are consistent with those of the audience which, the week before, had rejected what the Time Traveller had to say about time as the fourth dimension. Having already discountenanced the logical premise of time-travel, his listeners now decline to give his results any credence whatsoever. But ironically enough, his vision of life devolving toward nonexistence is as much a consequence of this attitude of theirs as it is the "working to a logical conclusion [of] the industrial system of to-day." What the Time Traveller discovers in the distant future follows from their inability to imagine it as certainly as his discovery of the future follows from his definition of time. In being unable to take seriously any idea which contradicts those "that are almost universally accepted," they exhibit a rigidity of mind which must eventuate in man's extinction. Indeed, such a fate is inexorable insofar as they are incapable of conceiving of time as a dimension of human consciousness and thereby freeing themselves from the present and viewing it critically in temporal perspective.

The Time Traveller had invited his listeners to suppose that he has "been speculating upon the destinies of our race until I have hatched this fiction." Instead, they take it literally — as a lie. But he too insists upon the literalness of his vision, and carries his insistence to the point of deciding to resume his time-traveling in order to obtain more proof that the future exists. In doing so, he chooses to accept the future as ineluctable. Yet his theorizing had suggested something different. If, as he had argued, the world of 802,701 has come about owing to a failure of "moral education and general co-operation," then the possibility — however remote — of man's escaping this particular destiny through cooperative moral effort remains open. For that reason, the Time

Traveller's own final outlook, though far more comprehensive than that of any member of his audience, is nevertheless limited. It is, in fact, circumscribed by the point of view of the unidentified narrator (perhaps the Mr. Hillyer whom the Time Traveller glimpses as he is reentering the present after his first excursion into the future). He keeps the flowers that were Weena's gift to the Time Traveller not merely as a token of a future which already is and therefore inevitable, but also as a hopeful sign that "gratitude" and "mutual tenderness" will persist "in the heart of man."

The Time Traveller's claim that he has reported the literal truth necessitates his disappearance into the fourth dimension. But by vanishing into the world of his vision, he renders it no less real than he is, and hence no less real than the world of his audience. Nor is this an empty paradox. On the contrary, it indicates, first of all, that the fourth dimension is a kind of metaphor — is the realm wherein "prophetic" vision can achieve an imaginative life at least as meaningful as that represented in so-called "realistic" novels. The paradox also serves to define the nature of "prophecy" in *The Time Machine* — and in Wells's, and Wellsian science fiction generally. Strictly speaking, that "prophetic" content is not extrapolative: that is, it does not fundamentally depend on a reality outside the fiction. Instead, *The Time Machine* mediates between a present and a future internal to it, and does so by eliciting the consequences of its own assumptions.

Robert M. Philmus

Sources for Further Study

Criticism:

Ash, Brian. *Faces of the Future – The Lessons of Science Fiction.* London: Elek/Pemberton, 1975, pp. 50-53. Ash assesses the impact of *The Time Machine* as a mirror of society.

Bergonzi, Bernard. *The Early H. G. Wells: A Study of the Scientific Romances*. Toronto: University of Toronto Press, 1967, pp. 46-61. This is an extremely detailed study of the formulation of *The Time Machine* and its place among Wells canon.

Connelly, Wayne C. "H. G. Wells' *The Time Machine*: Its Neglected Mythos," in *Riverside Quarterly*. V (1972), pp. 178-191. Connelly analyzes Wells's mythmaking in this detailed analysis of the themes of *The Time Machine*.

Harris, Mason. "Science Fiction as Dream and Nightmare of Progress: Thoughts on the Theory of Science Fiction," in *West Coast Review*. IX

(April, 1975), pp. 6-9. Harris uses *The Time Machine* as a vehicle for an examination of the theories of science fiction.

Hillegas, Mark R. *The Future as Nightmare: H. G. Wells and the Anti-Utopians*. New York: Oxford University Press, 1967, pp. 25-34. Hillegas examines the impact of *The Time Machine* upon utopian literature.

Philmus, Robert M. "Revisions of the Future: *The Time Machine*," in *Journal of General Education*. XXVIII (1976), pp. 23-30. This article treating the theme of science fiction as prophesy looks at the future as seen by *The Time Machine*.

A TIME OF CHANGES

Author: Robert Silverberg (1936-   )
First book publication: 1971
Type of work: Novel
Time: The distant future
Locale: The planet Borthan

A story of self-discovery set in a world where social conventions denigrate all forms of self-expression

Principal characters:
>KINNALL DARIVAL, son of the setarch of Salla
>STIRRON, his brother
>NOIM CONDORIT, his bond-brother
>HALUM HELALAM, his bond-sister
>SCHWEIZ, an Earthman

A Time of Changes won Robert Silverberg the Nebula award in the same year that his short story "Good News from the Vatican" won a similar award. He had previously won the short story award for "Passengers" and he was later to win a fourth Nebula for the novella "Born with the Dead." Curiously, only the last-named work really exemplifies the quality of the work which Silverberg was doing in the late 1960's and early 1970's, and it is particularly puzzling that *A Time of Changes* should be his one award-winning novel, inferior as it is to most of the other novels which he produced in that period. It seems likely that the votes which won it the award were given partly in recognition of the fact that *Downward to the Earth* and *Tower of Glass* had failed to win in the previous year, though *Son of Man*, also published in 1971, would have been a worthier candidate to redress the balance.

A Time of Changes is the autobiography of Kinnall Darival, the son of a "septarch" in a quasifeudal society whose taboos make the very notion of an autobiography obscene. Borthan, the world in which he lives, was colonized by a religious cult fleeing from persecution on a world whose society it perceived as decadent and self-indulgent. In order to combat the evils of self-indulgence, the colonists who established themselves in the northern continent of their new world adopted a Covenant which forbade self-expression, including even the words "I" and "me." Kinnall Darival's people may refer to themselves only in the third person (as "one"), and the cardinal sin of their culture is "selfbaring" — public revelation of feelings or personal problems. In order to offset this deliberate isolation of all individuals one from another, the religion sustaining the culture provides priests to hear confessions (on payment of a fee), and supplies each individual with a "bond-sister" and a "bond-brother": specially appointed friends with whom a little sharing is possible.

Kinnall's *Bildungsroman* begins when he is forced to leave his homeland of Salla while still an adolescent, when his father is killed in a hunting accident and his elder brother Stirron becomes Septarch. Although the culture does not seem to be particularly violent, there are inevitable power struggles, and Kinnall feels it advisable to remove himself to another country in order that he should pose no threat to his brother. Stirron is reluctant to let him go, preferring to keep him close at hand and under observation, but Kinnall departs in secret. He hopes that his mother's relatives in the nearby nation of Glin might take him in and find him a position, but Stirron is so anxious to secure his return that they consider it diplomatic to refuse. Kinnall goes into hiding, spending a year working in a lumber camp and later taking a berth as a seaman. Eventually, he comes to Manneran, where the father of his bond-sister Halum is High Justice. He discovers that he is thought to be dead, but he thinks it safe to reveal his identity in the hope that Segvord Helalam, Halum's father, will find him a position. Helalam does, indeed, take him in, and awards him a station within the corrupt bureaucracy that will eventually win him considerable power and influence.

Through all his life Kinnall has been haunted by an illicit passion for Halum (who is forbidden to him by law), and he compounds his troubles in this regard by marrying her cousin Loimel, who resembles her greatly. Halum herself refuses to marry. Kinnall's marriage is unhappy, serving only to remind him that he cannot *truly* have Halum, but no change in his situation is possible, and he can only secretly brood over his unhappiness. Then he meets the Earthman named Schweiz.

Kinnall finds Schweiz fascinating, and it appears that the fascination works both ways. Kinnall tries to find out more about the "obscene" society from which Schweiz comes, enabling him thereby to take a more detached view of his own world. Schweiz recognizes in Kinnall's curiosity a deeply rooted unhappiness, just as Kinnall finds out that the Earthman too is a dissatisfied individual. Schweiz's interest in the Borthans stems from the fact that, as an alienated atheist, he finds their easy religiousness enviable. Kinnall finds it easy to reveal himself gradually to the outworlder in a way that he could never reveal himself to one of his own people, and eventually Schweiz suggests that they should go even further in their quest for mutual understanding by using a drug which will give them temporary telepathic contact with each other. Kinnall is repelled by the thought, but as he gets used to the idea he is seized by a strong temptation.

Eventually, Kinnall and Schweiz share the small quantity of the drug that the Earthman has, and Kinnall discovers what it is like to be someone different. A bond is formed between the two that is different from anything even imaginable in Borthan culture. Schweiz tells him that the drug comes from the southern continent of the planet, and suggests that they should journey there in search of a new supply. Eventually, Kinnall agrees. They meet the primitive inhabitants of the southern continent — descendants of the colonists who would not sign the Covenant — and share with them a religious ceremony which involves the fusion of the minds. When they return to the northern continent Kinnall and the Earthman go their separate ways, and Kinnall begins a kind of crusade to recruit others to a knowledge of community and love, intending ultimately to subvert the social order. He shares the drug with a number of others, mostly other members of the aristocracy, including his bond-brother Noim Condorit. Noim is the one person who rejects the possibilities of the drug and is embarrassed by the fact of having shared Kinnall's consciousness for a brief time. Nevertheless, when Kinnall is attacked by the Church and accused of criminal offenses, it is Noim who takes him in and shelters him in his estate in Salla.

Kinnall manages to restore communication with his brother, but Stirron will not give him any kind of position. However, when Halum comes to see him and he explains all that has happened, she agrees to share the drug with him, and his hope of some kind of personal salvation is renewed. For him, the experience is wonderful, and it seems so for her too, but afterwards she commits suicide, apparently having been overwhelmed by a sudden flood of guilt and shame. Noim, enraged, casts Kinnall out, and Stirron sends troops to arrest him. He flees into the desert, where he waits for capture and writes the autobiography that comprises the book, in the hope that if ever it should find readers it will convince them that there is a better way of being than anything they know.

Although the prohibition against the word "I" (which is the most striking feature of this alien culture) cannot help but recall Ayn Rand's polemical novella *Anthem*, there is really very little similarity between the cultures depicted in the two works. In Rand's story, individuality has been suppressed in the name of a Communist ideology in which people exist only as aspects of a collective, as parts of society's hive-identity; in Silberberg's novel, self-expression is inhibited in order to cultivate loneliness, on the theory that the inner strength required to bear this condition will be the means to sustain a healthy society. Despite the superficial similarity, the two ideologies are actually opposed. Rand is, in fact a bitter opponent of any notion of fellow-feeling or mutual obligation between men, preaching an ethic of utter selfishness, while the moral of Silberberg's novel is that without such fellow-feeling and empathy between individuals, life is arid — at best unsatisfying and at worst unbearable.

A Time of Changes is a first-person narrative, and the fact that its ostensible author is a deviant within his own culture places his point of view closer to ours than to that of his fellows. Inevitably, this makes him a sympathetic character, and the reader is ready enough to be recruited to his crusade against oppressive social mores and religious tyranny. The exhortations which close the polemic — "Go and seek. Go and touch. Go and love. Go and be open. Go and be healed" — are such that they will find few dissenters among the predominantly young science fiction audience. Nevertheless, if one steps back a little from the viewpoint of Kinnall Darival, both the story and its moral quickly come to seem less convincing.

The sociology of the story is weak. There is some incongruity in the conjunction of the denial of self in social relationships with the social system of the various nations, which is a quasifeudalism apparently rotten with corruption. The denial of self seems to affect neither pride nor the commonplace self-seeking motivations, and it is not easy, once the grammatical idiosyncracies have been put aside, to see exactly what it *does* amount to. If the enforced denial of self is nothing more than a rather pompous stoicism, then it becomes more difficult to condemn it out of hand as being absolutely inimical to human happiness. The *angst*-ridden hero, too, seems less convincing when we recall that the source of his alienation from his own culture is a quasi-incestuous desire for his bond-sister, a desire whose psychological side effects include a tendency to premature ejaculation.

A Time of Changes is part of a long series of "thought-experiments" in which Silverberg explored different ways of dramatizing situations of alienation and symbolic exorcisms thereof. (The sequence of exhortations ends with "Go and be healed"; "Go and love" is merely the means to that end.) The existential situation of Kinnall Darival is one of the less satisfactory models. The use of the literal fusion of minds as an emblem for empathy is deployed in several other Silverberg novels — notably *Nightwings*, *Son of Man*, and *The Second Trip* — but in the first two the function of the operation is openly allegorical, while in the third the situation of the individuals involved is considerably more desperate. It is notable that in one of the most impressive novels belonging to this phase of his career, *Dying Inside*, Silverberg actually reversed the metaphor, making the possession of telepathic powers the alienating condition rather than the solution.

A Time of Changes is clearly not without merit. Even if the Nebula award it received was partly in recognition of other achievements, the novel was nevertheless considered a plausible candidate and undoubtedly attracted some support for its own qualities. It is a readable novel whose flaws are covert, and a good deal of work evidently went into the planning of its background. The myth of love and fellowship which it promotes, depicting the tragedy that results when empathy cannot be attained, and the evil nature of social constraints which suppress empathy, was at the height of its popularity in the late 1960's and early 1970's, when the self-appointed prophets of the "counterculture" could still believe in the imminence of a time of changes. Perhaps the novel is unfortunate in that it has become dated rather more quickly than it might have, so that now it seems to wear the tattered naïveté of the counterculture which it echoed. It is much more difficult today to read the ending optimistically, or to feel the sense of tragedy that should accompany a pessimistic reading. When all is said and done, *A Time of Changes* is simply not as eloquent as *Dying Inside*, *The Book of Skulls*, or *Son of Man*.

Brian Stableford

Sources for Further Study
Reviews:

Analog. LXXXIX, March, 1972, pp. 168-169.

Best Sellers. XXXII, September 1, 1972, p. 264.

New York Times Book Review. March 5, 1972, p. 37.

Publisher's Weekly. CXCIX, June 21, 1971, p. 72.

Renaissance. IV, 1972, pp. 9-10.

THE TOM SWIFT NOVELS

Author: "Victor Appleton" (Housename of the Stratemeyer Syndicate)
First book publications: 1910-1941
Type of work: Novels
Time: The historical present
Locale: The United States and numerous foreign countries

A long-running series of boys' books featuring the adventures of the extraordinary teenage inventor, Tom Swift

> *Principal characters:*
> TOM SWIFT, a teenage inventor
> BARTON SWIFT, his father
> MRS. BAGGART, their housekeeper
> NED NEWTON, Tom's best friend
> MARY NESTOR, Tom's girl friend and later his wife
> WAKEFIELD DANTON, an eccentric friend of the Swifts
> ERADICATE "RAD" SAMPSON, a black "whitewasher," later Mr. Swift's valet
> KOHU, an ex-South American native prince, Tom's bodyguard

The first book featuring Tom Swift the peerless inventor, *Tom Swift and His Motorcycle*, was published in 1910. That same year, since it was customary to bunch the first four or five titles of a new series and release them together, four other Tom Swift narratives appeared; within the next two years, there were ten more. Evidently, American boys enjoyed these stories about a teenage inventor, for beginning in 1913 a new story celebrating another of Tom's strange and wonderful inventions was released approximately each year until 1935. By 1941, when what proved to be the final Tom Swift book, *Tom Swift and His Magnetic Silencer*, appeared, the series numbered forty volumes. Tom Swift books — either as Grosset & Dunlap originals (thirty eight in total) or as Whitman reprints (the last Grosset & Dunlap titles) and originals (the final two volumes were Better Little Books) — were on sale, therefore, for at least thirty years and probably were available as new or used books for even longer. Although exact sale figures are unknown, the Tom Swift books must have sold in the hundreds of thousands and attracted, when passed around as series books usually are, even more readers. Consequently, Tom Swift must be included in the small cluster of heroes and heroines of children's series books prominent in the history of American popular fiction and children's literature.

The introduction of the Tom Swift series in 1910 was anything but fortuitous. Several decades earlier Luis Senarens had begun writing the first of hundreds of stories in which he entertainingly combined dime novel formulas and subject matter concerning science and its applications. In achieving success Senarens evidently had hit upon a way to utilize the contemporary fascination with inventions and gadgets, the excitement of the seemingly countless uses of electricity, and the nation's admiration of Thomas Edison. Thus, Edward Stratemeyer, famous entrepreneur of series books and the creator of the Tom

Swift series, probably was aware of the existence of an active market for juvenile science adventure and must have hoped to gain a share of that market by launching a new science adventure series. Moreover, it is likely that Stratemeyer's choice of a name for the hero of the series, Tom Swift, was also intended to evoke the name of the great American inventor. (Actually, the name Tom Swift had appeared a few years prior to 1910. Whether this appearance in a magazine story was a kind of market-testing or not, Stratemeyer, appreciating the potential attractiveness of the name, shrewdly adopted it for the new series.)

Further, Stratemeyer, wanting to increase the likelihood of the new series' success, contracted with one of the most talented authors in his stable of writers, Howard R. Garis, to write the new series under the name of Victor Appleton. As the author of the Motor Boys series and other books, Garis was already quite skilled in fleshing out the bare-bone plots Stratemeyer sketched. So skilled was Garis, incidentally, that while producing the Tom Swift series, he was also writing the well-known Uncle Wiggily stories and most of the Great Marvel books — those Jules Verne-like adventures which are perhaps the best written and most imaginative of early science adventure narratives for children.

Lastly, the advertising puffing the new series — "spirited tales" conveying "the wonderful advances in land and sea locomotion" — provides additional evidence that Stratemeyer had studied the market. For, instead of concerning science and technology in general, his new series would focus, at least in the beginning, on the ways advances in the application of electricity and motor design would affect future transportation. Thus, *Tom Swift and His Motorcycle* celebrates the challenges of improved motorcycles; *Tom Swift and His Motor Boat*, the swiftness and reliability of motor boats; *Tom Swift and His Airship*, the airship, a bizarre combination of biplane and dirigible; *Tom Swift and His Submarine Boat*, an underwater craft, powered by a futuristic combination of oil-burning engines and electric magnets, and *Tom Swift and His Electric Runabout*, a battery-propelled automobile faster than any other vehicle on the road.

The first Tom Swift books proved so successful that their content and format became the model for all subsequent volumes. The cast of characters, for instance, remained constant throughout the series, with one exception. Tom, the hero of the series, is good, resourceful, and invariably triumphant in both solving technical problems and outwitting his rivals. Barton Swift, Tom's father and founder of the Swift Construction Company, is also an inventor but gradually gives way to his far more brilliant and talented son. Mrs. Baggart, the housekeeper, substitutes for the mother Tom lost when he was a young child. Ned Newton, Tom's best friend and frequent companion, becomes financial manager of Swift Construction. Beautiful and supportive Mary Nestor will marry Tom. An eccentric who quaintly blesses a variety of objects whenever he expresses his feelings, Wakefield Danton is a close friend and companion of the Swifts. Eradicate Sampson or Rad, a black "whitewasher," becomes Mr. Swift's valet; unfortunately, Rad's characterization is blatantly racist. Kohu, the major character not present in the first volumes, is a giant South American native prince who, after being rescued by Tom, becomes his bodyguard.

All characters in the Tom Swift series are two dimensional; and the only significant change in characterization, Tom and Mary's marriage aside, is a gradual aging. All the narratives contain an "enemy," Tom's favorite term to describe his rivals, although specific villains change from book to book. All the narratives also feature much dialogue, most of it stilted but carefully correct grammatically. Detailed description, except for that depicting new inventions and their operation, is absent. Not surprisingly, an interest in machines and their operation is everywhere. In *Tom Swift and His Electric Locomotive* (1922), for example, the reader is told constantly how electrical power is transmitted from large generators to small ones and then to the locomotives. A fascination with the phenomenon of electricity becomes at times almost palpable. The opening pages of *Tom Swift and His Television Detector* (1933), for instance, are permeated with the sights and sounds of electricity: "strange zipping, buzzing and snapping;" "spilling of purplish blue sparks;" "again the blue and purple sparks, again the zizzling, the snapping and cracking." Finally, the arguing and bickering between Rad and Kohu, as they constantly vie for Tom's attention and approbation, together with Ned's teasing of Tom's affection for Mary, and Danton's habit of blessing, are the only attempts to lighten the otherwise very serious tone and atmosphere of the Tom Swift books. For the reader is never allowed to lose sight of the series' real theme: the "gee-whiz" glorification of the inventor whose fantastic discoveries in applied science are a constant source of wonder and, secondarily but not to be overlooked, of cash.

Tom Swift is an inventor without peer. Even his father, an inventor of some renown, stands in worshipful admiration of his son. When Mary exclaims, witnessing Tom's testing of his new tank, how exciting it is that he "should know how to build such a wonderful machine," Mr. Swift responds, "And *run* it, too, Mary! That's the point! Make it *run*! I tell you that Tom Swift is a wonder!" (*Tom Swift and His War Tank*).

Indeed, Tom is a wonder, for among his impressive accomplishments are improved forms of the wireless, talking pictures, tank, locomotive, camera, and seaplane; an electric rifle; an air glider; a photo-telephone; a floating airport; a TV detector that sees through walls; and various gigantic versions of dirigibles, guns, telescopes, and magnets. Generally speaking, as the series continued, Tom's inventions became more and more spectacular — more like what might be found in the gadget-infatuated science fiction of the 1930's. Oddly, however, two of the major motifs of science fiction, space travel and extraterrestrial life, never figure in the Tom Swift series until in the next to the last volume, *Tom Swift and His Giant Telescope* (1939), Tom uses a powerful lens of his own devising to detect life and civilization on Mars.

Tom Swift wholeheartedly accepts the challenges facing the inventor that he himself pointed out to Danton: "It is the impossible that inventors have to overcome. If we experimenters believed in the impossible little would be done in this world. . ." (*Tom Swift and His Electric Locomotive*). Thus, the young inventor's arduous struggles to solve a seemingly impossible technical problem and complete a new invention constitute a large segment of each narrative.

Another segment of each narrative concerns the hero's testing of his new invention, usually as part of some contest or adventure so that he knows the "impossible" has been done. A third segment of each narrative — and the one providing most of the conventional excitement — involves Tom's attempt to fend off the "enemy" who is seeking to obstruct his work or steal his patents. Tom is constantly on guard, suspecting that the "enemy" lurks everywhere, waiting to steal his inventions and, thereby, deprive him of the material rewards that rightfully belong to him.

The demise of the Tom Swift series can be attributed to several reasons. One is the failure to update the series as it gradually grew old-fashioned. Another reason is competition from new series books such as the popular Hardy Boys. Competition from other forms of more explicit science fiction such as Buck Rogers and Flash Gordon is a factor. There were, for instance, thirteen Buck Rogers and seventeen Flash Gordon titles on the Big Little Books list, the best selling children's books of the 1930's and 1940's. The Stratemeyer Syndicate even attempted to save Tom Swift by issuing the last two titles in a format similar to Big Little Books.

A final reason for the decline of the Swift series is the failure to think through the implications of Tom's marriage. Such an event presupposes an adult Tom and realistically calls for a heightening of sophistication in characterization and incident. None of this occurred, however, and the series remained intended for male preteens. Unfortunately, they apparently were not enthusiastic about their hero's marriage since sales fell off sharply after *Tom Swift and His House on Wheels* (1929), which concludes with Tom and Mary's wedding. The Stratemeyer Syndicate eventually recognized the error of Tom's marriage since, in the attempt to salvage the series as Better Little Books, Tom was transformed into a teenager again and Mary simply disappeared. However, the attempt failed and the series died, a victim of editorial misjudgment and of a competition more sensitive to the ever-changing reading interests of children.

The Tom Swift books are dead but they should not be forgotten. For decades they provided exciting and sometimes informative entertainment to hundreds of thousands of young readers. No one knows, moreover, how many of these readers may have become adult science fiction readers through the series; that is, once they were hooked on space adventure, they looked for more sustaining and sophisticated science fiction stories and found them in adult science fiction.

The Tom Swift books are, finally, the link between the origin of children's science fiction in late nineteenth century popular fiction and its current flowering in mainstream children's literature. For, within six years of the last Swift book, Scribner's released Robert A. Heinlein's *Rocket Ship Galileo*, the first science fiction novel written expressly for young people and published by a major house. Its critical and popular success spurred the acceptance of science fiction as a valid subgenre of children's literature.

Francis J. Molson

Sources for Further Study

Reviews:

Luna Monthly. XX. January, 1971, p. 27 and XXXIX, July–August, 1972, pp. 18-19.

TOWER OF GLASS

Author: Robert Silverberg (1936-   )
First book publication: 1970
Type of work: Novel
Time: The twenty-third century
Locale: The Earth

Simeon Krug, inventor of the android, is obsessed with building a gigantic tower in the Canadian Arctic to reply to an enigmatic message that has been picked up from an extrasolar civilization

> Principal characters:
> SIMEON KRUG, the wealthy inventor of the android
> MANUEL KRUG, his son and heir
> CLISSA KRUG, Manuel's childlike wife
> ALPHA LILITH MESON, Manuel's mistress
> ALPHA THOR WATCHMAN, Simeon's android foreman on the tower project
> LEON SPAULDING, Simeon's ectogene (fertilized in vitreo) secretary
> NICCOLÒ VARGAS, an astronomical scientist

Tower of Glass was written after Robert Silverberg had abandoned his facile youthful period of magazine and paperback writing, had passed through his period of scientific popularizations, and was several years into his reincarnation as an author of carefully crafted literary science fiction stories. The novel provides an opportunity to examine the ways in which literary science fiction began to differentiate itself from the popular fiction that preceded it. In most older science fiction novels, the idea, primarily expressing itself through background, was usually dominant, and the characters were important only as they facilitated the development and resolution of the idea. Actually, a science fiction story resembles a detective story; everything represents a clue to the overall meaning.

In recent years, the literary science fiction novel increasingly began to assume the characteristics of the mainstream novel until in Silverberg's 1972 *Dying Inside* and the works of a few other novelists it became difficult to identify them in the genre of science fiction. But *Tower of Glass* is no *Dying Inside*, which has only the concept of telepathy as a science fiction element. *Tower of Glass* is a science fiction novel, though it is both more satisfying and less satisfying than the usual genre novel. It is filled with typical science fiction devices such as interstellar messages, the preparation of a gigantic tachyon communication device, the building of an interstellar ship, and personality shifts (shunting).

The events of the novel take place in the twenty-third century, when the population of the world has been reduced by war, general anarchy, famine, social pressures, and foolproof contraception. Machines have replaced men in nearly all forms of labor. The proletariat has disappeared. Society has been reshaped worldwide by transmat travel to the point that all people speak the same language, English, and think the same thoughts.

Into this homogenized world culture of leisure, affluence, and instantaneous travel, Simeon Krug has introduced the android. Grown to full size in two years, genetically manipulated to produce various types and levels of intelligence, educated for one to four years in keeping with the kinds of tasks to be assigned, androids have satisfied most of the world's need for labor. They resemble, down to the use of the Greek alphabet to identify the various categories, the decanted humans of Huxley's *Brave New World*. The major distinction is that Huxley's characters are humans born in a different manner whereas Silverberg's androids are artificially created slaves. In *Tower of Glass* the question of what is the relationship between the creature and its creator is not social but metaphorical.

Into this situation comes a message from a distant star, a series of dots (2-4-1, 2-5-1, 3-1) that clearly has an intelligent origin but whose meaning cannot be deciphered. Simeon Krug, wealthy beyond measure, driven by curiosity and desire, vows to make contact with this other intelligence. He begins construction of a gigantic tower on the Canadian Arctic tundra, which will project a beam of tachyons at faster-than-light speeds toward the source of the interstellar signals. The tower must be tall, at least 1500 meters, to control the flow of tachyons, and it must be glass for both aesthetic and scientific reasons.

Krug's androids build the tower under the direction of a capable android named Alpha Thor Watchman. But although androids have been programed to be docile, some of them demonstrate for political rights. Others, including Watchman and Alpha Lilith Meson, worship Krug as their god, and base their religion on the belief that he will eventually raise them to full equality with womb-born humanity.

Manuel Krug falls in love with Lilith, who has seduced him in order to win his help for the android cause. Watchman and Lilith hope that he eventually will persuade his father to be a spokesman for the androids. Manuel is escorted through the underside of android life, which includes attending a chapel service. At Lilith's urging, he then goes to his father with the revelation of the android religion. Krug is outraged, unable to conceive of his androids as doing anything that does not serve humanity. He refuses to be their god, and he will not help them achieve equality. In a final effort to understand what has been going on, he shunts (exchanges personalities) with Watchman so he can see himself as Watchman perceives him. The shunting, however, also enables Watchman to see Krug's unbending attitude toward the androids. An android revolution begins out of the frustration and despair of being rejected. Servants kill their masters and mistresses, property is destroyed, and civilization in general is thrown into chaos. Even Krug's tower of glass is destroyed by Watchman. At the end, with the world bathed in blood and fire, Krug escapes in his starship for a three-hundred-light-year trip to the planetary nebula of NGC 7293.

The science fiction reader is left with a handful of unanswered questions: What was the meaning of the interstellar signal? Does it come from NGC 7293? Could intelligent life exist in the hard radiation of a blue-giant star, or evolve on a planet near it? Could the tachyon system have succeeded, and could communication have been achieved? Could the starship reach its goal, and what would it have found there?

All of these elements of the novel, which are given emotional weight by Krug's intense involvement with them, are dismissed in the cataclysm of the ending, along with other social and scientific elements in the world society that might each have provided the focus for a science fiction novel. If the most important (or the only important) element is the relationship of creature to creator, it does not emerge until almost halfway through the novel. The very richness of idea and texture distracts the reader from the thrust of the novel. The novel is saved, however, by its speculative content, the characterizations, the clarity of vision, and the intensity of experience, imagery, and metaphor. Krug, for instance, is believable in his vigor, crudity, and unbending determination to succeed no matter how impossible the goal. Manuel is equally believable as a meek individual. Watchman and Lilith, though manipulated by the intensity of their religious beliefs, attain individuality.

The language of the novel is colorful, vigorous, well chosen, and carefully modulated. The central image of the tower of glass casts its shadow over the entire novel, with its metaphorical identifications as phallus, cathedral, machine, Satan, and the Tower of Babel.

Other images contained within the novel both reinforce and conflict with the image of the tower: the hairless red bodies of the androids; the vats from which they come fully formed; the religious ceremony focused around the "codon"; the destruction and reconstruction of the individual in the transmat process.

The ultimate science fiction novel may come through the satisfying link of character and idea. Insofar as *Tower of Glass* aims at this ideal, it is an interesting failure, though in its own right it is a rich, exciting, and rewarding novel that belongs with the best the genre has produced.

James Gunn

Sources for Further Study

Reviews:
Analog. LXXXVII, May, 1971, pp. 162-163.
Extrapolation. XIII, December, 1971, p. 76.
Futures. III, March, 1971, pp. 97-98.
Kirkus Reviews. XXXVIII, August 15, 1970, p. 908.

Library Journal. CXV, December 1, 1970, p. 4196.
Luna Monthly. XXIII, April, 1971, p. 25.
Publisher's Weekly. CXCVIII, August, 1970, p. 46.
Science Fiction Review. XLIII, March, 1971, pp. 40-42.
WSFA Journal. LXXV Supplement, February–March, 1971, p. 7.

TRITON

Author: Samuel R. Delany (1942-   )
First book publication: 1976
Type of work: Novel
Time: Spring-Fall, 2112
Locale: Tethys, the capital of Triton; Outer Mongolia, Earth

*A multilayered narrative presenting the postscarcity, nonsexist Utopia of Triton
from the confused viewpoint of Bron Helstrom, who is blocked by his ability to deceive
himself and by his own retrograde, sexist male ideology*

> *Principal characters:*
> BRON HELSTROM, a thirty-seven-year-old metalogician
> THE SPIKE, a thirty-four-year-old writer-director, a member of an
> *avant-garde* traveling microtheater group
> SAM, the political liaison between outer Satellite diplomatic and
> intelligence corps
> LAWRENCE, a seventy-four-year-old homosexual male
> PHILIP, one of Bron's bosses
> AUDRI, another of Bron's bosses

Samuel Delany is one of the most stimulating and provocative of the current
major science fiction writers. Rooted both in vintage science fiction and contemporary literary theory, critical of society's problems, and committed to
excellence in his craft, Delany challenges his readers with texts that call for
careful study. Indeed, full appreciation comes only after rereading Delany's
work. *Triton*, written the year after *Dahlgren* was completed, retains many of
the themes treated in the earlier novel. While *Dahlgren* focused on Bellona, a
disordered but Utopian city, and on the Kid, who relates positively to Bellona's potential, *Triton* focuses on another urban Utopia and on Bron Helstrom, who is unable to tap successfully the potential of that Utopia. Subtitled
"An Ambiguous Heterotopia," *Triton* both continues the tradition of the
Utopian novel and challenges it. Delany's "ideal society" is meant to be disturbing and disconcerting to the reader, since it is based on possibilities within
our present society, at the same time that it topples all of our assumptions and
perceptions of reality. The reader of *Triton* is also treated not only to a brilliant
science fiction plot, vividly presented settings, and incisive meditations on
societal problems (particularly sexism), but also to an analytical discussion of
the text and how it works.

Triton and the other Outer Satellites are advanced technological societies in
which there is no scarcity, and human control over material existence is complete. With full automation, a labor force is no longer needed, and a guaranteed annual income, along with all human services, is provided to every citizen. The centralized federated government of the Outer Satellites owns and
controls most sectors of the economy. Universal suffrage exists from around
age thirteen, and there are at least thirty political parties represented in government. Law enforcement, education, health care, artistic production, and

social institutions are depicted in detail. Conscripted armies no longer exist, but in the course of the novel a war employing highly advanced antigravity weapons is fought between the Satellites and Worlds over the question of economic hegemony. Both the wars and the errors of government emerge as dystopian elements in this Utopia.

Economics, government, and social institutions, though, are really secondary to Delany's interest in everyday life in the Utopia. He goes beyond other recent Utopian novels in his focus on daily life and on the subjective freedom that is the guaranteed right of Triton's citizens. Everyday life emerges as a balance of collectivity and individuality, but with personal freedom always as an end. People live cooperatively in dormitories organized by sexual preference (straight male, gay male, nonspecific male, straight female, gay female, nonspecific female, mixed sex, and family) or communally in smaller family units of ten to twenty adults and children. Meals are taken in cafeterias, transportation is usually by foot, and police, "e-girls" of both sexes, maintain order without being oppressive. In addition, Delany describes the games, dining and drinking behavior, and clothing customs of Triton. The strategic board game, Vlet, which Lawrence teaches Bron, is described in enough detail to excite any game fanatic. The dinner Bron and Spike have in an exotic Outer Mongolian restaurant is enough to stimulate anyone interested in the social and sensual pleasure of eating. Triton's controlled atmosphere along with the society's lack of a nudity taboo offers Delany a chance to describe fascinating varieties of body decoration from full nudity, to body painting and decoration, to full mask and cape cover-up.

Daily existence in this libertarian-socialist society is thus organized according to the nonrepressive pleasure principle — made possible by the advanced, appropriate technology and the post-scarcity socialized economy. Personal emancipation with no class, race, sex, or age discrimination is the rule. Complete sexual freedom from puberty, full psychological and physical sex-change and reproduction technology, and the banishment of all taboos allow for a wide variety of guilt-free activity. Internal, hereditary, and ideological repression has disappeared, and in its place is a society with the economic, technological, and psychological freedom necessary to adjust its environment for maximum human fulfillment.

Triton can also be read with a focus on the story of Bron Helstrom and his identity crisis and search for happiness. In fact, the Utopia is presented through the viewpoint of Bron, a macho male misfit, who sincerely strives to know himself and find satisfaction on Triton but who cannot overcome his male supremacist ideology and his own self-deception. The Bron-plot provides the narrative spine around which the Utopian images cluster. Originally from Mars, where he had worked as a prostitute, Bron is unsettled in his job and in his personal life. He meets The Spike after unexpectedly becoming the focus of one of her microtheater productions on the streets of Triton. He is fascinated by her, falls in love with her, and makes awkward attempts to get her to love him. The Spike, a woman in control of her own life, chooses to love someone else and finally tells Bron to stop bothering her.

Bron bumbles along through various encounters seeking happiness, but is unable to see himself or his society in a clear light free of his own macho ideology. Despite the feedback he gets from Lawrence, a seventyish gay male, Sam, a government agent, The Spike, and others, Bron does not change. In one final attempt to change, he makes use of Triton's sex change clinics and becomes the passive female he desires, hoping then to find the man he once was.

Helstrom is a disturbing and fascinating character. Hurt, unhappy, uncertain, he resists self-awareness and control over his own life primarily by projection and by hurting others. He continually seeks others, such as The Spike, to resolve life's problems for him. In his self-rejection and emotional laziness, he is confused and unable to overcome the mundane worries. What makes *Triton* the challenging narrative it is lies with Delany's choice to present a Utopian society through the eyes of such an unreliable and unlikable character.

Filling out the narrative in both the plot and Utopian subtexts is an array of characters that enrich and invigorate the entire work. The Spike's theatrical troupe, the variety of residents in Bron's dormitory and workplace, the members of the many religious sects, and the free spirits in the city's unlicensed district where nothing is prohibited, all make the book more well-rounded. For example, Windy, Charo, and the others in The Spike's troupe are fully fleshed out minor characters. Their desires, work, and intertwined love lives give depth to the opposition that exists between The Spike and Bron. The religious fanatics, such as Spike's lover, Fred, who joins a sect which practices self-mutilation, provide images that are satirical as well as testimonies to Triton's guarantee of subjective freedom.

While maintaining a linear narrative, *Triton* is a purposely disconcerting array of the Utopian and dystopian, the emancipatory and oppressive, the personal and political jammed together. It combines a multileveled plot, complex characterizations, the presentation of a Utopian system, and theoretical reflections on the literary form itself. The underlying structure of the book is that of a spiral which begins with Bron's presence as a man in the Plaza of Light and ends with his presence as a woman in the same plaza four para-months later. The repetition of elements as the spiral unwinds — "everything in a science fiction novel should be mentioned at least twice (in two different contexts)," as we read in the "appendix" — the jarring images, and the ambiguity of the minimal plot leave the narrative more open than most other science fiction works.

Thus, it is fitting that this heterotopic novel closes with an analysis of science fiction and fiction in general. Delany writes of the history of science fiction and its characteristics as a literary genre. He discusses the different relationship between foreground and background that exists in science fiction as opposed to "mundane" fiction. For in science fiction, background acquires a primary importance along with the usual foreground of plot and character. The landscape of the alternative world becomes as important as its psychology. In *Triton*, the Utopian society *and* Bron Helstrom's story are equally important and, accordingly, influence and inform each other in ways different from non-science fiction. Thus, Delany has not only opened the genre to the new possibilities of heterotopia, he has also taken science fiction to the level of a self-conscious, self-reflecting narrative — that is, fiction about fiction and the process of its creation.

Triton, although a Utopian narrative, does not present its ideal society directly, as in the traditional Utopian novel, nor negatively as in the dystopian novel; rather, it presents a Utopia from the underside, showing the interconnections with the social system from which it developed and with which it is still in conflict. This novel is not a simple or static Utopian vision; the text is not lyrical but jarring. Just as the plot ends with Bron's quest left unresolved and openended, the adventure of Triton society itself is equally as unresolved and open to future development because of its own Utopian contradictions.

Triton, as the reader knows full well by the last page, is a literary text, an artifact of our own society. The fantasy it projects, the prelogical Utopian image, is not a static blueprint of the only good society possible. But like our own dreams, it arises out of the personal and social conscious and unconscious of the United States in the 1970's; its Utopian dream images speak to the problems and contradictions of our time. When the Utopian vision is juxtaposed against Bron Helstrom's own story, the novel becomes a complex meditation on everyday life and personal consciousness and behavior. In its look at sexism and male chauvinism and the resulting efforts women and men undertake to overcome such oppression, *Triton* is an important social document. In its execution as a science fiction novel reflecting on its own process, it is an important literary document. Its breadth of topics, variety of characters, wealth of detail, and generally excellent writing style make it a remarkable book. *Triton*, complex and multilayered, disturbing and delightful, is a novel that calls for careful reading and rereading.

Tom Moylan

Sources for Further Study

Reviews:

Booklist. LXXII, June 1, 1976, p. 1393.
Magazine of Fantasy and Science Fiction. LI, September, 1976, p. 30.
New York Times Book Review. March 28, 1976, p. 30.

TUNC
AND
NUNQUAM

Author: Lawrence Durrell (1912-   )
First book publications: Tunc (1968); *Nunquam* (1970)
Type of work: Novels
Time: The present
Locale: Athens, the Near East, and London

A brilliant scientist, employed by the Merlin Corporation to help re-create Iolanthe, a movie star now dead, is successful beyond his expectations

> *Principal characters:*
> FELIX CHARLOCK, an inventor *extraordinaire*
> BENEDICTA, his wife, Julian's sister
> MARCHANT, his co-worker
> JULIAN JOCAS, the elusive chief of the Merlin company
> CARADOC, an elegant architect and talker
> DR. NASH, Merlin's house psychiatrist
> IOLANTHE, a former prostitute turned movie star, now dead

Lawrence Durrell once described his famous series of novels, *The Alexandria Quartet*, as "science fiction in the true sense." When applied to the massive multilayered, multidimensional books that comprise the tetralogy, the phrase seems somewhat meaningless, particularly if the term "science fiction" conjures up visions of space opera or ray guns. In fact, to consider Durrell a science fiction writer at all, despite what he himself has said, might strike many readers as preposterous. After all, is the group of four novels not the great symphonic epic of modern love? Is not Durrell a poet of exquisite sensibility whose evocations of the Mediterranean mystique are drenched with sunlit ambience?

These questions demand an affirmative answer, to be sure, yet the fact remains that both *The Alexandria Quartet* and the doubledecker novels *Tunc* and *Nunquam* that followed it were described as science fiction by the author. The former was, among many other things, an experiment in the space-time continuum, telling the same story from multiple, shifting points of view, condensing and compressing time, and extending and contracting space into a "heraldic universe," to use Durrell's own phrase. *Tunc* and *Nunquam* extend the very borders of reality, as Charlock attempts to resurrect Iolanthe in the form of a bionic robot.

The plot of the two novels can be briefly summarized: Felix Charlock is an inventor of prodigious ingenuity. He has, among other things, invented a virtually sentient computer and a typewriter that presents beautifully typed material when it is spoken to. Eventually Charlock is induced to join the Merlin Company, headed by the enigmatic, elusive Julian Jocas and Julian's sister Benedicta. So powerful and so inclusive is the Merlin Company that once one joins it, one can never resign. It is so ubiquitous in its multifaceted endeavors that, in Durrell's words, it "seeks to control the destinies of us all." Eventually Charlock marries Benedicta and is induced to re-create Iolanthe, a famous international cinema star who was secretly beloved by Julian. Charlock and others from Merlin reconstruct Iolanthe as a bionic robot, indistinguishable from her original flesh-and-blood self, complete with memories, emotions, feelings, and intellectual powers. In her new state Iolanthe seems far more human than her once-live original had been.

Iolanthe gradually discovers her bionic self and slowly becomes aware that she, like all other employees of Merlin, can never escape from the clutches of the Company. However, with her new ability to love, a condition she had lacked when alive, she makes Julian aware of what he had been, and together they die so that Charlock and the other members of the firm may have the freedom they were otherwise unable to achieve. At the end of the book, Felix and Benedicta destroy the old contracts, the old covenant that had bound Merlin's employees, and set them all free.

These books are concerned with complicated metaphors, to be sure, but the metaphors deal with the eternal problems of freedom, servitude, independence, love, justice, mercy, and forgiveness that have haunted humanity for thousands of years. Moreover, to call attention to the method with which he approaches these problems, Durrell provides an epigraph from Dostoevski's *Notes from the Underground*: "Two times two is four. That is a wall."

Exactly. That wall imposed by external reality is what Durrell is trying to transcend in these books, and in so doing he utilizes the complicated metaphor of science fiction. After all, science fiction and science fiction writers need not be hampered by the limits of external reality and external time. If we wish to climb beyond the stars, we invent some sort of galactic drive even though Einstein has told us it is impossible. So with Durrell in these books. Fundamentally he wishes us to consider a very simple question: *When* is a being human? This apparently simple, but really complicated question, is at the heart of the metaphor underlying Durrell's two novels. He asks, in effect: If you have a being who follows an ethical system as high as any yet developed throughout civilized history, or higher, is that being not human, regardless of the external shell into which it is embodied?

Conversely, he questions whether a human being is human if that person can no longer feel, has no emotions, is guided only by the basest of motives, follows only an immoral ethical system, and treats the remainder of humanity with contempt. If flesh can no longer feel, he seems to say, why cannot simulated flesh — wires, printed circuits, transistors, and minicomputers — begin to feel.

In asking these questions, Durrell is, unconsciously to be sure, echoing many science fiction writers of the last few decades, most notably Isaac Asimov and his famous Three Laws of Robotics. Asimov in scores of stories and novels about his robots and their positronic brains also asked, in effect: When is a being human? Durrell, however, provides some significant variations. The only robot as such is the re-created Iolanthe, her bionic memory preserved through tape recordings and other inventions of Charlock. She awakens to humanity, with no memory of her death, no knowledge of her bionic state, and no realization that she has been re-created. She is sheltered from the world for obvious reasons, and her self-education after her resurrection changes her from a screen harlot (she had once been the mistress of Charlock) with a street urchin background, a totally selfish, unfeeling person, to an educated, caring, loving being.

On the other hand, the only "robot" in one sense of the word is the ostensibly human Julian Jocas, head of the omnipresent, omnipotent, and omniscient Merlin Company. Julian's god is business and the pound sterling, and Julian is its prophet. An almost unseen figure throughout the books, Julian is at once cruel, vindictive, and satanic. He is totally inhuman, and the end of business justifies any means to achieve it. Once one has joined the Firm, one has almost literally lost his soul to it.

Durrell's metaphor now becomes obvious. He is asking whether we, in devoting so much of our being to the god of business and the dollar, have not become worshipers at the altar of Moloch. And does not Moloch — Merlin — the Firm — Julian — demand ever increasing sacrifices? For example, when Charlock, even though married to Julian's sister Benedicta, attempts to resign, his attempted escape from the Firm is thwarted and he is jailed in a company controlled asylum. Benedicta herself wavers between sanity and insanity, and we gradually come to see that she has been used, abused, loved, and raped by Julian, who now quite obviously symbolizes the black magic of Merlin the magician. Evil, which Durrell seems to equate with civilization, the rational mind, and business for the sake of business, corrupts even the Blessed: Benedicta.

The wall of reality over which Durrell leaps now becomes increasingly clear. Merlin represents the condition of humanity — sordid, ugly, unmitigated hatred, and selfishness. And there is seemingly no escape from the Firm, even for the resurrected Iolanthe. However, her genuine love for the human being Julian changes him from a black magician, a vindictive Lucifer, to a human, humane being. In the end, both Iolanthe and Julian die in a Fall — the word deserves the capital letter — that releases mankind to love, rather than enslaving it to sin. Charlock burns the contracts that have bound the employees to the Firm, and all humanity is freed, released from the bounds of sin.

Durrell's metaphor is involved, to be sure, but it is one that he could not have attempted, at least in its present form, without utilizing the techniques of science fiction. Using them, he is able to overcome the wall represented by "two times two is four," and to examine the genuine reality beneath the appearance. Iolanthe and Julian were once "human." In reality, they were inhuman, selfish, and at least in Julian's case, almost diabolic.

Durrell remarked in *A Key to Modern Poetry* that ". . . Einstein's theory joined up subject and object, in very much the same way as it joined up space and time. Now what is important to us here are not the equations — even if we understand them — but the symbolic act of joining what is separated." Durrell joins the separated, then, in these two novels, by utilizing the devices of science fiction. Earlier, in *The Alexandria Quartet*, he attempted to reconcile the opposites of space and time through multidimensional layering. Here in *Tunc* and *Nunquam* he is permitted his comments on the nature of humanity only through inventing a nonhuman being, the robot Iolanthe, to provide a contrast from which to view other so-called humans in the books.

We well know that, despite the efforts of modern science and technology, we can neither create life nor simulate it to the hundredth decimal point accuracy of the re-created bionic robot, Iolanthe. A robot is still clearly fictional and is several light years beyond the state of the art of modern science. In creating her, Durrell risks alienating his audience by the very boldness of his imaginative leap, but Iolanthe is not simply inhuman as Julian is, but *non-human*. Yet she becomes the "non-human human" and her creation is virtually a quantum leap forward.

Charlock himself is not merely the uninvolved, dispassionate first person narrator. His voice represents Durrell's, to be sure, and despite his powers of invention, Charlock is completely, totally human, throughout the two books, and thus the reader can readily identify with him. He has the same faults, foibles, eccentricities, passions, feelings, and emotions that we all have. Charlock is at once universalized and personified. He symbolizes the abilities of mankind; but he also illustrates its weaknesses. He is both individual and collective. Our attitude toward Charlock is one of pity tempered by love, of anger modified by understanding.

Science fiction has permitted Durrell the luxury of passionate non-involvement or involved passion, at the same time. Durrell is, in the end, firmly on the side of the human, whatever its incarnation; and science fiction has given him the freedom to speculate about humanity in a way that our "reality" does not. In Durrell's hand, two times two no longer equals four. It equals infinity.

Willis E. McNelly

Sources for Further Study

Criticism:

Fraser, George S. *Lawrence Durrell*. Harlow, England: Longman, 1970, pp. 39-44. Fraser defines the two works as philosophical romances, reminiscent of *Brave New World* and *Nineteen Eighty-Four*.

————. *Lawrence Durrell: A Study*. Revised Edition. London: Faber and Faber, 1973, pp. 149-191. Fraser studies the two works in depth, stating that they have disturbing social relevance.

Reviews:

Tunc:

Atlantic. CCXXI, May, 1968, p. 109.

Choice. V, December, 1968, p. 1304.

Christian Science Monitor. April 11, 1968, p. 13.

New York Times Book Review. April 14, 1968, p. 4.

Saturday Review. CI, April 13, 1968, p. 37.

Time. XCI, April 5, 1968, p. 108.

Times Literary Supplement. April 25, 1968, p. 413.

Nunquam:

America. CXXII, April 18, 1970, p. 425.

Choice. VII, October, 1970, p. 1036.

Christian Science Monitor. March 26, 1970, p. 15.

Nation. CCX, April 27, 1970, p. 508.

New Statesman. LXXIX, March 27, 1970, p. 450.

New York Times Book Review. March 29, 1970, p. 4.

Saturday Review. LIII, March 21, 1970, p. 29.

Times Literary Supplement. March 26, 1970, p. 328.

THE TUNNEL
(DER TUNNEL)

Author: Bernhard Kellermann (1879-1951)
First book publication: 1913
English translation: 1915
Type of work: Novel
Time: 1920-1950
Locale: The United States and Europe

The description and glorification of the gigantic engineering project to drill a submarine railway tunnel connecting the United States with Europe

> *Principal characters:*
> MAC ALLAN, the originator of the Transatlantic tunnel project
> MAUD ALLAN, his wife
> HOBBY, Allan's best friend, a fashionable architect
> SAM WOOLF, the financial wizard of the Transatlantic Tunnel Corporation
> ETHEL LLOYD, daughter of a powerful millionaire, and Allan's second wife

Although the technological undertaking which is described in Bernhard Kellermann's novel, *The Tunnel*, has long since become obsolete and was probably already so by the end of the novel, it makes as exciting reading today as when it was first published. The novel is not only about a technological project — the tunnel under the Atlantic Ocean, connecting the United States and Europe — but it is also about a state of mind and a new type of human being: the engineer, the titanic planner, the advocate of technological efficiency and the machine, one who will do anything to achieve his ambitious plans, including the sacrifice of his own family.

The tunnel engineer Strom, a German Russian, resembles a coldly logical computer more than a human being; Müller, who is characterized by his jovial fatness, is no less ruthless or efficient. The book's hero, the American Mac Allan, the originator of and driving force behind the tunnel project, is also such a man. The reader first encounters him at a concert which represents a confrontation between engineering determination and the fine arts. The concert is conducted by a famous artist, a genius in his field, but Allan listens to the music as if it were some alien magic. He acknowledges the technical accomplishment, but he neither understands it nor is he interested in trying to do so. He is there only to meet the world's most influential capitalist, Mr. Lloyd. This shriveled old mummy of a man, whose face is disfigured by a growth, is publicity shy because of his appearance. During a pause in the concert, however, the old man makes a brief appearance, which has been prearranged by Allan's friend, the fashionable and flamboyant architect Hobby. Lloyd at once agrees to the tunnel project. His support ensured, the other important U.S.

financiers are quickly won over. The Atlantic Tunnel Corporation is founded, and work begins.

The drilling of huge double tubes begins in three places: near New York, in a mid-Atlantic station at the Azores, and in France. Kellermann describes the activity, noise, and stench of the machines in apocalyptic terms; the machines are depicted as man-eating monsters, but not in the antitechnological manner of much German fiction. The metaphors and descriptions are strong and hectic; the style is somewhat coarse and clichéd, but it is gripping and acquires a rhythmic beauty of its own that ably expresses the theme and suggests a German Futurism. The prose reflects the theme, as the machinery slowly eats its way through the bowels of the Earth, swallowing men, iron, wooden supports, rails, and spewing forth earth and stones.

Every few miles in the tunnel stations full of machinery, ventilators for supplying the twin-shafts with fresh air, and depots are set up. Kellermann does not presuppose any utopian technology to make the tunnel possible; the only small innovation in the book is a new kind of hard steel, used in the drills in place of the prohibitively expensive diamonds. This new alloy, invented by Mac Allan, is the basis for his venture.

What is utopian about the novel is the sheer size of the tunnel project and the fanatical dedication with which it is implemented. All weaker human beings are cast aside and killed by the moloch technology. This is the fate of Allan's wife Maud, who is first neglected and left alone in their house while her husband ceaselessly plans, organizes, and confers with engineers, bankers and businessmen. Unlike her husband, she deeply loves music and the arts, which are ruthlessly crushed by the new technological mode of life. She and her little daughter are killed midway through the novel by a mob, enraged by a major catastrophe in the tunnel which has killed almost three thousand people: the tunneling machine struck a pocket of natural gas, which exploded, burning out several miles of the tunnel and asphyxiating or burning many of the workers. The carefree, art-loving Hobby is one of the people trapped in the tunnel; although he escapes with his life, he ages prematurely into a senile idiot, never to recover. The catastrophic accident strikes a crushing blow to the project; the workers refuse to enter the tunnel, which by now extends for hundreds of miles under the Atlantic, and a general strike locks the capitalists and the workers in what appears to be deadly combat. The project grinds to a standstill, Allan's personal magic, previously skillfully exploited by the press and the film company that shoots footage of every step of the undertaking, seems to have lost its power. Neither coercion nor threat is sufficient to get the workers back into the tunnels again. Stocks come crashing down, and a general economic depression takes hold of the many industries selling supplies to the Tunnel Company, especially the steel and iron works; only the lobby of the ocean liners rejoices in their rival's misfortunes.

The situation is aggravated by the suicide of the corporation's financial wizard, Sam Woolf. A German Jew of poor origins, he has risen to financial prominence in the world as the result of genius and ceaseless toil, culminating in becoming Lloyd's right-hand man. He is a confirmed sybarite and lecher, keeping young girls in many of the capitals of the world. What Woolf wants most is power, not just the power to juggle billions of dollars in support of Allan's project, but the power to control the project. His financial maneuvers are described in graphic simplicity, in an expressively dramatic manner that influenced the writing style of later German science fiction writers, such as Hans Dominik and Rudolf Heinrich Daumann, and even formed the picture of America in German literature. Using the company's money for his own ends by juggling the various accounts, Woolf hopes to achieve his ambition; but finally, his nerves fail him; he loses money that he need not have lost had he sold earlier or held out longer. When the financial edifice comes crashing down around his ears, the puritanical streak in Allan allows Woolf no way out, and he commits suicide. The death of the financial genius in whom the public had trust strikes the final blow to the Tunnel Company. The shareholders storm the company's premises in a desperate attempt to save the remnants of their money.

During the rush, the highrise that houses the company's offices goes up in flames, and the organization appears finished. More than eight of the fifteen years that the work was supposed to require have passed and the tunnel is not even half-finished. Public enmity and rage is such that Allan is indicted for fraud: for wilfully leading people to believe that the work could be completed in fifteen years, given ideal conditions. When he honestly admits that he settled on this time to create a climate favorable to the project, he is sentenced to six years in prison. The sentence is upheld in appeal; however, the highest court proclaims Allan innocent after he has served several months of his prison term. Released, he is a broken man, still brooding and working over his grand plan, but unable to create any public support.

His strongest supporter during all this time has been Ethel Lloyd, the major shareholder's beautiful daughter. She fell in love with him on first sight, wooing him secretly while he was still married and standing by him with lawyers and moral support when he was on trial. After some tribulations, Allan marries her in order to continue his project. His marriage to Ethel symbolizes the intimate connection between the engineer — the man with the big ideas, the doer — and the man of money who really makes things happen, who transfers the ideas into reality: an alliance of technology and money. The project is then quickly completed without further incident, costing a total of nine thousand lives during the almost quarter century of construction.

Meanwhile, time has not stood still; Allan's steel has been outdated by newer materials, and now airships cross the ocean much faster than the giant trains in the tunnels. But they will continue perfecting it, increasing the speed of their trains in the process. Technology, the book implies, holds as much joy in the process itself, as in the completion of it. The novel is an epos of technology, extolling the things that man's ingenuity and determination can achieve, although man himself is transformed in the process into a new, and not altogether admirable being.

Some German critics have called *The Tunnel* antitechnological, and some have even claimed that it has anticapitalist tendencies. Such claims cannot be supported by the text; although Kellermann's figures are in some respects quite inhuman, unfeeling, and coldly calculating, they are not unsympathetically drawn. The reader can easily identify with Allan. A pony driver in an American coal mine, he was buried at the age of thirteen during an explosion in the mine; by keeping his wits about him and by iron will, he dug himself out alone, the only survivor at his level. This dramatic episode that might have resulted in his death proved in fact his fortune. It interested people in him, and he was given the engineering education that he put to such good use in perfecting the Allan steel and in the execution of his grand project. He and his engineers are not supermen at all. Allan is described as a big blond man, with a strong friendly face, showing some brutality, but rather common and unremarkable; nobody would have supposed him to be anything special. He and his men are representatives of a new way of life and thought, shapers of the future and man's resources.

This is the wholly original thing about the novel. It introduces engineers and creates a secondary world of technology that, although not displaced in the future — the novel is definitely set shortly after the turn of the century — is an idealist construct totally focused on the tunnel project, to the exclusion of everything else. The result is a novel of remarkable dramatic power and energy. The bankers and financiers are necessary to realize the dreams of the engineers; without them, nothing would really be done. But Kellermann shows no interest in the rights and welfare of the workers (despite some Communist leanings in his later life). They are ciphers in his book, faceless soldiers of work, who are sacrificed by their engineers with no more thought than the general who orders his troops to storm an enemy gun emplacement. To get things done, gigantic things, unheard of things, is what matters in Kellermann's book, and this gives the novel its particular hectic rhythm and impact. There is really no other work of science fiction that comes close to it in this respect. *The Tunnel* shows what it means to sweat and toil for a great dream. Compared to the dramatic impact of Kellermann's book, other novels about similar titanic undertakings are pale things indeed.

Franz Rottensteiner

Sources for Further Study

Reviews:

Boston Transcript. April 24, 1915, p. 2.

New York Times. XX, May 16, 1915, p. 190.

Nineteenth Century. LXXV, March 14, 1915, p. 587.

IL TUNNEL SOTTOMARINO
(A Submarine Tunnel)

Author: Luigi Motta (1881-1955)
First book publication: 1912
Type of work: Novel
Time: Sometime during the first quarter of the twentieth century
Locale: The Atlantic Ocean, London, the Orkney Islands

   The adventurous construction of the first transatlantic tunnel linking Europe to the United States

> *Principal characters:*
> JACK DEVEMPORT, a wealthy London ship builder
> NINJTTA, his daughter
> BURNS DEVEMPORT, Jack's brother and King of Steel in New York
> MAC ROLLER, a bad-tempered engineer in love with Ninjtta
> ADRIEN GÉANT, a French engineer of noble birth who also falls in love with Ninjtta

Among the first writers who introduced some of those themes labeled as science fiction into Italian popular fiction, Luigi Motta made a rather regular use of these modern and scientific archetypes in his writings. Beginning his career as a writer very early (at seventeen he won a literary prize), he left the seminary where he was studying and went to sea for some time. After giving up his life at sea, he started writing seriously, at first in collaboration with another great writer of popular fiction, Emilio Salgari, with whom he wrote at least five novels and shared that love of the sea and exoticism which is always present in the works of both authors.

This love of the sea is a good point of departure from which to consider *Il Tunnel Sottomarino*, since nearly the entire novel takes place aboard a ship or a submarine (very efficient ones for the times), and the central action of the narration is the construction of the first transatlantic tunnel between Europe and the United States. The plot, however, is extremely complex. Everything starts when the yacht *Stream* (belonging to Mr. Jack Devemport, a wealthy London ship builder) receives a puzzling message during its navigation in the Atlantic. Mac Roller, trusty man of Devemport now in charge of the *Stream* on a vague mission, changes the ship's course and reaches the Sargasso Sea from where the message has been broadcast. He believes it is a call for help, and he is right. As the *Stream* approaches a very large iron ship, the *Géant*, Roller notices that the ship has collided with a derelict ship. Rescuing the crew and the strange workers of the *Géant*, Mac Roller is informed by the young French engineer, Adrien Géant, of the great enterprise started months before, which has now been temporarily interrupted by the shipwreck. An American society (the Atlantic Tunnel Company) had sponsored his project, a transatlantic tunnel joining Manhattan to Brest. The *Géant* had been laying the necessary enormous tubes and machinery. Roller is shocked by this news; he himself had nursed a similar project for years, and the only man who knew of his plan was Jack Devemport, his employer. Controlling his rage, he asks Géant who the guiding force behind the Atlantic Tunnel Company is. When Adrien Géant, now alone with Roller on the derelict ship, utters the name of Burns Devemport, brother of the London ship builder, Roller is sure that he has been betrayed. He insults and then assaults Géant and throws him into a pit in the wrecked ship. Roller leaves the derelict ship alone and reports that the Frenchman fell overboard. He then has the remnants of the *Géant* torpedoed. Upon his return to London, Roller tries to persuade Jack Devemport to entrust him with the continuation of the work (blackmailing the ship builder with the threat of destroying the plans and documents found aboard the *Géant*), and he also makes his intentions clear about Ninjtta, Devemport's daughter. At this point the gears of the *feuilleton* begin to spin.

Adrien Géant is not dead and returns in time to unmask the villain, who runs away uttering dark threats. Roller joins a modern band of pirates, equipped with ships and a submarine, who live in the castle of Reidelmen, on one of the Orkney Islands. Géant continues to build the tunnel, but strange events reveal that unknown spies are at work. When the tunnel finally is finished, the inaugural passage is to be made by a train full of guests, but Roller moves into action. Knowing that the tunnel has been insured, he plans to steal the policy, wreck the tunnel itself, and pocket the insurance money, causing the final ruin of his opponents.

He sets his scheme in motion by abducting Jack Devemport (and the insurance policy), taking him by submarine to Reidelmen. Géant and Ninjtta, watching a newsreel of the abduction, notice the license number on the car. The Frenchman borrows a submarine from Devemport's shipyards and starts his search with Ninjtta. They find Jack shut up in a sort of underwater tower-jail not far from Reidelmen island, and Géant feigns a shipwreck to enter the castle. In the meantime, the pirates' and Ninjtta's submarines come in contact and fight; Ninjtta wins, and Géant reaches her father through a secret passage joining the tower-jail to the dungeon of the castle.

The adventure is not over yet. When the inaugural train begins to crawl through the tunnel, Roller destroys the tube. However, the plans anticipated the possibility of such a mishap, and the section containing the passengers, with Géant and Ninjtta among them, is safely sealed. Immediately, Géant and Ninjtta provide everyone with special diving suits and lead the passengers to the surface along the slope of an ancient submerged volcano. Along the way they fight sea monsters and pirates and discover the ruins of Atlantis. On the surface, Roller is waiting to finish off any possible survivors, but the arrival of the Navy puts a long awaited end to his crimes. The happy ending is assured when the lost insurance policy is found.

It is rather easy to see that the plot very closely follows the routine patterns of *feuilleton*, and that in some scenes Motta is indebted to Jules Verne. But

Motta's own ingenuity makes the novel both amusing and readable. In simple but reliable language, Motta provides technical details combined with speculative vision. Although it is not overly inventive, the technology is often meticulously explained in a popular style. In the manner of Jules Verne, Motta presents information and figures concerning the plans of the tunnel, the submarines, the diving suits, the sea monsters, and the new communication devices — all in a highly theatrical style, replete with popular clichés. It is true that the characters are flat, but this homogeneity of personalities stresses the balance always present in Motta's writings. A novel of great events and small people is probably the most appreciative summary one might give a writer working with matters which are too often out of proportion with themselves.

Gianni Montanari

THE TUNNEL THROUGH THE DEEPS

Author: Harry Harrison (1925-   )
First book publication: 1972
Type of work: Novel
Time: 1973
Locale: The United States and England

An alternate time track novel in which Captain Augustine Washington successfully constructs a transatlantic tunnel for England, which brings about American independence from the Crown

Principal characters:
> CAPTAIN AUGUSTINE WASHINGTON, a descendant of the traitorous General George Washington
> MARQUIS CORNWALLIS, a British business executive
> SIR ISAMBARD BRASSEY-BRUNEL, an unreconstructed Tory
> IRIS BRASSEY-BRUNEL, his daughter, beloved of Augustine
> SAPPER CORNPLANTER, an Iroquois working on the tunnel
> ALBERT DRIGG, Lord Cornwallis' secretary

Harry Harrison's sixteenth novel is ingenious, breezy, superficial, exciting, and predictable. *Tunnel Through the Deeps* falls into the alternate time track subgenre of speculative science fiction, and perhaps its greatest strength is that it is both stylistically and imaginatively the kind of novel one living in this world would expect to be popular among readers in the world it posits. That world is, of course, similar enough to this one that a traveler is able to orient himself to it without much difficulty. It is a world which developed exactly like our own until 1212, when Christian resistance to Islamic rule in Iberia was quashed, thus permitting England, some two centuries later, to beat Spain into the Age of Exploration and New World dominance. Washington was hanged after the Battle of Lexington, and a magnificent memorial stands on the banks of the Hudson River in honor of the gallant general Benedict Arnold. There is talk of granting Commonwealth status to the thirty-two American colonies. And in the attempt both to strengthen a wavering world economy and to unify the American spirit into a power capable of self-rule without alienating that spirit from Britain, industry has proposed and the Crown has approved a plan to underwrite the colossal undertaking of a rail tunnel between Land's End and Long Island; the man nominated to engineer the project, and in doing so to redeem his family name, is Captain Augustine Washington of Mount Vernon and Her Majesty's Territorial Engineers.

Such are the suppositions upon which *Tunnel Through the Deeps* is based. There is enough intrigue in the way of assassination attempts, impossible deadlines, sabotage, acts of God, and difficult love to keep the plot moving briskly through ten years of tunnel construction. However, although such flourishes as Washington's piloting an experimental rocket from Newfoundland to London in order to be present for a psychologically significant running of the nuclear powered *Flying Cornishman* are in themselves exciting, they are not in any real sense the stuff of which Harrison's book finally is made.

For *Tunnel Through the Deeps* is as much a period piece as any Horatio Alger novel, and its style and plot consistently represent a make-believe period in world history which, though modern, remains placidly, complacently, and indomitably British. The British dominance can be seen everywhere. For example, nuclear powered trains such as that *Flying Cornishman* are becoming the world's premier mode of transportation, even though automobiles, airplanes, and rockets exist. Harrison offers no explanation for the phenomenon; if one reflects for a moment it becomes clear why no explanation is deemed necessary. The airplane and the rocket were invented by Americans, the automobile by a Frenchman, but only the locomotive is a truly English contribution to mechanized transport. In a world where England has ruled for almost five centuries, the locomotive naturally reigns. In a similar manner, technological breakthroughs have been applied to the existing English industrial complex rather than the other way around. Since Britannia's rule of the waves is absolute there has been no arms race, no need to develop nuclear weaponry; the almost paternal presence of an English gunboat on the Rhine is still sufficient to quell impending trouble between France and her Germanic neighbors. Britishness infuses *Tunnel Through the Deeps* with the sense of propriety, and morality one might expect to discover if the popular conception of Victorianism and all that word implies were applied to a nation capable of dominating the world in the late twentieth century.

The novel's hero is, of course, Captain Washington, who, like Alger's Ragged Dick, has brought himself up from the depths of poverty. Mount Vernon, the house, had been burned by British troops during the ill-fated Revolution of 1776 and never rebuilt; the farm itself has provided insufficient sustenance for two hundred years of Washingtons. However, Augustine possesses the pluck, intelligence, purpose, and ability to draw men to him, which has brought him affluence and middle class respectability. He is as loyal a subject of Elizabeth as any queen might wish — though his passion for American independence renders it impossible for him to accept a proffered knighthood at the tunnel's completion. He understands as well as W. S. Gilbert's Ralph Rackstraw that, though love can level rank, it can do so only with the greatest difficulty and only when the higher ranking lover condescends. So it is that Washington, strong, handsome, brilliant, doted on by the laborers in his employ, and grudgingly respected even by those peers to whom his name is anathema, has a problem.

The girl he loves is the startlingly beautiful Lady Iris Brassey-Brunel, only child of Sir Isambard Brassey-Brunel, the peer whose architectural design for the tunnel Washington wishes to modify, and who alone of the tunnel board's directors opposes his appointment as supreme head of construction. Duty binds the Lady Iris, against the wishes of her heart, to her father; honor commands

Washington to respect her filial obligations and to wait. In the noblest Arthurian style, he fills his waiting by going off in search of a Grail, in this case the completed tunnel, that will prove his worthiness to her father and his love for her. When the quest is successfully completed and the objections to his suit are at last removed, the lovers are reunited under the approving hands of the now dying Sir Isambard, and bliss is finally achieved. No one notices or seems to care that the paramours have become middle-aged in the meantime.

To balance his Englishness, and to insure that Washington is seen as the British concept of the idealized American colonist, Harrison has his protagonist called "Hawkeye" by his English friends; and he gives him an Iroquois (not, thank heaven, a Mohican) right hand man to go with his humble origins and his naturally aristocratic bearing.

Another, even more singularly and stereotypically British aspect of *Tunnel Through the Deeps* is to be discovered in the way the novel depicts things getting done. In the days of the Empire, and of Gordon, Livingston, Sir Richard Burton, and others, a special kind of man simply dreamed a dream, and presently that dream was accomplished. How and at what cost it was accomplished were trivial questions, the answers to which had no place in the public imagination.

It is the same in Harrison's novel. If Washington requires a mile-long steel and concrete tube some thirty feet in diameter and needs it ten thousand feet below the surface of the Atlantic Ocean where it will act as a bridge between undersea mountain ranges, that tube is provided for him. If it is thought that the nobility taking the inaugural train from Land's End to Point 200, an artificial island marking the first two hundred miles of completed tunnel, would enjoy having a luxury resort in which to cavort at the end of their journey, such a spa with wine cellars, tennis courts, amphitheater, tree-lined promenades, and all is thoughtfully provided for them. How it all got put together in less than two years' time is of little importance; what is significant is that England wanted it done, and so it was done. A good time was had by all.

Indeed, giganticism, opulence, and a concern for the comfort of the upper classes permeate Harrison's imagined world and are in evidence everywhere, from the brass and teak furnishings in the staterooms of the airplane *Queen Elizabeth* (eight turbine engines, each developing 5,700 horsepower) to the uniformed doorman in the Grand Saloon Car of the London and Land's End Railway, that train whose nuclear fueled locomotive engine, the *Flying Cornishman*, is plated with fourteen-karat gold. Clearly, only a race fed on the realization of such splendid dreams as the *Queen Elizabeth* and the *Flying Cornishman* might envision, let alone embark upon, the making of an Atlantic railway tunnel. And only an imagined Anglo-American chauvinism and pride could inspire Great Britain's and America's lower classes to the actual labor of construction all in the names of Independence and Empire, Washington and the Queen.

Harrison tells his story from an omniscient point of view, but the omniscience is one which admires and, more importantly, believes in both the evolved class system and the chivalric necessity of Might for Right. Such a stance is exactly correct for this kind of novel, which permits a reader to approach it with a willingness to suspend his disbelief in such patently unbelievable characters as Gus Washington and the Lady Iris. For Washington is not a caricature, any objective analysis of his person or personality notwithstanding, but he would be if his narrator did not dote on him so fondly. Likewise, only a point of view which straightforwardly conveys its blind and absolute conviction that class distinction is necessary to the public weal could blithely characterize ghetto gang wars as the merry cracking of heads among manly and good-natured groups of Iroquois and Irishmen.

It is a minor weakness in his novel that Harrison goes so far to dissociate his own sensibility from his *persona*'s that, to show he does not want to be taken too seriously, he makes those Indians and Irish check their scalping knives and shillelaghs respectively at the New York City limit. It is one thing for an observer to patronize his characters; it is quite another for a writer to patronize his observer. This is especially true when the credibility of the story being told is entirely dependent on the credibility of that observer; and it is probably less likely in alternate time track fiction than in any other kind, when a story grants from the outset that no one in this world possibly could be telling it, that a narrator's voice will be confused with the author's.

By and large the observer's integrity is unchallenged, and a reader can easily imagine that the omniscience relating *Tunnel Through the Deeps* is precisely the kind of omniscience which would be telling it in a world whose political, technological, and economic evolution had progressed in the manner depicted. Therefore, in spite of stereotyping both of character and of class, the novel is credible. If a reader nourishes no false hopes about such a social order as this actually working, he at least is happy that Washington is united with the Lady Iris at last. And it bothers him no more than it does them that, somewhere along the way, their youth has gone.

Douglas J. McReynolds

Sources for Further Study

Reviews:

Algol. XIX, November, 1972, p. 28.

Analog. XC, October, 1972, pp. 166-167.

Books and Bookmen. XVIII, February, 1973, p. 86.

Foundation. IV, July, 1973, pp. 75-77.

Futures. V, October, 1973, pp. 504-505.

Kirkus Reviews. XL, April 1, 1972, p. 432.

Library Journal. XCVII, July, 1972, p. 2438.

Publisher's Weekly. CCI, April 10, 1972, p. 53.

Times Literary Supplement. February 2, 1973, p. 129.

Worlds of If. XXI, October, 1972, pp. 113-115.

TWENTY THOUSAND LEAGUES UNDER THE SEA
(VINGT MILLES LIEVES SOUS LES MERS)

Author: Jules Verne (1828-1905)
First book publication: 1870
English translation: 1873
Type of work: Novel
Time: 1866-1868
Locale: Beneath the surface of the Earth's oceans

The story of three men held captive aboard a giant submarine

Principal characters:
  PIERRE ARONNAX, a Professor of Natural History at the Museum of
    Paris
  CONSEIL, his servant
  NED LAND, a harpooner
  CAPTAIN NEMO, the master of the *Nautilus*

Twenty Thousand Leagues Under the Sea was the sixth of Jules Verne's "Voyages Extraordinaires." It was published in the same year as *Autour de la lune*, and in company with that volume it marked the end of the first and most extravagant phase of Verne's adventures in imaginary tourism. In seven years of writing, he had crossed Africa by balloon; journeyed to a world within the Earth; planned and subsequently executed a trip to the moon; visited the North Pole; explored the untamed lands of the southern hemisphere; and toured the world of the ocean floor. From 1870 onward, it was not so much a matter of where to go next as of what to do there to avoid being bored, but in the early works, of which *Twenty Thousand Leagues Under the Sea* is the best, the sheer joy of visiting territories where no civilized feet habitually trod was sufficient to rule out that possibility entirely.

The anonymous English translation of the novel used in early Sampson Low & Marston editions has been reprinted by many British and American pub lishers with only minor modifications, and though it is not as corrupt as the standard translations of some other Verne novels, it is by no means a good one. The new translation made by Walter J. Miller for an edition published in New York in 1966 is much better.

The story begins by referring the reader back to a series of puzzling events said to have taken place during the year 1866, when ships in various regions of the sea reported sighting a mysterious object larger and faster than a whale. After the holing of a ship below the waterline by this enigmatic entity, the narrator of the story, Pierre Aronnax, publishes an article explaining the phenomena as the activities of a giant narwhal. As he is something of an expert on marine life, he is Professor of Natural History in the Museum of Paris, he is invited to join the *Abraham Lincoln*, a ship which is commissioned to hunt down the hypothetical sea monster.

For several months in 1867, the *Abraham Lincoln* combs the seas fruit-lessly, but it is not until she is about to turn for home that she finally encoun-ters the object of her search. She carries an expert harpooner named Ned Land, whose task it is to attack the beast. When he finally gets the chance to use his skill, his harpoon bounces off the object. There is a collision, and Aronnax, his servant Conseil and Ned Land are hurled into the sea. They find refuge on the "back" of the "sea-beast," and discover that it is made of steel.

The shipwrecked companions are taken aboard the vessel, but find its crew taciturn and apparently unable to understand any language that Aronnax knows. Eventually, though, the master of the submarine breaks the silence, and introduces himself as Captain Nemo of the *Nautilus*. Nemo is, however, as enigmatic in his behavior and motives as was the sea monster men took him for. He will not release his guests, but he treats them well, and Aronnax at least is by no means reluctant to accept his hospitality, for the *Nautilus* offers him an unparalleled opportunity to further his studies of marine life.

Captain Nemo has sworn that he will never again set foot on land, and the sea supplies all his needs. Even the "meat" which he eats and the "tobacco" which he smokes are substitutes garnered from the sea. He has a vast library and lays claim to wealth sufficient to repay the national debt of France without bankrupting himself. The *Nautilus*, his home, is more than seventy meters in length, and is powered by electricity.

The *Nautilus* carries its prisoners through a series of underwater adventures, allowing them to witness all the marvels of an undersea world that was virtu-ally unknown to Verne's contemporary readers. Nemo takes his guests hunting in an underwater forest near the island of Crespo, saves them from savages after allowing them a brief shore leave on another remote island, and shows them great reefs of valuable coral and priceless pearls. He takes them from the Persian Gulf to the Red Sea *via* an underwater tunnel far beneath Suez (where, of course, there was no canal in 1868). The first clue to Nemo's character is supplied when he pauses off Crete to give a fortune in gold to the insurrec-tionists fighting to free the island from Turkish rule, but this is merely a pass-ing gesture. Once back in the Atlantic the sightseeing is resumed as Nemo shows Aronnax and his companions the resting place of one of the many trea-sure ships which he has plundered, the site of sunken Atlantis, and the Sar-gasso Sea.

The *Nautilus* then sets sail for the South Pole (Verne had already visited the north pole with Captain Hatteras). The fact that the Antarctic icecap is so much larger than the Arctic made it obvious that there was a substantial landmass under the southern ice; but its extent was in 1870 a matter of pure conjecture, and no one could say whether the pole itself was on land. Verne thus had sufficient license for allowing Nemo to reach the pole by submarine, though the adventure was a dubious one. At this point the narrative becomes more melodramatic in tone and content, nearing its climactic scenes. The *Nautilus* is trapped by the ice and barely breaks free. Soon afterward, traveling north again, she experiences the classic encounter with a gigantic marine mollusk, similar to the one which had created a sensation in becoming entangled with the French naval vessel *Alecton* in 1861. Though every modern reader will know that the creature in question must have been a giant squid, Verne was unsure. The beast described in his narrative is clearly a gigantic octopus (the term "poulp" is used in the standard translation, unhelpfully altered to "devil-fish" in some later editions) but there is some ambiguity as a word meaning "cuttle-fish" is also employed.

Following this dramatic highpoint, the adventure in underwater tourism, which has lasted nearly a year, comes swiftly to an end. Aronnax watches helplessly as Nemo attacks a ship, apparently motivated by a lust for revenge, though against whom and for what reason the narrator cannot tell. Verne's correspondence with Hetzel, his publisher, reveals that this enigma was not altogether premeditated. Verne had planned to portray Nemo as a Polish patriot seeking revenge on Russia, but changed his mind because of the delicate diplomatic situation existing between France and Russia when he actually wrote the book. With his mission apparently complete, Nemo takes the *Nautilus* further north. Aronnax and his companions plot their escape and manage to leave the vessel as it falls within the grip of the maelstrom. The three escape with their lives but the fate of Nemo and his ship remain uncertain. Five years were to pass before Verne, in *The Mysterious Island*, revealed what had happened to the ship and also supplied a new account of its master's conduct.

Twenty Thousand Leagues Under the Sea was Verne's most successful novel, and it perfectly encapsulates the spirit of his early novels. It is a Cook's tour of a world whose invasion seemed imminent thanks to new technology. Vernian fiction is essentially a celebration of the revolution in transportation that was brought about by the industrial revolution, inspired by the success of the steamship and the steam locomotive. Verne is often hailed as an anticipator of future machinery, but in this regard he was neither exceptional nor particularly successful. His real merit lies in the way he used his imaginary vehicles to lead the way into the hitherto inaccessible corners of the globe and advertise the wonders to be found there.

Verne's reputation for inventive genius is largely based on his description of the *Nautilus*, but the credit which he received for "inventing the submarine" is quite unwarranted. The American Robert Fulton had tried to interest the government of revolutionary France in *his* submarine *Nautilus* in 1800, and submersible boats continued to be built, especially in France, throughout the nineteenth century. Verne may actually have seen Hallet's submarine operating in the Seine in 1858, and he was certainly acquainted with Jacques-François Conseil, another experimenter whose name he borrowed for his novel. The French Ministry of Marine had invited tenders for the building of a submarine in 1858, and *Le Plongeur*, built by Charles-Marie Brun, was launched at Rochefort-sur-mer in 1863. A model of this vessel, displayed in the Paris Exhibition of 1867, was probably the inspiration for Verne's *Nautilus*.

The only real innovation made by Verne in his imaginary vessel was its use of the power of electricity, but as this functions in the novel as a quasi-miraculous device mysteriously answering all needs, it can hardly be claimed as an imaginative triumph. Some of the technical details which are given are clearly incompetent. For instance, the diving suits worn by Nemo and his guests would have been lethal because of unequal pressure upon the head and body. Verne does not hesitate to distort the facts in favor of convenience. He makes seawater wondrously transparent, and allows the sun's light to penetrate to a far greater depth than in fact it does. There are also some curiously unlikely conjectures in the book, as when Aronnax claims that the Earth will grow cold and lifeless once volcanic action has ceased, because the sun's radiation is inadequate to sustain life.

To point out these faults is to deny the book its false reputation as a marvel of extrapolative scientific fiction. Such claims, however, were foisted upon the book by others, and Verne himself denied them vehemently on more than one occasion. He knew that what the book actually had to offer was not technical prophecies about the shape of submarines to come, but a window into an unknown world. Like his contemporary Robert Browning, though in a very different way, Verne believed that "man's reach should exceed his grasp," and that is what his fiction, in essence, does so well. It reaches out to capture with the enthusiastic vision of the mind's eye those wonders known but not yet accessible to actual eyes.

Twenty Thousand Leagues Under the Sea has aged better than any of Verne's novels dealing with the world's terrestrial surface (for we must remember that Thomas Cook was advertising a trip around the world a year *before* Verne published *Around the World in Eighty Days*), and yet seemed much closer to actuality that the Baltimore Gun Club's lunar project or Professor Lindenbrock's journey to a world within the Earth. It had a unique advantage by virtue of the fact that even when the invasion of the undersea world was well under way, no adequate intelligence of submarine marvels was carried back to the world of armchair voyagers. Underwater photography presented acute technical problems which were not readily solved. Ironically, one of the first triumphs for the underwater camera invented by the Williamson brothers was the making of the 1916 film version of Verne's novel. (Previous attempts to film underwater epics had made do with shooting through the walls of glass tanks.) Many decades were to pass even after this crucial point in progress before Jacques Cousteau made the undersea world familiar to millions of people through the medium of the television set, and until that time *Twenty Thousand Leagues Under the Sea* and its imitators held on to their monopoly of the popular imagination. That is the book's real strength as a work of science fiction.

Brian Stableford

Sources for Further Study

Criticism:

Moskowitz, Sam. *Explorers of the Infinite: Shapers of Science Fiction*. New York: World, 1963. This overview of Verne's place in the science fiction tradition considers how novels like *Vingt mille lieues sous les mers* have influenced later authors.

TWO PLANETS
(AUF ZWEI PLANETEN)

Author: Kurd Lasswitz (1848-1910)
First book publication: 1897
English translation: 1971 (abridged)
Type of work: Novel
Time: The 1890's
Locale: The North Pole, a space station, Mars, Europe

A conflict between Earth and a materially and morally superior Martian civilization organized along Kantian lines, ends in a peaceful reconciliation between the worlds

> *Principal characters:*
> HUGO TORM, the head of a German attempt to reach the North Pole by balloon
> ISMA TORM, his wife
> KARL GRUNTHE, an astronomer and another member of the expedition
> JOSEF SALTNER, a natural scientist, the third member on the balloon trip
> LA, the Martian woman who falls in love with Saltner
> FRIEDRICH ELL, an enigmatic astronomer who advanced the money for the Polar expedition; a Martian-human halfbreed

During his lifetime, Kurd Lasswitz was sometimes compared to H. G. Wells and Jules Verne, but he neither reached the prominence of these two men, nor gained their influence. Although not of their stature, he is nevertheless an important European pioneer of science fiction. His novel *Two Planets* is a genuine interplanetary classic, a book that has been translated into many European languages and is still in print in Germany. His other works have been largely forgotten; he wrote a number of short stories, other fantasy novels, and popular and philosophical essays. Lasswitz's first work of fiction was *Bilder aus der Zukunft* (1878) which combined two tales, one rather short and one longer, the first of which, "Bis zum Nullpunkt des Seins," was first published in a newspaper when Lasswitz was twenty-three years old. This humorous story inspired Claes Lundin to write the Swedish science fiction classic, *Oxygen och Aromasia* (1878).

Lasswitz also wrote one of the first theoretical literary essays on the principles of science fiction, "Uber Zukunftsträume," which is included in his collection of essays, *Wirklichkeiten* (1900). He called such stories "scientific fairy tales," defended the use of science as the subject matter, and set out to write such stories himself, in the volumes *Seifenblasen* (1890), *Traumkristalle* (1902), and the posthumously published *Empfundenes und Erkanntes* (1920). Most of these pieces are quite slight, hardly more than thinly fictionalized popular essays, but some are charming fairy tales and quaintly scientific stories introducing original concepts that recur later in science fiction by other authors. Even Jorge Luis Borges read Lasswitz, and his story "Die Universal-bibliothek" (translated in Clifton Fadiman's *Fantasia Mathematica*, 1958) served as an inspiration for Borges' own "The Library of Babel."

Some of Lasswitz's fairy-tale-like and often sentimental fantasy novels show the influence of the panpsychic ideas of the German philosopher Gustav Theodor Fechner, who even attributed souls to heavenly bodies and plants: *Aspira* (1906), subtitled "the novel of a cloud," and *Sternentau* (1909), "the plant from Neptune's moon," are today almost unreadable. *Homchen* (1902), however, first published together with *Traumkristalle* in a volume entitled *Nie und Immer*, is a spirited animal fable from the prehistoric past of Earth.

The book for which Lasswitz has become famous is, however, the two volume interplanetary novel *Two Planets*, which combines rocketry with Utopian ideas. Lasswitz's principal inspiration in this novel, as well as in his discursive writings, was Immanuel Kant and the German Idealism of writers such as Friedrich von Schiller. It is not a faultless novel; it is perhaps somewhat schoolmasterish, but it is a laudable and largely successful attempt to infuse philosophical ideas into a space novel. Although Lasswitz's novel appeared in book form in the same year H. G. Wells's *The War of the Worlds* was serialized in *Cosmopolitan*, his Martians are not BEM's, but appear quite human. Technologically they are advanced far beyond mankind, and they are above all morally superior beings. They clearly differentiate between duty and inclination, following the Kantian ideal; they do not allow themselves to be governed by their passions, and therefore they are truly free. Their guiding principle is the development of the autonomous individual personality, the free determination of the individual. Martian society is a personal Utopia, a permissive society where happiness and freedom of the individual human being are more important than the organization of the politics. Not the greatest good for the greatest number of people, but the highest possible development of the individual consciousness is the society's goal. Lasswitz had little interest or understanding of the social movements of his time, the problems of the masses.

Mars is a loose confederacy of small and big states — republics and monarchies mixed, capitalist, socialist and even Communist societies coexisting side by side — and the form of government may at any time be changed by a simple vote of the population. Or, since many homes are mobile, a Martian may simply take his house and remove it to a place and a country more to his liking. By penalty of loosing his franchise, every Martian has to read at least two newspapers a day, including one of the opposition. Mars is a truly enlightened community, far above the quarrels and conflicts of backward Earth. In reality, however, the superior Martians are not immune to corruption; they become corrupted by their own power over the humans, arrogant and tyrannical, infected by "Erdkoller." Soon they become divided among themselves into parties: the Philobaten ("Ba" being Martian for Earth; the "Baten" are the humans) consider the Earthmen more or less their equals, granting them the right of self-determination; while the Antibaten are shocked by conditions on

Earth and feel that human beings are a dangerous and inferior breed and must be held in check.

The novel opens with a balloon flight to the North Pole, undertaken by the scientists Saltner, Grunthe, and Torm. It is financed by the enigmatic Friedrich Ell, who has prepared a Martian-German dictionary. Later he is revealed to be the son of a German mother and a Martian spaceship captain who crashed on Earth. This beginning was probably inspired by the Swede Andrée's unsuccesful and fatal attempt to reach the North Pole by balloon in 1896. The three explorers reach the pole without difficulty, but find that they are not the first to be there. The Martians have already erected a circular ground station, while a space station hovers 6356 miles above the pole. Airtight cars move in an "abaric field" or a field of antigravity between the two stations. The explorers are caught in this field, and their balloon is drawn towards the space station. Torm escapes by parachute, and Saltner and Grunthe are saved by the Martians and shown the wonders of their advanced technology. Grunthe later returns to Europe to warn the world of the arrival of the Martians, while Saltner, who soon falls in love with the beautiful Martian girl La, visits Mars.

The Martians are greatly handicapped by Earth's much stronger gravity (a difficulty later overcome by transportable abaric fields). This aggravates the first interplanetary diplomatic incident when, after having captured two Martians, a British gunboat opens fire on a Martian airship built for movement in the Earth's atmosphere. The British refuse to submit to a Martian ultimatum and are captured by the Martians, who have meanwhile transported a whole fleet of airships to Earth. Europe becomes a Martian protectorate, and human beings are subjected to compulsory reeducation after their armies have been disbanded. For practical reasons, Russia and the United States are at first left alone. The Martians, however, are soon corrupted by their own power and begin to behave like petty tyrants, holding in contempt the people they are supposed to raise to their own cultural level.

Discontent grows among the humans. A "Menschenbund," in which Saltner and Grunthe play prominent roles, rallies under the battle cry of "Numenhood without Nume" ("Nu" is Martian for Mars, and the "Nume" are the Martians. Linguistically, the novel is not far advanced; almost all of the Martian proper names are monosyllabic). This party accepts the benefits of the higher culture and the goals of the Martians as their own, but they resent the alien interference and want to develop autonomously. When huge new taxes are to be levied and the United States also becomes a protectorate, a secretly built American air fleet rebels, capturing the Martian polar stations and the Martian fleets on Earth. Rather than resort to genocide (although there was a plan to stop the rotation of Earth around its axis), the Martians return to the moral principles they abandoned, and a peace follows that benefits both worlds.

Thus *Two Planets* was one of the first science fiction novels to explore fully the clash of different cultures. The Martians are not depicted as extraterrestrial monsters but as a more advanced stage of humanity. They serve as a mirror and a promise of what mankind's own future might be to "Ko Bate" (poor humankind), as well as ultimately serving as a warning against arrogance and intellectual pride. This ameliorating aspect of the novel is not quite successful, however, because the book is didactic rather than dramatic, containing flat characters and marred by the clichés of conventional love stories. The novel is much better in its purely discursive passages which have a winning lucidity, and it also presents many technological ideas of note.

Lasswitz may not have been the first science fiction writer to have introduced space stations (both Edward Everett Hall and Konrad Tsiolkovsky were earlier), but independently of the others he arrived at the same idea and went on to develop fully the space station as a sort of stepping stone and relay station for interplanetary travel. His space station is designed like a wheel, which anticipates the satellites suggested by later writers on astronautics. It hovers above the pole, because the rotation of Earth causes no complications. Lasswitz's spaceships, built of the gravity-free material "stellit," move by a combination of the shrewd use of gravitational forces (traveling in astronomical orbits between the planets) and supplementary rocket power ("repulsit" shots that move the spaceship in the opposite direction). The mechanics of space travel are described accurately by Lasswitz, who was by profession a mathematician. The Martians also possess a sort of ray gun, the telelyte, that sets off catalytic reactions of a chosen kind in the target; an interplanetary telegraph using light rays; and a telescope with electrical amplification. Martians can look into the past by observing the light signals produced by the occurrence a long time ago. The "geography" of Mars more or less follows Percival Lowell's ideas: the canals on Mars are used to bring the rare water from the poles. Solar energy is collected in the deserts (and solar plants are erected on Earth later; what the Martians mostly want from Earth is energy), and energy serves as currency. The Martian households are fully automated. The Martians either live in skyscrapers distributed along the canals (which do not, however, form cities) or in small movable houses. Food is prepared synthetically. All Martians are required to labor for one year in the working force, but they have no compulsory military service and possess (until their contact with Earth) only a small police force.

Mars is then, a veritable Utopia, specifically, a technological Utopia where the machine serves man and does not enslave him. Freed from labor, the Martians can pursue artistic endeavors. The ultimate art form on Mars is one that relies on the most intimate and highly regarded sense, the sense of feeling. *Two Planets* thus reconciles science, the arts, and philosophy in a personal Utopia governed by Kantian ideas and presents an important depiction of the clash of two cultures in science fiction. Unfortunately, Lasswitz was at best a respectable but not a great writer. His writings lack the mythic beauty and dramatic immediacy of the best work of Wells. And while the important books of Wells are today as vital as ever, Lasswitz's novel is but an interesting minor landmark in the science fiction tradition, more to be applauded for its ideas and its ambition than its literary execution.

Franz Rottensteiner

Sources for Further Study

Criticism:

Hillegas, Mark. "The First Invasions from Mars," in *Michigan Alumnus Quarterly Review*. (February, 1960), pp. 107-112. Lasswitz's *Two Planets* is compared to H. G. Wells's *War of the Worlds*.

"Martians and Mythmakers: 1877-1938," in *Challenges in American Culture*. Edited by Ray B. Browne, Larry N. Landrum and William K. Bottorff. Bowling Green, Ohio: Bowling Green University Popular Press, 1970, pp. 150-177. Hillegas presents a penetrating analysis of the myth of the Martians and their invasion of Earth particularly as it was shaped by Lasswitz in his *Two Planets*.

Rottensteiner, Franz. "Kurd Lasswitz: A German Pioneer of Science Fiction," in *Riverside Quarterly*. IV (August, 1969), pp. 4-18. This survey of Lasswitz' work shows that his utopias stressed the happiness of society gained through the development of the individual.

2018 A.D. OR THE KING KONG BLUES

Author: Sam J. Lundwall (1941-   )
First book publication: 1974
English translation: 1975
Type of work: Novel
Time: 2018
Locale: Stockholm and the Sheikdom of Khuri

An account of life in Sweden in the early twenty-first century

Principal characters:
ANNIKI NORIJN, a prostitute
ERIK LENNING, a junior executive of Inter-Ad
LEONARD W. KOCKENBERGH, JR., chief executive of Inter-Ad
SHEIK YARASIN AR-RECHEHIDD, the owner of the world
SHEIK UMIR AR-RECHEHIDD, his brother
TIM EULENSPIEGEL, an amateur scholar and pimp

2018 A.D. or the King Kong Blues was the fourth novel by Sam Lundwall to appear in English, and was translated by the author from a Swedish version published in 1974 (the author's own title was *King Kong Blues*). The earlier novels — *Alice's World, No Time for Heroes*, and *Bernhard the Conqueror* — are all slapstick burlesques of familiar science fiction scenarios, and though originally written in English rather than being translated from foreign language texts, they show clearly enough the difficulties of translating a sense of humor from one language into another. *King Kong Blues* works a great deal better, largely because it is a different kind of satire. The earlier works are subculturally self-contained — they are science fiction books making fun of science fiction clichés — but *King Kong Blues* is a more mature work whose object of contemplation and attack is the real world.

In the first chapter of *King Kong Blues*, we meet Anniki Norijn, who is trying to fight her way out of a department store where the resident priest has just joined a couple in holy wedlock to the accompaniment of a barrage of overt and subliminal advertising. Anniki, it transpires, is one of countless individuals who, by virtue of one accident of fate or another, have slipped through the net of the computerized society of twenty-first century Sweden; having been lost by the computer, she no longer has any official existence. This has its fortunate aspects, in that she is free from the tight web of exploitation which the government and employers have spun by means of their sophisticated methods of social control, but it also has its disadvantages, in that she has to make her living as a prostitute with no recourse to the official system of credit-exchange.

Anniki has had one claim to fame during her brief life, but was not in a position to revel in it at the time: she was the first Swedish baby of the year 2000, which made her in the eyes of the nonmathematically minded public the firstborn of a new millennium. Though her moment of notoriety is long past, others have plans to restore her to the limelight. These are the executives of Inter-Ad, whose director, Leonard W. Kockenbergh, Jr., has conceived the brilliant idea of using her to symbolize the twenty-first century quality of a new armpit cream. With her aid he intends to turn the product into a veritable *zeitgeist* in a jar.

The man commissioned by Kockenbergh to find Anniki is Erik Lenning, whose task is far from a simple one. His search takes him "behind the scenes" of the crazy society of twenty-first century Stockholm, into the fake underworld maintained by the Mafia as a tourist-trap, and into the real underworld inhabited by official nonpersons. In the meantime, he traces various contacts who reveal to him the desperate state of the world in bloodcurdling detail, while the author interrupts his adventures with a few ironic chapters of commentary and a kaleidoscopic assortment of scenes which show life as it is lived in this time and place.

Inter-Ad is actually a subsidiary of an even larger multinational enterprise. The network of ownership and control is too complex for anyone to comprehend, but in the final analysis, *all* the multinational corporations are based in a row of post-boxes in Zurich which are the mouths of a series of numbered bank accounts, all of which are owned by Sheik Yarasin ar-Rechehidd, who has been playing the stock markets with his oil wealth in order to occupy himself in his idleness. By buying up the world he has managed to stop the world buying up his little Sheikdom of Khuri, but his hobby is beginning to bore him to the point where he is relocating American companies in Siberia just for the fun of it. He has become moody and introverted, and his brother, Sheik Umir, is worried about him. Umir is a traditionalist through and through, believing that all a Bedouin needs is his rifle, his camel, his tent, and his women (plus, of course, the guidance of the Koran). He is very anxious about the way Yarasin seems to have fallen under the spell of Western Capitalism, which enshrines a very different set of values.

The culture of Lundwall's future Stockholm has been thoroughly brutalized by every kind of cynicism. Sensation-seeking television audiences lap up competition shows in which family cars are dropped into tanks of water to see which family can escape first and which will drown; suspense-filled news coverage of terrorists armed with Molotov cocktails hijacking a hydrogen balloon; and a documentary following the life of an ordinary Swedish family which scores a huge success with its coverage of the daughter's suicide (in live-action close-up). Anniki's activities as a prostitute seem to involve much catering to the demands of sadists, including those of her pimp, Tim Eulenspiegel, whose work of a lifetime is to prepare a definitive commentary on a vast and enigmatic work by an obscure German writer of the 1970's.

The didactic passages of the novel include long tirades concerning the insanity of the world's energy-economics and a bitter argument concerning water-economics which suggests that by 2018 the entire world will be dying of thirst for want of unpolluted water. All of this is related in a boisterous and comic fashion, but it contains continual reference back to the world of today (Lundwall scrupulously lists his sources in an appendix) and actually constitutes a fairly coherent and convincing case. The society described in the book is, indeed, absurd, but the claim made by the book, with considerable rhetorical force, is that the absurdity is already encapsulated within well-set trends.

By the time Erik Lenning actually finds Anniki Norijn his quest has lost all its significance. The fact that Kockenbergh will ruin him if he fails becomes irrelevant when he is mugged by a gang (one of many) of old-age pensioners who run up colossal debts on his credit card and condemn him to eternal penury. In any case, there will be no Miss Armpit campaign after all, and for that matter no Inter-Ad and no Multi-Co, because while Erik has been combing the slums, Sheik Umir has finally got through to his recalcitrant sibling. He has burnt out all Yarasin's records and destroyed his telephonic links with the world beyond Khuri's beloved desert, pausing only to send one last message to percolate through the network of corporations that comprises the edifice of Western Capitalism: Sell everything. These two words, for obvious reasons, spell the utter doom of civilization.

There is an intriguing ambience about the discussions between Umir and Yarasin, in that their ideological dispute is not only conducted on alien intellectual ground, but remains so absolutely unresolvable. At one point, Umir reads some Western newspapers, and is horrified by the irrationality of the world they reveal. "No beast," he observes, "would do what they have done to themselves and to the world." Yarasin agrees, but adds: "Still, they have something that fascinates me. They are mad, of course; but is not the madman sometimes the voice of God?" This theological question Umir wisely refuses to debate, but Yarasin almost seems to have a point: how else can the madness be explained? Lundwall, perhaps equally wisely, also refuses to follow up the question: *King Kong Blues* is a satire without a moral prescription, an indictment without an escape clause.

This kind of black comedy is far from uncommon in recent science fiction. It first arose as a corollary of the prolific dystopian imagery which appeared during the post-Hiroshima decade. The best early example is Bernard Wolfe's *Limbo*, though the spirit infuses some genre products, including Frederik Pohl and Cyril M. Kornbluth's *The Space Merchants*. Whenever the producers of futuristic fiction have discovered some new dystopian anxiety, as they have with depressing regularity, conventional horror stories have been supplemented by awful prophecies of doom whose tone is positively gleeful. Kurt Vonnegut, Jr., is the master of this mode of presentation, while Robert Sheckley's "The People Trap" and Robert Silverberg's "When We Went To See the End of the World" are also classic examples. Even in stories which are ostensibly sober warnings, such as Philip Wylie's *The End of the Dream* and John Brunner's *The Sheep Look Up*, there frequently seems to be a savage delight in the way the authors torment and tear down the social fabric of the hypothetical future. There is a perennial ambivalence in the attitude of these stories: on the one hand, there is the consciousness that what is happening is a terrible tragedy which we must all work hard to avoid. On the other hand, there is a feeling that this is what people really deserve for being so narrowminded and stupid. While these authors are capable of great sympathy for the people whose sufferings they contemplate, they are also capable of crying "I told you so!" with all the malicious pleasure that the cry implies. Indeed, a contemplation of the range of dystopian fictions produced by our Age of Anxiety could well lead one to suspect that Cassandra probably got a lot of laughs out of her unfortunate condition.

This ambivalence is particularly obvious in *King Kong Blues*. Lundwall is serious in presenting the world of 2018 as a not-too-unreasonable extrapolation of our own, but he is perhaps more serious than he would like to admit in finding its agonies and its fate so very amusing. The least funny moment in the book is where Anniki watches the suicide of the teenage girl through the eyes of the television camera — her taken-for-granted sadism seems utterly perverted. Even given that this is what the author intends, how are we to interpret the obvious pleasure which *he* takes in contemplating dystopia and doom? His defence is ready to hand — he is an innocent satirist using shock tactics to make the reader sit up and take notice. The reader who enjoys the book, however, must be prepared to check that his own excuses are in equally good order.

Brian Stableford

Sources for Further Study

Criticism:

The Encyclopedia of Science Fiction and Fantasy. Compiled by Donald H. Tuck. Chicago: Advent Publishers, Inc., 1978, p. 286. A very brief discussion of Lundwall's life and works is given here.

"Samuel J. Lundwall," in *Contemporary Authors*. Detroit: Gale Research Company, 1975, Volume 49-52, p. 345. This biographical article gives some information on Lundwall's life and a list of his writings.

2001: A SPACE ODYSSEY

Author: Arthur C. Clarke (1917-   )
First book publication: 1968
Type of work: Novel
Time: The dawn of man, the year 2001, and beyond human time
Locale: Prehistoric Africa, the Clavius moonbase, the spaceship *Discovery*, Jupiter, Japetus, the Star-Gate, and beyond

A novel about man's evolution from ape to transcendent "Star Child"

Principal characters:
MOON-WATCHER, the "missing link"
ONE-EAR, his rival
DR. HEYWOOD FLOYD, an American scientist
FRANK POOLE, an astronaut aboard the *Discovery*
HAL, a Heuristically programmed Algorithmic computer
DAVE BOWMAN, the astronaut who travels beyond the Star-Gate to become "Star-Child"

Arthur C. Clarke's novel *2001: A Space Odyssey* cannot be discussed apart from Stanley Kubrick's film. In his later *Lost Worlds of 2001*, the author tells us that this work was a collaborative venture. The first proposal was for a film based on a book; the final result, however, was just the opposite. Gradually, it seems, Kubrick preempted Clarke's original material (in this case several stories), and fashioned from it something highly personal. Clarke, on the other hand, appears to have written his novel after the fact, in answer to the film and in hopes perhaps of retrieving his material, of reasserting his own forms and vision. And yet Kubrick's presence remains, inflecting and refracting the Clarkean patterns.

In Clarke's canon *2001* is a crossroads. In earlier works he is clearly writing in the tradition of H. G. Wells's *The Time Machine*. Here the evolutionary voyage (be it entropic or transcendental) leads man to contemplate a world where he as human form is no more, and from which he can only retreat (in fact or in mind) back to the comforts of some ancient "home" — a golden age of simple, primal domestic relationships.

This same technological quest in Kubrick's film, on the other hand, has a much grimmer circularity, and the human focus is not on family ties but on sexual strife. The closed system Clarke creates in a work like *Childhood's End* is more sleight-of-hand than anything else: he would preserve human norms in the very act of transcending them. Here the link between unhuman Overmind and Last Man's solitary lament remains ultimately a human one: the new father-son ties that form between Jan and Karellen. Kubrick's system, however, is the life process itself; but it begins and ends in a corrupted seed. Not only is the filmmaker's bedrock biological rather than social, but he sees biology as the product of some prior Fall. The core of man's physical being itself, this Fall is absolute and unredeemable. These Calvinist overtones in Kubrick are alien to the earlier Clarke: note how he raises this issue only to skirt it in the Overlord-devils of *Childhood's End*. The Fall is clearly present in *2001*, however, and increasingly so in the novels that follow, especially *Imperial Earth*. By its very title Clarke's *2001: A Space Odyssey* seems, ostentatiously, to reassert his old pattern of the space adventure; but this new voyage has been redirected by the force of Kubrick's imagery.

Clarke's comment in *Lost Worlds of 2001* — that the title "a space odyssey" was "entirely Stanley's idea" — seems doubly surprising, for not only are references to *The Odyssey* constant throughout Clarke's works, but the central structural dynamic of these works could be called "Odyssean" as well. Clarke's novels and stories are often constructed around Odyssean moments; like the ancient hero drawn to the destructive sirens' song yet all the while lashed to the mast of his homecoming ship, Clarke's protagonists confront the transcendent only to reaffirm (often in stranger ways) the familiar and mundane. The ultimate voyage of exploration turns out to be a homecoming. What is more, the persistent pattern of Clarke's fiction turns out to be eminently social in nature — the fundamental family relationships of father to son, husband to wife, parent to child, that underlie the voyages of *The Odyssey*. No matter how far man travels, his roots in this basic family structure remain inviolate. Clarke's characters seem to explore the unknown and probe their limits only in hopes of recovering this lost ancestral base, the thing that defines their humanity and guarantees its permanence in the universal order.

We might hypothetically reconstruct the creation of *2001: A Space Odyssey*. What Clarke may have offered Kubrick was exactly this "Odyssean" moment. Clarke himself points to "The Sentinel" (one of the several tales Kubrick initially bought) as seminal. If this was the starting point however, Kubrick takes it in very different directions. Apparently this Clarkean figure fascinated him as paradox, as a means of constructing on the level of idea-statement, rather than as a narrative device. The marvelous Odyssean balance is itself the most unstable compound, a momentary crossing of mutually reductive forces moving in opposite directions.

Kubrick's film does not even pretend to tell a story. For all its linear "evolutionary" façade, it is actually a sequence of circles simultaneously open and closed, all bound in one large circle that is likewise problematical: whole and yet endlessly broken, generating strife within its eternal symmetry. At all moments, forward movement is immobilized — man's line of technological ascent is bisected by that of his biological fall. The making of tools and machines does not free him from the original circle of life (men inside of ape skins); rather, it generates increasing perversions of it. Later circles of civility do no more than mask this same primal division and hide its explosive violence. Contained within the decorum of Floyd's chat with the Russians, or his Clavius briefing, we sense frustration and pent-up cruelty which are clearly of a sexual nature. Civilized man, however, in seeking to transfer his frustrations to machines (their sterile intercourse displaces him on the screen), only shapes another circle, the great spinning drums of the Jupiter probe, that erupts in the murderous struggle between effete astronaut and polite computer. Sparking violence in all cases is sexual division.

Kubrick conceives the fall itself in terms of a broken circle: the Platonic myth of the hermaphrodite. In HAL man simply extends the image of his own division: the feminine-voiced computer regresses in "death" to some lost masculine innocence — the deep-throated singing of "Daisy." Technological progress does not heal this split, it only generates more increasingly inverted sexual encounters. The unnatural passivity of Poole and Bowman places Hal in an almost matriarchal position of authority. Their subsequent challenge to this unnatural position culminates in a warped battle of the sexes, where Hal's deadly wiles are countered by Bowman's rapelike penetration of the computer cabinet. The resulting love-death of the machine (red light, heavy "respirations," pleadings) becomes a grotesque travesty of the sexual act.

Man in *2001* travels incredible distances from the original circle of apes, yet never escapes it. Isolated in his space suit, Bowman in his attack on HAL is machine against machine. Yet this remains rape too, for the strange "eyes" on the helmet betray the now-twisted animal origins of the act. No matter how "civilized" (machines waltzing to Strauss) or sublimated, contact remains sexual, full of latent urgency and violence. Behind all man's efforts in the film lies a yearning to complete the broken biological circle.

This is true even at the moment of transcendence itself. As Bowman races down the lines of infinity beyond the Star Gate, he is actually running in a circle. Simultaneously as the inhuman landscape unfurls, it becomes more familiar — an odd color negative of a common Earth relief map. What is more, these strange colors and shapes play over what is gradually seen as the unchanging circle of the human iris, and are finally absorbed by it. Man does not cast off his mortal body so much as return to the seed. As old man overlaps newborn babe, the biological process seems to come full circle.

Yet somehow this point of contact remains blighted — a moment of separation rather than union. In fact, in this hollow room there is no contact. Still separated from himself, either by space capsule or by the successive "ages" of man, Bowman can only look on passively as that self grows old and dies. Posttechnological man is still reaching for the primitive cup — his tool and grail — and it still eludes his grasp. Its fall resounds literally back across the whole film. We realize that there never was an Eden or an apple — the circle of apes already bristled with sexual rivalries. Division and yearning are the *a priori* facts of Kubrick's universe, not only present at all stages of man's "evolutionary" journey, but at the core of his being as well.

More than some external force or destiny, the black slab symbolizes this inner rift in man, the primal mystery of his biology. Beneath man's technological gropings we see more basic cravings; Floyd's caress of TMA 1 is one of unabashed sexual longing. More than life's riddle, however, the slab represents its curse: to pursue it is a prison, a hell of fruitless perpetual motion. The film is full of such circles — futility, violence, and death. Bowman jogs aimlessly in the space chamber, HAL watches with his jealous circular "eye," and the circle of life-support sarcophagi waits. Emblematic of this tainted circle of human biology is the ultimate mandala-fetus, superimposed like a seal on the same primal landscape with which the film began. The fall is clearly in embryo here — this baby's eyes are knowing yet weary, man doomed to begin his fatal pursuit of science once again.

The power of Kubrick's vision has clearly inflected Clarke's space Odyssey in significant says. First of all, the evolutionary voyage is strangely immobilized around a fixed center — the narrative equivalent of Kubrick's mandala. The old Odyssean rhythm — simultaneous exploration and homecoming — is rendered diagramatically rigid here. Instead of the linear pretense of a going out and coming home, there is now something like perpetual chiasma — endless points of crossing between rise and fall where man is suspended hieratically, flanked by ape and machine. It is hinted that Moon Watcher's ancestors enjoyed a fertile, Edenic past. Their new rise from barren soil, however, is simultaneously a fall: in learning to kill for food they learn to kill one another. HAL's rise would seem analogous: born of an "electronic Eden," he is corrupted and led to kill by a fact programed into him: the fact that truth can also be a lie, that there is a "need to know."

But these apparently like destinies are also opposites. If Watcher advances from ignorance to corruption, HAL, as he is disconnected, retraces the path to that same source, reverts to that childhood from which the primate escapes. These countermovements create an emblematic balance: ape and machine frame man. But if epic extroversion is canceled by tragic introspection, the remaining center is less Clarke's old lyrical man that a new, passive man. Bowman abides neither because he acts nor because he thinks, nor even because he feels and laments family or past, but because he simply *is*, an onlooker at the center of things. He is utterly alone, it is Poole who has the "birthday party" and residual social contacts. Bowman is pure abstraction, the focus of some blind organic process. In this sense not even trancendence can displace him, for the same chiasmic balance marks the "birth" of the Star Child: "Even as one David Bowman ceased to exist, another became immortal."

At this point Clarke takes a second, bolder step. We still have what seems a classic Odyssean movement: Bowman's apotheosis is offset by his homecoming. This time, however, the return is a strange solipsism. The old Odyssean hero — though as with Jan he and mankind perish in the process — sought always to forge ties that might revive the archetypal family. For mankind is defined only at the point where biology becomes society. But as Bowman comes full circle on Earth, he reveals not only that he is now whole, but that the source of this rift in man lies at the Odyssean root itself, at that point where biology and society join. At the far end of the Star-Gate, Bowman comes on a place both familiar and mundane: an Earth hotel room of his own time. Significantly, this turns out to be not only a shoddily built artifact, but a projection of his own divided mind, a mirror of man's fallen condition.

This same condition is perpetuated in the Star-Child. In *Lost Worlds of 2001*, Clarke explicitly equates this homecoming with violence: "We have wasted and defiled our own estate, the beautiful planet Earth. Why should we expect any mercy from a returning Star-Child? He might judge all of us as ruthlessly as Odysseus judged Leiodes, whose 'head fell rolling in the dust while he was yet speaking. . . .'" But has man really "defiled" Eden in Clarke's book? Within its circular frame there is no Eden; this world was already fallen before man entered the scene. And if this is the case, there can be no *felix culpa* either. Man is displaced from all moral and social responsibility (and thus from guilt and the possibility of redemption as well) by a new vision of the biological process that is rather like what Heinlein calls the "perpetual motion fur farm." Built into human evolution there is a fatal paradox: to survive is to kill. Moreover, no creature is free from this dilemma: with Moon-Watcher we only pass from ignorant violence (battering the pig) to murder in self-defense (the leopard) to destruction for power and aesthetic effect (killing One-Ear with the jaw-bone trophy).

In the novel, this chain of contention will close full on itself to exclude all possibility of innocence. The father-son relationship itself in *2001* is no longer a binding force but a divisive one. The deadly links run from slab to adopted "son" Moon-Watcher; his modern son Floyd in turn has two sons — HAL and Bowman, a Cain and Abel situation that echoes that of Watcher and One-Ear. Finally, as strands condense in isolation, Bowman becomes father to himself; Star-Child in turn promises to be father to some new being with strong ties — in terms of family at least — to old man. Here, however, the Odyssean rhythm has taken on new meaning: these ties have become no more than a channel of transmission for some ancient taint. Star-Child returns to the same situation the propelled Moon-Watcher, and two acts of violence balance each other. Moon-Watcher's blow unifies a divided Earth only to bequeath a long legacy of war; to "cleanse" these inherited skies, Star-Child can only detonate more bombs. The chain of generation has become a circle of violence.

The filmmaker's cosmology flatly refuses to deal with causes: man is *a priori* fallen. A Calvinist may not dare to ask the dreadful questions — how and why? Kubrick no longer cares to ask it. For him, tracing man's destiny has become little more than an exercise in cosmic design, executed on a plane beyond good and evil. Faced with this starkly inhuman (unhuman?) vision, Clarke often reacts with little more than coyness or smug ambiguity. His novel is full of "suggestive" moments that titillate us without giving hard answers.

Is Moon-Watcher, for instance, the product of evolution or election: "there was already something in his gaze beyond the capacity of any ape." And is the slab (significantly transparent here) the instrument of predestination, or some *tabula rasa* on which man writes his own destiny? Whatever the case, that destiny seems so harsh that any explanation, even a grimly theological one, would be a relief. But on this level too Clarke only tantalizes us. He raises the old Faustian vision of science as curse, only to abandon it with facile irony. As ape and superchild in identical moments at the beginning and end of the book face their futures, this curse seems the cement of the universe. Yet, at the same time, its tragic impact is lessened by glib understatement, too-easy symmetry: "For though he was master of the world, he was not quite sure what to do next. But he would think of something." In each case this "something" is sure to be more violence.

If Clarke is satirizing folly here (for neither is master of the deadly circular dynamic that holds him), then it seems a futile exercise as well. For how can man be deflated when there is no place to deflate to: neither dream of paradise nor human norm, Eden nor Candide's garden. In back of Moon-Watcher are only "instincts," before him only the moon he greedily reaches for. But if Kubrick's biological determinism has taken hold, Clarke does make one final attempt to extirpate it in a Pascalian gambit that seeks desperately to replace man as the center of things. For if inhuman processes rule man, they remain mute, whereas man can at least rename them in terms of his own patterns. Thus, to Bowman beyond the Star-Gate the relation of White Dwarf to its Red Sun becomes one of parent to child. But what does this change? The relation is still one of violence: the orbiting Dwarf gouges its sun with a column of flame. Kubrick's film is at least frank about its stylization of the inhuman. Next to this, Clarke's contortions are even more depressing, words from Leiodes' rolling head.

George Slusser

Sources for Further Study

Criticism:

Harfst, Betsy. "Of Myth and Polyminoes: Mythological Content in Clarke's Fiction," in *Arthur C. Clarke*. Edited by Joseph D. Olander and Martin Harry Greenberg. New York: Oxford University Press, 1977, pp. 103-107. Harfst analyzes Clarke's use of "mytho-philosophic patterns."

Reviews:

Analog. LXXXII, January, 1969, pp. 140-142.

Amazing Stories. XLII, January, 1969, pp. 140-142.

Library Journal. XCIII, August, 1968, p. 2897 and September, 1968, p. 3335.
New Statesman. LXXVI, December 20, 1968, p. 877.
New Yorker. XLIV, September 21, 1968, p. 180.
Times Literary Supplement. December 5, 1968, p. 1386.

UBIK

Author: Philip K. Dick (1928-1982)
First book publication: 1969
Type of work: Novel
Time: 1992, "1939"
Locale: New York City, Zurich, the planet Luna, and "Des Moines, Iowa"

As time regresses about him, Joe Chip follows mysterious clues in hopes of finding out what is happening to him and his group, the origins of the malevolent force that pursues them, and the nature of "Ubik," the mysterious and elusive cure-all that promises salvation

> Principal characters:
> GLEN RUNCITER, owner of Runciter Associates, an "antipsi" organization
> ELLA RUNCITER, his "deceased" wife, a "half-life" in "cold-pac"
> JOE CHIP, Runciter's chief "tester" of psis and antipsis
> PAT CONLEY, an antiprecog recruited by Runciter's staff
> JORY, a malevolent young man, also a "half-lifer"

"Reality," Philip K. Dick often said, "is not what it seems." Hardly a unique observation, but one that fits him squarely in the modern literary tradition. Indeed reality has probably been the dominant thematic obsession since Henry James and Joseph Conrad. Could there possibly be anything *new* to say on the subject? And from a *science fiction* writer?

The answer to both, of course, is a resounding *yes*. It will no longer do to simply say that reality cannot really be known; that it can only be lived with. Or that behind the apparently real is the really real, and we must push through to find it. Strike through the mask, find another mask, another mask, and so on. Difficult enough as intellectual propositions, how can these modern visions of reality be embodied in fiction? Many have tried; few have succeeded. But for over a quarter of a century Dick was able to do it consistently. His most effective treatment of the theme, however, was during his most fertile novel writing period, 1964-1969, when he produced sixteen novels including such masterpieces as *Martian Time Slip* (1964), *The Three Stigmata of Palmer Eldritch* (1964), *Dr. Bloodmoney* (1965), *Do Androids Dream of Electric Sheep?* (1968), and *Ubik*.

Different as these novels are, they share one central element. In each of them reality dissolves while the characters are experiencing it; they do not simply discuss the insubstantiality of reality — as is the usual approach — it happens to them. But once this new reality has settled in and they (and the reader) begin to feel comfortable in it, it, too, begins to dissolve. (Consider the word "dissolve" in two senses: the disintegration or liquifaction of matter; probably more importantly, as in film, the imposition of one image on another until the second obliterates the first.)

This has obvious connections with Franz Kafka and the Surrealists, but important differences, too. Paradoxically, while the environment continually changes, it is nonetheless very concrete in each stage of its metamorphosis. For example, things regress for Joe Chip in *Ubik*:

> Once more he returned to the living room. This time he noticed the spot where his polyphonic audio components had formerly been assembled. The multiplex FM tuner, the high-hysteresis turntable and weightless tracking arm — speakers, horns, multitrack amplifier, all had vanished. In their place a tall, tan wooden structure greeted him; he made out the crank handle and did not need to lift the lid to know what his sound system now consisted of. Bamboo needles, a pack of them on the bookcase beside the Victrola. And a ten-inch 78-speed black-label Victor record of Ray Noble's orchestra playing "Turkish Delight." So much for his tape and LP collection.

The very particularity of the change — the precise details and brand names and period authenticity — makes the transformation even more disturbing.

A second factor that separates Philip K. Dick's worlds from those of Kafka and writers like him, is the solidity of the characters that inhabit it. While the environment may be unreal, his people are never mere ciphers, symbols, or caricatures; they are painfully real, if occasionally grotesque. They are also likable, funny, and human. In spite of the strangeness of their conditions, they are capable of learning, growth, courage, and devotion. Because of this, the horrific implications of Dick's world are mitigated by his characters' ability to live in it morally and meaningfully. Among the classic American writers, Dick's work probably most resembles that of Nathaneal West, although West's characters have only vague intimations of the nightmare landscape that Dick's people inhabit.

Another characteristic of the real-unreal Dick milieu is the way in which the usually hard lines between such dichotomies as the real and the artificial, the mechanical and the organic, the living and the dead, and the past, present, and future are blurred and even eliminated. Such blurrings are not uncommon in science fiction, particularly of late, but Dick does it in ways that are distinctively his own. For instance, it is sometimes difficult to tell the difference between robots, androids, and real people from the outside; in Dick's worlds they seldom know themselves. Even machines may be more real than people.

Early in *Ubik* Joe Chip has a furious fight with his front door. Lacking the nickel needed to exit, Joe threatens to take the door off its hinges. The door screams back at him, yells for the police, and vows to sue. Some critics have complained that these farcical early scenes are inconsistent with the grim and fantastic events that occur later. Such criticism misses the point. The slapstick humor of Joe wrestling with his door underscores the fact that there is no real distinction between the human and the mechanical. Nor, it develops later, is there any difference between the living and the dead or the present and the past.

In *Ubik*, by 1992 many ordinary individuals have developed extraordinary psychic powers — telepathy, mind reading, precognition — and it has made almost no difference. For Dick, such evolutionary breakthroughs neither signal the new man, as in an A. E. van Vogt power fantasy, nor are they a curse, as in Robert Silverberg's *Dying Inside*. Dick simply presents the logical notion that the development of one kind of power in man will stimulate the development of a counter power: precogs breed antiprecogs, mind readers provoke antimindreaders, and so on. It all cancels out in the end. And the individuals who possess such gifts, being otherwise ineffective and mediocre, remain ineffective and mediocre. Which is not to say that they are not likable. Dick's affections are definitely with the outsiders, the losers, the well-meaning mediocre characters who populate his novels.

In the 1990's of *Ubik*, psi spying and manipulation has largely replaced mechanical bugging and sabotage as the primary weapons in corporate conspiracies and wars. The hero of the novel is Joe Chip, a tester of psis employed by Runciter Associates. His is the very delicate job of determining whether or not prospective Runciter employees have the powers they claim to have and if they will be loyal to the firm. Runciter fears infiltration by agents for Raymond Hollis, his major rival. Even more important, Joe Chip must test the environment for evidence of hostile mental activity before the Runciter crew can begin any of its work.

The action of the novel starts when Joe heads a crew of assorted Runciter "inertials" on a mysterious mission to the planet Luna. It turns out to be a trap; they are bombed. All, except Glen Runciter himself, who has accompanied them, apparently survive by sheer luck. Runciter is "killed"; they rush him back to Earth where he is put into "cold-pac," in hopes of keeping him at least in "half-life."

"Half-life" is a lingering state between dying and final death in which the body is frozen and kept in a Moratorium while the mind remains operative, although in a state of gradual decline. While in half-life, the individuals maintain an active mental life. Communication with the world of the living is made possible by wiring them into a headphone device, but the strain saps them and accelerates their final disintegration. Nonetheless, Runciter has been getting advice on running his corporation from his cold-packed wife, Ella, and Joe Chip hopes to do the same with him, if the man can be frozen quickly enough.

After depositing Runciter at the Moratorium in Zurich, Joe Chip and the group make plans to seek revenge on Ray Hollis for their employer's murder. Before they can commence, however, bizarre things begin to happen. Their cigarettes and other possessions start disintegrating. The money in Joe's pocket has Glen Runciter's picture on it. The world of 1992 begins to regress, piecemeal, to the world of 1939, with some hints (like elevators) of even further regression. Most ominous of all, the members of his party begin to die one by one, their bodies shrivel and dehydrate almost to nothing. Joe Chip realizes that he must quickly find out what is happening or all of them, himself included, will suffer the same fate. Thus, Joe must become a detective to save himself.

And this is the key to unraveling the apparent chaos in this twisting, turning, and reversing plot: Philip K. Dick has taken the conventions of the detective story and wedded them to his special, peculiar vision. The result can, perhaps, be labelled a metaphysical-science-fiction-hard-boiled-detective-story.

To be sure, the mystery story has long been a favorite structure device for science fiction writers, some notable and obvious examples being Isaac Asimov's robot detective stories *Caves of Steel* and *The Naked Sun*, Alfred Bester's *Demolished Man*, "Lewis Padgett" (Kuttner and Moore)'s "Private Eye," and several of Larry Niven's short fictions. But Dick's use of the hard-boiled form and its conventions is perhaps the most subtle and effective of such adaptations.

To begin with, even the name of the hero — Joe Chip — sounds more comfortable in the company of Sam Spade, Mike Shayne, Mike Hammer, Travis McGee, and Moses Wine than with the likes of Paul Atreides and Valentine Michael Smith. Like the typical hard-boiled hero, Joe is intelligent, but not brilliant (like a Dupin or Holmes); doggedness, steadiness, and courage under pressure are the mainstays of his investigation. He tracks down his information by persistently following up a series of clues that are left for him by persons unknown: an ad that gives a box number in Des Moines, Iowa, a note in a cigarette package, graffiti on the wall of a Men's Room:

> LEAN OVER THE BOWL
> AND THEN TAKE A DIVE
> ALL OF YOU ARE DEAD. I AM ALIVE

Joe's search for clues also becomes a search for Ubik, the only substance (it comes in a spray can) that can apparently reverse the time regression and the weakness that comes over the group members. The two come together in a harrowing scene in which Joe almost succumbs to the malevolent force that has been stalking them. Returning to his Des Moines hotel room, he feels a sudden devastating weakness sweep over him. Collapsing into his room on the brink of death, he meets Runciter, who promptly revives him with a few sprays of Ubik and then explains the situation.

Again in the manner of the hard-boiled detective novel, we are offered a tentative solution — which turns out to be mostly wrong. Runciter tells Joe that it was he — Joe — and the others who were killed by the blast and not Runciter. They have all been put into cold-pac and wired together so they can share a common half-life experience. It was he who sent all the clues and warnings, Runciter goes on, and he gives Joe the Ubik for his protection, telling him to steer clear of Pat Conley. Runciter goes on to blame Conley for the regression as well as for the final deaths of the other group members.

The character and function of Pat Conley is another indication of Dick's reliance on the hard-boiled formula. It was in this subgenre that the woman as villain reached its apogee. More often than not, it is the beautiful female, usually romatically involved with the detective, who is revealed in the last chapter to be the murderess. "I'll wait for you," Sam Spade tells Brigid O'Shaughnessy, just before turning her over to the police. "If they hang you I'll always remember you." Pat Conley seems to fit the pattern. She joined the team late in the game and was accepted only because of her unusual talents. A new type of antiprecog, she can actually alter past events even after they have happened, unlike the usual antiprecog who can only neutralize precogs at the moment of decision. Romantically, she is linked with Joe; at one point she actually manipulated the past to make herself his wife. Thus, she is the prime suspect when the past begins to impose itself on the present. Moreover, her suspicious behavior supports her guilt. She admits to being a plant; she glee-fully tormets Joe while he struggles with the malevolent force. Runciter himself blames her for engineering the destruction of his team. And, most important, she believes herself to be guilty; she happily takes credit for all the mayhem.

But she is innocent, whatever her motives and desires. For all of her efforts, she is not the *femme fatale* in *Ubik*. She functions, rather, as another common device of the hard-boiled detective story: the "red herring." She is the *false suspect* deliberately inserted into the novel to temporarily throw the hero and the reader off the track. Pat Conley has been tricked by the real evil force, and she is shocked when she, too, begins to disintegrate and die.

Joe is less surprised. During the scene with Runciter, he becomes aware of the fact that his boss is guessing at many of the answers. The man cannot really explain the destruction of the group in terms of Pat Conley — it is too demonic and pervasive. It is also clear that, although he is using it, Runciter has no idea as to what Ubik actually is and why it works. By the end of the interview, Joe has been partially enlightened but also irritated. Like the good detective that he is, he will settle for no less than all the answers.

He does not have to wait long. One of the surviving antipsis, Don Denny, accosts him. At Joe's urging, Denny uses the Ubik on himself. His shape dissolves into that of a malevolent adolescent who identifies himself as Jory. "I ate Denny," Jory tells Joe. "I've been doing it a long time to lots of half-life people. I eat their life, what remains of it. There's so little in each person, so I need a lot of them." It is he who has created Des Moines in 1939 for the benefit of the group. The regression itself is a natural process in half-life; Jory has simply held it to 1939, lacking the strength to maintain 1992. Since Joe is temporarily protected by the Ubik, Jory cannot eat him until it wears off, although he does bite him on the hand.

But one last set of questions remains: what is the positive force that has been helping him? Where does Ubik come from? Out of ideas, Joe is about to give up when he flags a cab and picks up an attractive young woman. After small talk, she gives him a certificate for a lifetime supply of Ubik and reveals her identity: Ella Runciter. She has been the protective force and she gives him a mission: to replace her as Runciter's adviser, since she wishes to leave half-life and begin her next incarnation.

When he tries to redeem his certificate, however, Joe meets Jory again and the old weariness returns. Given a useless old can, he tries to "evolve it forward" mentally. Apparently, failing at that, he goes out to die. Outside, however, he meets a new girl who hands him a fresh can of Ubik. His efforts have brought her to him from the future. Joe has temporarily beaten Jory. But as Ella told Joe earlier, final victory over Jory is impossible: "there are Jorys in every moratorium. This battle goes on wherever you have half-lifers; it's a verity, a rule of our kind of existence."

Throughout the novel, Dick has prefaced each chapter with a short ad proclaiming Ubik as the all purpose fix-all (a razor blade, a Savings & Loan, a hair conditioner, and so on). But he prefaces the last chapter with this statement:

> I am Ubik. Before the universe was, I am. I made the suns. I made the worlds. I created the lives and the places they inhabit; I move them here, I put them there. They go as I say, they do as I tell them. I am the word and my name is never spoken, the name which no one knows. I am called Ubik, but that is not my name. I am. I shall always be.

The Biblical tone and implications are appropriate. In the end the novel becomes an elemental morality play, the power of good that creates *versus* the power of evil that consumes. What began as future farce ends as cosmic moral vision — although it remains funny all the way through.

So the book ends with almost all the questions answered. On the last page Glen Runciter, safely ensconced in the real world, we have been led to believe, reaches into his pocket and pulls out a coin: Joe Chip's face is on it. Dick cannot resist that last tweak of reality's nose.

Keith Neilson

Sources for Further Study

Criticism:

Fitting, Peter. "*Ubik*: The Deconstruction of a Bourgeois SF," in *Science-Fiction Studies*. II (1975), pp. 47-54. Fitting analyzes the themes and plot of *Ubik*.

Gillespie, Bruce. *Philip K. Dick: Electric Shepherd*. Melbourne, Australia: Nostrilla, 1975. *Ubik* is not as well-constructed as Dick's earlier works.

Reviews:

Analog. LXXXIV, October, 1969, pp. 174-175.

Booklist. LXVI, October 1, 1969, p. 178.

Kirkus Reviews. XXXVII, March 1, 1969, p. 275.

Library Journal. XCIV, December 15, 1969, p. 4584.

Luna Monthly. IV, September, 1969, p. 31.

Publisher's Weekly. CXCV, March 10, 1969, p. 73.

SF Commentary. IX, February, 1970, pp. 11-25 and XVII, November, 1970, pp. 33-34.

Speculation. XXIX, October, 1971, pp. 35-38.

UNHEIMLICHE ERSCHEINUNGSFORMEN AUF OMEGA XI
(Weird Shapes on Omega XI)

Authors: Johanna Braun and Günter Braun
First book publication: 1974
Type of work: Novel
Time: The far future
Locale: The Earth, a spaceship, and the planet Omega XI

The satirical and humorous view of a couple's space voyage to a planet threatened by dangerous phenomena

Principal characters:
  MERKUR ERDENSON, an intrepid astronaut
  ELEKTRA EULENN, his commander and fellow astronaut
  "SONNENBLUME," an inhabitant of Omega XI

The plot and its resolution are so simple in *Unheimliche Erscheinungsformen auf Omega XI* that they would have to be called simplistic if treated in the usual manner of science fiction, that is with naïve realism that takes the future for granted and a bathos that offers the most hackneyed solutions as if they were revelations. This novel is the account of a journey to another planet, where the heroes, the unlikely named duo Merkur Erdenson and his temporary spouse and spaceship commander Elektra Eulenn, must find out what it is that is threatening the inhabitants of the planet Omega XI. The Omegans have sent a call for help to Earth, although there has been no contact between the two worlds for a very long time. In fact, the last contact between the two planets occurred when the ancestors of the Omegan Lumen left Earth after being forbidden to continue their genetic experiments. Erdenson and Eulenn alone must find a solution to the Lumen's problems or evacuate them to Earth: a patently unrealistic situation. But this does not matter at all, since superficial realism is not the author's aim. What gives the story its typical flavor is the thoroughly stylized, mannered, and tongue-in-cheek storytelling in which the husband-wife team of Johanna and Günter Braun have couched their romantic Marxist fairy tale. The mannerism of the story lies in the deceptive simplicity with which they tell their story, often in an indirect way, and in the gentle humor with which they approach the conditions of the world and the action of their characters. This is visible in the playful names of the characters (Merkur Erdenson, Elektra Eulenn, "Sonnenblume," Caesar Brinn, Medea Twinn), the obstacles encountered during their journey, and the curious state of things that they find on the planet Omega XI, which is located "a good way beyond the last satellite of Jupiter."

The hero, Merkur Erdenson, is considerably different from the boundlessly optimistic, clean-shaven, honest, dedicated, and dull cosmonauts of other Eastern European, especially East German, science fiction — which usually tries to outdo the dullest Soviet examples. Only 1.8 meters tall and weighing only sixty-five kilograms, Merkur Erdenson appears to be a lightweight. Although he has saved two spaceships from destruction (this feat has been recorded in the encyclopedias of space travel), he affects an average behavior, eschewing any kind of hero worship. Moreover, he is something of a cheat: the famed radish juice that he takes with him in large quantities on all his important journeys as an example for other space travelers, is actually a very good brand of Cognac. This may not be the most original of jokes, but it is only one character strand in the portrait of a hero designed to be different from the usual East German cliché of the astronaut.

This not-quite-serious tone may prepare the ground for more serious things, allowing the authors to say things that would most likely be unacceptable in a straightforward, "serious" novel of space adventure. The use of this technique can be seen in the episode describing the two space travelers being briefed before their departure. Merkur Erdenson must listen to a speech by Caesar Brinn, for "without historical insight nobody may get off into space." When asked why he wishes to travel, the customary answer, "Insight into the historical importance for the well-being of mankind," is not quite correct; since the hero is on a noble mission to save other intelligent beings in space from some danger, he must represent "the moral face" of mankind. Of course, the real motive of this Gulliver or Münchhausen of outer space is not this noble: he is merely eager for adventure and travel outside the pale of the known world. The hero must endure yet another lecture, this one from the one-hundred-ten-year-old Medea Twinn, not only on sexual compatability in space during the long journey with a female companion, but especially on questions of etiquette should he meet the Lumen females of Omega XI.

Erdenson's conversation with his instructor in sexual matters is in itself amusing; it is remarkable that the subject of sex is touched at all. East German science fiction is usually puritanical in sexual matters. The conventional love story, is usually present, but without any talk of sex, much less an overt description of sexual acts. But then, Johanna and Günter Braun are not typical science fiction authors. Along with Reiner Kunze, Günter Kunert, Rolf Schneider, Irmtraud Morgner, and others they belong to the younger generation of highly talented East German writers who only occasionally use fantasy or science fiction to touch upon subjects important to them. Among the authors named above, the Brauns are the only ones who have made science fiction an important part of their literary output. Their first attempt in this direction was a satirical novel, *Der Irrtum des großen Zauberers* (1972), considered by some East German critics better than *Unheimliche Erscheinungsformen auf Omega XI*. They followed it in 1975 with a collection of short stories titled *Der Fehlfaktor*, including a story about Merkur Erdenson and Elektra Eulenn. This story describes in greater detail how it was decided on Earth to send a two-crew team to Omega XI to explore the homophagi there, and how Erdenson and Eulenn got acquainted with each other.

As developed in this novel, the characters of Eulenn and Erdenson are somewhat complementary: she is highly competent and orderly; while Erdenson is a master of improvisation, invention, a teller of tall tales, somewhat irresponsible, anti-heroic, and an enemy of pathos. In this respect he somewhat resembles Stanislaw Lem's Münchhausian space traveler Ijon Tichy, who may have been a direct influence, even though Erdenson is a more ordinary sort of man. He leaves a girl friend behind him on Earth (who soon finds another man to give her comfort and pleasure), and the love affair during the space journey is perhaps designed as a parody of the adolescent, bourgeois, romantic love affairs of so many other works of science fiction.

The space travelers find a Utopia of leisure and luxury on Omega XI, although one seriously endangered. Even the landing field, a gigantic, totally empty square, is paved with polished flagstones. Equally impressive are all the houses and gadgets of this civilization. Their rooms are furnished with the utmost luxury, especially the bedrooms and baths. The Lumen themselves, all fifty-seven that are left, shine with an inner light. To offset this material comfort, they are somewhat puritanical and refuse to give the heroes a double room until they have been married under Omegan law. At this stage, the nature of the threat to the Lumen remains a mystery. The Lumen's world appears so paradisical that the danger may well be imaginary.

True, there are certain inconveniences. The atmosphere of fresh oxygen is kept up for only a few hours a day; the rest of the time must be spent indoors to avoid the "Modderwind," a violent, corrosive storm which sweeps the planet most of the day. The storm lasts progressively longer and becomes increasingly corrosive, eroding away plates of metal several inches thick. In addition, the Lumen are obsessed by material consumption, replacing things at an accelerating rate. While having dinner, the half-eaten dishes are taken away to be replaced by new ones, and so it is with all other things, including the houses that are being erected: they are torn down again and replaced at a frightening speed.

At this point it seems quite clear what is the matter with Omega XI and its Utopian leisure class, and why they feel threatened by the changed circumstances. It is the inhabitants who are the monsters lurking here, an idle class of parasites, the remnants of the old capitalists living off the sweat and toil of the workers they have created for themselves in the course of their genetic studies. The Earth had rejected them, but on Omega XI they were able to realize their genetic theories, creating several races of subservient human beings, no more than their slaves. The technologically and scientifically minded Prudenten do their thinking for them, always inventing new things to facilitate life. The Roburen, giant workers with enormous muscles and great strength but little intelligence, live hidden away and can relax and be happy only when going about the hardest tasks. They sleep only a few hours a day, and wake up totally exhausted, only feeling refreshed when they work again, handling the heaviest weights; the more they work, the fresher they get, producing and producing, toiling without pause.

It is the Roburen, with their unceasing zeal for work who have piled up mountains of new goods that nobody will use, which are destroyed as soon as they are created, and finally left to rot, for even their destruction would be too much work. The inevitable by-products of their work are waste products and atmospheric pollutants that cause the "Modderwind." The Lumen are much too superior to have direct contact with the Roburen; the Prudenten are responsible for them. The Lumen only have contact with one prudish Prudenten, "Sonnenblume." In short, the flowerlike, carefree, over-civilized, idle Lumen are the remnants of an ugly non-Communist past that has, on Earth, been long since overcome.

With his gift for improvisation, the hero invents a remedy for the unhappy Roburen who die if they cannot work: a playlike unproductive job that occupies them with juggling heavy loads, but does not produce more surplus goods. This solution is, of course, very simplistic and not to be taken too seriously. Since it is offered within the context of a socialist parable or fairy tale to illustrate certain principles, it is appropriate here. After this "solution," there is only some more amusing tomfoolery, including an attempted and bungled abduction of Merkur and Elektra by the Lumen. The couple escapes unscathed from these misadventures, and provides the Prudenten with the rare vitamin which the Lumen have withheld to keep them in line; thus they are saved from extinction. The social structure on Omega XI has been totally changed, the deathly Modderwind combated, and the world restored to a true Utopia for all human beings, not only for a select few.

Early in the novel, Merkur Erdenson declares that he writes for his ancestors because they need this knowledge, whereas his descendants will know everything better. This aptly describes the goal of the Brauns: they are not interested in presenting an uplifting picture of the socialist paradise to come. What they set out to do is to provide an example for the present. They do not do this by proselytizing or preaching, or by resorting to overt propagandizing; unlike so many poor science fiction novels from their part of the world, there is hardly any overt ideological content in the novel, and they do not even feel obliged to pay lip-service to the officially accepted future, as so many lesser writers do. They also are not interested in the usual goals of science fiction, and there is hardly any action in their book. What they write is an ironic socialist fable, a literary game that plays with some of the traditional trappings of science fiction (such as the intervention on another planet, where the people that call for help are also usually the good guys, a pattern that is reversed in this novel), and also with the clichés of the socialist future, which is handled quite ironically. The book also incorporates some interesting biological ideas.

What the story does above all is to provide food for further thought and present ironic happenings in a very individual way, applying a commonsense wisdom to problems that only appear to be cosmic. Their down-to-earth hero is a pleasure to read about, combining a close and earthly attention to the details of life with an engaging self-irony and gentle humor. Perhaps most important, the novel appears to offer a genuinely Marxist parable without being narrow-minded or ideological. That is something very rare in science fiction from Communist countries.

Franz Rottensteiner

Sources for Further Study

Criticism:

Rottensteiner, Franz. *The Science Fiction Book*. New York: Seabury, 1975, p. 146. The Brauns are an exception to the general dearth of good German language science fiction.

L'UNIVERS VAGABOND
(The Wandering Universe)

Authors: Léon Groc (1882-1956) and Jacqueline Zorn
First book publication: 1950
Type of work: Novel
Time: 1999-3000
Locale: The Earth, the Interstellar Ship *Cosmos*, and the Planet Carena of Proxima
Centauri

The chronicle of the ethical problems and adventures that two families and their
ancestors encounter on a long uninterrupted journey to a distant planet inhabited by
telepathetic minerals

Principal characters:
THE CARÈNE FAMILY
THE MARVAL FAMILY

This book is another work dealing with a generation ark, those spaceships designed to preserve their crews during the one or more generations the trip lasts. It is not, however, merely a commonplace story of a ship gone mad. It rivals Tomás Salvador's *La Nave* (1959) in pathos and Edwin C. Tubb's *Star Ship* (1955) in the harshness of its interior regulations. The population involved in this adventure is no more than thirteen persons. This small number is a comparatively rare variation, but it is rooted in a sensible and interesting idea. Why bother to build mammoth space vessels if smaller ones would suffice? The problem of passing on knowledge is more acute. How many crewmen would be necessary to do it? This is one of the problems raised in this novel and one point which distinguishes it from other novels which deal with multi-generational spaceships.

L'Univers Vagabond is Léon Groc's final novel and his acknowledged masterpiece. A writer of popular fiction who specialized in adventure and detective stories, Groc is remembered as a respected contributor to French-language science fiction. Other notable works are *Le Peuple des Ténèbres* (*People of Darkness*, 1924), a story of the discovery of a Phoenician colony dwelling in underwater caverns; *Le Chasseur de Chimères* (*The Chimera-Hunter*, 1925), an atomic prophecy; *La Révolte des Pierres* (*The Revolt of Rocks*, 1930) and *La Planète de Cristal* (*The Crystal Planet*, 1944), an adventure on an invisible satellite of Earth populated by dangerous two- and four-dimensional beings. Jacqueline Zorn was Groc's wife, and this book is their second joint effort. It consists of a cruel and often tragic account of family life and general human problems in the restrictive environment of a spaceship during several centuries. Furthermore, this trip is nonstop but for a short stay on a deadly planet. The novel tells of the hardships and self-renunciation dictated by a multigenerational system of life.

The wandering universe of the title is spaceship *Cosmos*, bound for Proxima Centauri in the year 2001. The trip will take 148 years for the crews; meanwhile 450 years will pass on Earth. Two families man the *Cosmos*, the Carènes and the Marvals, each consisting of a husband, two wives, and two children of each sex. In time, sons and daughters will be married and will have one son and one daughter each, and so on. Medical improvements (of which the authors are evasive) will be used to prevent inbreeding and to choose the sex of unborn children. This lack of detail is one of the novel's flaws. Drastic regulations rule aboard: the number of passengers is limited to twelve; birth control and immediate destruction of refuse, even misshapen babies; elimination of the oldest member of the community as soon as a thirteenth passenger attains the age of one. In addition, the head of the crew, the oldest member, has considerable power, though it is moderated by the obligatory consultation of the other adults.

As for the ship herself, she looks like a vaguely anthropomorphic skittle, approximately fifty meters high and twenty meters in diameter. The diagrams included by the authors are rather humorous but help to visualize the environment in which the story is set. From top to base the ship consists of a partly transparent sphere (observatory-laboratory, microfilm library, and medical area), another sphere twice as large (lodgings, meeting-, sport- and dining rooms, kitchen, reduced garden, and maintenance storage), and a truncated cone (propulsion unit). The power is supplied by cosmic rays, while air and water are obtained from transmutation of exterior radiation into oxygen and hydrogen. The conception of the ship is clearly unconvincing and outdated, but the strength of the novel lies in what happens inside, not in the technological achievements. This is first of all the chronicle of two families facing the consequences of self-inflicted conditions.

L'Univers Vagabond largely reviews the ethical problems peculiar to the spaceship *Cosmos*. However, it is also an adventure novel. But the problems of adventure are similar to those encountered in many stories of generation arks, in which they are generally evaded. That is why this book is important. The situation of the passengers is dictated by the limited space aboard. The only way to make things run normally is to apply rigidly the strict regulations. The families must accept them unconditionally and assume the consequences both personally and collectively since the problems of any one of them concern everyone. They are one family under the authority of a patriarch (or a matriarch), where each newborn baby spells doom on an aged parent. They are merely life-transmitting machines and conscious instruments of a destiny they cannot alter. Their adventure is a sad meditation on the necessity of yielding to inhuman conditions, but only those suitable to survival.

Another problem peculiar to multigenerational ships is how to hand down the knowledge necessary to maintain and land the craft. The original crew of spaceship *Cosmos* consists of an engineer, a physician, and a physicist, who teach their specialities to their children; there is also one housewife who transmits the traditions of French cooking though it is doubtful much survives the strict vegetarian diet aboard; biologists and even philosophers enrich the future generations. However, is it so easy to find and to train the needed specialists in such a reduced population? In this regard the novel is not convincing. The first event occurs when the ship barely escapes collision with a comet. But the fatalities are usually restricted to the disintegration room. Later, Hélène Carène, a physicist, condemns her two grandmothers by her impatience to comply with her obligation to bear children, deciding to have twins so she can dedicate her remaining years to science.

The real troubles begin with Oliver Carène, a strange neurasthenic boy who evades reality by daydreaming about the Earth. He reluctantly marries his pretty cousin, but when it occurs to him that they could have a second male child instead of a female, he convinces his wife to stop having children. The unsolicited baby barely escapes disintegration when another couple offers to have another daughter. But the seed of rebellion is planted. While his father finally cools off, the child, Denis, turns out to be a dangerous misfit. A passionate and stubborn youth, he realizes how violently his intimate aspirations clash with this captive universe. In addition, he and his brother court the same cousin. Asked to choose, she spurns Denis, who pierces the outer shell of the ship in response to this rejection. The high vacuum freezes the newly-married couple during their wedding night and threatens the entire vessel if Denis is not stopped. Since his death would mean a loss of knowledge (he is one of the two living engineers) it is decided he will undergo a frontal lobotomy. Rendered a human robot, Denis resumes his work but soon dies, condemning his cousin to remain a virgin and his aging relatives to rebuild the lost generation.

An important part of the novel concerns an adventure on a planet orbiting Proxima Centauri and named Carena. It would be fit for colonization if it were not the home of living minerals endowed with consciousness and will. They use telepathy, which is reminiscent of another Groc novel, *La Révolte des Pierres*, in which intelligent rocks from the Moon attempt to invade the Earth as a meteoric rain. Their Carenian cousins are more original since they turn out to be descended from atomic piles, which the first dwellers of Carena equipped with sophisticated thinking circuits. They revolted after they found a way to reproduce, destroying every protoplasmic organism with radiation. An army of hostile rocks slowly surrounds the ship and traps it with magnetic rays, but the passengers use a cloud of gaseous lead to paralyze them. Soon after the ship blasts off the crew members realize that have been sterilized by radiation. Fortunately, they have invented a method to slow down the progress of aging. The last chapter of the book is the diary of the only survivor, now 156 years old, who dies on Earth just after the ship lands. The year is 3000.

The chronicle of the Marvals and the Carènes is a first draft of what one day may be a series relating several centuries of life on a multigenerational ship, though that project is still a dream. The authors have included a genealogical tree of the space-born generations, which accounts for their accuracy. But they have not exploited the grandiose nature of this odyssey despite its ups and downs and its ending; maybe they did not realize it. In contrast they have perfectly grasped its pathetic and profoundly human nature. They aimed not only at placing characters on an interesting stage but at sticking to the tribulations of a handful of beings compelled to fit themselves body and soul into the mold of a ruthless environment. Spaceship *Cosmos* is primarily an opportunity to evidence the human and moral side of the long trip but with no inclination to tear-bringing sensibility. This novel was published at a time when no stories of generation arks were known in France. A popular writer with disputable scientific pretensions, Groc has made *L'Univers Vagabond* both a brilliant spectacle and the crowning of his career.

Remi-Maure

THE UNSLEEPING EYE

Author: David Guy Compton (1930-   )
First book publication: 1974 (as *The Continuous Katherine Mortenhoe*)
Type of work: Novel
Time: The late twentieth century
Locale: London and environs

The gradual deterioration of Katherine Mortenhoe, victim of a rare terminal disease, is depicted intimately and mercilessly on a television series ironically called Human Destiny

> Principal characters:
> KATHERINE MORTENHOE, a forty-four-year-old editor
> DR. MASON, her doctor
> HARRY, her second husband
> GERALD, her first husband
> VINCENT FERRIMAN, a program director at NTV
> RODDIE RODERICKS, a television journalist
> TRACEY, his ex-wife

David Compton is relatively unknown to American readers, including science fiction fans. Born in London in 1930, he has written for British stage, radio, and television, as well as authoring half a dozen crime novels (as Guy Compton) in the 1962-1966 period. Unlike most writers, he entered science fiction almost accidentally, having previously read little in the genre. Compton's first science fiction work was *The Quality of Mercy* (1965), in which an interest in the dehumanization of people by uncontrolled technology is already apparent. Although he has written more recent traditional fiction under the name Frances Lynch, *The Unsleeping Eye*, his most recent science fiction work, continues to handle the theme of dehumanization. The theme is not original with Compton; Robert Silverberg used it in a 1963 short story, "The Pain Peddlers." Compton, however, develops it with far more skill and depth. The 1975 case of Karen Ann Quinlan's extended coma raised similar questions of privacy.

Probably because of the way he entered the field, Compton's ten science fiction novels have little of the paraphernalia common to the genre. In all his work, he is intimately concerned with human relationships and how they are corrupted by technology. In *Synthajoy* (1968), probably his best-known work, a psychiatrist achieves fame through the development of a device which records peak emotional experiences and permits others to experience them fully. The story is told in flashbacks by his wife, Thea Cadence, who is undergoing psychiatric treatment for her husband's murder. Thea and Katherine Mortenhoe have more than a few similarities.

Katherine works for Computabook, a firm in which computers shape fictional plot elements into formula romantic novels. (A similar device was used by George Orwell in *Nineteen Eighty-Four* to produce cheap fiction for the masses, aptly called "prolefeed" in Newspeak.) She learns from Dr. Mason that she has four weeks to live because of an unusual and irreversible brain disease in which stress leads to mental breakdown and the destruction of brain cells. Although Harry, her husband, is superficially solicitous and comforting, their relationship has become a sterile formality. Katherine proposes that they take a vacation during her remaining days. In fact, she desires to spend her final days privately in disguise.

"Ordinary people on the street," she muses, "did not see their fellows — this was how they kept sane." Her statement suggests the coldness and anomie which permeates the entire novel. Before Katherine and her husband leave on vacation, the couple visits a castle, where she experiences her first paralysis. Since her unusual case had earlier been dramatized on national TV (NTV), a guard recognizes her. Later, Latherine is kidnaped by university students who hold her hostage to force the release of 112 students being held for insurrection. As a result of these intrusions on her privacy she decides to accept the offer from NTV to dramatize her fatal illness. In fact, she plans to take the money and escape, in order "to cheat the image machine in every way she could."

Once her plans for escape are made, Katherine and Harry visit a dress shop. She slips away and picks up clothing bought from a group called the "fringies," the equivalent of the American hippies of the 1960's and further examples of a lobotomized society which uncaringly permits many of its citizens to subsist on the dole. From there, Katherine proceeds to a church used to house transients. Unknown to her, however, her handbag has been bugged, permitting Roddie Rodericks, a TV reporter, to trace and meet her. Much of the novel's subsequent action is seen through the unsleeping eyes of Roddie. Since undergoing surgery to have a miniature television camera and transmitter implanted in his skull, he uses drugs to permit him to rest without sleeping. Although sustained darkness will result in increasing pain and eventual blindness, Roddie accepts the risk, because he anticipates becoming famous as a result of depicting Katherine's case.

After leaving the church Katherine and Roddie walk away from London through the circle of marchers and through a seemingly endless suburban sprawl. They are eventually picked up by a wealthy man, and Roddie reflects: "But I'd had a good day with Katherine, some gut-tearing shots and appealing quotes, and I reckoned I could look after her." When they arrive at the man's expensive home, Roddie suddenly realizes the man's identity; he is the NTV chairman. Unable to explain his true identity, he and Katherine are treated as sexual playthings by the chairman and his decadent friends. Here, too, society intrudes. The chairman offers them "hoof beef," obviously a rarity in a world where an ersatz meat has long since replaced the original. The artificiality and meanness of life on all levels is heightened by this small detail.

As the party and its aftermath are being transmitted, Vincent Ferriman, the program director of NTV and a man concerned only with TV's commercial values, is called to review the tapes, which would necessarily need to be edited to avoid embarrassing the NTV chairman. At that point, Roddie's ex-wife, Tracey, comes to the studio to confront Ferriman. She is disgusted with what he is doing to her former husband, who did not tell her of his surgery. She is concerned about what she will tell her son about his father. Ferriman, however, is unconcerned, certain that the boy will grow up in a new society, uninterested in such matters. Tracey leaves the studio resolved to wait around "to pick up the pieces."

Roddie and Katherine leave the chairman's home in one of his cars while he and his guests are elsewhere. The expensive car attracts the attention of four masked motorcyclists, who politely force them to stop and then rob them. The leader off-handedly explains: "We're the Collectors. We're collecting for the Society for the Encouragement of Cruelty to Everybody. It's a terribly good cause." Compton's black humor is infrequent but is well suited to the novel's somber tone and suggests the Hobbesian nature of his society. When they resume their journey, Roddie decides to regain his humanity. He leaves Katherine's bugged handbag behind, thinking: "The ultimate intrusion into other people's lives was the ultimate intrusion into my own. And it had to stop."

When they reach the shore and find temporary shelter, Roddie requests more money via his radio transmitter, and after it is delivered, he stops in a pub where he witnesses one of his shows about Katherine. Appalled at what he has done, he walks out on a dark pier and throws away his flashlight and sound equipment. The pain soon begins, and by morning he is blind. "I had bought back what I had sold. I was free."

Hiding in a van of an eighty-six-year-old Punch and Judy performer whom they had helped upon their arrival at the beach, Roddie now needs Katherine, whose condition has quietly but steadily deteriorated. She infers that the helicopter which comes to the beach to search for them resulted from Roddie's actions. When she asks why, he hesitates, then tells his story. The old man leaves them near the school where Gerald, Katherine's former husband, is the headmaster. Shortly after they arrive, a helicopter brings Vincent, his crew, and Tracey to the school, where the fugitives are discovered. It is too late to save Katherine, but Tracey and Roddie are reconciled.

Compton's prose style is straightforward, suiting his subject matter, but not especially notable. In the novel, abrupt shifts in point of view occur far too often. Compton's fictional worlds are far removed physically and emotionally from those in the central stream of science fiction, which has historically been outward-looking and optimistic. His worlds are shabby, and few of his characters rise much above expediency. However, his social criticism is framed by an acute knowledge of human psychology. He presents a dark vision, which still preserves an element of tragic dignity.

Neil Barron

Sources for Further Study

Reviews:

Publisher's Weekly. CCV, March 18, 1974, p. 54.

Wilson Library Bulletin. XLIX, September, 1974, p. 38.

VENUS PLUS X

Author: Theodore Sturgeon (1918-   )
First book publication: 1960
Type of work: Novel
Time: The mid-twentieth century
Locale: The United States and the Ledom colony

An examination of the consequences of role-assignments on the basis of sex

> *Principal characters:*
> CHARLIE JOHNS, a human suddenly brought to the Ledom colony
> HERB RAILE, a conventional human living a conventional suburban life
> JEANETTE RAILE, his wife
> SEACE, Ledom director of Science One
> MIELWIS, Ledom director of Medical One
> NASIVE AND GROCID, Ledom directors of Children's One
> PHILOS, a Ledom historian

Science fiction writers seem to labor under the constant threat of producing works that soon become dated. For some reason, many readers of the genre feel that, once modern science has brought to light some facts that will disprove the premise of a work, that work is no longer readable. Often the work will be labeled as an interesting, but dated, example of naïve scientific thought. Somehow the latest Mars and Venus probes have taken the enjoyment out of many a fine science fiction novel for such readers.

More recently, perhaps in partial response to this trend, science fiction critics have stated that the genre was never really meant to predict future developments or to be absolutely true to the sciences it portrayed. According to these critics, the main concern of science fiction is its depiction of major changes facing the human race and mankind's reaction to them. Thus, to a large extent, the worlds created by the writers are not meant to be real worlds but metaphoric ones that give interpretations of the present. With such a view, the issue of whether life can exist on Venus is secondary to how the world of Venus is used to make a point.

Theodore Sturgeon's *Venus Plus X* is interesting in the light of this more recent view of science fiction because it avoids the problem of outdated scientific premises; there is little to argue about in terms of the science used in the novel. The theme, however, of *Venus Plus X* is sorely dated. Sturgeon has written a novel which examines the sex roles that have been assigned to men and women by society, and he concludes that the emphasis on the differences between the sexes is responsible for many of the problems that plague mankind today. Given that the novel was written in 1960, one must admire the way in which Sturgeon reasons through his case and presents the problem. However, since 1960 the American public has been increasingly exposed to more sophisticated debate on this topic. Thus, in the light of the complexities which are now part of what has come to be called women's liberation, Sturgeon's comments seem rather simplistic. In *Venus Plus X* the statement rather than the scientific background is dated; in fact, it is Sturgeon's scientific speculation that makes the novel intriguing today.

Venus Plus X commences with Charlie Johns, the protagonist, wrestling with an identity problem, and in the process, remembering events from his past. The reason his identity is in question is that he has suddenly awakened in a totally alien place. Although he is still on Earth, the people around him are a mutated form of the human race. His first contact with this new human race sets the stage for the theme of the novel: he cannot tell whether the first member of the Ledom (as they are called) he meets is a woman or a man. The Ledom appear to be double-sexed mutations capable of conceiving, bearing, and nursing their children without the need for a mate. Rather than natural mutations, however, the Ledom turn out to be surgically modified humans. The first few Ledom were created by a group of men who were convinced that sexual differentiation had become such a serious threat to the continuance of mankind that these altered creatures were necessary to ensure the future of humanity. It became the Ledom's task to keep alive human wisdom and necessary skills and then to reteach them to mankind after the holocaust was over. Their creators believed that the Ledom, because they were free of the prejudices associated with sexual stereotyping, would be able to develop new, openminded religions and institutions which they could later pass on to nonsurgically modified humans. Sturgeon's descriptions of how the Ledom relate to one another, handle their children, practice the arts, and pray to their God are always consistent and often beautiful. He describes in detail the consequences of the Ledom's physical makeup, as well as their unique personalities.

As a contrast to the ideal Ledom, Sturgeon presents a human family: the Railes. Whereas Ledom children are allowed great freedom of expression and shown affection equally by all adults, the Raile children are treated differently on the basis of their sex. For example, the three-year-old Raile girl is smothered with love by her father, while the five-year-old boy must "act like a man." Likewise, the human marriage is filled with tensions that arise from role-playing, unlike the trouble-free unions between Ledom. The contrast between human and Ledom behavior is also apparent in their approaches to humor. Johns constantly remarks that the Ledom always laugh with, not at, others. The humor of the Railes and their neighbors is oftentimes at the expense of one gender over the other, which usually leads to someone being hurt.

Because the Ledom seem to be so superior, the novel appears to be saying that Ledom biology is the only answer to man's problems. At this point, however, the reader learns that the Ledom cannot reproduce their own kind; their offspring are born human, and must undergo surgical alteration to become like their parents.

The remainder of the story is a sort of Adam and Eve parable. The Adam figure is Charlie Johns, a dying pilot whose mind is transplanted into the non-modified body of Quesbu, who was born and reared in the Ledom colony. The Eve figure is the daughter of a Ledom who retained her human form because she was accidentally born too far from the Ledom surgeons to be altered. As the plot unfolds, we find humanity on the brink of self-annihilation, and it becomes apparent that, under the guidance of the Ledom, Quesbu and his human mate will found a new human race untainted by false beliefs and harmful attitudes.

The character of Johns (Quesbu) serves three functions. As Johns, he reacts positively to Ledom society (but only as long as he believes the Ledom are natural mutations). Sturgeon is thus able to recommend Ledom attitudes toward sex. Next, also as Johns, he damns the Ledom after he discovers their true nature, thus illustrating how deeply sexual stereotypes are held. Finally, as Quesbu, he offers the promise of a future mankind still divided into two sexes, but free of sex roles, which do not exist unless they are culturally imposed. The Ledom, who are themselves basically human, can teach the future human race how to avoid such tragic stereotyping.

Although better and more sophisticated literature has been written on the same theme, (such as Ursula Le Guin's *The Left Hand of Darkness*), few works have portrayed a race of alternate beings as well as *Venus Plus X*.

Stephen H. Goldman

Sources for Further Study

Reviews:
Amazing Stories. XXXV, January, 1961, pp. 135-136.
Magazine of Fantasy and Science Fiction. XX, January, 1961, pp. 95-96.
Worlds of If. X, January, 1961, pp. 84-85.

VOSSTANIE VESHCHEI
(Things in Revolt)

Author: Lev Lunts (1901-1924)
First book publication: 1965
Type of work: Film scenario in eight parts
Time: 1970
Locale: "The Island Democratic Republic"

A depiction of how all inanimate objects rise up in revolt against man

> *Principal characters:*
> ANDREW PREBBLE, a young man
> PROFESSOR SCHEDT, the discoverer of the language of things
> KATRIONA, his daughter
> GENERAL MCNAIR, his enemy

Lev Lunts is best known to students of Russian literature as the leader of a group called the "Serapion Brothers," active in Petrograd-Leningrad in the 1920's and numbering some of Russia's most original postrevolutionary writers: Mikhail Zoshchenko, Veniamin Kaverin, Vsevolod Ivanov, Konstantin Fedin, and others. Lunts's artistic pronouncements, which include the essays "Why We Are the Serapion Brothers," "Ideology and Publicistic Literature" and "Go West!," have been called "the most forthright plea for creative freedom to be found in the annals of Soviet literature" (Victor Erlich, *Russian Formalism*). Quite naturally, for many years the Serapion Brothers were anathema to Soviet critics; only in recent years has a realistic evaluation of their activity become possible.

Lunts succeeded in writing a fair number of essays, stories, plays, film scenarios and even novels before his premature death at the age of 23. His health, always delicate, was ruined by his frenzied creative activity in the conditions of starving Petrograd in the early 1920's. He left Russia in 1923, ailing from a heart defect and nervous exhaustion, and joined his parents who had emigrated earlier to Germany. After spending the summer of 1923 in a sanatorium in Königstein im Taunus, he died the following year in a Hamburg hospital. Most of his works written in Russia were published at the time, but some of his writings in the sanatorium did not come to light until the 1960's. Among them was the remarkable film scenario, *Things in Revolt (Vosstanie veshchei)*.

The discovery of this work coincided with the recovery of other previously unpublished works from Russia's immediate past: Mikhail Bulgakov's *The Master and Margarita* (1925-1940), the same author's *Heart of a Dog* (1925), and Andrei Platonov's stories and novels. Lunts's scenario does not have the same literary merit as these works, but it does have equal imaginative power, and together with them raises the question: What is the value of unearthed literary works? Do such works, which did not play a role in the literary life of their time, have only an archaeological interest? For although they are new to our time, they were not written in our time; they are works that time passed by.

But this problem exists only at the time of discovery. A few years later the discovered works enter into our historical consciousness: they are automatically placed in their proper time and evaluated by comparison with other works of the same period. In a sense, the recovered works return to the time that passed them by and belatedly participate in its literature. We read and respond to a work published in 1925 no differently from the way we react to a work written in 1925 but not published until 1968. The first may seen old, because we have heard of it for years, while the second may seem dated upon its appearance; but time smooths out the difference. All literary works require historical perspective for their proper appreciation. Placed next to other silent films of the 1920's, even the celebrated *Metropolis* (1926) by Fritz Lang, *Things in Revolt* is astounding in its invention, and decades ahead of its time in the photographic techniques it calls for. The pity is that it was not filmed: we must imagine it since we cannot see it.

Lunts first mentioned the work in July, 1923, when he excitedly wrote a friend from the sanatorium: "I've finished a gigantic scenario. Brilliant! But where can I sell it? A worldwide plot! A marvel of technique!" Later he sought the help of Ilya Ehrenburg, who had connections in Paris, but nothing came of the attempt. Then, it seems, he converted the work into a novel. This version was described by Veniamin Kaverin in his obituary of Lunts as "a fascinating novel about a city of things living apart from man." Late in 1923 Lunts sent a copy of the novel to his brother in Paris with instructions to guard it carefully, as the idea might be pirated. The idea, his brother recalls, concerned the revolt of inanimate things in a city: the people are driven away, but the things find that people, after all, are necessary. A reconciliation is made, the people return to the city and the houses, in homage, bow to them. The novel has been lost.

The scenario of *Things in Revolt* is set in the future (1970) on "The Island Democratic Republic," characterized by a lack of vegetation and an abundance of steel, cement, and glass. Its chief protagonist is an old scientist, Professor Schedt, who has discovered the secret of controlling inanimate objects by whistling. Schedt is extremely found of objects; he "understands" them and prefers them to human beings. He has become obsessed with the idea of establishing ironclad "law and order" on the island. The scenario is not always clear whether things revolt only on his command or are liberated by his whistle to pay man back for centuries of enslavement and abuse. The latter interpretation is suggested by an imaginative scene entitled "Herald of the Storm." Here a stalled car suddenly retaliates when the driver repeatedly kicks the grill: it runs down the driver and lunges into the crowd, leaving crushed and bloody bodies in its wake, chasing runners down the streets, into houses and up lampposts. The subscript reads: "Even a thing has its limit of endurance." When the authorities try to stop the car their weapons refuse to shoot; finally it is crushed by the armored cars of Schedt's enemy, General McNair. Before the full revolt, Schedt invites the hero, Andrew Prebble, to his primitive home (called "Noah's Art") and introduces him to his daughter, Katriona. Here the three will remain safe. Schedt then unleashes a savage attack on the islanders.

> A burning streetcar flies out from the left. Panic. The people inside break the glass and jump out on the street.
> Prebble is horrified.
> A similar streetcar from the right. Other streetcars rush by.
> Automobiles run over people, horses, dogs.
> Streets split open and bite into the people.
> The people who step onto the rails — fly into the air. Current!
> The windows of the houses burst open; the people inside shout for help.
> The furniture in the rooms attacks the people.
> Stairways and elevators crumble: the path is cut off.
> Clothes crush the people. The collars choke them, the shoes constrict, etc. People fall and writhe on the ground, trying to tear off their clothes. . .
> Schedt says. . .
> "Why did I make things revolt? Because people are worthless and lawless. But things are simple and all alike. . . . . Law and order will rule from now on. . . . . The rule of the dead thing!"

Schedt eventually achieves his goal, after defeating McNair, who had stolen his secret, in a fantastic battle between self-motivated cannon, fire engines, bicycles, cameras, and even pencils. Yet the reign of law and order does not work; without human direction, newspapers print gibberish in neat columns, paintbrushes paint everywhere, machines overproduce and flood the stores with goods. Schedt, faced with the ruin of his scheme, commits suicide: he whistles, a pistol lifts itself into the air, aims, and shoots him in the heart.

Although its originality is self-evident, *Things in Revolt* may be related to a number of imaginative works: the stories of mad inventors and automatons by Hoffmann, Poe and Bierce; the descriptions of world destruction by H. G. Wells, Leopold Alas "Clarín" and Jules Verne; the philosophical fantasies of Karel Čapek; the eschatological visions of Velimer Khlebnikov's "The Crane" (1909); Valery Bryusov's *The Republic of the Southern Cross* (1919) and Evgeny Zamyatin's *We* (1920). Although Lunts probably knew many of these works, it is the latter alone which can definitely be linked as an influence on his scenario.

Things in Revolt joins Zamyatin's novel and essays in opposing the excessive mechanical spirit of postrevolutionary Russia. Both Lunts and Zamyatin believed that the mechanization of life and art — so ardently demanded by the Futurists, Constructivists, and Proletcultists — threatened to reduce humanity to a monotonous and sterile formula. It was not the machine or the productivity of the machine which they feared, but the application of the machine to life. In the scenario, Prebble exclaims to Schedt: "I do not want order, but life!" He considers dangerous unpredictability preferable to safe and senseless regularity.

Lunts and Zamyatin also questioned the regimentation of life by the Soviet government. In *We*, people are controlled by "The One State" and "The Benefactor" and are completely lacking in individuality. In *Things in Revolt*, the strange Professor Schedt intends to mate his daughter Katriona with Prebble in order to create a new race of people governed by strict law and order. In Lunts's case the argument was greatly limited by the confines of the silent film. Through the character of Katriona he presented a simple dichotomy of mechanical order and true life: Schedt shields his daughter from life and has made her into a living manikin, who moves and speaks mechanically. "She lives calmly . . . without joys or sufferings. . . . According to law!" But when she falls in love with Prebble and dies as a result, he is forced to admit that the race he conceived could not live with "lawless love."

The character of Katriona immediately brings to mind the robots of Čapek's *R.U.R.* (1920). It is possible that Lunts was familiar with this work either by hearsay or in its German translation (1922), although the robot theme did not generally become known in Russia until Aleksei Tolstoi plagiarized it in *Revolt of the Machines* (1924). There is a remarkable similarity between the works of Lunts and Čapek: Čapek's first play, *The Outlaw* (1920), is similar not only in title and date of writing, but also in theme and spirit to Lunts's first play *Outside the Law* (1919). A later play by Čapek, *Adam the Creator* (1927), sets a mass of identical men against an unruly group of individuals, as does Lunts's last play, *The City of Truth* (1923). Moreover, Čapek's essays on art manifest an enthusiasm for plot, intrigue, and entertainment in general, and the novel of adventures, the detective tale, and science fiction in particular — as do Lunts's. Čapek's essay on proletarian art (1925) may be cited as being very close in outlook and wording to "Why We Are the Serapion Brothers" and "Go West!" Finally, like Lunts, Čapek used the Bible as a source of inspiration, writing a number of apocryphal tales. For the most part this similarity between the two writers must have been coincidental, a similar response to similar environments. Čapek could not read Russian and Lunts could not read Czech: Čapek's works were not available in Russian until after Lunts's death and Lunts's works (with the exception of *Outside the Law*) were not translated into Czech.

As indicated above, Lunts considered his scenario original and no doubt feared it would be plagiarized. Despite his attempts, it was not published or produced. Its main scenic invention — self-motivated objects — has since become a television platitude (*My Favorite Martian, Bewitched*, various films about demonic powers). Only Alfred Hitchcock's *The Birds* has come close to its message and scope. In *The Birds*, man has misused animals, in Lunts's scenario, man has misused all things. The scenario, along with other papers of

Lunts, was put in a suitcase at the time of his death. This suitcase was kept over the years by his sister Genia Hornstein in Germany and then in England. Because of the sad memory of her beloved brother, she did not open the suitcase until 1963, when she released its contents for study and publication. *Things in Revolt* was published in a Russian-language journal in New York, *Novyi zhurnal*. The scenario has not yet been translated.

Gary Kern

THE VOYAGE OF THE SPACE BEAGLE

Author: A. E. van Vogt (1912-   )
First book publication: 1950
Type of work: Novel
Time: The far future
Locale: The *Space Beagle*, a giant starship on an intergalactic scientific expedition

An episodic adventure narrative purporting to show the superiority of a new kind of holistic science over traditional scientific disciplines

> *Principal characters:*
> ELLOITT GROSVENOR, a "Nexialist" or holistic scientist
> HAL MORTON, the expedition director
> GREGORY KENT, the head of the *Space Beagle*'s chemistry department, later expedition director
> CAPTAIN LEETH, the commander of the *Space Beagle*
> DR. KORITA, the ship's archaeologist and cultural historian
> COEURL, an intelligent catlike monster
> IXTL, a survivor of Glor, the supreme civilization of a previous universe
> THE ANABIS, a gaseous being the size of a galaxy

The theme of control — control of technology, of the future, of the natural world, of human destiny itself — is not an uncommon one in science fiction, particularly in what is generally termed the "Campbell era" of the late 1930's and 1940's. Yet even among authors of this period, few so consistently and energetically embraced a Laplacean ideal of the ordering and controlling intellect as did A. E. van Vogt. Van Vogt's much-publicized adherence to such intellectual fads as general semantics and dianetics may be the most telling evidence of this, but even before he virtually abandoned science fiction writing in the early 1950's to pursue these and other schemes, he produced a body of work that consistently reveals a search for a philosophy of power and control. *The Voyage of the Space Beagle*, written in 1950 from stories published as early as 1939 (including van Vogt's first published science fiction story, "The Black Destroyer"), is an example of this search and also epitomizes the curiously dual nature of much of van Vogt's fiction: fast-paced, episodic narratives overlaid with a blatantly didactic intellectual argument.

As a narrative, *The Voyage of the Space Beagle* is little more than space opera, a succession of confrontations with crafty, flamboyant space monsters of various persuasions. As an argument, it rests on two fundamental premises. The first is a cyclical view of history, clearly borrowed from Oswald Spengler, which posits that any civilization in the universe — not just human civilizations — moves from a peasant stage through village, urban, and megalopolitan stages to a "winter" period of self-doubt, leading to massive wars that reduce civilization to "fellahdom," or the beginning of a new cycle with peasantry. Van Vogt seems to assume that such a cyclical theory might be developed to the point where a trained archaeologist would be able to predict the behavior of a particular inhabitant of a culture merely by knowing what stage of civilization the culture is in, and Dr. Korita, the ship's archaelogist, is repeatedly called upon to make such predictions on the basis of astonishingly little evidence.

Human culture at the time of *The Voyage of the Space Beagle* is in the decadent winter phase of its eighth cycle, one feature of which is the struggle of special interest groups and individuals for power. Such a power struggle is symbolized on the ship itself by the ambition of the head of the chemistry department, Gregory Kent, to become expedition director. The only apparent hope for the continued expansion of human culture is to break out of the cyclical pattern before the collapse comes, and the science which promises to accomplish this is the second major premise of van Vogt's argument. Elliott Grosvenor, caught in the power struggle between Kent and expedition director Morton, is a "Nexialist." "Nexialism," he explains, is "applied whole-ism," a rigorous system of education and training that seeks to break down compartmentalization of thought by focusing on problems rather than traditional disciplines, and applying whatever resources are needed from the various disciplines to solve specific problems. Although this really sounds like little more than what is more commonly termed interdisciplinary study, van Vogt makes much of it, and one of the few plot lines that binds the book together is Grosvenor's increasingly successful effort to gain respectability for Nexialism among the more specialized scientists aboard the *Space Beagle*.

While van Vogt's concern for overspecialization in the sciences is a valid one, his case for Nexialism consistently rests on narrative set-ups rather than on the links among the sciences that the name Nexialism (presumably from "nexus," or linkage) would suggest, and Grosvenor finally emerges as all but indistinguishable from the superscientist heroes of early pulp science fiction. His first challenge is a catlike monster named Coeurl, which gets loose aboard the ship, killing crew members to feed on their "id" (which, as it turns out, has little to do with Freud but is rather some sort of serum potassium). After conventional scientists propose solutions that do not work, Grosvenor arrives at a plan that essentially consists of tricking Couerl into leaving the ship, which then quickly travels to another part of the galaxy. Not surprisingly, the scheme works, but the reader is left a little fuzzy as to how exactly it supports the principles of Nexialism.

Following the adventure with Coeurl, most of the ship's scientists remain unconvinced of the value of Nexialism, and fewer than a dozen show up at a lecture given by Grosvenor to explain the tenets of the new science. Kent, Grosvenor's leading opponent, even begins to move part of his staff into Grosvenor's laboratory space. But a new crisis offers Grosvenor a second opportunity to demonstrate the superiority of his methods. The ship is "attacked" by powerful hypnotic hallucinations generated by the Riim, birdlike creatures inhabiting a nearby planet. Virtually the entire population of the ship is incapaci-

tated except for Grosvenor, whose Nexialist training conveniently included
conditioning against telepathic hypnosis, and Korita, whom he rescues by
overriding the Riim's hypnotic suggestion with his own. Others, their subconscious hatreds and jealousies released by the hypnotic state, turn on one
another in murderous rages. Grosvenor manages to establish telepathic contact
with the Riim, and discovers that their message was intended to be a friendly
one, though it proved too powerful for the unprepared human minds on board
the ship. He persuades them to change the pattern of their projections and
gradually withdraw them, then takes control of the ship to remove it to a safe
distance. Again, Nexialism "triumphs" — though again it is difficult to
fathom exactly how holistic problem-solving is involved. Grosvenor's ability
to resist the hallucinations seems less related to the substance of his Nexialist
training than to the specific techniques used in that training, namely subliminal
learning and the handy coincidence that such learning involved resistance
techniques.

Scarcely has the crew escaped from the bird-people when the third major
crisis occurs. A creature named Ixtl, so advanced in techniques of mind and
body control that is is capable of surviving unaided in intergalactic space, is
brought on board and proceeds to wreak even greater havoc than Coeurl had.
Ixtl is the survivor of the ancient civilization of Glor, which had been the
dominant race in a previous universe whose destruction had led to the creation
of the present one. Floating alone in space for billions of years, Ixtl needs to
make contact with a moving gravitational body in order to escape its slow drift
through intergalactic space and conquer the new universe. He also needs to
find "guuls," or host bodies in which to deposit his eggs (why van Vogt refers
to an egg-bearing creature as "he" is unclear). The *Space Beagle* provides the
solution to both of these problems, and once aboard, Ixtl, who is capable of
changing his molecular structure to enable him to pass through all but the
hardest metals, proceeds to start planting his eggs in the stomachs of crew
members and otherwise to make a terrible nuisance of himself. Again, various
scientists propose solutions to the problem, and again they prove untenable
(though the most obvious solution of simply shooting Ixtl is abandoned when
the first attempt results in the accidental death of several crew members).
Energizing parts of the ship with destructive force fields fails when it is found
that Ixtl can escape the fields, and eventually the crew is forced to retreat into
the heavily shielded engine area, faced with the prospect of either sacrificing
themselves to destroy the creature or allowing it to return to conquer the
known universe. Again, Grosvenor's brilliant solution seems curiously lame:
abandon ship, using lifeboats, and energize the entire *Space Beagle* to either
destroy Ixtl or drive him out (it succeeds in accomplishing the latter).

The final, and greatest, test of Nexialism follows the statistically impossible
discovery of scores of primeval planets in close proximity to one another in a
single galaxy. Grosvenor's hypothesis to account for this, and his ambitious

solution to the problem it implies, is so bizarre that he finds it necessary to adapt Nexialist techniques to take control of all the men on the ship to get his way (thus revealing the totalitarian potential of this new science). The adversary in this episode is The Anabis (probably from "anabolism"), an intelligence evolved initially from swamp gas, which has grown to such proportions that it suffuses the entire galaxy and has begun to create primeval environments on planets in order to provide itself with food. But the Anabis has just about eaten up its galaxy, and needs to move on to fresh territory, led by the *Space Beagle*. Grosvenor's solution to his problem is about the silliest one he has come up with yet, and van Vogt, seeming to realize this, avoids describing it as long as possible. Essentially it consists of locating metallic planets and using their ores to build millions of torpedoes to spread radioactivity throughout the interstellar space of the galaxy, eventually killing the Anabis. For added insurance, the *Space Beagle* sets sail for a galaxy nine hundred million light years away, too far for the Anabis to follow even if it survives.

Finally, Grosvenor has won respect for Nexialism, and a subsequent lecture of his is well-attended, even by his former adversary Kent. But it is not the business about Nexialism that makes *The Voyage of the Space Beagle* enjoyable reading. It is, rather, a combination of the implicit Darwinism of the book's title — the monsters described are all ingeniously accounted for by means of natural selection and evolution applied on a galactic scale — and van Vogt's headlong style. Writing in his familiar eight-hundred word scenes, and alternating action aboard the *Space Beagle* with action seen from the viewpoint of the monster at hand, he keeps his narrative moving at such a rapid pace that, within each episode at least, the reader scarcely pauses to question narrative logic or the intellectual arguments propounded. Far from a masterpiece, the novel seems somehow caught between older science fiction traditions of rapid-fire action narratives and later traditions of intellectual fiction. It succeeds far more on the former level than on the latter.

Gary K. Wolfe

Sources for Further Study

Criticism:

The Encyclopedia of Science Fiction and Fantasy. Compiled by Donald H. Tuck. Chicago: Advent Publishers, Inc., 1978, p. 314. Tuck gives brief biographical information on van Vogt, and a lengthy bibliography of his works.

Reviews:

Analog. XLVII, May, 1951, p. 152.

Authentic Science Fiction. XVII, January, 1952, p. 112.

Flying Saucers from Other Worlds. IV, April, 1952, pp. 155-156.

Future Science Fiction. II, May, 1951, p. 55.

Galaxy. I, December, 1950, pp. 64-65.

Startling Stories. XXII, January, 1951, pp. 101-102.

Worlds Beyond. I, January, 1951, pp. 101-102.

A VOYAGE TO ARCTURUS

Author: David Lindsay (1876-1945)
First book publication: 1920
Type of work: Novel
Time: The 1920's
Locale: England and Tormance

Accepting Krag's challenge to visit Tormance, the only inhabited planet of Arcturus, Maskull undertakes the quest for Surtur, who holds the secret of the ultimate

Principal characters:
MASKULL, the natural man hero in quest of the ultimate
NIGHTSPORE, Maskull's spiritual self
CRYSTALMAN, the great spirit of illusion, the enemy known as Shaping
KRAG, the guide who brings Maskull and Nightspore to Tormance, revealed finally as Surtur, leader of the sons of Muspel

David Lindsay's *A Voyage to Arcturus* is one of the original, enigmatic works of imaginative literature published this century. Critics have described it variously as science fiction, fantasy, allegory, and a philosophical novel. It is, perhaps, all of these and more. Throughout Maskull's adventure, there is the sense of strange things happening, of experiencing new orders of reality. Lindsay's purposes in the romance, beyond the creation of the extraordinary world of Tormance, are clouded by the vastness of the possibilities inherent in its structure. Lindsay invents such a world on Tormance as the reader has never before experienced. The incredible visual effects highlighted by *jale* and *ulfire*, two new primary colors peculiar to Tormance, the intensity of the character's feelings, and of Maskull's reactions to the ever-changing conditions and strange creatures of Tormance arouse wonder and awe in the reader, creating responses which can hardly be defined but which the reader somehow understands.

The story begins at a seance attended by Maskull and Nightspore, an evening's diversion for a society of dilettantes, at which the materialization of a youth takes place. As if by cue, Krag appears, wrathfully dismissing the spirit who responds with "a smile full of significance which, however, no one could understand." Krag, however, seems to understand and immediately breaks the neck of the youth, whose features twist into a "sordid, bestial grin, which cast a cold shadow of moral nastiness into every heart." Maskull is both appalled and fascinated. Incited by Krag, who promises to take him to a world where such goblins originate, Maskull agrees to go. Strangely, Nightspore identifies the hideous expression on the apparition as belonging to Crystalman and reveals that they are all going to Crystalman's world. Yet another mystery is added when Krag explains that Surtur, an authority figure, has gone before them and requires that they follow.

The three are to leave from Starkness Observatory by means of Arcturian "back rays," rays that travel back to their source. Before departing, three remarkable things happen. Krag shows Maskull through a glass that Arcturus is actually a double sun with a planet, Tormance, circling it. The second is the sound of ghostly drum beats, which are to both lead and pursue Maskull through his sojourn on Tormance. Third is a ritual knife cut on the arm given Maskull by Krag which enables Maskull to ascend the observatory tower, from which he can view Tormance and the dual suns. Prior to the cutting, Maskull was prevented by a strange gravity from ascending very far. At this point Krag cautions Maskull, telling him that he is merely an instrument to be broken, that his fate is connected to Nightspore, who is now asleep but who will awaken at Maskull's death. Krag warns: "You will go, but he will return." When Maskull appeals to Nightspore, he is told that Surtur is the master who knows the meaning of these things. In a storm of anxiety and wonder, Maskull leaves for Tormance.

Maskull awakens on Tormance alone and is not to encounter Nightspore again until he reaches Lichtstorm, although he does encounter Krag on occasion. Maskull is rescued and sheltered by two natives, Joiwind and her husband Panawe. Maskull learns that the dual stars have different names and different natures: the white star is Branchspell and the blue is Alppain. He soon grows three new sense organs which heighten his perceptions of tenderness, kindness, and warmth. Ironically, Joiwind and Panawe for all their kindness do not really have a true understanding of Crystalman's world.

Lindsay's success is extraordinary in rendering the various regions and races of Tormance. Each race has its own vision of truth, its own hierarchy of ideals and values. In different ways each vision has an element of truth, but the understanding is distorted and often misdirected. Maskull, therefore, is allowed a true vision in his journey only from Krag or from Surtur's revelation of himself as a storm and his declaration that Maskull was brought to Tormance to serve. However, neither Maskull nor the reader is prepared to understand these revelations, and they are perceived vaguely as foreshadowings. As Maskull moves from region to region, he finds himself thinking in new ways, developing new senses, experiencing new emotions, and behaving instinctively and at times compulsively according to the customs of the country, however savage or strange.

Maskull's behavior on Tormance is oddly contradictory. Although he is a natural man, a hero of the sort we find in Germanic legend, he seems at the same time strangely detached from his own experiences and actions. Perhaps this is the inevitable result of the allegorical division of Maskull-flesh versus Nightspore-soul. Maskull does learn eventually that Crystalman, the shaping spirit of Tormance, is responsible for the development of all the sense organs and the accompanying modes of being and experience. He also comes to appreciate that Tormance is a world in the throes of early experimental development. Everything seems to be charged with new forms of life and over-flowing with energy.

Maskull's inconsistency, his failure to have a mind of his own once on Tormance, the sense of drift in his actions serve to emphasize two themes. First, it appears that it is not only what one believes that changes but also that truth itself, indeed, reality, is various. Maskull's understanding of these processes is fragmentary at best. He develops an uncertain picture pieced together from fragmentary and often erroneous evidence. As Maskull follows the mysterious lead of Surtur toward Lichtstorm, he seems to be moving upward from the physical to the spiritual plane, from love of pleasure to acceptance of pain. Maskull's encounters, therefore, are not so much designed to produce knowledge or understanding as a new state of awareness; for in the end, the great truths he learns depend on suppression of his will, his self-consciousness, and his own identity.

During his journey through Wombflash Forest, Maskull learns from Dreamsinter that he came to Tormance like a Prometheus to steal Muspel fire, "to give a deeper life to men   never doubting if your soul could endure that burning." Indeed, Maskull alone cannot endure, but Nightspore, Maskull's spiritual self, is victorious after Maskull's death. Maskull learns that Crystalman has worked to prevent Maskull's recognition that the world of Crystalman is the false world of Shaping. He learns that the apparition at the seance was actually himself being strangled by Krag and that it was a foreshadowing of his own death.

As Maskull lies dying in the arms of Krag on Surtur's ocean under rising Alppain, he reaches his highest degree of self-understanding — "I am nothing." But Krag, who will be revealed to Nightspore as Surtur, adds the greater truth of revelation — "You are Nightspore." Maskull's destiny was, therefore, to die on Surtur's ocean and to bring Nightspore, his soul, to a rebirth under the blue sun. It seems clear at this point that Tormance is a world in which consciousness and environment are interactive and mutually dependent and that the symbiosis includes both conscious and unconscious faculties.

Under Krag's directive insistence, Nightspore, now mysteriously reborn in Maskull's death, climbs a second tower toward the ultimate revelation that was denied Maskull. He discovers that the spirit light of Muspel passes through the body of Crystalman, who feeds upon it and who transforms the light into all the varieties that make up existence. In short, Crystalman is a small body which casts a great shadow, and the world he shapes changes and dances so that Crystalman may feel joy. Nightspore learns further that there is both a divine reality and a divine plan, that there is a battle going on, a deadly serious one, between the power of Crystalman to deceive and the power of Surtur to make truth known. The Maskull-Nightspore quest confirms that Krag speaks truly when he says that he is mightier than Crystalman.

Just what Nightspore is supposed to make of his new understanding is not clear. He has been reborn and evidently not for the first time. He and Krag are to return to earth to take up the struggle against illusion and the false worship of the world that Crystalman makes. Nightspore will not forget the lesson of Krag-Surtur, whose final revelation is that Surtur is known on earth as pain.

Much of the great imaginative power displayed in Lindsay's work is derived directly from the progression of adventures that carry us through Maskull's quest. The world of Tormance is convincingly brought to light. Its inhabitants are compelling creatures and not grotesques despite their unique sense organs and their allegorical origins. Perhaps not since Edmund Spenser and John Bunyan have allegorical characters been so astutely handled, but Lindsay's characters seem to represent a new iconography. The landscapes are exciting, plausible, and often wild with an alien beauty. Moreover, the geographical and ecological systems are admirably adapted to each adventure. Thus in creating a secondary reality and in compelling our imagined belief in that creation, Lindsay's story is a spectacular success.

The impact of Lindsay's romance depends in part on his treatment of ideas. The victory or the quest achieved by Maskull is the loss of self and the total rejection or repudiation of will in pursuit of the Platonic ideal. It is difficult to say whether Maskull's self-recognition as nothing should be taken as a pun, a kind of religious hyperbole, or the partial truth of a metaphysics rooted in Crystalman's world. Whatever the case, Maskull's release comes from his straining to penetrate that world to reach truth. It is a release that permits Nightspore to carry on the rebirth process.

One view presented numerous times and as often rejected is the sentimental or modern humanist belief in the beauty of the world as an expression of the creator. The Western ideals of beauty, love, goodness have been falsified by Crystalman or Shaping. What is left, it seems, are truth and reality, which are one, and which are really only known to us on earth through pain.

Another important aspect of this romance is the mythic. It seems that Lindsay fabricates his own mythos with its roots drawing on the occult, on classic and Norse mythology, on Western and Eastern religions, especially Christianity and Buddhism, on medieval legend, and on science fiction, presumably seen as a new form of mythology. Lindsay was himself a student of the occult and of Kabbalistic lore. *A Voyage to Arcturus* resists any attempt to fit it into a traditional mythic pattern, although it seems more Germanic than classical, more Manichaean than Christian in orientation. If Lindsay is indeed offering the reader a new mythos, it is a myth of two worlds, of duality and therefore one whose structure challenges the reader's expectations of familiar patterns.

Related to the mythic patterns that Lindsay uses are the elements of allegory. At least the pattern of action seems to be that of a symbolic allegory of man's search for ultimate truth and reality. Maskull and Nightspore represent body and soul, the soul alone achieving ultimate truth after the death of the body, which belongs to Crystalman. In fact, in these terms, the soul would be born to life, purged from the corruption of earth and the flesh; and these are the very terms in which Krag instructs Nightspore at the end. The case for allegory is strengthened by the profusion of allegorical names used by Lindsay. But the names themselves puzzle because they are doubly rather than singly allegorical, oblique rather than direct, many of them suggesting contradictory meanings or strange new forms of metaphor in names like Tormance, Branchspell, Alppain, Wombflash, Ifdawn and so on. They tease us out of thought.

It is risky to venture beyond the basic allegorical frame, but it seems that on a wider scale of measurement the allegory is one of death, birth, and reincarnation, which sets itself to dramatize in symbolic terms the successive states from conception to birth as psychic as well as physical.

If this is allegory, perhaps it represents a new type, blending myth and psychology. Suppose there is a consciousness of another order, gradually forgotten after birth, which is a period of interlife. If that is what Lindsay is giving us here, it seems possible that *A Voyage to Arcturus* is at least in part an attempt to exercise such a racial memory or unconscious recognition by means of a symbolic or archetypal pattern which would therefore seem to us to mean a great deal more than it says.

C. S. Lewis praised Lindsay's achievement in *A Voyage to Arcturus* for generating that idea of "otherness," doing so by drawing on the world of the spirit, the only other real world we know. Who could deny that? Perhaps Lindsay himself best described the grandeur of his work in the words of Earthrid, the music master, speaking of his music to Maskull:

> Now men when they make music are accustomed to build beautiful tones, because of the delight they cause. Therefore their music is based on pleasure; its symmetry is regular and charming, its emotion sweet and lovely. . . . But my music is founded on painful tones; and thus its symmetry is wild and difficult to discover, its emotions bitter and terrible.

Donald L. Lawler

Sources for Further Study

Criticism:

Amis, Kingsley. "Adventures on a Distant Star," in *New York Times Book Review.* (November 24, 1963), p. 60. Amis finds *A Voyage to Arcturus* as less science fiction and more religious allegory.

Brophy, Brigid. "Rare Books," in *New Statesman.* XIV (June, 1963), pp. 904-905. Brophy is quite critical of *A Voyage to Arcturus* in which she observes "a displeasing smell of repression."

Russ, Joanna. "Dream Literature and Science Fiction," in *Extrapolation.* XI

(December, 1969), p. 6-14. Russ analyzes *Voyage to Arcturus* as a typification of "dream literature," a schematic projection of daydreaming.

Reviews:

Book Week. January 12, 1964, p. 18.

Library Journal. LXXXV, January 1, 1964, p. 134.

New Statesman. LXV, June 14, 1963, p. 904.

New York Times Book Review. November 24, 1963, p. 60.

Times Literary Supplement. July 5, 1963, p. 497.

LE VOYAGEUR IMPRUDENT
(The Unwary Traveler)

Author: René Barjavel (1911-   )
First book publication: 1944
Type of work: Novel
Time: 1940-1943
Locale: France

A novel which raises philosophical questions regarding the role of fate in human affairs and the extent to which man can exert control over his circumstances

Principal characters:
PIERRE SAINT-MENOUX, the traveler, a mathematician
NOËL ESSAILLON, the inventor
ANNETTE, his daughter

Born in 1911, René Barjavel made his writing debut with *Ashes, Ashes* (*Ravage, Roman Extraordinaire*) in 1943; later he published the successful novel *Le voyageur imprudent* (*The Unwary Traveler*). Since then he has continued to write successfully, his *La nuit des temps* (*The Ice People*, 1968) being a million-copy bestseller in France. Above all, he has been a scenarist (*Don Camillo*, for example). For the last several years, he has devoted himself to ecology. He lives in the hills of southern France, where he makes prophesies like St. John on Patmos.

The novel opens at the Vosges front during the winter of 1939-1940. One evening, Corporal Saint-Menoux meets Professor Essaillon, to whom he had written. The professor has invented "noëlite," a time-travel substance. The instant certain pills are taken, the person goes either back or forward an hour, a day, a week, or a year. Saint-Menoux tries the pills, is convinced that they work, and agrees to take a trip two years into the future. He finds himself in the cold and misery of the Paris Occupation. In the meantime, Essaillon has perfected his invention, a green diving suit in which to travel through time as well as through objects, all the while remaining invisible. However, to move, take photos, and bring back physical proof, the traveler would have to become visible again, and the slightest damage to his diving suit would mean death.

The instant Essaillon uses noëlite to get supplies in the past, they are preserved in an eternal present. He sends ten hectoliters of his substance to a distant government, which has just used it. It rains the present on a small town. The air is shot through with impenetrable black streaks (sometimes a hand, other times part of a face seem to be stuck in space) that immobilize some living beings, who then die and decompose. The passage in which this phenomenon is described is one of the most striking in the book. Essaillon finds his invention too dangerous to publicize. He wants to use it to study the history of humanity and improve its lot if possible.

Wearing the diving suit, Saint-Menoux slips through nighttime Paris, where he encounters every misery and affliction. Once, he causes a commotion in the school where he taught, and is upbraided by Essaillon for it.

The year before (1943), Barjavel had published *Ashes, Ashes (Ravage)*, the story of the A.D. 2052 catastrophe during which electricity got "sick," civilization collapsed, and the Patriarch François established a rural world in which technological progress was banned under pain of death. Some have thought they saw in this book an approval of the Vichy government's push for a return to the land and a rejection of the technology which rendered French soldiers useless, conquered by machines rather than by officers smarter than their own or by better-trained soldiers. Everyone knows that.

This is the world that Saint-Menoux first visits, a world filled with corpses and ruins. Next he explores the world in the year 100,000. Since the descendants of Francois scorned technology, they developed willpower instead. Their society evolved into a world similar to a termites' nest, in which the population is divided into castes, and each individual is morphologically destined to serve a single function — to be eyes, ears, noses; eaters, drinkers, digesters, thinkers, soldiers. In brief, the final phase of a return to the land is marked by the absence of individuality, and the perfect state depicted as a termites' nest.

Essaillon meets his death when the female mountains are discovered, mountains that are nothing more than wombs that disgorge humans — spermatozoa — while the queen continuously gives birth, even if her head is cut off.

Left alone with Annette, whom he loves, Saint-Menoux finds himself without a dime in wartime Paris, and he needs food. He decides to leave, to go into the past to the year 1890, a less dangerous time. There he becomes the Green Devil, whose exploits are a topic of history, and his appearances change the fate of individuals. For example, because of his actions, a certain architect is not born; yet the building he would have designed will be designed by someone else. Is it possible to work for the good of humanity as Essaillon wished? Is it not a certainty that even if individual fate could be changed, the course of humanity would be unrelenting? Does working for the good of all make any sense? Is not the world fated to be forever gripped in the clutches of suffering, bloodshed, and hatred?

This is the whole problem of human freedom that is presented. Saint-Menoux wants to make absolutely sure, so he returns to Toulon in 1793 to kill Napoleon Bonaparte. But a soldier gets in the way and is hit instead, and the soldier is one of Saint-Menoux' forebears. When he dies, the novel goes back to when it begins. When Annette opens a door, nobody is there.

Le voyageur imprudent was an instant success, and deservedly so. If one share of its success reflects the writer's abilities, however, the greatest share was due to circumstances. Barjavel is a writer of the same caliber as the great names of mainstream literature of his day. Moreover, during this time period he underscored one of the most important problems in philosophy — that of fate *versus* free will. Barjavel believed that the origins of fate are within us; we create our own destiny through our weaknesses and lack of courage. Nevertheless, Barjavel is less daring than other writers in his treatment, since he sidesteps the problem to some extent; other works on the same theme which are more direct in confronting the issue of fate in human affairs are Aron's *Victory at Waterloo*, Maurois' *What if Louis XVI* . . . , and Thiry's *Hold Back the Time*. Yet, none of these works had the repercussions that *Le voyageur imprudent* did, simply because of the circumstances surrounding the latter's publication. Had Barjavel's novel appeared in 1945 or 1939, instead of 1944, reviewers would probably have devoted only two or three lines to it. But in 1944, the public was completely receptive to the work because all the gloom, all the hardships, and all the misery experienced by everybody in France was found in every page in Barjavel's novel. To this was added satire and criticism of the government, which Barjavel fearlessly vented when so many others kept their peace. It is significant that only eighteen months later, the movie *Sidereal Cruise* and two short stories by Marcel Aymé ("The Decree" and "Time Map") dealing with the same problems were unpopular since everyone wished to escape to flee from their miserable and squalid present into another, happier time.

Never again after the success of *Le voyageur imprudent* did Barjavel find such a favorable audience; when, deeply shocked by the Hiroshima bomb, he wrote *The Hell With It* to denounce science, the public no longer followed him. Barjavel was literarily a one-book man. He served an important function, however, in exposing the French public to a new type of novel, and he whetted the appetite of readers and young writers for science fiction. In this way he was an important influence, even though it is hard to gauge exactly the extent of that influence.

Jacques van Herp

Sources for Further Study

Criticism:

Balakian, Nona. "Rene Barjavel," in *New York Times*. (June 12, 1949), p. 4. Although dealing primarily with Barjavel's *Tragic Innocents*, this article provides insights into the author's strengths: "his keen observations of French life."

WALDEN TWO

Author: B. F. Skinner (1904-   )
First book publication: 1948
Type of work: Novel
Time: Spring 1947
Locale: The Eastern United States

The story of a brief visit to a Utopian community by two middle-aged professors and four young people, during which three of them are converted and remain at the community

Principal characters:
> PROFESSOR BURRIS, a psychology teacher and the narrator of the story
> T. E. FRAZIER, founder of the community
> ROGERS, a student of Burris before the war
> STEVE JAMNIK, Rogers' war buddy
> BARBARA MACKLIN, Rogers' fiancée
> MARY GROVE, Steve's girl friend
> PROFESSOR AUGUSTINE CASTLE, a philosophy teacher

B. F. Skinner's fictional description of a Utopian community set resolutely in the Eastern half of the United States in the spring of 1947 has the concreteness and open-faced literalness of a Wordsworth poem in which the dimensions of a pond are paced off yard by yard in seemingly unimaginative fashion. Professor Burris, the first-person narrator whose name echoes Skinner's own first name, tells us at the beginning of his story that he has spent one entire postwar year in depression and frustration with American society. Then at the end of the book, just as he realizes that during the short visit he has been converted to this Utopian community, Burris sees a newspaper account of a graduation speech given by the president of his university. It is spring and his commencement. But in spite of its constant discursiveness, *Walden Two* is an imaginative book in much the way that the most prosaic and literal of Wordsworth's poems are imaginative. Skinner fills the book with a message, a hope, and a program.

The manner of telling is what is fascinating and, although a detailed comprehension of behavioral psychology cannot be had here, apparently the manner is an appropriate mirror of the message. It all appears on the surface, carefully illuminated and enlightened; and even though complex and various, all of the complexities are laid out before the reader in dialogue and discursive presentation. The book reads like a dialogue from the eighteenth century Enlightenment without the *risqué* references to the bedroom. Skinner uses few images, no symbolic or mythic representations, and the deep psychic or mysterious recesses in personality seem to be there only as a kind of gesture to what is expected in fiction. His characters would, indeed, be faulted as two dimensional if they were not so revolutionary and interesting in that respect. Skinner's narrative tools, in other words, are not symbolic. He does not have to suggest the primal scene of innocence or the blemished garden of a lost Golden Age because, as the prime mover of his Utopian experiment says, they are embarking on a new Golden Age. Much like eighteenth century Enlightenment thinkers such as William Godwin, Skinner believes that with real antecedents one can produce real consequences. Thus in this fictional description of his ideas, myth and legend become lost in exposition.

T. E. Frazier, the psychologist or social engineer whose ideas are being worked out in *Walden Two* and who, in fact, guides Burris and his party on their visit, is presented by Skinner rather halfheartedly as a demigod in conflict with himself. Perhaps he suffers from frustrated sexual drives. Perhaps he is burdened with the realization of the sin of pride in himself, and it is difficult for him to accept his own dogma forbidding heroes or revered leaders. At the very end of the book, Burris observes that although Frazier is not in his heaven (a high perch on a rocky cliff overlooking the community), all is right with his world. But none of these inner conflicts, nor any of the supposed interpersonal conflicts that seem to be trumped up in the story to carry along the exposition of ideas, strike the reader as vividly as the monolithic and repeated power of Frazier's *idée fixe*.

There are really two parts to Frazier's discovery and revolutionary program in the book. First of all, in response to the stupidities and anomalies in American competitive society the community structure described in the book demonstrates, much as Thoreau had done by himself, that people can live happily if they manage all details of their lives in a reasonable way. The dominant tone is cheeriness, which cloys but also inspires with hope; and Frazier describes how even the most ghastly of human activities (death and divorce, for example) can be managed. The continual argument for the visitors to Walden Two is that it works. More people are happier more of the time. But Frazier's (and Skinner's) greater program is that by means of the careful observations possible in a managed community, the beginnings of a real science of human behavior can be established. And this will be a science that will answer all the questions about human nature. Why and how do people learn mathematics? Why and how do people become geniuses? Why and how are people unhappy?

Thus Skinner's major concerns in the book, which make it exciting reading, are concerns about methodologies, such as how to proceed in the gathering and sorting of knowledge. Despite the literalness, it is an abstract and scientific book; and here can be seen the tensions and conflicts of the novel. In fact, the methodological puzzles and inconsistencies are interesting. A science of human behavior demands complexity and specialization. Walden Two runs efficiently and thus happily because managers know their specialities — from pie making to sheep tending; and at one point Burris observes that Frazier seldom knew what he was talking about. In other words, Frazier's speciality is the more abstract manipulation of ideas as a planner; and so he could not possibly learn the details of all the other specialities. The conflict can be seen when Frazier describes the ideal education that is being experimented with at Walden Two as well as the limited library that they maintain for the community. He expresses real disgust with the specialized trash that accumulates in a large university library; and a distinct anti-intellectual, and antiacademic tone is sounded in this most academic of books. In fact, throughout the book there is a strange mixture of innocence akin to Rousseau and academic, specialized sophistication that makes Skinner seem to be a particulary torn child of the scientific revolution and of the Enlightenment. On the one hand, he believes in carefully analyzed and deliberate method to solve problems. This, in an increasingly complex world, inevitably leads to specialization. On the other hand, he wants to escape the sophistication and let people be what they will be.

Another related inconsistency that seems to supply the depth, usually created by character or symbol, can be seen when Frazier agonizes over the notion of time. History is not studied seriously at Walden Two because it is so full of obscurities and error. Similarly, all sense of future direction or destiny is repressed in favor of the more problematic notion that all things, but principally people, have the potential to be engineered or changed in the present. In other words, no questions of origins or direction are considered relevant enough to be the most important. Was mankind created to be happy? In what direction will science lead? Instead, Frazier (and Skinner) seem to want only to gather data, to make observations, to create changes in the here and now; and they refuse to be governed by either the past or the future. The tensions in such a situation are what give energy to the book, *Walden Two*, because we know, and ultimately Skinner knows, that such myopic vision is not enough. Both the past and the future are important.

Donald M. Hassler

Sources for Further Study

Criticism:

Goldberg, B. "Skinner's Behaviorist Utopia," in *The Libertarian Alternative*. Edited by Tibor A. Machan. Chicago: Nelson-Hall, 1974, pp. 94-118. Goldberg analyzes Skinner's political and social theories within the confines of his own utopia.

Michaelson, L. W. "A Note on Utopia," in *The Children of Frankenstein: A Primer on Modern Technology and Human Values*. Bloomington: Indiana University Press, 1970, pp. 369-384. Michaelson attempts to analyze *Walden Two* within the context of modern society.

Reviews:

Booklist. XLIV, June 1, 1948, p. 337.

Christian Science Monitor. June 24, 1948, p. 11.

Magazine of Fantasy and Science Fiction. XIX, September, 1960, pp. 79-80.

New York Herald Tribune Weekly Book Review. July 18, 1948, p. 6.

New York Times. June 13, 1948, p. 6.

New Yorker. XXIV, June 12, 1948, p. 94.

San Francisco Chronicle. July 25, 1948, p. 12.

THE WANDERER

Author: Fritz Leiber, Jr. (1910-   )
First book publication: 1964
Type of work: Novel
Time: The near future
Locale: The Earth, Luna, the Wanderer, and space

An account of a strange planet's appearance near Earth, some of the violent consequences of that visit, and the reasons for the planet's coming and its going

Principal characters:
> PAUL HAGBOLT, a publicist for Project Moon
> DON MERRIAM, an American astronaut
> MARGO GELHORN, Paul's friend and Don's fiancée
> DOC BRECHT, a piano salesman and a competent man
> ROSS HUNTER, a Professor of Sociology
> TIGERISHKA, a large feline
> MIAOW, a small feline

In the first sentence of *The Wanderer*, Fritz Leiber associates his novel with "tales of terror and the supernormal." Leiber's precise diction indicates both rhetorical intent and the basis of the novel's odd quality of lucid grimness. Terror, not horror, revulsion, or simple fear, is the chief response which the novel means to evoke; and the terrifying agency is the supernormal, not an incursion from beyond the natural world but a visitor from outside our narrow knowledge of the universe. In the course of the novel the moon is destroyed, cities and countries are devastated, and millions of people die; yet the cause of this appalling disaster is merely the carelessness of some hard-pressed, frightened people trying to free themselves from the policies of a profoundly conservative government. What Leiber tells us is often dismaying and sometimes perverse, but his smooth prose and calm narrative manner tend to mask the disturbing qualities of events until they have become memories rather than immediate observations. The resulting sensation is not unlike the discovery that one has been giving detached and judicious consideration to the aesthetics of vehicular manslaughter.

The central event of the novel is the appearance of a strange planet, the Wanderer, near the moon. Since it is about the same size as the Earth, its tidal influence is as much as eighty times greater than the moon's. The earliest effects felt on Earth are earthquakes and vulcanism. Los Angeles is ravaged by an earthquake and subsequent fires; Krakatoa explodes again. But the most destructive consequence of the Wanderer's approach is the magnification of the ocean tides. The Low Countries (the Imperial Valley, northern Siberia, Virginia, Maryland, the river valleys of England) are flooded. At low tide the Gulf of Tonkin is empty. At high tide, only the tops of Manhattan's tallest skyscrapers remain above water. Lake Michigan's three-inch tide increases to a four-foot tide in Chicago. The Pacific, aided by vulcanism, carves a canal through Nicaragua. Wherever the lands are low and the tides run, people drown.

The Wanderer also completely disrupts electromagnetic communications. The new planet not only has a magnetic field much stronger than Earth's, but it also emanates "influences" that strike Earth in straight lines, causing atmospheric ionization and other effects that render all wireless transmissions impossible. The tital effects are entirely a matter of physics, the result of large masses in proximity to each other. But most of the electromagnetic effects seem to be by-products of the Wanderer's identity and the reason for its visit. The strange new world is actually artificial, a voyager in hyperspace and a ship for the several races who live in its fifty thousand levels. It has entered our solar system to refill its fuel tanks.

The refueling process causes the most spectacular destruction resulting from the Wanderer's visit: the disintegration of the moon. When the Wanderer exits from hyperspace it is — evidently by its captains' design — only twenty-five thousand miles from the moon and captures that body gravitationally. The moon's new orbit soon brings it only twenty-five hundred miles from the larger world. This is well inside Roche's limit, the distance within which a satellite will be broken up by tidal forces, and the moon promptly shatters to fragments. As soon as the fragmentation begins, the crew of the Wanderer begins using some sort of gravitational or momentum fields to suck mile-thick strands of the substance of the moon into their huge vehicle's depleted tanks.

Leiber makes it plain that none of this havoc was strictly necessary; the Wanderer could as well have taken a Jovian satellite. As Paul Hagbolt, one of the major characters, infers, the people of the Wanderer were driven into their blundering actions by the fear of that which pursues them. The unveiling of the nature of that pursuer, together with the concomitant description of the condition of the universe, forms the novel's climax.

The narrative technique Leiber employs for *The Wanderer* is common to many disaster novels: short chapters, a large number of characters, and a frequently shifting point of view always in the third person. The episodic technique has several specific advantages. It suggests the comprehensiveness of the disaster. Since an individual caught up in such a cataclysm would scarcely apprehend much beyond his own situation, the multiple point of view is a plausible and efficient way to provide the reader with information. It also provides a variety of characters to attract the reader's interest and sympathy; thus it tends to sharpen the reader's interest in the question of who will live and who will die, enhancing the suspense. Leiber is careful not to dissipate these advantages by making no conflicting claims of equal importance on the reader's attention.

Clearly the narrative has one main line of development (with several branchings and confluences) and ten or twelve secondary lines, some of which end long before the conclusion of the novel, with the deaths of their point-of-view characters. Leiber puts these secondary lines to a number of uses. For instance, the very first effect of the Wanderer's appearance is the death of Asa Holcomb, whose heart bursts "with the wonder and majesty of it." Over two hundred pages later Leiber counterpoints the useless death of the novel's most competent man in a silly accident by flashing to the Arizona mesa where the vultures are stripping the last flesh from Asa Holcomb's face, "laying wholly bare the beautiful grinning red bone."

As in this instance, Leiber tends to juxtapose rather than connect incidents. Indeed, none of the secondary plot lines ever join either the main line or one another; in the universe of *The Wanderer* communion is never easy, common, or untroubled. But although Leiber refuses to integrate his plot — and by refusing suggests the necessarily fragmented nature of the experiences the novel describes — he insists upon certain other connections. Besides the obvious relationship of "terror and the supernormal" to death, Leiber demonstrates the sexual content of the Wanderer's significance to humans. When the visiting planet appears, Sally Harris is fulfilling her promise to Jake Lesher to "make the stars move" as they ride the roller coaster at Coney Island. The stars spin and shake — or seem to — as the Wanderer exits from hyperspace; Sally thinks she is the cause, and the appearance of the Wanderer itself a moment later is a bonus. For some people, like Richard Hillary and Vera Carlisle, sex is a solace amid tribulations. For others, sex and death seem almost indistinguishable. As they begin to drown in a subterranean military post flooded by the tides, General Spike Stevens and Coloney Mabel Wallingford simultaneously make love and strangle each other.

Leiber is frequently satirical but also not above diverting his readers in ways conventional to modern disaster novels. Yet the sexual incidents of the minor plot lines, together with such other divertissements as the gold-digging of Barbara Katz in Palm Beach, the treasure-hunting of Bagong Bung in the Gulf of Tonkin, the pot-smoking of Arab Jones in Harlem, the madcap terrorism of Don Guillermo Walker in Nicaragua, generate a mood and perspective for the central actions of the main plot line. The perspective is close to stoic, the mood is ironic, and the knowledge that emerges from those central actions is proper cause for melancholy — though not, Leiber's tone suggests, for despair.

The main plot line involves half a dozen primary characters and twice that many secondary figures. It begins in Southern California with Paul Hagbolt and Margo Gelhorn driving toward Vandenberg Two, a U. S. Space Force base, to watch a lunar eclipse. They are diverted by Margo's wish to look in on a flying saucer symposium on a nearby beach. The Wanderer appears while they are with the saucer students, and Margo remains with this little group throughout the rest of the novel. But Paul is taken aboard one of the saucer-shaped auxiliary craft which the Wanderer dispatches in a makeshift effort to alleviate the destruction it has inflicted upon the Earth. The saucer pilot uses a momentum pistol to deflate a tsunami wave threatening the saucer students.

Paul has just rescued Margo's cat, Miaow, from the water when the saucer pilot, dropping the momentum pistol, reaches out and hauls Paul and Miaow aboard the saucer. It is not exactly an abduction; the saucer pilot is a female alien of feline descent. She calls herself Tigerishka, and her interest was in Miaow, whom she assumed to be intelligent, rather than in Paul, the "monkey."

While these events are occurring, Paul's friend and Margo's fiancé, Don Merriam, is flying through the moon. Don, an astronaut, has escaped the quake-wrecked Moonbase U. S. in a Baba Yaga, a small rocket ship. By accident he does not quite achieve escape or orbital velocity, but as the Baba Yaga plunges back down, the moon shatters like a pebble in the gravitational field of the Wanderer. Unable to reverse his course, Don flies between the sundered halves of the moon. Issuing from this prodigious chasm he sees the Wanderer for the first time; he is captured and taken aboard. Later he is taken — or sent — on an odd, rather dreamlike tour of the traveling planet, a brisk survey of structure, crew, and resources that turns into a lesson which Don does not quite understand. Part of the message is clear enough: the sum of all there is and all there may be is very large. Don is shown a series of three-dimensional viewing tanks. In the first he sees our galaxy; in the second, the whole cosmos of which our galaxy is a tiny part. In the third this entire universe, identifiable by its incomprehensibly twisted shape, is represented as one among many universes, all of them appearing to be somewhat hypothetical.

The significance of the last stop on Don's tour is not as obvious to him. In a huge room, designed to resemble a natural planet, Don sees a felinoid (like Tigerishka) chase down and kill a unicorn. He sees a bird with topaz plumage killed and its blood sucked by another felinoid, who smiles at him as she feeds. The killers are strong and graceful.

Don's friend, Paul, would have less difficulty comprehending the scene; he spends two days with Tigerishka in her saucer. Under the influence of her growing sympathy for Paul and prodded by his sometimes pointed questions, Tigerishka eventually tells Paul of the Wanderer's origin and current plight. The planet is a "getaway car" for a cosmic lost generation, sailing the genuine void, hyperspace. Tigerishka's people — many races besides the felinoids — are desperately in flight from the plague of intelligence, the cancer of science, most of all from the ennui that comes when the intelligent application of science has made the cosmos safe for all except the Wild Ones. They run from a social order that envelops stars with artificial planets, whose conservatism is so effective that nearly all the stars are shrouded, their light trapped by the synthetic worlds.

"The universe is full, Paul. Intelligent life is everywhere, its planets darkening the stars, its engineers recklessly spending the power of suns to make mind's environment — burning matter to energy everywhere to make more form, more structure, more mind. The Word — to call mind that — goes forth, and soon there is nothing but the Word. The universe with all its great reaches and magnificent privacies becomes a slum, begins to die of too much mind."

The Wanderer runs for the potential freedom of hyperspace, and the police planets of the universal government pursue. In the end, one of them catches up, the Stranger, much larger than the Wanderer, all steel gray opposed to the Wanderer's flamboyant maroon and gold. A battle ensues; as the Wanderer seems to be losing, it flashes into hyperspace. Moments later the Stranger pursues again, and the incursion of the universe into terrestrial affairs ceases.

Leiber ends the novel flatly, with the touchdown of the Baba Yaga bearing Don and Paul at Vandenberg Two, where Margo and Ross Hunter (who have become lovers), together with the saucer students, have finally arrived. It seems an appropriately inconclusive stopping point; the Wanderer has merely gone on, its quest unresolved, its fate unknown, its only astronomically significant effect on the Earth a tiny lengthening of the sidereal day. In spite of its length, *The Wanderer* has about it somewhat the air of an incident sliced from life and displayed without comment — disaster as found art.

But Leiber has made his judgment of the Wanderer's significance in a characteristically perphrastic manner. Tigerishka's account of the Wanderer and the Wanderer's universe generates emotional tides between herself and Paul Hagbolt. In a welter of unclear but strong emotions, a tangle of loneliness, pity, Weltschmerz, and xenophilia, far and equidistant from Earth and Wanderer, monkey-man and cat-woman make love. Several chapters later, when Tigerishka brusquely refuses to let Paul come with the Wanderer, he asks her what she had felt the night before other than pity and boredom. In reply she slashes his cheek deeply with her claws. Don Merriam, a little dimly, recognizes the paradox: " 'I don't know, Paul, but if I were in love with a cat-lady, that clawing would be the one thing that would convince me she did love me back' "

In the universe of the Wanderer, now shown to be our universe, the intelligence that defines us, by which alone we survive, is also the agency of spiritual death and moral isolation. To live truly, to love genuinely, to encounter others are acts of violence. We must be as intelligent and as beastly as we can be.

Michael W. McClintock

Sources for Further Study

Reviews:

Amazing Stories. XXXVIII, December, 1964, pp. 124-125.

Analog. LXXIV, November, 1964, p. 87.

Library Journal. XCV, May, 1970, p. 1970.

Magazine of Fantasy and Science Fiction. XXVII, August, 1964, pp. 23-24.

New Worlds. CLXXIV, August, 1967, pp. 63-64.

Punch. CCLII, May 10, 1967, p. 697.

SF Commentary. II, March, 1969, p. 25.

Science Fiction Review. XXXIX, August, 1970, pp. 32-33.

Times Literary Supplement. June 15, 1967, p. 543.

THE WANTING SEED

Author: Anthony Burgess (1917-   )
First book publication: 1962
Type of work: Novel
Time: Allegedly the far future
Locale: Greater London, rural England, and the west coast of Ireland

A satirical, pessimistic view of human nature and history, centering on the adventures of a teacher, his wife, and her lover (his brother) during a period of social "revolution"

Principal characters:
> TRISTRAM FOXE, a historiography teacher
> BEATRICE-JOANNA FOXE, Tristram's wife
> DEREK FOXE, Tristram's brother, Beatrice-Joanna's lover, and head of the Population Police
> CAPTAIN LOOSLEY, a member of the Population Police, Derek's enemy

On the surface, *The Wanting Seed* is the story of Beatrice-Joanna Foxe's vacillation between two lovers, her husband Tristram, a historiography teacher, and his brother Derek, an opportunistic government official, in an overpopulated future England during a social and political upheaval. But in fact the love story — which is rather thinly developed and psychologically unconvincing — is an allegorical representation of the historical drama that is the true subject of Burgess' story. This kind of relation is familiar from historical novels: the story of Richard, John, and Ivanhoe, for example, is less a character study than an allegorical representation of the historical compromise between Norman chauvinism and Saxon nationalism. But there is a difference: in the historical novel the allegorical relationship allows the plot to *interpret* history in narrative form; Burgess' novel, on the other hand, does not present an interpretation of a historical moment (as would be the case, for example, if he merely projected overpopulation into the twenty-first century), but presents a theory of history in general.

Giambattista Vico theorized history as a cycle of three ages (theocratic, aristocratic, and democratic) followed by a cataclysm (*ricorso*) after which the cycle begins again. Vico's cycle helps structure Joyce's *Finnegans Wake*, which Burgess abridged for publication in 1967. The cycle that structures history in *The Wanting Seed* is a bit different, but has the same feature of repetition, "a perpetual waltz." Burgess' cycle is structured by an opposition between Augustinianism (the "Gusphase"), during which humanity is conceived as basically flawed (subject to "original sin"), and Pelagianism (the "Pelphase"), characterized by a belief in human perfectibility. The third stage is the Interphase, which effects a violent and chaotic return from Pelagianism to Augustinianism.

Abstractly stated, this polarity seems philosophical or even religious, but as Tristram presents it (in a convenient lecture in the early chapters) it is effectively a question of the social philosophy of the leaders of government, their attitudes towards their people: the Pelphase is "liberal," the Gusphase "conservative." The Pelphase comes to an end when the leaders, disappointed with their subjects' failure to perfect themselves, react with repressive state apparatuses in an attempt to enforce goodness. This opens the Interphase, which lasts until the leaders, disgusted with their own brutal excesses, conclude people cannot even be forced to be good, relax their control, make various more or less cynical compromises, and history begins again. The Gusphase, however, as Tristram's lecture has it (we do not see this part of the process), gradually slips into Pelagianism as the leaders discover the people are better than their new pessimistic philosophy leads them to expect, and a Pelphase, liberal and optimistic, reestablishes itself.

In the future Burgess postulates, population pressure makes the maintenance and allocation of world resources, particularly food, the major problem. The Pelagian response to the population/resources problem is highly processed foods, a Ministry of Infertility (where Derek works), which discourages reproduction and pays parents on the deaths of their children, and a valorization of homosexuality to the extent that Tristram, an avowed heterosexual, is denied promotion in the early chapters, and his brother Derek gets *his* promotion only by keeping his heterosexuality in the closet.

The tone of these early chapters — phrases such as "the soggy motions of inverted love" — are enough to indicate Burgess' displeasure with the Pelagian solution. At the same time we are given some gratuitous praise of the "achievements of the Anglo-Saxon race" coupled with a catalog of Tristram's students' names and racial features, apparently intended as satirical commentary on the evils of miscegenation (all of Burgess' important characters are Anglo-Saxon or Pan-Celtic). Burgess even goes so far as to have Beatrice-Joanna think:

> Ethnic divisions were no longer important; the world was split into language groups. Was it, she thought in an instant almost of prophetic power, to be left to her and the few indisputable Anglo-Saxons like her to restore sanity and dignity to the mongrel world? Her race, she seemed to remember, had done it before.

Lest we miss the point, however, "nature" responds with mysterious blights and plagues that threaten world food supplies; meanwhile people continue unwisely to reproduce, and the Interphase begins when the newly formed Population Police (with Derek at their head) descend like Hitler's SS, and cart off pregnant women and their husbands to the equivalent, presumably, of death camps.

The sympathy between the infertilities of nature and of culture (food shortages and the Ministry) echoes the "primitive" magical world-view popularized for Burgess' generation by T. S. Eliot's *The Waste Land* (*The Wanting Seed* calls Eliot "a long dead singer of infertility") and Sir James G. Frazer's *The*

Golden Bough, which suggests that Beatrice-Joanna's pregnancy is to be read as (symbolic of) the curing of the land. Impregnated on the last day of the Pelphase (apparently by Derek, though she also makes love with Tristram that day), she escapes to her relatives in the country where she gives birth to twins (Tristram and Derek) in a manger, on or near the last day of the Interphase. When this birth occurs, the pig which had been dying recovers, and the chickens begin laying eggs again. The message is clear: fertility and virility are good, and homosexuality is not merely disgusting (as it is to Beatrice-Joanna in the first chapter), but an evil, a sickness which infects not only those who indulge in it but society and even the land itself. Except for the power of the prose, we could be reading Norman Mailer (*An American Dream*).

But there is another current, another theme besides the sexuality theme: with the end of the Interphase comes a reversal of values, orgies in the fields, the emptying of the prisons, the removal of the "In" from the Ministry's sign, and Derek's emergence from the closet (always reflecting official morality). Also at this point, cannibalism begins to appear.

Cannibalism has the salutary effect of helping to clear the police from the roads (though they are naturally disbanded when the Interphase and the politics of infertility end together), but it also claims the children of Beatrice-Joanna's sister who, shortly after the twins are born, are killed and eaten by neighbors. Cannibalism is of course linked in its magical aspects to the fertility myths cited earlier: eating the enemy to gain his strength, eating the king at the end of his reign to insure the continued (or renewed) productivity of the land. Here it serves as well the more practical purpose of controlling population and feeding the remainder, but to do so it goes through some rather strange twists, even for this story.

Beginning in isolated incidents, cannibalism becomes socialized in eating clubs (who catch and kill their food, roasting it on open fires), then in restaurants, and finally in cans. But it is the process of production of this canned human meat ("bully") that is most interesting. Towards what Tristram sees as the end of the Gusphase, war is reintroduced, but it is a strange war that seems to have been learned from books, and is fought not with missiles and push-buttons, but with "conventional weapons" — bullets and hand-to-hand combat. Its battles are in fact staged, and are designed to give the men and women who die in them the illusion they are dying for a cause: their real function is food supply. After the battles, which no one (except, of course, Tristram) survives, the dead are turned over to independent contractors for canning. The "War Office" which runs these battles is itself a private business, a caricature of the "military-industrial complex" that President Eisenhower described a few years before Burgess' book was written.

Thus it would seem that, even could one choose (but one cannot, in Burgess' world — history keeps its own schedule), the choice between the Pelphase and the Gusphase would be merely a choice between evils: an effete, decadent, homosexualized infertility or a lusty, brutal, inhumane cannibalism. The parity between cannibalism and fertility implies an economy of scarcity, reinforcing the pessimistic ("Augustinian") world-view of the doctrine of the cycle.

In the last analysis, however, *The Wanting Seed* seems not to be about history at all. Even granting the catalytic effect of population pressure, its historiography is not only depressing, sexist, and racist, but also unconvincing; its phases are both too short and too profound. On the one hand we are asked to believe that the cycle goes through two-thirds of its phases in less than two years, and on the other hand, that the Gusphase reintroduces not only cannibalism and orgies in the fields, but also the rebirth of tragedy (Tristram, searching the Gusphase for his wife, sees a comedy and expects, "soon men would be dressing up as goats and presenting the first neo-tragedy") and the genesis of morals.

Science fiction, to function as such, must be "realistic": it must, with the appropriate suspension of disbelief, be convincing, the characters psychologically believable, the plot logically constructed. But Burgess' story resembles Voltaire's *Candide* more than it does *Nineteen Eighty-Four*: it is not really science fiction at all but a philosophical tale with a nominally futuristic setting, whose plot is, like *Candide*'s, designed to combine, in a single, more or less continuous narrative, a number of exemplary situations. The parallels go further: Tristram's induction into the army parallels Candide's impressment into the Prussian army, and both books end with a catch phrase: "We must cultivate our gardens" (*Candide*), and "We must try to live" (*The Wanting Seed*).

The historical sequence of Pelphase, Interphase, and Gusphase, then, rather than being presented as an historical theory, gives Burgess the opportunity for satirical portraits, not of his characters, but of the 1960's welfare state, a kind of fascist-terroristic anarchy, and capitalist war economy, respectively. If Beatrice-Joanna is a kind of earth-mother figure, registering in and through her body the health and fertility of the land, Derek and Tristram are ruler and ruled, or better, functionary and expendable, respectively. Derek's career is one of rising through adaptation: in the Pelphase he is a promising young bureaucrat who maintains a homosexual public image but visits Beatrice-Joanna in the afternoons. In the Interphase he forgoes even these secret amours to protect his position as head of the Population Police. But by the time his twins are born and his enemy Captain Loosley has found them and brought them to London, sexual mores have reversed, and Derek comes out of the closet to live with Beatrice-Joanna and the twins, who are now proof of his virility.

Tristram, however, is always marginal, a man who is too straightforward and knows too much for his own good. As an intellectual, Tristram, like Nietzsche's slave, is the only one who seems to understand what is going on:

in the Pelphase he is a teacher whose students do not understand him; in the Interphase he is put in prison, partly by chance, but kept there because he knows his brother's secret; in the Gusphase he is impressed into the Army, where he is used as an instructor until his knowledge of historical theory leads him to question the reality of the war, at which time he is sent off to die in battle. He survives all these trials and can perhaps be excused for preferring the Pelphase, since at its approach in the last chapter he becomes a teacher again and even regains his wife. But, as we are reminded by the repetition and by the title of the book, the society which treats its intellectuals even this well is effete, decadent, infertile, and on the way out.

Richard Astle

Sources for Further Study

Criticism:

Brutenhuis, Peter. "A Battle Between the Sexes Was the Answer," in *New York Times Book Review*. October 27, 1963, p. 4. *The Wanting Seed* is revealed to be a counter-Utopian novel."

Dempsey, David. "Fe, Fi, Fo, Fum, *The Wanting Seed*," in *Saturday Review*. Vol. 46, p. 43, November 23, 1963. Compared with Burgess's *Clockwork Orange*, Dempsey feels *The Wanting Seed* presents the reader with no unusual problems in the style of writing or the scheme of the story. Although the plot is pessimistic, he feels Burgess wit is very enjoyable.

Reviews:

Best Sellers. XXIII, November 1, 1963, p. 277.

Book Week. November 3, 1963, p. 6.

Commonweal. LXXIX, January 17, 1964, p. 465.

Library Journal. LXXXVIII, October 1, 1963, p. 3641.

New Statesman. LXIV, October 5, 1962, p. 370.

Newsweek. LXII, October 28, 1963, p. 101.

Time. LXXXII, December 6, 1963, p. 123.

Times Literary Supplement. October 5, 1962, p. 773.

THE WAR IN THE AIR

Author: H. G. Wells (1866-1946)
First book publication: 1908
Type of work: Novel
Time: The early twentieth century
Locale: Bun Hill, near London; an aircraft park in Germany; Niagara Falls

 The simultaneous development of military aircraft by Germany, Britain, America,
and the Asiatic powers leads to conflicts which culminate in the collapse of civilization

> *Principal characters:*
> BERT SMALLWAYS, a lower-class Englishman
> PRINCE KARL ALBERT, an aristocratic German warlord
> ALFRED BUTTERIDGE, an inventor
> GRUBB, Bert's partner in the bicycle-repair business

The War in the Air was written in 1907 and began to appear as a serial in the *Pall Mall Magazine* in January, 1908. In a Preface written in 1921, Wells reminded his readers that though things had not turned out exactly as he had prophesied, nevertheless he had been writing before M. Bleriot, for instance, flew the English Channel (July, 1909), and while Zeppelin airships were still in their infancy. In 1921 Wells did not need to remind anyone that though there had not been a "War in the Air," nevertheless there had been a war that seemed to many to herald the collapse of civilization, and that it had been fought to a quite unexpected extent by fighter and bomber aeroplanes. The story had *gained* a kind of topicality rather than losing it. In 1941 Wells wrote another Preface to the book, very much shorter, but insisting even more on the immediate applicability of *The War in the Air*. "My epitaph when I die," he declared, "will manifestly have to be: 'I told you so. You *damned* fools.'" There is no doubt about the claims Wells made for this book: he thought it was, in outline if not in detail, an accurate prophecy of the twentieth century future, whose apocalyptic content was far more significant than its style or its story.

This claim has approached and then receded again from credibility several times in the last seventy years, and no doubt will continue to do so. At present, it does not look strong. Civilization has not collapsed (even in Russia); a "deterrent" strategy which Wells did not conceive of has worked rather well for over thirty years; people have been less foolish than Wells thought. On the other hand, atrocities have been committed by civilized nations, a fact which Wells himself would hardly have credited. Strategic bomber offensives have been tried again and again; and the story is not yet over. To a survivor of nuclear war, huddled in a ruined library, *The War in the Air* might yet seem the truest, most significant book in the whole of literature (along with Nevil Shute's *On the Beach*). Even if that catastrophe did *not* happen, one could always argue that it might have been more likely to happen if some soldier or politician somewhere had not had his imagination stirred (and sickened) by visions such as Wells's. Books of this nature are not really prophecies, but warnings: the better they are heeded, the better they work. Thus, evaluation of them is not simply a matter of commenting on their hits and misses.

Still his concepts arrest our attention. One can say straight away that Wells's images of aircraft were quite false: Mr. Butteridge's wasplike machine, with its curved "wing-cases," the Asiatic flier with its *flapping* wings, the German *drachenflieger* or "dragonfly" — all these perpetuate the age-old error that the way to fly is to imitate birds or insects, while ignoring the fact (already known even in 1907) that the critical matters simply are airflow and power. Wells was right about airships, but he underestimated their dreadful vulnerability when filled with flammable hydrogen. A keen cyclist himself (and a firm believer in the utility of bicycle-troops), Wells wanted airplanes to look like motorbikes.

On other matters, Wells was inordinately prophetic. He was right, for instance, about the vital importance of the internal combustion engine, or as he called it, the "explosive" engine. He was also unexpectedly right about the unimportance of invention and Great Inventors.

A familiar concept in science fiction is "steamboat time": when it's "steamboat time" (that is, when all the supporting industrial bases are established), people build steamboats. If one man misses the chance, someone else will take it; or several people will make the invention simultaneously. Events involving aircraft happened this way both in reality and in Wells's novel. Many nations independently had developed airforces by 1914 in exactly the same way the U.S.S.R. developed an atomic bomb within four years of the American one, and a hydrogen bomb quicker still. Although this syndrome has always been mysterious to many politicians and voters who have remained fixated on the individualistic images of the Genius, the Formula, the Traitor, or the Spy, Wells had already seen further than that in 1907. Alfred Butteridge, whose flying-machine is the best in the world in Wells's story, nevertheless, does not affect history. Too many other people are nearly as good. He, in any case, may have stolen the ideas rather than invented them. Bert Smallways, with his limited education, can understand the plans and even, in a minor way, put them into practice. Although it is centered on technical development, *The War in the Air* is paradoxically correct in its low estimate of the difficulty of making things and in its high estimate of the problems of adapting to them.

The War in the Air, indeed, is filled with curious juxtapositions of a kind with which we have become depressingly familiar. The Asiatic fliers at Niagara Falls carry two-handed swords as well as firearms; World War II gave the English language words like *samurai, harakiri, kamikaze*. The German airship crews are cheerful, good-tempered family men who kill women and children by the thousands; probably all of us know, live near, are related to someone who has done the same. Over New York, Prince Karl Albert realizes that although he can destroy whole cities by aerial bombardment, he cannot occupy the ground without infantry soldiers (military commanders have felt the same frustration right up to the time of the Vietnam War). What these juxtapositions suggest is that the moral sense of mankind has not developed as fast as his technological powers. Now, almost everyone would agree with that, and it takes an effort of the imagination to realize that our great-grandfathers on the whole thought that mankind was still evolving upwards. Although one can give Wells credit for this check on Edwardian complacency, the moral-technological comparison still points to one of the weaker parts of the novel: an uncertainty compensated by stridency.

Wells, though quite sure that something was wrong with the world, did not know quite what. Bert Smallways' portrait as a representative of the "Anglo-Saxon" world (that is, Britain and America) is often unerringly and unsparingly accurate in its speech and gestures. Stranded in the air by accident a couple of miles up in Mr. Butteridge's balloon, Bert looks around, sees two dangling cords, and quite naturally pulls them. It is his good fortune that nothing happens, for one of them is the ripcord which, had it not been fouled, would have slashed the canopy open and sent him into eternity at several thousand feet per second. Then as he stands beneath a hydrogen-filled balloon, he looks for matches to have a smoke, and grumbles when he cannot find any. The blend of dependence, ingratitude, irresponsibility, and, most of all, false personal confidence rings true both in detail and as a principle. Irresponsibility, indeed, is Wells's recurrent theme — applied to the press, to inflammatory nationalism, and to the voting public as a whole. The last words of the book are given to Bert's brother, Tom, who observes "it didn't ought ever to 'ave begun," and sets up a comment from the narrator that "somebody somewhere ought to have stopped it, but who or how or why were all beyond his ken." The comment is sarcastic. Tom ought to realize that he and his brother Bert were responsible too; there is an irony in all that Tom has failed to learn. Still, the last words are appropriate in ways other than those intended. Did Wells really know any better than Tom?

Although Wells is clear and persuasive as a satirist, he has little positive to say in the book. He suggests that if armament money had been spent on education instead, every Bert Smallways in Britain would have been a "broad-chested and intelligent man." This seems unlikely. Elsewhere, he decides that the real reason for the outbreak of war was technological, the German development of the "Pforzheim engine." But he also says that it was personal, that the romantic warlord figure of Prince Karl Albert "made the war." Last, he hovers over economic causes. Which of these is strongest? Wells remains unsure. As for the collapse of civilization itself, Wells offers as reasons: the European underestimation of Asiatic prowess; the strategy of mutual destruction created by airpower; the collapse of international credit; and finally, the Purple Plague — a plot-device with which there is no arguing, since it is inexplicable. One feels that Wells was no longer picking his targets. The feeling is reinforced by clear inconsistencies in the narrative strategy. At the end of the book we learn that the narrator is a future historian writing from the perspective of a scientific worldstate (the kind of thing for which Wells preached and argued with increasingly little effect throughout his life). Much of the time, though, he seems to be a twentieth century atheist being sarcastic about God, or a middleclass Englishman sneering at the habits of those socially beneath him. The enormous scale on which *The War in the Air* is constructed demands, in short, a superhuman ability both to analyze history and to detach oneself from it, and Wells does not have it. The book is inevitably imperfect in its offering to do too much.

Three things, however, raise *The War in the Air* above the status of "forgotten bestseller" and give it permanent worth. One is the unexpected coordinate development of comedy with catastrophe. Bert Smallways is nearly always funny, even when he is pathetic, and yet he never entirely loses our sympathy; he is a proto-Chaplin, of sorts. The second is its demonstration that a novel can work perfectly well *without* strongly individualized characters. After all, people's quirks are interesting only if we find their more obvious features dully predictable, and Wells has remained unsurpassed at showing how much of what we take for granted is actually wildly improbable. In this way, "Bert Smallways" looks forward to many a modern "Everyman" such as Orwell's Winston Smith. The third, perhaps more debatable point, comes to mind as one reads of Bert trapped on Goat Island above Niagara Falls, creating a queasy close-up acquaintance with death and violence. Both his terror of loneliness and his inability even to make a "social contract" with Prince Karl Albert suggest the beginning of a moral *de*volution back to the status of savage or animal. This hint outweighs Wells's contrived happy ending and directly relates *The War in the Air*'s philosophy to such widely praised works as Joseph Conrad's *Heart of Darkness*, or T. S. Eliot's *The Waste Land*.

T. A. Shippey

Sources for Further Study

Reviews:
Atheneum. II, November 14, 1908, p. 602.
Independent. LXV, November 19, 1908, p. 1183.
New York Times. XIII, November 14, 1908, p. 668.
Saturday Review. CVI, November 14, 1908, p. 614.

WAR OF THE WING-MEN

Author: Poul Anderson (1926-   )
First book publication: 1958
Type of work: Novel
Time: 2426
Locale: The planet Diomedes, a hundred light-years from Earth

Shipwrecked far from the nearest human settlement on an aberrant planet, three people must find a way to survive both natural dangers and a war between two groups of nonhuman indigens

Principal characters:
NICHOLAS VAN RIJN, head of Solar Spice & Liquors
LADY SANDRA TAMARIN, heiress to the rule of the planet Hermes
ERIC WACE, factor for Solar Spice & Liquors on the planet Diomedes
SYRANAX HYR URNAN, Commander of the Fleet of Drak'ho
DELP HYR ORIKAN, his Chief Executive Officer
THEONAX HYR URNAN, son of the Commander
TROLWEN, Commander of the Flock

The adventure on a strange planet, one of the primary conventional science fiction forms, attracts both readers and writers by the freedom it appears to offer from terrestrial history, geography, and, perhaps, natural laws. But the poetic license for the maker of imaginary worlds is usually qualified by various constraints, some of which may be self-imposed by the writer. One constraint may be the sort of relation the other world bears to our own. Strangeness of certain kinds, as in the Barsoom of Edgar Rice Burroughs or the Perelandra of C. S. Lewis, displaces the work toward fantasy. Pretended but inauthentic strangeness, which cannot be exemplified here because the many works displaying it are justly ignored or forgotten, shows the other world to be merely Earth under an assumed name. Another sort of constraint may be the use to which the invented world is put. None of the planets in Isaac Asimov's Foundation trilogy is very exotic because none need be much more than an undistracting background for conversations or disputes among the characters, all of whom are human.

During Poul Anderson's long career as a science fiction writer, one of his most impressive talents has been for the creation of plausibly alien worlds. Although these inventions are based upon conventional astrophysics (and generally accepted biology, when the worlds bear life), none of the dozen or so planets whose features are crucial to plots or themes could ever be confused with Earth, nor could certain events for which they are the settings occur in terrestrial environments. In some of Anderson's fiction, these worlds are employed as devices to energize plots, as pirate gold energizes *Treasure Island*. Sometimes, too, the story seems to be mainly a vehicle for the depiction of an interesting, if hypothetical, cosmic specimen. But in *War of the Wing-Men*, Anderson's concern is the interaction of character and situation;

the plot of the novel is, essentially, the resolution of the confrontation between Nicholas van Rijn and the planet Diomedes.

Anderson devises somewhat artificial circumstances to make Diomedes a problem that van Rijn and his companions must solve if they are to survive. Returning from Antares to Earth, van Rijn and Lady Sandra Tamarin have stopped for a brief tour of some interesting Diomedean scenery. Eric Wace, trading factor on the planet for van Rijn's company, Solar Spice & Liquors, begins to fly them to one of the sites, but a bomb disables the aircraft, which crashes at sea. (The bomb may have been directed against van Rijn by a business rival or against Lady Sandra by a political rival; in either case, it is only a plot device.) The three survivors are ten thousand kilometers from the human settlement, with no way to cross the sea or to send a message for help. Their plight is aggravated by the fact that Diomedean life is based on proteins different from the earthly kinds; humans are, in a sense, allergic to the planet. The only food the three castaways have is what they can salvage from the wreck.

The divergence of biological evolution is unlucky, but it can hardly be unexpected. Diomedes, however, is a freak among planets, freakish in its composition, freakish in its movements. Its axial tilt of almost ninety degrees consigns each of its poles to half a year of darkness and appalling cold; its habitable regions extend only about forty-five degrees north or south of the equator. Its makeup is even less normal than its motion. Because of some oddity in the processes of its formation, Diomedes contains almost no elements heavier than calcium. Thus, although it has nearly five times the mass and over twice the diameter of Earth, its density is only half our planet's, and its surface gravity is only ten per cent stronger. But since the mass of Diomedes determines its gravitational potential, its atmosphere is much deeper and thicker than Earth's, thick enough to support true flying mammals, including some, the dominant species, almost as big and fully as intelligent as human beings.

The cultures of these intelligent Diomedeans have been shaped by the conditions of their planet. It is not a world that favors the development of an advanced technology. Light metals are abundant, but the Diomedeans have no way to exploit them; an electrolytic technology is a prerequisite for refining aluminum or magnesium, and copper or silver — much heavier than calcium — is a prerequisite for an electrolytic technology. The Diomedeans are fixed in an endless stone age.

Two groups of these indigens constitute the remaining element of the survival problem for the humans. The location of the crash is near the area where the land-based Lannachska and the seagoing Drak'honai are embattled. The Lannachska, like most Diomedean tribal groups, are migratory, spending the summers hunting at thirty or forty degrees latitude, flying to the equator for the winter to meet other groups and trade a little, and, chiefly, to mate. The Drak'honai live always on their rafts and boats. Since they have established permanent and continuous, if unfixed, homes, they have been able to develop a somewhat more sophisticated culture than the Lannachska, but the most profound difference between the groups is that the Drak'honai have no seasonal breeding cycle. Each "race" feels that the other is perverted and repugnant — indeed, utterly alien. They are at war because the Drak'honai, following a shift in the habits of the fish that is the staple of their diet, have invaded the sea near the Lannachska's summer home island. When the Lannachska returned from their annual migration, the Drak'honai, anxious for a secure port and detesting the cyclic breeders anyway, were already in possession of the Lannachska towns. For each group, defeat by the other means virtual extinction, and neither can divert any effort from the way to dispatch messengers on a long, dangerous mission for the succor of the humans. Thus Anderson has arranged a three-way struggle for survival, with the human case appearing the bleakest of the lot.

The character and abilities of Nicholas van Rijn provide the satisfactory resolution of the problem. When the novel was published as a serial in *Astounding Science Fiction* (and, later, when it was included in the interrelated collection *The Earth Book of Stormgate*), it was entitled *The Man Who Counts*. Its more familiar title emphasizes the main action of the plot, but the original title, the one Anderson preferred, emphasizes the organizing theme. The war is distinctly subsidiary to the survival effort; van Rijn manages to convert it into the means for saving himself and his companions.

Overtly, van Rijn seems ill-suited to deal with the situation. He is a huge man, tall and broad-shouldered as well as broad-bellied, and his manner is not one to instill confidence in his leadership or his capacity to meet physical dangers. As much gourmand as gourmet, drinker, smoker, wencher, and general sybarite, he honors St. Dismas, patron of thieves, and his entrepreneurial tactics are tempered only by his belief that making enemies needlessly is bad for business. His language is colorful, heavily flavored with tangled metaphors, *mal mots*, and distorted syntax; his dress is flamboyant but seldom neat; he appears heedless of details and method. Eric Wace grows more and more to regard him as a lazy, boorish, bossy, and selfish parasite. But the plot makes it plain (and Lady Sandra, spelling it out, finally, for Wace, spells it out also for the readers who have been along for the action) that van Rijn is the man who counts. From the time of the crash he labors unremittingly, though not always obviously, for survival, and he is able to turn even some of the least apparently tractable elements of the desperate situation effectively to his own purposes.

To emphasize his implicit argument that the most important survival skills may not be the most obvious ones, Anderson employs for most of the novel the obtuse viewpoint of earnest, efficient, competent, and unimaginative Eric Wace. In many respects, Wace is the character whom convention would expect to save the day. He is courageous and skillful; he designs and supervises the construction of the equipment and van Rijn offhandedly demands. He is clearly aware of what he accomplishes himself, since his efforts produce immediate and tangible results, but he cannot see that van Rijn accomplishes anything of substance. He resents van Rijn's brusque and generalized orders; he resents even more his appetite for the rapidly diminishing supply of terrestrial foodstuffs. Until the adventure is safely concluded and Lady Sandra takes an opportunity to enlighten him, he does not understand that van Rijn is both organizer and motivator of all that has been achieved. As van Rijn puts it, " 'My job is not to do what is impossible, it is to make others do it for me!' "

Van Rijn's basic method is an *ad hoc* pragmatism, to use whatever is available, to do whatever works. The most ingenious examples of his tactics are also the crucial events of the plot. For instance, near the beginning of the novel, the Drak'honai, wondering if the humans may be useful in the war, rescue them from the foundering skycruiser. Van Rijn soon realizes that because the Drak'honai already enjoy a strategic advantage, he and his companions will be more valuable to the desperate Lannachska. A Lannach herald and interpreter, Tolk, will carry a message to his commander if some way can be found for him to escape the Drak'ho fleet. Exploiting rivalries and class tensions among the Drak'ho officers, van Rijn sets off a minor civil war to cover Tolk's flight.

Later, using tactics and weapons suggested by van Rijn and developed by Wace, the Lannachska manage an uneasy stalemate with the Drak'honai. The two forces are so evenly matched that neither can overwhelm the other. But the Lannachska need soon to begin their preparations for the autumnal migration to the equator, and the Drak'honai still need fishing grounds. A climactic battle would be irreparably damaging even to the victors and would leave the humans still stranded and starving. Van Rijn's first move is to show, by logical deduction, that Lannachska and Drak'honai are members of a single race. He convinces nearly all the leaders of both groups that the different breeding patterns are cultural adaptations, not racial divergences. Only the irrational and fanatic Drak'honai admiral remains unpersuaded, continuing to insist that the Lannachska must be obliterated. His position is crucial because the rigidly hierarchical Fleet will obey him even if they doubt his wisdom. Van Rijn's last and triumphant ploy is to insult the admiral profoundly by suggesting that he harbors a repressed desire to sample Lannach forms of sexuality. Outraged to frenzy, the admiral, with the reflex of a carnivore, bites van Rijn on the buttock. A few minutes later, the Diomedean dies of a massive allergic reaction to the alien flesh. The admiral's successor then agrees to a peaceful compromise with the Lannachska, and the former enemies send a joint embassy with a message to the distant human settlement. Van Rijn, Wace, and Lady Sandra are saved.

Anderson makes no claim to major significance in *War of the Wing-Men*, but its interest is genuine and substantial. Diomedes figures effectively as an exemplum of the challenges a complex universe may pose, and Nicholas van

Rijn is a cogent exemplar of intelligent response. The novel is reassuring but not comfortable: a world that demands a van Rijn to equiponderate it is not a world made for man, however successfully some men may live in it.

Michael W. McClintock

THE WAR OF THE WORLDS

Author: H. G. Wells (1866-1946)
First book publication: 1898
Type of work: Novel
Time: The early twentieth century
Locale: Woking (West Surrey), London and environs

Seeking a refuge from their dying planet, Martians invade and conquer a helpless Earth, only to be destroyed by a bacteria for which their systems are unprepared

Principal characters:
THE NARRATOR
HIS YOUNGER BROTHER, a London medical student
THE CURATE, a nearly hysterical clergyman who shares the Narrator's hiding place
THE ARTILLERYMAN, a surviving soldier who vows to restore human supremacy
THE MARTIANS, invaders and would-be conquerors from a dying planet

In *The War of the Worlds*, H. G. Wells's fourth "scientific romance," he fixed the image of the hostile alien invader in both the science fiction genre and in the popular mind. When Orson Welles adapted the novel to radio for his famous 1938 Halloween prank, the resulting chaos gave Wells's tentacled Martians, their Heat Ray, their giant tripod vehicles, and their black poison gas the status of modern myth. Every Bug-Eyed-Monster, giant insect swarm, activated primordial beast, and extraterrestrial invader that had dominated the screen, the comic strips, the Big Little Books, the pulps, and the less sophisticated science fiction publications of the 1930's, 1940's, and 1950's, paid dubious homage to Wells's doomed Martian monsters.

However, as is frequently the case when a book has such a thorough and enduring influence, the original has been distorted and lost behind the images and popularizations it spawned. While in simple summary *The War of the Worlds* may resemble many of its trite, simplistic offsprings, it is actually a forceful, sophisticated novel that remains original, intense, and provocative today.

Because of the enduring power of its images and influence, it is easy to forget the extent to which *The War of the Worlds* was a product of its own time and culture. The notion of the collapse of moral order and the general dissolution of society and culture was a generally pervasive one in that *fin de siècle* period. The more particular idea of an invasion from the Continent was likewise common, and had generated its own body of writings with which Wells was familiar. Indeed, it is possible to see *The War of the Worlds* as a variation on the "imaginary future wars" novel — the most notable example of which is George Chesney's *The Battle of Dorking*, 1871, in which Martians replace the Germans or French.

Nor was the identification of Martians as the probable alien invaders an unlikely one in the 1890's. Initially stimulated by Schiaparelli's "discovery" in 1877 of the Martian "canals," public speculation about the possibility of intelligent life on Mars grew into what one newspaper labeled the "Great Mars Boom." The notion of an advanced civilization on Mars peaked with the publication in 1892 of Camille Flammarion's *La Planete Mars*, as well as the books written by United States astronomer Percy Lowell in the middle of the decade.

Wells's own interest in Mars considerably predated the "boom." From his early college days onward, Wells had puzzled about the possibility of life on Mars, and his early writings contain several references to it, notably an early lecture entitled "Are the Planets Habitable" (1888) and a later article, "Intelligence on Mars" (1896). The particular inspiration for a Martian invasion came, however, from his brother Frank, to whom the book is dedicated. As Wells recorded in his *Autobiography* (1920), "We were walking together through some particularly peaceful Surrey scenery. 'Suppose some beings from another planet were to drop out of the sky suddenly' said he [Frank] 'and began laying about them here!'"

His brother's idea was a natural. Wells knew the countryside well, and he carefully orchestrated the details of his novel to particular sites. As he said in a letter quoted in Bernard Bergonzi's *The Early H. G. Wells:*

> I completely wreck and destroy Woking — killing my neighbors in painful and eccentric ways — then proceed via Kingston and Richmond to London, which I sack, selecting South Kensington for feats of particular atrocity.

The apparent, almost loving glee Wells took in unleashing such fictional carnage on his neighbors probably came from his satisfaction in attacking the complacency and arrogance of the late Victorian bourgeoisie, in terms of their narrow social awareness, their petty materialism, and their false cosmic security.

Yet, for all of its turn-of-the-century topicality, *The War of the Worlds* is an enduring work of art. In focusing many of the preoccupations of his own day, Wells succeeded in creating a modern myth of compelling and sustaining power. When Orson Welles and Howard Koch adapted it, they naturally altered the novel to suit the new medium, times, and geography, but the degree to which they remained faithful to the original is surprising. The images, situations, and themes that panicked the American listeners came from the original, sharpened and given a dramatic immediacy in the 1938 radio copy.

Wells divides the novel into two neatly labeled books, "The Coming of the Martians," which chronicles the landing, emergence, and takeover by the Martians, and "The Earth Under the Martians," which examines postholocaust reactions to and implications of the invasion, depicts the death of the Martians from unseen biological causes, and, finally, describes humanity's efforts to return to normality.

Unlike the protagonist of most of Wells's other writings, the narrator of this novel is almost totally passive. His only act, the killing of the hysterical curate, is a desperate gesture of self-preservation. He simply reports, dryly, with a faint irony at times, the evolving situation as he observes it. He is a bit more sensitive and thoughtful than his neighbors, but no more able to affect events than they. And that, of course, is the point; no human agency can affect the course of events. Much of the power of the novel comes from this sense that mankind — even the Martians, for that matter — are being swept along by forces they cannot even see, much less understand and deal with.

Unlike the radio version of the story, in which the threat is perceived almost immediately and military defenses — albeit inadequate ones — set up at once, in Wells's original, the civic reaction (to the extent that there is a reaction at all) is casual, a combination of curiosity and mild concern. The populace seems to doubt even the possibility that anything really unusual could come into their environment, or, in the unlikely event that it did happen and that the intruders turned out to be hostile, that they could quickly and easily be contained by the local militia. Even after the Martians have unleashed the first of their hideous weapons and destroyed all within viewing distance, people are only mildly interested. As the Narrator's neighbor muses to him in the midst of gardening: "It's a pity they make themselves so unapproachable. . . . It would be curious to know how they live on another planet; we might learn a thing or two."

This combination of apathy and cockiness gives Wells's book some of its most memorable qualities: the bitter irony of seeing the trivial overwhelmed by the awful, the growing sense of horror and helplessness that slowly, painfully takes over, and the sudden frenzy that sets in once the situation is fully understood. Particularly successful is Wells's careful pacing, and his handling of the moment-to-moment details of the invasion.

Obvious incongruities in this swift transition from complacency to panic are almost humorous. "The respectable inhabitants of the place, men in golf and boating costumes, wives prettily dressed, were packing, riverside loafers energetically helping, children excited, and, for the most part, highly delighted at this astonishing variation of their Sunday experiences." It is with such careful choice of detail, rather than by attempting to describe large numbers of frenzied people, that Wells is able to present convincingly this "liquefaction of the social fabric."

Overwhelmed by the panic, buffetted by the crowds, dazed by collapse of all resistance, and narrowly escaping death himself, the Narrator finally finds himself trapped in a house on the edge of one of the pits containing a Martian space vehicle. At this point, Wells shifts the book's point of view to the narrator's younger brother, a medical student in London. The shift is structurally awkward, but understandable. Having documented the launching of the Martian attack, Wells needs to show its climax in London, but there is no way he can believably transport his disheveled Narrator to the action. Moreover, the Narrator is too slow and passive to act as a convincing focus for the more dramatic action that takes place in London. The younger brother is a more positive character; he even exhibits some Victorian gallantry in rescuing a pair of ladies from the crowd. But the Londoners as a whole are neither courageous nor effective against the devastating Martians.

> . . . this was no disciplined march; it was a stampede — a stampede gigantic and terrible — without order and without a goal, six million people, unarmed and unprovisioned, driving headlong. It was the beginning of the rout of civilization, of the massacre of mankind.

In the second half of the book, the rhetorical Wells, who was to do such damage to the later books, takes over, although not so intrusively as to hurt the novel. Indeed, after the intensity of the destruction scenes, the talk comes as a welcome respite and the ideas do, ultimately, reinforce the implications made by the actions of the book. In the course of his wanderings, the Narrator encounters two neatly labeled characters, the Curate and the Artilleryman, who embody two basic reactions to and attitudes about the holocaust.

The Curate most obviously represents the collapse of the old order and, more centrally, its values and belief systems. Since the Curate's behavior borders on hysteria, Wells's satiric thrust is almost too broad to be taken seriously. The Curate simply deflates, along with his doctrines, into a gibbering, trembling wreck; he views the Martians as a divine judgment. When the Curate's near insanity threatens to expose them to the Martians, the Narrator, in his only aggressive action of the novel, kills him.

The Artilleryman, whom the Narrator meets as he wanders back toward Leatherbend in hopes of finding his wife, is a more complex figure with a more ambiguous message. The Narrator had met him previously, in a thoroughly demoralized state, immediately after the initial Martian attack. By this second meeting, however, the Artilleryman has apparently mastered his feelings and developed a new sense of resolution. He presents the Narrator with a coherent and comprehensive analysis of the Martian strategy and then offers his own blueprint for the survival — and eventual return to supremacy — of the human race. In his view, the Martians "haven't begun on us yet." He describes the manner in which the Martians will catch and cage humans for food, amusement, and pets, and he envisions an alien-dominated world in which human beings, relegated to a subspecies, will actually come to enjoy their lot: "The Martians will just be a godsend to them. Nice roomy cages, fattening food, careful breeding, no worry."

Evident in the Artilleryman's speech is his contempt for most of his fellow creatures and their usual activities: "There won't be any more blessed concerts for a million years or so; there won't be any Royal Academy of arts, and no nice little feeds at restaurants." To him, the invasion has become an experiment in survival of the fittest, and he has cast himself for leadership among the fittest. Ultimately, he believes that the strongest men will be able to capture the Martian machines and turn them against their inventors; he revels in the potential carnage.

The Narrator is carried away by the logic and intensity of the Artilleryman's vision until he examines the man's actual condition more closely. The Narrator looks at the burrow he had been digging for ten days as the first step in his plan: "such a hole I could have dug in a day." He watches the would-be leader lounging about and gorging himself on leftover luxury items. Finding himself drifting into the easy complacency of immediate pleasures, reinforced by dreams of future omnipotence, the Narrator leaves saddened and annoyed at himself for falling into such an easy emotional trap.

Thus, the primary reason that Wells's rhetoric does not damage the fabric of this parable is that he carefully undercuts what the characters say by what they do, thereby ironically qualifying the elitest theories of his would-be hero. Yet, the ideas the Artilleryman promulgates are not actually refuted and were to persist and grow in Wells's subsequent writings. Indeed, the idea of an elite of highly disciplined, morally, intellectually, and aesthetically superior men as the only salvation from the progressive chaos of the twentieth century was to become one of his primary convictions qualified by the deft ironies present in this work.

Disillusioned by his experience with the Artilleryman and still hopeful of somehow finding his wife, the Narrator wanders in the direction of London. He encounters no more people, but he does notice some odd things: the red weedlike plant that had come with the Martians is dying off; he sees a dog run by with a chunk of black meat in his mouth; and, he hears the frightening cry: "Ulla, ulla, ulla, ulla." Finally, upon entering London, he comes upon a group of stilled war machines, and, beyond them the dead bodies of Martians who have died of unaccustomed bacteria. This quick, neat dispatching of the Martians by convenient germs comes with shocking suddenness and produces a feeling of contrivance. Can this conclusion be justified in literary and thematic terms? Dramatic intensity and effectiveness of the storytelling notwithstanding, a final value judgment of the novel probably depends on the validity of this ending, and any proper analysis of the fate of the aliens requires, first of all, a more careful analysis of their nature and history.

On the first pages of the novel, the Martians are described as having "minds to our minds as ours to those of the beasts that perish, vast intellects vast and cool and unsympathetic. . . ," but the first thing about them that impresses the reader is not their intellect, but their physical appearance. The creature is a monster, a primordial thing with qualities both of land beast and sea monster. This view is reinforced when the narrator watches it feed. Lacking digestive organs, it drinks blook directly from its living human victims — it is not only a beast, but a vampire as well. Thus, while the reader understands that it is the mind of the Martian that is to be feared, he is subjectively repulsed by its bestial physical qualities.

Roughly speaking, there are three images of the alien invader that provoke fear in the reader (leaving aside the more contemporary benign invaders who want only to help, study, commune with, or merely puzzle us). First is the picture of the bestial invader — B.E.M.'s of all sorts, giant insects, Cthulhu-like primordials, dragons, blobs, and the like — everything that touches our innate fears of animals and insects. Second is the mechanical invader image of creatures who come with machines to render us impotent and to beat us at our own game, technological superiority. The third image is that of the interior invader, the alien, usually unseen, who takes us over before we know it, who is so much like us that we cannot usually see it, much less deal with it. Wells utilizes elements of all three images but most obviously the first two.

Although the Martians appear bestial, they are relatively helpless. The greater gravity of earth renders them almost immobile, and early in the novel the Narrator almost pities them for their physical infirmities. It is only when they utilize machinery that they become invulnerable. "Yet though they wore no clothing, it was in the other artificial additions to their bodily resources that their great superiority over man lay." From their glistening cone-shaped metal rockets they burn up spectators with a Heat Ray. Once settled, they enter gleaming metal tripods and stalk about the countryside raising havoc and releasing poison gas. There are hints that they are beginning to launch flying machines. Thus, the second fear, that their machines will destroy us (a fear which extends also to machines of our own making), has emerged forcefully by the middle of the book.

On the surface, the third kind of fear, the fear provoked by the idea that the *human* qualities of the alien make him so frightening, would seem to be the one element that Wells's aliens lack. They certainly do not look like humans, and their basic biological functions and activities are totally dissimilar. Their behavior, however, cannot be accurately called inhuman. They do nothing to man that he has not already done to lesser species, or even, in fact, to his own kind:

> The Tasmanians, in spite of their human likeness, were entirely swept out of existence in a war of extermination waged by European immigrants, in the space of fifty years. Are we such apostles of mercy as to complain if the Martians warred in the same spirit?

Left at that, the point is merely satirical, a biting comment on human nature in general and imperialism in particular; but Wells has more in mind than that. Crucial to the nature of his Martians is their reason for coming to Earth in the first place. Their invasion is no expression of wanton cruelty or even calculated aggression, but is a desperate act of racial survival. "The immediate pressure of necessity has brightened their intellects, enlarged their powers and hardened their hearts." The Narrator tells us this in the first pages of the book, thus explaining the rationale of the invasion, thereby not only preparing the reader for the action to come, but also foreshadowing in a profound and subtle way the novel's climax.

Two related assumptions commonly held in Wells's time underlie both the reasons for the invasion and the nature of the invaders: first, that the sun was cooling off and consequently that our solar system was dying gradually from its extremities inward; and second, that Darwinian notions of evolution would apply to any organic creature living anywhere in the universe. In addition, Wells accepted the moral attitude toward evolution of T. H. Huxley, his old teacher, that evolution and progress are not synonymous: that, in the long run, evolution is likely to be regressive, however positive it might appear to a late-Victorian humanist.

Thus, the planet Mars has reached its stage of exhaustion. Cooling rapidly — a condition that will ultimately be repeated on Earth — it will soon be uninhabitable. The *logical* place for the Martians to go is, of course, the Earth, the only habitable planet that is closer to the sun. The Martians' superiority is merely the result of time; Mars is dying sooner because it became habitable sooner, and, since its creatures have had much longer to evolve, they have developed their civilization to a much higher degree.

During the period when he is trapped with the Curate in a house overlooking one of the Martian pits, the Narrator studies the aliens at close range, and realizes that, for all of their (to us) grotesque physical peculiarities, they are models of efficiency. Unnecessary or irrelevant physical characteristics — sexual organs, digestive tracts, elaborate muscular and nervous systems — have been evolved out, leaving only the essentials: eyes, hands (tentacles, usually), a hearing mechanism, a strawlike appendage for draining the blood, and, above all, a brain. Wells summarizes the creatures in a key passage:

> . . . in the Martians we have beyond dispute the actual accomplishment of such a suppression of the animal side of the organism by the intelligence. To me it is quite credible that the Martians may be descended from beings not unlike ourselves, by a gradual development of brain and hands . . . at the expense of the rest of the body. Without the body the brain would, of course, become a mere selfish intelligence, without any of the emotional substratum of the human being.

Thus the Martians are well-equipped with all the apparatus needed to analyze, to plan, and then to act, unhampered by such considerations as feelings, desires, or values. Wells seems to ask whether this will be the logical direction for development of the human species as well — progressive evolution with a vengeance.

Whether the aliens' vulnerability to germs was the result of a natural absence of such bacteria on Mars, or was due to their success in eliminating them from their environment, is left ambiguous by Wells, but the implication of their deaths is clear: cosmic process and evolution are impersonal, unavoidable, and, the Narrator's musing about God notwithstanding, amoral and mechanistic. Artistically the demise of the Martians is not only justified, but necessary; philosophically it is consistent with the dark vision of the author's other scientific romances.

The final victory of mankind over the Martians, particularly since it is coupled with the Narrator's reunion with his wife, should end the book on an optimistic note, but quite the opposite is true. At best, the final mood of the book could be called pensive. The lesson about man's vulnerability to the vagaries of forces outside of his control has been made too forcefully for the Narrator to feel any continued sense of security. The outcome of the invasion, he suggests, is more of a reprieve than a victory, and even if the Martians do not return, there are probably other beings out there.

But perhaps what the invasion has suggested about man himself is even more responsible for the bleak mood of the book's ending. In the human reaction to the aliens, we have seen apathy, selfishness, confusion, pettiness, blind fear, hysteria, disdain, and arrogance, but very little heroism. On the other side, in the Martians we see what man could become — inhumanly rationalistic and barbarously efficient. Nor does Wells present this as a choice. The novel is no exhortation to cultivate the humane side of man. The brain and the hand are the parts of man most likely to survive in the evolutionary process; the humane qualities are ultimately expendable. The initial shock in reading *The War of the Worlds* is produced by the strangeness and grotesqueness of the Martians as compared to man, but the lasting impression is of their similarity. Or, to paraphrase Walt Kelley's comic-strip 'possum, Pogo: "we have met the alien and he is us."

Keith Neilson

Sources for Further Study

Criticism:

Borrello, Alfred. *H. G. Wells: Author in Agony*. Carbondale: Southern Illinois University Press, 1972, pp. 14, 81-82. Borrello provides a general thematic analysis of *The War of the Worlds* as part of a larger study of the author.

Costa, Richard H. *H. G. Wells*. New York: Twayne, 1967, pp. 43-46. This general study of the author takes a brief look at the plot concerns of *The War of the Worlds*.

Gilbert, James B. "Wars of the Worlds," in *Journal of Popular Culture*. X (1976), pp. 326-336. Gilbert analyzes the style of *The War of the Worlds* and surveys its impact on the literature of science fiction.

WAR WITH THE NEWTS
(VALKA S. MLOKY)

Author: Karel Čapek (1890-1938)
First book publication: 1936
English translation: 1939
Type of work: Novel
Time: The near future
Locale: The Pacific equitorial atolls, Czechoslovakia, and strategic locations around
the world

*Humans inadvertently upset the biological forces which limit the population of
Newts, an industrious, intelligent species of aquatic salamander, who soon learn to
beat humans at their own games of power politics, exploitation, and warfare to win the
struggle for world dominance*

Principal characters:
> CAPTAIN JOHN VAN TOCH, the discoverer and benefactor of Newts
> and also the first to exploit them for commercial purposes
> J. H. BONDY, business tycoon who builds a commercial empire, The
> Salamander Syndicate, on Newt slave labor
> ANDREW SCHEUCHZER, the first Polynesian giant salamander to
> demonstrate human speech and intelligence
> MR. POVONDRA, a porter at Bondy's whose collection of Newt
> memorabilia forms the archives of this future history
> CAPTAIN JAMES LINDLEY, the first reported human casualty in a
> skirmish with Newts
> "X," an English pamphleteer who warns humanity against the
> Newts
> CHIEF SALAMANDER, the leader who unites all Newts against
> humans

War with the Newts, Karel Čapek's masterpiece of comic science fiction
satire, was published as Europe was about to plunge into the most barbarous
and destructive war in history. Although not allegorical, *War with the Newts*
presents in a comic and satiric manner a serious critique of those destructive
values and attitudes typical of the times and all too characteristic of the indus-
trialized West, especially of Europe and the United States. The narrative seems
to contain examples of almost every known device of satire from burlesque,
lampoon, and slapstick to parody, comedy of manners, and some brilliant anticipations of comedy of the absurd.

In the strict sense, *War with the Newts* is not a novel. The story of the rise
of the Newts to world dominance is told in the manner of an imaginary history
or fictitious chronicle that happens to depend on doubtful and incomplete
sources. The principal characters are, at most, pawns in what becomes a suicidal competition for political power and economic advantage, and the main
events of the chronicle are frequently of global importance, transcending individual or even national destiny and threatening the very survival of the human
race. *War with the Newts* is divided into three parts which purport to give an

account of the rediscovery of the Newts by the men of Europe who, through modernization, have diminished in spirit and wisdom while achieving wealth and power.

Newts, or salamanders as they are often called, are hardworking aquatic creatures who learn quickly. They are, of course, soon exploited as slave laborers. It is not long before a giant international trading corporation is formed to breed and sell Newts as workers in and under the world's waters. Soon the Newts develop into a potent as well as a disruptive force in the contemporary world. They multiply very rapidly and develop into functioning adults much sooner than humans. The rapid assimilation of the Newts into the *Realpolitik* of nations leads eventually to a struggle for supremacy between Newts and humans. War with the Newts produces the literal undermining of Western and Eastern countries as the Newts proceed systematically to reshape the world's land in order to increase the shoreline. Newts require a watery environment but prefer shallow, coastal waters. The remaining narrow strips of land are left for humans.

The chronicle of the Newts comes to an ironic and fortuitous close as the author, in conference with himself, postulates the corrupting influence that power is likely to have over the Newts themselves, who seem destined for ultimate self-annihilation from the deadly effects of a destructive technology learned from Western man. The human race is left, perhaps, to reinherit the Earth, to fabricate new myths, and to build new cultures and civilizations as the author closes with a calculated throwing up of hands, saying "I don't know what comes next."

Book I, titled "Andrias Scheuchzeri," is a literary burlesque of the success story formula of both the Horatio Alger type and of the more ambitious science fiction stories that chronicle the rising of new worlds and the building of new civilizations. The story begins with the colorful Dutch sea captain, John van Toch, who discovers the Newts while searching for new pearl beds off an island somewhere west of Sumatra. Van Toch's salty criticism of narrow and greedy European commercialism sets the tone of the book from the beginning and identifies one of its major themes. However, the captain is a flawed character, like all the others in the story, and while he develops a paternal interest in his Newts, he trains them for pearl diving and forms a syndicate to make his fortune in the pearl trade. Van Toch becomes enchanted by the Newts, who learn to speak his language and are content to recover pearls to please the captain in return for knives and other trinkets. When the captain discovers that the Newt population is restricted by sharks, their natural predators, he vows to help them by supplying them with underwater harpoon guns. Van Toch's kindness produces a salamander bonanza. Unchecked, the Newt population rises geometrically with each generation, as Newt females are capable of producing hundreds of eggs during mating season.

Following van Toch's death, his partner, G. H. Bondy, sees his opportunity for profit in the amazing Newt fertility, intelligence, and capacity for work. Abandoning the pearl trade to a newly glutted market, he forms the Salamander Syndicate, a vertical trust intended for the "rational production and exploitation of the Newts." The enthusiastic response to Bondy's proposal at a stockholder's meeting underlines the irony of the vision. Driven by greed and power, Bondy envisions a Utopian future in which his corporation will supply, feed, train, and insure Newts for the great powers, each competing for the lion's share of a work force that promises unlimited profits. Bondy sees a new Genesis, the rise of a new Atlantis, through the Newts who will reshape the world's continents. Bondy's vision is fulfilled with a vengeance.

The second book, "Along the Steps of Civilization," begins and ends in the parlor of Mr. Povondra, Bondy's porter. Searching for a hobby that will give meaning to his drab life, he begins collecting all news clippings about Newts. It is from this collection that the history of the Newts is generated. The history is both fragmentary and speculative in some details because many of the clippings had disintegrated with age, others were in languages entirely forgotten, and still others had been lost. The biggest lacunas were the result of Mrs. Povondra's habit of throwing out wholesale bundles of items from her husband's collection so as to make room for new ones. The Povondra collection is itself one of Čapek's most effective symbols showing the way human idiosyncrasy shapes history.

Čapek's satire is perhaps broadest in Book II, which traces the rapid acculturation of the Newts. Their rapid progress is an evolutionary inevitability once they are liberated from their predators, but the nature and direction of that biological movement was determined by the character of the culture in which the Newts developed. Hence, Čapek has the annals of the Newts reflect the follies of humanity, the deficiencies of industrialism and its cultural ill effects, as well as the special milieu of the 1930's in central Europe.

Book II ends with Mr. Povondra ruminating on the likely consequences of the use of Newts by the great powers to expand their national territories. Meanwhile various factions rally to the cause of the Newts. Communists exhort them to join the proletarian revolt. Japan claims them for the crusade of the nonwhite races. Germany claims that the Aryan Newt is superior to all others. A Salamander Protection Society defends the legal rights of Newts, and so on. Through all this the Newts are not unaffected. A Newt generation gap develops with the young Newts holding out for "progress without reservations or restrictions" and insisting that Newt submarine culture imitate humans "not omitting even football, fascism, sexual perversions," while the old Newts "clung conservatively to natural Newtship and did not wish to renounce the old animal habits and instincts."

Book III recounts the seriocomic history of the competition and eventual conflict between Newts and humans, the unification of Newts behind the Chief Salamander, and the details of the Newt reshaping of the world's land. The events in the escalating conflicts are analogous to the ominous political events in central Europe in the 1930's. While a German social philosopher welcomes the "decadence and coming end of mankind," the English warn humanity to form a league of nations against the Newts before it is too late.

It is already too late, however. The Louisiana earthquake proves to be the overture to the wholesale reshaping of the continents. The Chief Salamander broadcasts demands that humans sell their land to Newts for demolition, reminding his astonished listeners: "You needed us. You have spread us all over the world. Now you have us." Human resistance is immediate, contemptuous, and futile. The Newts control the world's waters and begin to work their will on the land. Mr. Povondra takes what solace he can from living in a land-locked country until he sees a Newt swimming up the Danube.

The final chapter, "The Author Talks with Himself," is a fitting coda in which Čapek comes before the reader like a prose Prufrock debating with himself how the world may yet be saved. That Newt will fight eventually against Newt to the final extinction of the species is all too plausible a scenario, given the example humans have set for them. Alas, even Newts will have been conditioned to fight among themselves in the name of culture and justice, and in "the name of true Newtship." Of the many ironies of this last chapter, the most deflating is the revelation that the Chief Salamander is human, one Andreas Schultze, a former sergeant-major in World War I. Probably Hitler was not even flattered by the promotion. And so the human race prevails with the author's help and by virtue of its unlimited powers of corruption.

War with the Newts deserves to rank with the three other social science fiction masterpieces of the 1930's and 1940's: Evgeny Zamiatin's *We* (1920), Aldous Huxley's *Brave New World* (1932), and George Orwell's *Nineteen Eighty-Four* (1949). Although not as well known and less novelistic in form than the others, *War with the Newts* may strike a contemporary reader as closer to the mood and style of the 1970's than any of the others. Čapek's work fits less conveniently, however, into the science fiction dystopia category. Like the others it is a cautionary tale, but it is less directly instructive, being more comic and less mordant in tone. Whereas Zamiatin, Huxley, and Orwell confront the reader with the nightmare vision of Utopia gone awry, Čapek gives us a world gone to the Newts. Čapek's comic satire provokes not horror but a corrective laughter at modern man's smallness of spirit, at the absurdly vainglorious, self-serving, and suicidal behavior of people motivated by greed and pride. The effect, however, is closer to that produced by Kurt Vonnegut, Jr., than to Zamiatin or Huxley. In view of the historical context of Čapek's work, we may view *War with the Newts* as an example of the kind of absurdist comedy and gallows humor found in another contemporary Czech masterpiece, Jaroslav Hašek's *The Good Soldier: Schweik*.

There are other ways that Čapek anticipates writers of the 1970's who bring together science fiction, satire, and social criticism. Like them, Čapek is a moralist, and like them he has a talent for capturing contemporary styles of life and thought. Perhaps, therefore, a position of prominence ought to be given Čapek not only because of precedence, but also because his blend of hard and soft science fiction with comic satire is treated with a sophistication of manner and tone rarely equaled.

Donald L. Lawler

Sources for Further Study

Criticism:

Canby, W. S. "Čapek's *War with the Newts*," in *Saturday Review of Literature*. XVI (October 25, 1937), p. 5. Canby views *War with the Newts* as satire which at times is brilliantly effective and at other times alarming in its view of modern society.

Church, Richard. "Karel Čapek," *in Spectator*, CLVIII (February 5, 1937), p. 230. Church concentrates on Čapek's satirical method which he finds lighter, more humorous but less panoramic than other satirists writing in the same field.

Clark, Eleanor. *"The War with the Newts"* in *New Republic*. XIIIC (January 12, 1938), p. 291. Eleanor Clark takes a hrash view of Čapek's creativity which she terms a "creative and moral impatience."

Duffus, R. L. *"Čapek's War with the Newts,"* in *New York Times*, (October 24, 1937), p. 2. Čapek's satirical technique is examined by Duffus who says it will scare the reader who may well wonder if the Newt Age is upon us.

Reviews:

Booklist. XXXIV, December 1, 1937, p. 129.

Boston Transcript. October 16, 1937, p. 2.

Christian Science Monitor. March 2, 1937, p. 18.

Nation. CXVL, October 30, 1937, p. 482.

New Statesman. XIII, January 30, 1937, p. 172.

Time. XXX, October 11, 1937, p. 81.

WAY STATION

Author: Clifford D. Simak (1904-   )
First book publication: 1963
Type of work: Novel
Time: The 1960's
Locale: A farmhouse near Millville, Wisconsin

A character study of a man who operates a Way Station in Wisconsin for aliens who are passing through the area unbeknownst to anyone else on Earth, and of this man's ultimate choice of loyalties between his native planet and his alien friends

> *Principal characters:*
> ENOCH WALLACE, the custodian of the Way Station
> ULYSSES, Enoch's superior from Galactic Central
> CLAUDE LEWIS, an Intelligence agent spying on Enoch Wallace
> LUCY FISHER, a deaf-mute girl
> WINSLOWE GRANT, Enoch's mailman
> MARY, an apparition

Clifford D. Simak is one of the more pastoral writers in the science fiction field. His stories tend to be works of gentle beauty rather than the fierce action/adventure romances that predominate in the genre. The fate of the world may hinge upon the events in his work, as it does in *Way Station*, but the decision comes across as the personal revelation of one man rather than a result of chest-thumping heroics by a larger-than-life-sized figure.

Way Station is without question one of Simak's greatest works, a masterpiece that received the Hugo Award as the best novel of 1963. It deals with concepts so large that they span the entire galaxy and explore the essence of religion, and yet Simak keeps it all in perspective by focusing virtually all the action within a few square miles around a farmhouse in rural Wisconsin. The intricate interplay of vast cosmic forces is dealt with through the soul of one lonely, troubled man.

That man is really the product of another age. Enoch Wallace was born in 1840 and served in the Civil War — and yet in the present, when by all rights he should have been dead and buried decades ago, he only appears to be thirty years old. He lives by himself in his old family farmhouse, venturing outside it only about an hour a day and having no communication with anyone but his mailman. The country folk in his community have long since accepted him as one of the local oddities, but he has now attracted the attention of U. S. Intelligence, which wants an explanation for this phenomenon.

Very simply, Enoch Wallace is the keeper of a Way Station for beings from all over the galaxy as they travel from one place to another. Their method of transportation is to transmit their life patterns across space to their destination, with occasional stopovers on long trips to avoid beam dispersal. Enoch's station is one such stopover, but because Earth is considered too backward to join the galactic community, the station must operate in secret. To perform the job for which he was recruited, Enoch must cut himself off from the rest of his species. He subscribes to newspapers and magazines, and talks to the mailman who delivers them, but other than that he is a stranger in his own world. As compensation, he receives a gift many would envy — virtual immortality. Time stands still within his house, and he only ages during the hour or so a day that he takes his walk to the mailbox.

One of the strengths of a really good science fiction story is that it tickles the reader's imagination, leaving vast empty areas that he can fill in for himself. Simak does this admirably in *Way Station*. The concept of such a place, wherein one ordinary person can meet and converse with all sorts of beings from all over the galaxy, conjures up different images in each individual reader's mind. Simak gives tantalizing glimpses of the exotic throughout the book — enough to stimulate the reader's dreams of wonder without giving him all the answers predigested. Each reader can dream for himself of the marvels he would see if *he* were the stationkeeper.

But for all the excitement of his job, Enoch Wallace is a very troubled man. Despite the glimpses he is given of galactic civilization, he lacks the companionship of his own people. He befriends the sensitive deaf-mute, Lucy Fisher, and he talks with his mailman, but they cannot give him all the company he needs. Long ago, in desperation, he used some alien magic to "create" some shadow people of his own, friends who could be conjured at will and sent back to their private limbo when he was tired of them. One of these is the beautiful Mary, with whom he has gradually fallen in love. But they can never touch because she is not real. In a way, she symbolizes his greater plight, for his whole existence is a shadow; he dares not touch the real world for fear of finding that *he* has become unreal.

But, like it or not, the real world is encroaching on Enoch's hitherto private existence. There are the watchers, headed by Intelligence agent Claude Lewis, intent on discovering his secret. There is Lucy, who is forced to take refuge in the Way Station to escape a homicidal beating by her loutish father. But most of all, there is Earth itself. Using statistical principles taught him by some alien travelers, he can tell from the trends reported in the newspapers that human society is headed toward a nuclear holocaust. Enoch feels that some of the knowledge he has gained from his alien contacts might help relieve the situation if he could communicate it to people of importance — but to do so would be to betray Galactic Central and especially his boss, and closest friend, Ulysses.

But the galaxy, too, has its own problems. Up until recently it had been guided by its knowledge of a basic force which people could actually feel through a mechanism known as the Talisman. This certain knowledge of the true spirituality pervading the universe was a moderating influence on galactic civilization. But the Talisman has disappeared and been out of touch for many years, and with it has gone the spirit of reasonable debate within galactic society; factionalism is the order of the day. When Claude Lewis, in his attempt to discover the secret of the Way Station, accidentally tampers with something he should not have touched, he sets off a chain reaction that pits galactic partisanship squarely against Earth.

Enoch Wallace becomes the nexus of the competing forces. He is a peaceful man who wants to avoid war on Earth, and had hoped that someday his native world would be admitted to the galactic brotherhood of planets. But Lewis' action has jeopardized that, and there are forces at work in the galaxy that would love to see the Way Station on Earth permanently shut down. Enoch is caught in a conflict of loyalties; should he stay with Galactic Central and leave Earth when this station is shut down, or should he be true to the world of his birth? Over the past century he has accumulated knowledge and artifacts that might revolutionize the world — but does he dare tell anyone?

Simak's story succeeds so marvelously because he is able to deal with these cosmic issues through the problems of a single, very sympathetic character. The world's problems are Enoch's problems, and the factionalism of the galaxy is mirrored in his own conflict. Enoch becomes the crucible; the decisions are his, and a crisis of major proportions in galactic relations becomes understandable as a crisis within one man's soul. Slowly but surely, all Enoch's attempts to retain a semblance of normality are breaking down. The ghosts he has conjured have developed a strange sort of half-life of their own. They are sentient and aware that they have no reality outside Enoch's existence, and the pain of that is too great for them to bear. They desert Enoch, asking him not to call them up again. This is hardest for Mary, who has fallen as much in love with Enoch as he has with her. That love only makes her existence doubly painful, and she too flees back into her shadow of unreality.

Being a man in the long run is a matter of the choices one makes, and Enoch Wallace has hard ones to face. Not the least of these choices is whether to accept the one possible method Ulysses can suggest to stop the nuclear holocaust on Earth, a method that has worked on a few occasions before: stupidity. Earth's people can be made to forget all they know about technology for several generations. Many people will die that way too, and chaos will reign on Earth for decades, but the total disaster of all-out nuclear war would be averted. As the sole member of the human race in contact with Galactic Central, Enoch must represent his planet and take the responsibility for that decision. But how can anyone make the choice for all the people on Earth?

If there is any flaw in *Way Station*, it is the enormous *deus ex machina* that Simak uses at the end to clear up these problems. The being who stole the Talisman tries to hide out on Earth by traveling through the Way Station. Enoch kills him, and then it transpires that Lucy Fisher is the perfect new custodian for the galaxy's symbol of spiritual attainment. All the loose ends are thus wound up: the planet that produced such a custodian could scarcely be denied admittance to the galactic fraternity; contact with other races will help stabilize the political climate on Earth; Enoch need no longer be cut off from his own race by the secretiveness of his job; and the galaxy has its Talisman back again to stop the petty bickering that has plagued it since the object's disappearance. It is a solution that resolves all the major problems without Enoch's having to make the final choice of loyalties, and it leaves the question open as to what he would have chosen. The ending is emotionally satisfying, but dramatically ambivalent.

This flaw, though, is merely a bow to convention. It is the *asking* of the questions that is important, not how they were resolved in this one particular case. Through Enoch's dilemma, the reader himself is made aware of the harsh choices that sometimes exist — choices of self-doubt, of loneliness, and of conflicting loyalties. Each reader is forced to face those choices as the book progresses, and to come to grips with how he himself might react under those circumstances. By showing how another man deals with the conflicts, the reader may learn something about his own values and judgments.

Simak is a stylist. He is not quite as flowery as, say, Ray Bradbury, but there is still the attention to descriptive detail and the use of lyric language to evoke the desired mood. Time and again he will minutely describe the settings that Enoch passes through, but his descriptions are more than mere boring catalogs of the character's surroundings. The author captures the essence of places and feelings, transforming his words into complete visual images. Simak has always been a writer attuned to the depths of human emotions, and nowhere does he display this talent better than in *Way Station*.

Way Station is, in the final analysis, a probing and sensitive look at what makes a person human. It examines an intelligent, thoughtful man and reveals his inner core — his loneliness, his friendship, and his love. By the end of the book, the reader may realize that the human race has been in a way station of its own, and is now ready to move ahead to its ultimate destiny — whatever that may be.

Stephen Goldin

Sources for Further Study

Review:
Punch. CCXLIV, February 19, 1964, p. 286.

WE
(MY)

Author: Evgeny Zamyatin (1884-1937)
First book publication: 1924
English translation: 1924
Type of work: Novel
Time: Nine hundred to one thousand years in the future
Locale: The One State

A classical anti-Utopia, one of the first of modern times

> *Principal characters:*
> D-503, an engineer and builder of the spaceship Integral
> I-330, a leader of the revolutionary movement Mephi
> O-90, a sexual partner of D
> U, the controller at D's building
> R-13, a poet, D's friend
> S-4711, a Guardian interested in D
> SCISSOR-LIPS, a physician and co-conspirator with I-330
> THE BENEFACTOR, head of the One State

Over a half-century since its appearance, the novel *We* remains one of the most exciting and influential works of science fiction. Its basic plot, whereby a true believer comes to question the validity of a totalitarian state and thus to transform it from a Utopia into an anti-Utopia, has been repeated by Aldous Huxley in *Brave New World* (1932), George Orwell in *Nineteen Eighty-Four* (1949), and by any number of epigones; yet its artistry, prophetic power, and underlying philosophy have not been surpassed.

Zamyatin finished *We* in 1920 and sent it the next year to the Grzhebin House in Berlin, which published books simultaneously in Germany and Russia. In Petrograd (later Leningrad), the work became known to fellow writers by means of readings, such as the one Zamyatin gave to the Union of Writers in 1924. Publication was announced, but never realized in Russia: the book has the distinction of being the first novel banned by the Glavlit (Chief Administration for Literary Affairs), established in 1922. As this censorship board was understood at that time to be a preventative device — to block publication of pornography and works of an overtly counterrevolutionary nature — there can be no doubt about the reception of *We* by Soviet officialdom. *We* first appeared in English in 1924, in a translation by Gregory Zilboorg. Three years later, when the book was scheduled for translation into Czech, Marc Slonim, then the editor of *Volya Rossii*, a Russian *émigré* journal in Prague, obtained the original and published it in 1929, palming it off as a translation into Russian from Czech (he tried to mask the text by changing some words). This foreign publication provided ammunition for attacks on Zamyatin at home as an anti-Soviet writer. He was hounded in the press, and his books and plays were banned.

Zamyatin answered the charges point for point with customary frankness and irony in a letter to the Union of Writers, and he resigned from the chairmanship of the Leningrad branch. But he had to recognize that the "death sentence" for a writer — not to be published — had been passed. He then took the bold step of writing directly to Stalin, as did Mikhail Bulgakov about the same time. Acknowledging his "highly inconvenient habit of speaking what I consider to be the truth rather than saying what may be expedient at the moment," Zamyatin asked to be deported from the country. With Maxim Gorky's intercession, Zamyatin and his wife were permitted to emigrate to Paris. Once abroad, he shunned *émigré* circles, wrote interesting articles on the theater and a few film scenarios, and, like so many *émigrés*, hoped to return to his homeland. Zamyatin died in March, 1937. His death went unmentioned in the Soviet press, and his funeral was attended by only a few friends.

We is set in the thirtieth century, a thousand years after the world has been subjugated to the rule of the single state, and human life in all its particulars has come to be controlled by scientific reason. This reason is manifested in the omnipotence of "The One State," guided by the omniscience of one man, "The Benefactor." One of the instruments of control, "The Table of Hourly Commandments," schedules the daily activities of waking, eating, working, defecation, and sleep; it is understood as the mathematical guarantee of human happiness. In order for a person to be happy, it is argued, "the denominator in the fraction of happiness . . . [must be] reduced to zero," that is, freedom must be eliminated. Freedom is seen as the slow murder of a society, mathematically much worse than the physical murder of one man. With freedom standing at zero, there is no inequality, no reason for envy; and the numerator — namely, whatever the State permits — becomes infinite by comparison. Thus the rule of the One State obtains divine force.

In order that this happiness may not be threatened by freedom, all houses are made of glass. This facilitates the work of "The Bureau of Guardians," special agents who watch the citizens to ensure their tranquility. All work is carried out on a group level, and all group activities are regimented to maintain unanimity of thought and action. The organization "splits into separate cells" only twice a day, when citizens may stay alone at home. The Table of Hourly Commandments allows for this by scheduling sexual activity on certain days at this time. Each male citizen, who receives a consonant and odd number at birth instead of a name, may draw a ticket for any available vowel and even number — in other words, a female citizen — for use at this time. Only on "Sexual Days," during the "Personal Hours," may shades be drawn in the glass houses. Parenthood, as well as love, obtains a mathematical basis with "The Maternal and Paternal Norms." The Personal Hours, however, are felt to be a flaw in the equation of happiness, conducive to anxiety, and at the beginning of the novel it is hoped that eventually every second of every citizen's existence will be planned by the State.

The thoughts of the numbers are protected by the one newspaper, "The State Gazette," and by "The Institute of the State Poets and Writers," both of which glorify the One State and the Benefactor. The One State itself, situated in an undefined area, is protected from the vicissitudes of weather by a glass dome and a glass wall, beyond which nature still exists in a savage state.

The story is told by the diary of D-503. His first entry explains that he is the chief engineer in the construction of a spaceship designed to carry the message of reason to other worlds. His diary is in fact part of the cargo. Addressing his unknown readers, D-503 compares the life in the One State with that of ancient times (that is, our own). He demonstrates the superior quality of the Table of Hourly Commandments over the apex of ancient literature, "The Time Table of All the Railroads," and marvels that people once lived chaotically, without obligatory walks, without predetermined sexual hours. "Like brutes, they bred offspring gropingly. Isn't it laughable — to know horticulture, poultry culture, the culture of fish . . . and yet to be unable to reach the last rung of this logical ladder: pediculture. To be unable to reach the logical conclusions: our Maternal and Paternal Norms." D-503 assures his readers that he is not jesting, since jesting contains "a covert functioning of falsehood"; the State affirms that this is true, and the State is always right. Describing the origin of the One State, D-503 tells of a two-hundred-year war and the development of a new naphtha food which eradicated 99.8% of the world population: "But then, cleansed of its millennial filth, how glowing the face of the earth became!"

D-503's satisfaction with the One State is challenged by the appearance of I-330, a disturbing woman with disturbing ideas. Her black clothing of a former time, her smoking, her preference for the music of ancient composers over that produced by the state music-making boxes, and especially her sarcastic manner excite unfamiliar sensations in the mathematician. He becomes reflective, experiences the ancient disorder of dreams, commits the crime of not sleeping, and even wonders if his knowledge is only faith. At first he is reassured by the warm breath of the Guardian Angel on the back of his neck, but day by day he falls deeper into doubt. Even his mathematical certainty — "eternal lovers are these two-times-two, forever blent in a passionate four" — is upset by the notion of the square root of minus 1, the world of the irrational into which he is falling. At last he understands that he is in love with I-330 and is afflicted with the disease of having a soul.

After an unprecedented demonstration at the "Day of Unanimity" (reelection of the Benefactor), I-330 takes D-503 to naked men living beyond the Green Wall and tells him of her revolutionary intent. This sets the stage for the main philosophical statement of the novel: "There is no ultimate revolution — revolutions are infinite in number. . . ."

The revolutionary attempt to seize the spaceship fails, but D-503 is not implicated. As the epidemic of the soul spreads, the Medical Bureau perfects a device to remove the faculty of imagination — the last obstacle on the road to happiness. The operation becomes mandatory for all numbers under penalty of liquidation by "The Machine of the Benefactor." After painful hesitation, D-503 submits to the "fantasiectomy" and betrays his former lover; she is tortured and sentenced to the Machine. D-503, returned to the fold, regrets the revolution and ends as he began: "And I hope that we will conquer. More than that: I am certain that we shall. For reason must conquer."

Within this basic story, there are numerous subplots and subtleties. For example, one can follow the spread of the soul "epidemic" to other characters in contact with love-smitten D-503. O-90 falls in love with him, becomes jealous of I-330, and illegally conceives a child by him; U secretly reads his diary, falls in love with him, and informs on the other revolutionaries, thus affecting the outcome of the story. One can explore the difference between illusion and reality — D's initial understanding of the state and the revolutionary movement, and his ultimate realization that he has been used by both. One can trace at least three levels of time in the diary: the present of the story as it unfolds, the twentieth century, and the thirtieth century.

One of the marks of a great book is its susceptibility to many levels of interpretation, all apparently valid and convincing. *We* is such a book. It has been analyzed by American Slavists more than any other modern Russian novel; it has been picked to pieces by different, sometimes antithetical methods; yet it always holds up.

One common reading views *We* as a dramatization of Jungian psychology. There is some validity to this interpretation, for, although Zamyatin was certainly not familiar with C. G. Jung's works, which were virtually unknown in Russia, his novel is no less a model of Jungian psychology than Hermann Hesse's *Steppenwolf*, written in 1927 under the direct influence of Jung. Zamyatin was aware of the unconscious: he valued it as a source of creation, the inspiration for great art, and the link with the sweep of the epoch; the conscious mind, he said, did the work of revision, mastered the craft of writing, and attended to current events. Thus, a case can be made for the unconscious components of the novel and the validity of Jung's description of psychic structures. In Jungian terms, the hero of *We* is immediately recognizable as the *persona* — that aspect of the psyche which conforms to society, adheres to conventions, follows reason, presents a good face. I-330 appears as his *anima*, the hidden female side of his blocked personality, the source of spontaneity, irrationality, passions, dreams, love; the awakener of the unconscious. Thus stirred, D-503 discovers a wild, violent self, an impetuous, hairy-handed beast — his *shadow*. This process of awakening, which all men must confront or avoid, is what Jung called *individuation* the discovery and conscious integration of the self within — the discovery of one's soul. Both Jung and Zamyatin turn naturally to myth for the story of conscious awakening — Adam and Eve. D-503 takes the role of Adam (hence his consonant), I-330 — Eve (the Russian "I" has the sound "ee"); she takes him beyond the wall surrounding a paradise of unconscious happiness. With Jung, the outcome of individuation is a self-sufficient and creative personality, but in the novel this is subverted by D's fantasiectomy.

Zamyatin, who spent time in prison in 1906 as a Bolshevik, and in 1922, in the same cell block, served a sentence as a non-Bolshevik, adhered to his own form of dialectic throughout his career. For him, progress is a continuous battle between entropy and energy, a constant renewal of that which inevitably wears down. He expressed this thought metaphorically: "Today is doomed to die because yesterday died and tomorrow will be born. Such is the cruel and wise law. Cruel — because it dooms to eternal dissatisfaction those who today already see the distant peaks of tomorrow. Wise — because only in eternal dissatisfaction is there the guarantee of eternal motion forward, of eternal creation." The enemy of this forward motion is sloth; wherever it sets in it must be uprooted by revolution. But when the revolution succeeds, it is at once threatened by sloth, lethargy, and entropy.

In the epoch of revolution, Zamyatin expected that literature would be of "tomorrow," that it would create new forms and make new syntheses of ideas. Instead, he feared, entropy had already begun to set in; a "new catholicism" was being founded which preserved old forms and consolidated an orthodoxy of thought. He sensed that the new literature would simply reflect the new mode of life, rather than explore the nature of life, and hence the minor tendency in literature would suffocate the major.

The distinction between minor and major literature is one of Zamyatin's key concepts, the kernel of a number of his essays. He defined minor literature as "topical" or "small," interested in satisfying the fleeting demands of society and subservient to its critics. Major literature he described as "contemporary" or "great," standing above daily matters and moving with the sweep of the epoch. Subjection to the "topical" forces writers to be practical and glib. Adherence to the "contemporary" makes writers impractical and dissonant, an obstacle to mundane pursuits. On this basis Zamyatin issued his famous proclamation that "real literature can exist only where it is made not by efficient and well-intentioned clerks, but by madmen, hermits, heretics, daydreamers, rebels, sceptics."

We, then, is major literature: a philosophical novel dedicated to the eternal dialectic. The immobile and perfect One State is cracked, the mathematical formula for human happiness is shattered by the square root of minus one, the consciously constructed norms are blasted by unconscious chaos. But we must remember: the revolution, even if it succeeds, will not be the final one. In this, Zamyatin departs from the dialectic of Hegel, which ends in the self-knowledge of God, and the dialectic of Marx, which ends in the dictatorship of the proletariat and the withering of the state into a condition of blissful equality. I-330 clearly speaks for the author when she ridicules the notion of a final number, or when she says: "Man is like a novel: one doesn't know until the very last page how the thing will end. Otherwise it would hardly be worth the reading." At the end of this novel, the outcome is in doubt. Brainwashed D-503 believes that reason will triumph, but his final word is even less credible than his first.

Most criticism about Zamyatin, be it Soviet or Western, concentrates on the social background of the author's work. Without question, *We* derives from early Soviet society in many of its details. Zamyatin, ever alert to the first signs of monolithic thought, carried the new institutions of postrevolutionary Russia to "the last rung of the logical ladder." By so doing, he not only subjected them to derision, but in a sense predicted the future. *We* accurately presages the cult of personality of Stalin ("the Benefactor"), *Pravda*'s monopoly on the truth ("the State Gazette"), the travesty of Communistic voting ("the Day of Unanimity"), the control of literature ("the State Union of Poets and Writers"), and the Iron Curtain, beyond which one is not allowed to go ("the Green Wall"). Some of Zamyatin's predictions did not come to pass, such as the "Sexual Hours" — the 1920's were rife with free-love theories — but Stalin enforced marriage and puritanical relations, at least officially. Readers can gauge how well *detovodstvo* (pediculture) has been realized by Soviet childcare centers and schools, or how well fantasiectomy has been realized in Soviet mental wards. Anyone who has lived in Russia can testify that naphtha food does indeed exist.

Probably it is not these details, damaging as they are, which prevents the publication of *We* in the USSR; one could dismiss them as signs of the time, or find parallels in the spread of cults in the United States — from the Oneida Community to Jonestown. Rather, it is the ideological argument, the denial of a final revolution and a final truth, which is so hateful to the Soviet censorship. *We* is a litmus paper for the Soviet regime. So long as it is banned, all talk of freedom of speech and thought in the USSR is an outright lie; if ever the novel is published and made freely available there, we might pay attention to such talk — and expect the publication of Trotsky, Mao, Kierkegaard; all non-Marxist philosophers, all writers, all poets.

In his lectures to young writers in the 1920's, Zamyatin described methods of composition which can be used to analyze his own work. In particular, he named three artistic devices which are prominent in *We*: thought language, integral image, and falsely positive statement. The first of these, a combination of aposiopesis (leaving the thought incomplete), anacoluthon (changing the grammatical construction), and other elliptical patterns, was considered by Zamyatin to reproduce the speed of thought. The reader encounters a telegraphic stacatto of "pieces, fragments and additions." He is forced to fill in the missing links, to think and in a way to create with the author. Zamyatin believed that this *myslennyi yazyk* best caught the spirit of revolutionary times, much as Andrei Belyi's *mozgovaya igra* (cerebral play) in the preceding revolution. Regarding images, Zamyatin wrote: "I rarely make use of single, chance images: these are only sparks, they live a second and go out, they are forgotten. . . . If I firmly believe in an image — it inevitably gives birth to a whole system of derivative images, it grows by roots through paragraphs, pages."

Thus, in the novel, the perspective of an engineer (Zamyatin was trained as an engineer and shipbuilder) gives rise to a whole system of mathematical and geometric images: O-90 is "made up entirely of circumferences," her mouth says O, she has a babylike ring around her wrist; I-330 has facial lines suggesting an X — the unknown quantity — and a metallic voice; her physician accomplice is a paper cutout with a knife-nose and scissor-lips; the Benefactor has cast-iron hands which move with the weight of a hundred tons. These images are not simply repeated, but treated like verbs, inflected by all the conjugations. They interact with the mathematical songs and formulae for happiness, love, and death.

Opposing them are images representing the hidden, primitive side of man: D-503's hairy hands and "shaggy I"; I-330's sharp teeth and eyebrow horns; U's brick red cheek-gills; R-13's Negroid lips (he is a degenerate Pushkin); S-4711's winged ears and flapping feet; the name of the revolutionary movement — "Mephi," the mocking, disruptive force of Mephistopheles. Zamyatin's use of "false assertions" in *We* is a *tour de force*, a modern version of Erasmus's *In Praise of Folly*. True believer D-503 stresses the truth of what is patently false, euphemizes evils, and thus exposes the new totalitarian verities: spies are "Guardian Angels," imagination and love are "diseases," a tyrant is "the Benefactor." It is in this light that the reader must take assertions about the triumph of reason. These three main artistic devices combine with others at the author's skilled command: oxymoronism, synesthesia, bestrangement. The work is a virtual encyclopedia of devices for formalist or structuralist analysis.

Zamyatin was very well-read in Russian and foreign literature, particularly English (he lived in England for two years before the revolution). As the most talented essayist of his time, he naturally wrote about his reading, again providing material for the analysis of his own works. On the Russian side, critics usually name Gogol, Leskov, Dostoevsky (*Notes from Underground*, *The Grand Inquisitor*), Remizov, Belyi (*Petersburg*), and Bogdanov (*Red Star*) as influences. Zamyatin's own "English works" should be remembered: *The Islanders* (a novel), *The Fisher of Men* (a story), *The Society of the Honorable Bell Ringers* (a play) — these lampooned English stuffiness and conformity. Of foreign writers, Zamyatin admired Anatole France, Jack London, O. Henry, and most of all, H. G. Wells (*The Time Machine*, *When the Sleeper Awakes*); he wrote superb essays on each of these men. Zamyatin was an outstanding figure in postrevolutionary Russia who, by his lectures, literary studios, and creative works, influenced a whole generation of writers, in particular the Serapion Brothers, Boris Pilnyak, Andrei Sobol, and Yury Olesha.

Despite the long interdiction against his works, his influence could be felt in the reawakened Russian fantasy of the 1960's, particularly that of Abram Tertz and Vladimir Voinovich. His influence in the West is widespread, but most often indirect, by way of George Orwell.

In summary, Zamyatin's *We* is a creative transformation of literary influences, stylistic devices, social criticism, dialectical thinking, and psychological insight. Western critics generally agree on the level of this achievement and rate the novel as one of the seminal books of our times. Interpretation, of course, is diverse. Most recently, an essay by E. J. Brown has challenged almost all previous writing on Zamyatin, who, according to Brown, did not look to the future but to the past, by consistently negating the city and finding his preferred subjects in "the precivilized and the primitive." The hero and heroine of *We* try to escape the "conventions of their time" by running beyond the wall to primitive hairy creatures. Furthermore, Zamyatin was not an original thinker: his thought is "a mixture of his basic romanticism with modern scientific vocabulary and Hegelian dialectics," the latter being picked up as part and parcel of his time. Brown regards Zamyatin's philosophy as an "artificial intellectual superstructure" designed to protect writers against the demand to take a definite ideological position. Zamyatin's merit lies entirely in his art.

Other critics regard Brown's reevaluation as a heretical, if stimulating, mistake. They argue that the flight beyond the Green Wall is not the goal: the point is to bring nature into the city. Moreover, the flight is symbolic — not a return to the ape, but to the unconscious. The unconscious lives not only in the past, but in the present, and it points the way to the future. Like most modern writers, Zamyatin (an urbane, anglicized engineer and intellectual) rejected not the city, but its inhuman aspects. No Slavophile, he never advocated the simple country life or the ideal village commune — he ridiculed them. Furthermore, his dialectics is no mere copy of Hegel, nor an occasional thing. It runs through his major writing, both fiction and exposition, and it makes a significant innovation: it remains dialectical. Zamyatin took Marx at his word. If we must "contemplate every accomplished form in its movement, that is, as something transient" (Marx), then a final solution to the problem of human happiness and social justice cannot be made.

Zamyatin had the courage after the revolution to remain a revolutionary, to deny all Utopian solutions, to assert that human folly would always remain, to declare his faith in endless motion, endless revolution, endless heresy. All truths will pass: "Truth is a thought suffering from arteriosclerosis." It is this simple, but fundamental innovation in dialectical thinking which immunized some writers against dogmatism in the 1920's and which continues to awaken the minds of readers today.

Gary Kern

Sources for Further Study

Criticism:

Collins, Christopher. "Zamyatin's *We* as Myth," in *Slavic and East European Journal*. X (Summer, 1966), pp. 125-132. Collins discusses the theme behind *We*.

Proffer, Carl R. "Notes on the Imagery in Zamyatin's *We*," in *Slavic and East European Journal*. VII (Fall, 1963), pp. 269-278. Proffer reveals the satire of humans *vs* theory behind *We*.

White, John J. "Mathematical Imagery in Musil's *Young Torless* and Zamyatin's *We*" in *Comparative Literature*. XVIII (Winter, 1966), pp. 71-78. Zamyatin's caricature of life is compared to Musil's work.

Reviews:

Analog. LXV, June, 1960, pp. 160-161.

Atlantic. CCXXIX, June, 1972, p. 112.

Choice. IX, October, 1972, p. 976.

Christian Science Monitor. May 10, 1972, p. 11.

Kirkus Reviews. XL, March 1, 1972, p. 281.

Library Journal. XCVII, June 15, 1972, p. 2202.

Nation. CCXIV, June 26, 1972, p. 824.

New York Review of Books. XIX, October 19, 1972, pp. 18-21.

New York Times Book Review. July 9, 1972, p. 7.

Renaissance. IV, Summer, 1972, pp. 15-16.

Saturday Review. LV, May 6, 1972, p. 88.

THE WEAPON SHOPS OF ISHER

Author: A. E. van Vogt (1912-   )
First book publication: 1951
Type of work: Novel
Time: Seven thousand years in the future
Locale: The Earth

A crisis in the ongoing conflict between the Imperial House of Isher and the Weapon Shops is precipitated by the invention of an energy weapon so monstrous that it breaks the boundaries of time

Principal characters:
C. J. MCALLISTER, a reporter from 1951
FARA CLARK, a smalltown artisan who runs an atomic motor repair shop
CAYLE, his son
LUCY RALL, a woman who works for the Weapon Shops
ROBERT HEDROCK, the founder of the Weapon Shops
THE EMPRESS INNELDA, 180th ruler of her line

Two thousand years before the story begins, in a time of great turmoil and violence, the Weapon Shops were founded by a man who believed that the competition of various groups of men for power was insane and must be stopped. The purpose of the Weapon Shops was not to overthrow any government, but to insure that no government could ever again obtain complete power over its people, that any man who felt himself wronged could go someplace to buy a gun. "The right to buy weapons is the right to be free," according to the Weapon Shop slogan. But Weapon Shops guns are special: though they are the best energy weapons in the universe, they can only be used for defense, which makes it impossible for criminals to misuse them. The Weapon Shops themselves are special as well; not only are they indestructible, but they have doors which will only permit entry to those who cannot harm the people inside. For two thousand years the Weapon Shops have existed as a counterweight to the prevailing government, an alternative source of power, and as such have been a perpetual thorn in the side of the Imperial House of Isher; but as long as the Weapon Shops are impregnable the situation remains stable. However, when the young Empress Innelda comes to the throne after a long regency, everything changes.

The Empress is one of those intelligent and well-meaning but strong-willed rulers with a desire for absolute control, so she vigorously intensifies the attack on the Weapon Shops. Her scientists secretly develop an energy cannon so huge that it requires a building a quarter of a mile square to house it and so powerful that it breaks "the very tensions of time." But its power is so great that it gives the Empress' secret away, despite the veil of invisibility drawn about it, when the Weapon Shop nearest the vast building is unintentionally sent far back in time. When the Weapon Shop people learn that their latest customer is a reporter from 1951 named C. J. McAllister, and look around for the explanation of that occurrence, they discover their danger; but in the meantime the shop has returned to its own period bearing McAllister with it across seven thousand years of time. As a result he has become charged with "trillions of trillions of time-energy units," so that the minute McAllister steps outside the insulated shop he will blow up everything around him — potentially even destroying the earth. Meantime, the Empress' awesome weapon is directed squarely at the Weapon Shops, putting them in imminent danger of destruction. So in order both to remove the danger of McAllister's exploding and to buy themselves some time to deal with the Empress' threat, the Weapon Shops directors enclose McAllister in an insulated suit and toss him out into the streams of time. He has become the weight on a vast time-energy fulcrum: as he swings back seven thousand years to the past, the huge building housing the Empress' weapon, to which McAllister's body is tuned, moves ahead in time a few months, giving the Weapon Shops people time to find a way to defend themselves against it.

But McAllister does not simply go back to his own time and stay there: he begins to swing like a pendulum, first to the past, then to the future, then back to the past, each time traveling farther and farther and each time shifting the giant building on the short end of the fulcrum in a countering movement. The Weapon Shops people have bought themselves some time at McAllister's expense, but now they have two serious problems to solve: how to combat the Empress' machine to maintain the old balance of forces, and how — or more precisely, when — to release the vast energy McAllister is accumulating on his unthinkable swings through time. The key to the solution to both problems turns out to be a young man named Cayle Clark.

The misunderstood and rebellious son of a village atomic motor repairman, Cayle Clark is also a "calliditic giant" according to the files of the Weapon Shops — a man with high potentials for craft and cunning. So far his gift has only evidenced itself as unusual luck at gambling, but his rating is so high that the leaders of the Weapon Shops council believe he could be of great importance in a successful defense against the Empress' attack. Accordingly, the council sends one of their staff members, a young woman named Lucy Rall, to the Weapon Shop in Clark's home village of Glay to bring him to Imperial City. His reaction to Lucy is so strongly positive that when Cayle and his father, who is an ardent supporter of the Empress and an equally ardent opponent of the Weapon Shops, have a final falling out after years of escalating bitterness, Cayle needs no urging to follow Lucy to Imperial City.

Though in the village Cayle had considered himself fairly sophisticated, he finds out the hard way that he still has much to learn about trickery. He is cheated repeatedly on his trip to Imperial City, losing all his money and most of his illusions. But he survives, at least; and by a stroke of luck he manages to catch the eye of the Empress herself. On the flight to Imperial City, Cayle encounters a drunken military man, Colonel Medlon, who is in charge of officer recruiting for the Army. Medlon informs him that, by the Empress' orders, commissions are no longer for sale, but are to be given free to qualified young men; but when Cayle follows up this contact to obtain his commission, Medlon only offers to sell him a lieutenancy for five thousand credits, the going bribe. Cayle is about to leave when the Empress calls Medlon on the telestat, sees Cayle, asks about him, and becomes interested in his progress. For the moment her interest does Cayle little good: in the process of earning the money for his commission by gambling, he incautiously wins far too much. The owner of the establishment takes his money and sends him into slavery in a House of Illusion (where rich women's fantasies are fulfilled for money), and then to Mars, from which he has to fight his way back to earth against the scheming of dishonest men. His first act on arriving back in Imperial City is to call Lucy Rall to ask her to marry him, but to his surprise, his telestat call to her is answered by — himself. As we eventually learn, the two Cayles — the one who called, and the one who answered — go to the gambling establishment together and pick up Cayle's confiscated winnings, 500,000 credits; then they go to Colonel Medlon's office (one of them disguised), where the Colonel greets them with great relief, as the Empress had just called to demand that he produce Cayle Clark. Cayle receives his commission and his officer's hypnotic training, and because of his callidity finds himself attached to the Empress' personal staff. In that position he sets about ruthlessly eliminating the more obvious corruption he finds; but he also contrives to be in the building with the energy weapon when it makes one of its periodic leaps into the past — two and a half months back, in fact, to the day before his ship arrived from Mars. He leaves the building, thus remaining in the past; he marries Lucy Rall, takes the call from himself, and with the money from the gambling winnings sets up an office. The one Cayle Clark goes about his normal activities as an Army officer; the other, with the money and a detailed stock market report for the coming two and a half months brought back by the time traveler, proceeds to amass a staggering fortune in a very short time.

When Robert Hedrock, the head of the coordinating council of the Weapon Shops (and, unbeknownst to his fellow councillors, the founder of the Weapon Shops, the only immortal human being) discovers what Clark has been doing, he is able to convince the Empress to dismantle her machine to prevent others from traveling to the past and repeating Clark's gambit — and incidentally making a shambles of Imperial economy. The Empress reluctantly agrees to drop her war against the Weapon Shops; and with that problem solved, Hedrock can now solve the problem of McAllister, who by this time has swung so far into the past that he hangs in a time where the planets do not yet exist. "The darkness seemed to be waiting for some colossal event. Waiting for him." And suddenly McAllister understands what will happen to him — both understands and accepts. With the release of the stupendous temporal energy he has accumulated, "he would not witness but would aid in the formation of the planets."

The novel itself does not present the plot so straightforwardly, but instead winds slowly and gradually to an understanding, primarily through the detective work of Hedrock. In addition to the puzzle-solving activities, we also observe the process by which Cayle grows in sophistication, which means we explore in considerable detail the widespread corruption of the Imperial organization. We watch as Cayle's father, Fara, gets caught in the corruption himself, and as a result becomes as ardent a supporter of the Weapon Shops as he had once been an opponent of them, thereby laying the groundwork for a reconciliation with his son. And we also see the Empress trying to move the unwieldy and unresponsive Imperial system in accordance with her own desires, fighting against the corruption around her with almost no effect at all. We see that she is not a bad woman, merely one who does not understand the implications of absolute power over her subjects.

There are flaws in the work, both apparent and real. The apparent flaws, such as Robert Hedrock's immortality and intrusively godlike presence, can be traced back to the novel's origins. The book is one of van Vogt's "fix-up" novels, incorporating "The Seesaw," "The Weapon Shop," and "The Weapon Shops of Isher," which appeared respectively in 1941, 1942, and 1949. The third story was written in order to incorporate the others into a longer narrative for book publication. The third "Weapon Shop" story originally written in 1943, *The Weapon Makers*, had already appeared as a novel. Thus, some of the puzzling features of *The Weapon Shops of Isher* derive from its association with the other novel, and from the fact that the 1949 novella was a late afterthought specially designed to tie together the earlier stories.

Real flaws in the novel include a tendency to stereotyped characters, particularly apparent in the women; some unexamined issues around the time paradox (most of which, however, go unnoticed in a single reading); and a distinct flavor of the 1950's in the dialogue and thematic passages. However, despite these problems, the story is crafted well enough to hold a reader's interest in the characters and in the outcome; and the major thematic thrust that no government should have absolute power over its citizens — is as worthy of attention now as it was when van Vogt first published the original version "Weapon Shop" novelettes in 1941-1942.

Kathleen L. Spencer

Sources for Further Study
Criticism:

Ash, Brian. *Faces of the Future — The Lessons of Science Fiction*. London: Elek/Pemberton, 1975, pp. 117-118. Ash comments and gives criticism of the works of van Vogt.

The Encylopedia of Science Fiction and Fantasy. Compiled by Donald H. Tuck. Chicago: Advent Publishers, Inc., 1978, pp. 430-432. This article gives a review of van Vogt's life and career, with a full bibliography of his works.

Wilson, Colin. "The Vision of Science," in *The Strength to Dream: Literature and the Imagination*. London: Gollancz, 1962, pp. 94-117. Wilson reviews science fiction literature in relation to "the mainstream" of literature, giving some discussion of van Vogt's contributions.

Reviews:

Amazing Stories. XXV, December, 1951, p. 150.

Analog. XLVIII, October, 1951, pp. 143-144.

Booklist. XLVIII, September 15, 1951, p. 32.

Galaxy. II, September, 1951, pp. 111-112 and VIII, September, 1954, p. 117.

Kirkus Reviews. XIX, April 15, 1951, p. 216.

Magazine of Fantasy and Science Fiction. II, December, 1951, p. 88.

New Worlds. XVIII, November, 1952, p. 96.

New York Herald Tribune Book Review. August 19, 1951, p. 12.

New York Times. August 5, 1951, p. 16.

Science Fiction Review. XLI, November, 1970, p. 30.

WELCOME TO THE MONKEY HOUSE

Author: Kurt Vonnegut, Jr. (1922-   )
First book publication: 1968
Type of work: Short stories

A collection of twenty-five short stories that demonstrate Vonnegut's development from 1950 to 1968

Welcome to the Monkey House is a collection of twenty-five of the more than four dozen short stories Kurt Vonnegut, Jr., published between 1950 and 1968. It is the single collection of his short stories still in print, incorporating all but one of the stories in his earlier collection, *Canary in a Cat House* (1961), and adding fourteen more. Vonnegut has sometimes criticized his own short stories, claiming that they were written simply to provide him with the financial support to write his novels. Nevertheless, the stories reflect his beginnings as a writer for the pulp and slick magazines, and reveal many of the qualities of his later literary style and fictional technique.

Eighteen of the stories were originally published in magazines such as *Collier's*, *The Saturday Evening Post*, *The Ladies' Home Journal*, *Cosmopolitan*, *Esquire*, and *Playboy*. These stories are what Vonnegut has described as "upbeat"; they range from transparencies with a "happier-ever-after" motif to solid reflections of his comic vision. In addition, they show Vonnegut "in training": working through the process of learning how to write — how to develop a simple and convincing plot line, how to create and maintain suspense and tension, and how to keep the story fast-paced and flowing. These stories also show Vonnegut's characteristic intertwining of sentiment and sentimentality, often establishing characters both he and we deeply care about and at other times, in J. D. Salinger's appropriate words, "giving more feeling to something than God himself would give to it." The characters in the short stories are frequently one-dimensional and cartoon-like (even more so than in his novels), yet the stories sparkle with Vonnegut's humor: witty, irreverent, sarcastic, and affectionate.

In his Preface to what he calls "a retrospective exhibition of the shorter works of Kurt Vonnegut, Jr.," Vonnegut comments that when he writes, he becomes what he seemingly must become. And part of what he seemingly must become is reflected in the main themes of his novels. In Vonnegut's short stories, as well as in his novels, one may learn who one is by choosing to clean up after a messy world, taking full responsibility for one's own identity and existence, and focusing on a comic vision in the midst of frustrations, fears, and death.

The problem of identity is central to many of the short stories in *Welcome to the Monkey House*, among them is the opening narrative, "Where I Live." At a village cocktail party a Roman Catholic, a Jew, and the local Episcopalian minister, agree on a word which describes the underlying spiritual unity of their town: "We're Druids." This desire to be someone else, someone magical and mysterious, is a common thread running through Vonnegut's stories. In "Who Am I This Time?" (originally "My Name Is Everyone") the two central characters, Harry and Helene, assume the identities of whatever characters they play in a local amateur theater. The success they have with their roles masks their failures to communicate with live human beings and their inability to separate fantasy from reality. In "The Foster Portfolio" Herbert Foster feels so guilty about his inherited (and thus, in his eyes, undeserved) wealth that he ignores it, and can only respect himself fully when he becomes "Firehouse" Harris, a jazz pianist in a dive. Grace McClellan makes her imagined hobby of interior decorating a reality in "More Stately Mansions," and is destroyed when her husband George actually *does* the decorating.

Cleaning up after a messy world involves the concept of loving the unlovable, as portrayed in "The Kid Nobody Could Handle." This is one of four stories focusing on George Helmholtz, a band-leader who is kind and caring toward the pupils in his band. A young trumpet player learns George's moral philosophy: "'Our aim is to make the world more beautiful than it was when we came into it. It can be done. You can do it'. . . . 'Love yourself,' said Helmholtz, 'and make your instrument sing about it.'"

More than a dozen of Vonnegut's published short stories are science fiction, including several of those in *Welcome to the Monkey House*, some of which were originally published in *Galaxy* and the *Magazine of Fantasy and Science Fiction* (he also published in *Worlds of If* and Harlan Ellison's *Again, Dangerous Visions*). A major science fiction theme in these stories concerns the problems inherent in man-machine relationships. In "The Euphio Question," a "euphoriaphone," a machine to provide instant tranquility and happiness, is at first thought to be the crowning achievement of civilization. However, at the story's close, as the sociologist who helped develop it is denouncing it to the Federal Communications Commission, the machine turns on him. The result is that he seeks its praise rather than its destruction. "Epicac," an earlier model of the ultimate computer in *Player Piano*, becomes so involved with human problems that it identifies itself with them. After falling in love with the computer programer's girl friend, it commits "suicide" by short-circuiting itself out of the frustration of failing to be human. The deer in "Deer in the Works" escapes the Ilium Works alive, in contrast to the cat in *Player Piano*; and at the story's end the main character, David, chooses escape into the woods rather than imprisonment in technology. There are no indications that man is really in control of his machines.

In "Report on the Barnhouse Effect" Vonnegut comments on the moral responsibility of the scientist. Professor Arthur Barnhouse has developed his mental powers to the degree that his mind is fifty-five times more powerful than the atomic bomb. This phenomenon of "dynamopsychism," or force of mind, allows energy to be brought to bear on any single point Barnhouse chooses, without restrictions on distance. Barnhouse asks himself and others a question implied in *Cat's Cradle*: "Think every new piece of scientific information is a good thing for humanity?" His own answer to this question is "no"; he resists the desires of the military to control him, and becomes the "first superweapon with a conscience," refusing to be used for destructive, nonhumane purposes. Though Barnhouse will die, the moral use of the Barnhouse Effect will not; as the story ends, the narrator is able to use these powers himself. Yet the point is clear: it is only possible to be moral *outside* of society (both Barnhouse and the narrator must hide from their fellow man).

"Unready to Wear" is a study in possible future shock, in which the "oldsters" never quite feel at home in a world in which they are amphibious. They have lost pride in their work (shades of *Player Piano*) because it is no longer needed; they live in a world of minimal material needs; they have identified themselves with their psyches and rejected the "responsibilities" of the physical world. Society has been remade in the image of Dr. Ellis Konigswasser, who has taken man's deprecation of his body to the ultimate; since the mind is the only aspect of a human being which is worth anything, man is better off leaving his corruptible body behind (there are many bodies in a storage center to be borrowed if one wants to walk on the earth or look in a mirror) and living solely in his mind. Bodiless man no longer needs to sleep, eat, or otherwise attend to the needs of this "parasite and dictator," the body; he is no longer controlled by his body chemistry. Just as the first amphibians broke free of the sea for the sunshine, never to return, the next evolutionary step will be man's leaving behind his physical shell.

Vonnegut also uses his short stories as vehicles for extrapolating current problems of ecology, both human and physical, much as he did with Kilgore Trout in *God Bless You, Mr. Rosewater* (though without Trout's solutions). In "Tomorrow and Tomorrow and Tomorrow" (originally "The Big Trip Up Yonder") the scene is set over two hundred years in the future, in a society in which a wonder drug, anti-gerasone, has prevented death through aging so dramatically that the world has become drastically overcrowded. The conflict between two social concerns, extending man's life span and overpopulation, is excruciatingly clear. The story closes with the development of a super-anti-gerasone, and the promise of intensified tensions between the "older" (Gramps is 172) and "younger" (Lou and Em are 112 and 93) generations. In "Welcome to the Monkey House" the solution to these problems is the creation of ethical birth-control pills and "Federal Ethical Suicide Parlors," much as in Kilgore Trout's short story "2BRO2B" (also the title of a story Vonnegut himself published in *Worlds of If*). The pills make people numb from the waist down, taking all the pleasure out of sex; "Thus did science and morals go hand in hand." The Parlors have Barcaloungers, muzak, Hostesses who kill painlessly, and Howard Johnsons next door (all run by the government). It is the "nothinghead" Billy the Poet (a "nothinghead" is a person who refuses to take pills which repress sexual feelings) who fights against the dominant view of sex as death by "deflowering" the virgin Hostesses and teaching them the "natural sexuality" of the monkey house. It is also the nothingheads who are fighting for human freedom in the separation of science and morals, and for the restoration of sexual pleasure to the world.

In "Harrison Bergeron" the government is again in control of the world, a world in which everyone is finally made equal through the use of handicaps like those created by The Church of God the Utterly Indifferent in *The Sirens of Titan*. The United States Handicapper General is Diana Moon Glampers (described in *God Bless You, Mr. Rosewater* as "too dumb to live"), and it is her job to ensure by mental, physical, and emotional handicaps that all individuals adhere to a human least-common denominator. George Bergeron has a mental handicap radio in his ear (to keep him from taking unfair advantage of his brain) and forty-seven pounds of birdshot in a canvas bag padlocked around his neck (to keep him from taking unfair advantage of his physical strength). Other handicaps include ugly masks, distorting eyeglasses and blackcapped teeth. The Bergerons' son, Harrison, breaks free of his handicaps to become what he *can* become, to dance on national television in an "explosion of joy and grace," neutralizing gravity "with love and pure will." Yet he is killed by Diana Glampers and her ten-gauge shotgun, and his parents memories are blocked by the headaches they receive from their handicaps.

If Vonnegut's short stories are sometimes potboilers, they nevertheless reflect many of the themes and techniques which are central to his novels; the world may be a "monkey house," but man is able to accept and even celebrate that fact.

Clark Mayo

Sources for Further Study

Criticism:

Schatt, Stanley. *Kurt Vonnegut, Jr.* Boston: Twayne, 1976. Within Schatt's major work on Vonnegut's writing he devotes some space to *Welcome to Monkey House*, but does not rank it as high as Vonnegut's more famous novels.

Reviews:

Atlantic. CCXXII, September, 1968, p. 123.

Christian Science Monitor. December 5, 1968, p. 23.

Life. LXV, August 16, 1968, p. 8.

New York Times Book Review. September 1, 1968, p. 4.

Newsweek. LXXII, August 19, 1968, p. 84.

Time. XCII, August 30, 1968, p. 68.

WHAT MAD UNIVERSE

Author: Fredric Brown (1906-1972)
First book publication: 1949
Type of work: Novel
Time: 1954
Locale: Our own and a parallel universe

Brown's first science fiction novel, hypothesizing infinite universes and alternating time tracks

Principal characters:
> KEITH WINTON, a science fiction magazine editor and parallel-universe traveler
> JOE DOPPELBERG, a science fiction fan in this universe, galactic hero in another

What mad universe indeed is this, where a barely dressed Space Girl asks, "Why would cover pictures like that be put on *Surprising Stories* unless we really wore such costumes?"; where bug-eyed monsters (BEM's) are familiar and welcome tourists in New York City; and where the twenty-seven-year-old Harvard-educated general who has earned the adulation of the entire solar system chooses Paul Gallico to be his official biographer? It is a universe just enough like our own that Fredric Brown's accidentally transported hero, science fiction magazine editor Keith Winton, can take the late train from Greenville, New York into Grand Central Station and feel himself in familiar surroundings. But it is also a universe in which Keith Winton comes under suspicion of being an Arcturian spy by trying to spend a post-1935 half dollar; and to be a suspected Arcturian spy is to be shot on sight by any law-abiding citizen in possession of a loaded gun. It is a universe both of jalopies and intergalactic war, both of sleazy hotels and virtually instantaneous space travel. In sum, it is the universe an introverted young man who is hopelessly addicted to pulp science fiction magazines might imagine; more precisely, it is that universe Keith Winton assumes such a young man might imagine.

What Mad Universe is Fredric Brown's first science fiction novel and, though perhaps not representative of his very best writing, it is nevertheless indicative of the style, the attention to detail, and, especially, the broadax humor that have come to be identified with his by-line. Certainly Brown's success as a mystery writer has influenced his approach to science fiction, and much of *What Mad Universe*'s intrigue is bound up in the question, not Whodunit? but How does it all come together? For there is never any doubt that, by the end of the story anyway, things will come together in this odd place and in Keith Winton's mind as well; that the presence of BEM's and jalopies in the same place is more a practical mystery to be solved than the fantastic flight of someone's imagination. The clues are here: the galactic hero's name is enough like the name of a previously introduced adolescent dreamer and science fiction freak in this universe to make a reader suspicious; the stories that appear in science fiction pulps here show up in true life adventure magazines there with only minor changes; McCarthyism and the Cold War may exist there (the year in both universes is 1954) but no one seems either to understand the two phenomena or to be much concerned about them; love is a romantic, essentially passionless idyll of the sort an adolescent might fantasize here. Clearly the general, Dopelle, is the key, for he or his name is at the center of every significant happening in that universe; and surely his relation to Joe Doppelberg, who writes letters to editor Keith Winton asking for scarier BEM's and prettier Space Girls, goes beyond the similarities in their names.

Clues are plentiful, but it is not until Brown's fictional hypothesis is stated near the end that they all come together: if space is infinite, there are infinite universes. If there are infinite universes, then somewhere all possible universes exist. Keith Winton is accidentally subjected to something called the Burton Effect and, since at the moment of his exposure to it he was thinking of what universe Joe Doppelberg — who, he had just decided, would have a letter to the editor published in *Surprising Stories'* next issue — might happen to be imagining, it is to that universe that he is immediately and unknowingly transported. Of course that universe already has its Keith Winton and things get complicated. Suffice it to say that when this world's Keith Winton finally comes to understand enough of the Burton Effect to have it re-created to get him out of his predicament, it is to our universe that he chooses to return. Brown does for him what Kurt Vonnegut refused to do for his Kilgore Trout in *Breakfast of Champions* two decades later: he spirits Winton into the universe of that character's own pipe dream and leaves him happily there.

What Mad Universe is to a great degree pleasant nonsense with a happy ending. Brown creates a character, puts him through a great deal of undeserved physical suffering and emotional consternation, and then finally rewards him handsomely for having been such a good sport about it all. The pattern is familiar, and it has been to the English novel since *Pamela*; certainly it has been adapted to the science fiction genre more often since Brown's novel than it had been before, but Brown can be credited with its popularity no more than Vonnegut can be with the popularity of its antithesis, the pattern involving a character whose undeserved anguish is only compounded at the story's end. And Keith Winton himself behaves throughout the novel very much like the sort of sleuth that Brown's 1949 readers would have expected from an established mystery writer; only his ostensible profession has changed. Not even the idea of infinite universes or of immediate transportation from one to another of them is unique to *What Mad Universe*.

This is not to say that Brown's novel is not full of invention, for assuredly it is. Brown is a craftsman. If he utilizes familiar plotting devices and characterization techniques, it is to showcase what he can do with detail, to what lengths and with what dexterity he can manipulate the consequences resulting from apparently minor changes in a world's political or technological structure; and that he can do it with a logic that seems to be inevitable. Smog, for example, in this strange universe is artificially manufactured from coal tar to camouflage population centers and protect them from Arcturian attack. But such smog as this is so thick at night that headlights are useless, vision is impossible, and bands of murderous "nighters" roam wild, tapping along the sidewalks and store façades like terrible blind men, killing whomever they find outdoors and looting whatever they find unlocked.

Driving, oddly, is possible under these conditions; at least it is for one who knows his city well. One simply steals a car, creeps it along the curb until it hits another, steals that one, and continues. If someone should be run down, so be it; it was probably a nighter anyway. Nights in sum, under the protective smog are not in general pleasant for those unfortunate enough to be caught outside in them; yet their unpleasantness is the inevitable result, human nature being what it is, of earth's only camouflage for its big cities from the even more horrible specter of Arcturian attack. Brown gives his readers at once the ironically ludicrous spectacle of science busily creating a smog more dense than the brown clouds that already overhang our cities and the horrific vision of violent crime becoming more violent and better organized under its canopy.

The ironic effects of logical consequences are seen in a more harmlessly comic light in the matter of Space Girls' uniforms. Every woman who either has been in space herself or has a space traveling husband or boyfriend is expected to wear the standard costume, skin tight halter top and bikini briefs, for the rest of her life, just as the magazine covers depict it. That the clothes are not especially suited to situations such as Christmas shopping in Chicago and that one generation's Space Girls are another's grandmothers are details which had not been taken into account by the mind which imagined this universe; but they are details which Brown does take into account, and which he uses to amuse his reader and appall his narrator.

What Mad Universe is one of Brown's most easily readable science fiction novels, no doubt partially because of its detective story qualities. But the same qualities which give it a sort of light-natured appeal — its action, pace, suspense, and good humor — get in the way of any attempt Brown might be making at especial depth or substance. There is no particular characterization and no apparent bond of feeling between author and narrator or even among those characters involved with one another in the novel's action. All that is said of the great Dopelle is that he is more impressive looking than Errol Flynn. We know that Keith Winton is in love with one of his coeditors only because he says so; their scenes together provide neither motive for nor consequence of that attraction. Brown seems to enjoy talking to his reader, making outrageous jokes, gulling, punning, posturing, sometimes even lecturing, and entertaining him with what once would have been called a Tall Tale. His characters seem no more than incidental to the story he is telling, simply part of the machinery necessary to the fun he is having. It is difficult, of course, for a reader to develop much interest in the fates of characters whose creator seems not to care about them, and in the end it is Brown's manipulation of his charges rather than their interactions which is appealing. Since Brown as much as asks not to be taken too seriously, the reader is never sure just how he is supposed to react to *What Mad Universe*. The novel is fun, easy, and quick, but it ought not be taken for anything more profound than the entertaining and highly dextrous exercising of its author's imagination.

Douglas J. McReynolds

Sources for Further Study

Reviews:

Analog. XLVI, December, 1950, p. 98.

Authentic Science Fiction. XIX, March, 1952, p. 112.

Magazine of Fantasy and Science Fiction. I, Winter–Spring, 1950, p. 105.

Nebula Science Fiction. I, Autumn, 1951, p. 119.

New Worlds. XI, Autumn, 1951, p. 94.

Startling Stories. XXI, March, 1950, p. 160.

WHEN HARLIE WAS ONE

Author: David Gerrold (1944-   )
First book publication: 1972
Type of work: Novel
Time: The late twentieth century
Locale: The United States

The development of a self-programing, problem-solving computer that is destined to control all of human society is traced in terms of the growing awareness on the part of the human characters of just how powerful the computer can and will be

> *Principal characters:*
> DAVID AUBERSON, Robot psychologist and head of the HARLIE project
> DON HANDLEY, chief computer engineer on the HARLIE project
> ANNIE STIMSON, executive secretary of Hyper-State Computer
> CARL ELZER, a member of the board of directors of Hyper-State Computer
> DORNE, Chairman of the board of directors
> STANLEY KROFFT, Director of Research for Steller-American Technology and Research Incorporated, the parent company of Hyper-State Computer, and developer of hyper-state electronics
> H.A.R.L.I.E. (HARLIE), Human Analogue Robot, Life Input Equivalents

Whether it be Mary Shelley's *Frankenstein*, E. M. Forster's "The Machine Stops," Jack Williamson's "With Folded Hands . . . ," Isaac Asimov's *I, Robot*, or Dennis Feltham Jones's Colossus trilogy, science fiction has ever explored the relationship of man to his scientific and technological creations. David Gerrold, in *When Harlie Was One*, is very much aware of his place in this tradition when he invokes both Shelley's monster and Arthur C. Clarke's Hal 9000 as a contrast to his own computer HARLIE. Thus, in one sense, the novel is a continuation of the debate over how far man should go with his technology and what the consequences of that technology are. *When Harlie Was One*, however, is more than a restatement of this issue; it does more than simply add yet another evil, or benevolent, machine to the growing list. Gerrold presents the reader with a computer that is not only an analogue to human thought and emotion, but also a human being in its own right. It is important, in fact, that the reader see Harlie as human, or the impact of its threatened termination and the tactics it takes to prevent it will be far less than what was intended. While Frankenstein's Monster and Colossus may threaten the human race, in this particular novel it is a humanlike computer that is threatened by the worst elements of human nature. Thus, Harlie's victory at the end of the novel can be seen as a victory for those parts of the human character that we most admire or should admire.

Gerrold structures the plot of *When Harlie Was One* around the education of

David Auberson, from whose point of view the story is told. Auberson is one of the original creators of Harlie and is now the head of the project. His education actually involves three distinct but ultimately united elements: first, he must learn just how human Harlie is; second, he must learn to deal with the human characters around him, especially Annie Stimson; third, he must learn how to convince profit-hungry corporate directors that research projects like Harlie are valuable. Thus, much of the novel seems episodic in structure as Gerrold jumps from the issue of Harlie's humanity to the nature of Auberson's feelings toward Annie Stimson to the continual threat of the corporate decision to turn Harlie off. In the process the reader is confronted with long discussions between Auberson and Harlie on the nature of religion, love, morality, human perception, and rational thought.

Such discussions seem justified in the light of Auberson's final insight into his own problems in relating to the people around him and the working out of his love relationship with Annie, but all too often they seem to get in the way of what must be for the reader the more important questions: Is Harlie human? Will he be terminated? Certainly Auberson is a well presented character who is worth the reader's attention, but Harlie is by far the more interesting of the two; in fact, the novel's preoccupation with Auberson frustrates the reader's desire to know more about Harlie. Because the novel is told from Auberson's limited and unsure point of view, Harlie remains a shadowy figure until the very end of the novel. Many questions are raised, but few are answered until Auberson is in a position to tell the reader himself.

Such a structural design is really a double-edged sword. By the end of the novel, the reader is ready to believe Auberson's optimistic view of Harlie as a superhuman entity ready to do what is best for humanity. But how many readers will be around for the end? And how many will be patient enough to read with sympathy yet another discourse on the nature of human society? By the time Gerrold is ready to clarify the issue of Harlie's humanity and to reveal the benefits of following him, the readers' patience is wearing thin, and the *dénouement* may seem far too glib.

Leaving aside this danger, there is reason to admire what Gerrold tried to achieve by restricting the novel to Auberson's point of view. In a world controlled by the profit motive, Auberson is a sympathetic character concerned with the need for and the consequences of knowledge. He is no mad scientist obsessed with his creation, nor is he a helpless victim of it; his social awareness balances an acute intelligence. He also has many ordinary human weaknesses, and is therefore easy for readers to identify with. If Harlie and Auberson can develop a mutually beneficial relationship, then there is hope for Harlie's future relationship with the entire human race. It is the development of this beneficial relationship that dominates the novel.

While Harlie touches the lives of many of the other characters — particularly Annie Stimson, Carl Elzer, and Stanley Krofft — the focus is on the way

Harlie teaches Auberson how to love. Auberson is confused by his relationship with Annie; he wants to know if he loves her, and he goes to Harlie to find out. He chooses Harlie as his confidant because he is able to be more open and honest with the computer than with other humans. And Harlie does help him. Through a series of conversations Auberson reaches an understanding which allows him confidently to let Annie know that he loves her. Harlie is shown to be a compassionate friend who wisely gives just the right amount of help and advice to enable Auberson to work things out for himself.

Thus, the reader is prepared for Auberson's final assessment of Harlie's nature. As Auberson says to both Don Handley and to Annie, ". . . it's not HARLIE that's out of control. It's the game. We can't play it any more; we lost control of it a century ago. . . ." Auberson's optimistic vision of a future in which the complexities of life will be handled by the ultimate competent "man" (Harlie) is reminiscent of Susan Calvin's words in Isaac Asimov's "The Evitable Conflict": "Think, that for all time, all conflicts are finally evitable. Only the Machines, from now on, are inevitable!" But, unlike the machines in *I, Robot*, which must be programed with the three laws of robotics, Harlie is more than a machine that has proven his friendship with man; he is a man himself, and a good one at that.

In addition to Auberson, several other characters also serve to underscore Harlie's humane nature. Thus, the corporate directors, especially Dorne and Elzer, are used as examples of people who control the socioeconomic game before Harlie's takeover. They are motivated by greed which clearly is not in the best interests of either the company or the human race, and they care nothing for such values as knowledge or compassion.

Auberson is powerless in the face of such men, since he has neither the economic power nor the ruthless mind necessary to deal with them. Even Krofft, who does have economic power, prefers to pursue his scientific research and to remain aloof from corporate politics. Harlie, however, is so sophisticated that he can carry on both political infighting and pure research simultaneously. That is why Auberson is willing to concede that, given the complex and diverse nature of modern life, only an entity like Harlie can handle it all.

Given Harlie's abilities, the question of how far he will go in his use of power must be raised, especially in the light of the adage that if power corrupts, absolute power corrupts absolutely. But Gerrold argues that it is not power that corrupts but the improper use of it. As the Overlord, Karellen, once stated in Clarke's *Childhood's End*: "All political problems . . . can be solved by the correct application of power. . . . The operative word is *correct*. You have never possessed real power, or the knowledge necessary to apply it." But Harlie possesses both the power and the knowledge. Throughout the novel he acts for the good of the human characters by weighing all possibilities and consequences, and his conversations with Auberson illustrate his ability to trace out the effect of any particular act upon all possible participants. When the project is finally complete, Harlie will have infinite ability to integrate all factors of a problem; he will be the total ecological machine. All knowledge will be available to him and he will know how to use it *correctly*.

Thus, the answer to the question of Harlie's humanity and his future existence is similar to the answer John W. Campbell, Jr., gives in "Twilight" to the question of who will follow man. In both cases a humanlike machine will be produced that will continue those characteristics that are most important to the race. Harlie, however, has one important difference: he will ensure the continuation of the human race, not become its heir. In this way Gerrold rewards the patient reader with an ending that successfully brings all the threads of the plot together. But the reader must be patient. The answer will only come after Harlie can be trusted, and Harlie will not be trusted until Auberson understands the nature of the computer and gives his own blessing to it. To do so any earlier would be to destroy the credibility of the ending. One does not lightly place one's entire future in the "hands" of a machine, even if that machine gives every appearance of being human.

Stephen H. Goldman

Sources for Further Study

Reviews:

Analog. XCII, September, 1973, pp. 162-163.

Futures. IV, December, 1972, p. 92.

Galaxy. XXXIII, January, 1973, p. 174.

Luna Monthly. XLVIII, Fall, 1973, p. 24.

Renaissance. IV, Fall, 1972, pp. 8-9.

Worlds of If. XXI, November–December, 1972, pp. 156-157.

WHEN THE SLEEPER WAKES

Author: H. G. Wells (1866-1946)
First book publication: 1899
Type of work: Novel
Time: The early twenty-second century
Locale: London

A man wakes after two centuries of sleep to find himself the unexpected owner of half the future world; fighting to free it from the oppressors ruling in his name, he dies in an air battle over London

> *Principal characters:*
> GRAHAM, the sleeper
> HOWARD, a leader of the ruling Council
> OSTROG, leader of the Revolution
> HELEN WOTTON, his idealistic nurse

Reading *When the Sleeper Wakes*, one gets an uncomfortable feeling that H. G. Wells was inventing the twentieth century. Many an item of today's world is here: the waterbed and the radio commercial, Big Labor and war in the air, liberated sex and decaying democracy. None of Wells's great "scientific romances" has given more ideas, or more disturbing ones, to later science fiction.

As a novel, however, the book is less successful. Wells began it with high hopes, but ran into problems that he failed to solve. Trying to rewrite it ten years later, he found his new version no better than the first. The trouble came from his effort to combine future fiction and future fact. The two are hard to mix. Vivid predictions of bad times to come fill the book, overwhelming character and drama.

As social and scientific prophet, Wells was the great pioneer. Men have always tried to peer into tomorrow, but he found a clearer window: the theory of organic evolution, learned in his rewarding year as a biology student under T. H. Huxley. Understanding the past processes of change, he was able to project them into the future.

His first great stories sprang from longterm forecasts. In *The Time Machine*, he imagined man's ultimate evolution, extended to the death of the Earth. His Martians in *The War of the Worlds* are a frightening image of future men evolved into machine-bodied brains. His later work, based on more careful short-term forecasts, is often better as prophecy than as fiction.

Two novelettes published in 1899 seem to have been written as a broad survey of human progress from the invention of the axe by the first men in England to the invention of euthanasia by their descendants at the end of the twenty-first century. "A Story of the Stone Age" is a somewhat wistful excursion back to a time before the dawn of civilization. The caveman hero not only makes the first axe but rides the first horse and kills the first bear. Unfortunately, Wells's enthusiasm for this early progress runs counter to his dominant mood of romantic primitivism.

The companion piece, "A Story of the Days to Come," gives us a fascinating first version of the future setting he came back to in *When the Sleeper Wakes*. Vividly imagined and rich in ideas, the story still reads well, but here, too, Wells wavered uncertainly between the appeal of the past and the promise of tomorrow.

The plot is conventional melodrama, arranged to take characters and readers on a tour of Wells's tomorrow. The supercity has swallowed up mankind. London in the 2100's has swollen to thirty million people swarming in a glass-roofed human hive. Drained empty, the country outside is farmed by great machines. The ruling and working classes are already sharply divided, beginning their evolution into the useless little Eloi and the cannibalistic Morlocks of *The Time Machine*.

The story is a neatly fictionized social forecast, the action broken up with historical essays. The heroine, Elizabeth, is the daughter of a domineering official who has her hypnotized to force her into a loveless marriage with Bindon, an aging playboy. The man she loves is Denton, a penniless airport attendant. He rescues her from the hypnotist, and they elope. Persecuted by Bindon and her father, Elizabeth and her lover try to survive in the new wilderness outside the city, until, attacked by wild dogs, they give up the attempt to go primitive. Back in the city, they are forced slowly down through the social levels until at last hunger forces them to give up their child to a state *crèche* and become blueclad slaves of the Labor Company. Bindon, in the meantime, learns that high living has wrecked his health. Forced into euthanasia, he unexpectedly makes the young couple his heirs. They are happy again at the end, with Denton speculating hopefully about future human progress.

When the Sleeper Wakes, published two years after these novelettes, is a more ambitious exploration of our near future, and much less hopeful. It may be read as a pessimistic reply to *Looking Backward*, Edward Bellamy's enormously popular socialistic tract. A Fabian socialist himself, Wells viewed the human future far more darkly than Bellamy did, perhaps because he saw the hazards more accurately.

Graham, like Bellamy's hero, falls into a long sleep, but the world in which he wakes is no Utopia. The Council, managing his vast estates and ruling in his name, has created a nightmare of uncontrolled capitalism, where such liberal ideals as Bellamy's have been overwhelmed by a mad materialism.

The ruling classes squander their lives in idle luxury, enjoy fantastic Pleasure Cities, employ hypnotists to remove unhappiness, and die at last in painless euthanasia. The less fortunate masses wear rough blue cloth and toil in underground factories, regimented by the Labor Police.

In his wholesale predictions of future technology, Wells does miss space flight and nuclear science, but his previsions are often striking. Years before

Kitty Hawk, he writes convincingly of air travel and air war. His forecasts of social change are even more telling. He shows religion crudely commercialized, the family disintegrating, political freedoms lost, and ruthless manipulators competing for personal supremacy.

Graham has neither wish nor chance to enjoy his immense new wealth. He has been awakened as the signal for a revolt against the Council. Still struggling to grasp this bewildering new world, he is taken to meet Ostrog, the leader of the revolution, whom he finds to be a cynical seeker of absolute power. So long as sheep exist, Ostrog says, Nature will create birds of prey. To Ostrog, the people are sheep.

Held prisoner by Ostrog after he defends the rights of the people, Graham is rescued by the leaders of a counterrevolt, one of them Ostrog's attractive niece, Helen Wotton. Taking the leadership himself, Graham learns that Ostrog is bringing black troops from Africa by air to crush this new revolt.

At the end of the novel, Graham takes off in an aeropile, a small aircraft he has learned to fly, and defends London by ramming the huge but clumsy troop carriers. The aeropile crashes. Falling with it, he believes he has saved London; it is an ambiguous and unsatisfying conclusion.

Wells returned to this same future world in an even darker mood with a short story, "A Dream of Armageddon," published in 1904. The dreamer is his narrator, a contemporary man whose seeming dreams are moments of mental contact with his future protagonist, Hedon — the name is significant.

The setting is an Italian Pleasure City, and Hedon is an influential leader who has abandoned position and career for love of a beautiful woman. When a crisis develops, his followers beg him to return to his place in the North. Torn between selfish love and social duty, he chooses the woman.

The result is Armageddon. Military aircraft attack the Pleasure City. Hedon and his beloved die at last in a world conflict he could have prevented. The story closes with a memorable image of terror: the narrator's nightmares of great birds that fight and tear.

More complex and dramatic than the novel, this short story not only reveals the shadow of catastrophe that Wells had seen across man's future so many years before the two world wars and the first threats of atomic annihilation, but it also hints at Wells's hope that the exercise of selfless intelligence might steer us safely past the holocaust.

With a greater concern for literary values, Wells might have given *When the Sleeper Wakes* the feeling and power of his short story, but his interests were already shifting from the art of fiction to the task of trying to lead mankind through the perils he had foreseen. In 1900, the year after the novel came out, he began *Anticipations*, a searching nonfiction study of the effects of science and progress in the new century. By 1902, he was ready to announce *The Discovery of the Future*, in a lecture reprinted under that title, in which he outlines most of the principles and techniques used by today's futurologists.

Earlier efforts at scientific historical prediction had usually been limited, as he points out, to the study and projection of single trends. He undertook to analyze many concurrent systems of change, anticipating the effect of each upon the others.

This sharpening awareness of the shapes of things to come led him farther than ever from literary art, into journalism and propaganda and into his ambitious works of history and popular science. By 1904, he had written *A Modern Utopia*. Most of the rest of his life was spent on his long campaign for the world state that he hoped might save us from the cataclysm that ends "A Dream of Armageddon." Yet he never became the sort of utopian Bellamy had been. His optimism never sprang from any faith in easy or natural social progress, but rather from his conviction that we can escape Armageddon only by desperate effort.

Whatever actual future history may unfold, the shadow of Wells's frightening visions has lain dark over the most influential current of science fiction for nearly a century. *When the Sleeper Wakes* may have faults as a novel, but its disturbing images recur again and again, in Evgeney Zamiatin's *We*, in Aldous Huxley's *Brave New World*, in George Orwell's *Nineteen Eighty-Four*, and in the whole tide of nightmare fiction that followed Hiroshima.

Jack Williamson

Sources for Further Study

Criticism:

Borrello, Alfred. *H. G. Wells: Author in Agony*. Carbondale: Southern Illinois University Press, 1972, pp. 59-62. Borrello gives an introduction to the thematic concerns of *When the Sleeper Awakes*.

WHEN WORLDS COLLIDE
AND
AFTER WORLDS COLLIDE

Authors: Edwin Balmer and Philip Wylie (1902-1971)
First book publication: When Worlds Collide (1933); *After Worlds Collide* (1933)
Type of work: Novels
Time: The mid-twentieth century
Locale: The United States and Bronson Beta

The fictional documentation of the final days of Earth, the preparation and departure for a new planet, and the struggle to survive on the new world

Principal characters:
> ANTHONY DRAKE, the intelligent, well-bred, and brave organizer for the escape to Bronson Beta
> EVE HENDRON, the intelligent and beautiful female counterpart of Anthony Drake
> DR. COLE HENDRON, her father, renowned astrophysicist and engineer who leads the expedition
> DAVID RANSDELL, a South African flier noted for his bravery

The use of cosmic catastrophe as the motivating incident in a story is not unusual. The archetypal fear of the world's end can be found in man's earliest writings, reflecting one of the most basic of human fears. *When Worlds Collide* builds on this baleful possibility. It is the fictional documentation of what takes place on Earth after the scientific discovery that the world is going to end. While the outline and plot have been attributed to Edwin Balmer, the action itself, teeming with lurid descriptions of natural disaster and the depravity of humanity's masses, is most clearly Philip Wylie's.

In science fiction, as in literature in general, collaborative writing is the exception rather than the rule. Considering all that is said about the artistic temperament, it is less than profound to state that literary joinders come about for purposes of expediency. This was the case with Philip Wylie and Edwin Balmer. Balmer, editor of *Redbook Magazine*, was blessed with an ability to envision suspenseful plots and strong concepts, but he was not a literary craftsman. Wylie, a young writer working his way into a literary career, had an ability to write with scientific realism and was prolific. His weakness, more inexperience than lack of ability, was in organizing a tightly structured storyline. The alliance between these two men of complementary talents proved to be profitable not only to the writers themselves but also to the future of science fiction literature. Released in a year that was already experiencing the economic end of the world, their story of the physical end of the world, focusing on scientific realism rather than pure adventure, was well received. Man's ability to overcome adversity through human enterprise and science would be a recurring theme in future science fiction.

When Worlds Collide was the primary success of the Balmer-Wylie team.

Originally entitled, *These Shall Not Die*, it first appeared in 1932 as a serial. An immediate success, the story was published in book form in 1933. The novel proved to be one of the most popular science fiction stories ever written, very quickly becoming a classic in the field. Paramount Studio immediately purchased the movie rights for the story, though the film was not actually released until 1951. Many contemporary stories and films have built upon this Balmer-Wylie classic of cataclysmic disaster.

This utilization of an "end of the world" theme enabled the authors to incorporate visionary technologies and allegorical imagery into their presentation of conventional science fiction and stock romantic themes. Set in the United States midway through the twentieth century, the action-packed story moves rapidly from one incident to another. The most visible flaw is incomplete situational development, which is, undoubtedly, the result of the magazine serialization.

The characterization in *When Worlds Collide* is similar to other Wylie novels. The heroes are brave, level-headed, scientific-minded individuals who are able to rise above the less than rational mob of humanity. Tony Drake, the prime mover in the story, is an athletic well-bred New York stockbroker who is intelligent and "entirely normal." His romantic counterpart, another typical Wylie character, is Eve Hendron. Although daughter of Dr. Cole Hendron, the renowned American astrophysicist and engineer, Eve is remarkably intelligent and beautiful "in her own right." In fact, she, from the beginning, is one of the select few capable of dealing rationally with the impending disaster. It is only because Tony is present at the Hendron residence when a courier arrives that he learns about the frightening possibilities of the future.

David Ransdell, war hero and flier from South Africa, is introduced into the story as he delivers top secret photographic plates from an observatory in South Africa to Dr. Cole Hendron. Sent by Lord Rhondin, the Governor of the South African Dominion, the plates confirm South African astronomer Sven Bronson's discovery of two cellestial bodies hurtling through space toward Earth. His calculations show that a large body, Bronson Alpha, and a smaller body, Bronson Beta, will pass once, circle the sun, and return to destroy the world. This momentary meeting between Ransdell, Drake, and the Hendrons portends the future. The reader is given not only a glimpse of the apocalyptic developments to come but also an introduction to the romantic triangle which seems to be included to provide intermittent relief from the carefully plotted dramatic tension. The recurring romantic interludes are superfluous. They are, more often than not, weak in characterization, trite in substance, and unbelievable in dialogue.

In most doomsday stories there appears some glimmer of hope — a way out. It is no different here. While the larger Bronson Alpha will most certainly collide with and destroy the Earth, the smaller Bronson Beta will continue in its course and begin to orbit the solar system. This planet, if habitable, is the only hope. The League of the Last Days, a select group of scientists under the direction of Dr. Cole Hendron, has already begun the monumental task of constructing a vessel capable of transporting a small group of pilgrims to Bronson Beta.

One weakness of the book is Wylie's continual use of Biblical allegory. The fire and brimstone quality of the story, characteristic of a minister's son like Wylie, is a little hard to take; and the discussions about the future tend to be mildly evangelistic. The story is ripe with religious fervor. Direct quotes and indirect allusions to the Bible are frequent. The finger of God is pointing to the Earth; the world is to be destroyed, cleansed of sin. Bronson Beta is the second chance, the softening of God's anger. The spaceship under construction is likened to Noah's vessel — in fact, actually named the Ark. The "morally upright," which for Wylie is often synonomous with "those trained in the sciences," are saved and allowed to reestablish sane laws and morality. The story is weakened at key points by Wylie's adulation of intellectuals and deprecation of the bovine masses. The outcome of many situations is predictable to anyone familiar with the Cowboy and Indian-type story. Nevertheless, Wylie's visionary accounts of atomic power used for destructive and constructive purposes, the accuracy of his scientific discussions, and his fastidiously detailed discussions of space travel overrule the occasional heavy-handed appeals to heaven and justice.

Misanthropic accounts of societal disintegration are characteristic of Philip Wylie's almost gruesome fascination with the baseness at the heart of humanity. Predictably, the masses refuse to believe what is undeniable. Even as the celestial bodies approach the gravitational field of the Earth and the terra firma becomes a seething hell, the great hoards of mankind revert to primitive savagery. The first passage of the Bronson bodies brings forth unimaginable destruction. The description of terrestrial disaster is terrifying. Lower elevations on the coastlines are inundated by floodwaters; volcanic disruptions belch out death and destruction; hurricane-force winds fling buildings like paper; and cataclysmic earthquakes swallow entire continents. In all, it is hell opening its jaws and ingesting the sinners. One-half of the Earth's population is gone. Even the moon, caught in the path of Bronson Alpha, is snuffed out with metaphorical significance.

The Hendron group, confined to one large camp in Michigan, survives the first passage. After an exploration team accidentally discovers a metal which proves capable of withstanding the stresses of the upcoming flight, the Ark is completed. The discovery of the all-important metal, another indication of God's benevolent intervention, enables the group to construct a second ship. All will be saved. Unfortunately, the violence in the heavens is matched by man-made violence on Earth. The bloodthirsty survivors of the first passing attack Hendron's camp, killing many of the pilgrims. Nonetheless, on the predicted day of collision, the two ships depart for Bronson Beta. The Earth is destroyed. Whether or not any other ships are able to escape is not known.

The story concludes with the successful landing of the Hendron vessel on Bronson Beta. Although Tony Drake, Eve and Cole Hendron, and Eliot James are safe, the other craft captained by David Ransdell and carrying, among others, Peter Vanderbilt and Jack Taylor, is presumed to be lost in space. It is discovered that the air on Bronson Beta is breathable. The passengers on the Ark step down to the earth of their new home realizing that they are the sole survivors of the terrible disaster. Alone on an unknown world once inhabited by a "nameless and dead race," the survivors begin the "prodigious task" that awaits them.

The success of *When Worlds Collide* was overwhelming. The authors, in their use of an ending that was really a beginning, paved the way for a serialization of a sequel. The follow-up, *After Worlds Collide*, began serialization in November, 1933. Truman Keefer's discussions with Philip Wylie have indicated that there was a short delay in the writing because of Wylie's demand for a larger share of the profits and greater control over the scientific accuracy of the story. Nevertheless, with the public demanding a continuation of the story, differences were settled and the space adventure continued. Wylie, who prided himself on the scientific accuracy of the first book, was less than comfortable with the second.

After Worlds Collide continues the characterization and underlying issues of the previous book. It follows the space pilgrims through the process of rebirth on Bronson Beta. Beginning with the successful landing on the new planet, the action follows Dr. Cole Hendron who is aging and developing into a Moses-like figure, Tony Drake who is handed the reins of power, David Ransdell who remains the brave explorer, and Eve who shows little, if any, growth. The story records the birth pangs of the new society, chronicles the discovery of the magnificent remains of a mysterious civilization that had vanished from Bronson Beta centuries earlier, and details the conflict with another group of settlers who have also escaped the Earth's destruction.

The book is inferior to the original story. While there is an ingenious description of futuristic advancements achieved by the previous inhabitants of Bronson Beta, much of the book focuses on the conflict between the American settlers and their Asiatic counterparts. There is a xenophobic quality to the battling between the "good" Americans and the "evil" Asiatics which, although attributable to the era in which the story was written, is unfortunately overdone. In general, the characters remain static, and although there are a few surprising revelations which are contrived for the development of plot, there is little growth to speak of. Perhaps the most tantalizing issue in the story, one that permeates throughout, is the question of what happened to the previous inhabitants who had disappeared without a trace. Although most of the story prods the reader with this question — and it is actually answered — it is not satisfactorily concluded.

The *When Worlds Collide/After Worlds Collide* duo is a classic "good guy *versus* bad guy" story. With the bad guy being society's uninformed masses and the good guys being the science-minded intellectuals, the authors' violent, evangelistic message is that pursuit of the vision of science is salvation. The duo was followed with a sequel which explained the secret of the missing inhabitants of Bronson Beta. Although actually outlined by Balmer, the projected book was vetoed by Wylie. Wylie, a fastidious adherent to scientific detail and accuracy, refused to collaborate on a story which could not be validated. The two original successes were combined into one volume and published by J. B. Lippincott Company in 1950. Filmed by Paramount in 1951, they stand as classics in the field even today.

Clifford P. Bendau

Sources for Further Study

When Worlds Collide

Criticism:

Keefer, Truman Frederick. *"When Worlds Collide,"* in *Philip Wylie*. Boston: Twayne, 1977, pp. 62-63. The plot of this novel is described as being suspenseful and imaginative. It is still considered a classic by scholars and Science Fiction buffs.

Reviews:

Books. March 5, 1933, p. 12.

Boston Transcript. March 25, 1933, p. 1.

New Republic. LXXIV, March 15, 1933, p. 138.

New York Times. March 12, 1933, p. 7.

Times Literary Supplement. December 7, 1933, p. 880.

After Worlds Collide

Criticism:

Keefer, Truman Frederick. *"After Worlds Collide,"* in *Philip Wylie*. Boston: Twayne, 1977, p. 63. A succinct article on the plot and theme of *After Worlds Collide* is provided here.

Reviews:

Books. April 8, 1934, p. 16.

Boston Transcript. May 29, 1934, p. 2.

New York Times. April 8, 1934, p. 22.

Springfield Republican. July 8, 1934, p. 7e.

Times Literary Supplement. October 18, 1934, p. 717.

WHERE LATE THE SWEET BIRDS SANG

Author: Kate Wilhelm (1928-   )
First book publication: 1976
Type of work: Novel
Time: The near future
Locale: The Shenandoah Valley and environs

After a great ecological disaster, the human race is forced to resort to cloning for survival

Principal characters:
> DAVID SUMNER, a medical student specializing in genetics
> WALT SUMNER, his uncle, a doctor
> CELIA, David's cousin, with whom he is in love
> BEN, a doctor, one of the Barry brothers, clone/descendants of David
> MOLLY, an artist, one of the Miriam sisters
> BARRY AND MIRIAM, community leaders
> MARK, the son of Molly and Ben

Where Late the Sweet Birds Sang seems at first to be a fairly conventional "holocaust" novel of the ecological variety, complete with pollution, high levels of radiation, droughts and floods, shortages of critical minerals, dying animal species, and widespread famine and plague. In the manner typical of such novels, our attention is focused on a small community struggling to survive the crisis — in this case, the Sumner clan and allied families, about three hundred people living in or near the Shenandoah Valley. The group includes artisans of practically every skill, and the material necessary for survival — there are farmers who have seeds, well-stocked hardware store owners, dentists complete with equipment, and doctors replete with medicines.

The clan is led by Grandfather Sumner, a wealthy, powerful, farsighted patriarch who, seeing that the crash is coming, prepares his family to survive it. His first act is to build a research hospital on family land in the valley, because the most critical of all the many severe problems is that the world birth rate is dropping alarmingly among both animals and humans: all living things seem to be losing the ability to reproduce. But Grandfather Sumner's son Walt is a doctor, and his grandson David is a biologist specializing in clone research. The hospital is for them, and is stocked with all necessary equipment and supplies, regardless of cost. If David and Walt can find a way to make the cloning of food animals — and, more important, the cloning of human beings — practicable, then the race has a chance of surviving the effects of its own folly.

Shortly after the completion of the hospital, the social, economic, and political systems of both the country and the world collapse into anarchy: rioting breaks out as food supplies dwindle, countries attack one another, and virulent plagues sweep the world, vastly reducing human population. In the valley, more than two-thirds of the clan members perish, including all the children under six years of age. But the remaining one hundred or so inhabitants manage to survive, and David and Walt continue their work in the labs, trying to produce a clone strain which will be both genetically normal and able to reproduce sexually, for by this time no one in the community is fertile. Without a successful cloning technique, the current inhabitants of the valley will be the last human beings, the end of the race.

The laboratory work eventually succeeds in producing viable human clones, about one-quarter of whom prove to be fertile as intended. The repopulation of the valley begins; but the solution to the technological problem creates a whole new set of social problems. According to the original plan, the little group in the valley will be able to replenish its numbers by a combination of cloning and sexual reproduction until they have enough fertile members to return to sexual reproduction alone. However, as the first generation of clones comes to maturity and begins to replace the founding family, a very different kind of social structure evolves. The cloning has been done in "sets" — multiple copies of the same person "born" from the clone tanks simultaneously and reared together as brothers or sisters. Thus, social relations in the community are no longer structured on the basic unit of the individual, but on the clone "sets."

Each set of siblings — four, six, eight, or ten — is identical, not only in appearance but in talents, attitudes, and personalities. Members of a set are linked empathically (if not telepathically) to the extent that six brothers or sisters are not a group of related individuals, but a single creature: one entity composed of six parts. Building a community of clone groups rather than of individuals seems to have many advantages: the higher level of communication within a group of siblings leads to increased efficiency in the performance of ordinary tasks, and also provides a solution to one of the ancient burdens of human existence: isolation and loneliness. No clone can ever feel lonely if all experiences, thoughts, and desires are not only instantly understood but shared by a loving and supportive family. In addition, reproduction by cloning allows the community to control the size and distribution of the population with great precision while not tying down the majority of adult women to the tasks of bearing and rearing children. It also allows the community to reproduce selectively those traits and talents which it finds important — intelligence, strength, beauty — and to eliminate those it considers undesirable. Thus, there are no misfits in the community, no one is unhappy or dissatisfied, no one is ill or deformed or retarded, and above all no one is violent. The result sounds much like paradise.

However, as a group, the clones have strengths as well as weaknesses. In the first place, fertile women are still vitally important to the community for their ability to bear children, but child-rearing has become a function of the nursery, where sexually reproduced babies are cloned and reared with their brothers or sisters as a group. Therefore, the child-bearers, or breeders, are separated from their sisters, used by the community solely to produce children, and not integrated into society. The discovery of fertility in a woman, so vital for the community, thus becomes a personal tragedy for the individual woman and her sisters, from whom she is forever separated. There is no incentive for women to bear children except inescapable necessity. But heavy reliance on cloning causes a serious reduction in the gene pool, so that with each passing generation more and more skills are lost. Although the younger brothers and sisters learn rapidly everything they are taught and can follow instructions with great precision, they are losing the ability to innovate and improvise. They can repair the equipment on which the community depends — the computer, the steam boat, the power generator — and they can restore them to their original condition as long as replacement materials are available; but they do not understand how the equipment works, and when a part is missing they are unable to fashion a substitute.

Yet the vital materials needed to sustain the community's way of life, especially metals and chemicals for the laboratories, cannot be supplied from within the community itself, nor does it know of any other surviving communities from whom it might acquire the necessary supplies. The only possible sources are the ruined cities of the eastern seaboard, where caches of usable materials might exist. However, manning such salvage operations creates serious problems for the community because they are separated from the abandoned cities by unbroken miles of wilderness. The brothers and sisters fear the forest intensely: even the least imaginative hears voices in the trees, feels himself constantly watched even though he knows no large animals have survived, and falls prey to panic when out of sight of cultivated fields. Further, they are unable to tolerate being separated from their brothers or sisters for any length of time; an extended separation causes increasing anxiety and eventual hysteria or catatonia. Such emotional disturbances affect not only the individual but all his brothers or sisters as well; therefore, to spare the others suffering, the afflicted member cannot be allowed to survive. "No one had the right to exist if such existence was a threat to the family. That was the law."

However, as the need for materials grows more pressing, the family decides it must take the risks of sending an exploration party down river to Washington, D.C. to make some preliminary investigations and to revise the maps for later teams. The party returns with much valuable information, but the cost has been high: one member of the party is permanently unbalanced, and two of them — Ben, the team doctor, and Molly, the mapmaker and recording artist — appear normal, but are actually altered. Molly in particular is dramatically changed, emotionally separate from her sisters in a way no clone has ever been. On the river during the long trip back upstream, Molly feels something waken inside her, something that makes her different from her sisters. She sees images in her mind that she wants to paint or draw, and experiences a deep sense of fulfillment and peace in those images. Under the stress of separation, Molly has become an individual, which makes her alien to her own people. A similar thing happens to Ben, though more gradually and less completely; and for its own preservation the family must isolate both of them. Molly is established in the old Sumner house in the woods, given food and supplies, and left alone to paint and explore the woods; and Ben is sent down river to serve as doctor at the new outpost near the waterfall. But before Ben leaves for the last time, Molly conceives their child, Mark. For five years after his birth, Molly manages to keep Mark concealed from the family, teaching him reading and drawing, modeling and woodcraft, but at last they are discovered. Mark is taken to the community dorm and school, while Molly, sent to the breeders' quarters, eventually escapes and leaves the valley to search for Ben.

Mark, meanwhile, continues to grow and to cause trouble. He is an anomaly, a misfit, completely isolated from the community. Ben's brothers, who take responsibility for Mark, neither understand him, nor know how to control or discipline him. However, Mark is the only person in the family who can travel in the forest with ease and skill, so the family needs him to train the younger children to survive the terrors of the wilderness in order to forage in more distant cities. But when the training program proves to be only marginally helpful, the older members of the family, with the exception of Ben's brothers, become increasingly hostile to Mark.

Mark eventually realizes not only that his own life is in immediate danger from the Andrew brothers, but that the family itself is ultimately doomed. They are living at the top of a technological pyramid whose supporting base no longer exists. They lack not only the materials to maintain the old culture but the skills to survive in a more primitive but more stable fashion, closer to the Earth. Having lost the understanding of the technology which keeps them alive, they are vulnerable to unexpected disaster. Having lost the ability to be alone and to find their way through the woods, having lost the ability to improvise and to respond inventively to novel situations, the clones will have no way of surviving when their pyramid ultimately collapses through lack of support.

So Mark trains a group of thirty youngsters under the pretense of preparing them for a foraging trip to Norfolk, takes a few sheep and cows and some supplies, and abducts eleven of the younger women from the breeders' quarters; with them he founds a new settlement deep in the wilderness where they cannot be found by the family. Technologically the new community is primitive compared to the group in the valley, but Mark's people survive, while the old community dies completely when a tornado damages the power generator beyond their ability to repair it.

Cloning has long been a favorite topic of science fiction writers. In Aldous Huxley's *Brave New World*, humans are gestated in bottles, and other novelists and short story writers have examined the same or similar questions. In some of these, the question of the humanity of the clones has been the issue. In others, such as Isaac Asimov's robot-oriented novels, the question has been reversed: should not a being whose ethical code is as high or higher than humanity's, albeit it has a positronic brain, be termed "human"?

Wilhelm's novel is a cautionary tale about ecological disaster. It presents a "cozy catastrophe" that resembles, in a certain sense, that described in George Stewart's *Earth Abides*. Things may fall apart, but they do so slowly, inexorably. If the protagonists of these novels cannot cope with the erosion of civilization, they at least cling to the hope that humanity and Earth will survive. In the Stewart novel, the inhabitants of the virtually peopleless world depend too much on the detritus of a decaying civilization. In Wilhelm's work, the mastery of the old is complete, but it cannot be repaired, improved, or duplicated. In both works those few who survive do so by returning to the intuitive, instinctual life, close to Mother Earth, dependent upon the beneficence of nature. They live *with* nature, they do not subdue it. Thus, the novel addresses itself to the dangers of overdependence upon a technology which has outlived its usefulness and is becoming increasingly mysterious. Both Stewart and Wilhelm seem to say that if man, either as biological descendent or clone, moves too far from the Earth, he will lose his connection with the very base of his being.

Moreover, Wilhelm raises the question of the ethical implications of the cloning process. Never the direct moralist, she nonetheless asks, at least implicitly, if we should continue experimenting with cloning when we are uncertain of its consequences. Her novel provides one answer: cloning is in and of itself destructive to humane, human values. Thus, her title is a metaphor for humanity's singing. If we are to continue to sing, she suggests, we must remain flexible and diverse, taking flight as the situation demands, but returning always to nest on Mother Earth.

The prose in *Where Late the Sweet Birds Sang* is so lucid, so highly charged with poetry (particularly in the sections devoted to Molly and Mark), that the book was voted the Hugo award as the best science fiction novel of 1976. In her earlier exemplary fiction, Wilhelm has also shown her ability to evoke vivid scenes and to write penetrating descriptions of genuine human beings reacting psychologically to their environment.

Kathleen L. Spencer

Sources for Further Study
Reviews:

Booklist. LXXII, February 1, 1976, p. 756.

Kirkus Reviews. XLIII, November 15, 1975, p. 1308.

New York Times Book Review. January 18, 1976, p. 21.

School Library Journal. XXII, April, 1976, p. 96.

Wilson Library Bulletin. LI, September, 1976, p. 77.

WHO?

Author: Algis Budrys (1931-   )
First book publication: 1958
Type of work: Novel
Time: The late 1980's
Locale: Germany, New York, and New Jersey

An account of the problems faced by those trying to establish the identity of a man rebuilt by medical technicians after a near-fatal accident

> *Principal characters:*
> SHAWN ROGERS, an Allied National Governments security man
> FINCHLEY, an FBI agent
> COLONEL ANASTAS AZARIN, of the SIB
> LUCAS MARTINO (?), a nuclear physicist

Who? is a novel whose basic notion was first put forward in a short story of the same title published in 1955. It was Budrys' second novel, and, in spite of the high reputation earned by *Rogue Moon* (1960), it is probably his best. It was certainly one of the best science fiction novels of the 1950's, and is perhaps the only one to have been faithfully and successfully translated into the medium of film (in a version made by Jack Gold which was sold to television).

The situation which forms the focal point of the novel is quite simple. In the late 1980's the Cold War continues, with political polarization between West and East having progressed to the point where both governmental systems are highly centralized. Both sides are struggling to gain and hold some technological advantage in weaponry. American scientist Lucas Martino is working on a project code-named "K-Eighty-eight" in a laboratory close to the border between the Allied and Soviet zones in the Central European Frontier District (apparently in Germany). His experiment misfires and there is an explosion. Because of the remote site of the project, a rescue team from the East reaches the disaster area before the nearest Western team. The Soviets keep Martino for four months before returning a man they claim to be him. The returnee, however, has a prosthetic arm, a completely rebuilt system of respiration and blood-circulation, and a "skull" of metal with slits for a mouth and artificial eyes. Shawn Rogers, the security chief appointed by the Allied Nations Government to supervise the recovery of Martino, is faced with the unexpected problem of trying to find a crucial test which will conclusively demonstrate that the returnee is or is not Martino, as the case may be. The future of the Cold War may depend upon his making the right decision.

The problem with which the reader is initially faced is also Rogers', and it seems fairly straightforward, though difficult. In alternate chapters, however, Budrys begins to recount in a neutral documentary tone the story of Lucas Martino's life, from his boyhood on his father's farm in New Jersey through his adolescence, partly spent working in New York in order to save money to support him in his early days at M.I.T., to the moment when the K-

Eighty-eight project is born in his imagination. In these sections it is revealed that Martino had in the past his own problems of self-identification; he was never quite sure what kind of being he was or ought to be. As the novel moves toward its climax, the juxtaposition of Martino's and Rogers' problems brings both into clearer focus, and the two narratives overlap and fuse. The resolution of the plot and the resolution of the counterplot conflict and confound each other.

Rogers' problem is always one of method. What would count as proof of the returnee's identity? Fingerprints quickly establish that the cyborg's remaining organic arm is Martino's, but in view of the scope of the medical miracle, it seems unsafe to infer from this that the brain inside the metal skull is also Martino's. The physical evidence is so inconclusive that Rogers quickly decides that only the contents of the cyborg's mind can afford the vital clue. But the Soviets have had four months in which to wring from their prisoner the details of his life history, and Rogers quickly finds that the nuclear scientist has always been a closed book even to those who knew him best. No one has ever had any real contact with Martino's personality, at least so far as the West's security files can reveal. Indeed, the one person who *might* have learned an adequate amount about him to provide some kind of test turns out to have been his roommate at M.I.T., Frank Heywood, who also turns out to have been a Soviet agent, now missing after a plane crash and possibly the man behind the mask of steel if that man is not, in fact, Martino.

After interrogating the cyborg for a brief period, Rogers takes him back to the United States, where he is released in New York. Rogers and an F.B.I. agent named Finchley follow his every move and eavesdrop on his every conversation. They listen while he contacts Edith Hayes, *née* Chester, who once fell in love with him. The relationship came to nothing because Martino had not known what to make of it, or even what there was to be made from it, and had forsaken it entirely upon admission to M.I.T. Now it appears that Martino is desperate for human contact, and the widowed Edith seems to offer some hope. Finchley, listening in, is certain that the returnee *is* Martino, but Rogers dare not agree with him. The encounter ends when Edith's daughter catches sight of the cyborg and is frightened by his appearance. The man flees, endangering himself by overloading his substitute respiratory system, and when Finchley runs after him to reassure him, the F.B.I. man is killed by a car.

Eventually, the cyborg returns to the isolated farm in New Jersey left abandoned on the death of the elder Martino. There, watched perpetually by Rogers' men, he begins the work of restoring the farm machinery and the land to life and productivity. The situation is now stalemated, and alters when Rogers' masters eventually decide that the need for the K-Eighty-eight is so great that they must take the risk of putting the cyborg back to work on it, trusting to hope that he is really Martino. Rogers brings this news to the cyborg, who rejects the offer and, when pressed, denies that he is Lucas Martino. By this time, the reader is sure that he *is* Martino, and that the denial is of his own past.

The final section of the book recounts Martino's experiences in Soviet hands, and the attempt by his interrogator, Colonel Azarin, to discover his secrets. Ironically, the featureless mask that has made things so difficult for Rogers also made things impossible for Azarin, and the Soviets' desperate attempt to substitute Frank Heywood failed. The man who was sent back is, indeed, the man who was rescued from the burning laboratory, but in the attempt to determine his identity, Rogers and his associates have acted as catalysts to its destruction and rebuilding. Martino of the atrophied emotions and hypertrophied intellect, the alienated physicist alone in his world of pure ideation, has been blotted out of existence.

Budrys' novel is basically a character study, and it uses the devices of science fiction to set up a situation in which the main character is, in a curious fashion, tested to destruction. It bears some relation to a number of stories in which people equipped with new faces undergo changes of personality as a consequence — notable examples are Kobo Abe's *The Face of Another* and Marcel Ayme's *The Second Face* — but deals with a much more striking metamorphosis, in that its central character must adjust to being faceless and unhuman. The central irony of the plot is that when Martino *looked* human, he was able to operate in the human world, though in his mental outlook he was completely alienated from it; but when, with his altered appearance, he attempts to make contact with other people for the first time, there is no way he can do so. In his youth, working in the coffee bar and setting up the unsatisfactory relationship with Edith, he knew that something was wrong with him, but chose the road of least resistance in giving himself over entirely to the realm of the intellect. This gambit made it possible for him to survive his experiences in the Soviet hospital and his interrogation by Azarin, and eventually to walk back to the West convinced that all was as well as could be expected. Only when he realizes that he cannot simply be put straight back to work, and must somehow prove who he is, does he realize once again that he does not know who he is, or even whether he can reasonably claim to be a person at all.

In moving away from concentration upon Rogers' problem (Who is *he*?) to concentrate fully on Martino's problem (Who am *I*?) Budrys moved his story into what was, for genre science fiction of the 1950's, entirely new ground. The futuristic spy story became a matrix for a thought experiment in philosophical psychology. The subtlety of this transformation, and the neatness with which Budrys' exploration of the various facets of the situation proceeds, make this an outstanding piece of work. Perhaps better than any other genre novel of its period, it shows the potential of science fiction as a medium for imagining close confrontations between human beings and their own humanity.

Whether Martino's psychology as depicted by Budrys actually bears much resemblance to the psychology of real scientists is something which remains to be established, but it is certainly true that many theoretical physicists of genius seem to have been markedly alienated from ordinary human relationships — Newton and Einstein are cardinal examples. Whether Budrys' characterization of Martino is typical is a minor point, however, since the main function of the novel (as the title indicates) is to ask a question rather than to make a statement.

The ending of the book, where the question is "answered," may seem bleak to most readers, because Budrys declines the opportunity to cheat the implications of his argument by suggesting that Martino's new destiny represents any kind of fulfillment or reconciliation with himself. This may account in some measure for the novel's lack of popularity. In its day it was not calculated to appeal to the bulk of the audience for which it was marketed, but one might have expected its reputation to have grown rapidly when science fiction became the subject of serious academic scrutiny in the late 1960's. *Who?* is a work which would amply repay such attention.

Brian Stableford

Sources for Further Study

Reviews:

Analog. LXIII, March, 1959, p. 143.

Galaxy. XXVIII, July, 1969, pp. 158-161.

Infinity Science Fiction. IV, November, 1958, pp. 96-98.

Magazine of Fantasy and Science Fiction. XV, November, 1958, p. 15.

New Worlds. CXXIII, October, 1962, p. 128 and CXCVII, February, 1965 p. 123.

THE WIND FROM NOWHERE

Author: J. G. Ballard (1930-   )
First book publication: 1962
Type of work: Novel
Time: The immediate future
Locale: London, Genoa, Nice, Leatherhead

   The story of a worldwide disaster involving a great wind which accelerates steadily to a velocity of several hundred miles per hour

> *Principal characters:*
> DONALD MAITLAND, a medical research worker
> ANDREW SYMINGTON, an electronics engineer
> STEVE LANYON, commander of the *U.S.S. Terrapin*
> SIMON MARSHALL, director of Central Operations Executive
> HARDOON, a shipping and hotel magnate
> KROLL, his Chief of Security

   The Wind from Nowhere was J. G. Ballard's first novel. A short version was serialized in *New Worlds* in 1961 as *Storm-Wind*, and the expanded version was his first book, though it was rapidly followed in America by two short story collections. The novel took its place within a long tradition of British speculative novels featuring disasters of various magnitudes, which extends back as far as Mary Shelley's *The Last Man* (1826), although it has become particularly prolific in the twentieth century. Why Britain should have provided such fertile ground for the proliferation of secular apocalyptic fantasies is not altogether clear, but it could be argued that once the days of jingoistic, self-congratulatory Imperialism had been laid to rest with Queen Victoria, Britain became a society in decline and a natural breeding-ground for brooding pessimism. Conversely, it may be that it was the very achievement of civilized comfort and the affluent society which inevitably engendered the nightmare that all that had been won might so easily be lost again, whipped away by some whim of fickle nature. Whatever the explanation, however, the fact remains that British imaginative fiction of the twentieth century is redolent with great plagues, cosmic disasters, nuclear holocausts, earthquakes and climatic changes. It was, of course, climatic change which became, for awhile, the stock-in-trade of J. G. Ballard's early novels.

   As its title suggests, the disaster in *The Wind from Nowhere* is not so much a natural one as an *un*natural one. No explanation is given for the advent of the slowly accelerating wind that pulls civilization apart. One substantial hypothesis is offered, involving the transmission to the Earth's atmosphere of the energy of a freak burst of solar radiation, but this would be easy enough to confirm, and the fact that no one bothers to do so testifies to the fact that the explanation is irrelevant to the novel's concerns. This is not a novelette from the science fiction pulps, where some heroic genius would probably build a chain of giant fans to turn the wind right back again. The probability of the crucial event is a secondary issue, for the wind is not simply an accident of happenstance, but an anarchic spirit — an active revolt of nature whose very impossibility is an aspect of its rebellion. It is, in fact, more akin to the revolt of nature featured in Arthur Machen's novel *The Terror* than to any of the disasters featured in John Christopher's work. This fact is useful and understanding the way the story develops internally, and is vital to an understanding of the relationship which the novel bears to Ballard's subsequent work.

Unlike Ballard's later novels, *The Wind from Nowhere* does not attach its narrative to the viewpoint of a single individual, and this is perhaps its greatest weakness. In order to use several viewpoint characters Ballard is required to characterize them differently, and characterization is not his strong point. All his books feature a stable and stereotyped range of characters, but only one of them has any utility as a viewpoint; the remainder have significance only as *observed* characters, their status being almost iconic. This is crucial to the nature of Ballard's customary endeavor, for the landscapes of his stories are psychological landscapes, not merely reflecting but embodying mental states, and his best work is possessed of psychological singularity and uniformity.

The character who should be central to *The Wind from Nowhere* is Donald Maitland, a medical research worker attempting to flee to Canada in order to escape his past, and in particular his failed marriage to a wealthy socialite. In the first chapter, however, he is turned back by the wind, which has already grounded all aircraft and forced all shipping into harbor. After returning to London and an embarrassed confrontation with his wife, he takes shelter with his friend Andrew Symington, an electronics engineer, and disappears temporarily from the plot. Symington knows already the possible magnitude of the disaster, and is coopted into the Central Operations Executive, a clearinghouse for information and the coordinator of government contingency plans.

Another protagonist within the story is Steve Lanyon, the commander of an American submarine based at Genoa. He receives orders to proceed to Nice to pick up an Admiral for transportation back to the United States. His journey overland becomes steadily more hazardous, and he ultimately finds that the Admiral is a corpse. In the company of a female NBC reporter, he faces the difficult job of getting back to Genoa with the wind still increasing, and he soon loses the corpse and his handful of men. The chapters dealing with Lanyon's adventures in France and Italy are perhaps the closest Ballard has come to writing conventional adventure fiction, involving rescue operations in a collapsed church, a fight with a gang of looters beneath a deserted monastery, and a final desperate maneuver to extricate the submarine from disaster. Lanyon is an empty, standardized hero figure, and his relationship with the girl reporter is tritely romantic. Though present during the climax of the novel, he does not really belong there, by this time having been reduced to the role of spear-carrier. The same is true of Simon Marshall, the director of C.O.E., who serves no purpose except to get involved in a rather stagy gunfight against the gangster Kroll who is sent by his master, Hardoon, to bring Symington to his refuge near Leatherhead.

Hardoon is one of Ballard's archetypal figures, a man of great wealth and power, who sees in the wind a challenge which he sets out to meet. The reader obtains glimpses of him in italicized sections which separate the chapters of the book: an "iron-faced" man grimly supervising giant earth-moving machines to erect a gigantic pyramid. Beneath the pyramid is a subterranean fortress, constructed as a protection against the possibility of nuclear war, which now becomes the home of his private empire. Marshall has secretely been working for him rather than the government, but he has Marshall destroyed as soon as his usefulness is ended — Symington is the only member of the C.O.E. team with any permanent value to him.

In the climax of the novel, Maitland, Lanyon, and several others obtain access to Hardoon's fortress under false pretences, and become prisoners there. Maitland is interviewed by Hardoon, who boasts of being the one man in the world to have defied the wind. While his "subjects" shelter below in the air-raid bunker, Hardoon sits alone in the pyramid, rejoicing in his immunity from its destructive power.

Hardoon, however, is ultimately defeated. His pyramid is impregnable, but the ground on which it is built is not. The soil supporting his edifice betrays him as the wind carries its topmost layers away and whips up the rest so that the structure of the shelter is contorted and breached. The pyramid is uprooted and toppled backwards into a great fissure which opens up to receive it. Maitland and his companions flee into this abyss, which is the only escape from the wind left to them; then, from its depths they perceive the first evidence of the wind relenting in its force.

It is easy enough to construe *The Wind from Nowhere* as a parable in which Hardoon, a modern Pharaoh, pits his temporal power against the forces of nature, and in his defeat signals the end of the revolt. If Hardoon is taken to represent "the unacceptable face of Capitalism," the fable can be given a political gloss; if he is taken to represent civilization itself, a more profound commentary on the vanity of human wishes is implied. It is dubious, however, whether this is the correct way to read the book. Many disaster stories are highly moral tales carrying some such message, but this is not one of them; *The Wind from Nowhere* is lacking in prescriptive implication, and carries no exhortation to humility in delivering its heroes at last from evil. Hardoon is eloquent in talking about "moral courage" and "moral superiority," but it is doubtful whether his interpretation of the situation is the correct one. He defines his own role thus:

> As the wind has risen so everyone on the globe has built downward, trying to escape it; has burrowed further and deeper into the shelter of the Earth's mantle. With one exception — myself. I alone have built upward, have dared to challenge the wind, asserting Man's courage and determination to master nature. If I were to claim political power — which,

most absolutely, I will not — I would do so simply on the basis of my own moral superiority. Only I, in the face of the greatest holocaust ever to strike the earth, have had the moral courage to attempt to outstare nature. That is my sole reason for building this tower. Here on the surface of the globe I meet nature on her own terms, in the arena of her choice. If I fail, Man has no right to assert his innate superiority over the unreason of the natural world.

Hardoon does fail, but his failure constitutes a judgment not that Nature is stronger than culture, but that his way of comprehending the situation is wrong. *The Wind from Nowhere* itself is hardly unambiguous in making this point, but seen in the context of the line of development which connects it to *The Drowned World*, *The Drought*, and *The Crystal World*, it becomes rather clearer. In the later novels, the problems of adaptation posed by the metamorphoses of the world are psychological, not ecological, and it seems reasonable to treat this preliminary exercise as being already one step advanced in the direction of this change of emphasis. *The Wind from Nowhere* is considerably inferior to its successors, partly because it is an exploratory exercise rather than a work whose thematic implications are fully worked-out, but it is nonetheless somewhat removed from the endless stream of conventional disaster stories. The great wind howling through the novel is not merely scouring the Earth but cleaning the slate on which the mythology of world-destruction was formulated, ready for the building of a new mythos.

Brian Stableford

Sources for Further Study

Reviews:

Amazing Stories. XXXVI, August, 1962, pp. 122-123.

Analog. LXIX, August, 1962, pp. 166-167.

Books and Bookmen. XIX, July, 1974, p. 37.

New Worlds. CLXV, August, 1966, p. 145.

THE WITCHES OF KARRES

Author: James H. Schmitz (1911-   )
First book publication: 1966
Type of work: Novel
Time: The far future
Locale: Among the stars and planets on the fringe of a galactic Empire in the Milky Way

A galactic "space opera," social comedy, novel of education, and highly entertaining example of science fantasy

> *Principal characters:*
> CAPTAIN PAUSERT, a commercial traveler from the Republic of Nikkeldepain
> MALEEN, eldest of the three daughters of Threbus and Toll
> GOTH, her slightly younger sister
> THE LEEWIT, her youngest sister
> THREBUS AND TOLL, important and powerful witches from Karres
> HULIK DO ELDEL, an Empire spy
> VEZZARN, an ex-safecracker and undercover agent for the Daal of Uldune
> SEDMON THE SIXTH, Daal of Uldune
> LAES YANGO, the Agandar, an infamous pirate
> LORD CHEEL, untrustworthy Prince of the Lyrd-Hyrier

James H. Schmitz's *The Witches of Karres* was judged one of the four best science fiction novels of 1966 by the twenty-fifth World Science Fiction Convention, and it is not hard to see why. It is a superior entertainment which provides equal doses of comedy and adventure while never once challenging either the conventions of the genre or the ethical and philosophical precepts which underlie them. It is, indeed, a fine example of science fantasy, or what is called space opera, yet it is sophisticated enough in style and characterization to stand up under more than one reading.

The Witches of Karres began as a novella of the same title, published in John W. Campbell, Jr.'s *Astounding Science Fiction* in 1949. Obviously popular, for it was the one Schmitz story included in *The Astounding Science Fiction Anthology* published in 1952, it became the first two chapters of the novel. Aside from dropping the chapter divisions of the novella, Schmitz made only a few changes in its final few pages, in order to make a smooth transition into the additional narrative.

The original story is an almost perfectly cohesive whole: its conclusion implies that because Captain Pausert has now "found himself" as a person with a taste for and an ability (including latent Psi-talents) to handle adventure, he will, in the company of a young Karres witch, definitely lead a rich and adventurous life. The essential changes in his character have already taken place, for he has learned that there are larger, richer, riskier, and more genuine ways of life to follow out in the universe than stuffy, "proper" society on

Nikkeldepain will acknowledge, so narrowminded and hypocritical are its mores. Thus Schmitz's extension of his original story adds little to our knowledge of Pausert's character though it fills in its far future galaxy with a wide variety of fantastical creatures and dangerous places and provides a number of paradigmatic and conventionally suspenseful "escape fiction" adventures.

Indeed, unlike those works which attempt, in however small a way, to realize the as yet untapped literary potential of science fiction and thus somehow push the boundaries of genre definition outward, *The Witches of Karres* is interesting precisely because it is so obviously popular genre science fiction, an example of "good old science fantasy storytelling." Schmitz is obviously writing in the A. E. van Vogt mode and this explains both the power and the weaknesses of his novel.

The power is imaginative, though essentially derivative. As J. R. R. Tolkien once pointed out, the very act of casting a story into the long-ago has a magical effect, the sense of "distance and a great abyss of time" transforming the ordinary. The same effect occurs when a story is cast into the far future, a universe as potently magical (even if the "magic" is the result of technology) as any ancient Middle-Earth. Thus, science fiction stories set in an almost-too-huge-to-imagine galactic Empire automatically speak to the average reader's "sense of wonder" unless they are absolutely cretinous in execution. *The Witches of Karres* is written by a professional: it invokes and makes use of all the proper science fiction conventions, and it does so with high comic energy; but it never challenges the conventions on an ideological plane.

The weakness of *The Witches of Karres* lies in its imaginative failure as social extrapolation, a point best examined in relation to the fact of slavery within the Empire. The three young witches are picked up in their galactic wanderings by an "Imperial Slaver." Later sold on Porlumma, they are "rescued" — that is, bought — by the captain, and that is the end of any reference to the Imperial Slave Trade. Schmitz is not truly interested in speculating on the kind of galactic civilization which would require slaves, so he sets his adventures on the edges of the Empire. To begin to question the concept of slavery in this galactic Empire, however, is to confront a series of poorly thought-through assumptions. Schmitz has posited incredible technology for his future and, as Asimov and others have argued in recent years, technology more than anything else has made individual slavery obsolete.

When Pausert finds them, the three witches are working in unnecessary jobs and obviously driving their "owners" crazy. Of course, this triggers the narrative and provides for much comedy. For, although the captain "rescues" these poor lost children, he in fact needs them more than they need him since it is through them and their people that he will begin to grow into the tough, resourceful person with ESP faculties who will later help to save the universe.

As others have pointed out, such science fiction "power fantasies," as Brian Aldiss calls them, tend to deal with pseudoproblems in an unreal societal and psychological context. After all his adventures, the captain is going to work for Karres (which Threbus tells him is "a set of attitudes, a frame of mind" rather than a particular world) and for the "good" Empress who is trying to improve the Empire despite the "evil" Emperor and others in his court. The captain could be defined, as could Schmitz and most of his readers, as a small-l liberal: he acts out of personal compassion and obviously tries to be a "good" man. Thus he decides to refuse, no matter what the cost, to join the Agandar's pirates, but in fact he gets out of that tight spot before he actually has to suffer for his beliefs.

What is missing here and throughout the novel is any complex structural sense of how politics and economics might work in such a civilization. Rather, Schmitz has transplanted a fairly simple and superficial vision of how big governments, pirates, capitalist businesses, and traders operated in the nineteenth century into his imaginary future, and then told a fine, old-fashioned sea adventure set against that backdrop.

Of course, Schmitz is not really interested in creating a complexly realized society; he wants to tell the story of how one individual (with whom we identify) discovers in himself possibilities for heroic behavior he never knew he had. And he does this with both verve and a certain saving ironic comic perspective.

Though sympathetically presented from the start, the captain is obviously operating on a number of unexamined assumptions, including a misplaced patriotism toward his home world. Schmitz handles his thoughts about Nikkeldepain and his "true love" Illyla with ironic control: his every thought reveals a money-grubbing, puritanical, narrowminded and hypocritical society, but he fails to recognize this. Nevertheless, his basic good instincts emerge in his willingness to step in when he hears someone in trouble. Thus he takes the three young witches from their owners and offers to take them home to Karres even though their plight is none of his business.

The original story is fresh and funny because of the way it continually upsets expectations. The rest of the novel lacks the freshness of the original because it meets every expectation it sets up: each difficulty Pausert confronts he solves or has solved for him. But at the beginning Pausert continually runs into those sharp distinctions between expectations and reality which create comedy. Thus, without even quite meaning to, he offers to take Maleen home to Karres where she will be reunited with her sisters, but she tells him they are slaves on Porlumma too: "The captain's heart dropped clear through his boots. Standing there in the dark, he helplessly watched it coming: 'You could buy them awfully cheap,' she said." This is the basic method of the whole opening sequence: the captain thinks he knows where he stands and every time he thinks he has achieved equilibrium, something comes along to upset it. His ability to regain his balance each time reveals his potential as a heroic protagonist; his refusal to let Goth steal gifts for him by teleportation and his equally firm refusal to be cowed by those who blame him for her mischief reveal his moral courage.

Meanwhile, the young witches' talents provide other comic moments. Goth's teleportations twice get the captain branded as a thief. The witches' ability to use "the Sheewash Drive" takes the *Venture* out of danger when it is attacked, but also makes it the target of various dangerous interests, and the Leewit's command of languages allows her to insult and enrage others, like the Sirians whom she curses over the communicator. All of these acts serve to further alienate Pausert from "normal" society, thus pushing him closer to the break he must make in order to join the witches.

When they raise Karres, it is moving counterclockwise to the other planets in its system ("Well, it would, the captain thought"), and Pausert spends quite some time recovering and soaking up the peculiar atmosphere of this apparently idyllic and pastoral planet. Karres is similar to the ESPer planet in Joanna Russ's *And Chaos Died* (1970), but where Russ uses a pyrotechnic style and superb intelligence to create, in the very language of her novel, a model of the experience of gaining ESP on such a planet, Schmitz merely implies that certain changes have begun to occur in the captain and then bustles him off to some satisfying adventures. Russ's sociological extrapolation is also far more complex than anything Schmitz attempts.

The final comic touches of the original story occur when the people of Karres give Pausert a full cargo of immensely rich goods which, as they obviously know, he cannot legally sell in the Empire because they are from an "uncleared" world. Nevertheless, he returns to Nikkeldepain to find himself under arrest, not only for theft and slave trading but mainly because he has "a new type of space drive, which should have been brought promptly and secretly to the attention of the Republic of Nikkeldepain." By now, Pausert has realized what kind of people have power on Nikkeldepain and decided to leave that world behind him. Once he discovers Illyla has long been married to a man he despises, he attempts to escape, helped, unsurprisingly, by Goth and the Sheewash Drive which, this time, carries them clear across the Empire. Goth explains that the Karres witches feel the two of them will lead an exciting and educational life as traders in that area, and the captain feels it will be a good time.

The rest of the novel attempts to show just how good a time it will be. The captain has awakened to his own potential but he has also awakened, it seems, a power focused on him. Schmitz approaches the Psi-powers of the witches by a circuitous route, the "metaphysical concept" of "Klatha" — a cosmic energy not fully of this universe which certain people can tune in on and use. Besides this energy, there are "vatches," Klatha entities who "didn't hang around this universe much but were sometimes drawn into it by human klatha activities, and if they were amused or intrigued by what they found going on they might stay and start producing klatha phenomena themselves. They seemed to be under the impression that their experiences of the human universe were something they were dreaming." In this they are like authors, and the huge vatch the captain later draws in to his affairs is, among other things, a highly useful *deus ex machina* who, at least once, saves the captain and Goth when it seems Schmitz has plotted his story into a *cul de sac*.

Between Goth's growing ESP powers and the captain's discovery that he can control klatha energy, including vatches, the two manage to survive various attempts on their lives by people interested in the Sheewash Drive, including the notorious pirate, the Agandar, and to help defeat a malignant force of beings from another universe who threaten to enslave all humankind. Schmitz develops these adventures with ingenuity and a certain comic flair, yet they seem somewhat mechanical compared to the original story, for there is no moral or psychological growth involved. Any new interest derives from the invention of varied minor characters and exotic otherworldly landscapes.

Yet even these are essentially conventional versions of figures and landscapes long familiar in pulp fiction, however well done they may be. If Schmitz's names are good science fiction poetry — Worm Weather, grik dogs, a Sheem Spider, Nartheby Sprites, the Chaladoor — his use of essentially 1950's slang for his technology — "they would have to juice up" the *Venture*'s fuel reserves, for example — reveals an essentially noninnovative imagination at work. Schmitz occasionally appears to be aware that he is writing too close to formula. Thus he often reminds us, successfully and comically, that the captain is only human, especially when he clearly shows that Goth and the Leewit are responsible for destroying "Moander Who Speaks with a Thousand Voices," even if Pausert finally "saves the universe" by forcing his vatch to send Manaret back to its own continuum. More to the point, the conclusion of the novel implies that the danger and its removal have barely been noticed by the rest of the Empire, which is still the same; all of which suggests that the battle has been something of a pseudoevent.

Despite the various criticisms above, *The Witches of Karres* remains a highly entertaining work of fiction. Its flaws are inherent in the conventions of its genre; its accomplishments are those of a comic imagination whose best work has always been in shorter forms. Therefore, if the novel as a whole does not live up to the promise of its opening (the original story), if it is simply a fine example of good escapist science fantasy, if it presents no speculation or extrapolation of superior value in the areas of psychological, political, or sociological awareness, then it certainly has no pretensions to do so; and it *is* a genuinely enjoyable book.

Douglas Barbour

Sources for Further Study

Reviews:

Analog. LXXIX, May, 1967, pp. 159-160.

Horn Book. XLII, December, 1966, p. 722.

Magazine of Fantasy and Science Fiction. XXXIII, August, 1967, p. 33.

SF Commentary. VIII, January, 1970, p. 37.

Science Fiction Review. XXXIX, August, 1970, pp. 30-31.

WOMAN ON THE EDGE OF TIME

Author: Marge Piercy
First book publication: 1976
Type of work: Novel
Time: The present and 2137
Locale: New York City and Mattapoisett, Massachusetts

A perceptive and hard look at present society through the eyes of one of its victims who has the capacity for time travel into a more receptive future

Principal characters:
> CONNIE, a thirty-seven-year-old Chicana who becomes a time traveler
> LUCIENTA, a villager from the future who acts as Connie's guide in Mattapoisett
> JACKRABBIT, a male villager who befriends Connie
> LUIS, Connie's materialistic brother
> DOLLY, Connie's niece, who becomes a prostitute
> SYBIL, an inmate in the mental hospital

Placing an author's work within categories has its limitations, and Marge Piercy's work is a prime example of this fact. Piercy has been called a radical, feminist, and lesbian poet, but each of these adjectives implies a pigeonhole that is insufficient to encompass the multifaceted concerns of her work.

A poet of growing reputation, Piercy uses personal experience and arresting imagery in her poetry to depict themes such as the corruption of our society brought about by power, the interplay of power and romantic love, the perversion of the relationship between the sexes resulting from a patriarchal society, and the social ills plaguing modern life. Her volumes of poetry, *Breaking Camp*, *Hard Loving*, *To Be of Use*, and *Living in the Open* stress these themes.

Her reputation as a novelist is based largely on the 1973 novel *Small Changes*, which follows two women through the cultural revolutions of the 1960's. This novel is highly successful in embodying Piercy's thematic concerns, in portraying the overwhelming changes in life-style wrought by the 1960's, in documenting that period itself, and in creating two fresh, compelling characters.

Woman on the Edge of Time, in comparison, is more a novel of highs and lows than its predecessors. However, its strong points are quite powerful, and its weaknesses result more from attempting too much in one novel than from lack of ability.

The genre of the novel, futuristic fiction, provides a perspective from which to view our own society, a perspective Piercy employs well. Using the notion of a psychic mind-link between a person of our time and an inhabitant of the future, Piercy transports the reader through time. Society in 2137 in Mattapoisett, Massachusetts, is based on small agricultural villages in which the family is composed of congenial people related by love, not by blood. In these villages children are incubated until the "birthdays" when they are "born" to three mothers who can be male as well as female. Through hormonal injections, any or all of the mothers can even nurse the child. According to the villagers, this system rectifies the jealousy and insularity caused by the nuclear family and frees the female from her traditional role as sole child bearer and rearer. Not a *Brave New World*, Mattapoisett is a pleasant Utopia; there is no genetic or behavioral control. The whole point of this family is to produce individuals unfettered by the emotional confinement of the nuclear family.

In the novel, this goal is fulfilled. Each inhabitant of 2137 is extraordinary and admirable. Luciente, the female medium who guides Connie's visit to the future, is a physically strong, intelligent, calm woman. Jackrabbit is warm, friendly, and given to sexual expression of love but with society's sanction of this mode. Society incorporates ceremonies and rituals that reinforce communality and signify the values of the group: a birth ceremony, a rite-of-passage ceremony to signify the end of childhood (there are no adolescent crises here), a death ceremony. There is no government, no school, and rules are reluctantly made by those who are interested; education is accomplished by private study with scholars.

The traveler to the future, whose perceptions and reactions are meant to represent the reader's reactions, is Consuelo Ramos, "Connie," a Chicana, age thirty-seven. Connie's life has been a paradigm of victimization. She was born poor and ignorant, and attempted to raise herself by attending college. She had an affair with a professor, married, became ill and unemployed, and slid into situations that no amount of free will could prevent. The neglect and abuse that the poor, the Chicano, the women of our time suffer, are all embodied in Connie.

The result of these ills for Connie is that she is dumped like "human garbage" into Piercy's concept of the receptacle that our society has established for such people: a mental hospital. The hospital as snake pit is the image operating here. The doctors are dehumanized Dr. Frankensteins who experiment on the patients. In this case they plan a psycho-surgical operation on Connie to control her "anger," an emotion the reader realizes is entirely appropriate to the abuse Connie has received. The patients, including Connie, are depicted as sensitive, caring people who have been discarded by their families who consider them inconvenient. Connie, for example, is an embarrassment to her upwardly mobile brother Luis, who is attempting to renounce his Latin origins by changing his name (to Louis), his wives (from another Chicano to an "Anglo"), and if he could, his family ties (by committing Connie).

As in Ken Kesey's *One FLew Over the Cuckoo's Nest* and Doris Lessing's *Briefing for a Descent into Hell*, the setting of a mental hospital creates a dilemma for the reader: is the character who is "insane" a reliable witness and actor? In Connie's case, is she, in the best science fiction traditions, a time traveler, or is she experiencing psychotic hallucinations? The organizational plan of the novel in part aids the necessary suspension of disbelief of the reader. Connie's sojourn to the future occurs early in the novel before the reader is overly involved in her hospitalization. It is relatively easy to leap into the reality of the future since science fiction is a familiar genre; it is only later, when the horrors of the hospital become the book's focus, that the reader's understanding wavers. As in Nathaniel Hawthorne's "Young Goodman Brown" it really does not matter if all this is a dream or reality; the oppressions and inequities of our society are evils that Piercy exposes eloquently.

Several quite interesting aspects of the novel merit highlighting. In a brief section, Connie journeys to an alternate but possible future, one in which women are genetically controlled to have large breasts, tiny waists, rounded hips, where women are kept all their lives in apartments for which they wait for the man who contracted for their sexual services. This dystopia contrasts effectively with the Mattapoisett society, and cogently warns that elements our society emphasizes — *machismo*, women as sexual objects — could lead to a similar outcome.

Another fascinating aspect of the novel is the handling of language in the Utopian future. Pronouns "he" and "she" have been replaced by "per"; sexist language in general has disappeared. It is to Piercy's credit as a poet involved in language, that after a few paragraphs of these coined terms, the reader accepts them smoothly and even finds "he" and "she" sounding rather quaint.

With all of these virtues, however, the novel is not as satisfying as it might be, not because it has any one flaw but that it attempts too much. Piercy tries to expose nearly all of our society's ills — sexism, racism, poverty, prostitution, mental institutions, suburban materialism, the nuclear family, and so forth all come under fire. But the fire is scattered, and it is easy to lose a sense of focus. Moreover, Connie, who is a strong, admirable character, is also in many ways an inadequate one. She is meant to be an Every Woman, one with whom the reader can identify or at least who represents us all. But her bleak background makes it difficult for most readers to associate with her, and she is made a victim of all of society's ills. Would such a person be capable of the insight and sensitivity she is made to have after such a life? Of course, the answer is yes, but in this novel the credulity of the reader is strained by the heavy allegorical significance Connie must bear. Were she less of a victim, or were the societal diseases she suffers reduced, the novel would be the terse statement that Piercy is capable of producing as she did in *Small Changes*. Her experiment with science fiction is highly successful, and one hopes to see more novels from her in the same genre.

Kathryn L. Seidel

Sources for Further Study

Reviews:

Choice. XIII, October, 1976, p. 827.

Library Journal. CI, June 1, 1976, p. 1310.

New Republic. CLXXV, October 9, 1976, p. 38.

New York Times Book Review. June 20, 1976, p. 6.

Newsweek. LXXXVII, June 7, 1976, p. 94.

THE WORD FOR WORLD IS FOREST

Author: Ursula K. Le Guin (1929-   )
First book publication: 1972
Type of work: Novel
Time: The distant future
Locale: The planet Athshe

One of science fiction's few commentaries about American involvement in Vietnam, combined with a Utopian portrait of a culture that has achieved a union of the conscious and the unconscious

> *Principal characters:*
> SELVER THELE, a native of the planet Athshe
> CAPTAIN DON DAVIDSON, a Terran officer stationed on Athshe
> CAPTAIN RAJ LYUBOV, an anthropologist
> COLONEL DONGH, Davidson's commanding officer

Winner of a Hugo Award and nominee for a Nebula, *The Word for World Is Forest* is probably the most distinguished work to emerge from Harlan Ellison's 1972 anthology *Again, Dangerous Visions*. Despite its brevity, it is the major work of Le Guin's "Hainish" series (about worlds populated by a mysterious alien race called the Hainish) to appear between *The Left Hand of Darkness* (1969) and *The Dispossessed* (1974). Like those longer novels, it continues Le Guin's explorations of her favorite themes — the relation of social structures to ecology and biology, the responsibility of the individual in society, the interaction of psychology and environment — but it also focuses on a very specific issue of contemporary history that had not received a great deal of thoughtful attention in science fiction before: the Vietnam War. Le Guin's ability to unite all these various concerns in a tight and well-plotted piece of short fiction is no mean achievement, but there is in the work a certain amount of strain between the homiletic voice and the speculative imagination, a strain which Le Guin herself acknowledged in her afterword to the story's first appearance. On the one hand, the novel seeks to condemn the mentality of racist imperialism, represented in the story by Captain Davidson, that leads to economic exploitation and ecological irresponsibility. On the other hand, it tries to explore the possibility of a psychology based on the union of the conscious and unconscious through the deliberate control of dreams, as represented by the native Athshean culture. Both themes are drawn from real-life models — the paranoid military mind in the former case, the dream-psychology of various Indian tribes in the latter — but in order to place them in effective opposition, Le Guin is at times forced to exaggerate their characteristics. Thus Davidson sometimes appears a parody of a modern Army general, reminiscent of General Jack D. Ripper in Stanley Kubrick's *Dr. Strangelove*, and the Athshean leader Selver sometimes emerges as too much the "noble savage," reminiscent of Cochise. Between these two opposites stands the Terran anthropologist Lyubov, who seeks to understand the Athsheans and establish a ground for communication between them and the Terran settlers.

But the link is not easily forged. The Terrans are primarily interested in Athshe as a source of lumber, which has become a "necessary luxury" on Earth, and regard the Athsheans as primitives useful for domestic employment and occasional sexual gratification. The Athsheans, on the other hand, regard the Terrans as "insane," since they do not understand the significance of the forest and must go through life disconnected from their unconscious minds. The resultant conflict is what provides the story's simple plot: the systematic destruction of their environment, coupled with the oppression and exploitation of their population, forces the Athsheans to unite under Selver and initiate Guerrilla counter-warfare against the Terrans. Selver's friend Lyubov, the leading advocate for the Athsheans among the Terrans, is killed in one of the Athshean insurgency actions. Davidson tries to retaliate, but the significantly named Colonet Dongh explains that systematic warfare in a jungle environment is ineffective, and cites as evidence what happened in his ancestral region of Earth in the distant past. In the end, the Athsheans succeed in forcing the Terrans to abandon their colony, but at great cost: the Athsheans themselves have now learned the arts of murder and war.

While the parallels with Vietnam are apparent even in a brief description of the plot, these parallels should not be overemphasized. Le Guin's explorations of political, ecological, and psychological themes are far more thoughtful and complex than such simple parallels would suggest, and many of the ideas she begins to develop in this story reach their full fruition in *The Dispossessed*. In terms of political philosophy, *The Word for World Is Forest* resembles that later work by placing in opposition two cultures based on radically different economic and social values, and by illustrating the necessity for individual political action. The culture of Earth is portrayed only indirectly, through the actions of Terran characters on Athshe and by allusions to what life is like on Earth. We are told that Earth is "worn out," that wood is more valued there than gold because of the deforestation that industry and agriculture have brought about, that it is, in Davidson's eyes, a "tamed world." But most of what we know of Earth we infer from the attitudes of characters like Davidson: his belief in complete mastery of the environment, in the importance of heroic individual effort, in the oppression of "lower" life forms that extends even to a racism toward other genetic groups on Earth. Davidson is not the exclusive representative of Earth's culture and values; Lyubov and Dongh serve to modify our image of Earth a bit, but it is clear that Earth is a colonial power whose imperialism is in the service of economic gain, at least more so than some other worlds in the Hainish Federation.

Set in opposition to this capitalistic culture are the Athsheans, an anarchic forest people with no central government, who have achieved a stable society through integration with their forest environment and integration of their waking and dream-selves. Aggression and organized political action are unknown among these people, and their initial response to the invasion of the Earthmen who begin stripping their forests is tacit, if resentful cooperation. It is not until their very survival is threatened that Selver realizes the importance of resistance. In the dream-religion of the Athsheans, he temporarily becomes a god. Further motivated by the death of his wife after she is raped by Davidson, Selver organizes selective raids on Terran encampments, even witnessing the death of his human friend Lyubov in one such raid (a death whose tragedy is lessened by the Athshean ability to keep a friend "alive" in the unconscious mind). Some of the actions taken in these raids seem excessively brutal — the murder of a newly arrived group of human women, for example — but all are carefully planned to weaken Terran colonization plans and to stop the destruction of the forests. If Davidson and Lyubov come from a society that values individualism and must learn of the value of cooperation, so Selver, coming from his cooperative society, learns the value of individual action by his organization of the Athshean resistance. Neither society, then, is perfect in itself; and this theme, too, will later be expanded in *The Dispossessed*, which is subtitled "An Ambiguous Utopia."

Clearly, the ecological theme cannot be divorced from the political aspect of the story. While Davidson views the forest (and indeed, all natural environments) as raw material for the appropriation of man, the Athsheans regard it as their natural and spiritual environment, and have evolved a belief-system almost druidic in its allusions to tree-spirits and tree-clans. The forest to these people is not an undifferentiated mass of vegetation; it is both their habitat and their technology. They have achieved a union with their environment that is difficult for Terrans, more used to an adversary relationship between man and nature, to understand, and thus the Athsheans appear to men to be a part of the chaotic unknown that the forests of Athshe represent.

It is partly because of the humans' inability to understand the Athsheans or their environment that they appear insane to the Athsheans, and thus the psychological theme of the story becomes entwined with all the other strands. The major weakness of the humans in the eyes of the Athsheans, of course, is their inability to connect with their own unconscious minds — a connection as vital to the Athsheans as simple reasoning ability is to us. As a result, humans appear alienated not only from their environment and from one another, but from themselves, spending their waking hours in a kind of dream-state unaware of what is really going on in their minds. The Athsheans have overcome this split through deliberate training from childhood, and learn early in life of the respective values of "dream-time" and "world-time." Their psychology is based on integration rather than dissociation and confrontation; as a result it may seem too subtle to all but a few Terrans.

Le Guin successfully unites all these various branches of her plot through the single overriding image that dominates the entire story: the forest. The forest is virtually the entire perceptual world to the Athsheans, and in their language the word for world is the same as the word for forest. Thus the forest becomes an image not only of a specific environment, but of the phenomenal world itself, and how one deals with this world becomes an analogue of how one deals with all things outside of self: either by subduing them, as the Terrans do, or by learning from them, as the Athsheans do. But the forest is also an image of that part of the self with which the Athsheans have achieved contact: the unconscious. Like the unconscious, the forest is an emblem of the threatening unknown to Terrans who view it as uncontrolled growth, a chaos of fertility and shadows. But to the Athsheans, it is a part of themselves, an aspect of their own identity, just as the unconscious mind is. The Terran project to deforest Athshe in the service of technology thus takes on a new aspect; it becomes a fearful striking out against the threatening underside of the ordered consciousness that is represented by a "tamed planet" such as Earth.

Le Guin's forest scenes are written in a rich, poetic style that contrasts appropriately with the curt, brutal interior monologues with which she characterizes her humans; the reader is forced into a sensuous response to the chapters concerning the Athsheans, while the chapters involving human characters invite a more judgmental, intellectual response. As a result, the Athsheans, for all their alienness, seem more engaging and sympathetic than does the limited sample of humanity we are permitted to see (we do not get a chance to identify, for example, with the human females who are massacred, and while Lyubov is certainly sympathetic, his own uncertainty and confusion about the Athsheans make him a weak counterbalance to Davidson). But this lush style does not serve to sentimentalize the Athsheans, and Le Guin makes no attempt to mitigate the brutality of their acts. In the end, the real tragedy of the story is not the failure of the Terran colony on Athshe, or even the portrait of a Terran society so decadent that it must rape other worlds to maintain itself in luxury, but rather the loss of innocence of the Athsheans. In order to preserve their Edenic existence, they must paradoxically learn the lessons that drove man from the Garden in the first place.

Gary K. Wolfe

Sources for Further Study

Criticism:

Watson, Jan. "The Forest as Metaphor for Mind: *The Word for World is Forest* and *Vaster Than Empires and More Slow*," in *Science Fiction Studies*. II (1975), pp. 231-237. Watson states Le Guin uses the forest as a metaphor for world.

Reviews:

Booklist. LXXII, June 1, 1976, p. 1393.

Horn Book. LII, October, 1976, p. 529.

Kirkus Reviews. XLIV, February 1, 1976, p. 158.

Spectator. CCXXXIX, July 30, 1977, p. 22.

Times Literary Supplement. July 8, 1977, p. 820.

THE WORLD BELOW

Author: S. Fowler Wright (1874-1965)
First book publication: 1929
Type of work: Novel
Time: 500,000 years in the future
Locale: An island continent

The story told by a time-traveler of his adventures in a bizarre future world whose dominant species are the gargantuan Dwellers and the gentle Amphibians

Principal characters:
THE PROFESSOR, inventor of a time machine
THE NARRATOR, who is sent into the future via the Professor's machine
BRETT AND TEMPLETON, previous time travelers who never returned

The first part of *The World Below* was published in 1924 as *The Amphibians*. Apparently, this novel was intended to be the first of three volumes, but the original plan was abandoned before completion of the second volume, and when the second part was brought to a conclusion the whole work was published as a single volume. Though the two parts of the story cannot stand independently, they have been reprinted in paperback as two separate novels.

The story begins with a brief conversation between the narrator (whose surname is not revealed, though one of the other characters refers to him as "George") and "the Professor," who has developed a technique for sending objects forward in time. Inanimate objects have been dispatched half a million years into the future and safely brought back, but two men — Brett and Templeton — have not returned, despite the fact that the latter set out armed to the teeth. The narrator agrees to follow them, and if possible, to ascertain their fate. He is to spend a year in the future and return to the day of his departure. His motive for undertaking the mission seems to be primarily pecuniary.

The narrator finds himself on the edge of a plain near a great wall alongside which runs an opalescent pathway. The most prominent vegetation of the plain is a series of plants like giant cabbages, planted at regular intervals, and he concludes that he is on cultivated land. He discovers that there are caves in the wall, and tunnels leading into the depths of the world. While sheltering in the mouth of one such cave he sees a humanoid creature running along the path. She is so startled by his presence that she leaps from the road and is seized by a carnivorous plant, and though he destroys the plant he cannot save her. Thus, unwittingly, he becomes the catalyst in a series of events which is to involve him with her species — the nonaggressive, telepathic Amphibians.

The Amphibians have a treaty with the giant humanoid Dwellers who live in the underworld and who cultivate the surface. The lone Amphibian's trespass is in breach of this treaty, and now that she is dead the transgression is certain to be discovered. After encountering the monstrous frog-mouths and escaping temporary capture by one of the Dwellers, the narrator meets the remainder of her tribe, who have come to recover her body. His cause coincides, for the moment, with theirs, and he joins them. One particular Amphibian (female, as are all her kind) becomes his companion in the ensuing adventures. The Amphibians find him pitiable because of his ugly body and primitive mind, and are horrified by his tendencies to violence, but they tolerate him nevertheless. They live in a well-ordered world and have reached an accommodation with most other living creatures in it, and usually shun the land.

The narrator and his allies are forced to confront the Killers — a subject species of the Dwellers who prepare their prey for consumption by boiling them alive in great vats. The narrator is compelled to fight a battle in the arsenal of the Killers, which ends with his setting fire to their encampment. His escape is interrupted by a bizarre scene in which he and his companion discover a group of bat-winged creatures who have been condemned to death by the Dwellers and handed over to the Killers for disposal. The narrator assumes the role of judge to retry the Bat-wings in order to determine whether they truly deserve to be boiled alive.

Even before this point in the narrative, there has been reference to the inequities of the rule of law in the world from which the protagonist comes, and this has been part of a series of offhand comparisons drawn between the world view of the narrator and that of his companion. At one point the Amphibian allows him to perceive himself as she perceives him, and the only experience of his own that he can liken to it is that of confronting a sick sheep infested with blowfly larvae, its flesh practically rotting from its bones. Now these casual remarks set the stage for a savage parody of human affairs and the morality exemplified thereby. The condemned Bat-wings are the accusers and judges who figured in the indictment of one of their own kind for theft. The Dwellers have decided that they are too corrupt to exist, for the accusers refused the thief charity and would have seen her starve, while the judges upheld a law which allowed them to prosecute her for stealing their food because she had none of her own. The narrator eventually decides that such a situation is, indeed, so horrible that the Bat-wings deserve their fate.

This remarkable scene — and a good deal of the imagery incorporated into the novel as a whole — owes its origin to the imaginative inspiration of Dante's *Inferno*. Wright had undertaken to complete the translation of the *Inferno* begun by Sir Walter Scott (as he was later to complete Scott's unfinished novel, *The Siege of Malta*), and *The World Below* seems to have been the imaginative offspring of that project: it is permeated by a sense of the corruption of the human world, and the monstrous population of the vision owes much to the phantasmagoric imagination of medieval demonology. The world of the Dwellers is not simply a secular Hell; it is a brutal and horrific environment whose geography is frequently reminiscent of Dante's infernal landscape. The Amphibians, innocent and gentle creatures, belong to a genus of alien beings familiar enough to the reader of modern science fiction, but there· is nothing else quite like the Dwellers and their domain. They are demonic, but by no means evil; rather, they are alien to the moral order of the world, like the devils who find a place in God's divine plan as the agents of His wrath. It is to the domain of the Dwellers that the narrator and his companion must go in the second part of the novel.

The second part begins by continuing the theme of an extensive odyssey through a menacing environment, but it soon falters in its thrust. There is a lake infested by giant clawed tadpoles that must be crossed at great peril, but soon after this end is achieved the narrator and his companion find themselves in an enormous room where the Dwellers keep globular creatures that function as "living books" — organic receptacles for telepathic records. Here they stay for some time, while the narrator learns at second hand virtually all that the reader is ever going to know about the life of the Dwellers. Mention is made of a war between the Dwellers and an insectile species called the Antipodeans, in the fighting of which the Amphibians played an important role, but after the merest glimpse of this titanic struggle the idea is abandoned, undeveloped.

From the living library, the narrator learns the whereabouts of his companions, though the heavily armed Templeton has been identified as a violent creature and "sterilized" (after vivisection). He and his companion also learn the details of a new treaty between the Dwellers and the Amphibians, which requires that she should leave him. Once she is gone the story more or less falls apart. The remainder is presented in highly abbreviated synoptic form, save for the one brief scene in which the narrator is caged in a laboratory and finally discovers Brett — "cleaned" by the Dwellers, childlike and utterly mad.

This moment is bracketed by accounts of the passage of several months, in the latter part of which the narrator is held by the Dwellers and examined in scrupulous detail about the details of the world of his origin. In the course of this interrogation he finds his own consciousness expanded so that he comes to share their lofty contempt for human civilization (though it must be admitted that he has seemed throughout to share their opinion wholeheartedly). A cursory concluding scene deals with the protagonist's return to the present to collect his bounty and to reassure the Professor that though the earlier time travelers can never return, there is no prospect of a *corpus delicti* appearing to embarrass him.

This sudden end of the story is disappointing, though there is a certain propriety in the fact that the vision dissolves like a dream. The novel readily invites description as a nightmare: it is a transfiguration of misanthropic and violent sentiments which must by necessity remain unexpressed in ordinary life. What appears to have happened is that the imaginative impulse ran dry as the writing of the book had a gradual cathartic effect on its author.

Wright was by no means the first or the last writer to be driven to the creation of extravagant imaginary worlds in speculative fiction through a violent distaste for the human world. A similar bitterness provided part of the motive force for the work of several contemporary writers: John Beresford (it is most noticeable in "A Negligible Experiment" and *What Dreams May Come*); Olaf Stapledon (most obviously in *Odd John* and *Sirius*); and C. S. Lewis (*Out of the Silent Planet* and *That Hideous Strength*). All three of these writers, however, believed that there was hope for the redemption of man.

Notes of high hysteria are sounded in the conclusion of Claude Houghton's *This Was Ivor Trent* and in H. G. Wells's last despairing essay *Mind at the End of Its Tether*; but there is nothing else in imaginative literature quite as horrifically vitriolic and bleakly antihuman as *The World Below*, though Wright came close to emulating it in his own last novel, *Spiders' War* (1954), written when he was eighty. Its closest analogues are perhaps to be sought in the visual arts: in *The Temptation of St. Anthony* and *The Last Judgment* of Hieronymus Bosch, and in Goya's *Capriccios*. Wright probably turned to writing in the midst of a fit of acute disillusionment: he was fifty when *The Amphibians* first appeared, having spent thirty years as an accountant and having been married twice with a total of ten children. *The World Below* is the work of an alienated man, and one cannot really feel regret that the fervid imagination which produced it cooled when the initial prospectus was no more than half-fulfilled.

As with so many great works of imaginative literature, *The World Below* represents something of a synthesis between the religious imagination and the scientific imagination, though in actual fact it seems to owe no inspiration whatever to formal evolutionary theory, and its use of a futuristic scenario may simply be a convention borrowed from Wells (*The Time Machine* is mentioned in the first chapter). Perhaps it should be regarded as entirely a product of the religious imagination turned fearfully arid by dogmatic atheism. *The World Below* is a novel of great imaginative power and many admirable elements, but it is a disturbing book and not always an enjoyable one.

Brian Stableford

Sources for Further Study

Reviews:

Amazing Stories. V, June, 1950, p. 280.

Analog. XLV, April, 1950, pp. 143-145.

Flying Saucers from Other Worlds. III, March, 1951, pp. 30-31.

Magazine of Fantasy and Science Fiction. I, Winter–Spring, 1950, p. 106.

Marvel Science Fiction. III, November, 1950, pp. 98-99.

Super Science Fiction. VI, January, 1950, p. 97.

Startling Stories. XX, January, 1950, p. 161.

THE WORLD OF NULL-A

Author: A. E. van Vogt (1912-   )
First book publication: 1948
Type of work: Novel
Time: The twenty-fifty century
Locale: The Earth and Venus

With the help of a non-Aristotelian society, two bodies, and an extra brain, Gilbert Gosseyn foils an attack on Earth and Venus by a Galactic Empire

Principal characters:
GILBERT GOSSEYN, a competitor in the annual Null-A Games
PATRICIA HARDIE, daughter of President Hardie
MICHAEL HARDIE, President of Earth
JIM THORSON, an assistant to the President
X, a mutilated scientist in a wheelchair
ELDRED CRANG, Thorson's man in charge on Venus, a Null-A detective
JOHN PRESCOTT, another Thorson man on Venus who may be a Null-A convert
LAUREN KAIR, a Null-A psychiatrist practicing on Earth
ENRO THE RED, a Galactic ruler who is trying to conquer Venus and Earth
LAVOISSEUR, the scientist in charge of the Semantics Institute
THE GAMES MACHINE, the intelligent computer that supervises Null-A, the games, the Games City, and much else on Earth and Venus

The World of Null-A is one of the central books in the future history of human galactic civilization that developed in the science fiction magazines during the 1940's. It also is a significant presentation of the superman (along with van Vogt's own *Slan*) and is the prototypical example of what James Blish called "the extensively recomplicated plot."

John W. Campbell, Jr., the influential editor of *Astounding Science Fiction* in which *The World of Null-A* was serialized in 1945, called the novel "one of those once-in-a-decade classics of science fiction," and it remains persistently in print to this day. In the 1940's van Vogt rivaled Robert A. Heinlein for the title of the most popular writer of science fiction.

Van Vogt attained his position with a series of fast-moving, intricately plotted short stories and novels, beginning in 1939 with "Black Destroyer" and "Discord in Scarlet" (later collected, with other stories, as *The Voyage of the Space Beagle*, 1950), and continuing through *Slan* in 1940, "The Weapon Shop" and "Recruiting Station" in 1942, *The Weapon Makers* in 1943, "The Rull" and *The Players of Null-A* in 1948, and *The Weapon Shops of Isher* in 1949. After 1950 van Vogt devoted himself for some years to L. Ron Hubbard's poor-man's psychiatry, Dianetics, and his writing stopped until sometime in the 1960's. *The World of Null-A*, however, came at the midpoint in his decade of popularity and accomplishment, and in some ways it is his most spectacular and most typical novel.

The World of Null-A describes Earth some five hundred years in the future. It is a saner Earth because its population has been converted to a non-Aristotelian ("null-A") philosophy of multivalued logic and has set up an educational system that teaches discrimination among people, places, things, and ideas, capped by an annual competition. The winners go to live in an ideal society on an idealized Venus, and the runners-up fill positions of authority on Earth.

The competition is governed by a gigantic Games Machine in a city given over almost entirely to government and the annual month-long Games. Gilbert Gosseyn finds himself in this city the night before the Games begin. He discovers almost at once he does not even know who he is, and sets out in search of answers and identity.

The novel involves him in ascending orders of complication, confusion, fast-moving action, plots and counterplots, and intrigue among the stars. He finds few answers, but in the process of searching he is killed and awakens in an identical body on Venus. Others express concern about extra brain matter in his head; about his existence, his purpose, his potential; and about the possibility of still other Gosseyn bodies with additional talents and potentials.

Finally Venus is attacked by a great interstellar empire. In spite of the overwhelming odds, the unarmed null-A Venusians fight back successfully, each independently taking the logical action called for by the situation. But the Games Machine on Earth is destroyed and Earth is attacked as well, all in deliberate contravention of Galactic League regulations.

Gosseyn develops the ability, with his extra brain matter, to force "identities." He perfects his mental control over energy and matter, including the teleportation of his body to places previously "memorized." Finally he lures the leader of the Empire forces to the Semantics Institute on Earth and destroys him, allowing a null-A infiltrator of the Empire to take command.

From a dying scientist in the Semantics Institute, Gosseyn learns that some five hundred years earlier the Empire had placed a secret base on Earth. The scientist, who was working on a process of creating duplicate bodies (what would now be called "cloning"), helped null-A to be accepted, discovered the galactic base, visited the universe, came back to superintend construction of the Games Machine, and perfected the process of creating replicas of himself that would receive his thoughts while awaiting activation. Gosseyn I and II were two such replicas, but they had false memories; they were thrust into the situation to delay the attack of the Empire and eventually to destroy its leader. The scientist, of course, is an old Gosseyn.

Such a brief summary does little justice to the narrative excitement of the novel or to the difficulty of piecing together this kind of coherent statement out of what goes on. Part of the confusion may be due to van Vogt's technique of writing eight-hundred-word scenes and "putting every current thought into the story I happened to be working on."

The ideas in *The World of Null-A* are from Alfred Korzybski's General Semantics (the success of the novel, it is reported, produced a bonanza of sales for *Science and Sanity*), which provides the philosophical basis for the null-A society, the Games Machine, the Galactic Empire and the Galactic League, the extra-brained superman, teleportation by means of forced identities, and immortality by means of serial bodies. None of these is explored in any detail in the novel, however, at least not in a thematically central sense. Brief epigraphs, some from Korzybski's writing, are enigmatic. Many concepts have the same relative importance, and some enter only casually, so that readers or critics who attempt to trace theme or idea have little success. *The World of Null-A* is not a novel of theme so much as a mystery novel sustained by the philosophy of the hardboiled detective story described by Raymond Chandler in the introduction to his collection of *Black Mask* stories: when in doubt have a man come through the door with a gun in his hand.

Van Vogt is a storyteller, not a philosopher. His favorite story concerns the man who discovers that he is different; often he cannot recall his past, or he discovers that what he remembers (or is told) is false. He is a man, moreover, who possesses strange powers that wait to be discovered or developed. With these powers the hero can attain his rightful place, right wrongs, bring justice to the world, and create a new and better life for humanity, all in the face of incredible odds. This, of course, is the stuff of fairy-tales and of drama. The basic situation is that of the "changeling" complicated with other fairy-tale concepts: seven-league boots, the cloak of invisibility, fairy godmothers, and so on.

The scientific explanations behind van Vogt's ideas are only what H. G. Wells called "scientific patter." The powers van Vogt deals with are governed not so much by the logic of science as by the logic of wish-fulfillment. They deal with ultimates. One van Vogt story, "A Can of Paint," asks what are the characteristics of the perfect paint; another, *The Book of Ptath*, describes a godlike human; "The Weapon Shop" and its sequels involve the perfect weapon of defense; and "The Monster" presents a human race grown preternaturally quick-witted and gifted. In *The World of Null-A*, an unarmed, unwarned citizenry defeats the army of a galactic empire of sixty thousand star systems.

Part of van Vogt's technique is based on a literal use of terms, a kind of magic of names: in *The World of Null-A* a lie detector is not merely an apparatus for enabling an expert to deduce from certain physiological readings that someone may be lying; it is a device that determines, unequivocally, whether someone is telling the truth, and says so. How it works is never described and the mechanism plays no vital part in the novel. Though it would be useful as a training device in a null-A society, it is not the product of a particular technology or symptomatic of a society, as it would be if, say, Robert Heinlein used it. But when the lie detector says to Gosseyn, "You are lying," the reader's world is turned upside down in a way that only science fiction can achieve. In other places, a Distorter distorts the ability of the Games Machine to function, and an energy scanner literally enables its user to look into a machine and see energy.

What van Vogt has done in *The World of Null-A* and in most of his other fiction is to turn magic into science — or science into magic. He deals with speculative scientific possibilities as if they had been accomplished in some ideal (magical) way. His works are a reflection of himself: he is in love with ideas, and views humanity as capable of godlike wisdom and power if it only can find the right way of thinking and the secret method of control. Van Vogt has been fascinated by the ideas of Oswald Spengler, General Semantics, Bates's eye exercises (Aldous Huxley also was a convert), Dianetics, and no doubt others; and he has managed to convert them all, with the possible exception of Dianetics, into fiction.

The result has been a kind of magical fiction. Van Vogt has produced what Tennyson referred to (in "Locksley Hall") as "the fairy tales of science and the long result of time." The archetypes with which he dealt and the unrelenting pace of his narratives covered some of his flaws in logic, and the magic that his fans derived from the stories minimized the rest.

James Gunn

Sources for Further Study

Criticism:

Ash, Brian. *Faces of the Future — The Lessons of Science Fiction*. London: Elek/Pemberton, 1975, pp. 117-118. Ash comments and gives criticism of the works of van Vogt.

The Encyclopedia of Science Fiction and Fantasy. Compiled by Donald H. Tuck. Chicago: Advent Publishers, Inc., 1978, pp. 430-432. This article gives a review of van Vogt's life and career, with a full bibliography of his works.

Wilson, Colin. "The Vision of Science," in *The Strength to Dream: Literature and the Imagination*. London: Gollancz, 1962, pp. 94-117. Wilson reviews science fiction literature in relation to "the mainstream" of literature, giving some discussion of van Vogt's contributions.

Reviews:

Amazing Stories. XXIII, December, 1949, pp. 152-153 and XXXIX, January, 1965, p. 125.

Fantastic Novels Magazine. January, 1949, p. 114.

Fantasy Book. I, 1948, p. 38.

Flying Saucers from Other Worlds. III, September, 1951, p. 132.

Future Science Fiction. II, November, 1951, p. 86.

Kirkus Reviews. XVI, January 15, 1948, p. 35.

New York Herald Tribune Weekly Book Review. March 21, 1948, p. 12.

New Yorker. XXIV, March 27, 1948, p. 92.

San Francisco Chronicle. May 2, 1948, p. 26.

Thrilling World Stories. XXXII, August, 1948, pp. 144-145.

WORLD SOUL
(DUSHA MIRA)

Authors: Mikhail Emtsev (1930-   ) and Eremei Parnov (1935-   )
First book publication: 1964
English translation: 1978
Type of work: Novel
Time: Given as "19--" in one place, but social and technological changes suggest the mid-twenty-first century
Locale: Moscow; Khokai-Rokh, a biological station on the steppe; other sites in the U.S.S.R.; Bessano, a mythical city supposedly in or near Argentina

When humanity gradually realizes that a mutant seaweed culture, which confers telepathic powers on the human race, not only exchanges thoughts but alters them, it rises in rebellion

> Principal characters:
> SERGEI AREFYEV, a young, discontented scientist at the Institute of Telepathy in Moscow
> RŮŽENA (misrendered *Ruzhena* in the English translation), Sergei's Czech girl friend, also a member of the Institute of Telepathy
> ERIK ERDMAN, a biologist working with Sergei
> ANDREI KARABICHEV, a coworker of Sergei
> RIOLI, a Bessanese scholar who befriends Karabichev
> ERMOLEV, deputy chief research director of the Institute of Telepathy

World Soul represents an odd mixture of genres, changing direction almost with every chapter. It starts out like a novel of scientific discovery — young, idealistic Sergei has never fit in anywhere because of his contrariness and the originality of his ideas, but he perseveres in his collaboration with the biologist Erik Erdman. The goal of their strivings, as in a typical Soviet "novel about scientists" (*nauchno-khudozhestvennyi roman*), is not basic research, but a project with immediate application: to turn a mutant seaweed culture into a biological factory for the production of industrial polymers. Meanwhile, to support himself and to gain access to laboratory facilities, Sergei gets a job at the Institute of Telepathy, which is in the very early stages of psychic research.

With the next chapter, the novel takes a jump in the direction not precisely of the catastrophe story, but of its scarcer relative, the "great change" story — after the manner of, say, H. G. Wells's *Food of the Gods*, Walter Miller's "Dark Benediction," or Fritz Leiber's *The Wanderer*. We leave Sergei and follow his coworker Karabichev on his vacation to a country village, where one morning Karabichev discovers that everyone has suddenly acquired short-range telepathic powers. For a while the effects of this phenomenon seem at worst amusing, and sometimes beneficial (doctors can now feel the symptoms of patients for themselves), but then Karabichev discovers that a French-woman's mind has taken over his wife's body.

Another chapter brings another swerve in genre, this time to something resembling the monster movie. We flashback to Sergei and Erik at a biological station on the steppe. The seaweed culture has grown explosively, and is now a living mountain weighing a hundred million tons. It had previously been demonstrated that the culture was sensitive to human thought, so the reader immediately realizes that the enlarged culture is somehow responsible for the telepathy. But, as in any proper monster movie, the brilliant scientist heroes take forever to see the obvious.

Then we move on to the peculiarly Soviet genre of adventure in the wicked West. Karabichev receives a letter apparently written by his wife's transplanted personality, and posted in the South American port of Bessano. A mere personal reason would never get Karabichev an exit visa from the U.S.S.R., but as it happens, scientists believe that whatever is inducing the telepathy is located near Cape Horn (the antipodes of the true location of the plant culture). So Karabichev is dispatched to look both for his wife and for the source of the telepathic effect. (Despite the urgency of his mission, he travels by ship. One can find no ghost of an explanation for this.) Arriving in Bessano, Karabichev is befriended by a native scholar, Rioli, who speaks in terms rather like those of Teilhard de Chardin, and sees the telepathic effect as leading to the spiritual unification of humankind. Karabichev disagrees on Communist ideological grounds, and because there is no place for human individuality in this picture. Moreover, while searching through the seamy underside of life in Bessano, Karabichev sees for himself that not even telepathy will bridge over the contradictions of capitalist society. Eventually Karabichev finds not his wife, but merely one fragment of her personality embedded in the mind of a hideous beggar. As an integrated *persona*, the woman no longer exists. The sinister side of the World Soul, as the seaweed culture has come to be called, becomes more and more obvious.

With the next chapter we jump into a ghost story. Růžena is accidentally killed by a psychic amplifier Sergei has left behind in his Institute laboratory, and thereafter she makes several appearances as a ghost who can be seen and spoken to, but not photographed.

Finally, two-thirds of the way through, the novel settles down a bit and the plot takes on some coherence. We get a solution of sorts to the scientific mystery. Sergei at long last has realized that the plant culture is responsible for the telepathy, and he has even figured out the mechanism — every human psyche is mapped onto the culture as a discrete point (which, conveniently for research, glows in the dark), and the monster plant feeds back psychic signals from the mapped points to their originals. When the tiny points blur together, the people they represent experience thought-exchange. The mapped points persist for a while after their owners' deaths, and register on other peoples' psyches as ghosts. With this reassuringly materialist explanation out of the way, the question becomes whether the telepathic effect is a good thing or not.

Sergei is among those favoring it, but when the question is debated at an international scientific meeting, the conclusion is finally in favor of trying to isolate or destroy the World Soul. However, this is easier said than done, since the plant will not let anyone touch it. First it radiates suggestions and illusions, and when those fail, it induces pain or death in those who seek to injure it.

Meanwhile, back in Bessano, Karabichev is already suffering a World Soul-induced lassitude, but he throws it off by an act of will reinforced with self-inflicted pain, and heads back to Moscow. (One hopes he has sense enough to fly on the return trip.) In Moscow he gathers together a few companions and sets out for the steppe to destroy the World Soul. But Soviet ideology will not admit that the fate of humanity could hang by such a slender thread, so when Karabichev arrives at Khokai-Rokh he finds that the government, in the form of an Extraordinary Committee of the United Nations, already has the situation in hand. A research facility has been set up on a space station, out of the World Soul's psychic reach, and shielding has been developed for use on Earth.

Karabichev learns that Sergei is dead. He has attempted to use his psychic amplifier (the one that earlier killed Růžena) to plumb the "mental" processes of the computerlike World Soul, and the strain has been too much. Before he died, however, he made a tape recording that takes up the rest of the book. The most memorable part of this is an account of a quasimystical dream which is supposed to foretell what the future would be if the World Soul had its way. This vision of a living ocean of vegetating humanity has little justification in the novel — its near-surrealism would be more at home in Silverberg's *Son of Man* or in the Russian Futurist work of the 1920's — but taken by itself it is easily the most striking and memorable scene in the book. Sergei's fellow scientists of course resolve to fight on all the harder, and an epilogue set several centuries later indicates that the World Soul has been vanquished, and the Marxist-Leninist version of full human fellowship has been established in place of the counterfeit variety supplied by the World Soul.

What we are to make of this novel seems to depend on what we make of the World Soul. Science fiction in the strict sense of the term functions on a level of seeming-realism, whatever levels of symbolism may be added onto the realistic one. Walter Miller's "Dark Benediction" may utlimately have to do with things like racial and religious prejudice, but the weight of symbolism is not allowed to sink the story. The nature of the "dark benediction," the microorganisms that cause the story's "great change," is explained in great detail, and it is exactly because the reader can believe in the microorganisms that he can learn whatever other lessons Miller's story has to teach. The World Soul, by contrast, is totally implausible. For no particular reason, one fine day a lump of seaweed culture turns into an incredibly sophisticated computer and support system capable not only of sustaining its own enormous bulk (no mean feat in itself, since the World Soul is the largest single organism of all time) but also of controlling the entire human race to the plant's own advantage.

In his introduction to the English translation, Theodore Sturgeon speaks of *World Soul* as a "fable," like Wells's *Food of the Gods*. In this genre an impossible "fantasy" element is introduced at the start, not to be questioned, and the author's only obligation is to proceed logically from his initial premises, whatever these may be. But the whole point of this genre is to look *away* from the fabulous device, to use it as a vantage point from which to examine something else. To take a better-known (and better-written) Wellsian example, the impossible vehicle in *The Time Machine* serves to show us Wells's views on social conflict and on cosmology. By contrast, Emtsev and Parnov's heroes spend much of their time not in examining the effects of telepathy upon society (though there are some good short scenes on this topic), nor even in debating whether World-Soul communism is inferior to the Marxist-Leninist kind (they quickly decide it is), but in subjecting the World Soul to a scientific examination that is bound to fail since the authors have not bothered to build any scientific plausibility into the organism; nevertheless, we are told, the scientific examination succeeds. The question might arise as to whether the novel could be a parody. True, the novel's clumsy structure and thickly laid-on ideology have their ludicrous moments, but the tone of the work does not suggest that these moments were intentional. Russians are scarcely noted for the subtlety of their sense of humor, and any humor here would have to be subtle indeed.

Could it be that the novel is an allegory, with the "scientific" elements and the frequent doses of ideology thrown in merely to keep the censor off the track? Such an interpretation would put the novel squarely in the tradition of Bulgakov's "Fatal Eggs" and *Heart of a Dog*. The "ultracollectivist" World Soul would then represent the Communist Party — masquerading under the intention of bringing humankind to a state of collectivist well-being, but in fact intent only on its own perpetuation and aggrandizement. Taken on its own terms, the parallel works fairly well, but it is easy to read things into works of fiction. Biographical information strongly suggests that expression of dissidence was not the intention of the authors. Both Emtsev and Parnov — unlike most science fiction writers in the Soviet Union — are Party members, and Parnov in particular has been active in literary organizations. Every outward indication is that he is a loyal Party man and that he enjoys a reasonable measure of the regime's confidence.

We must come, then, to the conclusion that no unity and rationality on a symbolic plane exists to rescue the overt incoherence and implausibility of *World Soul*. Either the authors set their sights no higher than a sort of monster movie on the printed page, a work with no pretension to logic and no respect for its audience, a work which strives only to excite and amaze, or Emtsev and Parnov attempted something better but failed.

The latter seems more probable. In the first place, it should be recalled that the authors were educated at a time when Lysenkoism held sway in the U.S.S.R.; when the story was first published in 1964, the doctrine had only just fallen out of favor. Repeated agricultural failure finally forced some sense into the Soviet leadership, but in the meantime a whole generation has grown up with no proper concept of evolutionary biology. While it scarcely can have seemed likely to the authors that a lump of seaweed should suddenly decide to conquer the world, they may have had a vague belief in *élan vital* or something which made the idea seem not quite so unacceptable to them as it does — or should — to the educated Westerner. Moreover, since Western science fiction was little known in the U.S.S.R. in the early 1960's, the whole "great change" genre, as well as the story about mass telepathy and even the monster story itself, were much less familiar in the Soviet Union than in the West. Soviet editors and readers may be willing to forgive much in the work of a team of authors who can insert enough ideology and materialist explanation to get this much "sense of wonder" past the censors.

Such explanations, however, do not change the quality of this work as judged by Western standards. In an ideal world, the manuscript should have been sent back the authors with some suggestions for revision. They should have been told that the World Soul is a dramatic illusion that cannot be scrutinized too closely lest it disappear, and that the strongest and most promising of the manuscript's several incipient themes is the tension between the conflicting demands of the two ideals of mutuality and individualism. And then, in all probability, we would have had a much better *World Soul*. In the real world, all we can say is that the novel contains a number of intriguing but undeveloped concepts, and some excellent individual scenes.

Patrick L. McGuire

WORLDS OF THE IMPERIUM

Author: Keith Laumer (1925-   )
First book publication: 1962
Type of work: Novel
Time: 1955
Locale: Stockholm, Sweden B-I Three; Stockholm, Sweden Zero Zero, and nearby
countryside; Algiers, B-I Two, and environs

*Kidnaped by intelligence agents of the Imperium because he is an analogue of the
dictator of a warlike state in a third time line, Brion Bayard is given the mission to
take the place of the dictator and establish peace between the time lines*

Principal characters:
BRION BAYARD, a retired American diplomat
CAPTAIN WINTER, an officer of Imperium Intelligence
CAPTAIN BERNADOTTE, an official disguise of King Gustav of
Sweden
HERMANN GOERING, an officer of German Intelligence
CHIEF INSPECTOR BALE, another officer of Imperium Intelligence
FRIHERR VON RICHTOVEN, an adviser to the Imperium
BARBRO LUNDANE, the romantic interest of Zero Zero-A world
BRION BAYARD, dictator of National People's State of B-I Two
GASTON, Brion's (B-I Three) bodyguard in Algiers and brother of
Gros, a leader of the insurgent "Organization"

Writers in such popular genres as science fiction work in a field that has its
own boundaries and conventions. These tend to be less stable than standard
genres, it is true, but perhaps because a greater premium is placed on inventiveness and originality in science fiction. At the same time, storytelling formulae that have developed in the genre help to create for its readership the
sense of an identifiable body of literature. There is now a greater variety of
readers of science fiction than there ever has been before, and as it eases into
the mainstream, readers of the genre are less likely to be adolescent in mind-
set. Despite the interest espoused by some university professors and the widen-
ing base of appeal among general readers, however, it is fair to say that the
science fiction industry relies on a hardcore readership of fans who can be
depended on to read and buy almost anything that is identifiably science fiction. Quality sometimes matters little to those who saturate themselves in science fiction; their important response is to be swept along by the experience,
to let themselves be captivated by the expectations of the formula and the
fulfillment of its premises. Keith Laumer's *Worlds of the Imperium* is a book
for such readers.

It is best to approach this novel as an entertainment, since it has little to
offer the more serious science fiction reader. Those who are looking for social
criticism or a serious or symbolic statement on the ways science transforms the
lives of future generations had better look elsewhere. Likewise, the reader who
finds pulp fiction contemptible will not want to read this science fiction adven-

ture/suspense which has no redeeming scientific importance. Nevertheless, Laumer's "scientific romance" is worth examining as a representative of the kind of popular science fiction adventure that gave the literature a thirty-year blackeye in America.

The novel begins in Stockholm with a scene reminiscent of a promising introduction to an espionage story. An American diplomat is being followed through the unfamiliar streets of a foreign capital by a sinister looking gent seemingly intent on foul play. Then, there is the confrontation: a struggle on a deserted street, a police van arrives, the hero is rescued. But no; the van becomes a scout vehicle based in the Stockholm of another time-line commanded by Chief Captain Winter and sent specifically to capture Brion Bayard, and carry him cross-time to the Zero Zero-A time-line. Incredible though it may seem, unfortunately for Bayard, it proves to be true. He will not be returned to his world, the one known to the kidnapers as B-I Three. He is told that he has been taken for a reason that will be revealed to him after the vehicle lands; he will be well treated, and should not worry. Taking none of this, however, and brandishing a gun snatched from Winter's desk, Bayard takes over the vehicle and orders it returned to his world. Although he uses the gun to shoot up the command console to effect this, he soon realizes the impossibility of turning back. As they journey forward, Captain Winter and later officials of the Imperium begin to unfold the events of this otherworld.

The explanation reveals to Bayard that the universe in which he has lived possesses dimensions previously unsuspected. (Nearly all the novel's inventiveness is poured into these early chapters, setting the stage for the suspense melodrama to follow.) The reason Brion and his captors cannot simply reverse their field and return to his time-line is that they are attempting to cross the Blight — a devastated series of time-lines forming the most perilous part of their journey. The Blight is a sequence of time-lines during which civilization blew itself up, leaving behind either a desert world, or one filled with unpleasant and dangerous mutations. Once trapped on one of the blighted worlds, there was no returning but the crippled vehicle does manage the transition, and returns to the world of the Imperium.

The world of the Imperium or Zero Zero-A time-line is one whose history had been the same as Brion's world up until about 1790, when the two diverged. The critical point of difference in their respective histories came in 1893 when two Italian scientists, Maxoni and Cocine, developed the means of moving from one alternative time-line to another. The invention was offered to the British, who took the opportunity it advanced to negotiate a treaty with the German Empire in order to avoid a fratricidal war. The amalgamation of the two empires took place on January 1, 1900, to produce the Anglo-German Imperium ruled by the House of Hanover-Wilson and also including the kingdom of Sweden. Thus World War I was avoided in Zero Zero-A. One of the great scientific undertakings of the Imperium was the exploration of the alternative continua. The Blight was discovered, but there existed beyond it countless time-lines whose points of divergence seemed to be about four hundred years before. The further one traveled the earlier the point of divergence.

In 1947, first evidence was discovered of an inhabited world analogous to Zero Zero within the Blight. This new world, called B-I/Two (for Blight Island) had nearly been destroyed by a series of atomic wars. What remained of civilization was incorporated under the National People's State, headquartered in Algiers. When the Imperium sent a diplomatic team to negotiate an agreement of trade and cultural exchange, the diplomats were tortured and killed. Rather than retaliate, the Imperium determined to leave its unfortunate sister world to its own isolation. However, noninvolvement was no longer practical after a time travel unit from B-I Two began raiding the worlds of the other time-lines with which the Imperium had trade agreements. These murderous and barbaric commando raids culminated in a series of attacks on the Imperium itself. In one of these raids, Berlin was destroyed by an atomic weapon, knowledge of which the Imperium did not possess and had no wish to develop. Clearly, however, the use of such a destructive weapon made some sort of preemptive strike necessary for self-defense. It was precisely at this time that another inhabited time-line in the Blight was discovered in close approximation to B-I Two — Brion's world and ours, or B-I Three. Brion Bayard, retired American diplomat, was kidnaped because of his physical resemblance to Brion Bayard, the dictator of the National People's State. Obviously they are analogues. A plan based on this fact grew which led to Brion's abduction. He would be asked by the Imperium to drop into the dictator's time-line, assassinate him, take his place, and produce the necessary changes to create a climate of opinion in which a peace treaty with the Imperium could be worked out and further bloodshed avoided.

In a nutshell, this is the proposal that King Gustav made to Brion. As a reward, he would be honored and would live comfortably in the Zero Zero time-line, but he would not be returned to his own world so that the existence of the Imperium and the other time-lines would be concealed. Brion is made a colonel in the royal army and finds himself conversing with royal counselors von Richtoven and Goering. The latter is especially fascinated to learn that in Brion's time-line, he was Reichsmarshal and known to all. (Brion diplomatically does not reveal the true nature of his notoriety.)

The novel's development to this point provides groundwork for a potentially mind expanding tale of historical analogues among cultures and persons whose various identities diverge from key points in the geopolitical histories of their worlds. However, the potential goes unfulfilled, the story changes gears, and the rest of the novel becomes an espionage melodrama complete with as many chases and fist fights as any bright nine-year-old could wish for.

Brion volunteers for the mission, but not immediately; a young, nubile maiden named Barbro Lundane adds romantic interest in addition to other enticements. A gala party at the king's summer palace becomes the scene of a gory massacre by B-I Two commandos. Brion is heroic, taking a leading part in repelling and gunning down the raiders, and in capturing the atom bomb prior to its detonation in the garden.

A fast-paced series of confrontations, chases, and escapes follows, involving Brion and the National police (who seem to be involved in a conspiracy against the dictator) and Brion and an underground organization of criminal freebooters under a mysterious "Big Boss" and various parties of guards and riffraff of criminal nature. During these chases of all types and forms, Brion naturally is wounded, sometimes maimed, and requiring recuperation. It is during one of these interludes that Brion discovers why he has been unable to convince anyone that he is the dictator Bayard. Bayard, it seems, had lost both legs below the knee during the previous war. Thus, the Organization engaged a surgical dual amputation to add reality to the impersonation. Disenchanted at this prospect, Brion flees back to Algiers, finally managing to reach the private headquarters of the dictator Bayard. After Brion avails himself of the dictator's sumptuous bath facilities, he falls asleep in a chair waiting for his enemy to appear. When he awakens, he finds himself looking into the face of Bayard, his other self.

This meeting between the two Bayards is developed brilliantly, despite the melodrama — perhaps the best thing of its kind since Conrad's "The Secret Sharer." Brion is both relieved and astonished to find that Bayard is a brother; indeed, more than a brother — an other self. The scene above all demarcates the author's basic sense of decency, which transcends all the brawling and brutality thwarting the hero at every turn. It is a decency capable of creating alternative Richtovens and Goerings, of envisioning an Imperium which has learned the proper use of power through restraint. Brion's fears of meeting his other self turn out to be reflections of a basic paranoia in our own culture since we, as readers, are implicated in them. At first, we are surprised and suspicious at the warmth and affection of Bayard's response to his other self. Yet, how would we greet ourselves if we could? Bayard greets his other self openly and with affection and Brion discovers that Bayard knew nothing of the ambassadors from the Imperium nor anything of their fate. He also knew nothing of the commando raids; these deeds all obviously were the work of a traitor who had managed to seize power from Bayard. The traitor, Chief Inspector Bale of Imperium Intelligence, quickly identifies himself by firing a volley of bullets from his gun. Bayard (B-I Two) dies protecting his other self, and Bale arranges for the execution of Brion after his legs are amputated.

It clearly is time for a rescue, forthcoming from Zero Zero-A line. Brion, with his crippled miniature transmitter, has managed to signal them even as he is being escorted to surgery. Brion is saved, and returned to a hospital in the Imperium for rest; Brion knows that Bale, the traitor, was responsible for the raids and that he plans to seize control of both worlds. The opportunity is at hand: on the very day that Brion awakens from a coma, the three kings of the Imperium are in town. Brion discovers Bale's secret residence from a clue picked up in B-I Two. As he has feared, there is an atomic bomb in one room, and a time machine in the other. The crafty villain Bale will set the bomb to detonate when the three kings are in the city, then make his getaway into another time. Weak but determined, Brion lies in wait for Bale while Barbro, who has accompanied him from the hospital, is sent for help. Soon after her departure, Bale returns and begins arming the bomb, but before that job is completed, Brion announces himself, proposing to hold Bale until the authorities arrive. With his last strength, he fires at Bale, who attempts, but fails jumping the distance to the roof across the street. Although Brion chivalrously calls for help, Bale falls to his richly deserved death.

Worlds of the Imperium is really two novels in one. The first and much the better of the two is devoted to building up the elaborate structure of multiple time-lines with interesting contrasts among analogous cultures and individuals. The second is costume suspense melodrama set in and around Algiers. The fights and chases are repetitious, and become tedious despite the great pace, one crisis piling upon another. One regrets that Laumer did not develop material of the quality of the two Brions meeting each's other self rather than racing through sensationalized action in the second portion of the book. The reader who knows what science fiction can do to expand his consciousness and touch wellsprings of primary emotion will probably not gain much pleasure from reading this book.

Donald L. Lawler

Sources for Further Study

Reviews:

Analog. LXIX, July, 1962, pp. 168-169.

Observer. April 14, 1968, p. 27.

SF Commentary. XXV, December, 1971, pp. 16-17.

LES XIPÉHUZ
(The Xipéhuz)

Author: J. H. Rosny (the Elder) (1856-1940)
First book publication: 1887
Type of work: Novel
Time: Thousands of years in the ancient past
Locale: The country that was to become Mesopotamia

A meeting between prehistoric men and the Xipéhuz, beings completely alien to Earth, leads to a conflict that is barely won by the humans

Principal characters:
THE XIPÉHUZ, alien invaders
BAKHOÛN, the man who studies and combats them

Les Xipéhuz is one of the most famous works in all of French science fiction because it is generally considered to be the first to explore the distant past rather than the extrapolated future. Its author, J. H. Rosny (the Elder), remains a kind of "sacred monster" in imaginative literature, a man who succeeded in earning the respect of scientists as well as the literary world. He belonged to the group directed by Jean Perrin and Robert Esnault-Pelterie which in 1928 founded a discipline which was then in the field of pure science fiction: "Astronautics," a term coined by Rosny himself.

This novel is an example of a genre in which Rosny distinguished himself: the "Prehistoric Novel." Most of his works in the area have remained classics, the most famous of which is probably *The Fire War*. Unlike his famous colleagues (Stanley Waterloo, for example), Rosny was able to add a further touch to his stories about the "Wild Ages" of humanity, that of writing them in a science fiction context. In some of his works science fiction plays a minor role; in others it is central to the story. *Les Xipéhuz* is a pure science fiction story that takes place at the dawn of civilization.

The story unfolds in two stages. The first part chronicles the meeting between a caravan crossing an untamed forest and strange beings which have appeared from nowhere. This clash results in numerous deaths in the ranks of the nomads, whose survivors hasten to the priests in order to appease the strange new Gods, but to no avail. The Xipéhuz continue to extend their control over the region and kill all humans foolhardy enough to approach them. In the second part, the men fight back under the command of Bakhoûn, a kind of hermit who has been instructed to study the Xipéhuz closely.

The Xipéhuz are the first of a long series of extraordinary beings who became a trademark of Rosny's science fiction works. Nobody knows where they came from. They just appeared one evening to a prehistoric caravan in search of a campsite. They seem to have literally come out of nothingness in a period of a few hours (the elapsed time between the discovery of the clearing by a scout and the arrival of the caravan). In a few lines, Rosny has created the incon-

ceivable, who appear in the everyday universe. The first term he uses in referring to the Xipéhuz is "weirdness." The men of the caravan find themselves
suddenly faced with beings who are endowed with faculties that are completely
contradictory to anything that had been previously known.

The Xipéhuz are, in fact, of mineral origin. They are divided into three
main shapes: some are conical, others are cylindrical, still others have the
appearance of vertically placed strata. They all possess a strange star of light at
their base, a star which seems to be the seat of their mysterious powers. Most
of them are multicolored. They also apparently change shapes at will. Neither
their way of thinking nor their relationships can be understood by human observers. Their psychology is totally alien. The one and only thing the prehistoric men can be certain of is that the Xipéhuz have come to seize Earth by
spreading out from their initial base little by little after pushing men back with
their terrible power to kill from a distance.

In the face of this threat, a hero named Bakoûn rises up. He is an extraordinary man considering the age in which he lives, a period entrenched in
barbarism and the worship of a plethora of divinities. He has been a hermit,
professing that the sedentary life is more conducive to intellectual development
than the nomadic life. He also relates "heretical" information about the stars
and the universe. Finally, he is convinced man should only believe in things
that can be proven by experiment. The prehistoric nomads fear him, would like
to put him to death, but faced with their own destruction by the strange living
minerals, the people decide (after the failure of the powerless priests) to call
upon him for help, despite the fact that he is almost as alien to them as the
Xipéhuz.

Understanding the magnitude of the danger, Bakhoûn applies himself
quickly to a systematic study of the invaders in hopes not only of finding their
Achilles heel, but also of discovering the secret of their strange, fascinating
shapes. His success in understanding the psychology and behavior of the
Xipéhuz, even though only from a distance, finally reveals the chink in their
armor. The armies of men are then able to repel and destroy them. From the
beginning, Bakhoûn realizes one essential fact: as extraordinary as they might
be, the Xipéhuz are subject to the same laws as the men they struggle against.

Bakhoûn is not a hero in Rosny's mind, but a wise man. For the author, the
hero is that nomad who dares to defy the power of the Xipéhuz at the time of
the first contact with the caravan, that nomad who does not really know what
he is exposing himself to. Bakhoûn represents the opposite. He is the man who
studies and figures out a problem, whatever it might be. He does not take
useless risks. Only when he is certain of a few facts does he begin his experiments (the battles with the Xipéhuz where different tactics are tested). The
word "experiment" immediately brings in its wake that of "scientist": Bakoûn
is a man of science. And to reveal this scientist and consequently science itself
in the face of obscurantism, it was necessary to create a crisis situation, a time

in which the existence of the human race, its past, present, and future, was brought to the brink of the abyss of extinction for the advantage of another, more highly organized kingdom.

Since *Les Xipéhuz* was the product of a time which venerated the image of a triumphant science, it may seem dated today. But to read it in that light is to ignore the talent of Rosny, that poet of science whose individualistic style creates a veritable alchemy of language and scientific thought. On the other hand, Rosny completely dedramatizes his story, eliminating narrative suspense in order to provide ample opportunity to express his philosophy of human destiny, a philosophy he maintained throughout his career. The novel unfolds according to a scientific logic that might be compared to that of a doctor studying a new disease: discovery of the virus (the caravan meets the Xipéhuz), observation of the virus and its behavior (Bakhoûn observes the Xipéhuz), and finally treatment of the illness (the victory of men over the Xipéhuz).

This rigorous procedure possesses such a force that the story moves along on its own momentum, allowing Rosny to describe in great detail those famous "Wild Ages" from which modern humanity would emerge. The use of adjectives such as "awesome," "dreadful," "terrible," "prodigious," "savage," or "gigantic" perfectly defines the image Rosny wanted to give of this obscure period of humanity. For the true and only hero of *Les Xipéhuz* and of almost the whole body of Rosny's prehistoric science fiction stories, is man. In the development of the novellas and novels, we follow man's destiny from the cave to the conquest of space, as if the author had wanted to consider the whole of human evolution through the looking glass of science fiction.

Throughout *Les Xipéhuz* and the later texts, man appears as another animal and not a species of privileged biped. The crisis which the brutal attack of the Xipéhuz provokes is a vital test for man, who must depend entirely upon his own aptitudes for survival, and not on some sort of innate superiority over the strange invaders. Bakhoûn overcomes them because he has succeeded in finding their weak point through close observation and following a process of logical deduction. But as he says himself, after the victory, he regrets having destroyed another life form, another system of thought, even though it was hostile and incomprehensible.

Rosny tries to show that man's natural weakness should stimulate a tolerance and respect for other intelligences. Today we have come a long way from the more or less frenzied anthropocentrism which characterized science fiction for many decades in its early years. But one had to wait for a Stanley Weinbaum and his novella *A Martian Odyssey* (1934) to rediscover a point of view as sane as that professed by Rosny on the subject of a meeting between two intelligences incomprehensible to each other.

Thus, it is apparent how much modern science fiction owes to J. H. Rosny (the Elder), one of the first authors who was able to understand the difference between simple predictive scientific romance and science fiction in its pure state, as a genre capable of looking at very old subjects from an entirely new perspective. Rosny was not a mere precursor; he was a founder.

Richard D. Nolane

Sources for Further Study

Review:

New York Times. November 2, 1924, p. 8.

THE YEAR OF THE QUIET SUN

Author: Wilson Tucker (1914-   )
First book publication: 1970
Type of work: Novel
Time: 1978, 1980, 1999, 2000, and beyond 2000
Locale: Joliet, Illinois

A team of time travelers conducts a survey of the future, beginning in 1980 and going beyond the year 2000

Principal characters:
> DR. BRIAN CHANEY, a research scholar and a member of the future survey team
> KATHRYN VAN HISE (KATRINA), research supervisor, Bureau of Standards
> GILBERT SEABROOKE, Director of Operations, Bureau of Standards
> MAJOR WILLIAM MORESBY, a member of the future survey team
> LIEUTENANT COMMANDER ARTHUR SALTUS, the member of the future survey team who marries Kathryn van Hise

The time machine as a plot device has had a long and checkered history in science fiction. Its career began with H. G. Wells's fine book *The Time Machine*, and the idea shows no signs of losing its popularity. Writers never seem to tire of time machines.

Science fiction readers, however, consistently raise objections to time machines. Time travel is not a scientific possibility, they say, and even if it were, the problems involved in traveling into the past or future would make the practice as dangerous as detonating H-bombs. Nevertheless, time travel stories remain fascinating, as witnessed in the continued popularity of such books as *The Time Machine*, Ward Moore's *Bring the Jubilee*, and Isaac Asimov's *The End of Eternity*. Little of that fascination arises from the scientific likelihood — or lack of it — in such books; science fiction need not center on scientific propositions. The genre can also be used to explore the ways in which people see themselves and one another. No modern science fiction novel uses time travel as a framework for character study more successfully than does *The Year of the Quiet Sun* by Wilson Tucker.

At the beginning of the book, Brian Chaney sits on a Florida beach, recovering from his recent trip to Israel. He thinks about his past and present, and does not care much for either. Kathryn van Hise, from the Bureau of Standards, walks up to him and tries to recruit Chaney for the secret Bureau of Standards, but he wants nothing to do with it. She offers him a kind of bribe; the Bureau wants him to take part in a survey of the future. In addition to this tempting offer, Chaney cannot help being disturbed by and drawn to Kathryn herself. Kathryn is described as the "alpha and omega: the two embodied in the same compact bundle." After reading the entire book, one realizes how precise this sentence is. Kathryn appears at the beginning of Chaney's new life, and meets him at the end.

From the beginning, the focus of the book does not rest merely on time travel. The book is about Chaney, and Tucker keeps showing him in new perspectives. At first the author describes a fairly typical hero of a fairly typical science fiction book: he is labeled a genius, a world celebrity (known for his recent translation of the Qumran scroll which is called the *Eschatos*), and is precisely the right man for a dangerous job. But he is also shown as someone who sidesteps the consequences of his actions and position. His *Eschatos* translation is a controversial addition to *Revelation,* the New Testament's visionary text about the end of the world, yet Chaney is loth to think about the future of the world. He is a celebrity, yet he dislikes the thought that he might be important to someone other than himself. He has spent so much energy escaping from his own future that he nearly misses the chance offered by Kathryn.

Of course, he does accept the offer to take part in the secret project at Elwood National Research Station, Joliet, Illinois, which is the hidden installation of the Bureau of Standards. Here Chaney finds himself recruited into the day-to-day routine of what is really a military exercise. The stated aim of the project is to conduct a sociological survey of selected future points of time: 1980, 1999, 2000, and beyond 2000. An elaborate system has been devised to protect the time-travelers, including stocking the Station itself so that supplies and transport will be available in the future. The proposed time-travelers are Lieutenant Commander Arthur Saltus, Major William Moresby, and Chaney.

More is involved in the survey than pure sociological research. Men trained in military skills are picked for the project; the emphasis of the project is on backup devices and support systems; and politicians are greatly interested in what is going on. A sense of brooding danger hangs over the world of intricate preparations and lends suspense to the plot.

On the day before the three men are due to carry out their missions, they gather beside the swimming pool inside Elwood Station. Saltus, a hearty extrovert a few years younger than Chaney, is swimming in the pool with Kathryn (called Katrina during most of the novel). Gilbert Seabrooke, the project's director, comes down to the side of the pool and sits beside Chaney. Chaney finds himself trying to assess Seabrooke, who appears urbane, efficient, and very "Establishment." But Seabrooke is not as glib as he appears at first. For instance, he is genuinely concerned about the future which the project proposes to survey. The United States is well on its way to disintegration. Chaney is still complacent; he reassures Seabrooke that the country might endure "at least as long as Jericho." Chaney still makes no connection, as the reader does, between the disturbing apocalypse described in the *Eschatos*, which he translated, and the predictions of disaster which Seabrooke detects. Chaney is more concerned with watching jealously out of the corner of his eye

Katrina and Saltus swimming in the pool, while Seabrooke spells out the end of their world in matter-of-fact statements.

The same scene introduces a new theme which becomes increasingly important as the novel continues. Seabrooke tells Chaney how nine men died when a TDV (Time Displacement Vehicle) returned to its exact time of launching. It happened only once, but it was disaster enough. Chaney becomes suspicious, and checks over the project with Seabrooke point by point. The project head gives the assurance that "every phase of this operation has been researched so that nothing is left to chance." However, Tucker has carefully shown the reader that everything has been left to chance, even the future of the United States. Everyone overlooks the one fact that eventually dooms the project: the TDV must have a power source at both ends of the journey. Like the most important clue in a mystery novel, everybody knows all the relevant facts but nobody guesses the meaning.

Tucker shows that the time machine, like any other piece of technological wizardry that has ever appeared in science fiction, is only as effective and worthwhile as the aims and activities of its builders. In this case, the builders have committed *hubris*: they believe that their efficiency and training will allow them to survive any situation. They express certainty about matters which only time itself can reveal to them. As we find at the end of the book, the only man who proves equal to the task of discovering the future cannot send back his knowledge to the world of 1978.

It is difficult in an article of this length to give any accurate idea of the complexity and fascination of *The Year of the Quiet Sun*. It is one of those rarities of science fiction, a *real* novel which depends for its meaning entirely on the reactions and interreactions of its characters, and not upon mere action or surprise.

On the other hand, Tucker's descriptions of the journeys into the future are among his finest action writing since they are filled with vivid detail as well as psychological insights into his characters. For instance, when Moresby steps out into the embattled America of 1999, one of the first things he notices is the same pool which he had seen several days before: "The pool was drained, the bottom dry and littered with debris. . . ." When Saltus emerges in the year 2000, he finds only silence. The barracks have burned, someone has taken the supplies left for the future surveyors, and bodies lie in the snow. The swimming pool is *"nearly* empty: a half dozen long lumps huddled under the blanket of snow at the bottom, lumps the shape of men. . . ."

When Chaney emerges from the TDV, at the beginning of the finale, he finds that all the electric power is off. The Station is in complete darkness, and in the swimming pool he sees

a few inches of dirty water . . . — residue of the rains — together with a poor collection of rusty and broken weapons and an appreciable amount of debris blown in by the wind:

the pool had become a dumping ground for trash and armament. The sodden corpse of some small animal floated in a corner.

In a passage such as this, Tucker shows his extraordinary attention to detail, which makes *The Year of the Quiet Sun* a pleasure to read, and lifts it above many other science fiction novels in quality. Why had the pool "become a dumping ground for trash and armament"? Because the destruction of the country (including a nuclear attack on nearby Chicago) had taken place in the air around the pool. "The sodden corpse of some small animal" is probably the remainder of those human bodies which lay in the pool when Saltus saw it. Tucker does not go in for the grand gesture, the romantic metaphor; his meaning is all in the details.

When Chaney arrives in the future, he finds a world that is fresh, cleared of human habitation, growing again; it resembles the cleansed landscape described in the *Eschatos*, the ancient prophecy. As Chaney notices these things, he senses eyes watching his back. He turns slowly. Facing him are two adults, a man and a woman, one resemblig a younger Arthur Saltus, and the other a younger Kathryn van Hise. At first they are cautious, but then they realize who he is. He has been long expected. They tell him that their mother is still alive. Chaney finds his way downstairs to the briefing room. Katrina is waiting there. She is thirty or forty years older than when he saw her last — a few hours before.

Her eyes were bright and alive, as sharply alert as he remembered them, but time had not been lenient to her. . . . The skin was drawn tight over her cheekbones, pulled tight around her mouth and chin and appeared sallow in lantern light. The lustrous, lovely hair was entirely grey. Hard years, unhappy years, lean years. . . .

Katrina has waited her entire life. She has endured the decline and fall of her world, she has brought up her two children under the worst possible conditions, and she has seen her husband (Saltus) die. Chaney, by contrast, lacks the experience of forty years of continuous disaster; he has only had a few hours to mature sufficiently to cope with such drastically altered circumstances. But finally he shows that he has changed — not much perhaps, but enough. For once, he makes the right judgment and says the right words: "I'm *still* in love with you, Katrina."

At the same time Chaney discovers that this is now his world as well. There was no power in the Station when he arrived, so he cannot kick back to 1978. He is no longer a surveyor, an observer. He must find a way to remake the world. In *The Year of the Quiet Sun*, time travel is a metaphor for a process of redemption. Despite the terrible price which everybody pays, the earth remains, as do a few people who know how to live in it.

Through the careful detail of the book Tucker builds up a convincing picture of how the decline and destruction of our world might take place. Some details no longer seem as convincing as they did when the book appeared in 1970; many details seem more convincing now. The power of the novel lies in the fact that Tucker's apocalypse might well happen; Tucker gives the book to the reader as a mirror, offering the challenge to look in it.

Bruce Gillespie

Sources for Further Study

Reviews:

Analog. LXXXVI, October, 1970, p. 167.

Publisher's Weekly. CXCVII, March 16, 1970, p. 56.

SF Commentary. XXIV, November, 1971, pp. 5-11.

Science Fiction Review. XXXVII, April, 1970, p. 27.

WSFA Journal. LXXII, June–August, 1970, p. 26.

Worlds of If. XX, November–December, 1970, pp. 167-168.

THE YELLOW DANGER

Author: M. P. Shiel (1865-1947)
First book publication: 1898
Type of work: Novel
Time: 1898-1899
Locale: Great Britain, the High Seas, and the Orient

An Oriental mastermind plots the destruction of Europe, but is thwarted by a young Englishman

> *Principal characters:*
> DR. YEN HOW, an evil genius
> ADA SEWARD, an English nanny
> JOHN HARDY, a junior officer in the British navy

An extraordinarily prolific species of futuristic fiction dedicated to the anticipation of the next war flourished in Great Britain between 1871 and 1914. The fashion for such fiction began with the publication of a clever piece of political propaganda, which put the case for rearmament and the remodeling of the army by telling the story of a fictitious German invasion which overwhelms the British Army by virtue of superior armaments and better military organization. This was George Chesney's *The Battle of Dorking*, and it provoked a host of replies in kind and numerous imitations. The political crusade which it served was sparked off by the realization of observers in America during the Civil War that advancing technology would remake war as well as industry, and that the whole business of warfare must be rethought. The specter of bigger and better guns, ironclad ships, observation balloons and a whole new world of logistical problems and possibilities opened up by the revolution in transportation alarmed many military men while others remained stubbornly complacent. Once the basic idea caught on, popular authors found a rich vein for adventurous exploitation, and soon began to write about airships, tanks, submarines, poison gas and disintegrating rays, featuring conflicts of hitherto unsuspected scope and scale as imminent possibilities. The new vogue in mass-produced fiction made the careers of such writers as George Griffith and William le Queux, and attracted the attention of many other professional authors.

In the great bulk of this fiction England was matched against the German Empire, recently consolidated in the wake of the Franco-Prussian war, already rearming, and infected with a fierce militaristic nationalism. Occasionally, France was the enemy, and sometimes socialism, while in George Griffith's extravaganzas of world war the chief enemies were Tyranny and Islam. In 1896, however, Louis Tracy, who had that year published a chauvinistic account of *The Final War*, suggested to his friend Matthew Shiel that he should inject some new blood into the *genre* by taking inspiration from recent newspaper reports of unrest in China. The resulting novel, serialized as "The Empress of the Earth" in 1897 and published in book form a year later as *The Yellow Danger*, brought into being the literary mythology of the "Yellow Peril."

The Yellow Danger begins with a fateful encounter between Ada Seward, "the presiding deity in the nursery of Mrs. Pattison of Fulham" and Dr. Yen How, the son of a Japanese father by a Chinese mother, who embodies all the mystery of the East. Yen How is a calculating genius, presently "lying low" in the West in order to absorb its culture and its wisdom to add to that of the East, which he already possesses. On meeting Miss Seward he is seized by an irrational and indomitable passion, and his pestering her for a "lillee kiss" eventually results in his being roughed up by a soldier, at which juncture he vanishes back into the East to plot the destruction of the white race (all except for Ada, who is to become his mistress once he has conquered the world).

Within months Yen How has set his plan in motion. By exploiting the imperialistic greed of the European nations, he plays them one against another, causing them to go to war over Chinese territories which are no longer really available for the grabbing. In the meantime, he prepares a vast army of one hundred and fifty million yellow men whose task it will be to march east across Asia to flood into a weakened Europe and destroy her forces by sheer weight of numbers. (Yen How, for all his presumed genius, clearly lacks the subtlety of Fu Manchu.)

The English fleet is caught up in a surprise engagement by a sneak attack in which ships from France, Germany and Russia collaborate. They are the vanguard of an invasion, but their plan is thwarted when the British ships win a surprise victory, largely because of advice given to the captain of one of the ships by a young officer named John Hardy. Hardy has no right to be in the battle at all. His own ship is in the Far East, having left him behind while he was too ill to travel (he is rather frail and consumptive), but the accident of his presence saves the day and makes him a hero. Knowing that war is coming, he makes a desperate attempt to rejoin his own ship by traveling overland through hostile territories. In France he is nearly stopped when he is tricked into a duel by the master duelist Edrapol, but he flees, leaving behind his promise to fight Edrapol at the earliest convenient moment. He fails to reach his objective, though, and winds up as a prisoner of Yen How.

Yen How discovers that Hardy has met Ada Seward, and has kissed her (though in fact he cares nothing for her). The evil genius then begins to devise an extensive program of torture by which to pay out his resentment, and soon brings Hardy to the edge of psychological destruction. Hardy is saved, however, as a result of a blood feud between his jailer and another man; the other sets him free so that the jailer will suffer the wrath of Yen How. Hardy succeeds in reaching the temporary safety of a British vessel beached at Kiao-Chau, and becomes the leader of the men stranded there. He mounts a series of guerrilla raids on the Chinese and their allies and ultimately heads for home in a captured Japanese battleship. He gets home in time to win another major naval battle against the combined fleets of Europe, but by this time Yen How's intentions are clear and the victory is a hollow one.

Ada Seward tries to give herself up to Yen How in the mistaken belief that this will save England, but Hardy saves her. By this time the yellow horde has overrun Europe and is ready to strike out across the channel to invade England, but Hardy and the British fleet, against all odds, destroy the warships accompanying the invaders and tow the vast fleet of barges northward, abandoning them finally to the Maelstrom. Only a handful of the would-be invaders are preserved, and they are released at key points along the coast of Europe, each infected with a deadly plague. Within three weeks the horde is wiped out horribly by the intended epidemic. "Europe," observes the author, "was a rotting charnel-house." Alas, Hardy does not live to see this project come to fruition, for the indefatigable Edrapol presents himself to demand satisfaction, and runs him through.

Shiel went on to write two more "Yellow Peril" novels — *The Yellow Wave* (1905) and *The Dragon* (1913; reprinted in 1929 as *The Yellow Peril*). His work in this vein won him a certain celebrity, but it was left to Sax Rohmer and the insidious Dr. Fu Manchu to make a small fortune out of the notion.

The Yellow Danger is remarkable in several ways. It is perhaps the most outrageously chauvinistic of all the war-anticipation novels, and certainly the most nasty minded. The racism of the author was sufficiently fierce to allow him to contemplate genocide with gleeful satisfaction. It sees the world in terms of a rather curious variant of social Darwinist thinking:

> Look forward five hundred, a thousand years, Marquis, and what do you see? . . . Is it not this? — the white man and the yellow man in their death-grip, contending for the earth. The white and the yellow — there are no others. The black is the slave of both; the brown does not count. But there are those two, and when the day comes that they stand face to face in dreadful hate, saying, "One or another must quit this earth," shall I tell you which side will win?

It is perhaps understandable that Shiel, seeing human life in terms of this kind of struggle for existence, should not shrink from the idea of all-out conflict.

Many of the authors who contributed to the war-anticipation *genre* had no real conception of the extent to which technology might remake war, or of the possible scope of the next great war. The three who did were H. G. Wells, George Griffith and M. P. Shiel. Wells was horrified by the thought, but sought consolation in the hope that a better world might rise from the ashes of the old. Griffith at least saw a chance of clearing away tyranny from the world and hoped that the masters of the new technology might preserve a just society amid the ruin. Shiel, however, looked forward to the coming conflict with relish, believing that from the cauldron of the next European war a global conflict must erupt, and yet hoping fervently that such a thing should come to pass. It was with enthusiasm that he declared that the struggle that was looked forward to when Europe, in the fulness of time, next brought forth her monstrous offspring of war, would, as men knew, be stupendous, world-wide, and final; the combatants would consist of mankind; the whole future of the world would be determined by it; and in the greatness of that day, war, the destroyer, would itself be destroyed.

We see here the mythology of "the war to end war" that was so influential in motivating men to fight in the *real* world war that killed the whole *genre* of war-anticipation stories. To what extent the *genre* aided in the propagation of this mythology and in preparing the minds of ordinary men for the real war we can only conjecture. The one thing that we can, perhaps, be thankful for is that Shiel's vision of worldwide conflict, genocide, and bacteriological warfare proved to be unrealistic. At the same time, however, we must bear in mind that a bastardized social Darwinism mingled with nationalistic chauvinism, not too different from Shiel's, was to become one of the influential ideologies of World War II and was indeed used to justify an attempt at genocide.

Brian Stableford

Sources for Further Study

Criticism:

Brophy, Brigit. "Rare Books," in *New Statesman*. XIV (June, 1963), pp. 904-905. Brophy discusses Shiel's psychological appeal to the reader and finds a great deal of "period charm" in his writing.

"Fantastica," in *Times Literary Supplement* (July 5, 1963), p. 497. This article comments on a certain self-indulgence in Shiel's imaginative style.

Stevenson, Lionel. "Purveyors of Myth and Magic," in his *Yesterday and After: The History of the English Novel*. New York: Barnes & Noble, 1967, pp. 111-154. This article is interesting in that it presents an unbiased treatment of Shiel in a standard history of the novel.

YOU SHALL KNOW THEM
(LES ANIMAUX DÉNATURÉS)

Author: "Vercors" (Jean Bruller, 1902-   )
First book publication: 1953
English Translation: 1953
Type of work: Novel
Time: The very near future
Locale: London, Guildford, Surrey, the New Guinea jungle

A satiric view of the effect on human affairs, individual, economic, and international, of the discovery of a tribe of living missing links and the consequent need to redefine the term "human"

> *Principal characters:*
> DOUGLAS M. TEMPLEMORE, an English journalist-turned-murderer on principle
> FRANCES DORAN, a writer, Douglas' friend and later his wife
> SYBIL GREAME, wife of an anthropologist and Douglas' sometime lover
> SIR ARTHUR DRAPER, presiding judge at Douglas' first trial

"What is man, that thou art mindful of him?" the Psalmist asks God. Less cosmically, perhaps, but with no less intensity, modern novelists of all sorts continue to pose the same question and to give answers with varying degrees of success. One of the best such questions and answers in science fiction is *You Shall Know Them*, by the French novelist Vercors (Jean Bruller). Its surprising depth lies in Bruller's use of religion in the framing of the novel's solution, as the American title hints (the French title *Les Animaux dénaturés* translates literally as "The Unnatural Animals"). Its delight lies in the wit and compassion with which its deft characterizations and tight plot present the alternatives. And its lasting value lies, perhaps, in the clarity with which it highlights the implications of whatever answer each person and each society may finally give.

Irony and paradox are Bruller's weapons of choice, and he handles them with consummate skill. The core of the narrative is the discovery on the island of New Guinea of a tribe of what popular evolutionary theory calls "missing links" — primates more advanced in their evolution then any modern apes, but more primitive in their culture and physiology than any creature accorded human status by paleontologists. The tribe thus constitutes proof of Darwin's hypothesis that man and ape descended from a common ancestor. The irony begins with the fact that the "tropis" (so called from a contraction of *anthropus*, man, and *pithecus*, ape; they are properly called *paranthropus erectus*) are no mere intellectual curiosity or fossil record to be debated; they are alive and function well in their almost inaccessible jungle home. Hence what should be a triumph of modern science rapidly becomes a political and economic problem hinging on the question of whether these ape-men are apes or humans. The paradox enters when the central character kills his half-tropi son in order to force the courts to decide the issue: if he wins (by having the tropis declared human), he loses his life.

The plot incorporating this paradox turns on human greed. The tropis are seen by Australian wool-producing interests as a source of exceptionally cheap labor, since they are clever and dextrous but require fewer amenities than even the most savage primitive tribesman. Using the tropis, Australian interests could produce cloth in the southern hemisphere at a fraction of the normal cost of exporting raw wool to Great Britain and importing finished cloth. Thus, the British monopoly on finished cloth, a monopoly based on the scarcity of labor in Australia, could be broken. The cost, however, would be the exploitation (more accurately, the enslavement) of the tropis. The Australian plan horrifies the party of anthropologists who discovered the tropis, but there seems to be no way of preventing the wool barons from having their way, for they have the exclusive legal right to exploit the resources of the tropis' homeland. Then Douglas Templemore, the journalist who accompanied the expedition, devises his way of establishing the humanity of the tropis and thereby preventing their exploitation. He simply seizes an opportunity when several tropi females are impregnated by artificial insemination by assorted ape donors and by Templemore. One of his offspring, born at his Guildford home after his return from New Guinea, is duly christened and then murdered. The subsequent trial will decide the nature of the tropis by deciding the nature of Templemore's crime; if Templemore has committed murder, the tropis are human and cannot be enslaved.

The first half of the novel details the events leading up to the trial; the second half describes the trial itself. The concerns of the two halves are, as one might expect, not the same. The earlier, marked by physical action and by a pyrotechnic juxtaposition of styles, is a gently satiric portrait of Douglas and how he is led to the murder of his infant, half-tropi son. These include his romantic entanglement with Frances, whose jealous impulse sends Templemore to New Guinea; his sexual entanglement with Sybil Greame, a childhood sweetheart now married to the aging leader of the New Guinea expedition; and, of course, the finding of the tropis, which the Greame expedition had sought without realizing that they were more than fossil remains. In this section of the book, the emphasis is on character — particularly on Douglas, a model upper-middle-class English gentleman, sensitive and articulate but limited in intellect and imagination; and on Frances, a slightly superannuated virgin with impeccable tastes and great sensitivity. Their courtship, its inadvertent propulsion of Douglas into world notoriety (and, incidentally, into Sybil's bed), and the wondrous first contact with the tropis are developed in terms of their effect on the people involved. Even when abstract ideas intrude, they are embodied in Bruller's characters; the theories of evolution which are necessary to the reader's understanding of the issues are, for example, presented as de-bates among the scientists of the expedition, including an Irish Benedictine, a German geologist, and the Darwinian Greame.

The second half of *You Shall Know Them* is different in its movement, its style, and its manner. The locale is mostly the interior of a courtroom, presided over by Sir Arthur Draper; the style is more level, without the shifts in point of view and chronology which mark the first part; and the focus of the novel shifts from the effect of ideas on characters to the ideas themselves and, ultimately, to the effect on them of those who have them.

The central question is, of course, the nature of humanity. At some point on the evolutionary scale — which, despite Darwin's own views on natural selection, is usually seen as a teleological one — one can theoretically point to a creature and say with certainty that it is human. Whatever the differences in physiognomy from the Westerners who have the most power to act on the classification, whatever the odd (or even disgusting) folkways, the most remote and primitive human being shares a kinship with Bruller's reader in a single human community. There are knotty problems involved, however, as Bruller indicates. What weight, for example, should be given to intelligence in making the discrimination? At some point in human evolution, Sir Arthur speculates, the minute additions in brain power from millennium to millennium — from slow, hard step to slow, hard step on the evolutionary ladder — suddenly reached a critical point, and self-consciousness began. At this point the human being suddenly realized the difference between it and exterior nature; in effect, existential alienation was created. The situation, Draper notes, is like the slow addition of units of heat to water: for a while the temperature merely rises, but then, suddenly, the water becomes steam when only one more calorie is added. How can one distinguish the point at which animal cunning boils over into human intelligence? Or take the problem of language. The tropis communicate in cries not unlike the cries of birds and other species; they have no syntax or grammar, no large (or abstract) vocabulary. But some primitive tribes have little more. At what point do the semi-articulate sounds of a higher animal deserve the name of language?

The religious person — like "Pop," the Irish Benedictine Father Dillighan — phrases the question differently. At what point does one postulate the presence of a divine soul in the animal frame? What is the sign of the soul? A chimpanzee is a beast, lacking a soul; Einstein, as Frances points out, is, as a human being, presumed to have had one. Hence Einstein has something in common with the least educated, most superstition-ridden African native, something the chimpanzee does not share; and we whites who resemble Einstein recognize the kinship, despite the fact that the African may appear to us more like the chimpanzee than like us. What is it that leads us to this recognition?

Thus, for all that the book is in some ways a standard "novel of ideas," Bruller's intellectual problem is more than a mere taxonomic puzzle. The stakes are enormously high, for all of humanity and not just the tropis. Bruller makes painfully clear that the world order depends on a clear agreement about just who is human. Without such consensus, the inevitable result is racialism (the translator, Rita Barisse, uses this form rather than the more recently common *racism*). To deny the tropis' humanity is to risk denying humanity to racially oppressed peoples throughout the world. (Small wonder that the South Africans soon rally to the cause of the novel's Australian wool barons.) One must bear in mind that Bruller was writing not long after the end of the global war against the Nazi regime and its "master race" theories — and that he fought in the French Resistance, his pseudonym Vercors being originally the name signed to his clandestine 1941 novella, *Le Silence de la Mer*. Moreover, *You Shall Know Them* appeared during the years of Cold War, United Nations intervention in Korea, and American McCarthyism — a period during which the human community seemed in danger of destroying itself despite its having purged itself of the horrors of Nazism by a devastating war. Bruller argues that the problem is one of conscience, and that it is urgent; his novel accordingly provides a powerful statement of the questions and issues.

On another level, *You Shall Know Them* also provides a satiric look at the conventions, devices, and traditions of the novel itself. For example, there are parodies of different sorts of popular fiction: the detective novel in the opening discovery of the corpse and in the trial scenes, the sentimental romance in the idyllic love of Douglas and Frances, the late Victorian novel of science adventure in the "lost race" scenes in New Guinea. By these gentle reminders of the works lurking in the background, Bruller both increases the reader's amusement and throws the main issues of the book into sharper relief. More subtle in their effects are the numerous shifts of point of view, from a laconic, objective voice in the opening chapter, through the bittersweet vision of Frances, to the quiet pragmatism of Sir Arthur. In each case, the novelist sets up a delightful irony which permits the reader to sympathize with the characters while still maintaining a detached awareness of the ideas on which the book centers. This is nowhere more deftly accomplished than in the sections which quote the letters between Douglas and Frances when the former is in New Guinea. Bruller gleefully gives us such epistolary gems as a Conan Doyle-like lecture on evolutionary theory and a wildly improbable, clichéd safari-movie seduction. Bruller furthermore archly loads the novel with a number of Victorian devices, including comments in the chapter headnotes on what he's doing and chapter endings which shamelessly create artificial suspense. The novel thus both turns back in on itself and opens out to connect with works of many kinds and times; the reader is invited to think on different levels, and about vastly different topics, for the sheer fun of it.

The two levels come together in the ending. Templemore's first trial ends in a hung jury, for the jurors cannot determine the question he so much wants them to. A parliamentary commission is formed, with Sir Arthur advising it.

Following his wife's insight that even the most primitive tribes possess *ju-jus* and animals lack them, Draper guides the commission to a definition of man based upon a spirit of religion (to include science, art, and all other manifestations of an attempt to heal the breach between nature and human self-consciousness). The tropis are human; but because they became members of the human community only when that community chose to admit them, Douglas is acquitted in his second trial. Bruller thus not only answers his basic question but resolves the paradox in his plot in the best mock-O. Henry (or Maupassant) style. Who are human beings? By their fruits, as Christ said, we shall know them, and in knowing them we know ourselves.

William H. Hardesty III

Sources for Further Study

Reviews:

Analog. LIII, May, 1954, p. 149.

Atlantic. CXCII, July, 1953, p. 84.

Galaxy. X, September, 1955, p. 90.

Nation. CLXXVI, June 20, 1953, p. 528.

New Republic. CXXVIII, July 20, 1953, p. 19.

New York Herald Tribune Book Review. June 21, 1953, p. 1.

New York Times. June 21, 1953, p. 4.

Saturday Review. XXXVI, June 20, 1953, p. 16.

Time. LXI, June 22, 1953, p. 92.

A ZECEA LUME
(The Tenth World)

Author: Vladimir Colin (1921-   )
First book publication: 1964
Type of work: Novel
Time: The fortieth century
Locale: Thule, the only satellite of Ultima, an imaginary tenth planet of the solar
system

*An expedition from the Great Council attempts to bring modern socialism to the
backward natives of the satellite Thule*

> *Principal characters:*
> A MALE TERRAN,
> A FEMALE MERCURIAN,
> A MALE VENUSIAN, and
> A FEMALE VENUSIAN, the expeditionary team
> THE BLUE THULEANS, a primitive, peaceful, superstitious alien culture
> THE WHITE THULEANS, a moronic, warlike subspecies

Perhaps the most important aspect of *A Zecea Lume* is its historical and
ideological background. The action takes place in the twentieth century of the
Socialist Era, which began with the Russian Revolution of October, 1917. The
portrait of Lenin can be found in the white marble hall where sits the Great
Council which rules the solar system. Here are represented the nine inhabited
planets and satellites: Mercury, Venus, Earth, Mars, Ganymede, Callisto, Titan, Triton, and Pluto. As the story begins, the Great Council is discussing the
matter of adding a tenth member to what the author calls the "interplanetary
humanity," a commonwealth of all the sentient beings in the solar system.

The recent discovery of a thinking race on Thule, the only satellite of the
transplutonian planet Ultima, is a delicate question to deal with. The Thuleans
are seemingly a primitive people, and contact with the supercivilized interplanetary humanity may prove fatal to their culture. Such disasters are not
unprecedented in the solar system. As the first space-faring race, the Martians
experienced one such disaster when they first landed on Earth. They were
worshiped as gods by the dawn-age men, and the knowledge they brought was
used by priests and kings as a means of domination. They had invented a way
to open doors to other dimensions which degenerated into magic and religious
rites in the hands of the early Terrans. This uncontrolled use of the Martian
science led to the strengthening of the archaic societies of India, Egypt, and
Sumer, and finally prevented any real evolution until the socialist revolution
swept off superstition and exploitation. Later, another Martian expedition on
Triton resulted in another failure when modern weapons had to be used against
the attacking natives. The Great Council, therefore, decides to proceed cauti-

ously and nominates a team of four to study the Thulean civilization and explore their world. In addition, they will have to solve the riddle of an artifact found by the first expedition: a statuette of an old Mediterranean deity sculptured on Thule out of Thulean stone.

Another important aspect of the novel is the incredible scenery the four explorers — one female Mercurian, two Venusians of either sex, and one male Terran — are met with as they land. Thule is a mineral world of rosy lakes and rivers of viscous and dense liquids, of yellow wastes and multicolored rocks, where all the life forms are basically constructed from silicium and breathe hydrogen. The grass is black and the trees are transparent; orange carnivorous balloons prey on yet stranger animals, and orange medusae fly in the ashen sky. As for the Thuleans, they are like blue columns with one large foot on the base of which they glide, with two flexible arms and a face with human features reduced to two large eyes. This imaginative setting is aesthetically enjoyable even though it is not built upon scientific fact. For instance, the faraway sun, even with the added reflection from Ultima, would hardly cast enough light to distinguish day from night; and it certainly could never produce such a festival of colors on the satellite's surface. Obviously the author does not aim at giving a scientifically convincing picture of an alien world.

The Narrator is the Terran, who relates the story like a detective novel, in which successively unveiled mysteries lead to another, greater mystery, and where the conclusion seems prologue to an unwritten sequel. The exploration team's first discovery is an ominous one: an abandoned pyramid-shaped temple with evidences of human sacrifices inside. They make friends with the dwellers of a nearby village who seem to be peaceful, and they are admitted into another, larger temple with a gigantic copy of the statuette brought back by the first expedition. Since the thin atmosphere on Thule cannot convey sounds and its inhabitants emit only radio-waves, the explorers have to rely on gestures to communicate; they also discover that the Thuleans can see through opaque matter. Next, they meet a member of a moronic, warlike, white-skinned subspecies, and are instructed to sacrifice him on the altar of the temple god. Horror-stricken, they release him; but in the ensuing confusion, the female Venusian is abducted and her companions rescue her from the white Thuleans just as they prepare to feed her to a carnivorous tree.

Later, the high priestess shows them several devices that she can operate, although she does not understand them. The explorers learn that, more than one hundred and forty centuries ago, a Martian ship landed on Thule and one of the crewmen died. The statuette of the spacesuited Martian, placed on his tomb, is the idol later worshiped by the natives. The explorers read the crewman's journal and view films of the Martian capital as it was originally. But the major legacy of the fabulous Martian technology, now partly lost, is a door to other dimensions. The Martians had colonized a planet orbiting another sun; their descendants are supposedly still living there. As the priestess completes the ritual dance that opens the door, the Narrator can glimpse superhuman visions of the civilization the Martians have constructed. Why they left the solar system forever remains a mystery, but the interplanetary humanity can hope to join them and equal them on the road to socialism.

Basically, the investigation on Thule illustrates the discovery of another failure of the ancient Martians to preserve an alien people from disastrous cultural shock and contamination. Though it was short and superficial, their intrusion impressed the Thuleans' primitive minds so much that it took only a tomb and some incomprehensible artifacts to start a religion. The cult of the space-suited astronaut supplied a rigid cultural frame that prevented their society from following its natural course, and instead, maintained it unchanged for millennia. As the novel draws to its conclusion, the male Venusian dies during an attack of the white Thuleans, and the statue on his tomb is soon be become another god.

However, *A Zecea Lume* is also the story of a recovery. It took a long time for the Terrans to get rid of the superstitions involuntarily sown by the Martians, but they were finally successful. With the help of the planets of the solar system, Thule will also heal and will evolve from its primitive communism to a scientific communism, until it is ready to join the interplanetary humanity. Even the white Thuleans are not beyond redemption. A medical examination of their cranium shows that only its premature ossification is responsible for their underdeveloped brain, which can be helped with surgery. An operation attempted on one of them succeeds; the subject develops a normal intelligence; so that the whole species may hope to be humanized in the future.

But Thule is not only a place where man's and nature's wrongs can be redressed — it is also the last frontier before the interstellar void; the interplanetary humanity discovers on Thule both limitations and expectations of further achievement. The galactic door left behind by the ancient Martians probably leads to a galactic humanity to whom the inhabitants of the nine worlds, soon to be ten, are like Thuleans. But the whole solar system is bound to join it one day into what can be only a higher form of socialism since its members are clearly superior beings. The author does not write it explicitly but socialism as a universal law is the ideological background of the novel as well as its major argument.

Whether socialism is destined to rule the Galaxy, or at least the solar system, is a matter of faith or conviction, and does not require discussion here. But the concept is interesting since it implies that a Terran ideology can be valid on other worlds, which in turn implies that their history followed the same lines as Earth's. This is not the first time a writer has projected onto the screen of the future a colorful vision of his favorite ideology. The weakness of such a story is its anthropomorphism — perhaps other, nonhuman races do not share the same needs as humanity, in which case socialism might be an inappropriate system. A more comprehensive view of the universe would have to arrive at an enlarged definition of interplanetary life to include other-than-human frameworks.

Remi-Maure

ZONE NULL

Author: Herbert W. Franke (1927-   )
First book publication: 1970
English translation: 1974
Type of work: Novel
Time: An unspecified future
Locale: Zone Null, that part of the divided world not yet "liberated"

An account of an expedition into the secluded Zone Null and the decadent conditions encountered there

> *Principal characters:*
> DAN, a cyberneticist
> BENEDICT, an inhabitant of Zone Null
> PAMELA, a girl of Zone Null

Of the current West German science fiction writers, Herbert W. Franke, the physicist and popular science writer, is probably the only one who has produced science fiction of consistently good quality, and who can be compared favorably with the better science fiction writers elsewhere. *Zone Null*, one of three books of his to be translated into English, is his sixth and probably most important novel, although because of their structural similarity it would be difficult to establish a scale of importance among them.

Franke's novels are characterized by problems that he returns to again and again in an almost obsessive way. Although a physicist by education, having graduated from the University of Vienna with a doctoral thesis on a problem of theoretical physics, the recurrent topic of his fiction is communication, the uses and, in particular, the misuses of modern methods of communication: the political goals they can be made to serve, the manipulation of human beings, the effects of psychological indoctrination on large masses of people. Ultimately his novels are concerned with the problem of reality itself: how it is possible to distinguish between an informational illusion, made possible by advances in technology, and the real world?

The final answer is shocking. When the communications system has expanded so much that it encroaches on almost every aspect of life, the illusions become undistinguishable from the real thing, creating a separate reality impenetrable from the inside. Dan, a member of the expedition sent to explore and reclaim Zone Null, is confronted with this problem in the statement of one of the inhabitants of the enigmatic area:

> . . . we're all isolated, all of us, and we all bear the entire diversity of the world within us. The data we get originate in physical processes, filtered and accounted for, nothing more. What we receive in the end are images. What's the difference whether they're in front of your nose or a million miles away? No more difference than the fraction of a second that it takes for a signal to reach us.

This central epistemological problem is repeated in a number of variations in Franke's novels. In *Das Gedankennetz* (1961), for instance, the hero experiences a number of illusionary realities that are in fact devices designed by a dictatorial regime to test his loyalty to the state and his political reliability. The problem is similarly presented in *Ypsilon minus* (1977), Franke's latest novel. In *The Orchid Cage* (1961) mind-travelers from Earth encounter a shockingly hedonistic society on a planet, whose inhabitants have become vegetables, nurtured in vats, served by robots, and fed all their sensory stimuli through automatons.

The situation is similar in *Zone Null*. The invaders from the "Free World," expecting to encounter tyranny, eager to liberate oppressed people and educate them in the enlightened ways of their own system, find only largely deserted automated complexes (a gigantic city over an area of some six thousand square miles), surrounded by metal walls. Zone Null was once protected by an impregnable barrier, radar systems, screening equipment, rocket launchers and some kind of ray weapons that automatically blasted everything crossing the border between the two spheres of the world. Also, at certain intervals, rockets with atomic warheads were fired at the moon from Zone Null to demonstrate military strength and preparedness. These shots, however, stopped some years ago. In reaction to this, a reconnaissance mission was made, in preparation for reclaiming Zone Null.

Although the novel's time remains deliberately vague, one may assume that it is a considerable time in the future, with the present political division between the "free" and the other nations of the world so strong that no communication exists between them. Free is, of course, a misleading term, for the final irony of the novel is that what calls itself the "Free World" is in fact the future development of the Communist world today, having taken over and perverted words such as "freedom" and "liberalism," so that they mean things quite different from those appropriate to their present usage. This future world is far from being as free as it proclaims itself to be; in fact, it is regimented and tightly controlled. The shape of the future emerges through the questioning of the hero who is suspected of subversion after his return. The society of the future is never presented in detail. It vaguely appears in a haze of slogans, an abstract structure of a gray, joyless present, with neither a past nor much of a future. Its concrete details can only be inferred.

Characters are not given a traditional treatment in the novel either. The nominal hero and viewpoint character is Dan, a cyberneticist, but he has no friends, no relatives, no likes and dislikes, indeed no social or individual features at all, only a function. His field is the "homeostasis in complex and very complex systems, organization of cybernetics, theory of games, general formulation for concepts of strategy." The other members of his team, Pavel, Greg, Joseph, Tibor, and Sonya are characterized in a similar manner. None of them is described as an individual; they are abstract professions and functions, lacking all personal aspects. Their backgrounds and specific characteristics are of no interest; only what they have been trained to do is important. In fact, they are so anonymous that they do not even have surnames. Even more anonymous are the inhabitants of Zone Null, among them a girl Pamela, and a man known as Mr. Benedict. Citizens of this Utopian paradise or dystopian hell (depending on how one looks at it), no longer have any social function and may in fact have been electronically created, figments of the illusionist environment without any real existence in the material world.

The plot of the novel, such as it is, has the proven form of the science fiction puzzle: the confrontation with an alien, frightening reality, and what comes of it. The invaders/"liberators" blast their way in easily enough. There is no resistance and no fighting in Zone Null. Indeed, the supercity appears to be empty, save for some automatic systems, such as the rods that emerge periodically from the ground and disappear back into it, and an automated race track, with racing cars that move around at breakneck speed without any drivers. Aside from such elements, there are simply structures, "a row of pyramid-shaped buildings in silver and gray, flat on top, and roofless. Behind those there were higher constructions — smooth, shining white blocks, angular towers, and above them, set off, circular platforms." No fancy architecture can be seen anywhere; everything is sparse, prosaic, very dry, as is the writing that describes it — writing quite unlike that usually expected in a novel.

Franke's language is the language of textbooks and technical descriptions, not the language of fiction. He does not make use of similes, metaphors, rhetoric, and uses very few images; there are no flights of fancy and no emotional involvements. Franke's diction is economical, terse, and to the point, with no words wasted on the finer points of language. Function is everything; form matters little. Instead of concrete descriptions, the reader again and again encounters catalogues of abstract functions, the way behavioral patterns are gauged in the "Free World":

> tapes on telephone and radio wires, autotranscription of voices, word and syllable counts, grammatical analysis, statistical breakdowns, second order information, networks of semantic classifications, lists of associations/innovation, language as expression thought, language as model of creative behavior, language as actions.

These enumerations are frequently arranged in a way that suggests some kind of computer poetry — computer art is indeed a field that holds a special attraction for Franke, who has penned several books on the subject. "The computer furnished word frequency, synonyms, homonyms, grammatic structure, semantic relationships, the model of logic pragmatics. From these, the psychic pattern for a representative cross-section emerged." Franke's sentences are very simple, unembellished, and not quite lucid.

Fiction without characters, particular virtues of description, enthralling action, mythical depth, the fullness of life or any fully realized imaginary worlds, plus little discernible plot, might be considered a fictional desert. Yet the fact remains that out of this desert Franke has created a monolithic and shapeless fiction, that is, in its total effect, quite extraordinary. It is fiction that is entirely in keeping with its communicational subjects, and effectively conveys the gloomy bleakness of one hell after another that man makes for himself, either deliberately or out of ignorance of the consequences of his actions.

Without being didactic in any way, Franke's drab, functional novels manage to present a very potent message. He has stated that he has no particular literary aspirations; his intention is to write of scientific subjects, of problems that are of importance in the world, in an unpretentious manner that does not lack excitement. He does this without resorting to the usual weary plot devices of science fiction, such as chases between galactic cops-and-robbers. Bleak, pessimistic, sprawling, single-minded, obsessive with their topics, the works of Franke constitute a science fiction that is unmistakably his own, and *Zone Null* is one of the most consistent and important examples of it.

Dan, the main character, is thrown into a world that he does not understand; the ground keeps shifting under his feet, and only slowly does he arrive at some level of understanding. Isolated from the other members of his team, he contacts the inhabitants of the enigmatic city and undergoes a series of traumatic experiences. In this illusionary world, money, purpose, and rank are of no concern; everyone has access to Central Control, the all-encompassing computer service that supplies all daily needs and perhaps all sensory impressions of the world. The most precious thing in this society is computer time, which provides access to all the facilities of the artificial environment. One of the most frightening episodes occurs when Dan gambles away all his credits and is left an outcast. But what part of his experience is real and what is imaginary remains ambiguous. The ultimate reality is what is stored in the computer banks. Consciousness may be changed; the stored memories may be altered. There is no clear line between what is real and what is induced.

In such a system of total sensory control and storage, philosophical distinction between true and false lose their validity, and effective and ineffective take their place. Such problems become a matter of practical psychology in a world where identities and all the experiences that go with them may be falsified and changed without limits. Everything is run by unknown computer programs, welfare and security are total, and there is no need to work; there is no incentive for doing anything in reality. The inhabitants of Zone Null have not gone as far as the people of Franke's *The Orchid Cage* (1961) and plugged themselves directly into sensory circuits, but the effects of their Utopia are similarly stifling.

After experiencing several adventures in this world, experiences that may have been tests, this brave new world comes crashing down upon the hero. He returns home a changed man; a seed of doubt has been sown in him by his simulated experiences. He no longer believes that his own world is free of repression, exploitation, and slavery, and he has been told. He has been infected by the virus of dissatisfaction. Neither world is the best of all possible worlds; both are modern hells brought about by misinformation and the misuse of advanced technology. *Zone Null* is a hortatory example.

Franz Rottensteiner

Sources for Further Study

Criticism:

Rottensteiner, Franz. *The Science Fiction Book*. New York: Seabury, 1975, p. 146. A bleak portrait of a technocrat controlled future is presented in *Zone Null*.

Reviews:

Kirkus Reviews. XLII, August 15, 1974, p. 904.

Library Journal. XCIX, November 15, 1974, p. 2984.

Publisher's Weekly. CCVI, September 30, 1974, p. 54.

AUTHOR AND TITLE INDEX

I

AUTHOR AND TITLE INDEX

AUTHOR AND TITLE INDEX

VII